# PHILIP'S
# EASYREAD Britain

GW00640698

First published in 2006 by
Philip's a division of
Octopus Publishing Group Ltd
2–4 Heron Quays, London E14 4JP
www.philips-maps.co.uk
First edition 2006
First impression 2006
Cartography by Philip's
Copyright © 2006 Philip's

Ordnance Survey®

This product includes mapping data licensed from Ordnance Survey®, with the permission of the Controller of Her Majesty's Stationery Office. © Crown copyright 2006. All rights reserved. Licence number 100011710

To the best of the Publisher's knowledge, the information in this atlas was correct at the time of going to press. No responsibility can be accepted for any errors or omissions or their consequences. The representation in this atlas of any road, drive or track is no evidence of the existence of a right of way.

Data for the speed cameras provided by PocketGPSWorld.com Ltd.

Information for Tourist Attractions in England supplied by the British Tourist Authority / English Tourist Board.

Information for National Parks, Areas of Outstanding Natural Beauty, National Trails and Country Parks in Wales supplied by the Countryside Council for Wales.

Information for National Parks, Areas of Outstanding Natural Beauty, National Trails and Country Parks in England supplied by the Countryside Agency.

Data for Regional Parks, Long Distance Footpaths and Country Parks in Scotland provided by Scottish Natural Heritage.

Gaelic name forms used in the Western Isles provided by Comhairle nan Eilean.

Data for the National Nature Reserves in England provided by English Nature.

Data for the National Nature Reserves in Wales provided by Countryside Council for Wales. Darparwyd data'n ymwneud â Gwarchodfeydd Natur Cenedlaethol Cymru gan Gyngor Cefn Gwlad Cymru.

Information on the location of National Nature Reserves in Scotland was provided by Scottish Natural Heritage.

Data for National Scenic Areas in Scotland provided by the Scottish Executive Office. Crown copyright material is reproduced with the permission of the Controller of HMSO and the Queen's Printer for Scotland. Licence number C02W0003960.

Printed by Toppan, China

## Contents

This directory includes properties belonging to, or associated with, The National Trust, English Heritage, The National Trust for Scotland, Scottish Heritage, Historic Royal Palaces and The Royal Horticultural Society. They are listed alphabetically by county.

## Symbols

National Trust property
**Sudbury Hall**
- Castle
- Historic house
- Other buildings
- Church, chapel etc
- Garden
- Park
- Countryside
- Coast
- Archaeological site
- Industrial heritage
- Events
- Farm / farm animals
- Nature reserve
- Mill
- Country walk
- Guided tours

National Trust for Scotland property
**The Hill House**

English Heritage property
**Rievaulx Abbey**
- Christian heritage
- Castle / fort
- Historic house
- Romantic ruin
- Roman
- Garden / park
- Industrial monument
- Antiquity

Historic Royal Palaces property
**HRP The Banqueting House**

Royal Horticultural Society garden
**RHS Harlow Carr**

RHS partner garden, see page X
**Yalding Organic Gardens**

Historic Scotland property
**HS Elgin Cathedral**

# England

## Bath and North East Somerset

*See also* Somerset, North Somerset

### Prior Park Landscape Garden
A beautiful and intimate 18th-century landscape garden, created by local entrepreneur Ralph Allen with advice from the poet Alexander Pope and 'Capability' Brown, and set in a sweeping valley with magnificent views of the city of Bath. **Ralph Allen Drive, Bath BA2 6BD ☎01225 833422** 43 C6

### Sir Bevil Grenville's Monument
Commemorates the heroism of a Royalist commander and his Cornish pikemen at the Battle of Lansdown. **4m NW of Bath, on N edge of Lansdown Hill, near road to Wick.** 43 B6

### Stanton Drew Circles and Cove
A fascinating assembly of three stone circles, two avenues and a burial chamber makes this one of the finest Neolithic religious sites in the country. **Circles: E of Stanton Drew village; Cove: in garden of Druid's Arms. ☎0117 975 0700 for details.** 43 C5

### Stoney Littleton Long Barrow
This Neolithic burial mound is about 30 metres (100 feet) long and has chambers where human remains once lay. **1m S of Wellow off A367.** 43 D6

## Bedfordshire

### De Grey Mausoleum
A remarkable treasure-house of sculpted tombs and monuments from the 16th to 19th centuries, dedicated to the de Grey family of Wrest Park. **Flitton, attached to church, on unclassified road 1½m W of A6 at Silsoe. ☎01525 860094. Access through Flitton Church.** 84 D2

### Houghton House
Reputedly the inspiration for 'House Beautiful' in Bunyan's Pilgrim's Progress, the remains of this early 17th-century mansion still convey elements that justify the description, including work attributed to Inigo Jones. **1m NE of Ampthill off A421, 8m S of Bedford.** 84 D2

▲ Wrest Park Gardens, Bedfordshire English Heritage Photographic Library

### Wrest Park Gardens
Over 90 acres of wonderful gardens originally laid out in the early 18th century, including the Great Garden, with charming buildings and ornaments, and the delightfully intricate French Garden, with statues and fountain. The house, once the home of the de Grey family whose Mausoleum at Flitton is nearby, was inspired by 18th-century French chateaux. **¾m E of Silsoe off A6, 10m S of Bedford. ☎01525 860152** 84 D2

## Berkshire

### Ashdown House
A 17th-century house built by 1st Lord Craven and dedicated to Elizabeth, sister of Charles I, who became Queen of Bohemia. The great staircase, rising from hall to attic, is impressive and the house contains important portraits of the Winter Queen's family. **Lambourn, Newbury, Berkshire RG17 8RE ☎01793 762209** 45 A6

### Basildon Park
Beautiful Palladian mansion built by John Carr for Francis Sykes. The interior is notable for its original delicate plasterwork and elegant staircase as well as the unusual Octagon Room. Extensive parkland with waymarked trails. **Lower Basildon, Reading, Berkshire RG8 9NR ☎0118 9843040** 47 B4

### Donnington Castle
Built in the late 14th century, the twin towered gatehouse of this castle survives amidst some impressive earthworks. **1m N of Newbury off B4494.** 46 C2

## Bristol

*See also* Gloucestershire, North Somerset

### Temple Church
The handsome tower and walls of this 15th-century church defied the bombs of World War II. The graveyard is now a pleasant public garden. **In Bristol, Temple St off Victoria St.** 43 B4

## Buckinghamshire

### Ascott
Ascott is the creation of Leopold de Rothschild. Anthony de Rothschild, Leopold's son, introduced the exceptional oriental porcelain collection that is so prominent a feature of this house. There are also collections of 18th-century English furniture and paintings. A giant sundial forms the highlight of the garden's topiary work. **Wing, nr Leighton Buzzard, Buckinghamshire LU7 0PS ☎01296 688242** 66 A3

### Claydon House
Manor house famous for its 18th-century rococo interiors. Features of the house include the unique Chinese Room and parquetry Grand Stairs. Occupied by the Verney family for over 380 years, the house has mementoes of their relation Florence Nightingale, a regular visitor. **Middle Claydon, nr Buckingham, Buckinghamshire MK18 2EY ☎01296 730349** 66 A2

### Cliveden
Grade I listed garden set in a spectacular estate overlooking the River Thames. Series of gardens each with its own character, featuring topiary, statuary, water gardens and a formal parterre. Other highlights include the Octagon temple, woodland and riverside walks. **Taplow, nr Maidenhead, Buckinghamshire SL6 0JA ☎01628 605069** 48 A2

### Hughenden Manor
Home of Queen Victoria's trusted prime minister Benjamin Disraeli from 1848 until his death in 1881. Most of his books, furniture and pictures remain in this his private retreat away from the rigours of life in London. Beautiful walks in the surrounding garden, park and woodlands. **High Wycombe, Buckinghamshire HP14 4LA ☎01494 755573** 66 D3

### Princes Risborough Manor House (tenanted)
A 17th-century red-brick house with Jacobean oak staircase. House and front garden by written arrangement only with tenant. **Princes Risborough, Buckinghamshire HP17 9AW ☎Regional Office 01494 528051** 66 C3

### Stowe Landscape Gardens
One of the finest Georgian landscape gardens, made up of valleys and vistas, narrow lakes and rivers with more than 40 temples and monuments designed by many of the leading architects of the 18th century. **Buckingham, Buckinghamshire MK18 5EH ☎01280 822850** 82 D3

### Waddesdon Manor
RHS Members: free Mar, Sept, Oct. Open: 3 Mar-31 Oct, Wed-Sun and Bank Holiday, 10am-5pm. 3 Nov-23 Dec, Wed-Sun 11am-5pm. **Nr Aylesbury, Buckinghamshire HP18 0JH ☎01296 653226** 66 B2

### Waddesdon Manor
Waddesdon Manor, designed in the style of a French Renaissance chateau, was built in the 1870s by Baron Ferdinand de Rothschild. The interior evokes 18th-century France and is furnished with panelling, furniture, carpets and porcelain, many of which have a royal French provenance. There is an important collection of English 18th-century portraits by Gainsborough and Reynolds, rooms devoted to Sevres porcelain and Baron Ferdinand's 18th-century panelling. In the garden a rococo-style aviary houses exotic birds. **Waddesdon, nr Aylesbury, Buckinghamshire HP18 0JH ☎01296 653226** 66 B2

### West Wycombe Park
Perfectly preserved rococo landscape garden created by Sir Francis Dashwood. The house is among the most theatrical and Italianate in England, its facades formed as classical temples. The interior has Palmyrene ceilings and decoration, with pictures, furniture and sculpture. **West Wycombe, Buckinghamshire HP14 3AJ ☎01494 513569** 66 D3

### West Wycombe Village and Hill
Chilterns village with buildings spanning several hundred years. The hill, with its fine views, is surmounted by an Iron Age hill fort and is part of the original landscape design of West Wycombe Park. It is now the site of a church and the Dashwood Mausoleum. **West Wycombe, Buckinghamshire ☎(Hughenden Estate Office) 01494 755573** 66 D3

## Cambridgeshire

### Anglesey Abbey Garden and Lode Mill
Jacobean-style country house built on the site of a 12th-century Augustinian priory. Home to many notable paintings and collections including clocks and tapestries. Surrounded by a beautiful landscape garden and arboretum which has year-round floral interest. **Lode, Cambridgeshire CB5 9EJ ☎01223 810080** 86 A1

### Denny Abbey and the Farmland Museum
Remains of a 12th-century Benedictine abbey founded by the Countess of Pembroke which, at different times, also housed the Knights Templar and Franciscan nuns. **6m N of Cambridge on A10. ☎01223 860489** 85 A6

### Duxford Chapel
A mediaeval chapel once part of the Hospital of St John. **Adjacent to Whittlesford station off A505. ☎01223 443000** 85 C6

### Houghton Mill
This five-story timber-built watermill is set on the island in the Great Ouse and has intact machinery which is still operational. Milling takes place on Sundays and Bank Holiday Mondays, with the flour for sale. Riverside meadows offer marvellous walks. **Houghton, Cambridgeshire PE28 2AZ ☎01480 301494** 101 D4

### Isleham Priory Church
Rare example of an early Norman church. It has survived little altered, despite being later converted to a barn. **In Isleham, 16m NE of Cambridge on B1104. ☎Regional office 01223 582700** 102 D2

### Peckover House and Garden
A lovely Georgian brick town house with a charming Victorian walled garden including summerhouses, Victorian fernery and an orangery. **North Brink, Wisbech, Cambridgeshire PE13 1JR ☎01945 583463** 101 A6

### Wicken Fen National Nature Reserve
Britain's oldest nature reserve and a unique fragment of the wilderness that once covered East Anglia. A haven for birds, plants, insects and mammals alike, the Fen can be explored by the traditional wide droves and lush green paths, and there is a boardwalk nature trail giving access to several hides. **Lode Lane, Wicken, Ely, Cambridgeshire CB7 5XP ☎01353 720274** 86 A1

### Wimpole Hall, Garden, Park and Home Farm
The largest house in Cambridgeshire, its facades date from the first half of the 18th century when visitors included Swift and Pope. There is an impressive library and also a Chapel with painted decorations. Home Farm presents a living museum of agriculture with ancient farm implements and many rare breeds, all housed in the thatched farm buildings. **Arrington, Royston, Cambridgeshire SG8 0BW ☎01223 206000** 85 B5

## Cheshire

### Arley Hall and Gardens
RHS Members: free throughout open period, excluding special event days. Open: 9th Apr-28th Sept, Tue-Sun and Bank Holidays, 11am-5pm, Oct – weekends only. **Arley, Northwich, Cheshire CW9 6NA ☎01565 777353** 128 A1

### Beeston Castle
Standing majestically on sheer, rocky crags which fall sharply away from the castle walls, Beeston has possibly the most stunning views of the surrounding countryside of any castle in England and the rock has a history which stretches back over 4,000 years. **11m SE of Chester on minor road off A49 or A41. ☎01829 260464** 127 D5

### Bluebell Cottage Gardens and Lodge Lane Nursery
RHS Members: free throughout open period. Open: May-Aug, Sat-Sun and Bank Holidays, 12-5pm **Bluebell Cottage, Lodge Lane, Dutton, nr Warrington, Cheshire WA4 4HP ☎01928 713718** 127 B5

### Chester Castle: Agricola Tower and Castle Walls
Set in the angle of the city walls, this 12th-century tower contains a fine vaulted chapel. **Access via Assizes Court car park on Grosvenor St.** 127 C4

### Chester Roman Amphitheatre
The largest Roman amphitheatre in Britain. Used for entertainment and military training by the 20th Legion, based at the fortress of Deva. **On Vicars Lane beyond Newgate, Chester.** 127 C4

### Cholmondeley Castle
RHS Members: free Jun. Open: Apr-Sept, Wed, Thur, Sun and Bank Holidays, 11.30am-5pm. **Malpas, Cheshire SY14 8AH ☎01829 720383** 127 D5

### Dunham Massey
Georgian house with Edwardian additions set in a wooded deer park. Fine furniture, paintings and outstanding Huguenot silver. The moat provides power for a working Jacobean mill. The large garden contains an 18th-century orangery, a Victorian bark house and well house. **Altrincham, Cheshire WA14 4SJ ☎0161 941 1025** 128 A2

### Little Moreton Hall
Arguably the finest example of a timber-framed manor house in the country, Little Moreton Hall remains exceptional among half-timbered houses of its time. **Congleton, Cheshire CW12 4SD ☎01260 272018** 128 D3

### Lyme Park
The exterior of Lyme Hall, one of the largest houses in Cheshire, is a splendid example of Palladian architecture containing Mortlake tapestries, Grinling Gibbons carvings and a unique collection of English clocks. The garden encompasses a sunken parterre, Victorian-style formal bedding, a lake, herbaceous borders and Wyatt Conservatory. **Disley, Stockport, Cheshire SK12 2NX ☎01663 762023/766492** 129 A4

### Quarry Bank Mill & Styal Estate
Set in a country park with riverside and woodland walks, Quarry Bank Mill is a Georgian cotton mill, built in 1784 by Samuel Greg, and restored as Europe's largest working textile museum. The Apprentice House garden is a fascinating example of a Victorian utilitarian garden, growing fruits, vegetables and herbs using the same methods as 150 years ago. **Wilmslow, Cheshire SK9 4LA ☎01625 527468** 128 A3

**The Quinta Arboretum and Nature Reserve**
RHS Members: free throughout open period. Open: all year during daylight hours, except Christmas Day. **Swettenham Village, nr Congleton, Cheshire CW12 2LD** 01477 537698 128 C3

**Rode Hall Gardens**
RHS Members: free throughout open period. Open: 7-22 Feb, daily, 12pm-4pm. Apr-Sept, Tue-Thu and Bank Holidays, 2-5pm. **Church Lane, Scholar Green, Cheshire ST7 3QP** 01270 882961/873237 128 D3

**Sandbach Crosses**
Rare Anglo-Saxon stone crosses carved with animals, dragons and biblical scenes, dominating the centre of the market square. **Market Square, Sandbach.** 128 C2

**Tatton Park**
One of the most complete historic estates open to visitors in England. The 19th-century Wyatt house, set in an extensive deer park, contains the Egerton family collections and specially commissioned Gillow furniture; servants' rooms and cellars. The gardens contain authentic Japanese and Italian gardens. Also, the Tudor old hall and a working 1930s farm. **Knutsford, Cheshire WA16 6QN** 01625 534400 128 A2

**Tatton Park Gardens**
RHS Members: free throughout open period (gardens only). Open: 27 Mar-3 Oct, Tue-Sun, 10am-6pm, 4 Oct-25 Mar, Tue-Sun, 11am-4pm. **Tatton Park, Knutsford, Cheshire WA16 6QN** 01625 534400 128 A2

## Cornwall

**Antony**
One of Cornwall's finest early 18th-century houses. The garden contains The National Collection of Day Lilies, magnolias and summer borders. Also of note is an 18th-century dovecote and the 1789 Bath Pond House. **Torpoint, Plymouth PL11 2QA** 01752 812191 6 B3

**Ballowall Barrow**
In a spectacular position, this is an unusual Bronze Age chambered tomb with a complex layout. **1m W of St Just, near Carn Gloose.** 2 B1

**Carn Euny Ancient Village**
The remains of an Iron Age settlement. **1¼m SW of Sancreed off A30.** 2 C2

**Chysauster Ancient Village**
A deserted Romano-Cornish village with a 'street' of eight well-preserved houses, each comprising a number of rooms around an open court. **2½m NW of Gulval off B3311.** 07831 757934 **for details.** 2 B2

**Cornish Mines and Engines**
Cornwall's engine houses are dramatic reminders if the time when the shire was a powerhouse of tin, copper and china clay mining. Two great beam engines originally powered by high-pressure steam, can be seen. The site also includes the Industrial Discovery Centre at East Pool. **Pool, nr Redruth, Cornwall TR15 3NP** 01209 315027 3 A4

**Cotehele**
Built 1485-1627, and home of the Edgcumbe family for centuries, the house contains original furniture, armour and a remarkable set of tapestries and other textiles. There is a series of formal gardens near the house and a richly planted valley garden. **St Dominick, nr Saltash, Cornwall PL12 6TA** 01579 351346 6 A3

**Dupath Well**
A charming granite-built well house set over a holy well of c.1500 and almost complete. **1m E of Callington off A388.** 6 A2

**Glendurgan Garden**
Set in a wooded valley rich in fine trees and rare and exotic plants, Glendurgan is one of the great sub-tropical gardens of the South West. The 1833 laurel maze, and the 'Giant's Stride' (a pole with ropes to swing from) are unusual and popular features. **Mawnan Smith, nr Falmouth, Cornwall TR11 5JZ** 01326 250906 3 C5

**Halliggye Fogou**
One of several strange underground tunnels, associated with Iron Age villages, which are unique to Cornwall. **5m SE of Helston off B3293 E of Garras on Trelowarren estate.** 3 C5

**Hurlers Stone Circles**
These three Bronze Age stone circles in a line are some of the best examples of ceremonial standing stones in the South West. **½m NW of Minions off B3254.** 10 D3

**King Doniert's Stone**
Two decorated pieces of a 9th-century cross with an inscription believed to commemorate Durngarth, King of Cornwall, who drowned c.875. **1m NW of St Cleer off B3254.** 6 A1

**Lanhydrock**
Magnificent late-Victorian country house with extensive servants' quarters, gardens and wooded estate. The gatehouse and north wing survice from the 17th century, but the rest of the house was rebuilt following a disastrous fire in 1881. One of the most fascinating and complete late-19th-century houses. **Bodmin, Cornwall PL30 5AD** 01208 265950 5 A5

**Launceston Castle**
Set on the motte of a Norman castle and commanding the town and surrounding countryside, this mediaeval castle controlled the main route into Cornwall. The shell keep and tower survive. **In Launceston.** 01566 772365 10 C4

**The Levant Mine & Beam Engine**
In its tiny engine house perched on the cliff edge, the famous Levant beam engine is steaming again after sixty idle years. A short underground tour takes you from the miners' dry to the man engine shaft via a spiral staircase. Also on view are the winding and pumping shafts and the newly restored electric winding engine. **Trewellard, Pendeen, nr St Just, Cornwall** 01736 796993 2 B1

**Pendennis Castle**
Henry VIII's fortress at the mouth of the Fal boasts Second World War secret underground defences. Attractions include the re-constructed Second World War Battery Observation Post housing range-finding equipment, a First World War Guard House, 16th-century keep with a recreated working gun-deck, plus a hands-on discovery centre, tearoom and gift shop. **On Pendennis Head, Cornwall, 1m SE of Falmouth.** 01326 316594 4 D3

**Penhallam**
Ruins of a mediaeval manor house surrounded by a protective moat. **1m NW of Week St Mary, off minor road off A39 from Treskinnick Cross (10 minute walk from car park).** 10 B3

**Probus Gardens**
RHS Members: free Aug-Oct. Open:3 Nov-28 Feb, 1-24 Dec, Mon-Fri, 10am-4pm (or dusk if earlier), 3 Mar-31 Oct, daily, 10am-5pm (or dusk if earlier). **Probus, Truro, TR2 4HQ** 01726 882597 4 C4

**Restormel Castle**
**1½m N of Lostwithiel off A390.** 01208 872687 5 A6

**St Breock Downs Monolith**
A prehistoric standing stone, originally about 5 metres (16 feet) high, set in beautiful countryside. **On St Breock Downs, 3¾ m SW of Wadebridge off unclassified road to Rosenannon.** 5 A4

**St Catherine's Castle**
A small fort built by Henry VIII to defend Fowey Harbour. **¾ m SW of Fowey along footpath off A3082.** 5 B6

**St Mawes Castle**
Set in the wonderful location alongside the pretty fishing village of St Mawes, with delightful landscaped gardens and extensive views of the coastline. The castle is the most perfectly preserved of Henry VIII's coastal fortresses, complete with its commons. Gift shop. **In St Mawes on A3078.** 01326 270526 4 D3

**St Michael's Mount**
Rocky island crowned by mediaeval church and castle, accessible by boat or foot at low tide. Oldest surviving buildings date from the 12th century. The mansion house has fascinating rooms on display from different eras including the mid-18th-century gothic-style Blue Drawing Room. **Marazion, nr Penzance, Cornwall TR17 0EF** 01736 710507 2 C3

**Tintagel Castle**
The mystical Tintagel Castle, renowned as the birthplace of the legendary warrior leader, King Arthur, is English Heritage's top Cornish site. A site of outstanding natural beauty, groups can explore the remains of the 13th century castle on the mainland and walk the narrow and rugged trail across the wild and windswept Tintagel Island for spectacular views. Remains of the castle, built by Richard, Earl of Cornwall, include steep stone steps and stout walls. Recent excavation works at

▲ Wicken Fen, Cambridgeshire Tim Gartside / Alamy

the site resulted in a dramatic find: a 1500 year old piece of slate, bearing the name ?rtognou,' refuelling speculation about links with King Arthur. **On Tintagel Head ½m along uneven track from Tintagel, no vehicles.** 01840 770328 9 C6

**Tintagel Old Post Office**
One of the most distinctive buildings in Cornwall, this small 14th-century manor is full of charm and interest. Restored in the fashion of the Post Office it was for nearly 50 years. **Tintagel, Cornwall PL34 0DB** 01840 770024 9 C6

**Trebah Garden**
RHS Members: free throughout open period. Open: all year, daily, 10.30am-5pm. **Mawnan Smith, nr Falmouth, Cornwall TR11 5JZ** 01326 250448 3 C5

**Tregiffian Burial Chamber**
A Neolithic or early Bronze Age chambered tomb by the side of a country road. **2m SE of St Buryan on B3315.** 2 C2

**Trelissick Garden**
Tranquil garden set on many levels containing a superb collection of exotic plants. Beautifully positioned at the head of the Fal estuary with ferry links to Falmouth, Truro and St Mawes. Stunning panoramic views of the area and woodland walks beside the river. Year round garden colour. **Feock, nr Truro, Cornwall TR3 6QL** 01872 862090 4 D3

**Trengwainton**
Sheltered garden with exotic trees and shrubs, leading up to a terrace and summer houses with splendid views across Mount's Bay to The Lizard. Walled gardens contain unusual species. **Nr Penzance, Cornwall TR20 8RZ** 01736 363148 2 B2

**Trerice**
Elizabethan manor house containing fine fireplaces, interesting clocks and Stuart portraits. The highlight is the magnificent Great Chamber with its splendid barrel ceiling. The garden has unusual plants and an orchard full of old varieties of fruit trees. History of lawn-mower exhibition in hayloft. **Nr Newquay, Cornwall TR8 4PG** 01637 875404 4 B3

**Trethevy Quoit**
An ancient Neolithic burial chamber, consisting of five standing stones surmounted by a huge capstone. **1m NE of St Cleer near Darite off B3254.** 6 A1

**Trevarno Estate Gardens and the National Museum of Gardening**
RHS Members: free 1 Jan-8 Apr, 1 Nov-31 Dec. Open: all year, daily, 10.30am-5pm. Closed Christmas and Boxing Day. **Trevarno Manor, Helston, Cornwall TR13 0RU** 01326 574274 3 C4

**Trewithen Gardens**
RHS Members: free Jul-Sept. Open: Mar-Sept, daily (Sun only Apr, May), 10am-4.30pm. **Grampound Road, Truro, Cornwall TR2 4DD** 01726 883647 4 C4



## Cumbria

**Acorn Bank Garden and Watermill**
Surrounded by ancient oaks and high sandstone walls, this is the largest culinary and medical herb collection in the north of England. **Temple Sowerby, nr Penrith, Cumbria CA10 1SP** 017683 61467 165 C4

**Ambleside Roman Fort**
Remains of a 1st- and 2nd-century fort were built to guard the Roman road from Brougham to Ravenglass. **200 yds W of Waterhead car park, Ambleside.** 154 A2

**Beatrix Potter Gallery**
This exhibition of original sketches and watercolours painted by Beatrix Potter for her children's stories changes annually. The 17th-century building, the model of Tabitha Twitchit's shop, was once the office of Beatrix's husband and gives an interesting insight into an Edwardian law office. Close by is Hill Top where Beatrix lived and wrote many of her stories. **Main Street, Hawkshead, Cumbria LA22 ONS** 015394 36355 154 B2

**Bow Bridge**
Late mediaeval stone bridge across Mill Beck, carrying a route to nearby Furness Abbey. **½m N of Barrow-in-Furness, on minor road off A590 near Furness Abbey.** 153 C6

**Brougham Castle**
These impressive ruins on the banks of the River Eamont include an early 13th-century keep and later buildings. Its one-time owner Lady Anne Clifford restored the castle in the 17th century. **1½m SE of Penrith on minor road off A66.** 01768 862488 164 C3

**Brough Castle**
Dating from Roman times, the 12th-century keep replaced an earlier stronghold destroyed by the Scots in 1174. **8m SE of Appleby S of A66.** 165 D5

**Carlisle Castle**
Sitting proudly on the highest point above the River Eden, Carlisle Castle has guarded the western end of the Anglo-Scottish border for over nine centuries. It was first built after William II relieved Carlisle of two centuries of Scottish domination in 1092. Since then it has often been the scene of turbulent conflict between the two nations, being fought over fairly constantly until the union of the crowns in 1603. It then fell into Scottish hands again during the Civil War and the Jacobite Rising 100 years later. **In Carlisle, Cumbria** 01228 591922 175 C6

**Castlerigg Stone Circle**
Possibly one of the earliest Neolithic stone circles in Britain. **1½m E of Keswick.** 163 B5

**Clifton Hall**
The surviving tower block of a 15th-century manor house. **In Clifton next to Clifton Hall Farm, 2m S of Penrith on A6.** 164 C3

**Countess Pillar**
An unusual monument, bearing sundials and family crests, erected in 1656 by Lady Anne Clifford to commemorate her parting with her mother in 1616. **1 m SE of Brougham on A66** 164 C3

**Dalemain Historic House and Gardens**
RHS Members: free 20th Apr-16th May. Open: 28th Mar-21st Oct, Sun-Thur, 10.30am-5pm (4pm Sept and Oct). House open 11am-4pm (3pm Sept and Oct). **Dalemain, Penrith, Cumbria CA11 0BH** 01768 486450 164 C2

**Fell Foot Park**
Fell Foot is a Victorian garden with space for children to play, and leisure facilities in season. There are magnificent views of the Lakeland fells. The park has access to the lakeshore where there are boats for hire and fine picnic areas. **Newby Bridge, Ulverston, Cumbria LA12 8NN** 015395 31273 154 C2

**Furness Abbey**
In a peaceful valley, the red sandstone remains of a wealthy abbey founded in 1123 by Stephen, later King of England, are at the end of an ancient route from Bow Bridge. There is an exhibition and a museum contains fine stone carvings. **1½m N of Barrow-in-Furness, on minor road off A590.** 01229 823420 153 C6

▲ Carlisle Castle English Heritage Photo Library

**Gondola**
The grand Victorian elegance of Steam Yacht Gondola and her plush interior evoke memories of a bygone age. Gondola provides a relaxing passenger service on Coniston Water in the heart of the Lake District. **NT Gondola Bookings Office, The Hollens, Grasmere LA22 9QZ** ☎015394 41288 154 B2

**Hardknott Roman Fort**
One of the most dramatic Roman sites in Britain. The fort, built between AD120 and 138, controlled the road from Ravenglass to Ambleside. There are visible remains of granaries, the head-quarters building and the commandant's house, with a bath house and parade ground outside the fort. **9m NE of Ravenglass, at W end of Hardknott Pass.** 163 D5

**Hill Top**
Beatrix Potter wrote her famous children's books in this little 17th-century farmhouse. The original settings of several of the illustrations for her books can be found in the house. Timed entry system **Nr Sawrey, Ambleside, Cumbria LA22 OLF** ☎015394 36269 154 B2

**Holker Hall Garden**
RHS Members: free Apr-Oct (excluding special event days). Open: 28 Mar-31 Oct, Sun-Fri, 10am-6pm (last entry 4.30pm), closed Sat. **Cark-in-Cartmel, nr Grange-over-Sands, Cumbria LA11 7PL** ☎01539 558328 154 D2

**King Arthur's Round Table**
A prehistoric circular earthwork bounded by a ditch and an outer bank. **At Eamont Bridge, 1m S of Penrith.** 164 C3

**Lanercost Priory**
Augustinian priory founded c.1166. The church's nave contrasts with the ruined chancel, transepts and priory buildings. **Off minor road S of Lanercost, 2m NE of Brampton.** ☎01697 73030 176 C3

**Mayburgh Henge**
An impressive prehistoric circular henge, with banks up to 4½ metres (15 feet) high, enclosing a central area of one and a half acres containing a single large stone. **At Eamont Bridge, 1m S of Penrith off A6.** 164 C3

**Muncaster Castle**
RHS Members: free 1 Jul-7 Nov. Open: all year, daily, 10.30am-5pm. **Ravenglass, Cumbria CA18 1RQ** ☎01229 717614 153 A4

**Penrith Castle**
A 14th-century castle set in a park on the edge of the town. **Opposite Penrith railway station.** 164 C3

**Piel Castle**
The ruins of a 14th-century castle, accessible by boat from Roa Island. 144 A2

**Ravenglass Roman Bath House**
The walls of the bathhouse are among the most complete Roman remains in Britain. **¼m E of Ravenglass, off minor road leading to A595.** 153 A4

**Shap Abbey**
The striking tower and other remains of this Premonstratensian abbey stand in a remote and isolated location. **1½m W of Shap on bank of River Lowther.** 164 D3

**Sizergh Castle & Garden**
Mediaeval house built by the Strickland family. Exceptional series of oak-panelled rooms culminating in the Inlaid Chamber. Portraits, fine furniture, and ceramics are on display alongside the family photographs. The garden features include two lakes and a superb rock garden. **Nr Kendal, Cumbria LA8 8AE** ☎015395 60951 154 C3

**Stott Park Bobbin Mill**
Working mill, built in 1835. It is typical of the mills in the Lake District which supplied the spinning and weaving industry in Lancashire. **½m N of Finsthwaite near Newby Bridge.** ☎01539 531087 154 C2

**Townend**
Townend is one of the finest examples of vernacular domestic Lake District architecture. Its contents reflect a fascinating accumulation by a wealthy farming family gradually rising in society. In the unique little library are first editions of Milton and throughout the house an impressive range of carved oak furniture. **Troutbeck, Windermere, Cumbria LA23 1LB** ☎015394 32628 154 A3

**Wetheral Priory Gatehouse**
A Benedictine priory gatehouse, preserved after the Dissolution by serving as the vicarage for the parish church. **On minor road in Wetheral village, 6m E of Carlisle on B6263.** 176 D2

**Wordsworth House**
The birthplace of the poet William Wordsworth. This Georgian house is preserved in an 18th-century style, and costumed interpreters provide an insight into the daily life of the family and their servants. The house includes many personal effects. The garden referred to in 'The Prelude' has a terrace walk overlooking the River Derwent. **Main Street, Cockermouth, Cumbria CA13 9RX** ☎01900 824805 163 A4

## Darlington

*See also* County Durham

**Raby Castle Gardens**
RHS Members: free throughout open period (excluding special event days). Open: May and Sept, Wed and Sun, 11am-5.30pm, Jun-Aug, Sun-Fri, 11am-5.30pm and Bank Holidays (Sat to following Wed, 11am-5.30pm). **Staindrop, Darlington, County Durham DL2 3AH** ☎01833 660202 166 C4

## Derbyshire

**Arbor Low Stone Circle and Gib Hill Barrow**
A fine Neolithic monument, this 'Stonehenge of Derbyshire' comprises many slabs of limestone. **½m W of A515 2m S of Monyash.** ☎**01629 816200 (Site managed by Peak District National Park Authority)** 129 C6

**Bluebell Arboretum and Nursery**
RHS Members: free throughout open period. Open: Mar-Oct, Mon-Sat, 9am-5pm, Sun, 10.30am-4.30pm, Nov-Feb, Mon-Sat, 9am-4pm (closed 24th Dec-4th Jan and Easter Sunday). **Annwell Lane, Smisby, Derbyshire LE65 2TA** ☎01530 413700 114 D1

**Bolsover Castle**
An enchanting and romantic spectacle, situated high on a wooded hilltop dominating the surrounding landscape. Built on the site of a Norman castle, this is largely an early 17th-century mansion. Explore the 'Little Castle' or 'keep', a unique celebration of Jacobean romanticism with its elaborate fireplaces, panelling and wall paintings. There is also an impressive 17th-century indoor Riding House, built by the Duke of Newcastle, and ruins of great state apartments. **Off M1 at junction 29, 6m from Mansfield. In Bolsover, 6m E of Chesterfield on A632.** ☎01246 822844 131 B4

**Calke Abbey**
Vivid example of a great house in decline with extraordinary contents, historic park and restored garden. The house contains the spectacular natural history collection of the Harpur Crewe family and interiors that are essentially unchanged since the 1880s. **Ticknall, Derby, Derbyshire DE73 1LE** ☎01332 863822 114 C1

**Hardwick Hall**
A spectacular Elizabethan house built for the ambitious and formidable Bess of Hardwick – the richest woman in England after the queen. Elizabethan and later furniture, tapestries, needlework and embroidery on display. Walled courtyards enclose fine gardens, orchards and a herb garden. Historic parkland with rare breeds of sheep and cattle. **Doe Lea, Chesterfield, Derbyshire S44 5QJ** ☎01246 850430 131 C4

**Hardwick Old Hall**
This large ruined house, finished in 1591, still displays Bess of Hardwick's innovative planning and interesting decorative plasterwork. **9½m SE of Chesterfield, off A617, from J 29 of M1.** ☎01246 850431 131 C4

**Hob Hurst's House**
A square prehistoric burial mound with an earthwork ditch and outer bank. **From unclassified road off B5057, 9m W of Chesterfield.** 130 C2

**Kedleston Hall**
Built between 1759 and 1765 for the Curzon family. The house boasts the most complete sequence of Adam interiors in England, with the state rooms retaining their great collections of paintings and original furniture. Beautiful surrounding parkland with a series of lakes and cascades. **Derby, Derbyshire DE22 5JH** ☎01332 842191 113 A7

**Nine Ladies Stone Circle**
Once part of the burial site for 300-400 people, this Early Bronze Age circle is 15 metres (50 feet) across. **From unclassified road off A6, 5m SE of Bakewell.** 130 C2

**Peveril Castle**
There are breathtaking views of the Peak District from this castle, perched high above the pretty village of Castleton. **On S side of Castleton, 15m W of Sheffield on A6187.** ☎01433 620613 130 A1

**Sudbury Hall**
Late 17th-century house with superb interiors including woodcarving by Grinling Gibbons, plasterwork and murals by Louis Laguerre and a fine collection of portraits. The Great Staircase is one of the most elaborate of its kind. Several rooms featured in the BBC's Pride and Prejudice. **Sudbury, Derbyshire DE6 5HT** ☎01283 585305 113 B5

**Sutton Scarsdale Hall**
The dramatic hilltop shell of a great early 18th-century baroque mansion. **Between Chesterfield and Bolsover, 1½m S of Arkwright Town.** ☎01604 735400 131 C4

**Wingfield Manor**
Huge, ruined, country mansion built in mid-15th century. Mary Queen of Scots was imprisoned here in 1584 and 1585. The manor has been used as a film location for 'Peak Practice' and Zeffirelli's 'Jane Eyre'. **17m N of Derby, 11m S of Chesterfield on B5035 ½m S of South Wingfield. From M1 – Junc. 28, W on A38, A615 (Matlock Road) at Alfreton and turn onto B5035 after 1½m.** ☎01773 832060 130 D3

## Devon

**A la Ronde**
A unique 16-sided house built on the instructions of two spinster cousins, Jane and Mary Parminter, on their return from a grand tour of Europe. Completed c.1796, the house contains many collections brought back by the Parminters. **Summer Lane, Exmouth, Devon EX8 5BD** ☎01395 265514 13 C5

**Arlington Court**
A house full of collections, a stable block with horses and one of the finest carriage collections in the country. Walks through colourful gardens, grounds and woods, all set in miles of beautiful North Devon countryside. **Arlington, nr Barnstaple, Devon EX31 4LP** ☎01271 850296 25 A7

**Bayard's Cove Fort**
A small artillery fort built before 1534 to defend the harbour entrance. **In Dartmouth, on riverfront.** 8 B2

**Berry Pomeroy Castle**
**2½m E of Totnes off A385.** ☎01803 866618 8 A2

**Blackbury Camp**
An Iron Age hillfort, defended by a bank and ditch. **1½m SW of Southleigh off B3174 / A3052.** 14 B1

**Bowhill**
A mansion of considerable status built c.1500 by a member of the Holland family. **1½m SW of Exeter on B3212.** ☎0117 975 0700. 13 B4

**Bradley (tenanted)**
A small 15th-century medieval manor house with original decoration set in woodland and meadows. **Newton Abbot, Devon TQ12 6BN** ☎01626 354513 12 D3

**Buckland Abbey**
Buckland Abbey holds the secret to over 700 years of history. Medieval monks established a Cistercian monastery. Sir Richard Grenville converted the Abbey into a dwelling place. Later, Sir Francis Drake lived at Buckland during the turbulent period of the Armada. **Yelverton, Devon PL20 6EY** ☎01822 853607 6 A3

**Castle Drogo**
The last castle to be built in Britain, this 20th-century home designed by Sir Edwin Lutyens incorporates modern conveniences with a medieval atmosphere. The garden is colourful from spring to autumn. A huge, circular croquet lawn is available for visitors. **Drewsteignton, nr Exeter, Devon EX6 6PB** ☎01647 433306 12 B2

**Clovelly Court**
RHS Members: free Mar and Oct. Open: Mar-Oct, daily, 10am-4pm **Clovelly, nr Bideford, Devon EX39 5SZ** ☎01237 431200 24 C4

**Coleton Fishacre House and Garden**
This garden, developed by Rupert and Lady Dorothy D'Oyly Carte, lies in a stream-fed valley amid the spectacular scenery of this National Trust coast. The subtropical climate and sheltered location provides a superb setting for the large collection of tender and exotic plants, started in the 1920s. The house reflects the Arts and Crafts tradition but has refreshingly modern interiors. **Coleton, Kingswear, Dartmouth, Devon TQ6 0EQ** ☎01803 752466 8 B3

**Compton Castle**
A fortified manor house with curtain wall, built between the 14th and 16th centuries by the Gilbert family. It was the home of Sir Humphrey Gilbert (1539-83), coloniser of Newfoundland and half-brother of Sir Walter Raleigh: the family still lives here. **Marldon, Paignton, Devon TQ3 1TA** ☎01803 875740 8 A2

**Dartmouth Castle**
This brilliantly positioned defensive castle juts out into the narrow entrance to the Dart estuary, with the sea lapping at its foot. It was one of the first castles constructed with artillery in mind and has seen 450 years of fortification and preparation for war. **1m SE of Dartmouth off B3205, narrow approach road.** ☎01803 833588 8 B2

**Docton Mill and Gardens**
RHS Members: free Mar, Apr, Sept, Oct, and any Sat May-Aug. Open: Mar-Oct, daily, 10am-6pm **Lymebridge, Hartland, Devon, EX29 6EA** ☎01237 441369 24 C3

**Finch Foundry**
Fascinating 19th-century forge, powered by three water wheels. The forge produced sickles, scythes and shovels for both agriculture and mining, and is in the centre of the picturesque village of Sticklepath with countryside and river walks adjoining. **Sticklepath, Okehampton, Devon EX20 2NW** ☎01837 840046 12 B1

**Grimspound**
This late Bronze Age settlement displays the remains of 24 huts in an area of four acres enclosed by a stone wall. **6m SW of Moretonhampstead off B3212.** 12 C2

**Hound Tor Deserted Mediaeval Village**
Remains of three or four mediaeval farmsteads, first occupied in the Bronze Age. **1½m S of Manaton off The Ashburton Road. Park in Hound Tor car park, ½m walk.** 12 D2

**Killerton**
The house, built in 1778, is furnished as a comfortable family home. Upstairs, the Paulise de Bush collection of costumes from the 18th century to the present day is displayed in a series of period rooms. The spectacular hillside garden is beautiful throughout the year. **Broadclyst, Exeter, Devon EX5 3LE** ☎01392 881345 13 A4

**Kirkham House**
A well preserved, mediaeval stone house, much restored and repaired. **In Kirkham St, off Cecil Rd, Paignton.** ☎0117 975 0700. 8 A2

**Knightshayes Court**
Designed by William Burges and built in 1869, a rare example of the architect's High Victorian Gothic style. Of equal beauty is the glorious garden which owes much to the late Sir John and Lady Joyce Amory, who devoted themselves to its development. **Bolham, Tiverton, Devon EX16 7RQ** ☎01884 254665 27 D4

**Lundy Island**
An unspoilt island, with rocky headlands and fascinating animal and bird life, with no cars to disrupt the peace. The small island community includes a tavern, shop, castle and church. **Bristol Channel, Devon EX39 2LY** ☎**01237 431831 www.lundyisland.co.uk** 24 A2

**Lydford Castles and Saxon Town**
Standing above the gorge of the River Lyd, this 12th-century tower was notorious as a prison. The earthworks of the original Norman fort are to the south. **In Lydford off A386 8m S of Okehampton.** 11 C6

**Lydford Gorge**
The Gorge is perhaps best known for its spectacular White Lady Waterfall, a 100 foot cascade of water, and the Devil's Cauldron, a whirlpool of water where the River Lyd rushes through a series of potholes. **The Stables, Lydford Gorge, Lydford, nr Okehampton, Devon EX20 4BH** ☎01822 820320/820441 11 C6

**Merrivale Prehistoric Settlement**
Two rows of standing stones stretching up to 263 metres (864 feet) across the moors, together with the remains of an early Bronze Age village. **1m E of Merrivale.** 11 D6

**Okehampton Castle**
The ruins of the largest castle in Devon. There is a picnic area and there are also lovely woodland walks. **1m SW of Okehampton town centre.** ☎01837 52844 11 B6

**Overbecks**
A beautiful garden with many rare plants, shrubs and trees from around the world and with spectacular views over the Salcombe estuary. The elegant Edwardian house contains collections of local photographs and inventions by its former owner, Otto Overbeck. **Sharpitor, Salcombe, Devon TQ8 8LW** ☎01548 842893 7 D6

**RHS Rosemoor**
Rosemoor is a garden acclaimed by gardeners throughout the world. You do not have to be a keen gardener to appreciate the beauty and diversity of Rosemoor. Whatever the season, the garden is a unique and enchanting place that people return to time and again for ideas, inspiration or simply to enjoy a marvellous day out. The Spiral, Square and Foliage and Plantsman's Gardens demonstrate the many contrasting forms, textures and colours that can be found in garden plants, providing plenty of ideas and inspiration to take away with you. **Great Torrington, North Devon** ☎01805 624067 25 D6
**Open all year, except Christmas Day, from 10am. Closes at 6pm Apr to Sept and 5pm Oct to Mar. One mile south of Great Torrington on the A3124.**

**Royal Citadel**
A dramatic 17th-century fortress, with walls up to 21 metres (70 feet) high. **At E end of Plymouth Hoe.** ☎0117 975 0700 6 B3

**Saltram**
Magnificent Georgian house standing high above the River Plym, set in gardedns and landscaped parkland. The house features some of Robert Adam's finest rooms, original Chinese wallpapers and exceptional paintings. The predominantly 19th-century gardens contain an Orangery and several follies. **Plympton, Plymouth, Devon PL7 1UH** ☎01752 333500 7 B4

**Shute Barton (tenanted)**
One of the most important surviving non-fortified manor houses of the Middle Ages. Begun in 1380 and completed in the late 16th century, then partly demolished in the late 18th century, the house has battlemented turrets, late Gothic windows and a Tudor

gatehouse. Access to most parts of the interior by guided tour only. **Shute, nr Axminster, Devon EX13 7PT** 01297 34692 14 B2

### Tapeley Park
RHS Members: free 8 Jun-8 Jul. Open: 18 Mar-1 Nov, Sun-Fri, 10am-5pm. **Instow, nr Bideford, Devon EX39 4NT** 01271 342558 15 B5

### Totnes Castle
A superb motte and bailey castle, a fine example of Norman fortification. **In Totnes, on hill overlooking town.** 01803 864406 8 A2

### Upper Plym Valley
Scores of prehistoric and mediaeval sites covering six square miles of ancient landscape. **4m E of Yelverton.** 7 A4

### Watersmeet House
A fishing lodge, built c.1832 in a picturesque valley has been a tea-garden since 1901 and is the focal point for several beautiful walks. **Watersmeet Road, Lynmouth, Devon EX35 6NT** 01598 753348 26 A2

## Dorset

### Abbotsbury Abbey Remains
The remains of a cloister building of this Benedictine abbey, founded in 1044. **In Abbotsbury, off B3157, near churchyard.** 15 C5

### Abbotsbury Sub-Tropical Gardens
RHS Members: free Oct-Feb. Open: all year, daily, 10am-6pm (dusk in winter). Closed over Christmas and New Year. **Abbotsbury, Weymouth, DT3 4LA** 01305 871387 15 C5

### Brownsea Island
Brownsea Island is a beautiful wildlife haven in the middle of Poole Harbour, reached via a short crossing by boat. Lord Baden-Powell held his first scout camp on this island. **Poole, Dorset BH13 7EE** 01202 707744 17 C4

### Chiffchaffs
RHS Members: free throughout open period. Open: Mar-Oct, Wed and Thur, 2-5pm. Also open some Sundays. Please call the garden for further details. **Chaffeymoor, Bourton, Gillingham, Dorset, SP8 5BY** 01747 840841 30 B1

### Christchurch Castle and Norman House
Early 12th-century Norman keep, and Constable's house, built c.1160. **In Christchurch, near Priory.** 17 B5

### Clouds Hill
A tiny isolated brick and tile cottage, bought in 1925 by T.E. Lawrence (Lawrence of Arabia) as a retreat. The austere rooms inside are much as he left them and reflect his complex personality and close links to the Middle East. **Wareham, Dorset BH20 7NQ** 01929 405616 16 B2

### Corfe Castle
Majestic thousand year old castle rising above the Isle of Purbeck. Defended during the Civil War by Lady bankes, the castle fell to treachery from within and was substantially destroyed afterwards by the parliamentarians. Many fine Norman and early English features remain. **Wareham, Dorset BH20 5EZ** 01929 481294 16 C3

### Cranborne Manor Garden
RHS Members: free throughout open period. Open: Mar-Sept, Wed only, 9am-5pm. **Cranborne, Wimborne, Dorset, BH21 5PP** 01725 517248 31 D4

### Fiddleford Manor
Part of a mediaeval manor house, with a remarkable interior. **1m E of Sturminster Newton off A357.** 30 D2

### Hardy's Cottage
The small cob and thatch cottage where novelist and poet Thomas Hardy was born in 1840 and from where he would walk to school every day in Dorchester, three miles away. It was built by his great-grandfather and is little altered since. See also Max Gate. **Higher Bockhampton, nr Dorchester, Dorset DT2 8QJ** 01305 262366 16 B1

### Jordan Hill Roman Temple
Foundations of a Romano-Celtic temple enclosing an area of about 22 square metres (240 square feet). 15 C6

### Kingston Lacy
The 17th-century house houses a magnificent collection of Old Masters; the celebrated 'Spanish Room', panelled in gilded leatherwork and hung with Spanish paintings; and a ceiling shipped home from Venice. **Wimborne Minster, Dorset BH21 4EA** 01202 883402 16 A3

### Kingston Maurward Gardens
RHS Members: free throughout open period. Open: 5 Jan-19 Dec, daily, 10am-5.30pm. **Kingston Maurward, Dorchester, Dorset DT2 8PY** 01305 215003 15 B7

### Kingston Russell Stone Circle
A Bronze Age stone circle of 18 stones. **2m N of Abbotsbury, 1m along footpath off minor road to Hardy Monument.** 15 C5

### Knoll Gardens
RHS Members: free Apr-Oct. Open: all year (except over Christmas and New Year), daily, 10am-5pm (or dusk if earlier). **Hampreston, nr Wimborne, Dorset BH21 7ND** 01202 873931 17 A4

### Knowlton Church and Earthworks
The ruins of this Norman church stand in the middle of Neolithic earthworks, symbolizing the transition from pagan to Christian worship. **3m SW of Cranborne on B3078.** 31 D4

### Lulworth Castle
An early 17th-century romantic hunting lodge, Lulworth Castle became a fashionable country house set in beautiful parkland during the 18th century. Gutted by fire in 1929, the exterior is now being restored by English Heritage. **In east Lulworth off B3070, 3 miles NE of Lulworth Cove.** 0845 450 1051 16 C2

### Maiden Castle
This is the finest Iron Age hill fort in Britain. The earthworks are enormous, with a series of ramparts and complicated entrances. **2m S of Dorchester. Access off A354, N of bypass.** 15 C6

### Mapperton Gardens
RHS Members: free throughout open period. Open: Mar-Oct, daily, 2-6pm. **Nr Beaminster, Dorset DT8 3NR** 01308 862645 15 B5

### Max Gate (tenanted)
Designed by poet and novelist Thomas Hardy who lived here from 1885 until his death in 1928. The house contains several pieces of his furniture. **Alington Avenue, Dorchester, Dorset DT1 2AA** 01305 262538 15 C7

### The Nine Stones
Remains of a prehistoric circle of nine standing stones constructed about 4,000 years ago. **1½ m W of Winterbourne Abbas, on A35.** 15 B6

### Portland Castle
One of Henry VIII's best-preserved coastal forts, Portland Castle was in use up to the Second World War. There are superb views over the harbour, a gift shop and tearoom. **Overlooking Portland harbour, off A354.** 01305 820539 15 D6

### Sherborne Old Castle
The ruins of this early 12th-century castle are a testament to the 16 days Cromwell took to capture it during the Civil War. It was then abandoned. **½m E of Sherborne off B3145.** 01935 812730 29 D6

### St Catherine's Chapel
A small stone chapel, set on a hilltop, with an unusual roof and small turret used as a lighthouse. **½m S of Abbotsbury by pedestrian track from village off B3157.** 15 C5

### Winterbourne Poor Lot Barrows
Part of an extensive 4,000-year-old Bronze Age cemetery. **2m W of Winterbourne Abbas, S of junction of A35 with minor road to Compton Valence. Access via Wellbottom Lodge – 180 metres (200 yards) E along A35 from junction.** 15 B5

## County Durham
*See also* Darlington

### Auckland Castle Deer House
A charming building erected in 1760 in the park of the Bishops of Durham so that deer could shelter and find food. **In Auckland Park, Bishop Auckland, N of town centre on A68.** 167 B5

### Barnard Castle
The substantial remains of this large castle stand on a rugged escarpment overlooking the River Tees. You can still see parts of the 14th-century Great Hall and the cylindrical 12th-century tower. 01833 638212 166 D3

### Bowes Castle
Massive ruins of Henry II's tower keep, three storeys high and set within the earthworks of a Roman fort. **In Bowes Village just off A66, 4m W of Barnard Castle.** 166 D2

### Derwentcote Steel Furnace
Built in the 18th century, the earliest and most complete steel-making furnace to have survived. Closed in the 1870s, it has now been restored and opened to the public. **10m SW of Newcastle on A694 between Rowland's Gill and Hamsterley.** 01207 562573 178 D3

### Egglestone Abbey
Picturesque remains of a 12th-century abbey. **1m S of Barnard Castle on minor road off B6277.** 166 D3

### Finchale Priory
These beautiful priory ruins, dating from the 13th century, are in a wooded setting beside the River Wear. **3m NE of Durham, on minor road off A167.** 0191 386 3828 167 A5

## Essex

### Audley End House and Gardens
Just a short drive from Cambridge, Audley End House is set within a magnificent eighteenth century park designed by "Capability" Brown. The interior of the mansion remains unaltered since the early 1700s, reflecting past generations of style. Highlights of Audley End are the Great Hall, reception rooms designed by Robert Adam and the Victorian appearance of Lady Braybrooke's Sitting Room. Works of art by Canaletto and Van Goyen can be seen. The newly restored laundry and kitchen give an insight into life below stairs. Outside, the organic kitchen garden is being restored to how it was during its Victorian hey-day, with box-edged paths, trained fruit and a magnificent 170-foot long vine house. An artificial lake created with water from the River Cam runs through the estate and there is a restored 19th century parterre, Robert Adam's elegant Tea Bridge and the classical Temple of Concord. There are two tearooms and a gift shop. **1m W of Saffron Walden, Essex on B1383 (M11 exits 8, 9 Northbound only, and 10).** 86 D1

### The Beth Chatto Gardens
RHS Members: free Feb-Mar. Open: Mar-Oct, Mon-Sat, 9am-5pm, Nov-Feb, Mon-Fri, 9am-4pm. **Elmstead Market, Colchester, Essex CO7 7DB** 01206 822007 71 A4

### Bourne Mill
This unusual little Tudor building is an exotic hotch-potch of stones, some from Roman remains. Built as a fishing lodge in Tudor times, the mill changed from cloth milling to corn in about the 1850s. **Bourne Road, Colchester, Essex CO2 8RT** 01206 572422 71 A4

### Coggeshall Grange Barn
Originally part of the Cistercian monastery of Coggeshall, this is one of the oldest timber-framed barns in Europe, dating from around 1140. **Grange Hill, Coggeshall, Colchester, Essex CO6 1RE** 01376 562226 70 A2

### Glen Chantry
RHS Members: free throughout open period. Open: 2 Apr-25 Sept, Fri and Sat, 10am-4pm. **Ishams Chase, Wickham Bishops, nr Witham CM8 3LG** 01621 891342 70 B2

### Hadleigh Castle
The curtain wall and two towers of this 13th-century castle survive almost to their full height. **¾m S of A13 at Hadleigh.** 01760 755161 51 A5

### RHS Hyde Hall
Hyde Hall is set on a hilltop amongst rolling hills of arable crops. This 28-acre garden combines environmental and sustainable practices with the high standards of horticulture for which the RHS gardens are renowned. Highlights include the widely acclaimed Dry Garden; the inspirational colour-themed Herbaceous Border, demonstrating the art of ornamental horticulture; the commemorative Queen Mother's Garden and the model Garden for Wildlife. Hyde Hall's long association with roses is very much in evidence, with the many varieties thriving in the heavy Essex clay soil and high light levels. A comprehensive range of courses, demonstrations and walks is held throughout the year. Contact the garden direct to receive a copy of the Events Programme. **Rettendon, Chelmsford, Essex** 01245 400256 70 D1
**Open all year, except Christmas Day, from 10am. Closes at 6pm Apr to Sept and 5pm or dusk Oct to Mar. Seven miles southeast of Chelmsford and signposted from the A130.**

### Lexden Earthworks and Bluebottle Grove
Parts of a series of earthworks, once encompassing 12 square miles, which protected Iron Age Colchester and were subsequently added to by the conquering Romans. **2m W of Colchester off A604.** 01206 282931 **(Site managed by Colchester Borough Council)** 70 A3

▲ Batsford Arboretum, Gloucestershire John Bower/Alamy

### Mistley Towers
The remains of a church designed by Robert Adam and built in 1776. It was unusual in having towers at both the east and west ends. **On B1352, 1½m E of A137 at Lawford, 9m E of Colchester.** 01206 393884. **(Site managed by Mistley Thorn Residents Association)** 88 D2

### Paycocke's (tenanted)
This fine half-timbered merchant's house dating from c 1500 is evidence of the wealth generated by the wool trade in the 15th and 16th centuries. It contains unusually rich panelling, woodcarving and examples of the lace that Coggeshall was famous for. Attractive cottage garden. **West Street, Coggeshall, Colchester, Essex CO6 1NS** 01376 561305 70 A2

### Prior's Hall Barn
One of the finest surviving mediaeval barns in south-east England and representative of the aisled barns of north-west Essex. **In Widdington, on unclassified road 2m SE of Newport, off B1383.** 01799 522842 86 D1

### Rainham Hall (tenanted)
Conveniently close to the Thames, this elegant Georgian house was completed in 1729 for prosperous merchant, John Harle. Built in the domestic Dutch style, with dormers in the hipped roof, the interior has hardly changed. Bookings by written application to the tenant. **The Broadway, Rainham, Essex RM13 9YN** 01708 555360 50 A2

### St Botolph's Priory
The nave, with an impressive arcaded west end, one of the first Augustinian priories in England. **Colchester, near Colchester Town station.** 01206 282931 **(Site managed by Colchester Borough Council)** 70 A3

### St John's Abbey Gate
This fine abbey gatehouse, in East Anglian flintwork, survives from the Benedictine abbey of St John. **On S side of central Colchester.** 71 A4

### Tilbury Fort
The largest and best preserved example of 17th-century military engineering in England, commanding the Thames and showing the development of fortifications over the following 200 years. Exhibitions, the powder magazine and the bunker-like 'casemates' demonstrate how the fort protected London from seaborne attack. There's even a chance to fire an anti-aircraft gun! **½m E of Tilbury off A126.** 01375 858489 50 B3

### Waltham Abbey Gatehouse and Bridge
A late 14th-century abbey gatehouse, part of the cloister and 'Harold's Bridge'. **In Waltham Abbey off A112.** 01992 702200 68 C3

## Gloucestershire

### Batsford Arboretum
RHS Members: free Jan-Sept and Nov-Dec. Open: 1st Feb-mid Nov, 10am-5pm. Mid Nov-1st Feb, 10am-4pm. Closed Christmas Day. **Batsford Park, Moreton-in-Marsh, Gloucestershire GL56 9QB** 01386 701441 81 D4

### Belas Knap Long Barrow
Neolithic long barrow surrounded by a stone wall. The chamber tombs, where the remains of 31 people were found, have been opened up so that visitors can see inside. **2m S of Winchcombe, near Charlton Abbots, ½ mile on Cotswold Way.** 63 A6

### Blackfriars
A small Dominican priory churchwith original 13th-century scissor-braced roof. **In Ladybellegate Street off Southgate Street and Blackfriars Walk, Gloucester.** 0117 975 0700. 63 B4

### Chedworth Roman Villa
Remains of one of the largest Romano-British villas in the country. Set in a wooded Cotswold combe, over a mile of walls survive, fine mosaics, bathhouses and hypocausts can also be seen. The museum houses objects from the villa and an audio-visual presentation gives an insight into its history. **Yanworth, nr Cheltenham, Gloucestershire GL54 3LJ** 01242 890256 01242 890544 63 B6

### Cirencester Amphitheatre
A large well-preserved Roman amphitheatre. **Next to bypass W of town – access from town or along Chesterton Lane from W end of bypass onto Cotswold Ave. Park next to obelisk.** 63 B6

### Great Witcombe Roman Villa
The remains of a large villa. Built around three sides of a courtyard. **5m SE of Gloucester, off A417, ½m S of reservoir in Witcombe Park.** 63 B4

### Greyfriars
Remains of a late 15th-early 16th-century Franciscan friary church. **On Greyfriars Walk, behind Eastgate Market off Southgate St, Gloucester.** 63 B4

### Hailes Abbey
13th-century Cistercian abbey, set in wooded pastureland, with examples of high quality sculpture in the site museum. **2m NE of Winchcombe off B4632.** 01242 602398 80 D3

### Hidcote Manor Garden
An Arts and Crafts garden on a hilltop. A series of small gardens within the whole, separated by walls and hedges of different species. Hidcote is famous for rare shrubs, trees, herbaceous borders, 'old' roses and interesting plant species. **Hidcote Bartrim, nr Chipping Campden, Gloucestershire GL55 6LR** 01386 438333 81 C4

### Kingswood Abbey Gatehouse
The 16th-century gatehouse, with a richly carved mullioned window. **In Kingswood off B4060 1m SW of Wotton-under-Edge.** 62 D3

### Lodge Park
Rare 17th-century grandstand and Cotswold country estate. Situated on the picturesque Sherbourne Estate, Lodge Park was created in 1634 by John 'Crump' Dutton. The interior of the grandstand has been reconstructed to its original form. Much of the village if Sherbourne is owned by the Trust. **Sherborne, Cheltenham, Gloucestershire GL54 3PP** 01451 844130 64 B2

▲ Osborne House, Isle of Wight English Heritage Photographic Library

**Mill Dene Garden**
RHS Members: free Apr and Oct. Open: Apr-Oct, Tue-Fri and Bank Holidays, 10am-5.30pm, Sundays 2pm-5.30pm for June sculpture exhibitions. **Blockley, Moreton-in-Marsh, Gloucestershire GL56 9HU 01386 700457** 81 D4

**Notgrove Long Barrow**
A Neolithic burial mound with chambers for human remains opening from a stone-built central passage. **1½m NW of Notgrove on A436.** 64 A1

**Nympsfield Long Barrow**
A chambered Neolithic long barrow 30 metres (90 feet) in length. **1m NW of Nympsfield on B4066.** 63 C4

**Odda's Chapel**
A rare Anglo-Saxon chapel attached, unusually, to a half-timbered farmhouse. **In Deerhurst (off B4213) at Abbots Court SW of parish church.** 63 A4

**Offa's Dyke**
Three mile section of the great earthwork built by Offa, King of Mercia 757-96, from the Severn estuary to the Welsh coast as a defensive boundary to his kingdom. **3m NE of Chepstow off B4228. Access via Forestry Commission Tidenham car park. 1m walk (way marked) down to Devil's Pulpit on Offa's Dyke. (Access suitable only for those wearing proper walking shoes; not suitable for very young, old or infirm).** 62 C1

**Over Bridge**
A single-arch masonry bridge spanning the River Severn, built by Thomas Telford 1825-27. **1m NW of Gloucester city centre at junction of A40 (Ross) and A419 (Ledbury).** 63 B4

**Snowshill Manor**
Snowshill Manor is no ordinary Cotswold manor house but the setting for Charles Paget Wade's collection of craftsmanship. You will see English, European and Oriental furniture, musical instruments, clocks, toys and other collections. The delightful garden is now organically managed. **Snowshill, nr Broadway, Gloucestershire WR12 7JU 01386 852410** 80 D3

**St Briavel's Castle**
A splendid 12th-century castle now used as a youth hostel. **In St Briavel's, 7m NE of Chepstow off B4228. 01594 530272** 62 C1

**St Mary's Church**
A Norman church with superb wall paintings from the 12th-14th centuries. **1m N of Kempley off B4024, 6m NE of Ross-on-Wye.** 79 D4

**Uley Long Barrow (Hetty Pegler's Tump)**
Dating from around 3000 BC, this 55 metre- (180 foot-) long Neolithic chambered burial mound is unusual in that its mound is still intact. **3½m NE of Dursley on B4066.** 62 D3

**Westbury Court Garden**
A formal water garden with canals and yew hedges, laid out between 1696 and 1705. It is the earliest of its kind remaining in England, restored in 1971 and planted with species dating from pre-1700, including apple, pear and plum trees. **Westbury-on-Severn, Gloucestershire GL14 1PD 01452 760461** 62 B3

**Westonbirt The National Arboretum**
RHS Members: throughout open period. Open: all year, daily, 10am-8pm (dusk if earlier). **Westonbirt, Tetbury, Gloucestershire GL8 8QS 01666 880220** 44 A2

**Woodchester Park**
This secret wooded valley, formerly an 18th-century park with five lakes, was first opened to the public in 1996. There are waymarked trails (steep and strenuous in places) through delightful scenery with spectacular views. **The Ebworth Centre, Ebworth Estate, The Camp, Stroud, Gloucestershire GL6 7ES 01452 814213** 63 C4

## Hampshire

**Bishop's Waltham Palace**
This mediaeval seat of the Bishops of Winchester once stood in an enormous park. Wooded grounds still surround the mainly 12th- and 14th-century remains, including the Great Hall and three-storey tower, as well as the moat which once enclosed the palace. **In Bishop's Waltham 5m from junction 8 of M27. 01489 892460** 32 D4

**Calshot Castle**
From the 20th century, the fort has been part of a Royal Navy and RAF base. Henry VIII built this coastal fort to command the sea passage to Southampton. **On spit 2m SE of Fawley off B3053. 02380 892023** 18 A3

**Flowerdown Barrows**
Round barrows of a Bronze Age burial site which were once part of a larger group. **In Littleton, 2½m NW of Winchester off A272.** 32 B3

**Fort Brockhurst**
This was a new type of fort, built in the 19th century to protect Portsmouth with formidable fire-power. Largely unaltered, the parade ground, gun ramps and moated keep can all be viewed. Opens occasionally for pre-booked guided tours. **Off A32, in Gunner's Way, Elson, on N side of Gosport. 02392 378291** 19 A4

**Fort Cumberland**
Constructed in the shape of a wide pentagon by the Duke of Cumberland in 1746 and perhaps the most impressive piece of 18th-century defensive architecture remaining in England. Opens occasionally for pre-booked guided tours. Please telephone for details. **In the Eastney district of Portsmouth on the estuary approach via Henderson Road, a turning off Eastney Road, or from the Esplanade. 02392 378291** 19 B5

**Furzey Gardens**
RHS Members: free Mar-Oct. Open: all year, daily (except Christmas and Boxing Day), 10am-5pm (dusk in winter). **School Lane, Minstead, nr Lyndhurst, Hampshire SO43 7GL 02380 812464** 32 D1

**Hinton Ampner Garden**
Set in superb countryside, the garden combines formal design and informal planting, producing delightful walks with many unexpected vistas. The house contains fine Regency furniture, 17th-century Italian pictures and porcelain. **Bramdean, nr Alresford, Hampshire SO24 0LA 01962 771305** 33 C4

**Hurst Castle**
This was one of the most sophisticated fortresses built by Henry VIII, and later strengthened in the 19th and 20th centuries, to command the narrow entrance to the Solent. There are two exhibitions in the castle, and two huge 38-ton guns from the fort's armaments. **On Pebble Spit S of Keyhaven. Best approached by ferry from Keyhaven, telephone 01590 642500 (June-Sept, 9am-2pm) for ferry details. 01590 642344** 18 C2

**King James's and Landport Gates**
These gates were once part of the 17th-century defences of Portsmouth **King James's Gate: forms entrance to United Services Recreation Ground (officers) on Barnaby Road; Landport Gate: as above, men's entrance on St George's Rd.** 19 B5

**Mediaeval Merchant's House**
Life in the Middle Ages is vividly evoked by the brightly painted cabinets and colourful wall hangings authentically re-created for this 13th-century town house, originally built as shop and home for a prosperous wine merchant. **58 French Street, Southampton, ¼m S of city centre just off Castle Way (between High St and Bugle St). 02380 221503** 32 D3

**Mottisfont Abbey Garden, House and Estate**
The setting of this 12th-century Augustinian Priory is one of great beauty and tranquillity. The grounds contain a magnificent collection of huge trees. The Priory became a house after the Dissolution of the Monasteries in the 16th century. The National Collection of Old-Fashioned Roses is housed in the walled garden. **Mottisfont, nr Romsey, Hampshire SO51 0LP 01794 340757** 32 C2

**Netley Abbey**
A 13th-century Cistercian abbey converted in Tudor times for use as a house. **In Netley, 4m SE of Southampton, facing Southampton Water. 02392 581059** 18 A3

**Northington Grange**
Magnificent neoclassical country house, built at the beginning of the 18th century. **4m N of New Alresford off B3046. 01424 775705** 33 B4

**Portchester Castle**
A residence for kings and a rallying point for troops, this grand castle has a history stretching back nearly 2,000 years. There are Roman walls, the most complete in Europe, substantial remains of the castle and an exhibition telling the story of Portchester. **On S side of Portchester off A27, Junction 11 on M27. 02392 378291** 19 A5

**Royal Garrison Church**
Originally a hospice for pilgrims, this 16th-century chapel became the Garrison Church after the Dissolution. **On Grand Parade S of Portsmouth High St. 02392 378291** 19 B5

**Sandham Memorial Chapel**
This red-brick chapel was built in the 1920s for the artist Stanley Spencer to fill with murals of his experiences in the First World War. Inspired by Giotto's Arena Chapel in Padua, this impressive project took five years to complete and is arguably Spencer's finest achievement. The chapel is set amidst lawns and orchards with views across Watership Down. **Burghclere, nr Newbury, Hampshire RG20 9JT 01635 278394** 46 C2

**Silchester Roman City Walls and Amphitheatre**
The best preserved Roman town walls in Britain, almost one-and-a-half miles around, with an impressive, recently restored amphitheatre. **On minor road 1m E of Silchester.** 47 C4

**Titchfield Abbey**
Remains of a 13th-century abbey overshadowed by a grand Tudor gatehouse. **½m N of Titchfield off A27. 01329 842133** 18 A4

**The Vyne**
16th-century house and estate reflecting changing styles and tastes over 500 years. The house acquired a portico in the mid-17th century (the first of its kind in England) and contains a fasinating Tudor chapel, Palladian staircase and a wealth of fine furniture. Attractive grounds and woodland walks. **Sherborne St John, Basingstoke, Hampshire RG24 9HL 01256 881337** 47 D4

**Wolvesey Castle (Old Bishop's Palace)**
One of the greatest mediaeval buildings in England, the Palace was the chief residence of the Bishops of Winchester. Its extensive ruins still reflect their importance and wealth. The last great occasion was on 25th July, 1554 when Queen Mary and Philip of Spain held their wedding breakfast in the East Hall. **¼m SE of Winchester Cathedral, next to the Bishop's Palace; access from College St. 01424 775705** 32 C3

## Herefordshire

**Arthur's Stone**
Impressive prehistoric burial chamber formed of large blocks of stone. **7m E of Hay-on-Wye off B4348 near Dorstone.** 77 C7

**Berrington Hall**
This elegant Henry Holland house was built in the late 18th century and is set in parkland designed by 'Capability' Brown. The delicate beautifully decorated interior holds great collections of furniture and paintings as well as a nursery, Victorian laundry and Georgian dairy. Attractive walled garden. **Nr Leominster, Herefordshire HR6 0DW 01568 615721** 78 A3

**Croft Castle**
Croft Castle is an imposing country house containing fine Georgian interiors and furniture. There are restored walled gardens and a park with a magnificent avenue of ancient Spanish chestnuts and panoramas across the once turbulent border country. **Nr Leominster, Herefordshire HR6 9PW 01568 780246** 78 A2

**Edvin Loach Old Church**
Peaceful and isolated 11th-century church remains. **4m N of Bromyard on unclassified road off B4203.** 79 B4

**Goodrich Castle**
Remarkably complete, magnificent red sandstone castle with 12th-century keep and extensive remains from the 13th and 14th centuries. **5m S of Ross-on-Wye off A40. 01600 890538** 62 A1

**Longtown Castle**
An unusual cylindrical keep built c.1200, with walls 4½ metres (15 feet) thick. There are magnificent views to the Black Mountains. **4m WSW of Abbey Dore.** 61 A5

**Mortimer's Cross Water Mill**
Intriguing 18th-century mill, still in working order, showing the process of corn milling. **7m NW of Leominster on B4362. 0121 625 6820** 78 A2

**Rotherwas Chapel**
This Roman Catholic chapel dates from the 14th and 16th centuries and features an interesting mid-Victorian side chapel and High Altar. **1½m SE of Hereford on B4399.** 78 D3

**The Weir**
Delightful riverside garden particularly spectacular in early spring, with fine views over the River Wye and Black Mountains. **Swainshill, nr Hereford, Herefordshire HR4 7QF Regional Office 01981 590509** 78 C2

**Wigmore Castle**
Fortified since the 1060s, the present ruins date from the 13th and 14th centuries. The castle was dismantled during the Civil War, and remains very much as it was left then. **11m NW of Leominster, 14m SW of Ludlow off W side of A4110.** 78 A2

## Hertfordshire

**Ashridge Estate**
This magnificent estate runs along the main ridge of the Chiltern Hills. There are woodlands, commons and chalk downland, supporting a rich variety of wildlife and offering walks through outstanding scenery. The Visitor Centre comprises a shop, tea shop and facilities. **Ringshall, Berkhamsted, Hertfordshire HP4 1LX 01442 851227** 67 B4

**Berkhamsted Castle**
The extensive remains of a large 11th-century motte and bailey castle. **By Berkhamsted station. 01442 871737** 67 C4

**Old Gorhambury House**
The remains of this Elizabethan mansion illustrate the impact of the Renaissance on English architecture. **¼m W of Gorhambury House and accessible only through private drive from A4147 at St Albans (2m).** 67 C6

**Roman Wall**
**On S side of St Albans, ½m from centre off A4147.** 67 C6

**Shaw's Corner**
An early 20th-century house, and the home of George Bernard Shaw from 1906 until his death in 1950. The rooms remain much as he left them with many literary and personal effects on show. Shaw's writing hut is hidden at the bottom of the garden, which has richly planted borders and views over the Hertfordshire countryside. **Ayot St Lawrence, nr Welwyn, Hertfordshire AL6 9BX 01438 820307** 68 B1

## Isle of Wight

**Appuldurcombe House**
The fine 18th-century baroque-style house retains its elegant east front and stands in its own ornamental grounds, designed by 'Capability' Brown. **½ m W of Wroxall off B3327. 01983 852484** 18 C4

**Bembridge Windmill**
Dating from around 1700, Bembridge is the only windmill to survive on the island. Much of the wooden machinery can still be seen. **High Street, Bembridge, Isle of Wight PO35 5SQ 01983 873945** 19 C5

**Carisbrooke Castle**
From time immemorial, whosoever controlled Carisbrooke controlled the Isle of Wight. The castle sits at the very heart of the island, and has been a fixture since its foundation as a Saxon camp during the 8th century. **1¼m SW of Newport, Isle of Wight. 01983 522107** 18 C3

**The Needles Old Battery**
Victorian gun battery perched on the tip of the Isle of Wight. The Battery retains two original gun barrels and the laboratory and position-finding cells have been restored. A 60 yard tunnel leads to dramatic views of The Needles rocks and the Dorset coastline. Exhibitions also highlight the intriguing past as a rocket testing site. **West Highdown, Totland, Isle of Wight PO39 0JH 01983 754772** 18 C2

**Old Town Hall, Newtown**
17th-century town hall set in the once small, now tranquil village of Newtown, once the setting for often turbulent elections. An exhibition depicts the exploits of 'Ferguson's Gang', an anonymous group of Trust benefactors in the 1920s and 1930s. **Contact Custodian, Ken Cottage, Upper Lane, Brighstone, Isle of Wight PO30 4AT 01983 531785** 18 B3

**Osborne House**
Osborne House was 'a place of one's own, quiet and retired', for Queen Victoria and Prince Albert. They found tranquillity on the Isle of Wight, far from the formality of court life at Buckingham Palace and Windsor Castle. The house they built was set among terraced gardens and filled with treasured mementoes. Victoria died at Osborne in 1901, still mourning her beloved Albert, who had died in middle age. Visit the newly refurbished Durbar Wing with its exquisite collection of Indian items. **1m SE of East Cowes, Isle of Wight. 01983 200022** 18 B4

**St Catherine's Oratory**
Affectionately known as the Pepperpot, this 14th-century lighthouse stands on the highest point of the island. **¾m NW of Niton.** 18 D3

**Yarmouth Castle**
This last addition to Henry VIII's coastal defences was completed in 1547. It houses exhibitions of paintings of the Isle of Wight and photographs of old Yarmouth. **In Yarmouth adjacent to car ferry terminal. 01983 760678** 18 C2

## Isles of Scilly

**Bant's Carn Burial Chamber and Halangy Down Ancient Village**
In a wonderful scenic location lies this Bronze Age burial mound with entrance passage and chamber. **1m N of Hugh Town.** 2 E4

**Cromwell's Castle**
This 17th-century round tower was built to command the haven of New Grimsby. **On shoreline, ¾m NW of New Grimsby.** 2 E3

**Garrison Walls**
Take a pleasant walk along the ramparts of these well-preserved walls and earthworks, built as part of the island's defences. **Around the headland W of Hugh Town.** 2 F3

**Harry's Walls**
An uncompleted 16th-century fort. **¼m NE of Hugh Town.** 2 E4

**Innisidgen Lower and Upper Burial Chambers**
Two Bronze Age cairns, about 30 metres apart. **1¾m NE of Hugh Town.** 2 E4

**King Charles's Castle**
At the end of a bracing coastal walk to the northern end of Tresco you will find the remains of this castle built for coastal defence. **¾ m NW of New Grimsby.** 2 E3

**Old Blockhouse**
The remains of a small 16th-century gun tower. **On Blockhouse Point, at S end of Old Grimsby harbour, near New Grimsby.** 2 E3

**Porth Hellick Down Burial Chamber**
Probably the best-preserved Bronze Age burial mound on the Islands, with an entrance passage and chamber. **1½ m E of Hugh Town.** 2 E4

## Kent

**Bedgebury**
RHS Members: free throughout open period. Open: all year, daily, 10am-5pm **The National**

Pinetum, Goudhurst, Cranbrook, Kent TN17 2SL 01580 211781 37 C5

**Broadview Gardens**
RHS Members: free Sept, Oct. Open Apr-Oct, daily, 10am-5pm (4pm Sun). **Hadlow, Tonbridge Kent, TN11 0AL 01732 853211** 36 A4

**Brogdale Horticultural Trust**
RHS Members: free Easter-Nov except festivals. Open: Mar-Nov, daily, 10am-5pm, Nov-Mar, daily, 10am-4pm. **Brogdale Road, Faversham, Kent ME13 8XZ 01795 535286/535462** 52 C2

**Chartwell**
The home of Sir Winston Churchill from 1924 until the end of his life. The rooms have been left as they were in his lifetime. Two rooms are given over to a museum for his many gifts and uniforms. Terrace gardens descend towards the lake; the garden studio containing many of Sir Winston's paintings is also open. **Mapleton Road, Westerham, Kent TN16 1PS 01732 868381** 50 D1

**Conduit House**
The Conduit House is the monastic waterworks which supplied nearby St Augustine's Abbey. **Approximately 5-10 minutes' walk from St Augustine's Abbey. Situated within the new St Martin's Heights housing estate, St Martin's Avenue, Canterbury.** 52 D3

**Deal Castle**
Crouching low and menacing, the huge, rounded bastions of this austere fort, built by Henry VIII, once carried 119 guns. It is a fascinating castle to explore, with long, dark passages, battlements, and a huge basement with an exhibition on England's coastal defences. **SW of Deal town centre. 01304 372762** 53 D5

**Dover Castle**
Explore secret wartime tunnels deep beneath the White Cliffs. See the cramped conditions of the 1940s underground military hospital, telecommunications station and barracks. In the Keep, a Henry VIII exhibition recreates preparations for a visit by the Tudor king in 1539 and a Siege of 1216 exhibition shows Dover Castle under siege from the French. Other attractions include the royal chapel and Princess of Wales' Royal Regiment Museum. Restaurant, coffee shop and tea bar, gift shops and a free land train. **On E side of Dover. 01304 211067.** 39 A5

**The Home of Charles Darwin (Down House)**
Charles Darwin was perhaps the most influential scientist of the 19th century. It was from his study at Down House that he worked on the scientific theories that first scandalized and then revolutionized the Victorian world, culminating in the publication of the most significant book of the century, 'On the Origin of Species by means of Natural Selection', in 1859. His home for forty years, Down House was the centre of his intellectual world and even now his study remains full of his notebooks and journals, and mementoes. The house has been restored so that you can visit Darwin's much-loved family home in the tranquil Kent countryside. **In Luxted Road, Downe, Kent, off A21 near Biggin Hill. 01689 859119** 50 C1

**Dymchurch Martello Tower**
One of many artillery towers which formed part of a chain of strongholds intended to resist invasion by Napoleon. **In Dymchurch. Access from High Street, not from seafront. 01304 211067** 38 C3

**Emmetts Garden**
A hillside garden originally laid out around the turn of 19th century, with a fine collection of trees and shrubs, noted for its outlook with good views of the Weald of Kent. **Ide Hill, Sevenoaks, Kent TN14 6AY 01732 751509** 50 D1

**Eynsford Castle**
One of the first stone castles built by the Normans. **In Eynsford off A225.** 50 C2

**Faversham: Stone Chapel**
The remains of a small mediaeval church incorporating part of a 4th-century Romano-British pagan mausoleum. **1¼m W of Faversham on A2.** 52 C1

**Goodnestone Park Gardens**
RHS Members: free Apr, May, Sept, excluding special events. Open: 31 Mar-22 Sept, Mon, Wed, Thur, Fri, 11am-5pm. Sun 12-6pm. **Goodnestone Park, nr Wingham, Canterbury, Kent CT3 1PL 01304 840107** 53 D4

**Horne's Place Chapel**
This 14th-century domestic chapel was once attached to the manor house. The house and chapel are privately owned. **1½m N of Appledore. 01304 211067.** 38 B1

**Ightham Mote**
Ightham Mote is a beautiful moated manor house set in a wooded valley. Ranged around the cobbled centre courtyard are the old gatehouse, Great Hall, chapel and the Jacobean drawing-room. Lovely garden and woodland walks. **Ivy Hatch, Sevenoaks, Kent TN15 0NT 01732 810378** 36 A3

**Kit's Coty House and Little Kit's Coty House**
Ruins of two prehistoric burial chambers. **W of A229 2m N of Maidstone.** 51 C4

**Knights Templar Church**
Standing across the valley from Dover Castle are the foundations of a small circular 12th-century church. **On the Western Heights above Dover.** 39 A5

**Knole**
One of the great treasure houses of England with fascinating historic links to kings, queens and nobility. Thirteen superb staterooms are laid out much as they would have been. Rare furniture, tapestries and works by Gainsborough, Van Dyck and Reynolds are on display. **Sevenoaks, Kent TN15 0RP 01732 450608/462100** 36 A3

**Lullingstone Roman Villa**
The villa, discovered in 1939, was one of the most exciting finds of the century. Dating from c.100 AD, but extended during 300 years of Roman occupation, much is visible today. **½m SW of Eynsford off A225 off junction 3 of M25. Follow A20 towards Brands Hatch. 01322 863467** 50 C2

**Maison Dieu**
Part of a mediaeval complex of Royal lodge, almshouses and hospital, it is much as it was 400 years ago. It contains an exhibition about Ospringe in Roman times. **In Ospringe on A2, ½m W of Faversham. 01795 534542** 52 C1

**Milton Chantry**
A small 14th-century building which housed the chapel of a leper hospital and a family chantry. It later became a tavern and, in 1780, part of a fort. **In New Tavern Fort Gardens E of central Gravesend off A226. 01474 321520** 50 B3

**Old Soar Manor**
The remains of a late 13th-century knight's manor house, comprising the two-storey solar and chapel. There is an exhibition to visit. **1m E of Plaxtol. 01732 810378** 36 A4

**Penshurst Place and Gardens**
RHS Members: Apr, Sept, Oct. Open: 6-27 Mar, weekends, 10.30am-6pm, 28 Mar-31 Oct, daily, 10.30am-6pm. **Penshurst, Nr Tonbridge, Kent TN11 8DG 01892 870307** 36 B3

**Quebec House**
One of Britain's greatest military heroes, James Wolfe, spent his childhood here. The 17th-century house is full of mementoes of his victory at Quebec when he defeated the French by scaling the Heights of Abraham above the town. **Westerham, Kent TN16 1TD Chartwell Office 01732 868381** 36 A2

**Reculver Towers and Roman Fort**
Standing in a country park, a 12th-century landmark of twin towers and the walls of a Roman fort. **At Reculver 3m E of Herne Bay. 01227 740676** 53 C4

**Red House**
Designed in the late 1850s by Philip Webb for William Morris, one of his co-founders in the Arts and Crafts Movement, Red House is a landmark in the history of domestic architecture. The gardens inspired many of Morris's wallpaper patterns. **Red House Lane, Bexleyheath, Kent DA6 8JF 01494 559799** 50 B1

**Richborough Roman Amphitheatre**
Ditch associated with the nearby 3rd-century castle. **1¼m N of Sandwich off A257, Junction 7 of M2, onto A2. 01304 612013 for details.** 53 D5

**Richborough Roman Fort**
This fort and township date back to the Roman landing in AD 43. The fortified walls and the massive foundations of a triumphal arch which stood 25 m (80 ft) high still survive. **1½m N of Sandwich off A257. 01304 612013** 53 C5

**Rochester Castle**
Built on the Roman city wall, this Norman bishop's castle was a vital royal stronghold. **By Rochester Bridge (A2), Junction 1 of M2 and Junction 2 of M25. 01634 402276** 51 C4

**St Augustine's Abbey**
This impressive abbey is situated outside the city walls and is sometimes missed by visitors. At the abbey, you can also enjoy the museum and free interactive audio tour. **In Longport ¼m E of Cathedral Close. 01227 767345** 52 D3

**St Augustine's Cross**
19th-century cross, in Celtic design, marking the traditional site of St Augustine's landing in 597. **2m E of Minster off B29048.** 53 C5

**St John's Commandery**
A mediaeval chapel, converted into a farmhouse in the 16th century. **2m NE of Densole off A260. 01304 211067 for details.** 39 A4

**St John's Jerusalem (tenanted)**
A large garden, moated by the River Darent. The house is the former chapel of a Knight's Hospitallers' Commandery, since converted into a private residence. Access to chapel and garden only. **Sutton-at-Hone, Dartford, Kent DA4 9HQ Ightham Mote 01732 810378** 50 B2

**St Leonard's Tower**
An early and particularly fine example of a Norman tower keep, built c.1080 by Gundulf, Bishop of Rochester. **On unclassified road W of A228. 01732 870872** 37 A4

**Scotney Castle Garden and Estate**
Often described as the most romantic garden in England, the ruins of the small 14th-century castle are reflected in its moat, forming the backdrop to a garden of breathtaking beauty and considerable importance to the garden-historian. **Lamberhurst, Tunbridge Wells, Kent TN3 8JN 01892 891081** 37 C4

**Sissinghurst Castle Garden**
Of international acclaim, this connoisseur's garden was created by the late Vita Sackville-West and her husband, Sir Harold Nicolson. A series of small enclosed romantic gardens or 'outdoor rooms' are the spring garden, orchard, white garden and herb garden. Also the study where Vita Sackville-West worked, and the Long Library. **Sissinghurst, nr Cranbrook, Kent TN17 2AB 01580 710701** 37 C6

**Smallhythe Place**
Legendary actress Ellen Terry lived here for nearly 30 years, from 1899 until her death in 1928. The house is a museum of the great actress's career and includes many personal and theatrical mementoes from the greats of Victorian drama. Beautiful cottage grounds house the Barn Theatre. **Smallhythe, Tenterden, Kent TN30 7NG 01580 762334** 37 D6

**Stoneacre (tenanted)**
A half-timbered mainly late 15th-century yeoman's house, with great hall and crownpost, and restored cottage-style garden. **Otham, Maidstone, Kent ME15 8RS 01622 862157** 37 A6

**Stone Chapel**
See Faversham: Stone Chapel. 52 C1

**Sutton Valence Castle**
The ruins of a 12th-century stone keep. **5m SE of Maidstone in Sutton Valence village on A274.** 37 B6

**Temple Manor**
The 13th-century manor house of the Knights Templar. **In Strood (Rochester) off A228.** 51 B4

**Upnor Castle**
Well preserved 17th-century castle, built to protect Queen Elizabeth I's warships. **At Upnor, on unclassified road off A228. 01634 718742** 51 B4

**Walmer Castle and Gardens**
Walmer Castle is the official residence of the Lord Warden of the Cinque Ports, an ancient title previously held by Her Majesty, Queen Elizabeth the Queen Mother. Created for her is a garden featuring topiary, a 95-foot pond, an E-shaped box parterre and mixed borders. Other garden highlights are a working kitchen garden, herbaceous border, croquet lawn and woodland walk. Tea room and shop. **On coast S of Walmer, Kent, on A258. Junction 13 off M20 or from M2 to Deal. 01304 364288** 53 D5

▲ **Down House, the home of Charles Darwin, Kent** English Heritage Photo Library

**Western Heights**
Parts of moat of 19th-century fort built to fend off a French attack. **Above Dover town on W side of Harbour. 01304 211067** 39 A5

**The White Cliffs of Dover**
The gateway to Britain, the White Cliffs of Dover are internationally famous. A Gateway visitor centre has spectacular views and introduces the visitor to five miles of coast and countryside. Visitors can also tour South Foreland Lighthouse, a distinctive landmark used by Marconi for his first ship-to-shore radio experiments. **Langdon Cliffs, Dover, Kent CT16 1HJ 01304 202756** 39 A5

**Yalding Organic Gardens**
RHS Members: free throughout open period. Open: May-Sept, Wed-Sun, 10am-5pm, Apr and Oct, weekends and Bank Holidays, 10am-5pm. **Benover Road, Yalding, Maidstone, Kent ME18 6EX 01622 814650** 37 B5

## Lancashire

**Gawthorpe Hall**
Elizabethan house set in tranquil grounds in the heart of urban Lancashire, resembles the great Harwick Hall. The Long Gallery is hung with portraits of society figures from the 17th century. International collection of needlework, lace and costume assembled by Rachel Kay-Shuttleworth. **Padiham, nr Burnley, Lancashire BB12 8UA 01282 771004** 146 D2

**Goodshaw Chapel**
A restored 18th-century Baptist chapel with all its furnishings complete. **In Crawshawbooth, 2m N of Rawtenstall, in Goodshaw Avenue off A682. 0161 242 1400 for details.** 137 A7

**Rufford Old Hall**
Evidence suggests that William Shakespeare performed here for owner Sir Thomas Hesketh in the Great Hall of this, one of the finest 16th-century buildings in Lancashire. The house contains fine collections of 16th- and 17th-century oak furniture, arms, armour and tapestries. **Rufford, nr Ormskirk, Lancashire L40 1SG 01704 821254** 136 B3

**Warton Old Rectory**
Rare mediaeval stone house with remains of the hall, chambers and domestic offices. **At Warton, 1m N of Carnforth on minor road off A6.** 154 D3

**Whalley Abbey Gatehouse**
The outer gatehouse of the nearby Cistercian abbey. There was originally a chapel on the first floor. **In Whalley, 6m NE of Blackburn on minor road off A59.** 146 D1

## Leicestershire

**Ashby de la Zouch Castle**
The impressive ruins of this late-mediaeval castle are dominated by a magnificent 24-metre (80-foot) high tower, split in two during the Civil War, from which there are panoramic views of the surrounding countryside. **In Ashby de la Zouch, 12m S of Derby on A50. 01530 413343** 114 D1

**Jewry Wall, Leicester**
One of the largest surviving lengths of Roman wall in the country. Over 9 metres (30 ft) high, it formed one side of the civic baths' exercise hall. **In St Nicholas St Leicester, W of Church of St Nicholas. 0116 225 4971 (Site managed by Jewry Wall Museum)** 98 A2

**Staunton Harold Church**
Built by Sir Robert Shirley in an open act of defiance to Cromwell's Puritan regime, set in beautiful parkland. The church survives, little changed. **Ashby-de-la-Zouch, Leicestershire LE65 1RW 01332 863822** 114 D1

## Lincolnshire

**Belton House**
The serenity of Belton House has made it a favourite for royal visitors. Built late in Charles II's reign, the interiors are exuberantly baroque, with a stunning collection of Old Masters.There are formal gardens, orangery and magnificent landscaped park. **Grantham, Lincolnshire NG32 2LS 01476 566116** 116 B2

**Bolingbroke Castle**
Remains of a 13th-century hexagonal castle, birthplace of Henry IV in 1367 and besieged by Parliamentary forces in 1643. **In Old Bolingbroke, 16m N of Boston off A16. 01529 461499 Site managed by Heritage Lincolnshire)** 134 C3

**Gainsborough Old Hall**
A large mediaeval house with a magnificent Great Hall and suites of rooms. **In Gainsborough, opposite the Library. 01427 612669** 141 D6

**Gunby Hall (tenanted)**
A red-brick house with stone dressings, built in 1700 and extended in the 1870s. Contemporary stable block, walled garden, lawns and borders. **Gunby, nr Spilsby, Lincolnshire PE23 5SS Regional Office 01909 486411** 135 C4

**Lincoln Mediaeval Bishop's Palace**
The remains of this mediaeval palace of the Bishops of Lincoln are in the shadow of Lincoln Cathedral. You can climb the stairs to the Alnwick Tower, explore the undercroft and see the recently established Contemporary Heritage Garden. **In Lincoln, S side of Lincoln Cathedral. 01522 527468** 133 B4

**Sibsey Trader Windmill**
An impressive tower mill built in 1877, with its machinery and six sails intact. Flour milled on the spot can be bought there. **½m W of village of Sibsey, off A16 5m N of Boston. 01205 750036** 134 D3

**Tattershall Castle**
Dramatic 15th-century red brick tower with six floors to explore. Built for Ralph Cromwell and later restored by Lord Curzon,

the building contains four great chambers with enormous Gothic fireplaces, tapestries and brick vaulting. Spectacular views across the fens from the battlements. **Tattershall, Lincolnshire LN4 4LR** 01526 342543 134 D2

### Tattershall College

Remains of a grammar school for church choristers, built in the mid-15th century by Ralph, Lord Cromwell, the builder of nearby Tattershall Castle. **In Tattershall (off Market Place) 14m NE of Sleaford on A153.** 134 D2

### Woolsthorpe Manor

Small 17th-century manor house, birthplace of Sir Isaac Newton. He formulated some of his major works here during the Plague years. Newton's ideas can be explored in the Science Discovery Centre. Outside are orchards, paddocks and farm buildings, with rare breed sheep and hens. **23 Newton Way, Woolsthorpe-by-Colsterworth, Lincolnshire NG33 5NR** 01476 860338 116 C2

## North Lincolnshire

### Gainsthorpe Mediaeval Village

One of the best preserved deserted mediaeval villages in England. **On minor road W of A15 S of Hibaldstow 5m SW of Brigg (no signs).** 142 C1

### Normanby Hall Victorian Walled Garden

RHS Members: free throughout open period. Open: all year, daily, 10.30am-5pm (4.30 in winter). Closed Christmas Day, Boxing Day, New Year's Day. **Normanby Hall Country Park, Normanby, Scunthorpe, North Lincolnshire DN15 9HU** 01724 720588 141 B6

### St Peter's Church

One of the most studied churches in England, with its Anglo-Saxon tower and baptistry, mediaeval nave and chancel, and 15th-century church. **In Barton-upon-Humber.** 01652 632516 142 A2

### Thornton Abbey and Gatehouse

Remains of an Augustinian priory including a beautiful octagonal chapterhouse. Most impressive is the 14th-century gatehouse, recognised as one of the grandest in Europe. **18m NE of Scunthorpe on minor road N of A160; 7m SE of Humber Bridge on minor road E of A1077.** 142 B3

## Liverpool

### Mendips

Home of John Lennon between the ages of five and 23, restored to how it would have been at the time. Access only by pre-booked guided minibus tour, which also visits Paul McCartney's childhood home, 20 Forthling Road. Donated to the National Trust by Yoko Ono. **Woolton, Liverpool** 0151 708 8574 **(am tours) 0151 427 7231 (pm tours)** 127 A4

### Speke Hall, Garden & Estate

One of the most famous half-timbered houses in the country. Originally built in 1530 its Great Hall and priest hole date from Tudor times. William Morris wallpapers, Jacobean plasterwork, as well as a fully-equipped Victorian kitchen and servants' hall. Also, restored Victorian farm building with restaurant, shop and visitor reception. **The Walk, Liverpool L24 1XD** 0151 427 7231; **Infoline (local rate) 08457 585702** 127 A4

## London

### Apsley House

Designed and built by Robert Adam between 1771 and 1778 for Baron Apsley. Known for the Duke of Wellington's magnificent art collection. **149 Piccadilly, Hye Park Corner, London.** 020 7499 5676 49 B5

### HRP The Banqueting House

The Banqueting House was built between 1619 and 1622 during the reign of James I. Designed by Inigo Jones, it is the only surviving building of the vast Whitehall Palace, destroyed by fire nearly 300 years ago. The palace has seen many significant royal events including the only execution of a British monarch – Charles I in 1649. The Banqueting House is a welcome retreat away from the bustle of the city, and a hidden treasure for anyone interested in art and architecture. Its Rubens ceiling paintings are stunning examples of the larger works of the Flemish master and its classical Palladian style sets the fashion for much of London's later architecture. 0870 751 5178 49 A5

**How to get there**

Westminster (District, Circle and Jubilee lines), Embankment (Bakerloo, Northern, District and Circle Lines)
3, 11, 24, 53, 88, 112
Charing Cross

### Blewcoat School Gift Shop

The building was in use as a school until 1926, bought by the Trust in 1954 and restored in 1975. This is the NT London gift shop and information centre. **23 Caxton Street, Westminster, London SW1H 0PY** 020 7222 2877 49 B5

### Carlyle's House

Thomas Carlyle and his wife Jane lived in this 1708 Queen Anne terraced house, close to the Thames in Chelsea from 1834 to 1881. Opened in 1895 as a literary shrine it contains some of the Carlyle's furniture, books, pictures and personal possessions. **24 Cheyne Row, Chelsea, London SW3 5HL** 020 7352 7087 49 B5

### Chiswick House

Close to the centre of London lies one of the first and finest English Palladian villas, surrounded by beautiful gardens. It was designed by the third Earl of Burlington, one of the foremost architects of his generation and a great promoter of the Palladian style first pioneered in England by Inigo Jones. Today you can enjoy the house and its lavish interiors before stepping outside into the classical gardens – a perfect complement to the house itself. **Burlington Lane, London W4. Tube: Turnham Green** 020 8995 0508 49 B5

### Coombe Conduit

Built by Henry VIII to supply water to Hampton Court Palace, three miles away, Coombe Conduit consists of two small buildings (one now a ruin) connected by an underground passage. **Coombe Lane, on the corner of Lord Chancellor's Walk.** 020 8942 1296 49 C5

### Eltham Palace

A fascinating blend of a mediaeval royal palace and a 1930s' Art Deco country house. Step from the 15th-century Great Hall, straight into the lost pre-War world with a suite of striking Modernist interiors. **¾m N of A20 off Court Yard, SE9.** 020 8294 2548 49 B7

### Fenton House

Handsome 17th-century merchant's house set in the winding streets of Hampstead village. Houses an outstanding collection of porcelain, needlework pictures, Georgian furniture, and the Benton Fletcher collection of early keyboard instruments, most of which are in working order. **Windmill Hill, Hampstead, London NW3 6RT** 020 7435 3471 49 A5

### George Inn

The only remaining galleried inn in London, famous as a coaching inn during the 17th century, and mentioned by Dickens in 'Little Dorrit'. The George Inn is leased and run as a public house. **The George Inn Yard, 77 Borough High Street, Southwark, London SE1 1NH** 020 7407 2056 49 B6

### Ham House

Outstanding Stuart house built on the banks of the River Thames in 1610 and enlarged in the 1670s. Ham House contains rare survivals of the 17th century including exquisite closets, furniture, textiles and paintings. **Ham, Richmond TW10 7RS** 020 8940 1950 49 B7

### HRP Hampton Court Palace

With its 500 years of royal history, Hampton Court Palace has something to offer everyone. Set in sixty acres of world-famous gardens, the Palace is a living tapestry of history from Henry VIII to George II. From the elegance of the recently restored 18th-Century Privy Garden to the domestic reality of the Tudor Kitchens, visitors are taken back through the centuries to experience the palace as it was when royalty was in residence. Costumed guides and audio tours provide inside information on life in the royal households, and free family trails encourage a closer look at the palace, with the chance of a prize at the end. In the summer months horse-drawn carriages offer a sedate trip around the stunning gardens. 0870 752 7777 49 C4

**How to get there**

Wimbledon (District Line) for connecting train from Waterloo to Hampton Court, or Richmond (District Line) then R68 bus
111, 216, 411, 416, 451, 461, 513, 726, 267 (Sundays) Green Line coach 415 and 718
Hampton Court station, 32 minutes from Waterloo via Clapham Junction
River launch From Westminster, Richmond or Kingston upon Thames
The palace is on the A308 close to the A3, M3 and several exits of the M25

**Helpful hints**

Wear comfortable shoes as the cobbles can be very hard on the feet. Drop in to the information centre when you arrive; staff there will help you to plan your visit. During the summer, gardeners, housekeepers, flower arrangers and the vine keeper all regularly give informal presentations of their work.

**Timing your visit**

Recommended visit time 4 hours

| | |
|---|---|
| Henry VIII's State Apartments | 30 mins |
| Tudor Kitchens | 40 mins |
| The King's Apartments | 45 mins |
| The Queen's State Apartments | 30 mins |
| The Georgian Rooms | 30 mins |
| The Wolsey Rooms and Renaissance Picture Gallery | 30 mins |
| The Palace Gardens | 45 mins |
| The Maze | it depends... |

### Jewel Tower

One of two surviving buildings of the original Palace of Westminster, the Jewel Tower was built c.1365 to house the personal treasure of Edward III. It was subsequently used as a storehouse and government office. The exhibition, 'Parliament Past and Present', and accompanying video provide a fascinating account of the Houses of Lords and Commons. **Opposite S end of Houses of Parliament (Victoria Tower).** 020 7222 2219 49 B5

### HRP Kensington Palace State Apartments

Situated in the peaceful surroundings of Kensington Gardens, Kensington Palace was the residence of William III and Mary II, and later the childhood home of Queen Victoria. The magnificent State Apartments include William Kent's elaborate trompe l'oeil ceilings and the Cupola Room where Queen Victoria was baptised. There is a stunning presentation of Royal Court and Ceremonial Dress dating from the 18th century, which allows visitors to participate in the excitement of dressing for court – from invitation to presentation, and also a dazzling selection of dresses owned and worn by HM Queen Elizabeth II. Multi-language sound guides are available. 0870 751 5170 49 B5

**How to get there**

Queensway (Central Line), Notting Hill Gate (District, Circle and Central Lines), High Street Kensington (District and Circle Lines), Gloucester Road (District, Circle and Piccadilly Lines)
9, 12, 33, 49, 52, 52a, 88, C1

### Kenwood

Standing in splendid, landscaped grounds on the edge of Hampstead Heath, Kenwood contains the most important private collection of paintings ever given to the nation, the Iveagh Bequest. Among the finest is the 'Self-Portrait' by Rembrandt and 'The Guitar Player' by Vermeer, and also other works by such eminent British artists as Gainsborough, Turner and Reynolds. The outstanding neo-classical house was remodelled by Robert Adam, 1764-79 and English Heritage has restored his original colour scheme in the Entrance Hall. Outside, the landscaped park forms the perfect setting for the concerts that are held here in summer. **Hampstead Lane, London, NW3.** 020 8348 1286 49 A5

### London Wall

The best preserved piece of the Roman Wall, heightened in the Middle Ages, which formed part of the eastern defences of the City of London. **Near Tower Hill Underground station EC3** 49 A6

### Marble Hill House

A magnificent Thames-side Palladian villa built 1724-29 for Henrietta Howard, Countess of Suffolk, set in 66 acres of parkland. The Great Room has lavish gilded decoration and architectural paintings by Panini. The house also contains an important collection of early Georgian furniture, the Lazenby Bequest Chinoiserie collection and an 18th-century lacquer screen. **Richmond Road, Twickenham.** 020 8892 5115 49 B4

### Morden Hall Park

A green oasis in the heart of suburbia, the park has hay meadows, wetlands, a collection of old estate buildings and an impressive rose garden with over 2,000 roses. The River Wandle meanders through the parkland and the old Snuff Mill is now used as an education centre. **Morden Hall Road, Morden, London SM4 5JD** 020 8545 6850 49 C5

### Osterley Park

Neo-classical house with beautiful Adam interiors, one of Britain's most complete examples. The magnificent 16th-century stables survive largely intact. The house is set in extensive park and farm land, complete with Pleasure Grounds and neo-classical garden buildings. **Jersey Road, Isleworth, Middlesex TW7 4RB** 020 8232 5050 48 B4

### Sutton House

A unique survival in London's East End, built in 1535 by Sir Ralph Sadleir. Although altered over the years it remains an essentially Tudor house. Oak-panelled rooms and carved fireplaces survive intact and an exhibition tells the history of the house. **2 and 4 Homerton High Street, Hackney, London E9 6JQ** 020 8986 2264 49 A6

### HRP HM Tower of London

A palace and fortress for over 900 years, the Tower's bloody legends and its renown worldwide as the repository of the Crown Jewels make it a 'must see' site on the visitor map. Once inside, free Yeoman Warder tours leave from the front entrance every half an hour, and there are costumed guides giving special presentations in the Medieval Palace. The original Tower of London, the White Tower, has recently been refurbished and is home to the Royal Armouries collection including Henry VIII's armour. New events and exhibitions take place throughout the year and for families, family trails take children on a special path through the Tower with a prize for all those who complete it. 0870 751 5177 49 A6

**How to get there**

Tower Hill station (District and Circle Lines)
15, 25, 42, 78, 100
Fenchurch Street station, London Bridge station Docklands Light Railway (DLR): Tower Gateway station

**Timing your visit**

| | |
|---|---|
| Recommended visit time | 3 hours |
| A Yeoman Warder tour 1 hour | |
| The Crown Jewels | 35 mins |
| Crowns and Diamonds | 20 mins |
| The Medieval Palace | 25 mins |
| The Bloody Tower | 10 mins |
| The Beauchamp Tower | 20 mins |
| The White Tower and Royal Armouries | 30 mins |

### Wellington Arch

Step inside this splendid London landmark and take in spectacular views of the capital from the viewing platforms. Gaze over surrounding parks to the Houses of Parliament, Big Ben and the London Eye, and see the mounted Horse Guards as they ride through the Arch's majestic columns every day. Beneath the magnificent Quadriga – the largest bronze sculpture in England – Wellington Arch houses exhibitions on the monuments, statues and memorials of London. **Hyde Park Corner.** 020 7930 2726 49 B5

### The Wernher Collection at Ranger's House

One of the finest and most unusual 19th-century mixed art collections in the world, containing over 650 exhibits collected by millionaire diamond dealer Sir Julius Wernher. Highlights include Renaissance jewellery, carved medieval, Byzantine and Renaissance ivories, Limoges enamels and immaculate Sevres porcelain. **Chesterfield Walk, Greenwich, SE10.** 020 8853 0035 49 B6

### Winchester Palace

Remains of the Great Hall of this 13th-century town house of the Bishops of Winchester, damaged by fire in 1814. **Near Southwark Cathedral, at corner of Clink St and Storey St, SE1.** 49 B6

## Middlesbrough

*See also* Redcar and Cleveland

### Ormesby Hall

Mid-18th-century Palladian mansion, noted for its fine plasterwork and carved wood decoration. The Victorian laundry and kitchen are especially interesting and there is a large model railway exhibition on show. Attractive garden and holly walk. **Ormesby, Middlesbrough TS7 9AS** 01642 324188 168 D3

▼ Hampton Court Palace ©HRP

## Norfolk

**Baconsthorpe Castle**
Remains of the gatehouses of a large 15th-century fortified manor house. **¾m N of village of Baconsthorpe off unclassified road 3m E of Holt.** 120 B3

**Binham Priory**
Extensive remains of a Benedictine priory. **¼m NW of village of Binham. 01328 830362** 120 A1

**Binham Wayside Cross**
Mediaeval cross marking the site of an annual fair held from the reign of Henry I until the 1950s. **In Binham on village green adjacent to Priory.** 120 B1

**Blakeney Guildhall**
The surviving basement of a large 14th-century building, probably a merchant's house. **In Blakeney off A149.** 120 A2

**Blickling Hall, Garden and Park**
Magnificent Jacobean house famed for its spectacular long gallery, superb plasterwork ceilings and fine collections of furniture, pictures and tapestries. Extensive parkland and gardens full of colour throughout the year. **Blickling, Norwich, Norfolk NR11 6NF 01263 738030** 120 C3

**Burgh Castle**
A Roman fort built in the late 3rd century as one of a chain to defend the coast against Saxon raiders. **At far W end of Breydon Water, on unclassified road 3m W of Great Yarmouth.** 105 A5

**Caister Roman Site**
The remains of a Roman fort, including part of a defensive wall, a gateway and buildings along a main street. **Near Caister-on-Sea, 3m N of Great Yarmouth.** 121 D7

**Castle Acre: Bailey Gate**
The north gateway to the mediaeval planned town of Acre with flint towers. **In Castle Acre, at E end of Stocks Green, 5m N of Swaffham.** 119 D5

**Castle Acre Castle**
The remains of a Norman manor house, which became a castle with earthworks, set by the side of the village. **At E end of Castle Acre, 5m N of Swaffham.** 119 D5

**Castle Acre Priory**
The great west front of the 12th-century church of this Cluniac priory still rises to its full height and is elaborately decorated, whilst the prior's lodgings and porch retain their roofs. The delightful herb garden, re-created to show herbs used in mediaeval times for both culinary and medicinal purposes, should not be missed. **¼m W of village of Castle Acre, 5m N of Swaffham. 01760 755394** 119 D5

**Castle Rising Castle**
A fine mid 12th-century domestic keep, set in the centre of massive defensive earthworks, once palace and prison to Isabella, 'She-Wolf' Dowager Queen of England. **4m NE of King's Lynn off A149. 01553 631330** 118 C3

**Church of the Holy Sepulchre**
The ruined nave of a priory church of the Canons of the Holy Sepulchre, the only surviving remains in England of a house of this order. **On W side of Thetford off B1107.** 103 C4

**Cow Tower**
A circular brick tower, which once formed part of the 14th-century city defences. **In Norwich, near cathedral. 01603 212343** 104 A3

**Creake Abbey**
The ruins of the church of an Augustinian abbey. **1m N of North Creake off B1355.** 119 B5

**East Ruston Old Vicarage**
RHS Members: free Sept, Oct. Open: 28 Mar-30 Oct, Wed, Fri, Sat, Sun and Bank Holidays, 2-5.30pm. **East Ruston, Norwich, NR12 9HN 01692 650432** 121 C5

**Fairhaven Woodland and Water Garden**
RHS Members: free Feb-Apr and Oct. Open: all year, daily, 10am-5pm (9pm, Wed and Thur, May-Aug). Closed Christmas Day. **School Road, South Walsham, nr Norwich NR13 6DZ 01603 270449** 121 D5

**Felbrigg Hall Garden and Park**
17th-century country house with fine hall containing its original 18th-century furniture, one of the largest collections of Grand Tour paintings by a single artist and an outstanding library. The Walled Garden has been restored and features a working dovecote and the National Collection of Colchicums. **Felbrigg, Norwich, Norfolk NR11 8PR 01263 837444** 120 B3

**Grime's Graves**
These remarkable Neolithic flint mines, unique in England, comprise over 300 pits and shafts. The visitor can descend some 10m (30ft) by ladder into one excavated shaft, and look along the radiating galleries, where the flint for making axes and knives was extracted. **7m NW of Thetford off A134. 01842 810656** 103 C4

**North Elmham Chapel**
Remains of a Norman chapel converted into a fortified dwelling and enclosed by earthworks in the late 14th century by the notorious Bishop of Norwich, Hugh le Despencer. **6m N of East Dereham on B1110.** 120 C1

**Oxburgh Hall, Garden and Estate**
15th-century moated manor house with magnificent gatehouse and accessible priest's hole. Rooms show mediaeval austerity through to neo-Gothic Victorian comfort and include a display of embroidery by Mary, Queen of Scots. Attractive gardens feature a French parterre, walled orchard and kitchen garden. **Oxborough, King's Lynn, Norfolk PE33 9PS 01366 328258** 102 A3

**Row 111 House Old Merchant's House and Greyfriars' Cloisters**
Two 17th-century Row Houses, a type of building unique to Great Yarmouth, containing original fixtures and displays of local architectural fittings salvaged from bombing in 1942-43. Nearby are the remains of a Franciscan friary, with rare early wall paintings, accidentally discovered during bomb damage repairs. **Great Yarmouth, head for South Quay along riverside and dock, ½m inland from beach. Follow signs to dock and south quay. 01493 857900** 105 A6

**Sheringham Park**
One of Humphry Repton's most outstanding achievements, the landscape park contains fine mature woodlands, and the large woodland garden is particularly famous for its spectacular show of rhododendrons and azaleas (flowering at its best mid-May to June). There are stunning views of the coast and countryside from the viewing towers and many delightful waymarked walks. **Upper Sheringham, Norfolk NR26 8TB 01263 821429** 120 A3

**St Olave's Priory**
Remains of an Augustinian priory founded nearly 200 years after the death in 1030 of the patron saint of Norway, after whom it is named. **5½m SW of Great Yarmouth on A143.** 105 A5

**Thetford Priory**
The 14th-century gatehouse is the best preserved part of this Cluniac priory built in 1103. The extensive remains include the plan of the cloisters **On W side of Thetford near station.** 103 C4

**Thetford Warren Lodge**
The ruins of a small, two-storeyed mediaeval house. **2m W of Thetford off B1107.** 103 C4

**Weeting Castle**
The ruins of an early mediaeval manor house within a shallow rectangular moat. **2m N of Brandon off B1106.** 102 C3

## Northamptonshire

**Canons Ashby House**
Tranquil Elizabethan manor house set in beautiful gardens. Home of the Dryden family since its construction. Canons Ashby has survived unaltered since c 1710. The atmospheric interior contains wall paintings and Jacobean plasterwork of the highest quality. **Canons Ashby, Daventry, Northamptonshire NN11 3SD 01327 861900** 82 B2

**Chichele College**
Parts of a quadrangle remain of this college for secular canons, founded in 1422. **In Higham Ferrers, on A6. 01933 314157. (Site managed by East Northamptonshire Council)** 83 A6

**Cottesbrooke Hall Gardens**
RHS Members: free throughout open period. Open: 5th May-end Jun, Wed, Thur and Bank Holiday Mon, 2-5pm. Jul-Sept, Thur and Bank Holiday Mon, 2-5pm. For details of opening times of house, please contact Cottesbrooke Hall. **Cottesbrooke Hall, Cottesbrooke, Northamptonshire NN6 8PF 01604 505808** 99 D4

**Eleanor Cross, Geddington**
One of a series of famous crosses erected by Edward I to mark the resting places of the body of his wife, Eleanor. **In Geddington, off A43 between Kettering and Corby.** 99 C5

**Kirby Hall**
Outstanding example of a large, stone-built Elizabethan mansion, begun in 1570 with 17th-century alterations. The fine gardens are home to beautiful peacocks. **On unclassified road off A43 4m NE of Corby. 01536 203230** 99 B6

**Lyveden New Bield**
The shell of an uncompleted 'lodge' or garden house, begun c.1595 by Sir Thomas Tresham, and designed in the shape of a cross. The exterior incorporates friezes inscribed with religious quotations and signs of the Passion. **Nr Oundle, Peterborough, Northamptonshire PE8 5AT 01832 205358** 100 C2

**Rushton Triangular Lodge**
Extraordinary building built by the Catholic Sir Thomas Tresham on his return from imprisonment for his religious beliefs. Completed in 1597, it symbolizes the Holy Trinity. It has three sides, three floors, trefoil windows and three triangular gables on each side. **1m W of Rushton, on unclassified road 3m from Desborough on A6. 01536 710761** 99 C5

## Northumberland

**Aydon Castle**
One of the finest fortified manor houses in England, built in the late 13th century. Situated in a position of great natural beauty, its remarkably intact state is due to its conversion to a farmhouse in the 17th century. **1m NE of Corbridge, on minor road off B6321 or A68. 01434 632450** 178 C2

**Belsay Hall, Castle and Gardens**
The beautiful honey-coloured stone from which Belsay Hall is built came from its own quarries in the grounds. Those quarries have since become the unusual setting for one of a series of spectacular gardens. They are the property's finest feature, deservedly listed Grade I in the Register of Gardens. The house itself was innovative, when built between 1810 and 1817 in a style derived directly from Ancient Greece. **In Belsay, Northumberland, 14m NW of Newcastle on A696. 01661 881636** 178 B2

**Berwick-upon-Tweed Barracks**
**On the Parade, off Church St, Berwick town centre. 01289 304493** 198 A4

**Berwick-upon-Tweed Castle**
Remains of 12th-century castle **Adjacent to Berwick railway station, W of town centre, accessible also from river bank.** 198 A3

**Berwick-upon-Tweed Main Guard**
Georgian Guard House near the quay. An exhibition celebrates the 150th anniversary of the railway coming to Berwick-upon-Tweed. **Surrounding Berwick town centre on N bank of River Tweed.** 198 A3

**Berwick-upon-Tweed Ramparts**
Remarkably complete, 16th-century town fortifications, with gateways and projecting bastions. **Surrounding Berwick town centre on N bank of River Tweed.** 198 A4

**Bide-a-Wee Cottage Gardens**
RHS Members: free throughout open period (excluding group visits outside normal opening hours). Open: 24th Apr-28th Aug, Wed and Sat only, 1.30pm-5pm **Stanton, Netherwitton, Morpeth, Northumberland NE65 8PR 01670 772262** 178 A3

**Black Middens Bastle House**
A 16th-century two-storey defended farmhouse, set in splendid walking country. **200yds N of minor road 7m NW of Bellingham; access also along minor road from A68.** 187 D6

**Brinkburn Priory**
This late 12th-century church is a fine example of early Gothic architecture. **4½m SE of Rothbury off B6344. 01665 570628** 189 D4

**Cherryburn**
Cottage and farmhouse, birthplace of Northumberland's greatest artist, wood engraver and naturalist Thomas Bewick. The 19th-century farmhouse plays host to an exhibition on Bewick's life and work. Occasional printing demonstrations take place in the adjoining barn. **Station Bank, Mickley, nr Stocksfield, Northumberland NE43 7DD 01661 843276** 178 C2

## Hadrian's Wall

**Hadrian's Wall, World Heritage Site**
**Cumbria, Northumberland**
Stretching across northern England from the Solway Firth in the west to the Tyne in the east, Hadrian's Wall divided the 'civilized' world of the Romans, from the northern tribes beyond. Emperor Hadrian, who came to Britain in 122, was unusual in that he believed consolidation to be more glorious than new conquest. The Wall was the physical manifestation of his strategy, a defensive barrier linking the existing system of forts and watchtowers along the Stanegate road **West of Hexham, the Wall runs roughly parallel to the A69 Carlisle-Newcastle-upon-Tyne road, lying between 1-4 miles North of it, close to the B6318.** 177 C5

**Banks East Turret**
Cumbria
Well-preserved turret with adjoining stretches of Wall and fine views. **On minor road E of Banks village, 3½m NE of Brampton.** 176 C3

**Benwell Roman Temple**
Tyne and Wear
Remains of small temple, surrounded by modern housing. **Immediately S off A69 at Benwell in Broomridge Ave.** 179 C4

**Benwell Vallum Crossing**
Tyne and Wear
The sole remaining example of an original stone-built causeway across the ditch of the Vallum earthwork that ran parallel to the Wall. **Immediately S off A69 at Benwell in Broomridge Ave.** 179 C4

**Birdoswald Roman Fort**
Cumbria
Almost on the edge of the Irthing escarpment, there is visible evidence of the granaries, the west gate and, most importantly, the east gate, which is among the best-preserved on the Wall. **2¾m W of Greenhead, on minor road off B6318. 01697 747602** 176 C4

**Black Carts Turret**
Northumberland
A 460 metre (500 yard) length of Wall and turret foundations, with magnificent views to the north. **2m W of Chollerford on B6318.** 177 B6

**Brunton Turret**
Northumberland
Well-preserved 2½ metre (8 foot) high turret with a 20 metre (70 yard) stretch of Wall. **¼m S of Low Brunton on A6079.** 178 C1

**Cawfields Roman Wall**
Northumberland
A concentration of Roman sites – camps, turrets, a fortlet, and Milecastle 42 – along with a particularly fine, consolidated stretch of the Wall, and one of the best-preserved sections of the Vallum earthwork and ditch. **1¼m N of Haltwhistle off B6318.** 177 C4

**Chesters Bridge**
Northumberland
Fragments of the bridge that carried Hadrian's Wall across the North Tyne are visible on each bank. The most impressive remains are on the east side, across from Chesters Fort, where a short stretch of the Wall itself leads from the broad splay of the bridge's east abutment, and ends at a gatehouse tower. **¼m S of Low Brunton on A6079.** 177 B7

**Chesters Roman Fort**
Northumberland
Originally built to guard a Roman bridge, it was one of a series of forts added to Hadrian's Wall as the result of a change of plan during construction. Its six-acre plot would have held a cavalry regiment of around 500 men. The four principal gateways are well preserved, as are the short lengths of Hadrian's Wall adjoining them. The entire foundation of the headquarters building is visible, with a courtyard, hall, regimental temple and strongroom clearly laid out. Down by the river the changing rooms, steam range and bathing rooms of the garrison's bath house are extremely well preserved, as is the Roman bridge abutment on the opposite bank of the river. **1¼m W of Chollerford on B6318. 01434 681379** 177 C7

**Corbridge Roman Site**
Northumberland
Originally the site of a fort on the former patrol road, Corbridge evolved into a principal town of the Roman era, flourishing until the 5th century. The large granaries, with their ingenious ventilation system, are among its most impressive remains. Corbridge is an excellent starting point to explore the Wall. **½m NW of Corbridge on minor road, signed Corbridge Roman Site. 01434 632349** 178 C1

**Denton Hall Turret**
Tyne and Wear
Foundations and 65 metre (70 yard) section of Wall. The turret retains the base of the platform on which rested the ladder to the upper floor. **4m W of Newcastle city centre on A69.** 178 C3

**Hare Hill**
Northumberland
A short length of wall standing nine feet high. **¾m NE of Lanercost, off minor road.** 176 C3

**Harrow's Scar Milecastle**
Cumbria
Remains linked to Birdoswald Fort by probably the most instructive mile section on the whole length of Hadrian's Wall. **¼m E of Birdoswald, on minor road off B6318.** 176 C4

**Heddon-on-the-Wall**
Northumberland
A fine stretch of the Wall up to two metres (six feet) thick, with the remains of a mediaeval kiln near the west end. **Immediately E of Heddon village, S of A69.** 178 C3

**Housesteads Roman Fort**
Northumberland
Housesteads occupies a commanding position on the basalt cliffs of the Whin Sill. One of the twelve permanent forts built by Hadrian c. 124, between milecastles 36 and 37, Housesteads is the most complete example of a Roman fort to be seen in Britain. To the east of Housesteads, Knag Burn Gate, constructed in the third century, was an alternative way through the wall when the north gate in the fort itself fell out of use. It is one of only two isolated gates – all the rest are found at forts and milecastles. This gate and some of the Wall have been partially reconstructed, and much has been consolidated, to give one of the most coherent pictures of the Romans and their great works in Britain. **2¾m NE of Bardon Mill on B6318. 01434 344363** 177 C5

**Leahill Turret and Piper Sike Turret**
Northumberland
Turrets in the section of Wall west of Birdoswald, originally constucted for the turf wall. **On minor road 2m W of Birdoswald Fort.** 176 C3

**Pike Hill Signal Tower**
Cumbria
Remains of a signal tower joined to the Wall at an angle of 45 degrees. **On minor road E of Banks village.** 176 C3

**Planetrees Roman Wall**
Northumberland
A 15-metre (50-foot) length of narrow wall on broad foundations, showing extensive rebuilding in Roman times. **1m SE of Chollerford on B6318.** 178 C1

**Poltross Burn Milecastle**
Northumberland
One of the best-preserved milecastles, with part of a flight of steps to the top of the Wall and the remains of the gates, enclosing walls and barrack blocks. **Immediately SW of Gilsland village by old railway station.** 176 C4

**Sewingshields Wall**
Northumberland
Largely unexcavated section of Wall. Remains of Sewingshields Milecastle and Turret and Grindon and Coesike Turrets. **N of B6318, 1½m E of Housesteads Fort.** 177 B6

**Temple of Mithras, Carrawburgh**
Northumberland
Remains of a third-century temple and facsimiles of altars found during excavations. **3¾m W of Chollerford on B6318.** 177 B6

**Walltown Crags**
Northumberland
One of the best-preserved sections of the Wall, snaking over the crags to the turret on its summit. **1m NE of Greenhead off B6318.** 177 C4

**Willowford Wall, Turrets and Bridge**
Northumberland
One thousand yards of Wall, including two turrets, leading to bridge abutment remains. **W of minor road ¾m W of Gilsland.** 176 C4

**Winshields Wall**
Northumberland
Very rugged section of the Wall, including the highest point at Winshields Crag. **W of Steel Rigg car park, on minor road off B6318.** 177 C5

❦ **Cragside House, Gardens and Estate** ▣▣▣▣▣▣
Cragside was the first house in the world to be lit by hydro-electric power, with state-of-the-art hydraulics powering both the revolutionary new lift systems and internal telephones. The formal Victorian Garden is a short walk from the house. You can also explore the 1,000 acre estate. **Rothbury, Morpeth, Northumberland NE65 7PX** ☎01669 620333 188 C3

⌗ **Dunstanburgh Castle** ◯
An easy coastal walk leads to the eerie skeleton of this wonderful 14th-century castle, which is sited on a basalt crag more than 30 metres (100 feet) high. **8m NE of Alnwick, on footpaths from Craster or Embleton.** ☎01665 576231 189 A5

⌗ **Edlingham Castle**
This complex ruin has defensive features spanning the 13th-15th centuries. **At E end of Edlingham village, on minor road off B6341 6m SW of Alnwick.** 189 C4

⌗ **Etal Castle** ⊙
A 14th-century border castle located in the picturesque village of Etal. There is a major award-winning exhibition about the castle, border warfare and the Battle of Flodden, which took place nearby in 1513. **In Etal village, 10m SW of Berwick.** ☎01890 820332 198 C3

❦ **Farne Islands** ▣▣▣
The islands provide a summer home for over 20 different species of seabirds including puffin, eider ducks and four species of tern. Large colony of grey seals. St Cuthbert died on Inner Farne in 687 and there is a chapel built to his memory in the 14th-century that can be visited. **Northumberland** ☎01665 721099 199 C6

❦ **George Stephenson's Birthplace** ▣▣▣▣
A small stone tenement built c 1760 to accommodate mining families. The furnishings are circa 1781, when George Stephenson was born. The room in which he was born is open to visitors. **Wylam, Northumberland NE41 8BP** ☎01661 853457 178 C3

❦ **Lindisfarne Castle** ▣▣▣▣
Romantic 16th-century castle perched on a rocky crag and accessible by the causeway at low tide. Originally a tudor fort it was converted into a private house in 1903 by the young Edwin Lutyens. Small rooms of intimate decoration and design overlook the charming walled garden. **Holy Island, Berwick-upon-Tweed Northumberland TD15 2SH** ☎01289 389244 199 B5

⌗ **Lindisfarne Priory** ▣
Founded in AD635, the site of one of the most important centres of early Christianity in Anglo-Saxon England. **On Holy Island, Northumberland, only reached at low tide across causeway (tide tables at each end).** ☎01289 389200 199 B5

⌗ **Norham Castle** ⊙
Set on a promontory in a curve of the River Tweed, this was one of the strongest of the border castles, built c.1160. **Norham village, 6½m SW of Berwick-upon-Tweed on minor road off B6470 (from A698).** ☎01289 382329 198 B3

⌗ **Prudhoe Castle** ⊙
Set on a wooded hillside overlooking the River Tyne are the extensive remains of a 12th-century castle, with gatehouse, curtain wall and keep. **In Prudhoe, on minor road off A695.** ☎01661 833459 178 C3

❦ **Wallington** ▣▣▣▣▣▣▣
Magnificent mansion with fine interiors such as the beautiful rococo plasterwork and interesting collections of dolls' houses, paintings and ceramics. Set in extensive parkland influenced by 'Capability' Brown who went to school in the village. Beautiful walled garden and delightful estate walks. **Cambo, Morpeth, Northumberland NE61 4AR** ☎01670 773600 178 A2

⌗ **Warkworth Castle and Hermitage** ⊙
The magnificent eight-towered keep of Warkworth Castle stands on its hill above the River Coquet, dominating all around it. A large and complex stronghold, it was home to the Percy family who at times wielded more power in the North than the King himself. Most famous of them all was Harry Hotspur (Sir Henry Percy), immortalised in Northumbrian ballads and Shakespeare's Henry IV, several scenes of which were set at Warkworth. **In Warkworth, Northumberland 7½m S of Alnwick on A1068.** ☎01665 711423 189 C5

## Nottinghamshire

❦ **Clumber Park** ▣▣▣▣▣▣
Vast area of parkland with a superb serpentine lake at its heart and the longest avenue of lime trees in Europe. Formerly home to the Dukes of Newcastle, the house was demolished in 1938, but many fascinating features remain such as the Gothic Revival Chapel and walled kitchen garden. **The Estate Office, Clumber Park, Worksop, Nottinghamshire S80 3AZ** ☎01909 476592 131 B6

✿ **Felley Priory**
RHS Members: free throughout open period. Open: all year, Tue, Wed and Fri, 9am-12.30pm. Mar-Oct, every 2nd and 4th Wed, 9am-4pm, every 3rd Sun 11am-4pm. **Underwood, Nottinghamshire NG16 5FL** ☎01773 810230 131 D4

⌗ **Mattersey Priory** ▣
Remains of a small Gilbertine monastery founded in 1185. **Rough access down drive ¾m long, 1m E of Mattersey off B6045, 7m N of Retford.** 132 A2

❦ **Mr Straw's House** ▣▣
A semi-detached house built at the turn of last century, belonging to William Straw and his brother, Walter. The interior has been preserved since the death of their parents in the 1930s with 1920s wallpaper, furnishings and local furniture. **7 Blyth Grove, Worksop, Nottinghamshire S81 0JG** ☎01909 482380 131 A5

⌗ **Rufford Abbey** ▣
The remains of a 17th-century country house, built on the foundations of a 12th-century Cistercian abbey. **2m S of Ollerton off A614.** ☎01623 822944 131 C6

## Oxfordshire

⌗ **Abingdon County Hall**
This 17th-century public building was built to house the Assize Courts. **In Abingdon, 7m S of Oxford in Market Place.** ☎01235 523703 65 D5

❦ **Buscot Park** ▣▣▣
A late 18th-century house with pleasure grounds set within a park. **Estate Office, Buscot Park, Faringdon, Oxfordshire SN7 8BU** ☎0845 3453387 🖷01367 241794 64 D3

⌗ **Deddington Castle**
Extensive earthworks conceal the remains of a 12th-century castle. **S of B4031 on E side of Deddington, 17m N of Oxford on A423.** 82 D1

❦ **Farnborough Hall (tenanted)** ▣▣▣
A classical, mid 18th-century stone house. The entrance hall, staircase and two principal rooms are shown; the plasterwork is particularly notable. Superb landscaped garden. **Banbury OX17 1DU** ☎01295 690002 82 C1

❦ **Great Coxwell Barn** ▣
A 13th-century monastic barn, stone-built with stone-tiled roof and interesting timber construction. **Great Coxwell, Faringdon, Oxfordshire** ☎**Coleshill Office 01793 762209** 64 D3

❦ **Greys Court** ▣▣▣
This picturesque house has a beautiful courtyard and one surviving tower dating from 1347. The house has an interesting history and was involved in Jacobean court intrigue. Outside features include a Tudor wheel-house, walled gardens full of old-fashioned roses and an ice-house. **Rotherfield Greys, Henley-on-Thames, Oxfordshire RG9 4PG** ☎01491 628529 47 A5

⌗ **Minster Lovell Hall and Dovecote** ◯
The handsome ruins of Lord Lovell's 15th-century manor house. **Adjacent to Minster Lovell church, 3m W of Witney off A40.** 64 B4

⌗ **North Hinksey Conduit House**
Roofed reservoir for Oxford's first water mains, built in the early 17th century. **In North Hinksey off A34, 2½m W of Oxford. Located off track leading from Harcourt Hill; use footpath from Ferry Hinksey Lane (near station).** 65 C5

⌗ **North Leigh Roman Villa** ⊙
The remains of a large and well-built Roman courtyard villa. **2m N of North Leigh, 10m W of Oxford off A4095.** 65 B4

## The Royal Horticultural Society

### Step into a world of inspirational gardens with the RHS

The RHS is the UK's leading gardening charity, dedicated to advancing horticulture and promoting good gardening. Membership is at the heart of the RHS, since without member support we would be unable to fulfill many of our charitable aims. These include providing expert advice and information, training the next generation of gardeners, helping school children learn about plants, and conducting research into plant pests and environmental issues affecting gardeners.

**Join today and enjoy the privileges of RHS membership…**

**Free entry** with a guest to RHS gardens Wisley in Surrey, Rosemoor in Devon, Hyde Hall in Essex and Harlow Carr in North Yorkshire

**Free Access** to partner gardens. There are over 100 inspirational gardens to visit throughout their opening season or at selected periods.

**RHS flower shows**. Privileged entry and reduced rate tickets for RHS shows; Chelsea, Hampton Court Palace, Tatton Park, plus free entry to London and Wisley Flower Shows.

**Free monthly magazine**. Receive monthly the RHS members' magazine for free (RRP £3.95). Full of practical advice, ideas and inspiration.

**FREE advice**. Invaluable support and answers to your gardening questions all year round.

**FREE seeds**. You can apply for seeds harvested from RHS gardens. (There is a small postage & packaging charge).

**Flower shows**. Reduced admission to BB Gardeners' World Live and the Malvern Spring and Autumn Garden and Country Shows.

**RHS Plant Selector**. Privileged information on over 4,500 plants at www.rhs.org.uk

**Special events**. Reduced price tickets to hundreds of lectures, tours workshops and events around the UK.

**Support the RHS and secure a healthy future for gardening.**

### How to join the RHS

To join the RHS and enjoy all of the benefits of membership please call 0845 130 4646 and quote 1557. Lines open from 9am to 5pm, Monday to Friday or visit our website at **www.rhs.org.uk**

⌗ **Rollright Stones** ⓘ
Three groups of stones, known as 'The King's Men', 'The Whispering Knights' and 'The King Stone', spanning nearly 2,000 years of the Neolithic and Bronze Ages. **Off unclassified road between A44 and A3400, 2m NW of Chipping Norton near villages of Little Rollright and Long Compton.** 81 D5

⌗ **Rycote Chapel** ▣
Lovely 15th-century chapel, with exquisitely carved and painted woodwork. **3m SW of Thame off A329.** ☎01424 775705 66 C1

⌗ **Uffington Castle, White Horse and Dragon Hill** ⓘ
A group of sites lying along the Ridgeway, an old prehistoric route. There is a large Iron Age camp enclosed within ramparts, a natural mound known as Dragon Hill and the spectacular White Horse, cut from turf to reveal chalk. **S of B4507, 7m W of Wantage.** 45 A7

✿ **Waterperry Gardens**
RHS Members: free Sept. Open: all year, daily, 9am-5pm. **Wheatley, Oxford OX33 1JZ** ☎**01844 339254 (office), 01844 339226 (shop)** 66 C1

⌗ **Wayland's Smithy** ⓘ
Near to the Uffington White Horse lies this evocative Neolithic burial site, surrounded by a small circle of trees. **On the Ridgeway ¾m NE of B4000 Ashbury-Lambourn road.** 45 A6

## Redcar and Cleveland

*See also* Middlesbrough

⌗ **Guisborough Priory** ▣
An Augustinian priory. The remains also include the gatehouse and the east end of an early 14th-century church. **In Guisborough town, next to parish church.** ☎01287 633801 168 C4

## Rutland

✿ **Barnsdale Gardens**
RHS Members: free throughout open period Open: Mar-May and Sept-Oct, daily, 9am-5pm; Jun-Aug, daily, 9am-7pm; Nov-Feb, daily, 10am-4pm. **The Avenue, Exton, Oakham, Rutland LE15 8AH** ☎01572 813200 116 D2

⌗ **Lyddington Bede House** ▣
Originally one wing of a medieval rural palace belonging to the Bishops of Lincoln. Although it is not known when it was first built, the land was certainly owned by the church in the time of William the Conqueror. The property was seized by the Crown in 1547 and was passed on to Lord Burghley who turned it into an almshouse for the poor in the 1600s. Visitors can wander through the bedesmen's rooms with their tiny windows and fireplaces, as well as the Great Chamber which features a beautiful ceiling cornice. An on-site audio tour reconstructs some of the major changes during the past 700 years, and outside there is a small herb garden. **Next to church in Lyddington, 6m N of Corby, 1m E of A6003.** ☎01572 822438 99 B5

## Shropshire

⌗ **Acton Burnell Castle** ◯
The warm red sandstone shell of a fortified 13th-century manor house. **In Acton Burnell, on unclassified road 8m S of Shrewsbury.** 94 A3

❦ **Attingham Park** ▣▣▣
Elegant mansion built in 1785 for the 1st Lord Berwick, designed by George Steuart with a picture gallery by John Nash. Magnificent rooms housing beautiful collections of furniture and paintings. Other features include park, walks, organic open farm and play area. **Shrewsbury, Shropshire SY4 4TP** ☎01743 708162 94 A3

❦ **Benthall Hall (tenanted)** ▣▣▣
The exterior of Benthall Hall has changed little since it was built in the 16th century. The early 17th-century interior includes an intricately carved oak staircase, decorated plaster ceilings and oak panelling. The intimate garden is sheltered and enclosed by trees. **Broseley, Shropshire TF12 5RX** ☎01952 882159 95 A4

⌗ **Boscobel House and the Royal Oak** ⊙✺
Fully refurnished and restored, the panelled rooms, secret hiding places and pretty gardens lend this 17th-century timber-framed hunting lodge a truly romantic character. King Charles II hid in the house and the nearby Royal Oak after the Battle of Worcester in 1651 to avoid detection by Cromwell's troops. Today there is a farmhouse with dairy, farmyard and smithy, and an exhibition in the house. **On minor road from A41 to A5, 8m NW of Wolverhampton.** ☎01902 850244 95 A6

⌗ **Buildwas Abbey** ▣
Set beside the River Severn, against a backdrop of wooded grounds, are extensive remains of this Cistercian abbey begun in 1135. **On S bank of River Severn on B4378, 2m W of Iron Bridge.** ☎01952 433274 95 A4

⌗ **Cantlop Bridge** ⊙
Single-span cast-iron road bridge over the Cound Brook, designed by the great engineer Thomas Telford. **¾m SW of Berrington on unclassified road off A458.** 94 A3

⌗ **Clun Castle** ◯⊙
The remains of a four-storey keep and other buildings of this border castle. **In Clun, off A488, 18m W of Ludlow.** 93 C6

❦ **Dudmaston** ▣▣▣▣
This late 17th-century house of mellow red brick contains collections of modern art and sculpture. The house is surrounded by an extensive and impressive lakeside garden with a colourful rockery and woodland walks. **Quatt, nr Bridgnorth, Shropshire WV15 6QN** ☎01746 780866 95 C5

⌗ **Haughmond Abbey** ▣
**3m NE of Shrewsbury off B5062.** ☎01743 709661 111 D4

⌗ **Iron Bridge** ⊙
The world's first iron bridge and Britain's best-known industrial monument. Cast in Coalbrookdale by local ironmaster Abraham Darby, it was erected across the River Severn in 1779. **In Ironbridge, adjacent to A4169.** 95 A4

⌗ **Langley Chapel** ▣
This small chapel, standing alone in a field, contains a complete set of early 17th-century wooden fittings and furniture. **1½m S of Acton Burnell, on unclassified road off A49, 9½m S of Shrewsbury.** 94 A3

⌗ **Lilleshall Abbey** ▣
Extensive and evocative ruins of an abbey of Augustinian canons, including remains of the 12th- and 13th-century church and the cloister buildings. **On unclassified road off A518, 4m N of Oakengates.** ☎**0121 625 6820 (Regional Office)** 111 D6

⌗ **Mitchell's Fold Stone Circle** ⓘ
Bronze Age stone circle, set on dramatic moorland and consisting of some 30 stones of which 15 are visible. **16m SW of Shrewsbury W of A488.** 93 B7

⌗ **Moreton Corbet Castle** ◯⊙
A ruined mediaeval castle with the substantial remains of a splendid Elizabethan mansion. **In Moreton Corbet off B5063, 7m NE of Shrewsbury.** 111 C4

⌗ **Old Oswestry Hill Fort** ⓘ
An impressive Iron Age fort of 68 acres defended by a series of five ramparts, with an elaborate western entrance and unusual earthwork cisterns. **1m N of Oswestry, accessible from unclassified road off A483.** 110 B1

⌗ **Stokesay Castle** ◯⊙✺
The finest mediaeval manor house in England, situated in peaceful countryside. The castle now stands in a picturesque group with its own splendid timber-framed Jacobean gatehouse and the parish church. **7m NW of Ludlow off A49.** ☎01588 672544 94 C2

⌗ **Wenlock Priory** ▣
The ruins of a large Cluniac priory in an attractive garden setting featuring delightful topiary. There are substantial remains of the early 13th-century church and Norman chapter house **In Much Wenlock.** ☎01952 727466 95 A4

⌗ **White Ladies Priory** ▣
The ruins of the late 12th-century church of a small priory of Augustinian canonesses. **1m SW of Boscobel House off unclassified road between A41 and A5, 8m NW of Wolverhampton.** 95 A6

✿ **Wollerton Old Hall Garden**
RHS Members: free Apr, May, Sept. Open: Easter-Aug, Fri, Sun and Bank Holidays, 12-5pm, Sept, Sun only, 12pm-5pm. **Wollerton Market Drayton, Shropshire TF9 3NA** ☎01630 685760 111 B5

⌗ **Wroxeter Roman City** ⊙
The excavated centre of the fourth largest city in Roman Britain, with impressive

remains of the 2nd-century municipal baths. **At Wroxeter, 5m E of Shrewsbury on B4380.** 01743 761330 94 A3

## Somerset

*See also* Bath and North East Somerset

**Barrington Court**
An enchanted formal garden influenced by Gertrude Jekyll and laid out in a series of 'rooms'. The Tudor manor house was restored in the 1920s by the Lyle family and is let to Stuart Interiors as showrooms with antique furniture for sale. **Nr Ilminster, Somerset TA19 0NQ** 01460 241938 28 D3

**Butter Cross**
A mediaeval stone cross. **Beside minor road to Alcombe, 350m (400 yds) NW of Dunster parish church.** 27 A4

**Cleeve Abbey**
One of the few 13th-century monastic sites where you will see such a complete set of cloister buildings. **In Washford, ¼m S of A39.** 01984 640377 27 A5

**Coleridge Cottage**
The home of Samuel Taylor Coleridge for three years from 1797, with mementoes of the poet on display. It was here that he wrote 'The Rime of the Ancient Mariner', part of 'Christabel' and 'Frost at Midnight'. **35 Lime Street, Nether Stowey, Bridgwater, Somerset TA5 1NQ** 01278 732662 28 B1

**Dunster Castle**
Ancient castle with fine interiors and sub-tropical gardens. Dramatically sited on a wooded hill, a castle has existed here since at least Norman times. The building was remodelled in 1868-72 by Antony Salvin for the Luttrell family, who lived here for 600 years. **Dunster, nr Minehead, Somerset TA24 6SL** 01643 821314 27 A4

**Dunster Working Water-Mill**
Built on the site of a mill mentioned in the Domesday Survey of 1086, the present mill dates from the 18th century and was restored to working order in 1979. Note: the mill is a private business and all visitors, including NT members, pay the admission charge. **Mill Lane, Dunster, nr Minehead, Somerset TA24 6SW** 01643 821759 27 A4

**Farleigh Hungerford Castle**
Ruins of a 14th-century castle with a chapel containing wall paintings, stained glass and the fine tomb of Sir Thomas Hungerford, the builder of the castle. **In Farleigh Hungerford 3½m W of Trowbridge on A366.** 01225 754026 44 D2

**Forde Abbey Gardens**
RHS Members: free Oct-Feb. Open: all year, daily, 10am-4.30pm. **Chard, Somerset, TA20 4LU** 01460 221290 14 A3

**Gallox Bridge**
A stone packhorse bridge with two ribbed arches which spans the old mill stream. **Off A396 at S end of Dunster.** 27 A4

**Glastonbury Tribunal**
A well-preserved mediaeval town house. **In Glastonbury High St.** 01458 832954 19 B5

**Lytes Cary Manor**
A manor house with a 14th-century chapel, 15th-century hall and 16th-century great chamber. Rescued from dereliction by Sir Walter Jenner who refurbished the interiors in period style. Several estate walks. **Charlton Mackrell, Somerton, Somerset TA11 7HU** Regional Office 01458 224471 29 C5

**Meare Fish House**
A simple, well-preserved stone dwelling. **In Meare village on B3151.** 29 A4

**Montacute House**
Built in the late 16th century, this is a magnificent Elizabethan mansion in the tranquil setting of Montacute village. The garden includes colourful mixed borders and formal landscapes. **Montacute, Somerset TA15 6XP** 01935 823289 29 D4

**Muchelney Abbey**
The well-preserved remains of the cloisters and abbot's lodging of this Benedictine abbey **In Muchelney 2m S of Langport.** 01458 250664 28 C4

**Nunney Castle**
A small 14th-century moated castle which is distinctly French in style. **In Nunney 3½m SW of Frome, off A361 (no coach access).** 30 A1

**Stembridge Tower Mill**
The last thatched windmill in England, overlooking the Somerset Levels. **High Ham, Somerset TA10 9DJ** 01458 250818 28 B4

**Tintinhull Garden**
Tintinhull Garden is a delightful walled garden divided into separate areas by clipped hedges. Closer to the house stands the impressive cedar court. **Farm Street, Tintinhull, Yeovil, Somerset BA22 9PZ** 01935 822545 29 D5

**Yarn Market**
A 17th-century octagonal market hall. **In Dunster High St.** 27 A4

## North Somerset

**Clevedon Court**
Outstanding 14th-century manor house built by Sir John de Clevedon, features include a massive 13th-century tower and great hall. Home to fascinating collections such as striking Eltonware pots, vases and Nailsea gloass. There is a beautiful terraced garden. **Tickenham Road, Clevedon, North Somerset BS21 6QU** 01275 872257 42 B3

**Tyntesfield**
Magnificent Gothic-Revival country house with original furnishings and decor, acquired by the National Trust in June 2002, following a public appeal. Access only by pre-booked guided tours. **Wraxall, Somerset BS48 1NT** 0870 458 4500 43 B4

## Staffordshire

**Biddulph Grange Garden**
A rare and exciting survival of a high Victorian garden, designed by James Bateman. Specimens from his extensive collections are set out in a series of connected 'compartments'. Tunnels and pathways lead to gardens inspired by countries from around the world. **Grange Road, Biddulph, Stoke-on-Trent, Staffordshire ST8 7SD** 01782 517999 128 D3

**Croxden Abbey**
Remains of a Cistercian abbey founded in 1176. **5m NW of Uttoxeter off A522.** 113 B4

**The Dorothy Clive Garden**
RHS Members: free Jul-Aug. Open: 14 Mar-31 Oct, daily, 10am-5.30pm.. **Willoughbridge, Staffordshire TF9 4EU** 01630 647237 111 A6

**Moseley Old Hall**
An Elizabethan house with later alterations. Charles II hid here after the Battle of Worcester and the bed in which he slept is on view, as well as the ingenious hiding place he used. The small garden has been reconstructed in 17th-century style with formal knot garden. **Moseley Old Hall Lane, Fordhouses, Wolverhampton, Staffordshire WV10 7HY** 01902 782808 96 A2

**Shugborough**
Complete historic estate with late 17th-century mansion, 19th-century model farm and servants' quarters. Seat of the Earls of Lichfield, the house contains collections of china, silver, paintings and furniture. Farm houses a working watermill, dairy and rare breeds of farm animal. **Milford, nr Stafford, Staffordshire ST17 0XB** 01889 881388 112 C3

**Wall Roman Site (Letocetum)**
The remains of a staging post, alongside Watling Street. Foundations of an inn and bath-house can be seen, and there is a display of finds in the site museum. **Off A5 at Wall near Lichfield.** 01543 480768 96 A3

## Suffolk

**Bury St Edmunds Abbey**
A Norman tower and 14th-century gatehouse of a ruined Benedictine abbey, church and precinct. **E end of town centre.** 87 A4

**Flatford: Bridge Cottage**
Flatford remains very much as John Constable saw and painted it 150 years ago. The thatched Bridge Cottage, upstream from Flatford Mill and right on the bank of the River Stour, is now restored and contains an exhibition on John Constable. **Flatford, East Bergholt, Colchester, Suffolk CO7 6UL** 01206 298260 88 D1

**Framlingham Castle**
A superb 12th-century castle. From the continuous curtain wall, linking 13 towers, there are excellent views over Framlingham and the charming reed-fringed mere. At different times, the castle has been a fortress, an Elizabethan prison, a poor house and a school. **In Framlingham on B1116.** 01728 724189 88 A3

**Ickworth House, Park and Garden**
The eccentric Earl of Bristol, created this equally eccentric house, started in 1795 to display his European collection of art. A wonderful collection of paintings includes works by Titian, Gainsborough and Velazquez. The Georgian silver collection is considered the finest in private hands. There are many Mediterranean species in the unusual, Italianate garden. 'Capability' Brown parkland with many ancient oaks and beech trees. **Horringer, Bury St Edmunds, Suffolk IP29 5QE** 01284 735270 87 A4

**Landguard Fort**
An 18th-century fort, with later additions. There is a museum featuring displays of local history. **1m S of Felixstowe near docks.** 01394 277767 (evenings) 88 D3

**Lavenham: The Guildhall of Corpus Christi**
Early 16th-century timber-framed Tudor building, originally the hall of the Guild of Corpus Christi, overlooks and dominates the market place. Displays of local history, farming, industry and the development of the railway, and a unique exhibition of 700 years of the medieval woollen cloth trade. **Market Place, Lavenham, Sudbury, Suffolk CO10 9QZ** 01787 247646 87 C5

**Leiston Abbey**
The remains of this abbey for Premonstratensian canons include a restored chapel. **1m N of Leiston off B1069.** 89 A5

**Lindsey Chapel**
A little 13th-century chapel with thatched roof and lancet windows. **On unclassified road ½m E of Rose Green, 8m E of Sudbury.** 87 C5

**Melford Hall**
A turreted brick Tudor mansion, little changed since 1578 with the original panelled banqueting hall, an 18th-century drawing room, a Regency library and Victorian bedrooms, showing fine furniture and Chinese porcelain. There is also a special Beatrix Potter display and a garden. **Long Melford, Sudbury, Suffolk CO10 9AA** 01787 379228 87 C4

**Moulton Packhorse Bridge**
Mediaeval four-arched bridge spanning the River Kennett. **In Moulton off B1085, 4m E of Newmarket.** 86 A2

**Orford Castle**
A royal castle built for coastal defence in the 12th century. A magnificent keep survives almost intact with three immense towers reaching to 30m (90 feet). Inside a spiral stair leads to a maze of rooms and passageways. **In Orford on B1084 20m NE of Ipswich.** 01394 450472 89 C5

**Saxtead Green Post Mill**
A fine example of a post mill, where the superstructure turns on a great post to face the wind. The mill, which ceased production in 1947, is still in working order. **2½m NW of Framlingham on A1120.** 01728 685789 88 A3

**Sutton Hoo**
One of the most fascinating and important archaeological finds in this country's history. A fascinating story of Anglo-Saxon pagan kings, ship burials, treasure and warriors is revealed. **Sutton Hoo, Woodbridge, Suffolk IP12 3DJ** 01394 389700 88 C3

**Theatre Royal**
Built in 1819 by William Wilkins, a rare example of a late Georgian playhouse with fine pit, boxes and gallery. A working theatre presenting a year-round programme of professional drama, comedy, dance, music, mime, pantomime and amateur work. Closed from August 05-November 06 for restoration. **Westgate Street, Bury St Edmunds, Suffolk IP33 1QR** 01284 769505 87 A4

## Surrey

**Clandon Park**
This is a remarkable combination: a Palladian (1730s) house with its magnificent Roman-style marble hall; the Gubbay collection of porcelain, furniture and needlework; Ivo Forde collection of Meissen Italian comedy figures; fine English 18th-century furniture; the Museum of Queen's Royal Surrey Regiment and to cap it all a Maori house in the garden. **West Clandon, Guildford, Surrey GU4 7RQ** 01483 222482 34 A3

**Claremont Landscape Garden**
One of the earliest surviving English landscape gardens. Lake, island with pavilion, grotto, turf amphitheatre, viewpoints and avenues. The first gardens were begun c 1715 and later the delights of Claremont were famed throughout Europe. **Portsmouth Road, Esher, Surrey KT10 9JG** 01372 467806 48 C4

**Dapdune Wharf**
The old boat-building site for the Wey and Godalming Navigations, Dapdune Wharf has a collection of associated buildings that have been restored and refurbished to tell the fascinating story of this historic waterway. **Wey Navigations Office, Guildford, Surrey GU1 4RR** 01483 561389 34 A2

**Farnham Castle Keep**
A motte and bailey castle, once one of the seats of the Bishop of Winchester, which has been in continuous occupation since the 12th century. **½m N of Farnham town centre on A287.** 01252 713393 34 B1

**Hatchlands Park**
A handsome mansion built in the 1750s for Admiral Boscawen, hero of the Battle of Louisburg. The mansion houses Adam interiors and the Cobbe Collection of keyboard instruments. Set in beautiful Repton park offering a variety of walks. Small Gertrude Jekyll garden. **East Clandon, Guildford, Surrey GU4 7RT** 01483 222482 34 A3

**Loseley Park**
RHS Members: free May and Sept (excluding special event days). Open: May-Sept, Wed-Sun, 11am-5pm. House open Jun-Aug. **Guildford, Surrey GU23 1HS** 01483 304440 34 B2

**Oakhurst Cottage**
A small 16th-century timber-framed cottage, restored and furnished as a simple labourer's dwelling. Delightful cottage garden with Victorian plants. **Hambledon, nr Godalming, Surrey GU8 4HF** 01483 208477 34 C2

**Polesden Lacey**
Polesden Lacey is still a peaceful country estate, surrounded by trees and green pasture. The house, an elegant Regency 'villa', was luxuriously furnished in Edwardian times by society hostess, the Hon. Mrs Greville. Her collection of furniture, paintings, porcelain and silver is remarkable. Lovely walled garden and stunning walks through the North Downs. **Nr Dorking, Surrey RH5 6BD** 01372 458203/452048 35 A4

**Runnymede**
Attractive area of riverside meadows, grassland and broad-leaved woodland, rich in flora and fauna and part-designated SSSI. It was on this site in 1215 that King John sealed Magna Carta, an event commemorated by the American Bar Association Memorial and John F Kennedy Memorial. **Egham, Surrey** 01784 432891 48 B3

**Waverley Abbey**
First Cistercian house in England, founded in 1128. **2m SE of Farnham off B3001 and off junction 10 of M25.** 34 B1

**Winkworth Arboretum**
Tranquil hillside woodland with sweeping views, established in the 20th century, now contains over 1,000 different shrubs and trees, many of them rare. Fantastic spring displays and autumn colour. Ideal place for picnics and circular walks. **Hascombe Road, Godalming, Surrey GU8 4AD** 01483 208477 34 B2

**Wisley**
Whatever the season, Wisley demostrates British gardening at its best with 240 acres of glorious garden. For 100 years the garden has been a centre of gardening excellence with visitors benefiting from the knowledge and experience of experts. Highlights of the garden include the Mixed Borders, the Country Garden, the magnificent Rock Garden, and the Alpine Houses. In addition you can visit the spectacular Piet Oudolf borders, with their modern approach to perennial planting, or Battleston Hill, alight with colour in spring, which leads on to the Trials Field with more than 50 trials each year. Everyone has their favourite area of Wisley, and the whole garden is a living encyclopaedia for all gardeners, however experienced they are. **Wisley, Woking, Surrey** 01483 224234 34 A3

**Open all year, except for Christmas Day, from 10am to 6pm (opens 9am weekends, closes 4.30pm in winter). 20 miles southwest of London on the A3, junction 10 off the M25.**

## East Sussex

**1066 Battle of Hastings, Battlefield and Abbey**
It was here in 1066 that the Battle of Hastings took place. The Abbey was built by William the Conqueror in 1070 as penance for the slaughter – the high altar marks the spot where Harold fell. There is an interactive tour around the battlefield and a 'Prelude to Battle' exhibition plus a gift shop. **In Battle, East Sussex, at S end of High St.** 01424 773792 23 A5

**Alfriston Clergy House**
Alfriston Clergy House was the first building to be acquired by the Trust in 1896. This mediaeval thatched cottage is set in a pretty cottage garden in an idyllic setting beside Alfriston's Parish church. **The Tye, Alfriston, Polegate, East Sussex BN26 5TL** 01323 870001 22 B3

**Bateman's**
Beautiful 17th-century house, home of Rudyard Kipling from 1902 to 1936. Many of the rooms, including his book-lined study, are as Kipling left them. Delightful grounds with roses and wildflowers run down to the small River Dudwell with its watermill. **Burwash, Etchingham, East Sussex TN19 7DS** 01435 882302 37 D4

**Bayham Old Abbey**
Ruins of a house of 'white' canons, founded c.1208, in an 18th-century landscaped setting. The Georgian House (Dower House) is also open to the public. **1¾m W of Lamberhurst off B2169.** 01892 890381 36 C4

**Bodiam Castle**
One of the most famous and evocative castles in Britain, Bodiam was built in 1385, both as a defence and a comfortable home. The exterior is virtually complete and the ramparts rise dramatically above the moat below. Enough of the interior survives to give an impression of castle life, and there are spiral staircases and battlements to explore. **Bodiam, Robertsbridge, East Sussex TN32 5UA** 01580 830436 37 D5

**Camber Castle**
A rare example of an Henrician fort surviving in its original plan. (Site managed by Rye Harbour Nature Reserve.) **Access by a delightful 1m walk across fields, off the A259, 1m S of Rye off Harbour Road.** 01797 223862 **for further information.** 23 A7

**Lamb House (tenanted)**
Home of the writer Henry James from 1898 to 1916 where he wrote the best novels of his later period. **West Street, Rye, East Sussex TN31 7ES** Regional Office 01372 453401 37 D7

**Monk's House (tenanted)**
A small village house and garden, and the home of Leonard and Virginia Woolf from 1919 until Leonard's death in 1969. **Rodmell, Lewes, East Sussex BN7 3HF** 01372 453401 22 B2

**Pevensey Castle**
William the Conqueror landed at Pevensey on September 28, 1066. Today you can see the ruins of the mediaeval castle including remains of an unusual keep enclosed within its walls, originally dating back to the 4th-century Roman fort Anderida. **In Pevensey off A259.** 01323 762604 22 B4

**Sheffield Park Garden**
Internationally renowned landscape garden laid out in the 18th century by 'Capability' Brown. The original four lakes form the centrepiece. Fantastic spring and autumn displays of colour, winter walks can also be enjoyed in this garden for all seasons. **Sheffield Park, East Sussex TN22 3QX** 01825 790231 36 D2

**Sheffield Park Garden**
RHS Members: free throughout open period. Open: Jan, Feb, weekends, 10.30am-4pm (or dusk), Mar-Dec, Tue-Sun and Bank Holidays, 10.30am-6pm (4pm or dusk Nov, Dec). **Sheffield Park, East Sussex TN22 3QX** 01825 790231 36 D2

## West Sussex

**Borde Hill Garden**
RHS Members: free Jan, Feb, Nov, Dec. Open: all year, daily, 10am-6pm (or dusk if earlier). **Balcombe Road, Haywards Heath, West Sussex RH16 1XP** 01444 450326 35 D6

▲ Baddesley Clinton, Warwickshire National Trust Photo Library / Andrew Butler

**Boxgrove Priory**
Remains of the Guest House, Chapter House and church of a 12th century priory. 20 B2

**Bramber Castle**
The remains of a Norman castle's gatehouse, walls and earthworks. **On W side of Bramber village off A283.** 21 A4

**Nymans Garden**
Great Sussex Weald garden developed in the 20th century by three generations of the Messel family. Nymans garden still retains much of its distinctive family style in the historic collection of plants, shrubs and trees. Messel family rooms are opened during the main season. **Handcross, nr Haywards Heath, West Sussex RH17 6EB** 01444 400321 35 D5

**Nymans Garden**
RHS Members: free throughout open period. Open: 18 Feb-31 Oct, Wed-Sun and Bank Holidays, 11am-6pm (or dusk). Nov-Feb, Sat and Sun only, 11am-4pm. Closed 1 and 2 Jan 2006. **Handcross, nr Haywards Heath, West Sussex RH17 6EB** 01444 400321 35 D5

**Petworth House and Park**
Magnificent 17th-century mansion set in a beautiful park, landscaped by 'Capability' Brown. The house contains the Trust's finest and largest collection of pictures with works by Turner, Van Dyck and Reynolds, as well as fine furniture by Grinling Gibbons. **Petworth, West Sussex GU28 0AE** 01798 342207 34 D2

**Standen**
Built in the 1890s by the architect Philip Webb, whose friendship with William Morris led to the house being decorated with many of the famous designer's textiles and wallpapers. There is also a good collection of contemporary furniture, pottery and pictures. Fine views over the Sussex countryside. **East Grinstead, West Sussex RH19 4NE** 01342 323029 36 C1

**Uppark**
A fine late 17th-century house, re-opened after major restoration following a fire in 1989. There is an important collection of paintings formed by members of the Fetherstonhaugh family. Below stairs attractions include extensive servants' rooms where the mother of H.G. Wells worked as housekeeper. **South Harting, Petersfield, West Sussex GU31 5QR** 01730 825415 33 D6

**Wakehurst Place**
This magnificent garden is leased to the Royal Botanic Gardens, Kew who maintain it. Wakehurst Place offers a unique blend of education, conservation and science. Here you can see four comprehensive National Collections plus rare plants from the Himalayas and the southern hemisphere. Temperate trees from across the continents and several lakes and ponds. **Ardingly, nr Haywards Heath, West Sussex RH17 6TN** 01444 894066 35 C6

## Tyne and Wear

**Bessie Surtees House**
Two 16th- and 17th-century merchants' houses. One is a remarkable and rare example of Jacobean domestic architecture. **41-44 Sandhill, Newcastle.** 0191 269 1200 179 C4

**Gibside**
One of the north's finest landscapes, much of which is SSSI. Gibside is a forest garden with miles of river and woodland walks. There are several outbuildings including a Palladian chapel. The estate is the former home of the Queen Mother's family, the Bowes-Lyon. **Nr Rowlands Gill, Burnopfield, Newcastle-upon-Tyne NE16 6BG** 01207 541820 178 D3

**Hylton Castle**
A 15th-century keep-gatehouse, with a fine display of mediaeval heraldry adorning the facades. **3¾m W of Sunderland.** 179 D5

**St Paul's Monastery and Bede's World Museum**
The home of the Venerable Bede, partly surviving as the chancel of the parish church. The monastery has become one of the best-understood Anglo-Saxon monastic sites. **In Jarrow, on minor road N of A185.** 0191 489 7052 179 C5

**Souter Lighthouse**
Striking Victorian lighthouse, boldly painted in red and white hoops. The first lighthouse to use alternating electric current, the most advanced lighthouse technology of its day. The engine room, light tower and keeper's living quarters are all on view. CCTV shows the view from the top for those unable to climb. **Coast Road, Whitburn, Sunderland SR6 7NH** 0191 529 3161 179 C6

**Tynemouth Priory and Castle**
The castle walls and gatehouse enclose the substantial remains of a Benedictine priory founded c.1090 on a Saxon monastic site. **In Tynemouth, near North Pier.** 0191 257 1090 179 C5

**Washington Old Hall**
Delightful stone built 17th-century manor house, which incorporates parts of the original mediaeval home of George Washington's direct ancestors. Displays on George Washington as well as collections of oil paintings and delftware. Tranquil Jacobean garden. **The Avenue, Washington Village, Tyne and Wear NE38 7LE** 0191 416 6879 179 D5

## Warwickshire

**Baddesley Clinton**
Picturesque mediaeval moated manor house dating from the 15th century. The interiors reflect the house's history as a haven for persecuted Catholics with no fewer than three priest-holes. There is a delightful garden with stewponds, a lake walk and nature walk. **Rising Lane, Baddesley Clinton Village, Knowle, Solihull, Warwickshire B93 0DQ** 01564 783294 97 D5

**Charlecote Park**
Superb Tudor house and landscaped deer park. Home of the Lucy family for over 700 years. The rich early Victorian interior contains many important objects from Beckford's Fonthill Abbey. The property has strong associations with both Queen Elizabeth and Shakespeare. **Warwick, Warwickshire CV35 9ER** 01789 470277 81 B5

**Coughton Court**
One of England's finest Tudor houses. It has important connections with the Gunpowder Plot and contains priests' hiding places. Some notable furniture, porcelain and portraits. There are two churches, a tranquil lake, riverside walk and formal gardens. **Nr Alcester, Warwickshire B49 5JA** 01789 400777 80 A3

**Kenilworth Castle**
England's largest castle ruin has been linked with many great names in history, including Henry V and Elizabeth I. Once one of the most important castles in the area, Kenilworth's key features include the Norman keep, reconstructed Tudor gardens and the remains of John of Gaunt's Great Hall. Tea room and gift shop. **In Kenilworth, Warwickshire** 01926 852078 97 D5

**Packwood House**
Dating from the 16th-century, Packwood House has been extended and much changed over the years. This fascinating timber-framed house contains a wealth of fine tapestries and furniture. Cromwell's general, Henry Ireton, slept here the night before the Battle of Edgehill in 1642. The superb gardens are noted mainly for their yew topiary and Carolean Garden and the renowned herbaceous borders. **Lapworth, Solihull, Warwickshire B94 6AT** 01564 783294 97 D4

**Upton House**
The house, built of a mellow local stone, dates from 1695, but the outstanding collections it contains are the key attraction. These include paintings by Old Masters, Brussels tapestries, Sevres porcelain, Chelsea figures and 18th-century furniture. The garden is also of great interest, with the National Collection of Asters, a large kitchen garden, a water garden and pools with ornamental fish. **Nr Banbury, Warwickshire OX15 6HT** 01295 670266 81 C6

## West Midlands

**Halesowen Abbey**
Remains of an abbey founded by King John in the 13th century, now incorporated into a 19th-century farm. **Off A456 Kidderminster road, 6m W of Birmingham city centre.** 96 C2

**Ryton Organic Gardens**
RHS Members: free throughout open period. Open: all year (closed Christmas week), 9am-5pm. **Ryton-on-Dunsmore, Coventry CV8 3LG** 024 7630 3517 97 D7

**Wightwick Manor**
Victorian manor house, one of a few surviving built and furnished under the influence of the Arts & Crafts Movement. The many original William Morris wallpapers, fabrics and Pre-Raphaelite paintings remain. An attractive garden reflects the style and character of the house. **Wightwick Bank, Wolverhampton, West Midlands WV6 8EE** 01902 761400 95 B6

## Wiltshire

**Avebury**
See: Avebury Stone Circles, The Sanctuary, Silbury Hill, West Kennet Avenue, West Kennet Long Barrow and Windmill Hill. 45 C5

**Avebury**
One of the most important megalithic monuments in Europe. The great stone circle is approached by an avenue of stones. West of Avebury, the Iron Age earthwork of Oldbury Castle crowns Cherhill Down, along with the conspicuous Lansdowne Monument. **Nr Marlborough, Wiltshire SN8 1RF** Answer-phone 01672 539250 45 C5

**Alexander Keiller Museum, Avebury**
Alexander Keiller put together one of the most important prehistoric archaeological collections in Britain, and this can be seen in the Avebury Museum. **In Avebury 7m W of Marlborough.** 01672 539250 45 C4

**Avebury Manor and Garden**
A much-altered house of monastic origin, the present buildings date from the early 16th century. The topiary and flower gardens contain mediaeval walls, ancient box and numerous 'rooms'. **Nr Marlborough, Wiltshire SN8 1RF** 01672 539250 45 B4

**Avebury Stone Circles**
Complex, gigantic and mysterious, the Circles were constructed 4,500 years ago, originally comprising more than 180 stones. **In Avebury 7m W of Marlborough.** 45 C5

**Bradford-on-Avon Tithe Barn**
A mediaeval stone-built barn with slate roof and wooden beamed interior. **¼m S of town centre, off B3109.** 44 D2

**Bratton Camp and White Horse**
A large Iron Age hill fort. **2m E of Westbury off B3098, 1m SW of Bratton.** 44 D3

**Chisbury Chapel**
A thatched 13th-century chapel rescued from use as a farm building. **On unclassified road ¼m E of Chisbury off A4 6m E of Marlborough.** 45 C6

**Corsham Court Gardens**
RHS Members: free throughout open period. Open: 20th Mar-30th Sept, Tues-Thur and weekends, 2-5pm, 1st Oct-19th Mar, weekends only, 2-4pm. Closed Dec. **Corsham Court, Corsham, Wiltshire SN13 0BZ** 01249 701610 44 B2

**The Courts Garden**
One of Wiltshire's best-kept secrets, this is the English garden style at its best, full of charm and variety. The garden includes topiary, water features and fine specimen trees under-planted with spring bulbs. A kitchen garden has been created. **Holt, Bradford-on-Avon, Wiltshire BA14 6RR** 01225 782340 44 C2

**Dyrham Park**
Beautiful baroque country house set in garden and parkland, designed by Talman for William Blathwayt, Secretary at War during the reign of William III. Fine collection of Dutch decorative arts on display include delftware, paintings and furniture. **Nr Chippenham, Wiltshire SN14 8ER** 0117 937 2501 43 B6

**Great Chalfield Manor**
Charming 15th-century manor house enhanced by a moat and gatehouse with beautiful oriel windows and a great hall. The garden, designed by Alfred Parsons, has been replanted and compliments the manor. **Nr Melksham, Wiltshire SN12 8NH** 01225 782239 44 C2

**Hatfield Earthworks**
Part of a Neolithic enclosure complex 3,500 years old. **5½m SE of Devizes off A342 NE of village of Marden.** 45 D4

**Lacock Abbey**
The abbey was founded in 1232, and was converted into a country house in the mid 16th century. The Museum of Photography commemorates the achievements of a former resident of the Abbey, William Fox Talbot, inventor of the modern photographic negative. The 13th-century village is also cared for by the National Trust. **Lacock, nr Chippenham, Wiltshire, SN15 2LG** 01249 730227 44 C3

**Ludgershall Castle and Cross**
Ruins of an early 12th-century royal hunting palace and a late-mediaeval cross. **On N side of Ludgershall off A342.** 45 D6

**Mompesson House**
A perfect example of an 18th-century house, and one of the most distinguished in the Cathedral Close. A peaceful garden with traditional herbaceous borders, provides an oasis of peace in the city centre. **The Close, Salisbury, Wiltshire SP1 2EL** 01722 335659 31 C5

**Netheravon Dovecote**
A charming 18th-century brick dovecote with most of its 700 or more nesting boxes still present. **In Netheravon, 4½m N of Amesbury on A345.** 31 A5

**Old Sarum**
Originally an Iron Age hillfort, the 56-acre site was once a major settlement in the area, occupied by the Romans, Saxons and Normans. It was one of William the Conqueror's great palaces and site of the first Salisbury Cathedral. Gift shop. **2m N of Salisbury, Wiltshire off A345.** 01722 335398 31 B5

**Old Wardour Castle**
The unusual hexagonal ruins of this 14th-century castle are on the edge of a beautiful lake, surrounded by landscaped grounds, which include an elaborate rockwork grotto. **Off A30 2m SW of Tisbury.** 01747 870487 30 C3

**Pound Hill Garden**
RHS Members: Jul-Oct. Open: Garden: Mar-Oct, daily, 2-5pm Nursery: Feb-Dec, daily, 10am-5pm. **Pound Hill, West Kington, nr Chippenham, Wiltshire SN14 7JG** 01249 783880 44 B2

**The Sanctuary**
Possibly 5,000 years old, The Sanctuary consists of two concentric circles of stones and six of timber uprights. **Beside A4, ½m E of West Kennet.** 45 C5

**Silbury Hill**
An extraordinary artificial prehistoric mound, the largest Neolithic construction of its type in Europe. There is no access to the hill. **1m W of West Kennet on A4.** 45 C5

**Stonehenge, World Heritage Site**
Visitors from all over the globe are fascinated by the mystery surrounding the ancient stone circle of Stonehenge in Wiltshire, English Heritage's most visited historic attraction and a World Heritage Site. With the first phase built over 5,000 years ago, speculation still surrounds the purpose of the monument, which is aligned with the rising and the setting of the sun. As the focal point of a landscape filled with prehistoric ceremonial structures, it is generally acknowledged that only a sophisticated society would have the design and construction skills needed to build Stonehenge and its surrounding monuments. But whether Stonehenge was built by a sun-worshipping culture or as part of a huge astronomical calendar, remains unknown. An inclusive audio tour is available in nine languages and a gift shop and refreshments are available. **2m W of Amesbury, Wiltshire on junction A303 and A344/A360.** 0870 333 1181 31 A5

**Stourhead**
Stourhead garden is one of the most famous examples of the early 18th-century English landscape movement. Sheets of water reflect splendid mature trees, temples, a classical bridge, and a grotto. The house contains a wealth of Grand Tour paintings and works of art, together with furniture designed by Chippendale the Younger. **The Estate Office, Stourton, Warminster, Wiltshire BA12 6QD** 01747 841152 30 B1

**West Kennet Avenue**
An avenue of standing stones, which ran in a curve from Avebury Stone Circles to The Sanctuary, probably dating from the late Neolithic Age. **Runs alongside B4003.** 45 C5

**West Kennet Long Barrow**
A Neolithic chambered tomb, consisting of a long earthen mound containing a passage with side chambers, and with the entrance guarded by a large stone. **¾m SW of West Kennet along footpath off A4.** 45 C5

**Westwood Manor (tenanted)**
A 15th-century stone manor house, altered in the early 17th century, with late Gothic and Jacobean windows and fine plasterwork. There is a modern topiary garden. **Bradford-on-Avon, Wiltshire BA15 2AF** 01225 863374 44 D2

**Windmill Hill**
Neolithic remains of three concentric rings of ditches, enclosing an area of 21 acres. **1½m NW of Avebury.** 45 B4

**Woodhenge**
Neolithic ceremonial monument of c. 2300 BC, consisting of a bank and ditch and six concentric rings of timber posts, now shown by concrete markers. **1½m N of Amesbury, off A345 just S of Durrington.** 31 A5

## Worcestershire

**Bredon Barn**
A 14th-century mediaeval threshing barn, beautifully constructed of local Cotswold stone and noted for its dramatic aisled interior and unusual stone chimney cowling. **Bredon, nr Tewkesbury, Worcestershire** Regional Office 01985 843600 80 D2

**Brockhampton Estate**
A late 14th-century moated manor house, with an attractive detached half-timbered 15th-century gatehouse, a rare example of this type of structure. Also the ruins of a 12th-century chapel. **Bringsty, Worcestershire WR6 5TB** 01885 482077 79 B4

**Croome Park**
Croome was 'Capability' Brown's first complete landscape, making his reputation and establishing a new parkland aesthetic which became universally adopted over the next fifty years. **NT Estate Office, The Builders' Yard, High Green, Severn Stoke, Worcestershire WR8 9JS** 01905 371006 80 C1

**The Fleece Inn**
A medieval farmhouse in the centre of the village, containing family collection of furniture. It became a licensed house in 1848 and remains largely unaltered. **Bretforton, nr Evesham, Worcestershire WR11 5JE** 01386 831173 80 C3

### The Greyfriars
Built in 1480 for a Worcester brewer on a site next to a Franciscan friary. The Greyfriars remains a good example of a wealthy merchant's home of the late Middle Ages with early 17th- and late 18th-century additions. Interesting textiles and furnishings add character to the panelled rooms. An archway leads through to a delightful garden. **Friar Street, Worcester, Worcestershire WR1 2LZ** 01905 23571 79 B6

### Hanbury Hall
This homely William & Mary-style house is famed for its fine painted ceilings and staircase. Other fascinating features include an orangery, ice house, pavilions and working mushroom house. The stunning garden and parkland provide beautiful views of the surrounding countryside. **Droitwich, Worcestershire WR9 7EA** 01527 821214 80 A2

### Leigh Court Barn
Magnificent 14th-century timber-framed barn, built for the monks of Pershore Abbey. **5m W of Worcester on unclassified road off A4103.** 79 B5

### Witley Court
In its heyday, the gardens and vast mansion (destroyed by fire in 1937) regularly hosted royalty and society. A parterre garden is also being created, as is a wilderness garden. Gift shop. 01299 896636 79 A5

## York

### Clifford's Tower
Standing high on its mound in the city of York, Clifford's Tower is one of the few vestiges of the pair of castles built by William the Conqueror after his victory in 1066. **In Tower St.** 01904 646940 149 B5

### Treasurer's House
Elegant town house, originally home to the treasurers of York Minster and built ovber a Roman road. The house was carefully restored between 1897 and 1930 by local industrialist Frank Green, with rooms presented in a variety of historic styles. **Minster Yard, York YO1 7JL** 01904 624247 149 B5

## East Riding of Yorkshire

### Burnby Hall Museum and Gardens
RHS Members: free Apr-Sept. Open: 29th Mar-28th Sept, daily, 10am-6pm. **The Balk, Pocklington, York YO42 2QE** 01759 302068 149 C7

### Burton Agnes Gardens
RHS Members: free throughout open period. Open: Apr-Oct, daily, 11am-5pm. **Burton Agnes Hall, Burton Agnes, Driffield, East Yorkshire YO25 4NB** 01262 490324 150 A3

### Burton Agnes Manor House
Rare example of a Norman house, altered and encased in brick in the 17th and 18th centuries. **In Burton Agnes village, 5m SW of Bridlington on A166.** 150 A3

### Howden Minster
Elaborate ruins of the mediaeval chancel and chapter house (viewable only from the outside) attached to the large cathedral-like Minster, now the parish church. 141 A5

### Skipsea Castle
Extensive earthworks of an abandoned, fortified mediaeval borough, attached to a Norman motte and bailey castle. **8m S of Bridlington, W of Skipsea village.** 151 B4

## North Yorkshire

### Aldborough Roman Site
The principal town of the Brigantes, the largest tribe in Roman Britain. The delightfully located remains include parts of the Roman defences and two spectacular mosaic pavements. A museum displays local Roman finds. **¾m SE of Boroughbridge, on minor road off B6265 within 1m of junction of A1(M) and A6055.** 01423 322768 148 A3

### Beningbrough Hall and Gardens
Georgian mansion built in 1716 containing one of the most impressive baroque interiors in England. Over 100 portraits on loan from the National Portrait Gallery can be seen. Other features include a fully equipped Victorian laundry, delightful walled garden and interesting wood sculptures. **Beningbrough, York, North Yorkshire YO30 1DD** 01904 470666 148 B4

### Byland Abbey
A hauntingly beautiful ruin set in peaceful meadows in the shadow of the Hambleton Hills, and once one of the great northern Cistercian monasteries. The Abbey has a splendid collection of decorated mediaeval floor tiles. **2m S of A170 between Thirsk and Helmsley, near Coxwold village.** 01347 868614 159 D4

### Duncombe Park
RHS Members: free throughout open period (house and garden). Open: 13th Apr-24th Oct, Sun-Thur, please telephone for times. **Helmsley, York, North Yorkshire, YO62 5EB** 01439 770213 159 C5

### Easby Abbey
Substantial remains of the mediaeval abbey buildings stand in a beautiful setting by the River Swale near Richmond. The abbey can be reached by a pleasant riverside walk from Richmond Castle. **1m SE of Richmond off B6271.** 157 A5

### Fountains Abbey and Studley Royal Water Garden
One of the most remarkable places in Europe, this World Heritage Site comprises the spectacular ruin of a 12th-century Cistercian abbey, an Elizabethan mansion and one of the best surviving examples of a Georgian water garden. Elegant ornamental lakes, avenues, temples and cascades provide a succession of dramatic eye-catching vistas. St Mary's Church provides a majestic focus to the medieval deer park, home to 500 deer. **Fountains, Ripon, North Yorkshire HG4 3DY** 01765 608888 148 A1

### RHS Harlow Carr
For over 50 years Harlow Carr has provided a garden setting to assess the suitability of plants for growing in the north. Now, as the first northern RHS garden, and with exciting future developments planned, the garden is "Growing to inspire". The woodland and arboretum are havens for wildlife, whilst the spectacular summer swathe of candelabra primulas along the famous streamside will delight adults and children alike. With scented, herb and foliage themed gardens, extensive vegetable and flower trials, contemporary grasses border and much more, both the keen gardener, and those just wanting a relaxing day out, will find Harlow Carr a place of magic and beauty. **Harlow Carr, Crag Lane, Harrogate** 01423 565418 148 B1 **Open all year from 9.30am to 6pm (or dusk if sooner). Just off the B6162 (Otley Road) 1½ miles from the centre of Harrogate. U Helmsley Castle 3**
The ruins of this 12th-century castle are situated on the edge of the market town of Helmsley. Set amid massive earthworks, it makes a dramatic sight. New exhibition and audio tour. 01439 770442 159 C5

### Kirkham Priory
The ruins of this Augustinian priory, including a magnificent carved gatehouse, are set in a peaceful and secluded valley by the River Derwent. **5m SW of Malton on minor road off A64.** 01653 618768 149 A6

### Marmion Tower
A mediaeval gatehouse with a fine oriel window. **N of Ripon on A6108 in West Tanfield.** 157 D6

### Middleham Castle
This childhood home of Richard III stands controlling the river that winds through Wensleydale. The massive 12th-century is one of the largest in England, and offers splendid views of the surrounding countryside from the battlements. **At Middleham, 2m S of Leyburn on A6108.** 01969 623899 157 C5

### Millgate House
RHS Members: free Apr-Oct. Open: 16 Feb-30 Mar, Sun, 12pm-4pm (weather permitting or by appointment). Apr-Oct, daily, 10am-5.30pm. **Richmond, North Yorkshire DL10 4JN** 01748 823571 157 A5

### Mount Grace Priory
The ruins of this 14-century priory are the best of any of the 10 Carthusian monasteries in Britain. A reconstructed monk's cell and herb garden offer visitors a glimpse into the daily lives of the mediaeval residents. **12m N of Thirsk, 7m NE of Northallerton on A19.** 01609 883494 158 B3

### Newby Hall and Gardens
RHS Members: free throughout open period (except special event days). Open: 1 Apr-26 Sept, Tue-Sun and Bank Holidays, 11am-5.30pm. **Ripon, North Yorkshire HG4 5AE** 0845 450 4068 148 A2

### Nunnington Hall
A delightful, mainly 17th-century, manor house on the banks of the River Rye. A magnificent panelled hall, fine tapestries, china and the Carlisle collection of miniature rooms. The delightful walled garden is a rare survival from the 17th-century which still bears traces of the original formal layout. **Nunnington, nr York, North Yorkshire YO62 5UY** 01439 748283 01439 748284 159 D5

### Parcevall Hall Gardens
RHS Members: May-Aug. Open: Apr-Oct: daily, 10am-6pm. **Skyreholme, Skipton, North Yorkshire BD23 6DE** 01756 720311 147 A4

### Pickering Castle
A splendid motte and bailey castle, once a royal hunting lodge. It is well preserved, with much of the original walls, towers and keep. There is an exhibition on the castle's history. **In Pickering 15m SW of Scarborough.** 01751 474989 159 C7

### Piercebridge Roman Bridge
Remains of the stone piers and abutment of a Roman timber bridge over the River Tees which once led to Piercebridge Roman Fort. **At Piercebridge, 4m W of Darlington on B6275.** 167 D5

### Richmond Castle
Built shortly after 1066 on the orders of William the Conqueror, this is the best-preserved castle of such scale and age in Britain. The magnificent keep, which dominates the town, provides breathtaking views over the River Swale and is reputed to be the place where the legendary King Arthur sleeps. The site's military history, including its use as a prison for First World War conscientious objectors, is explored further in a special exhibition, as well as being reflected in the contemporary heritage garden. **In Richmond.** 01748 822493 157 A5

### Rievaulx Abbey
Rievaulx was the first Cistercian Abbey to be founded in the north of England and became one of the most powerful monasteries in Europe. The atmospheric spiritual ruins were once home to the greatest spiritual writer of the Mediaeval Ages, St Aelred, who described it as 'everywhere peace, everywhere serenity, and a freedom from the tumult of the world'. A special exhibition examines the commercial activities of the monks and shows how religion blended with business, with the Abbey at the centre of a mediaeval-style "industrial revolution". **In Rievaulx, North Yorkshire 2¼m W of Helmsley on minor road off B1257.** 01439 798228 159 C4

### Rievaulx Terrace and Temples
One of Yorkshire's finest 18th-century landscape gardens. Vistas over Rievaulx Abbey (English Heritage) to Ryedale and the Hambleton Hills. The two mid-18th-century temples include the Ionic Temple, intended as a banqueting house with elaborate ceiling paintings and fine furniture. **Nr Helmsley, North Yorkshire YO62 5LJ** 01439 798340 159 C4

### Ripley Castle Gardens
RHS Members: free throughout open period. Open: all year, daily, 9am-5pm (4.30pm during winter). **Ripley, nr Harrogate, North Yorkshire HG3 3AY** 01423 770152 148 A1

### Scarborough Castle
There are spectacular coastal views from the walls of this enormous 12th-century castle. The buttressed castle walls stretch out along the cliff edge and the remains of the great rectangular stone keep still stand to over three storeys high. There is also the site of a 4th-century Roman signal station. The castle was often attacked, but despite being blasted by cannons of the Civil War and bombarded during World War I, it is still a spectacular place to visit. **Castle Rd, E of town centre.** 01723 372451 161 C4

### Spofforth Castle
Manor house with fascinating features including an undercroft built into the rock. Once owned by the Percy family. **3½m SE of Harrogate, off A661 at Spofforth.** 148 B2

### Stanwick Iron Age Fortifications
The tribal stronghold of the Brigantes, whose vast earthworks cover some 850 acres. **On minor road off A6274 at Forcett Village.** 167 D4

### Steeton Hall Gateway
A fine example of a small, well-preserved 14th-century gatehouse. **4m NE of Castleford, on minor road off A162 at South Milford.** 148 D3

### Stillingfleet Lodge Nurseries
RHS Members: free throughout open period. Open: May-Sept, Wed and Fri, 1-4pm. **Stewart Lane, Stillingfleet, North Yorkshire YO19 6HP** 01904 728506 149 C4

### St Mary's Church Studley Royal
Magnificent Victorian church, designed by William Burges in the 1870s, with a highly decorated interior. **2½m W of Ripon off B6265, in grounds of Studley Royal estate.** 01765 608888 148 A1

### Thorp Perrow Arboretum and Woodland Garden
RHS Members: free Mon-Fri (excluding Bank Holidays and event days) throughout open period. Open: Mar-mid-Nov, daily, dawn-dusk. **Bedale, North Yorkshire DL8 2PR** 01677 425323 157 C6

### Wharram Percy Deserted Mediaeval Village
One of over 3,000 deserted villages to have been identified from the foundations of over 30 houses still visible. The remains of the mediaeval church still stand. **6m SE of Malton, on minor road from B1248 ½m S of Wharram le Street.** 150 A1

### Wheeldale Roman Road
This mile-long stretch of Roman road, still with its hardcore and drainage ditches, runs across isolated moorland. **S of Goathland, W of A169, 7m S of Whitby.** 159 B7

### Whitby Abbey
These moody and magnificent ruins offer dramatic views over the town and harbour. A superb new visitor centre and museum helps visitors discover key periods in the site's history – from the Synod of 644 who decided on the date of Easter to the inspiration behind Bram Stoker's fictional classic Dracula. **On cliff top E of Whitby in North Yorkshire** 01947 603568 169 D7

## South Yorkshire

### Brodsworth Hall
Brodsworth Hall offers a unique opportunity to see the faded grandeur of a Victorian country house with much of the original decorating scheme surviving – from the grand reception rooms and private quarters to the cluttered Victorian kitchen. Outside, the gardens have undergone a programme of restoration and are a copybook example of 1860s design. Tearoom and shop. **In Brodsworth, South Yorkshire, off A635 Barnsley Road, from junction 37 of A1(M).** 01302 722598 140 C3

### Conisbrough Castle
The spectacular white circular keep of this 12th-century castle is the only one of its kind in England and is a fine example of mediaeval architecture. **NE of Conisbrough town centre off A630, 4½m SW of Doncaster.** 01709 863329 140 D3

### Monk Bretton Priory
Sandstone ruins of a Cluniac monastery founded in 1153, including remains of the 14th-century gatehouse. **1m E of Barnsley off A633** 140 C1

### Roche Abbey
Fine remains of a Cistercian monastery now set in a Lancelot 'Capability' Brown landscaped valley. **1½m S of Maltby off A634.** 01709 812739 140 D3

## West Yorkshire

### East Riddlesden Hall
A charming 17th-century West Yorkshire manor house with embroideries, pewter and a fine collection of Yorkshire oak furniture. The tranquil walled garden overlooking a grass maze has now been restored to its original design. **Bradford Road, Keighley, West Yorkshire BD20 5EL** 01535 607075 147 C4

### Harewood House
RHS Members: free Mar-Jun, excluding weekends, Bank Holidays and special event days. Open: Feb-Oct, daily, 10am-6pm. **Harewood, Leeds, West Yorkshire, LS17 9LQ** 0113 218 1010 148 C2

### Nostell Priory
18th-century architectural masterpiece with Adam interiors and fine collections set in a landscaped park. Built by James Paine on the site of a mediaeval priory, the priory houses one of England's best collections of Chippendale furniture, as well as an outstanding art collection. **Doncaster Road, Nostell, nr Wakefield, West Yorkshire WF4 1QE** 01924 863892 140 B2

# Scotland

## Aberdeenshire

### Castle Fraser, Garden and Estate
**Off A944, 4m north of Dunecht and 16m west of Aberdeen**
Approaching Castle Fraser, you're certain to be impressed by the magnificent tower with its distinctive turrets. Dating from 1636, this is one of the grandest Castles of Mar. Inside the Great Hall, fine furniture, paintings and embroideries powerfully evoke the past. In the grounds, enjoy the secluded walled garden and woodland walks. Children will love the adventure playground. Courtyard tearoom, shop, plant sales. **Sauchen, Inverurie AB51 7LD** 01330 833463 245 A4

### HS Corgarff Castle
A 16th-century tower house converted into a barracks for Hanoverian troops in 1748. Its last military use was to control the smuggling of illicit whisky between 1827 and 1831. Still complete and with star-shaped fortification. **8m W of Strathdon village.** 01975 651460. 243 B5

### Craigievar Castle
**On A980, 26m west of Aberdeen**
Standing just as it did when completed in 1626, this fine example of Scottish Baronial architecture, rising seven storeys high, appears almost to grow out of the rolling hills. Walking the grounds, you can enjoy the panoramic views of the countryside. Please note that the castle itself will be closed until spring 2007 for restoration work, but the grounds will remain open. **Alford AB33 8JF** 013398 83635 244 B2

### Crathes Castle, Garden and Estate
**On A93, 3m east of Banchory and 15m west of Aberdeen** With its intriguing round towers and overhanging turrets, Crathes is a fine example of a 16th-century tower house, home to the Burnett family for over four centuries. The magnificent gardens, with their massive yew hedges and colourful herbaceous borders, were recently judged one of the three best in Britain. The gardens and estate, with fascinating waymarked trails, are ideal for a family day out. Circular mill restaurant, wildlife exhibition, shop, plant sales centre, picnic area, adventure playground. **Banchory AB31 3QJ** 01330 844525 245 C4

### Drum Castle, Garden and Estate
**Off A93, 3m west of Peterculter, 8m east of Banchory and 10m west of Aberdeen**
A visit to Drum Castle is a little like striding across the centuries. It includes a 13th-century keep, with adjoining Jacobean mansion house and several 'modern' additions by Victorian lairds. The castle holds a superb collection of paintings and furniture, and for keen gardeners there is a splendid collection of roses in the Garden of Historic Roses. For children there are woodland trails and a play area. Shop and tearoom. **Drumoak, nr Banchory AB31 5EY** 01330 811204 245 B4

### Fyvie Castle
**Off A947, 8m south-east of Turriff and 25m north-west of Aberdeen**
The appeal of Fyvie Castle spans the centuries. Some parts date from the 13th century, while the opulent interiors are Edwardian. Art lovers will recognise paintings by Raeburn and Gainsborough, and military enthusiasts will appreciate the impressive collection of arms and armour. Take a leisurely stroll around the lake, or visit the restored racquets court and bowling alley. Tearoom and shop. **Fyvie, Turriff AB53 8JS** 01651 891266 256 C2

### Haddo House
**Off B999, near Tarves, 19m north of Aberdeen**
Imagine life amongst the Scottish nobility when you visit this elegant country house, once the home of the Earls and Marquesses of Aberdeen. The distinctive Georgian exterior leads into sumptuous Victorian interiors. You're also free to wander amongst the terrace gardens and country park beyond, with lakes, walks and monuments. Tearoom and shop. **Ellon AB41 7EQ** 01651 851440 256 C3

### HS Huntly Castle
A magnificent ruin consisting mainly of a palace block erected in the 16th and 17th centuries by the Gordon family. **In Huntly.** 01466 793191. 255 B6

### HS Kildrummy Castle
Though ruined, the best example in Scotland of a 13th-century castle, with a curtain wall, four round towers, hall and chapel. The seat of the Earls of Mar, it was dismantled after the 1715 Jacobite Rising. **10m W of Alford.** 01975 571331. 244 A1

**HS Kinnaird Head Lighthouse**
Built in 1787 within a 16th-century tower house, Kinnaird Head was the first lighthouse built by the Northern Lighthouse Company. **On a promontory in Fraserburgh.** 01346 511022. 269 C5

**Leith Hall, Garden and Estate**
**On B9002, 1m west of Kennethmont and 34m north-west of Aberdeen**
This fine mansion house stands as a living monument to the Leith family who lived here for almost 300 years. You can find out more about how they lived when you wander through the elegantly furnished rooms. Outside you can explore the estate trails or lose yourself among the colourful herbaceous borders. Period tearoom, picnic area, bird hide. **Huntly AB54 4NQ** 01464 831216 255 D6

**Leith Hall and Garden**
RHS Members: free throughout open period. Open: all year, daily, 9.30am-sunset. House open Easter weekend, May-Sept, Fri-Tue, 12pm-5pm. **(National Trust for Scotland) Huntly, Aberdeenshire AB54 4NQ** 01464 831216 255 D6

**Mar Lodge Estate**
**Off A93, 6m west of Braemar via an unclassified road; parking at Linn of Dee**
Located in the heart of the Cairngorms, Mar Lodge offers a wealth of interest for walkers and nature lovers. The estate contains four of the five highest mountains in the UK as well as remnant Caledonian pine forest. There is a rich variety of wildlife and bird life including red deer, red squirrels and golden eagles, and walks to suit all abilities. Ranger-guided walks are also available. **Braemar AB35 5YJ** 013397 41433 **Ranger Service: 013397 41669** 242 D3

**Pitmedden Garden**
**On A920, 1m west of Pitmedden village and 14m north of Aberdeen**
Gardeners will appreciate Pitmedden not only as a beautifully kept garden, but also as a unique historical re-creation. The Great Garden follows elaborate 17th-century parterre designs with thousands of colourful bedding plants. There are also woodland walks, fine herbaceous borders, topiary and a herb garden. The Museum of Farming Life close by brings the agricultural past to life. Tearoom, shop, picnic area. **Ellon AB41 7PD** 01651 842352 256 D3

**HS Tolquhon Castle**
Built for the Forbes family, Tolquhon has an early 15th-century tower. It is noted for its highly ornamented gatehouse. **15m from Aberdeen off the Pitmedden – Tarves Road.** 01651 851286. 256 D3

## Angus
*See also* Dundee

**Angus Folk Museum**
**Off A94, in Kirkwynd, Glamis, 5m south-west of Forfar**
A fascinating glimpse into traditional Scottish rural life. Housed in a group of 18th-century buildings, the folk museum's collection offers an insight into the realities of life as a local land worker. It includes farming tools, domestic objects and the restored 19th-century 'Glenisla' hearse. **Kirkwynd, Glamis, Forfar, Angus DD8 1RT** 01307 840288 232 D1

**HS Arbroath Abbey**
The substantial ruins of a Tironensian monastery, founded by William the Lion in 1178. Parts of the abbey church and domestic buildings remain. This was the scene of the Declaration of Arbroath of 1320, which asserted Scotland's independence from England. **In Arbroath.** 01241 878756. 233 D4

**Barry Mill**
**North of Barry village, between A92 and A930, 2m west of Carnoustie, 9m east of Dundee**
Enjoy the splash of the waterwheel, the rumble of the machinery and the smell of the grinding corn in this 19th-century mill, working on a demonstration basis. There's an exhibition on the historical role of the mill, and a delightful walkway along the mill lade. Milling demonstrations normally take place on Sunday afternoons and for pre-booked parties. **Barry, Carnoustie, Angus DD7 7RJ** 01241 856761 221 A5

**HS Edzell Castle and Garden**
Very beautiful complex with a late-medieval tower house incorporated into a 16th-century courtyard mansion. The carved decoration of the garden walls is unique in Britain. **At Edzell, 6m N of Brechin.** 01356 648631. 232 B3

**Finavon Doocot**
**In Finavaon, off A90**
Largest doocot in Scotland, with 2,400 nesting boxes. Believed to have been built by the Earl of Crawford in the 16th century. 232 C2

**House of Dun and Montrose Basin Nature Reserve**
**3m west of Montrose on the A935**
This handsome house, dating from 1730, was once the home of Lady Augusta FitzClarence, daughter of William IV and the actress Mrs Jordan. Don't miss her royal mementoes, or the superb plasterwork by Joseph Enzer in the saloon. The surrounding estate includes a woodland walk and a recreated Victorian walled garden. Visitors have access to the Montrose Basin Nature Reserve. Restaurant, shop and picnic area. **Montrose, Angus DD10 9LQ** 01674 810264 233 B4

**JM Barrie's Birthplace and Camera Obscura**
**A90/A926, in Kirriemuir, 6m north-west of Forfar.**
A great afternoon out for children of all ages. JM Barrie, the creator of Peter Pan, was born here in 1860, one of ten children. Barrie established his first theatre in the outside wash-house. There's an imaginative exhibition about the author and 'Pirates' Workshop' for children. Look out for the crocodile in the garden! Tearoom and picnic area. The fascinating camera obscura, one of only three in the country, was a gift to the town from JM Barrie. From the top of Kirriemuir Hill you can enjoy superb views of the surrounding countryside **9 Brechin Road, Kirriemuir, Angus DD8 4BX** 01575 572646 232 C1

## Argyll and Bute

**Arduaine Garden**
**On A816, 20m south of Oban and 18m north of Lochgilphead.**
A favourite destination for gardeners all year round. The perennial borders at Arduaine are magnificent throughout the season, but in late spring and early summer the rhododendrons and azaleas really come into their own. Stroll through the woodland and enjoy the views from the coast, or relax in the water garden. **Arduaine, nr Oban, Argyll PA34 4XQ** 01852 200366 213 A5

**HS Bonawe Iron Furnace**
Founded in 1753 by a Lake District partnership, this is the most complete charcoal-fuelled ironworks in Britain. Displays illustrate how iron was made here. **Close to the village of Taynuilt.** 01866 822432. 227 C5

**Burg**
**Isle of Mull, Argyll and Bute. By footpath, 5 miles W of Tiroran, off B8035 on north shore of Loch Scridain.**
These 1,405 acres of Mull, with high cliffs known as 'The Wilderness', were bequeathed by Mr A Campbell Blair of Dolgelly in 1932. MacCulloch's Fossil Tree, possibly 50 million years old, is beyond Burg Farm and can be reached at low water with difficulty. A 7-mile walk on a path which becomes very rough and precipitous culminates in a steep descent to the beach by an iron ladder. 224 D3

**Crarae Garden**
**On A83, 15m north of Lochgilphead and 10m south of Inveraray**
Crarae, on the banks of Loch Fyne, is a beautiful woodland glen with tumbling waterfalls. Trees and shrubs from all over the world thrive here throughout the year, and in the spring the rhododendrons burst into life. Shop, refreshments, picnic area. **Crarae, Inveraray PA32 8YA** 214 C2

**HS Dunstaffnage Castle and Chapel**
A very fine 13th-century castle enclosure, built on a rock, with nearby ruins of a chapel of exceptional architectural refinement. **By Loch Etive, 3½m from Oban.** 01631 562465. 226 C3

**Geilston Garden**
**On A814 at west end of Cardross, 18m north-west of Glasgow**
A delight for garden enthusiasts. This 200-year-old walled garden has shrub borders, lawns and a herbaceous border that bursts into spectacular colour in summer. There are enchanting woodland walks along Geilston Burn. A wide range of market garden crops can be seen growing in the popular vegetable garden. This produce is also offered for sale to visitors. Produce sales and picnic area. **Cardross, Dumbarton G82 5HD** 01389 849187 204 A3

**Geilston Gardens**
RHS Members: free throughout open period. Open: Apr-Oct, daily, 9.30am-5pm. **(National Trust for Scotland) Cardross, Dumbarton G82 5EZ** 01389 849187 204 A3

**Glencoe and Dalness**
**Off A82, 17m south of Fort William**
Glencoe is a dramatic location in every sense. This spectacular landscape was the setting for the notorious massacre of th MacDonalds by government soldiers in 1692. Find out about the glen's remarkable history, landscape and wildlife at the Trust's eco-friendly Visitor Centre. The glen is also a walker's paradise – from gentle strolls to challenging climbs for experienced mountaineers. Cafe, shop and picnic area. **NTS Visitor Centre, Glencoe, Argyll PA49 4LA** **Centre:01855 811307 Ranger:01855 811729** 237 D5

**The Hill House**
**Off B832, between A82 and A814, 23m north-west of Glasgow**
Anyone with a passion for design and architecture will love this house, commissioned in 1902 but still looking startlingly modern. Mackintosh and his wife Margaret MacDonald also designed the interiors and fittings, including the exquisite writing cabinet recently acquired by the Trust and now in its original setting from April to July. Look out for the changing exhibitions of contemporary design. Mackintosh shop and Contemporary Design shop, tearoom. **Upper Colquhoun Street, Helensburgh G84 9AJ** 01463 673900 215 D5

**Iona**
**By ferry from Fionnphort, Isle of Mull (A849)**
In AD 563 Columba and his followers arrived here from Ireland to extend in Scotland and the north of England the gospel which had first been introduced by St Ninian at Whithorn in AD 397. 224 D1

# Historic Scotland

## How to join Historic Scotland

For immediate membership you can join at any staffed Historic Scotland property, on-line at www.historic-scotland.gov.uk or by phoning +44 (0)131 668 8999 • Historic Scotland, Longmore House, Salisbury Place, Edinburgh EH9 1SH 0131 668 8800

**HS Iona Abbey and Nunnery**
One of Scotland's most historic and sacred sites, Iona Abbey was founded by St Columba and his Irish followers in AD 563. A celebrated focus for Christian pilgrimage, Iona retains its spiritual atmosphere and remains an enduring symbol of worship. **On the Island of Iona, public ferry from Fionnphort, Mull.** 01681 700512 224 D1

**HS Rothesay Castle**
A remarkable 13th-century, circular castle of enclosure. A favourite residence of the Stewart kings. **In Rothesay, Isle of Bute.** 01700 502691. 203 B5

**Staffa National Nature Reserve**
**11 km (7 miles) northeast of Iona.**
Romantic and uninhabited island, famous for its basaltic formations, the best known of which is Fingal's Cave. Immortalised by Mendelssohn in his celebrated Hebrides overture, its cluster columns and seemingly man-made symmetry give the cave a cathedral-like majesty. Visitors have included the artist J M W Turner, and poets and writers Keats, Wordsworth, Tennyson and Sir Walter Scott. 224 C2

**Tighnabruaich Viewpoint**
**On A8003, north-east of Tighnabruaich**
The indicators, attributed to the Trust and the Scottish Civic Trust, were erected by a Trust supporter in memory of two brothers, who gave generously of their time to the work of the Trust. 203 A4

**Torosay Castle and Gardens**
RHS Members: free Apr-Jun and Sept-Oct. Open: all year, daily, 9am-sunset. **Torosay Castle, Craignure, Isle of Mull PA65 6AY** 01680 812421 226 C2

## North Ayrshire

**Brodick Castle, Garden and Country Park**
**Ferry from Ardrossan to Brodick (connecting bus to castle) and Claonaig, Kintyre to Lochranza (ferry enquiries 0870 565000)**
Brodick Castle, with origins in Viking times, has everything – heritage, horticulture and activity. For antique-lovers, the castle is packed with artefacts telling Brodick's story. Gardeners will love exploring the estate, with its famous rhododendron collection. Still in the mood for walking? Discover woodlands, waterfalls and wildlife along trails around the Country Park, or tackle the rugged clopes of Goatfell. Licensed terrace restaurant, coffee shop, shop, plant sales centre, picnic area, adventure playground. **Isle of Arran KA27 8HY** 01770 302202 191 B6

**Goatfell**
**Isle of Arran**
Goatfell is the highest peak on the Isle of Arran, with impressive views. Trust property includes part of Glen Rosa and Cir Mhor; fine rock climbing and ridge walking. 203 D4

## South Ayrshire

**Bachelors' Club**
**In Tarbolton, off A77 south of Kilmarnock and off A76 at Mauchline. 7½m north-east of Ayr**
A chance to find out more about Scotland's most famous poet, Robert Burns. In this thatched 17th-century house, Burns and his friends hotly debated the topics of the day before drinking their fill at the inn next door. **Sandgate Street, Tarbolton KA5 5RB** 01292 541940 193 C4

**HS Crossraguel Abbey**
The 13th-century remains, which are remarkably complete and of high quality, include the church, cloister, chapter house and much of the domestic premises. **2m S of Maybole.** 01655 883113. 192 E2

**Culzean Castle and Country Park**
**12m south of Ayr, on A719, 4m west of Maybole, off A77**
Culzean Castle occupies a stunning location with spectacular views across the Firth of Clyde; it is surrounded by acres of ornamental gardens and parkland. Inside the castle, look out for the Oval Staircase, the Circular Saloon and the impressive armoury. Afterwards enjoy the delicious Scottish produce in the Home Farm restaurant or take home some plants from the Country Park shop. Ranger service, full events programme including special children's events, adventure playground, deer park, licensed restaurant. **Maybole KA19 8LE** 01655 884455 192 E2

**HS Dundonald Castle**
A fine 13th-century tower built by Robert II incorporating part of an earlier building. The king used the castle as a summer residence until his death in 1390. **In Dundonald, off the A759.** 01563 851489. 192 B3

**Souter Johnnie's Cottage**
**In Kirkoswald, A77, 4m south-west of Maybole**
A visit to Souter Johnnie's cottage is like stepping into one of Burns' poems. The shoemaker who inspired the character Souter Johnnie in Burns' Tam O'Shanter lived and worked here. The much-loved poem comes to life in the garden, where life-sized stone figures of the characters sit in the restored alehouse. **Main Road, Kirkoswald KA19 8HY** 01655 760603 192 E2

## Clackmannanshire

**Alloa Tower**
**Off A907 in Alloa, Clackmannanshire 6m east of Stirling**
A fascinating view inside the ancestral home of the Earls of Mar, whose portraits still look down from the walls of the tower. Parts of the structure date back to medieval times and you can still see the original dungeon, well and roof-beams contrasting with the elegant staircase added in the 18th century. **Alloa Park, Alloa, Clackmannanshire FK10 1PP** 01259 211701 208 A1

**HS Castle Campbell**
Traditionally known as the 'Castle of Gloom'. The oldest part is a well-preserved 15th-century tower, around which other buildings were constructed, including an unusual loggia. **At the head of Dollar Glen.** 01259 742408. 208 A2

**Dollar Glen**
**Clackmannanshire. Off A91, north of Dollar.** This wooded glen provides spectacular walks to Castle Campbell. During or after rain the path can be dangerous. Dogs must be kept strictly under control and on leads during lambing season. 208 A2

▼ **Black Rock cottages, Glencoe, Argyll and Bute** National Trust Photo Library / Andrew Butler

# The National Trust for Scotland

## How to join The National Trust for Scotland

For immediate membership you can join at almost all of the Trust's properties or shops. Alternatively contact The National Trust for Scotland, 28 Charlotte Square, Edinburgh EH2 4ET
☎0131 243 9300 ☎0131 243 9301 wwww.nts.org.uk

**Menstrie Castle**
**Off A91 in Menstrie, 5m north-east of Stirling**
Not Trust property, but the Trust, in co-operation with the then Clackmannanshire County Council, played a large part in saving it from demolition. It was the birthplace of Sir William Alexander, James VI's Lieutenant for the Plantation of Nova Scotia, and an exhibition in the Nova Scotia Commemoration Room tells the story of this ill-fated scheme. Castle Road, Menstrie FK11 ☎01259 211701 207 A6

## Dumfries and Galloway

**Broughton House and Garden**
**Off A711/A755**
Cross the threshold of Broughton House and enter the world of well-known Scottish artist EA Hornel, one of the 'Glasgow Boys'. Now open to the public after a period of conservation, this fine 18th-century town house was bought by Hornel in 1901 and became his home and studio. Today, you can admire his paintings and those of his fellow artists throughout the house and gallery. See how the design and colours of the garden reflect the artist's vision through a series of charming 'outdoor rooms'. **12 High Street, Kirkcudbright DG6 4JX** ☎01557 330437 173 C4

**HS Caerlaverock Castle**
One of the finest castles in Scotland, on a triangular site surrounded by moats. Its special features are the twin-towered gatehouse and the Nithsdale Lodging, a Renaissance range dating from 1638. **8m SE of Dumfries.** ☎01387 770244. 174 B3

**HS Cardoness Castle**
The well-preserved ruin of a tower house of 15th-century date, the ancient home of the McCullochs. **1m SW of Gatehouse of Fleet.** ☎01557 814427. 172 D3

**HS Dundrennan Abbey**
The beautiful ruins of a Cistercian abbey founded by David I. Mary Queen of Scots spent her last night on Scottish soil here. **6½m E of Kirkcudbright.** ☎01557 500262. 173 D5

**Gatehouse of Fleet**
**Dumfries and Galloway. Off A75.**
Venniehill: a field with hilltop viewpoint at the west end of the main street. The Murray Isles: two small uninhabited islands in the Islands of Fleet, Wigtown Bay, off Carrick Point. 172 C4

**HS Glenluce Abbey**
Cistercian abbey founded in 1192. The remains include a handsome early 16th-century chapter house. **2m N of Glenluce village.** ☎01581 300541. 170 B3

**Glenwhan Garden**
RHS Members: free 1 Aug-30 Oct. Open: All year, daily, 10am-5pm. **Dunragit, by Stranraer, Wigtownshire DG9 8PH** ☎01581 400222 170 B3

**Grey Mare's Tail Nature Reserve**
**On A708, 10m north-east of Moffat**
A magnificent upland area, reaching from the waterfall that cascades into the Moffat Valley, up steep slopes to Loch Skeen and cor-ries beyond. Home to rare upland plants and a variety of wildlife. This landscape, shaped by human activity since the Iron Age, offered refuge to the 17th-century Covenanters. Guided walks are available in summer. Video link to peregrine falcon nest site. 185 A4

**HS MacLellan's Castle**
A castellated town house built by the then provost of Kirkcudbright from 1577, with particularly good architectural details. **In the centre of Kirkcudbright.** ☎01557 331856. 173 C4

**HS New Abbey Corn Mill**
A carefully renovated water-powered oatmeal mill, in working order, and demonstrated regularly to visitors in the summer. **In New Abbey village.** ☎01387 850260. 174 B2

**Rockcliffe**
**Off A710, 7m south of Dalbeattie**
A beautiful stretch of coastline for wandering and exploring. Includes a network of paths, among them the Jubilee path from Kippford to Rockcliffe, with guided walks available in summer. There's a huge variety of plants and flowers to see, as well as the Rough Island bird sanctuary and the Mote of Mark ancient hill fort. 173 C6

**HS Sweetheart Abbey**
Splendid ruin of a late 13th- and early 14th-century Cistercian abbey founded by Dervorgilla, Lady of Galloway. **In New Abbey village, 7m S of Dumfries.** ☎01387 850397. 174 B2

**Thomas Carlyle's Birthplace**
**Off M74, 5½m south-east of Lockerbie**
A fascinating insight into the life and work of writer and historian Thomas Carlyle. He was born here in 1795 and the house is furnished in period style with an intriguing collection of portraits and Carlyle's personal belongings. **The Arched House, Ecclefechan, Lockerbie DG11 3DG** ☎01576 300666 175 A4

**Threave**
**Off A75, 1m west of Castle Douglas**
A fascinating spot for garden enthusiasts. Wander around the rose garden and the walled garden with its splendid glasshouse collection. In spring, see the gardens come alive with nearly 200 varieties of daffodil. Meanwhile in Threave House discover past times with the Maxwelton Collection of household objects. Or see a live video link with the estate's bird life from the Countryside Centre. Licensed terrace restaurant, shop, plant sales centre. **Castle Douglas DG7 1RX** ☎01556 503702 173 B5

**HS Threave Castle**
Massive tower built in the late 14th century. Round its base is an artillery fortification built before 1455, when the castle was besieged by James II. It is on an island, approached by boat, followed by a long walk. **3m W of Castle Douglas.** ☎07711 223101. 173 B5

**Threave Garden and Estate**
RHS Members: free Apr, May, Sept, Oct. Open: all year, daily, 9am-sunset. Visitor Centre open Feb, Mar and Nov, Dec, daily 10am-4pm; Apr-Oct, daily, 9.30am-5.30pm. **(National Trust for Scotland), Castle Douglas, Dumfries and Galloway DG7 1RX** ☎01556 502575 173 B5

**HS Whithorn Priory and Museum**
Site of the first Christian church in Scotland, founded as 'Candida Casa' by St Ninian in the early 5th century. The priory was built over the church for remonstratensian canons in the 12th century and became the cathedral church of Galloway. In the museum is a fine collection of early Christian stones. **In Whithorn.** ☎01988 500508. 171 C6

## West Dunbartonshire

**HS Dumbarton Castle**
Spectacularly sited on a volcanic rock, this was the site of the ancient capital of Strathclyde. The most interesting features are the 18th-century artillery fortifications, with 19th-century guns. **At Dumbarton.** ☎01389 732167. 205 A4

## Dundee

*See also* Angus

**Dundee University Botanic Garden**
RHS Members: free throughout open period. Open: Mar-Oct, daily, 10am-4.30pm, Nov-Feb, daily, 10am-3.30pm **University of Dundee, Riverside Drive, Dundee DD2 1QH** ☎01382 647190 220 B3

## Edinburgh

**Caiy Stane**
**In Caiystane View, off B701, Oxgangs Road, Edinburgh**
This 9ft (3m) tall prehistoric cup-marked stone, also known as General Kay's Monument, or the Kel Stone, traditionally marks the site of an ancient battle, perhaps between the Picts and the Romans. 209 D5

**HS Craigmillar Castle**
Built round an L-plan tower house of the early 15th century, Craigmillar was much expanded in the 15th and 16th centuries. It is a handsome ruin, and includes a range of private rooms. **2½ m SE of central Edinburgh, to E of Edinburgh to Dalkeith Road.** ☎0131 661 4445. 209 C5

**HS Edinburgh Castle**
The most famous of Scottish castles has a complex history. The oldest part dates from the Norman period; there is a Great Hall built by the James IV; the Half Moon battery was built by Regent Morton in the late 16th century; the Scottish National War Memorial was formed after World War I. The castle also houses the crown jewels (Honours) of Scotland, the history of which is described in a new exhibition. Also see the famous 15th-century gun, Mons Meg. Attractive restaurant with spectacular views over the city. **In the centre of Edinburgh.** ☎0131 225 9846. 209 C5

**The Georgian House**
**Charlotte Square, 2 mins from west end of Princes Street.**
On the opposite side of Charlotte Square to No 28 Charlotte Square, home of the NTS, at No 7 is the Georgian House, a vivid recreation of life in late 18th century Edinburgh. Experience a taste of high society and the fascinating 'below stairs' life of servants who made this elegant lifestyle possible. **7 Charlotte Square, Edinburgh EH2 4DR** ☎0131 226 3318 209 C5

**Gladstone's Land**
**On Edinburgh's Royal Mile, near the castle**
A window onto 17th century Edinburgh life. Antique lovers will be fascinated by this Old Town apartment, featuring authentic decoration and period furniture as well as a fine collection of Dutch paintings. Don't forget to look up and admire the remarkable painted ceilings. Experience the 17th century-style shopping in the reconstructed 'luckenbooth' cloth shop. **477B Lawnmarket, Edinburgh EH1 2NT** ☎0131 226 5856 209 C5

**Malleny Garden**
**In Balerno, near Edinburgh, off Lanark Road (A70).**
The 17th-century house (not open to the public) was built for Sir James Murray of Kilbaberton about 1635, with two Georgian reception rooms added in 1823. The walled garden is dominated by four 400-year-old clipped yew trees and a large collection of old-fashioned roses. It also has the National Bonsai Collection for Scotland. Extensive woodland. **Balerno EH14 7AF** ☎0131 449 2283 209 D4

**Newhailes**
**Off A6095, Newhailes Road, Musselburgh**
A mellow, untouched late 17th century house and designed landscape. The rococo interior has many original decorations and furnishings. It's easy to imagine famous figures from the Scottish Enlightenment gathered in the library with their hosts the Dalrymples, many of whom appear in the fine collection of portraits and paintings. The historic landscape surprises with unexpected features that inspire reflection. Shop and courtyard cafe. **Newhailes Road, Musselburgh EH21 6RY** ☎0131 653 5599 209 C6

**No 28 Charlotte Square**
**Edinburgh, 2 mins from west end of Princes Street**
Sample the best of Scotland's heritage in the New Town with a visit to the Trust gallery. There's a fine collection of 20th-century works by the Scottish Colourists, and a wonderful display of Regency furniture. Temporary exhibitions are advertised separately. Relax in the coffee house and the courtyard garden, or enjoy light lunches in the bistro. Licensed bistro, coffee house, gift shop, New Interiors Collection shop. **28 Charlotte Square, Edinburgh EH2 4ET** ☎0131 243 9300 209 C5

## Falkirk

**HS Blackness Castle**
Built in the 1440s, and massively strengthened in the 16th century as an artillery fortress, Blackness was an ammunition depot in the 1870s. It was restored by the Office of Works in the 1920s. **4m N of Linlithgow, on a promontory in the Forth estuary.** ☎01506 834807. 208 B3

**The Pineapple**
**Off A905, then off B1924, 1m west of Airth; 7m east of Stirling**
A bizarre structure in the shape of a pineapple, built in 1761 as a garden retreat. Now an oasis for wildlife, including bats and the great crested newt, with a car park, pond and woodland. An orchard of crab-apple trees has been planted in the walled garden. 208 B1

## Fife

**HS Aberdour Castle**
A 14th-century castle, extended in the 16th and 17th centuries with splendid residential accommodation and a terraced garden and bowling green. There is a fine circular dovecote. **In Aberdour.** ☎01383 860519. 209 B4

**HS Dunfermline Abbey and Palace**
The remains of a Benedictine abbey which was founded by Queen Margaret in the 11th century. The foundations of her church are under the superb, Romanesque nave, built in the 12th century. Robert the Bruce was buried in the choir, now the site of the present parish church. **In Dunfermline.** ☎01383 739026. 208 B3

**Falkland Palace and Garden**
**A912 in the village of Falkland, 11m north of Kirkcaldy, 10m from M90, junction 8**
A landmark building in the life of Mary, Queen of Scots. Set in the gentle scenery of the Royal Burgh of Falkland in the Kingdom of Fife, Falkland Palace was the hunting lodge of the Royal Stuarts. It is a stunning example of Renaissance architecture and contains sumptuous interiors from the 16th century. Stroll around the beautiful gardens and visit the Real Tennis court built in 1539. Shop and plant sales centre. **Falkland, Cupar, Fife KY15 7BU** ☎01337 857397; Shop: 01337 857918 220 D2

**Hill of Tarvit Mansionhouse and Garden**
RHS Members: free (garden) throughout open period. Open: all year, daily, 9.30am-sunset. **(National Trust for Scotland) Cupar, Fife KY15 5PB** ☎01334 653127 220 C3

**Hill of Tarvit Mansionhouse and Garden**
**Off A916, 2m south of Cupar**
A fine early 20th-century home and a treat for collectors and antique lovers. The house was rebuilt in 1906 by renowned Scottish architect Sir Robert Lorimer for a Dundee industrialist. It contains a superb collection of furniture, porcelain and paintings. Lorimer also designed the terrace gardens. The grounds contain one of the largest mixed borders in the country and some delightful woodland walks. Shop, tearoom, plant sales centre. **Cupar, Fife KY15 5PB** ☎01334 653127 220 C3

**HS Inchcolm Abbey**
The best-preserved group of monastic buildings in Scotland, founded in about 1123, and including a 13th-century octagonal chapter house. **On an island on the Firth of Forth, opposite Aberdour. Ferries from South Queensferry and North Queensferry.** ☎01383 823332. 209 B4

**Kellie Castle and Garden**
**On B9171, 3m north of Pittenweem**
A truly atmospheric castle dating back more than six centuries. Kellie was restored by the Lorimer family in the late 19th century and today you can see furniture designed by Sir Robert Lorimer, magnificent plaster ceilings, painted panels and a mural by Phoebe Anna Traquair. Don't miss the exhibition on sculptor Hew Lorimer and the late-Victorian organic garden. Shop and tearoom. **Pittenweem, Fife KY10 2RF** ☎01333 720271 221 D5

**Kellie Castle and Garden**
RHS Members: free throughout open period. Open: all year, daily, 9.30am-sunset. Castle open Easter weekend and Jun-Sept, daily 1pm-5pm. **(National Trust for Scotland) Pittenweem, Fife KT10 2RF** ☎01333 720271 221 D5

**Royal Burgh of Culross**
**Off A985, 12m west of Forth Road Bridge and 6m west of Dunfermline**
Wandering among the old buildings and cobbled streets of this picturesque royal burgh on the River Forth is like stepping back into the 16th and 17th centuries. You can explore the splendid refurbished palace and gardens dating from 1597, and find out more about this historic town from the video in the palace. Shop and tearoom. ☎01383 880359 208 B2

**St Andrews Botanic Garden**
RHS Members: free throughout open period. Open: all year, daily, 10am-7pm (Oct-Apr, gardens close at 4pm). **Canongate, St Andrews KY16 8RT** ☎01334 477178 221 C5

**HS St Andrews Castle and Visitor Centre**
Ruins of the castle of the Archbishops of St Andrews, dating in part from the 13th century. Features include a 'bottle dungeon', and mine and counter-mine tunnelled during the siege that followed the murder of Cardinal Beaton in 1546. Visitor Centre with shop and major exhibition depicting the history of the castle and cathedral. **In St Andrews.** ☎01334 477196. 135 C7 221 C5

**HS St Andrews Cathedral**
Remains of the largest cathedral in Scotland, and of the priory's domestic ranges. The precinct walls are particularly well-preserved. **In St Andrews.** ☎01334 472563. 221 C5

## Glasgow

**Holmwood**
**Signposted from Clarkston Road, B767, 4m south of Glasgow city centre**
The villa was the finest domestic work of Glasgow architect, Alexander 'Greek' Thompson, and was completed in 1858. Inside, see conservation work bringing the original ornamentation and decoration back to life and discover more from the exhibition and audio tour. Attractive riverside grounds. Shop and refreshments. **61-63 Netherlee Road, Cathcart, Glasgow G44 3YG** ☎0141 637 2129 205 C5

**Hutchesons' Hall**
**Ingram Street, near south-east corner of George Square, Glasgow**
A chance to look inside one of Glasgow city centre's landmark buildings. The Hall was completed in 1805 and remodelled 70 years later to create the elegant interior you can see today. The exhibition, Glasgow Style, contains work for sale by young designers from this vibrant city. Contemporary Design shop, Interiors Collection shop. **158 Ingram Street, Glasgow G1 1EJ** ☎0141 552 8391 205 B5

**Pollok House**
**3m south of Glasgow city centre. Off M77 junction 1, follow signs for Burrell Collection**
One of Glasgow's most elegant houses, home to the Maxwell family for nearly six centuries. The interiors are amazing, from the magnificent mahogany and marble hallway to the extensive servants' quarters. Collectors will love the famous paintings, silver and ceramics. Enjoy a stroll in the grounds, perhaps after a wonderful lunch in the Edwardian Kitchen restaurant! Varied events programme. Licensed Edwardian Kitchen restaurant, Servants' Hall tearoom (weekends), gift shop, food shop. **Pollok Country Park, 2060 Pollokshaws Road, Glasgow G43 1AT** ☎0141 616 6410 205 B5

**The Tenement House**
**Buccleuch Street, Garnethill, three streets north-west of Sauchiehall Street, near Charing Cross**
A fascinating view of turn-of-the-century tenement life fozen in time. This Victorian tenement was the home of a shorthand typist for more than 50 years. Little has changed in the flat since the early 20th century and many of the fittings are original, including the splendid kitchen range, along with the other family items on display. **145 Buccleuch Street, Glasgow G3 6QN** ☎0141 333 0183 205 B5

## Highland

**Abriachan Gardens**
RHS Members: free throughout open period Open: Feb-Nov, daily, 9am-5pm. **Loch Ness Side, by Inverness, IV3 8LA** ☎01463 861 232 252 C1

**Balmacara Estate and Lochalsh Woodland Garden**
**A87, adjoining Kyle of Lochalsh**
Wandering around this charming crofting estate reveals many delights. There are spectacular views across to Skye and Applecross. The beautiful village of Plockton is an Outstanding Conservation Area, and the old steadings in Balmacara Square have been restored to provide workshops for local crafts, a delicatessen and an interactive Visitor Centre. Enjoy quiet lochside walks at the Lochalsh Woodland Garden. **Lochalsh House (NTS), Balmacara, Kyle IV40 8DN** ☎01599 566325 249 D4

**Canna**
**Inner Hebrides. Cruises from Mallaig and Arisaig.**
The most westerly of the Small Isles, Canna is 4½ miles long and 1 mile wide and is one of the most interesting islands in the Hebrides for scenic, agricultural, scientific and historical reasons. 246 D1

**Cawdor Castle Gardens**
RHS Members: free May, Jun, Sept, Oct. Open: 1st May-10th Oct, daily, 10am-5.30pm. **Cawdor Castle, Nairn, Highland, IV12 5RD** ☎01667 404401 253 B4

### Corrieshalloch Gorge National Nature Reserve
**A832/A835 at Braemore**
This spectacular gorge, one of the finest examples in Britain of a box canyon, is 200ft deep. The river which carved this channel through hard metamorphic rock, plunges over the Falls of Measach. The suspension bridge, downstream from the falls, was built by John Fowler, joint designer of the Forth Railway Bridge. **262 C4**

### Culloden
**Highland**
Culloden is one of the most poignant and haunting battlegrounds in the British Isles. Here, on a sleet-filled April morning in 1746, Jacobite forces were brutally crushed by government troops, ending Bonnie Prince Charlie's dream of restoring the crown to the Stuarts. You can relive the battle through the Visitor Centre presentations or wander among evocative memorials on the battlefield itself. Restaurant, speciality Scottish bookshop, battlefield tours. **NTS Visitor Centre, Culloden Moor, Inverness IV2 5EU** **01463 790607 252 B3**

### Dunrobin Castle Gardens
RHS Members: free throughout open period. Open: Apr, May and 1st-15th Oct, daily, 10.30am-4.30pm, Jun-Sept, daily, 10.30am-5.30pm **Golspie, Sutherland KW10 6SF** **01408 633177 274 D2**

### Falls of Glomach
**Highland. North-east of A87.**
One of the highest waterfalls in Britain, set in a steep narrow cleft in remote country. The best approach is from the Dorusduain car park, by path, allow 5 hours for round trip. Or, for the very fit only, leave car by the Ling bridge, at the north end of Loch Long, for a long walk along Glen Elchaig before making a steep climb to the Falls; allow 8 hours. **250 D2**

### HS Fort George
A vast site and one of the most outstanding artillery fortifications in Europe. It was planned in 1747 as a base for George II's army, and was completed in 1769. Since then it has served as a barracks. There are reconstructions of barrack rooms in different periods and a display of muskets and pikes. **11m NE of Inverness, by the village of Ardersier.** **01667 460232 252 A3**

### Glenfinnan Monument
**On A830, 18m west of Fort William**
Set in superb scenery at the head of Loch Shiel, this monument to Jacobite clansmen stands close to the spot where Bonnie Prince Charlie raised his Standard in 1745. There's an exhibition and commentary on the Jacobite campaign, and from this spot you can see the viaduct that features in the Harry Potter films. Shop and tea room. **NTS Information Centre, Glenfinnan PH37 4LT** **01397 722250 238 D3**

### Inverewe Garden
**On A832, by Poolewe, 6m north-east of Gairloch**
A mecca for garden enthusiasts, Inverewe is an oasis of exotic plants bursting with vibrant colour. Rhododendrons from the Himalayas, eucalypts from Tasmania, Olearia from New Zealand, and other species from such far-flung places as Chile and South Africa all flourish here, in a display that changes with the seasons, so it's always worth a repeat visit. Licensed Woodside Restaurant, extensive shop, plant sales centre. **Poolewe IV22 2LQ** **01445 781200 261 B5**

### Kintail and West Affric
**North of A87, 16m east of Kyle of Lochalsh**
This is magnificent territory for walking. There are ten Munros in the area, which includes the Five Sisters of Kintail and the Falls of Glomach. Keen-eyed naturalists may be able to spot red deer, eagles and an amazing variety of other wildlife. **249 D6**

### Miller House and Hugh Miller's Cottage
**Via Kessock Bridge and A832, in Cromarty, 22m north-east of Inverness**
The Trust is proud to present an entirely new museum portraying every aspect of the great Cromarty writer and geologist, Hugh Miller. Situated in Miller House, a handsome Georgian villa, the museum features three floors of exhibitions covering Miller's life from harsh toil as a stonemason to national fame as a scientist, church reformer and campaigning editor. **Church Street, Cromarty IV11 8XA** **01381 600245 264 D3**

### Shieldaig Island
**Highland**
This 32-acre island is almost entirely covered in Scots pine which once formed vast forests covering much of the Scottish Highlands. **249 A5**

### Strome Castle
**Highland. Off A896.**
Ruined castle, romantically situated on a rocky promontory jutting into Loch Carron. First recorded in 1472 when it was a stronghold of the Lords of the Isles, it later belonged to the MacDonnells of Glengarry. Following a quarrel with Kenneth MacKenzie, Lord of Kintail, it fell in 1602 after a long siege and was blown up. **249 C5**

### Torridon
**A896, 9m south-west of Kinlochewe, Wester Ross**
Climbers, geologists and naturalists are all drawn to the Torridon estate, which contains some of Scotland's most formidable scenery. Learn more about the area at the Countryside Centre and Deer Museum, and see herds of red deer and Highland cattle kept nearby. **01445 791368 249 A6**

### HS Urquhart Castle
Standing above Loch Ness, this was one of the largest castles in Scotland, having fallen into decay after 1689. Most of the existing buildings date from after the 16th century. **On Loch Ness, near Drumnadrochit.** **01456 450551. 252 D1**

## Inverclyde

### HS Newark Castle
The oldest part of the castle is a tower built soon after 1478, with a detached gatehouse. The main part was added in 1597-9 by Patrick Maxwell. **In Port Glasgow.** **01475 741858. 204 A3**

## South Lanarkshire

### HS Bothwell Castle
The largest and finest 13th-century stone castle in Scotland, much fought over during the Wars of Independence. Part of the original circular keep survives, but most of the castle dates from the 14th and 15th centuries. **In Bothwell, approached from Uddingston, off the B7071.** **01698 816894. 194 A1**

### Cameronians' Regimental Memorial
**Off A70, in Douglas, South Lanarkshire**
Statue of the Earl of Angus who was the first Colonel of the Cameronian Regiment which was raised at Douglas in 1689. The statue is situated at the north edge of the village. **194 C3**

### HS Craignethan Castle
The oldest part is a tower house built by Sir James Hamilton of Finnart in the 16th century, defended by an outer wall pierced by gun ports, and by a wide and deep ditch with a most unusual 'caponier' – a stone vaulted chamber for artillery. **5½m NW of Lanark.** **01555 860364. 194 B3**

### The David Livingstone Centre
**Leave the M74 at junction 5 – join A725 – take the A724 to Blantyre.**
Scotland's most famous explorer was born here in a one room tenement in 1813. Today his birthplace commemorates his life with a fascinating exhibition including personal belongings and a new sculpture of Livingstone and the Lion. There's plenty to do for families – dressing up, jigsaws and even a lion hunt. Shop, cafe and adventure playground. **165 Station Road, Blantyre G72 9BT** **01698 823140 194 A1**

### Kittochside, The Museum of Scottish Country Life
**Between A726 and A749; from M74, junction 5 and from M77, junction 3**
A chance to experience first-hand the traditional way of life on a Scottish farm. Created in partnership with the National Museums of Scotland, this is a living museum of farming over the last 300 years. The farm itself is worked using techniques and equipment from the 1950s and there are many other special events highlighting country life. **Stewartfield Way, East Kilbride G76 9HR** **01355224181 205 C6**

## East Lothian

### HS Dirleton Castle and Gardens
The oldest part of this romantic castle dates from the 13th century. It was rebuilt in the 14th century and extended in the 16th century, when the gardens were established. **In the village of Dirleton.** **01620 850330. 210 B2**

▲ **Skara Brae Prehistoric Village, Orkney** David Lyons / Alamy

### Inveresk Lodge Garden
**A6124, south of Musselburgh**
This attractive terraced garden and 17th-century lodge (which is not open to the public) were presented to the Trust in 1959 by Mrs Helen E Brunton. Fine Edwardian conservatory. **24 Inveresk Village, Musselburgh, East Lothian EH21 7TE** **0131 665 1855 209 C6**

### Preston Mill and Phantassie Doocot
**Off A1, in East Linton, 23m east of Edinburgh**
There has been a mill on this site for centuries, and the present stone buildings date from the 18th century. The water-wheel and the grain milling machinery it powers are relatively modern and the mill continued in commercial use until 1959. The conical-roofed kiln, red pantiles and groupings of the buildings are popular with artists. **East Linton, East Lothian EH40 3DS** **01620 860426 210 C2**

### HS Seton Collegiate Church
The chancel and apse of this lovely building date from the 15th century, and the transepts and steeple were built by the widow of Lord Seton, who was killed at Flodden in 1513. **1m SE of Cockenzie off Edinburgh – North Berwick Road.** **01875 813334. 209 C7**

### HS Tantallon Castle
Remarkable fortification with earthwork defences, and a massive 14th-century curtain wall with towers. Interpretative displays include replica guns. **3m E of North Berwick.** **01620 892727. 210 B2**

## West Lothian

### House of the Binns
**Off A904, 4m east of Linlithgow.**
Home of the Dalyell family since 1612, the house contains a fascinating collection of portraits, furniture and porcelain, revealing the family's lives and interests through the centuries. A walk around the grounds will reward you with panoramic views over the River Forth. **Linlithgow, West Lothian EH49 7NA** **01506 834255 208 C3**

### HS Linlithgow Palace
Magnificent ruin of a great royal palace, set in its own park. All the Stewart kings lived here, and work commissioned by James I, III, IV, V and VI can be seen. The great hall and the chapel are particularly fine. **In Linlithgow.** **01506 842896. 208 C3**

## Midlothian

### HS Crichton Castle
A large and sophisticated castle, of which the most spectacular part is the range erected by the Earl of Bothwell between 1581 and 1591. **2½ m SW of Pathhead.** **01875 320017. 209 D6**

## Moray

### HS Balvenie Castle
A castle of enclosure first owned by the Comyns with a curtain wall of 13th-century date. Added to in the 15th and 16th centuries and visited by Mary Queen of Scots in 1562. **At Dufftown.** **01340 820121 254 B4**

### Brodie Castle
**Off A96 4½m west of Forres and 24m east of Inverness**
This 16th-century castle is packed with enough arts and antiques to keep connoisseurs happy all day. It houses a major art collection, as well as porcelain and fine furniture. In springtime the grounds are carpeted with daffodils, making for pleasant walking. Meanwhile the children can enjoy storming the play fort and special quizzes. Tearoom, shop; available for weddings/corporate events. **Brodie, Forres IV36 0TE** **01309 641371 253 A5**

### HS Dallas Dhu Distillery and Visitor Centre
A perfectly preserved time capsule of the distiller's art. Built in 1898 to supply malt whisky for Wright and Greig's 'Roderick Dhu' blend. Video presentation and a glass of whisky to end your visit. **About 1m S of Forres off the Grantown Road.** **01309 676548. 253 A6**

### HS Elgin Cathedral
The superb ruin of what many think was Scotland's most beautiful cathedral. Much of the work is in a rich late 13th century style, much modified after the burning of the church by the Wolf of Badenoch in 1390. The octagonal chapter house is the finest in Scotland. **In Elgin.** **01343 547171. 266 C3**

### HS Spynie Palace
Residence of the Bishops of Moray from the 14th century to 1686. The site is dominated by the massive tower built by Bishop David Stewart (1461-77). **2m N of Elgin, off the A941.** **01343 546358. 266 C3**

## Orkney

### HS Bishop's and Earl's Palaces
The Bishop's palace is a 12th-century hall-house, later much altered, with a round tower begun by Bishop Reid in 1541. A later addition was made by the notorious Patrick Stewart, Earl of Orkney, who built the adjacent Earl's Palace between 1600 and 1607 in a splendid Renaissance style. **In Kirkwall.** **01856 871918. 282 F5**

### HS Broch of Gurness
Protected by three lines of ditch and rampart, the base of the broch is surrounded by a warren of Iron Age buildings. **At Aikerness, about 14m NW of Kirkwall.** **01856 751414. 282 E4**

### HS Maes Howe Chambered Cairn
The finest megalithic tomb in the British Isles, with a large mound covering a stone-built passage and a large burial chamber with cells in the walls. Of Neolithic date, broken into during Viking times, with Viking runes carved on the walls. **About 9m W of Kirkwall.** **01856 761606. 282 F4**

### HS Skara Brae Prehistoric Village
The best-preserved group of Stone Age houses in Western Europe. The houses contain hearths, stone furniture and drains, and give a remarkable picture of life in Neolithic times. **19m NW of Kirkwall.** **01856 841815. 282 F3**

## Perth and Kinross

### Ben Lawers National Nature Reserve
**Mountain Visitor Centre, off A827, 6m north-east of Killin**
Climb to the summit of Ben Lawers, the central Highlands' highest mountain, on a clear day and it's possible to enjoy views as far as Ben Lomond and Glencoe to the west, and the high Cairngorms to the north. For naturalists, its slopes are home to a rich variety of birds and mountain plants. The Trust is pioneering habitat restoration here and you can find out more from the Visitor Centre exhibition. Shop. **01567 820397 217 A6**

### Branklyn Garden
**A85, Perth.**
With its fine collection of rare and unusual plants, this enchanting little garden attracts gardeners and botanists from all over the world. Among the rhododendrons, alpines, herbaceous, and peat gardens, look out for the vivid blue Himalayan poppy. Shop and plant sales. **116 Dundee Road, Perth PH2 7BB** **01738 625535 219 B6**

### Craigower
**1½m north of Pitlochry, off A924**
A bracing walk to the summit viewpoint (1,335ft) will reveal splendid views of Pitlochry and Loch Faskally below, along Lochs Tummel and Rannoch and across Rannoch Moor to Glencoe. **230 C3**

### Dunkeld and the Hermitage
**12m north of Perth on A9**
There's an air of timeless tranquillity about the village of Dunkeld. Here you can wander among restored 17th-century houses and drop into the Ell Shop, named after the weaver's measure fixed to the wall. At The Hermitage, one mile west, a woodland walk leads to Ossian's Hall, an 18th-century folly overlooking the dramatic Falls of Braan. **Ell Shop, The Cross, Dunkeld PH8 0AN** **The Hermitage: 01350 728641 230 D4**

### HS Huntingtower Castle
Two fine and complete towers, of the 15th and 16th centuries, now linked by a 17th-century range. There are fine painted ceilings. **2m W of Perth.** **01738 627231. 219 B5**

### Killiecrankie
**On B8079, 3m north of Pitlochry**
Here, where the Highlands meet the Lowlands, you can enjoy this spectacular, deep river gorge, cloaked in ancient woodlands, and discover the story of the Jacobite victory at the Battle of Killiecrankie in 1689. The Visitor Centre features exhibitions and natural history displays. A camera link with the woodlands shows nesting or feeding birds. The Ranger Service offers guided walk in summer. Shop, snack bar, picnic area. **NTS Visitor Centre, Killiecrankie, Pitlochry PH16 5LG** **01796 473233 230 B3**

### Linn of Tummel
**On B8019, 2m north-west of Pitlochry**
Enjoy a quiet walk through the woodlands to the meeting place of the rivers Garry and Tummel. Here you can see a very early example of a fish-pass. Before the building of the hydro-electric scheme, this allowed salmon making their way upstream to bypass the Falls of Tummel. **230 C3**

### HS Loch Leven Castle
Late 14th-century tower on one side of an irregular courtyard. Mary Queen of Scots was imprisoned here in 1567 and escaped in 1568. **On an island in Loch Leven, accessible by boat from Kinross.** **07778 040483. 219 D6**

### HS Meigle Sculptured Stone Museum
A magnificent collection of 25 sculptured monuments of the Celtic Christian period, one of the finest collections of Dark Age sculpture in Western Europe. **In Meigle.** **01828 640612. 231 D6**

### Scone Palace
RHS Members: free Sept, Oct. Open: Apr-Oct, daily, 9.30am-5.45pm. **Perth, Perthshire PY2 6BD** **01738 552300 219 B6**

## Renfrewshire

### Weaver's Cottage
**M8 junction 28a, A737, follow signs for Kilbarchan, 12m south-west of Glasgow**
Built in 1723, this cottage still has the atmosphere of a pre-Industrial Revolution home and workplace. See authentic domestic objects in their original settings, and watch weavers and spinners work on traditional looms and wheels. The cottage garden includes some interesting archaeological finds. There are costumed guides and activi-

ties for children too. **The Cross, Kilbarchan PA10 2JG** 01505 705588 205 B4

## East Renfrewshire

### Greenbank Garden
**Flenders Road, off Mearns Road, Clarkston. Off M77 and A726, 6m south of Glasgow city centre**
A source of inspiration for suburban gardeners, this unique walled garden has a fine collection of plants and design features, fountains and a woodland walk. Pick up practical advice from one of the gardening demonstrations or join us for other special events throughout the year. Tearoom, shop, plant sales centre, special disabled visitor centre. **Flenders Road, Clarkston, Glasgow G76 8RB** 0141 616 5216 205 C5

## Scottish Borders

### HS Dryburgh Abbey
Both beautifully situated and of intrinsic quality, the ruins of Dryburgh Abbey are remarkably complete. Much of the work is of the 12th and 13th century. Sir Walter Scott and Field Marshal Earl Haig are buried in the abbey. **5m SE of Melrose, near St Boswells.** 01835 822381. 197 C4

### Harmony Garden
RHS Members: free throughout open period. Open: Easter, Jun-Sept, Mon-Sat, 10am-5pm, Sun 1-5pm. **(National Trust for Scotland) St Mary's Road, Melrose, Borders TD6 9LJ** 01721 722502 197 C4

### Harmony Garden
**In Melrose, opposite the Abbey.**
The name says it all, Harmony Garden, surrounded by walls and screened by trees, has an unmistakable aura of peace and serenity. It's a special place to wander and enjoy the simple pleasures of the flowers, fruits and vegetables growing here. **St Mary's Road, Melrose TD6 9LJ.** 197 C4

### HS Hermitage Castle
A vast and eerie ruin in a lonely situation, of the 14th and 15th centuries. Mary Queen of Scots made her famous ride there to meet the Earl of Bothwell. **In Liddesdale, 5½m NE of Newcastleton, off the B6399.** 013873 76222. 186 D3

### HS Jedburgh Abbey and Visitor Centre
One of the abbeys founded by David I and the Bishop of Glasgow in about 1138 for Augustinian canons. The church is mostly in Romanesque and early Gothic styles and is remarkably complete. **In Jedburgh.** 01835 863925. 187 A5

### HS Melrose Abbey
Probably the most famous ruin in Scotland, founded around 1136 as a Cistercian abbey by David I, and repeatedly wrecked in the Wars of Independence. The surviving remains of the church are 15th century and of an elegance unique in Scotland. The Commendator's house contains displays relating to the abbey's history and to the Roman fort at Newstead. **In Melrose.** 01896 822562. 197 C4

### Priorwood Garden and Dried Flower Shop
**Off A6091, in Melrose, adjacent to Abbey.**
Priorwood is a centre for the unique craft of dried-flower arranging. The flowers used are grown in the gardens here and preserved using techniques from ancient Egypt. You can learn more about the craft, buy flowers from the shop, or simply relax in the sheltered gardens. Gift shop, dried-flower shop, food shop, picnic area. **Melrose TD6 9PX** 01896 822493 197 C4

### Robert Smail's Printing Works
**Innerleithen, 6m east of Peebles.**
A living insight into the history of print. Robert Smail's is a working print shop preserved just as it was a century ago. You can still see the presses in action, try your hand at traditional typesetting amd pick up authentic replica Victorian prints from the shop. **7/9 High Street, Innerleithen EH44 6HA** 01896 830206 196 C2

### St Abb's Head National Nature Reserve
**Off A1107, 2m north of Coldingham**
For birdwatchers and wildlife enthusiasts, St Abb's Head is a landmark site. This National Nature Reserve is home to thousands of cliff-nesting sea birds and offers a spectacular vantage point to watch them wheeling and diving into the North Sea. Find out more about the special exhibition or join a ranger-guided walk. 018907 71443 211 D6

### HS Smailholm Tower
A simple rectangular tower in a good state of preservation. It houses costume figures and tapestries relating to Sir Walter Scott's 'Minstrelsy of the Scottish Borders'. **Near Smailholm village, 6m NW of Kelso.** 01573 460365. 197 C5

## Shetland

### Fair Isle
**Accessible in summer by regular sailings of the mail boat from Grutness, on Shetland. Flights from Tingwall (Lerwick) airport and Kirkwall, Orkney.**
One of the most isolated inhabited islands in Britain. The Fair Isle Knitting Co-operative sells island knitwear world-wide. Important for the study of birds, flora and fauna, for its traditional crofting practices and for conservation of the environment. Additional crafts now include traditional wooden boatbuilding and the manufacture of stained glass windows. 285 L3

### HS Jarlshof Prehistoric and Norse Settlement
An very important site with a complex of ancient settlements within three acres. The oldest is a Bronze Age village of oval stone huts. There is an Iron Age broch and an entire Viking settlement. The visitor centre has new displays on Iron Age life and a history of the site. **At Sumburgh Head, about 22m S of Lerwick.** 01950 460112. 285 N5

### Unst and Yell
**Shetland. Ferry from Aberdeen to Lerwick, then (via two ferries) by hired car or bus.**
The estate of Unst and Yell, at the northern tip of Shetland and Britain, extends to 3,830 acres. Most of the land is in agricultural use and there is a first-class Shetland pony stud. Scenically the three west coast areas of Woodwick, Collaster and Lund are outstanding, with undulating hills, low rocky coastline, beaches, cliffs and voes. The area is of geological, botanical and ornithological importance. There is an interesting wood – the only one on Unst – at Halligarth. 284 B8

## Stirling

### Bannockburn
**Off M80/M9 at junction 9, 2m south of Stirling.** Here in 1314 King Robert the Bruce routed the English forces to win freedom for the Scots. In the Heritage Centre close to the Borestone, Bruce's command post, you can experience the epic encounter through an exciting audio-visual show and exhibition. You can even see the battle through Bruce's eyes by trying on a reproduction of his battle helmet. Shop and cafe. **Glasgow Road, Stirling FK7 0LJ** 01786 812664 207 A5

### Ben Lomond
**B837, at Rowardennan, 11m beyond Drymen, off A811**
Rising from the east shore of Loch Lomond to a height of 3,193ft (974m), Ben Lomond offers exhilarating walking and spectacular views across the Loch Lomond and Trossachs National Park. Walking routes, including the low-level Ardess Hidden History Trail, are available from the Information Centre and it's also possible to arrange ranger guided walks. **Ardess Lodge, Rowardennan, by Drymen G63 0AR** 01360 870224 215 B6

### Bucinch and Ceardach
**In Loch Lomond.**
These two small, uninhabited islands in the loch, between Luss and Balmaha, were presented by Col Charles L Spencer of Warmanbie, Dumfries, in 1943. 206 A1

### Cunninghame Graham Memorial
**Stirling. Off A81, in Gartmore**
Cairn to the memory of R B Cunninghame Graham of Ardoch, distinguished Scottish author. It was erected in 1937, a year after his death, at Castlehill, Dumbarton. Moved to Gartmore in 1981. 206 A3

### HS Doune Castle
A late 14th-century courtyard castle built for the Regent Albany. Its most striking feature is the combination of keep, gatehouse and hall, with its kitchen in a massive frontal block. **In Doune.** 01786 841742. 218 D2

### HS Inchmahome Priory
A beautifully situated Augustinian monastery founded in 1238, with much of the original 13th-century building surviving. **On an island in the Lake of Menteith, approached by boat from Port of Menteith.** 01877 385294. 217 D5

### Moirlanich Longhouse
**Off A827, 1m north-west of Killin.**
An outstanding example of a traditional cruck frame cottage and byre, dating from the mid-19th century. Little altered and retaining many original features such as the box beds. A small shed adjacent displays a rare collection of working clothes found in the longhouse, and an exhibition interprets the history and restoration of the building. 217 A5

### HS Stirling Castle
The grandest of all Scottish castles. The Great Hall and the Gatehouse of James IV, the marvellous Palace of James V, the Chapel Royal remodelled by James VI, and the artillery fortifications of the 16th and 18th centuries, are all of outstanding interest. Medieval kitchens and introductory display now open. **In Stirling.** 01786 450000. 207 A5

## Western Isles

### HS Black House
A traditional Lewis thatched house, with byre, attached barn and stackyard, complete and furnished. **In Arnol village, Lewis.** 01851 710395. 288 C4

### Mingulay, Berneray and Pabbay
**Western Isles**
The last of the population of this remote group of islands left in 1912, leaving behind a precarious existence based on crofting, fishing and fowling. Mingulay and Berneray are Site of Specific Scientific Interest, and all the islands have significant archaeological sites, with large parts of Mingulay and Pabbay being designated as Scheduled Ancient Monuments. 286 H1

### St Kilda National Nature Reserve
**41m west of North Uist**
The main island of Hirta maintained its population until 1930, when the islanders were evacuated at their own request. Each year, Trust work parties using volunteer labour conserve and repair buildings and carry out archaeological work. 287

# Wales

## Anglesey

### Plas Newydd
Home of the Marquess of Anglesey, this elegant house was redesigned by James Wyatt in the 18th century and is a mixture of classical and Gothic. Exhibition on Rex Whistler and his largest paintings are on display. Fine spring garden, Australasian arboretum and woodland walk. **Llanfairpwll, Anglesey LL61 6DQ** 01248 714795 123 D5

## Carmarthenshire

### Dinefwr
A landscaped park and mediaeval deer park, home to the ancient White Park Cattle since the 9th-century. The 12th-century Castle of Dinefwr, the home of the Princes of Deheubarth, and part of Newton House are also open. **Llandeilo, Carmarthenshire SA19 6RT** 01558 823947 58 C3

### Dolaucothi Gold Mines
These unique Roman goldmines are set amid wooded hillsides overlooking the beautiful Cothi Valley on the Dolaucothi Estate. The Trust's Exhibition Centre and Miners' Way vividly illustrate the ancient and modern mine workings. **Pumsaint, Llanwrda, Carmarthenshire SA19 8RR** 01558 650177 58 A3

### National Botanic Garden of Wales
RHS members: free Jan-Mar, Oct-Dec. Open: 25 Oct-31 Mar, daily, 10am-4.30pm, 1 Apr-24 Oct, daily, 10am-6pm. Closed Christmas Day. **Llanarthne, Carmarthenshire SA32 8HG** 01558 668768 57 A5

## Ceredigion

### Llanerchaeron
18th-century Welsh gentry estate set in the beautiful Dyffryn Aeron. A self-sufficient estate – evident in the dairy, laundry, brewery and salting house, as well as the Home Farm buildings. Today it is a working organic farm. **Nr Aberaeron, Ceredigion SA48 8DG** 01545 570200 74 C3

## Conwy

### Aberconwy House
Dating from the 14th-century, Aberconwy House is the last remaining medieval merchant's house in the old walled town of Conwy. Each room shows a different moment in time, reflecting the taste and character of some of the families who lived there. **Castle Street, Conwy LL32 8AY** 01492 592246 124 B2

### Bodnant Garden
Bodnant covers nearly 100 acres on a slope looking down to the River Conwy and across to Snowdonia. Above is a series of Italianate-style terraces and formal lawns whilst below, in a wooded valley, a stream runs through the secluded wild garden. Magnificent 200-year-old native trees. Bodnant holds the National Collections of Rhododendrons, Magnolias and Eucryphias. **Tal-y-Cafn, Colwyn Bay LL28 5RE** 01492 650460 124 B3

### Bodnant Garden
RHS Members: free throughout open period. Open: 13th Mar-31st Oct, 10am-5pm, last admission 4.30pm. **Tal-y-Cafn, nr Colwyn Bay, Conwy LL28 5RE** 01492 650460 124 B3

### Conwy Suspension Bridge
Designed and built by Thomas Telford, the famous engineer, this elegant suspension bridge was completed in 1826, replacing the ferry. **Conwy LL32 8LD** 01492 573282 124 B2

### Ty Mawr Wybrnant
Situated in the beautiful and secluded Wybrnant Valley. Ty Mawr was the birthplace of Bishop William Morgan, first translator of the entire Bible into Welsh. The house has been restored to its probable 16th-/17th-century appearance, with a display of Welsh bibles. **Penmachno, Betws-y-Coed LL25 0HJ** 01690 760213 124 D2

## Gwynedd

### Penrhyn Castle
This dramatic neo-Norman castle was built by Thomas Hopper between 1820 and 1845. The extraordinarily grand staircase and extravagant stone carving of the interior create an almost cathedral-like atmosphere. The restored Victorian kitchens and servants' rooms complete the Penrhyn story. **Bangor, Gwynedd LL57 4HN** 01248 353084 123 C6

### Plas Yn Rhiw
Small 16th-century manor house with Georgian additions, rescued from neglect by the Keating sisters in 1938. Delightful garden with interesting flowering trees and shrubs. Spectacular views from the grounds across Cardigan Bay. **Rhiw, Pwllheli, Gwynedd LL53 8AB** 01758 780219 106 D2

## Neath Port Talbot

### Aberdulais Falls
For over 400 years this famous waterfall has provided the energy for industry from the first manufacture of copper in 1584 to the later tinplate works. Today the Turbine House provides access to an interactive computer, fish pass and display panels. **Aberdulais, Neath SA10 8EU** 01639 636674 40 A2

## Pembrokeshire

### Colby Woodland Garden
Woodland garden set in a tranquil and secluded valley. Gentle strolls or extensive walks to explore the estate. A haven for bird watchers and gardeners alike. **Amroth, Narberth, Pembrokeshire SA67 8PP** 01834 811885 56 B1

### Picton Castle and Woodland Gardens
RHS Members: free Apr-Sept (gardens and gallery only, excluding event dys). Open: Apr-Oct, Tue-Sun and Bank Holidays, 10.30am-5pm. **Haverfordwest, Pembrokeshire SA62 4AS** 01437 751326 55 C6

### Tudor Merchant's House
A late 15th-century example of domestic town architecture, characteristic of the stone building tradition found in south west Wales. Furnishings and fittings recreate the atmosphere of the house when a Tudor family was in residence. **Quay Hill, Tenby, Pembrokeshire SA70 7BX** 01834 842279 56 B1

## Powys

### Powis Castle & Garden
Mediaeval castle rising dramatically over the world-famous garden. Laid out under the influence of French and Italian styles, it retains original lead statues, an Orangery and an aviary. The castle houses a magnificent collection of paintings, furniture, tapestries and he Clive Museum of treasures from India. **Welshpool, Powys SY21 8RF** 01938 551929 93 A6

## Wrexham

### Chirk Castle
Magnificent 14th-century fortress of the Welsh Marches completed in 1310. Chirk's rather austere exterior belies the comfortable and elegant staterooms inside. Features include the mediaeval tower and dungeon, 18th-century Servants' Hall and beautiful gardens. **Chirk, Wrexham LL14 5AF** 01691 777701 110 B1

### Erddig
Atmospheric house and estate, vividly evoking its family and servants. Stunning state rooms display most of their original 18th- and 19th-century furniture and furnishings. Beautiful and extensive outbuildings include the kitchen, laundry, bakehouse, stables and sawmill. **Wrexham LL13 0YT** 01978 355314 110 A2

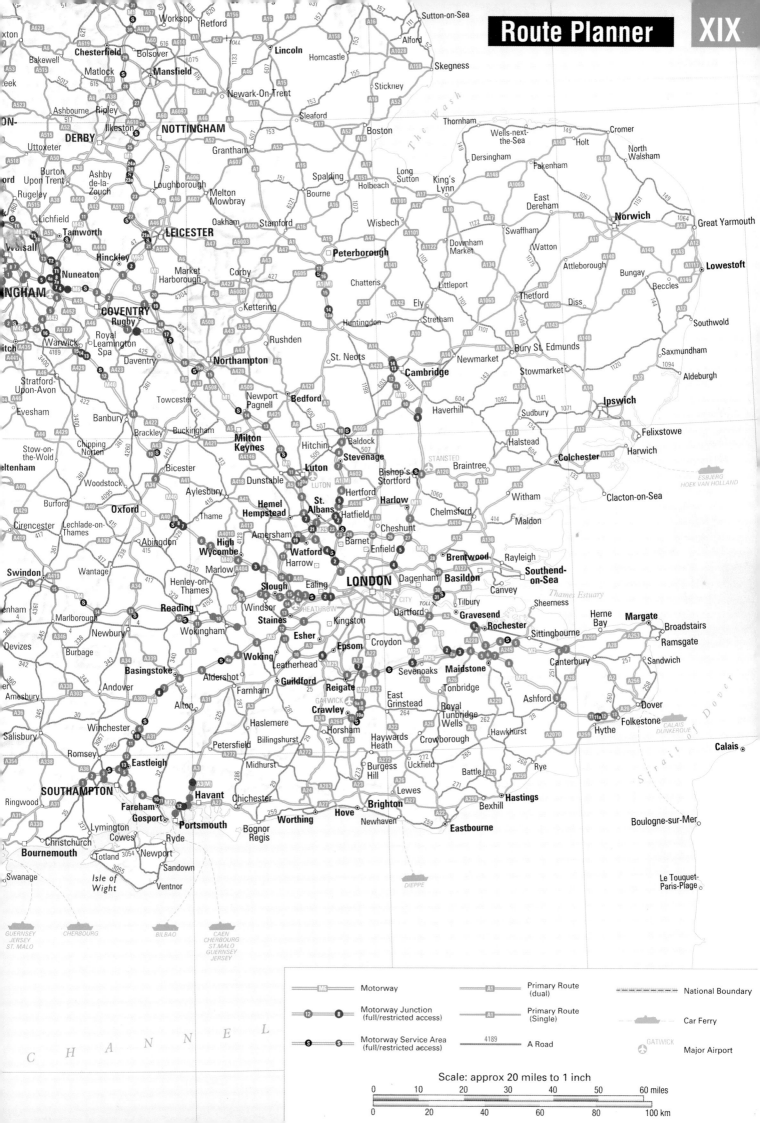

**Scale: approx 20 miles to 1 inch**

| | Motorway |
| | Motorway Junction (full/restricted access) |
| | Motorway Service Area (full/restricted access) |

Primary Route (dual)
Primary Route (Single)
A Road

National Boundary
Car Ferry
Major Airport

## Restricted motorway junctions

| M1 | Northbound | Southbound |
|---|---|---|
| 2 | No exit | No access |
| 4 | No exit | No access |
| 6a | No exit | No access |
|  | Access from M25 only | Exit to M25 only |
| 7 | No exit | No access |
|  | Access from M10 only | Exit to M10 only |
| 17 | No access | No exit |
|  | Exit to M45 only | Access from M45 only |
| 19 | No exit to A14 | No access from A14 |
| 21a | No access | No exit |
| 23a | Exit to A42 only |  |
| 24a | No access | No access |
| 35a | No access | No exit |
| 43 | No exit to M621 northbound |  |
| 48 | No exit to A1 southbound |  |

| M2 | Eastbound | Westbound |
|---|---|---|
| 1 | Access from A2 eastbound only | Exit to A2 westbound only |

| M3 | Eastbound | Westbound |
|---|---|---|
| 8 | No exit | No access |
| 10 | No access | No exit |
| 13 | No access to M27 eastbound |  |
| 14 | No exit | No access |

| M4 | Eastbound | Westbound |
|---|---|---|
| 1 | Exit to A4 eastbound only | Access from A4 westbound only |
| 2 | Access to A4 eastbound only | Access to A4 westbound only |
| 21 | No exit | No access |
| 23 | No access | No exit |
| 25 | No exit | No access |
| 25a | No exit | No access |
| 29 | No exit | No access |

| M4 | Eastbound | Westbound |
|---|---|---|
| 38 |  | No access |
| 39 | No exit or access | No exit |
| 41 | No access | No exit |
| 41a | No exit |  |
| 42 |  | Exit to A483 only |

| M5 | Northbound | Southbound |
|---|---|---|
| 10 | No exit | No access |
| 11a | No access from A417 eastbound | No exit to A417 westbound |

| M6 | Northbound | Southbound |
|---|---|---|
| 4a | No exit | No access |
|  | Access from M42 southbnd only | Exit to M42 only |
| 5 | No access | No exit |
| 10a | No access | No exit |
|  | Exit to M54 only | Access from M54 only |
| 11a | No exit / access | No access / exit |
|  | No access to M6 Toll |  |
| 20 | No exit to M56 eastbound | No access from M56 westbound |
| 24 | No exit | No access |
| 25 | No access | No access |
| 30 | No exit | No access |
|  | Access from M61 | Exit to M61 |
|  | northbound only | southbound |
| 31a | No access | No exit |

| M6 Toll | Northbound | Southbound |
|---|---|---|
| T1 |  | No exit |
| T2 | No exit / access | No access |
| T5 | No exit | No access |
| T7 | No access | No exit |
| T8 | No access |  |

| M8 | Eastbound | Westbound |
|---|---|---|
| 8 | No exit to M73 northbound | No access from M73 southbound |
| 9 | No exit | No exit |
| 13 | No exit southbound | No access |
| 14 | No access | No access |
| 16 | No exit | No access |
| 17 | No exit | No access |
| 18 |  | No exit |
| 19 | No exit to A814 eastbound | No access from A814 westbound |
| 20 | No access | No access |
| 21 | No access | No exit |
| 22 | No access | No exit |
|  | Access from M77 only | Exit to M77 only |
| 23 | No exit | No exit |
| 25 | Exit to A739 northbound only | Exit to A739 northbound only |
|  | Access from A739 | Access from A739 |
|  | southbound only | southbound only |
| 25a | No access | No access |
| 28 | No access | No access |
| 28a | No exit | No access |

| M9 | Eastbound | Westbound |
|---|---|---|
| 1a | No exit | No access |
| 2 | No access | No exit |
| 3 | No exit | No access |
| 6 | No access | No exit |
| 8 | No exit | No access |

| M11 | Northbound | Southbound |
|---|---|---|
| 4 | No exit | No access |
| 5 | No access | No exit |
| 9 | No access | No exit |
| 13 | No access | No exit |
| 14 | No exit to A428 westbound | No exit |
|  |  | Access from A14 westbound only |

Continued on page XXIII

# Restricted motorway junctions

Continuation from page XXI

| M20 | Eastbound | Westbound |
|---|---|---|
| 2 | No access | No exit |
| 3 | No exit | No access |
| | Access from M26 eastbound only | Exit to M26 westbound only |
| 11a | No access | No exit |

| M23 | Northbound | Southbound |
|---|---|---|
| 7 | No exit to A23 southbound | No access from A23 northbound |
| 10a | No exit | No access |

| M25 | Clockwise | Anticlockwise |
|---|---|---|
| 5 | No exit to M26 eastbound | No access from M26 westbound |
| 19 | No access | No exit |
| 21 | No exit to M1 southbound | No exit to M1 southbound |
| | Access from M1 southbound only | Access from M1 southbound only |
| 31 | No exit | No access |

| M27 | Eastbound | Westbound |
|---|---|---|
| 10 | No exit | No access |
| 12 | No access | No exit |

| M40 | Eastbound | Westbound |
|---|---|---|
| 3 | No exit | No access |
| 7 | No exit | No access |
| 7a | No exit | No access |
| 13 | No exit | No access |
| 14 | No access | No exit |
| 16 | No access | No exit |

| M42 | Northbound | Southbound |
|---|---|---|
| 1 | No exit | No access |
| 7 | No access | No exit |
| | Exit to M6 northbound only | Access from M6 northbound only |
| 7a | No access | No exit |
| | Exit to M6 only | Access from M6 northbound only |
| 8 | No exit | Exit to M6 northbound |
| | Access from M6 southbound only | Access from M6 southbound only |

| M45 | Eastbound | Westbound |
|---|---|---|
| M1 junc 17 With A45 (Dunchurch) | Access to M1 southbound only No access | No access from M1 southbound No exit |

| M49 | Southbound | |
|---|---|---|
| 18a | No exit to M5 northbound | |

| M53 | Northbound | Southbound |
|---|---|---|
| 11 | Exit to M56 eastbound only | Exit to M56 eastbound only |
| | Access from M56 westbound only | Access from M56 westbound only |

| M56 | Eastbound | Westbound |
|---|---|---|
| 2 | No exit | No access |
| 4 | No exit | No access |
| 7 | | No access |
| 8 | No exit or access | No exit |
| 9 | No access from M6 northbound | No access to M6 southbound |
| 15 | No exit to M53 | No access from M53 northbound |

| M57 | Northbound | Southbound |
|---|---|---|
| 3 | No exit | No access |
| 5 | No exit | No access |

| M58 | Eastbound | Westbound |
|---|---|---|
| 1 | No exit | No access |

| M60 | Clockwise | Anticlockwise |
|---|---|---|
| 2 | No exit | No access |
| 3 | No exit to A34 northbound | No exit to A34 northbound |
| 4 | No access to M56 | No exit to M56 |
| 5 | No exit to A5103 southbound | No exit to A5103 northbound |
| 14 | No exit to A580 | No access from A580 |
| 16 | No exit | No access |
| 20 | No access | No exit |
| 22 | | No access |
| 25 | No access | |
| 26 | | No exit or access |
| 27 | No exit | No access |

| M61 | Northbound | Southbound |
|---|---|---|
| 2 | No access from A580 eastbound | No exit to A580 westbound |
| 3 | No access from A580 eastbound | No exit to A580 westbound |
| | No access from A666 southbound | |
| M6 junc 30 | No exit to M6 southbound | No access from M6 northbound |

| M62 | Eastbound | Westbound |
|---|---|---|
| 23 | No access | No exit |

| M65 | Eastbound | Westbound |
|---|---|---|
| 1 | No access | No exit |

| M66 | Northbound | Southbound |
|---|---|---|
| 1 | No access | No exit |

| M67 | Eastbound | Westbound |
|---|---|---|
| 1a | No access | No exit |
| 2 | No exit | No access |

| M69 | Northbound | Southbound |
|---|---|---|
| 2 | No exit | No access |

| M73 | Northbound | Southbound |
|---|---|---|
| 2 | No access from M8 or A89 eastbound | No exit to M8 or A89 westbound |
| | No exit to A89 | No access from A89 |
| 3 | Exit to A80 northbound only | Access from A80 southbound only |

| M74 | Northbound | Southbound |
|---|---|---|
| 2 | No access | No exit |
| 3 | No exit | No access |
| 7 | No exit | No access |
| 9 | No exit or access | No access |
| 10 | | No exit |
| 11 | No exit | No access |
| 12 | No access | No exit |

| M77 | Northbound | Southbound |
|---|---|---|
| M8 junc 22 | Exit to M8 eastbound only | Access from M8 westbound only |
| 4 | No exit | No access |
| 6 | No exit | No access |
| 7 | No exit | No access |
| 8 | No access | No access |

| M80 | Northbound | Southbound |
|---|---|---|
| 3 | No access | No exit |
| 5 | No access from M876 | No exit to M876 |

| M90 | Northbound | Southbound |
|---|---|---|
| 2a | No access | No exit |
| 7 | No exit | No access |
| 8 | No access | No exit |
| 10 | No access from A912 | No exit to A912 |

| M180 | Northbound | Southbound |
|---|---|---|
| 1 | No access | No exit |

| M621 | Eastbound | Westbound |
|---|---|---|
| 2a | No exit | No access |
| 4 | No exit or access | |
| 5 | No exit | No access |
| 6 | No access | No exit |

| M876 | Northbound | Southbound |
|---|---|---|
| 2 | No access | No exit |

| A1(M) | Northbound | Southbound |
|---|---|---|
| 2 | No access | No exit |
| 3 | | No access |
| 5 | No exit | No access |
| 44 | No exit, access from M1 only | Exit to M1 only |
| 57 | No access | No exit |
| 65 | No access | No exit |

| A3(M) | Northbound | Southbound |
|---|---|---|
| 1 | | No access |
| 4 | No access | No exit |

| A38(M) | Northbound | Southbound |
|---|---|---|
| With Victoria Road (Park Circus) Birmingham | No exit | No access |

| A48(M) | Northbound | Southbound |
|---|---|---|
| M4 Junc 29 | Exit to M4 eastbound only | Access from M4 westbound only |
| 29a | Access from A48 eastbound only | Exit to A48 westbound only |

| A57(M) | Eastbound | Westbound |
|---|---|---|
| With A5103 | No access | No exit |
| With A34 | No access | No exit |

| A58(M) | Southbound | |
|---|---|---|
| With Park Lane and Westgate, Leeds | No access | |

| A64(M) | Eastbound | Westbound |
|---|---|---|
| With A58 Clay Pit Lane, Leeds | No access | No exit |
| With Regent Street, Leeds | No access | No access |

| A74(M) | Northbound | Southbound |
|---|---|---|
| 18 | No access | No exit |
| 22 | No access | No exit |

| A167(M) | Northbound | Southbound |
|---|---|---|
| With Camden St, Newcastle | No exit | No exit or access |

| A194(M) | Northbound | Southbound |
|---|---|---|
| A1(M) junc 65 Gateshead Western Bypass | Access from A1(M) northbound only | Exit to A1(M) southbound only |

## Road map symbols

| | |
|---|---|
| M6 | Motorway, toll motorway |
| 4 — 5 | Motorway junction – full, restricted access |
| S — S | Motorway service area – full, restricted access |
| = = = = = | Motorway under construction |
| A453 | Primary route – dual, single carriageway |
| S — ◎ — ⬦ | Service area, roundabout, multi-level junction |
| 4 — 5 | Numbered primary route junction – full, restricted access |
| = = = = = | Primary route under construction |
| | Narrow primary route |
| **Derby** | Primary destination |
| A34 | A road – dual, single carriageway |
| ============ | A road under construction |
| | Narrow A road |
| B2135 | B road – dual, single carriageway |
| ============ | B road under construction |
| | Narrow B road |
| | Minor road – over 4 metres wide, under 4 metres wide |
| ============ | Minor road with restricted access |
| 2 | Distance in miles |
| ╪===╪ | Tunnel |
| TOLL | Toll, steep gradient – arrow points downhill |
| | National trail – England and Wales |
| | Long distance footpath – Scotland |
| —•— | Railway with station |
| —×—)—–— | Level crossing, tunnel |
| —•— | Preserved railway with station |
| | National boundary |
| | County / unitary authority boundary |
| 🚢 🚤 | Car ferry, catamaran |
| 🚢 🚤 | Passenger ferry, catamaran |
| 🚢 🚤 | Hovercraft, freight ferry |
| CALAIS 1:15 Ferry | Ferry destination, journey time – hrs : mins |
| ············ | Car ferry – river crossing |
| ✈ ✈ | Principal airport, other airport |
| | National park |
| | Area of Outstanding Natural Beauty – England and Wales National Scenic Area – Scotland |
| | forest park / regional park / national forest |
| | Woodland |
| | Beach |
| | Linear antiquity |
| - - - - - | Roman road |
| ⬚ ✕1066 | Hillfort, battlefield – with date |
| ☀ 🍁 795 | Viewpoint, national nature reserve, spot height – in metres |
| ⚑ ▲ ◎ | Golf course, youth hostel, national sporting venue |
| ⛺ 🚐 🚐 | Camp site, caravan site, camping and caravan site |
| 🛒 P&R | Shopping village, park and ride |
| 29 | Adjoining page number – road maps |

### Road map scale 1: 150 000 or 2.37 miles to 1 inch

```
0    1    2    3    4    5   6 miles
0  1  2  3  4  5  6  7  8  9  10 km
```

## Approach map symbols

| | |
|---|---|
| M6 | Motorway |
| | Toll motorway |
| 6 — 5 | Motorway junction – full, restricted access |
| S | Service area |
| | Under construction |
| A6 | Primary route – dual, single carriageway |
| S | Service area |
| ○ | Multi-level junction |
| ◎ | roundabout |
| = = = | Under construction |
| A195 | A road – dual, single carriageway |
| B1288 | B road – dual, single carriageway |
| | Minor road – dual, single carriageway |
| | Ring road |
| 📷 | Speed camera – single |
| 📷 | Speed cameras – multiple |
| 3 | Distance in miles |
| —•— | Railway with station |
| —⊕— | Tramway with station |
| M ⊖ ⟷ • | Underground or metro station |
| | Congestion charge area |

## Town plan symbols

| | | | |
|---|---|---|---|
| | Motorway | | Bus or railway station building |
| | Primary route – dual, single carriageway | | Shopping precinct or retail park |
| | A road – dual, single carriageway | | Park |
| | B road – dual, single carriageway | 🏠 | Building of public interest |
| | Minor through road | 🎭 🎥 | Theatre, cinema |
| → | one-way street | P ♿ | Parking, shopmobility |
| | Pedestrian roads | Bank | |
| | Shopping streets | ⊖ West St • | Underground, metro station |
| —🚉— | Railway with station | H | Hospital |
| ++++ City Hall ++++ | Tramway with station | ⧽ | Police station |
| | | PO | Post office |

## Tourist information

| | | |
|---|---|---|
| † Abbey, cathedral or priory | ⬛ Castle | Ⓐ Picnic area |
| 🏛 Ancient monument | 🏰 Church | 🚂 Preserved railway |
| 🐟 Aquarium | 🎪 Country park England and Wales | 🏇 Race course |
| 🏛 Art gallery | ⚘ Scotland | 🏺 Roman antiquity |
| 🐦 Bird collection or aviary | 🐴 Farm park | ⚘ Safari park |
| | ✽ Garden | 🎡 Theme park |
| | ⛵ Historic ship | Tourist information centre |
| | 🏠 House | 🅘 open all year |
| | 🏠 House and garden | 🅘 open seasonally |
| | 🏁 Motor racing circuit | 🐘 Zoo |
| | 🏛 Museum | ✦ Other place of interest |

### Relief

| Feet | metres |
|---|---|
| 3000 | 914 |
| 2600 | 792 |
| 2200 | 671 |
| 1800 | 549 |
| 1400 | 427 |
| 1000 | 305 |
| 0 | 0 |

### Speed Cameras.

Fixed camera locations are shown using the 📷 symbol.

In congested areas the 📷 symbol is used to show that there are two or more cameras on the road indicated.

Due to the restrictions of scale the camera locations are only approximate and cannot indicate the operating direction of the camera. Mobile camera sites, and cameras located on roads not included on the mapping are not shown. Where two or more cameras are shown on the same road, drivers are warned that this may indicate that a SPEC system is in operation. These cameras use the time taken to drive between the two camera positions to calculate the speed of the vehicle.

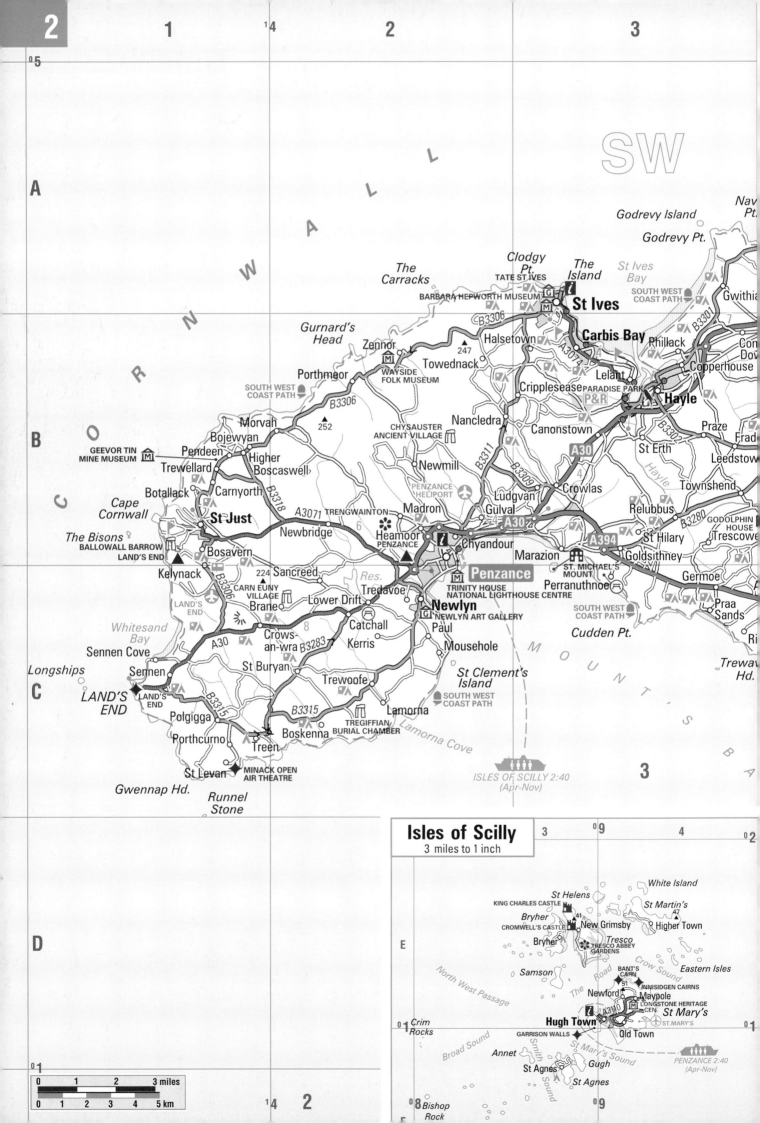

4 5 6

11 11

A A

SR SS

10 10

SW SX

B B

*Fire Beacon Pt.* Be

BOSCASTLE
HARBOUR

Bosc

Trevalga

CASTLE
*Tintagel Hd.*
OLD POST OFFICE
TINTAGEL Bossiney

TINTAGEL Tintagel

Treknow Trewarmett
*B3263*

*Start Pt.* Trebarwith

C C

Treligga

SOUTH WEST
COAST PATH Delabole

Valley Truckle

*Port Isaac
Bay* Helstone

Port
*Pentire Pt.* Isaac
Port Quin Port Gaverne St Teath
*Port Quin
Bay* Treveighan
LONG CROSS *B3267*
New Polzeath Trelights Pendoggett A39
*Gulland Rock* *Padstow
Bay* Polzeath St Endellion Trelill Michaelstow
Trebetherick 10
St Minver Trewethern St Bre
*Gunver Hd.* St Kew Row
Crugmeer Pityme Chapel St Tudy
*TREVOSE HEAD* PRIDEAUX Amble St Kew
PLACE Rock Highway We Ordbridg
Trevone D D
TREYARNON BAY Constantine **Padstow** Blisla
*Constantine
Bay* Bay St *Camel*
Merryn Bodieve
Treyarnon Shop Trevanson **Wadebridge** St Mabyn
SOUTH WEST Little *Camel*
COAST PATH Petherick St PENCARROW
Porthcothan Whitecross Breock Egloshayle HOUSE Helland
*B3276* St Helland
*Park Hd.* St Issey *A389*
Penrose Ervan Tredinnick *A39* 6 Burlawn
Rumford St Jidgey Washaway *Bodmin
RARE BREEDS Forest*
4 CENTRE 5 A30
St Eval CREALY GREAT STREOCK DOWNS Cardi
Trenance ADVENTURE MONOLITH
PARK

AIRFIELD
D-DAY MEMORIAL
Whitehall
West
Grinstead
Kent Street
Cowfold
Broomer's
Corner
B2135
A24
West
End
B2116
Wineham
35
Bolney
Wivelsfield
Wivelsfield
Green
North
Common
A2036
B2112
A273
Goose
Green
Dial
Post
Partridge
Green
Twineham
JUMPING
COURSE
Sayers
Common
BURGESS
HILL
Chailey
South
Street
A275
Spear
Hill
7
B2116
B2133
Blackstone
Albourne
WASHBROOKS
FARM CENTRE
Hurstpierpoint
Hurst Wickham
DITCHLING
COMMON
Plumpton
Green
Thakeham
West
End
Henfield
Woodmancote
B2117
Hassocks
B2036
PLUMPTON
DITCHLING
MUSEUM
Chiltington
East
Chiltington
Ashington
B2139
A283
Rock
Wiston
Ashurst
A281
A281
B2112
Keymer
Ditchling
Streat
Westmeston
Cooksbridge
Offham
A275
Washington
238
Small Dole
A2037
206
A273
A23
Clayton
Pyecombe
Plumpton
B2116
195
MT. HARRY
Lew
A24
Steyning
Bramber
Poynings
Fulking
DITCHLING
BEACON
248
1264
Wallands Park
H
ST. MARY'S
HOUSE
Upper
Beeding
216
Edburton
TRULEIGH HILL
217
Saddlescombe
DEVIL'S DYKE
D O
22
A27
Findon
Botolphs
Coombes
2
Mile
Oak
Brighton and
Hove
Brighton
Patcham
Coldean
Stanmer
6
Falmer
Kingston
near Lewes
Iford
A280
184
N
S
Westdene
P&R
Withdean
N
S
Castle Hill
Rodm
High
Salvington
3
North
Lancing
A27
Portslade
West
Blatchington
A270
Preston
MANOR
Preston
Moulsecoomb
Bevendean
BRIGHTON
Woodingdean
B
South
Salvington
Sompting
Lancing
SHOREHAM
Kingston
by-Sea
Southwick
A259
Portslade-
by-Sea
6
MUS &
ART GAL
Royal Pavilion
Kemp
Town
Ovingdean
Telscombe
Broadwater
A2032
4
South
Lancing
SHOREHAM-
BY-SEA
HOVE
BRIGHTON
Brighton
Sea Life
A259
Rottingdean
Saltdean
A259
East
Worthing
MARLIPINS MUSEUM
VOLK'S
ELECTRIC
RAILWAY
MERCHANTS QUAY
Telscombe Cliffs
Goring-
by-Sea
West
Worthing
Worthing
Peacehaven
10
C
22
TV
D
8

1    21    2    3    4

15

A

B

C

D

11

**North West Point**

**North East Point**

**LUNDY MARINE NATURE RESERVE**

142

**LUNDY**

*ILFRACOMBE 2:15*
*BIDEFORD 2:15*
*CLOVELLY 1:30*

**South West Point**

**Surf Point**

*LUNDY 1:30*

B I D E F O

N    O    R    T    H

**HARTLAND POINT**

**SS**

*Windbury Pt.*

**Titchberry**

**CLOVELLY VILLAGE**

**Clovelly**

*Hartland Quay*

**Stoke**

B3248

**Higher Clovelly**

**Hartland**

**SOUTH WEST COAST PATH**

**Philham**

**Buck's Cross**

**THE MILKY W**
**NORTH DEVO**
**BIRD OF PREY**

**Milford**

**ELMSCOTT**

**Eddistone**

**Elmscott**

**Tosberry**

**Woolfardisworthy**

*Hartland Forest*

**Almin**
**Cro**

**South Hole**

*Knaps Longpeak*

**Welcombe**

235

**Meddon**

**Ash**

**Woolley**

**Gooseham**

**Eastcott**

**Youlstone**

**West P**

156

**Morwenstow**

**Dinworthy**

*Higher Sharpnose Pt.*

A39

**KILLARNEY SPRINGS FAMILY LEISURE PARK**

**Shop**

**Bradworth**

**Woodford**

**BROCKLANDS ADVENTURE PARK**

**Bradworthy Cross**

*Lower Sharpnose Pt.*

14

*Waldon*

**Kilkhampton**

**Alfardisworthy**

**Coombe**

**Soldon Cross**

**Stibb**

10

*Strat*

**3**

22

**Poughill**

**DUNSDON**

**Holsw Beac**

1   2   2   3   4

5

## A

North West Point
North East Point

LUNDY MARINE
NATURE RESERVE
142

**LUNDY**

ILFRACOMBE 2:15
BIDEFORD 2:15
CLOVELLY 1:30

South West Point

Surf Point

## B

LUNDY 1:30

BIDEFO

## C

NORTH

HARTLAND POINT

Windbury Pt.

Titchberry

**SS**

Hartland Quay

Stoke

CLOVELLY VILLAGE
Clovelly

Hartland
B3248
Higher Clovelly

Philham

SOUTH WEST
COAST PATH

Buck's Cross
THE MILKY W
NORTH DEVO
BIRD OF PREY

Milford
Eddistone

**ELMSCOTT**
Elmscott
Tosberry

Woolfardisworthy

*Hartland Forest*
Almin
Cr

## D

South Hole

Knaps Longpeak

Welcombe   235

Meddon

Ash

Gooseham
Woolley

West P

156
Eastcott
Youlstone

Dinworthy

*Higher Sharpnose Pt.*

Morwenstow
Shop
**A39**

KILLARNEY SPRINGS
FAMILY LEISURE PARK

Bradworth

Woodford
BROCKLANDS
ADVENTURE
PARK

Bradworthy Cross

*Lower Sharpnose Pt.*

14

Waldon

Kilkhampton

Coombe
Alfardisworthy

Stibb

**10**

Soldon Cross

0   1   2   3 miles
0   1   2   3   4   5 km

2

3

4

Strat

DUNSDON

Poughill

Holsw
Beac

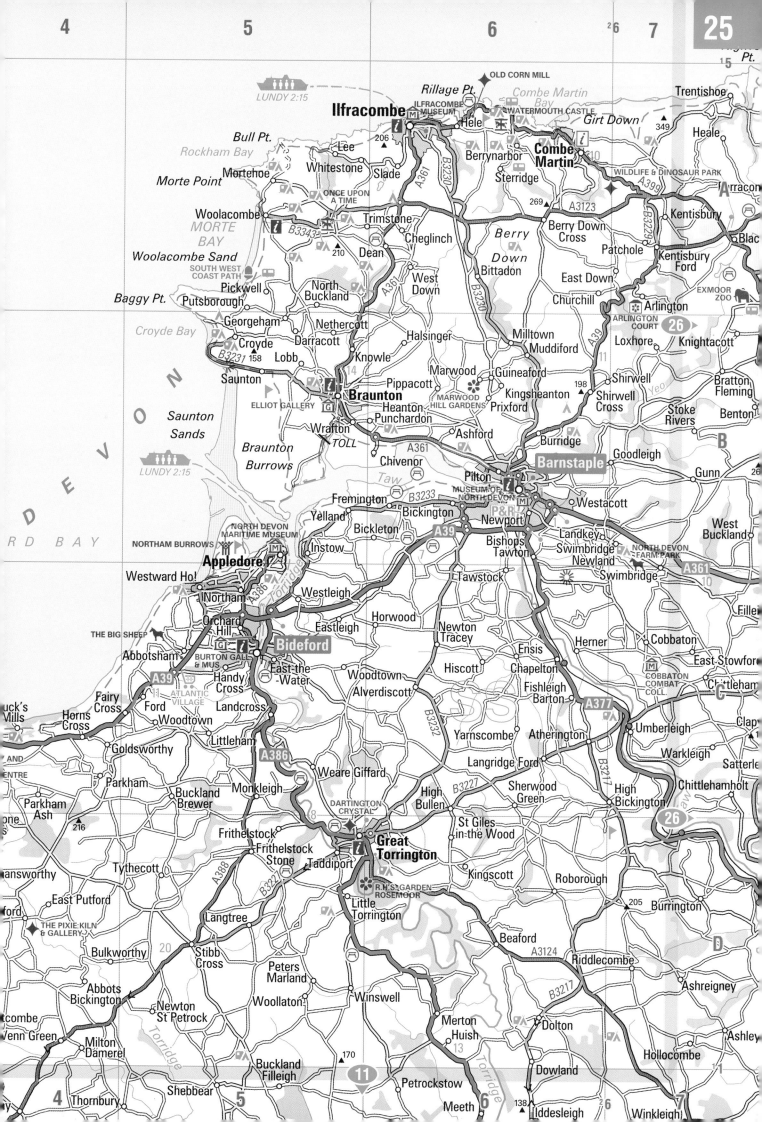

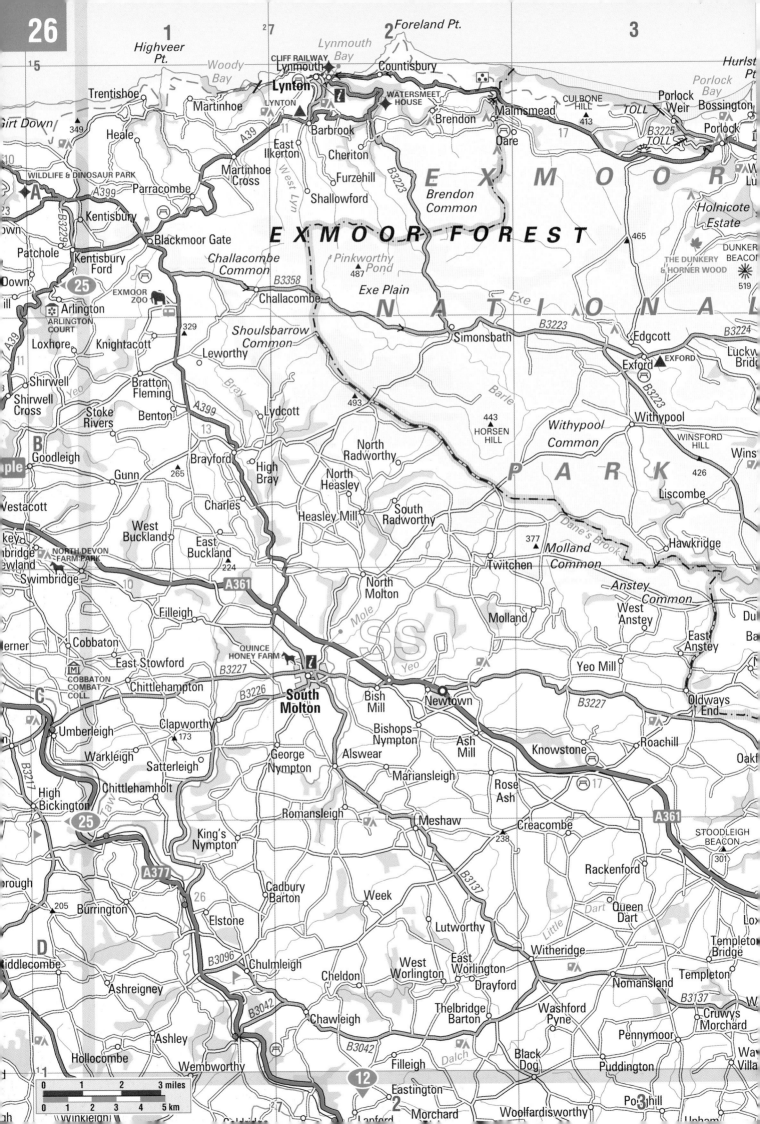

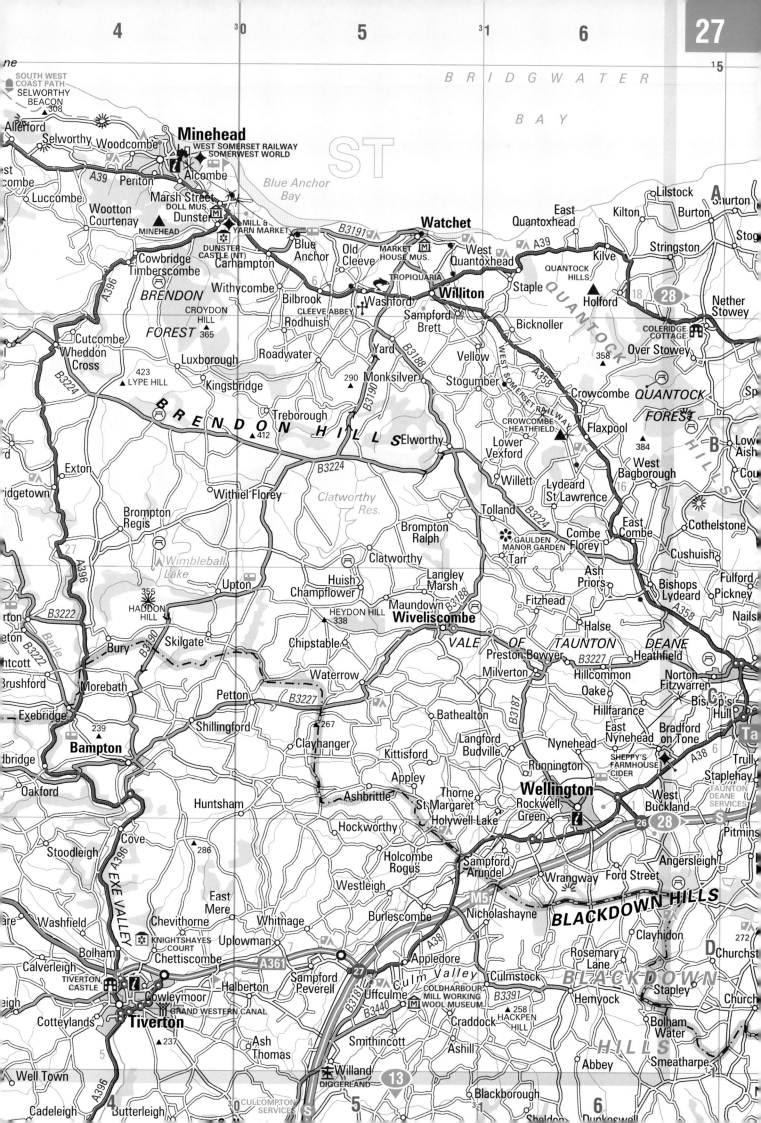

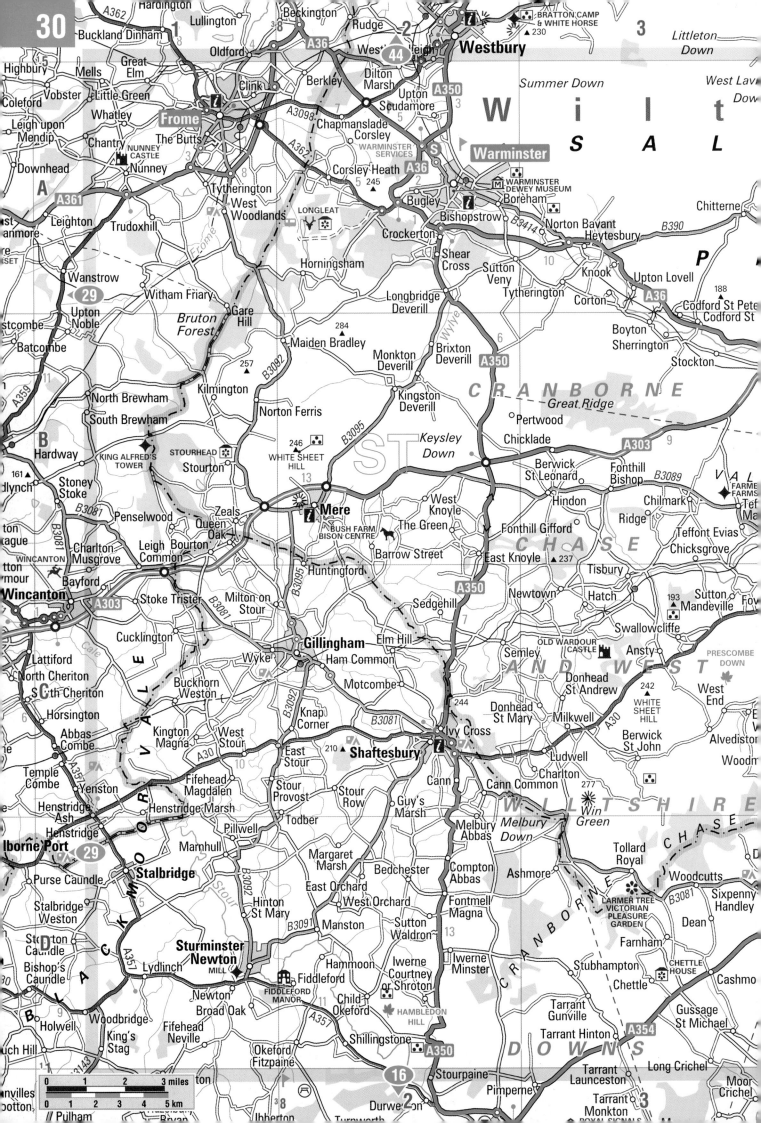

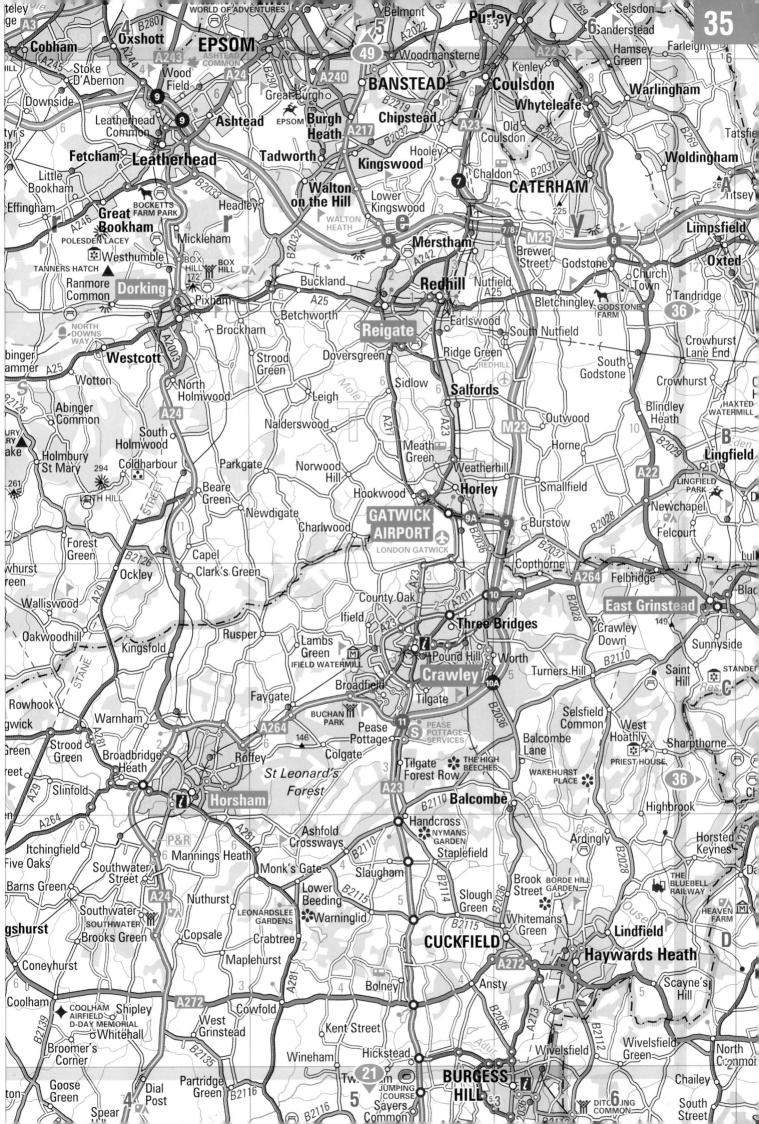

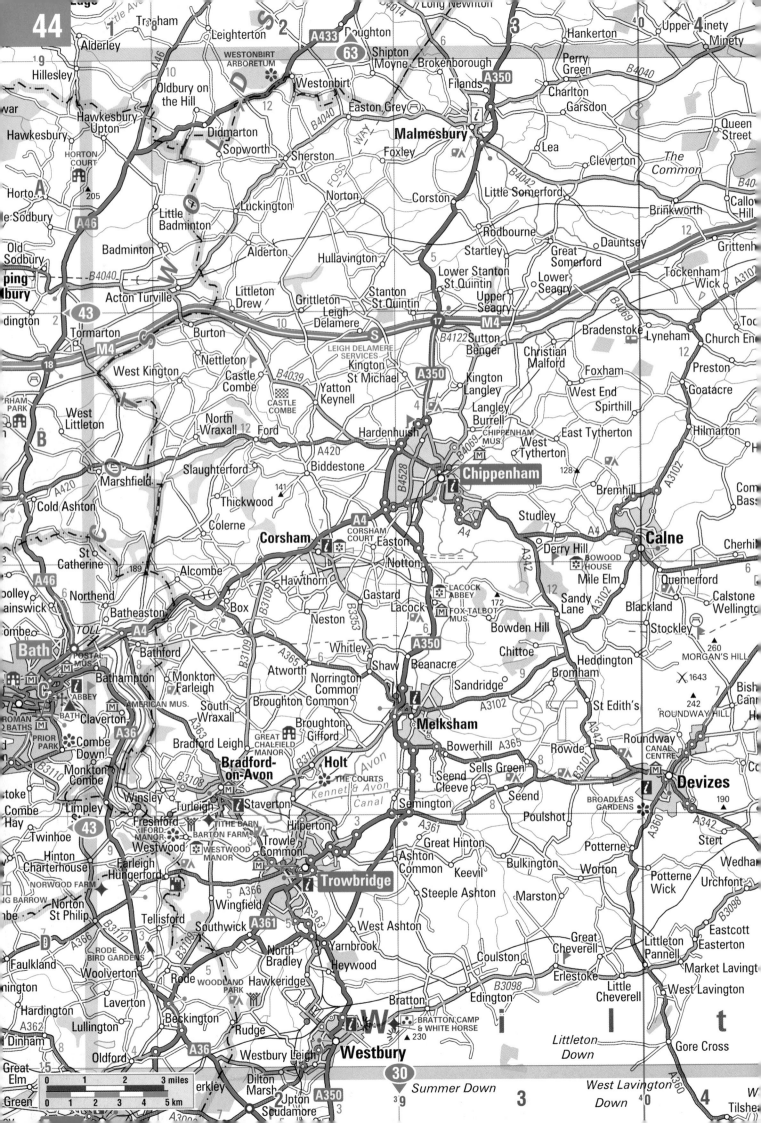

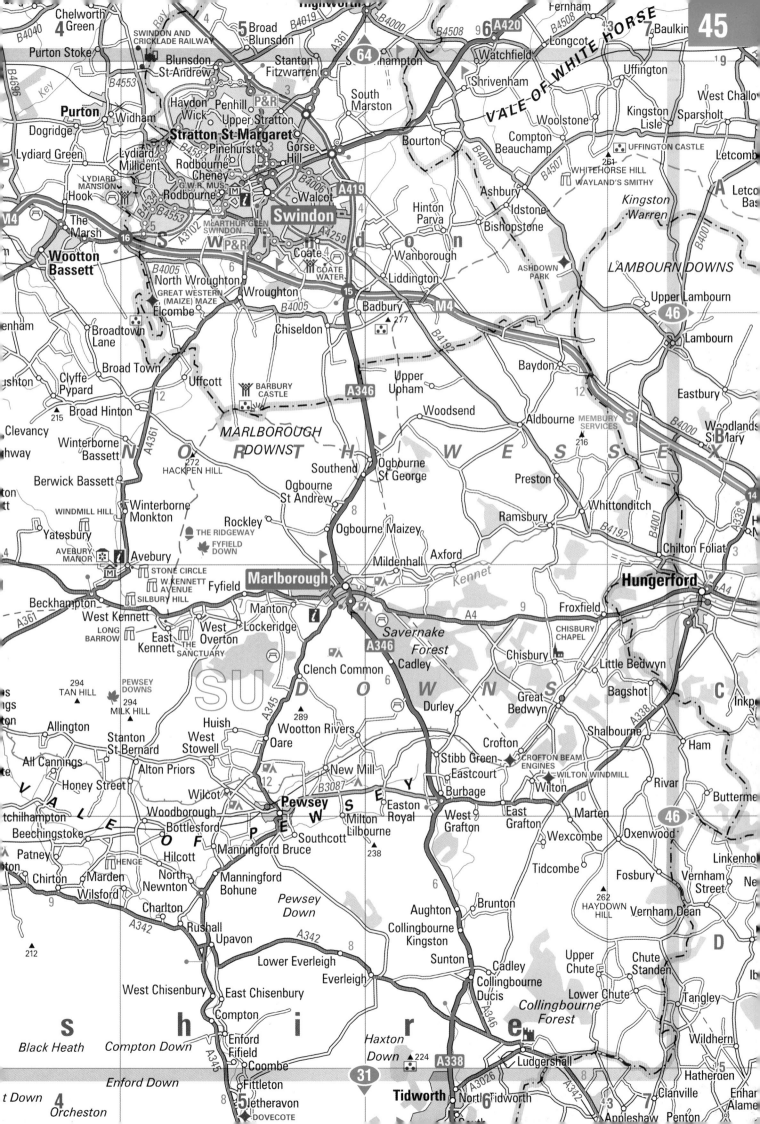

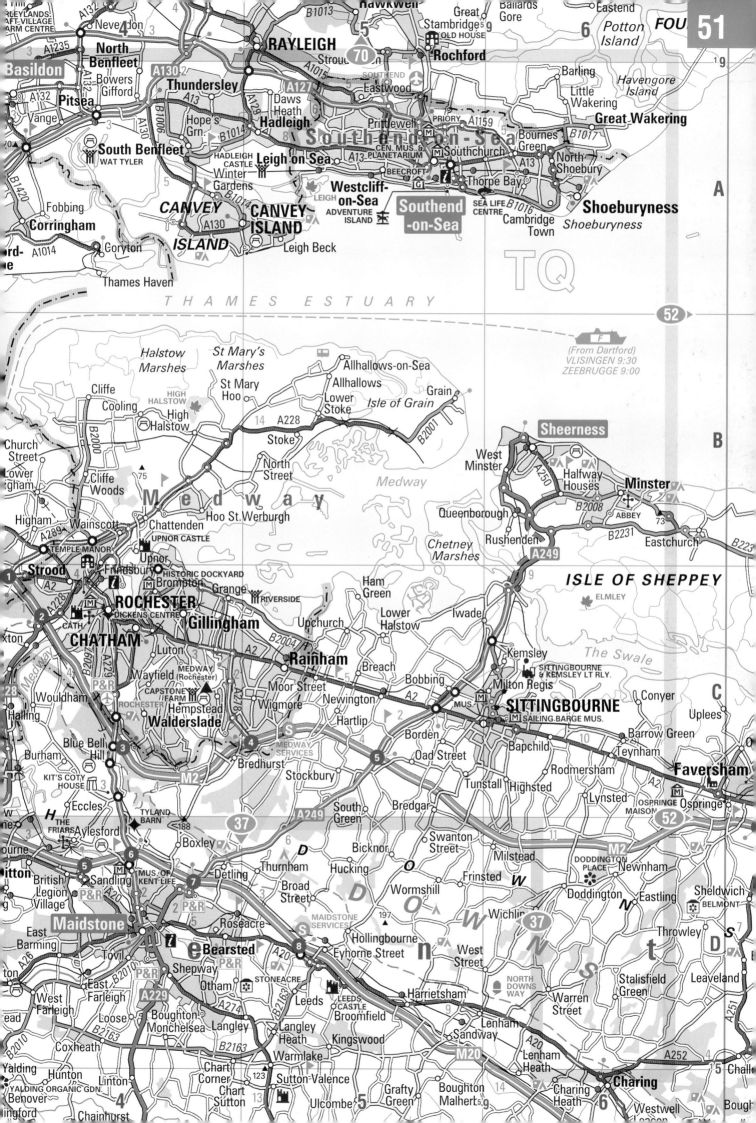

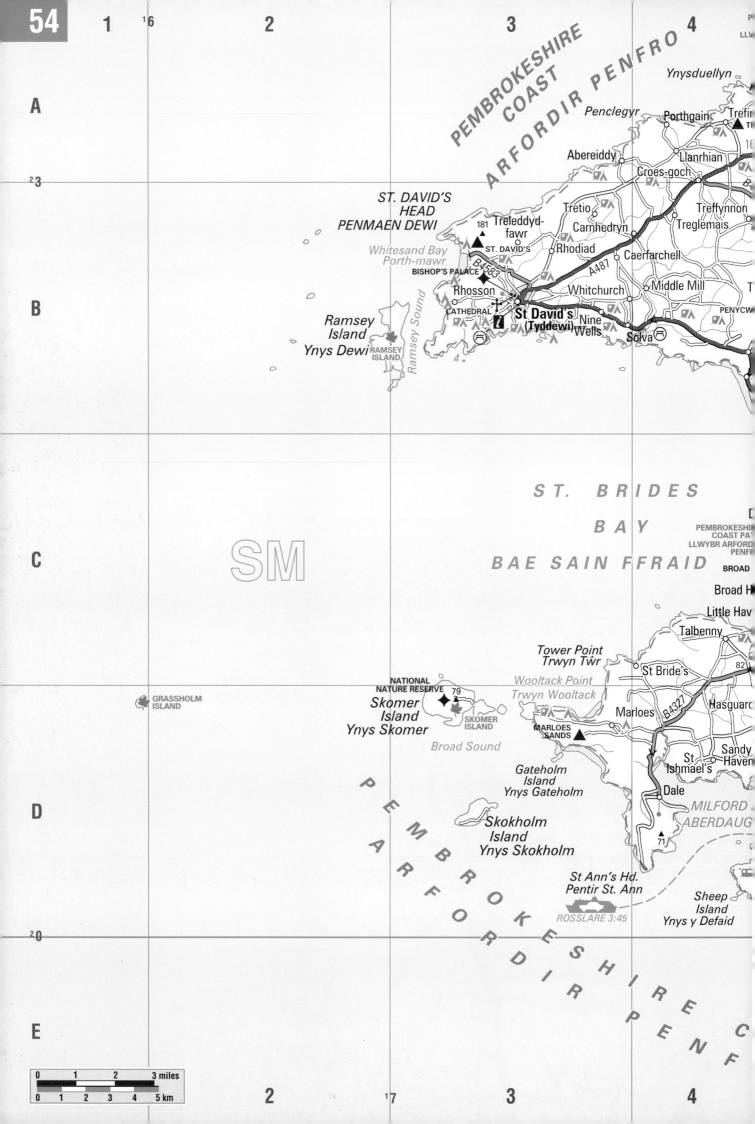

**1** ¹6 **2** **3** **4**

**A**

PEMBROKESHIRE COAST
ARFORDIR PENFRO

Ynysduellyn

Penclegyr

Porthgain Trefi

²3

Abereiddy
Llanrhian
Croes-goch

ST. DAVID'S
HEAD
PENMAEN DEWI

Tretio

Treffynnon

Treleddyd-
fawr
181 ▲

Carnhedryn

Treglemais

Whitesand Bay
Porth-mawr

▲ ST. DAVID'S

Rhodiad

**B**

Ramsey
Island
Ynys Dewi

RAMSEY
ISLAND

Ramsey Sound

BISHOP'S PALACE

Rhosson

CATHEDRAL

St David's
(Tyddewi)

Nine
Wells

Solva

Caerfarchell

Middle Mill

Whitchurch

PENYCW

4.

ST. BRIDES

BAY

BAE SAIN FFRAID

PEMBROKESHI
COAST PAT
LLWYBR ARFORD
PENF

BROAD

**C**

SM

Broad H

Little Hav

Talbenny

82

GRASSHOLM
ISLAND

Tower Point
Trwyn Twr

St Bride's

NATIONAL
NATURE RESERVE

Wooltack Point
Trwyn Wooltack

79

Skomer
Island
Ynys Skomer

SKOMER
ISLAND

Marloes

B4327

Hasguard

MARLOES
SANDS ▲

Broad Sound

Gateholm
Island
Ynys Gateholm

St
Ishmael's

Sandy
Haven

**D**

Skokholm
Island
Ynys Skokholm

Dale

MILFORD
ABERDAUG

71 ▲

P
A
R
F
O
R
D

St Ann's Hd.
Pentir St. Ann

Sheep
Island
Ynys y Defaid

²0

ROSSLARE 3:45

**E**

P
E
M
B
R
O
K
E
S
H
I
R
E

C
F

0   1   2   3 miles
0  1  2  3  4  5 km

**2** ¹7 **3** **4**

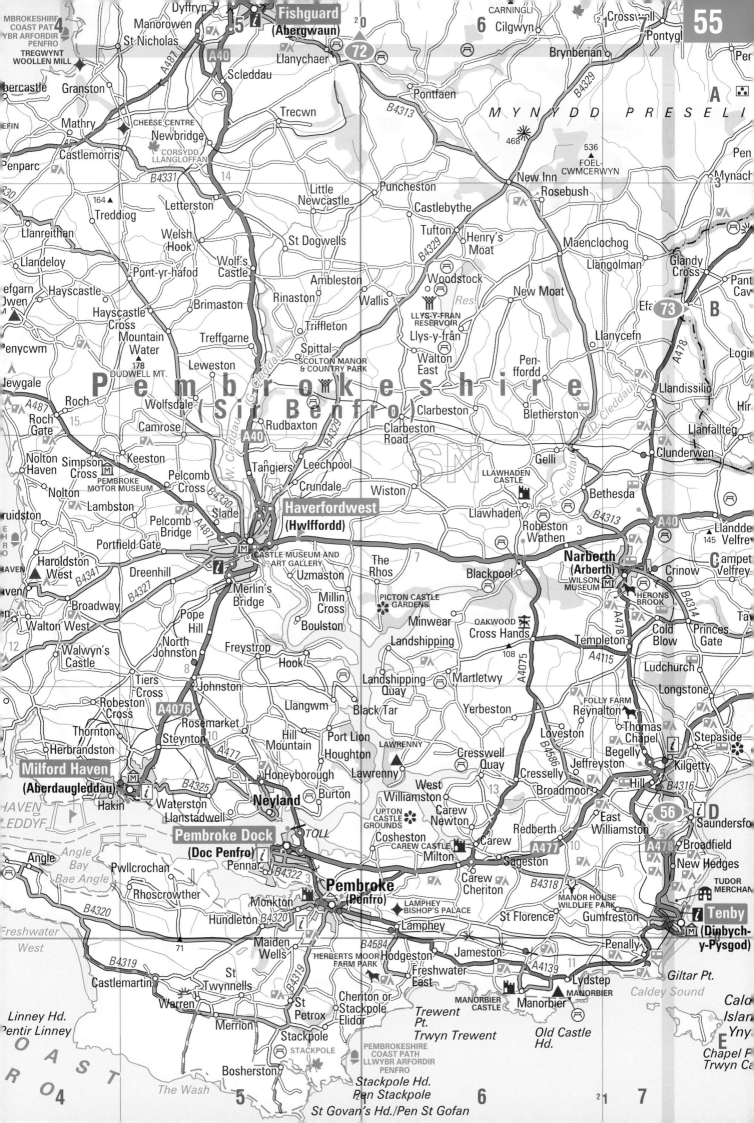

Swerford · Newington · St Michael · Clifton · Souldern · Cottisford · Newton Purcell

Nether Worton · Hempton · Deddington · M40 · Fritwell · Baynard's Green · Hardwick · Hethe · Chetwode

Great Tew · Over Worton · Duns Tew · North Aston · Somerton · Fewcott · Ardley · Stoke Lyne · Fringford · Stratton Audley

Little Tew · Ledwell · Middle Aston · Upper Heyford · Bucknell · Caversfield · Twyfor

Heythrop · Sandford St Martin · Middle Barton · Steeple Aston · Highfield · Woodfield · Bicester · Marsh

Church Enstone · Westcott Barton · Steeple Barton · Lower Heyford · Caulcott · Middleton Stoney · Chesterton · Bicester Village · Launton

Enstone · Gagingwell · Kiddington · Glympton · Tackley · Kirtlington · Weston-on-the-Green · Bletchingdon · Ambrosden · Wendlebury · Blackthorn · Lower Arncott

Taston · Over Kiddington · Wootton · STREET · Charlton on Otmoor · Murcott · Merton · Upper Arncott · Piddington

Charlbury · Stonesfield · Fawler · Woodstock · Bunkers Hill · Shipton on Cherwell · Thrupp · Hampton Poyle · Oddington · Islip · Noke · Horton-cum-Studley · Boarstall · Brill

Ramsden · Combe · Bladon · Begbroke · Kidlington · Murcott · Beckley · Little Oakley

Whiteoak Green · East End · North Leigh · Long Hanborough · Yarnton · Woodeaton · Elsfield · Stanton St John · Forest Hill · Ickford · Waterperry

Hailey · New Yatt · Freeland · Church Hanborough · Cassington · Wolvercote · Barton · Holton · Waterstock

Witney · Cogges · South Leigh · Eynsham · Wytham · Summertown · Marston · Headington · Wheatley · Shotover · Holton

High Cogges · Swinford · Farmoor · Botley · Oxford · University · Cowley · Horspath · Oxford Services

Hardwick · Sutton · Stanton Harcourt · West End · North Hinksey · New Hinksey · Cowley · Cuddesdon · Great Milton

Yelford · Brighthampton · Standlake · Northmoor · Cumnor · Chawley · South Hinksey · Littlemore · Denton · Garsington · Tiddin

Shifford · Bessels Leigh · Eaton · Wootton · Boars Hill · Kennington · Sandford on Thames · Little Milton · Little Ha

Duxford · Appleton · Lamborough Hill · Foxcombe Hill · Toot Baldon · Marsh Baldon

Longworth · Netherton · Cothill · Sunningwell · Radley · Nuneham Courtenay · Chislehampton · Stadhampton

Fyfield · Tubney · Shippon · County Hall · Clifton Hampden · Burcot · Drayton St Leonard · Berinsfield · Chalgrove · Newington · Brightwell Baldwin

Southmoor · Kingston Bagpuize · Frilford · Marcham · Caldecott · ABINGDON · Culham · Dorchester · Berrick Salome · Warborough · Roke

Pusey · Charney Bassett · Lyford · Garford · Drayton · Sutton Courtenay · Long Wittenham · Little Wittenham · Shillingford

West Hanney · East Hanney · Steventon · Milton · Appleford · Didcot Railway Centre · Brightwell cum Sotwell

Goosey · Denchworth · Milton Hill · Rowstock · Harwell · Didcot · Wallingford · North Moreton

East Challow · Ardington · East Hendred · Grove · West Hendred · East Hagbourne · South · Crowmarsh Gifford

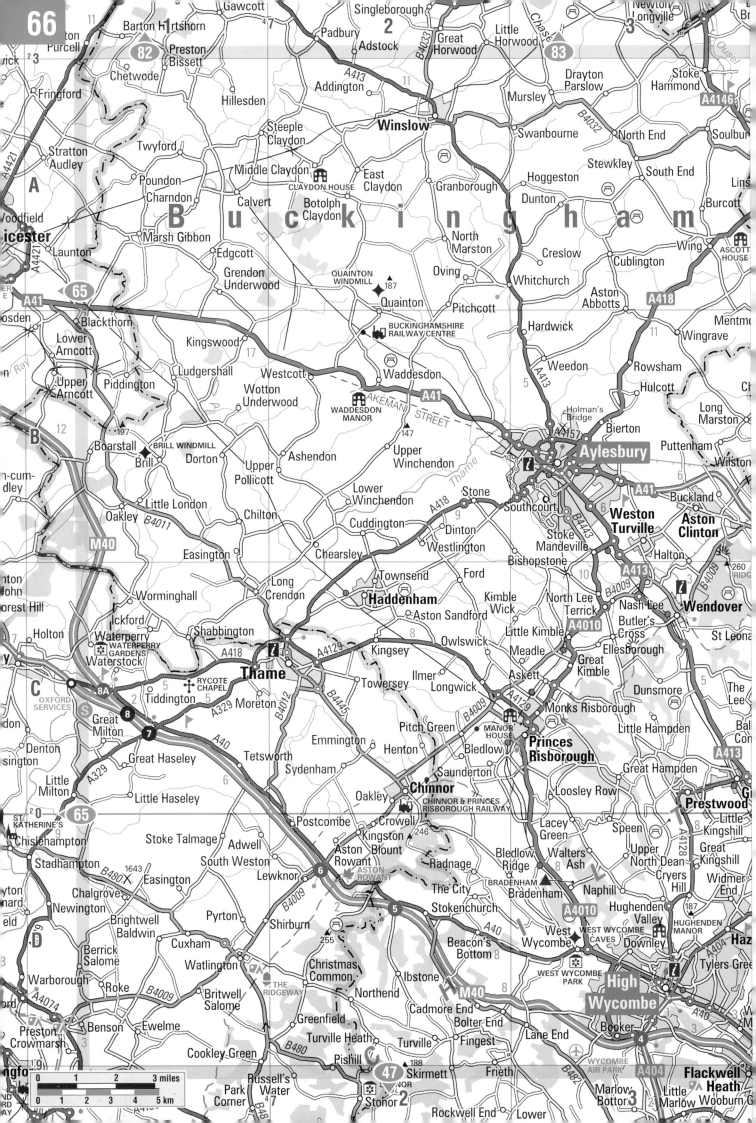

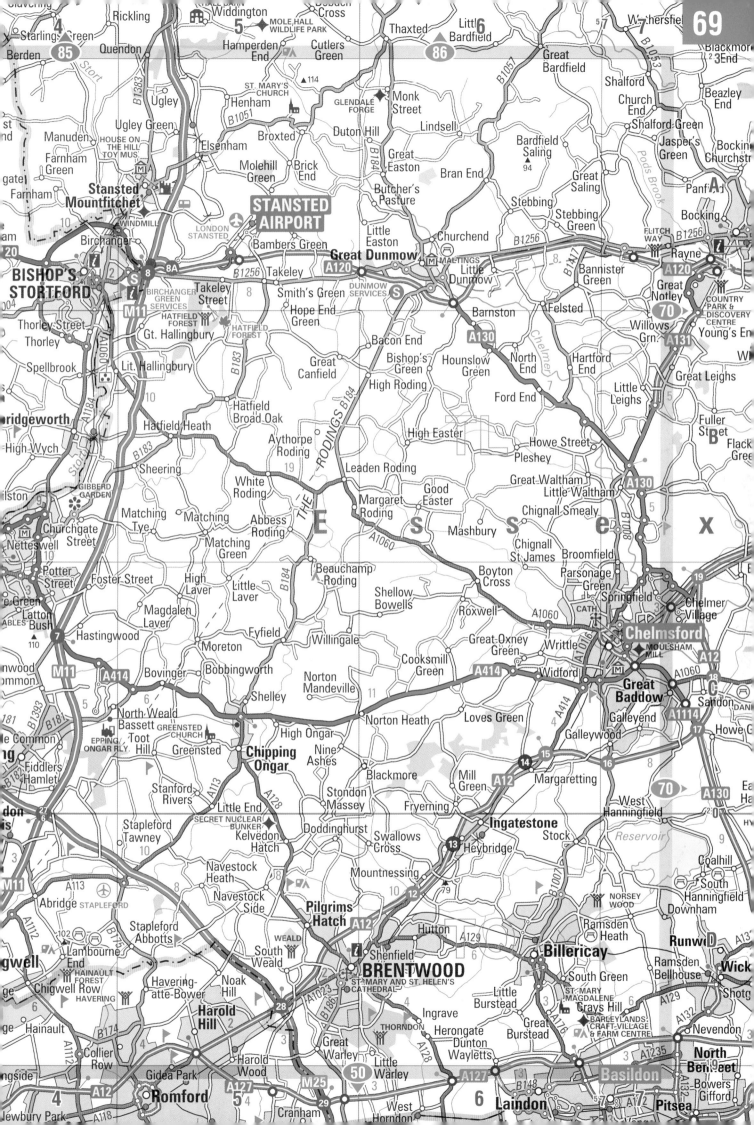

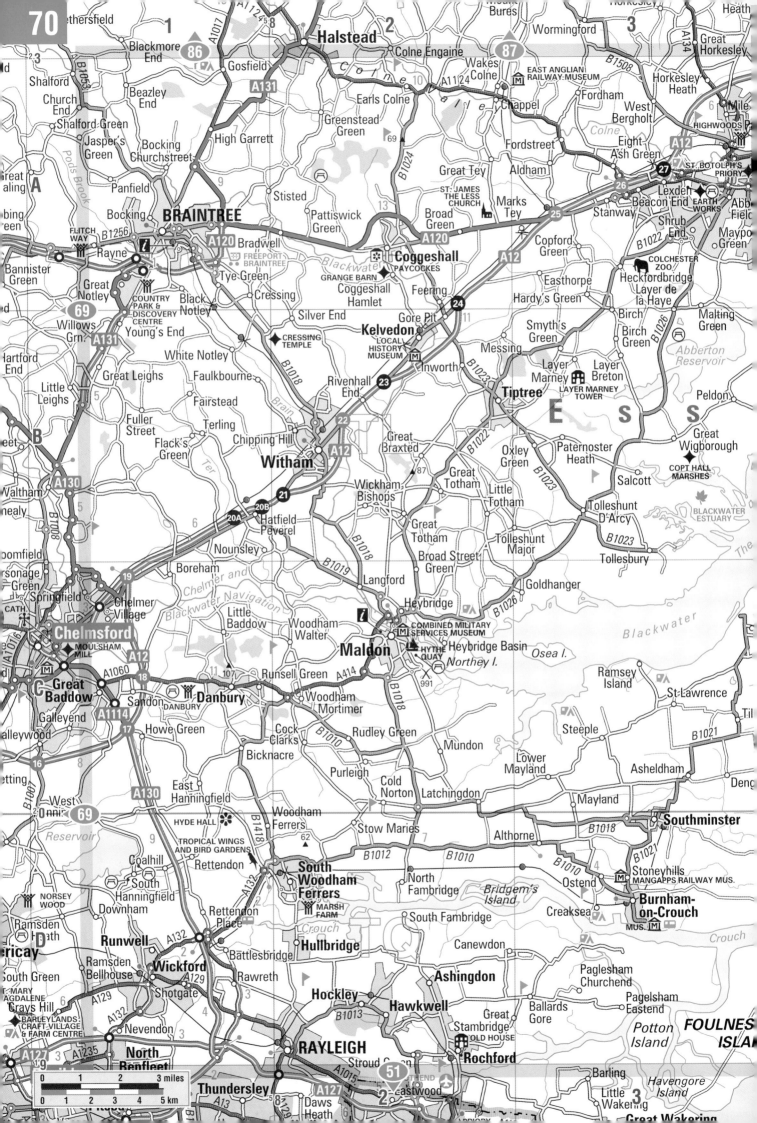

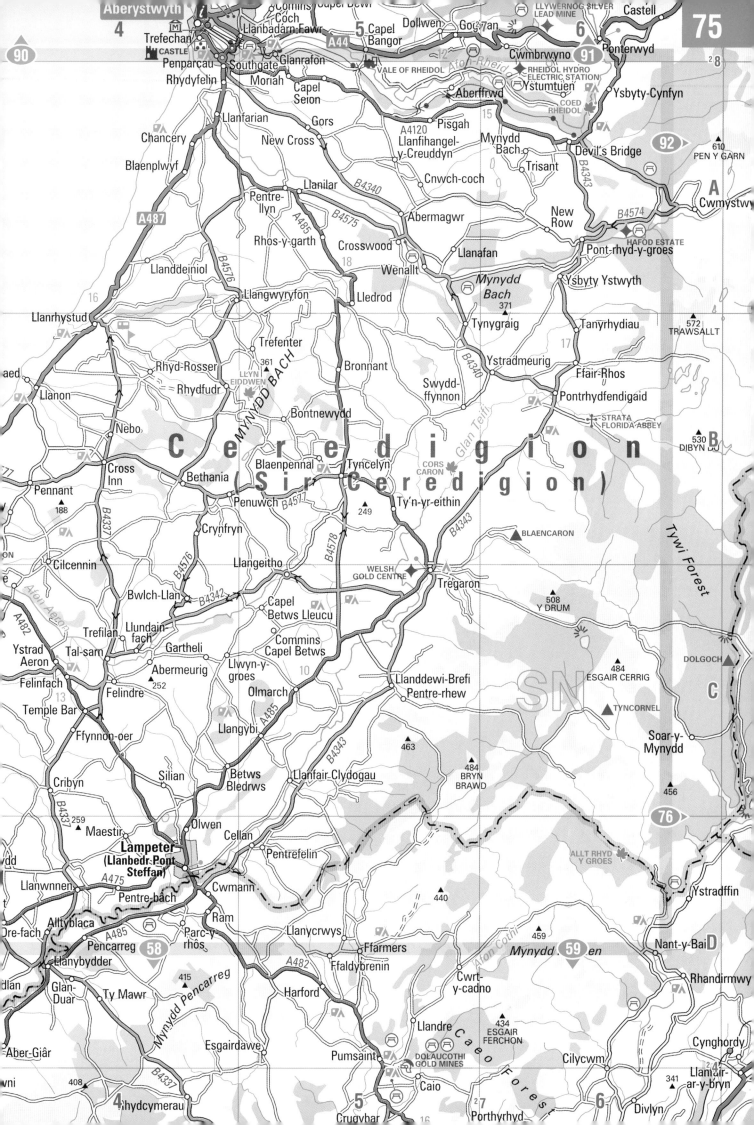

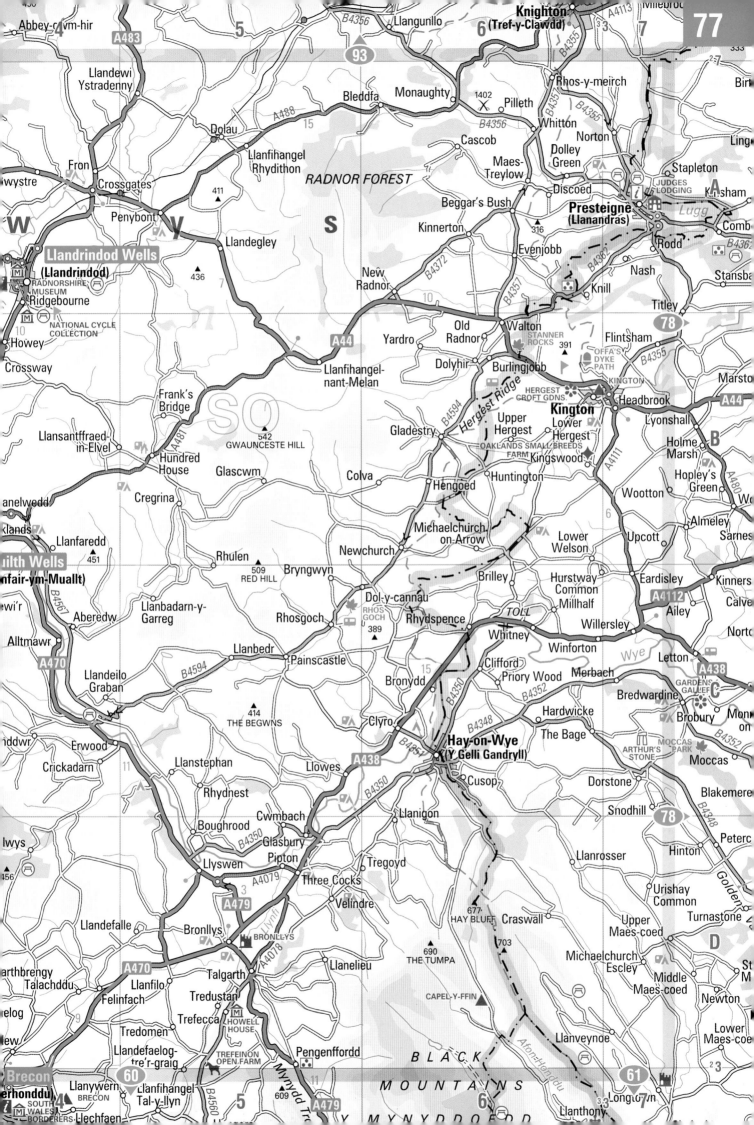

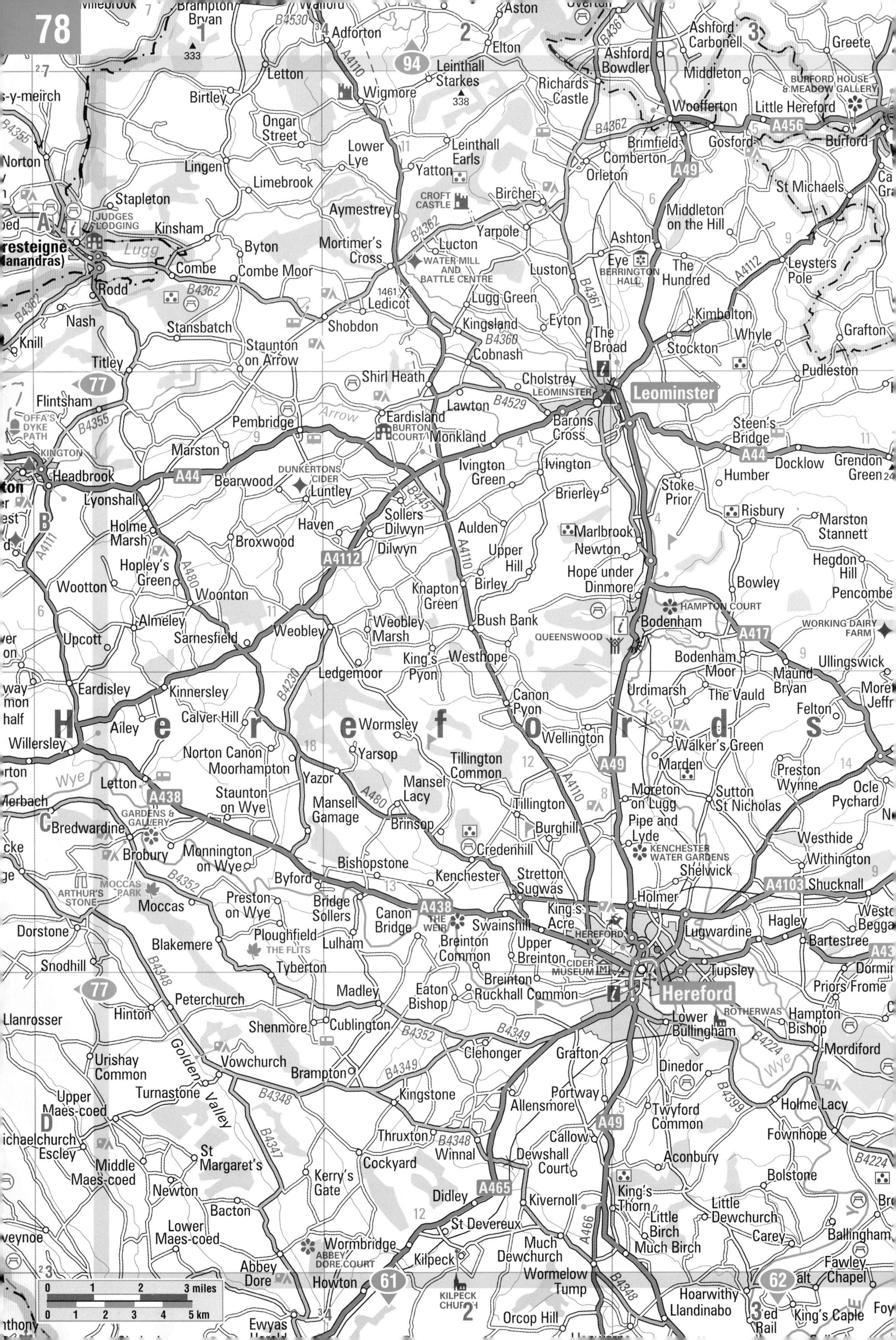

Brampton Bryan
Aston
Overton
Ashford Carbonell
Greete
Adforton
Elton
94
Leinthall Starkes
Ashford Bowdler
Middleton
BURFORD HOUSE & MEADOW GALLERY
Letton
Wigmore
Richards Castle
Woofferton
Little Hereford
Birtley
Ongar Street
Leinthall Earls
Brimfield
Comberton
Gosford
Burford
Lower Lye
Yatton
Orleton
A49
St Michaels
Lingen
Croft Castle
Bircher
Ashton
Middleton on the Hill
Stapleton
Aymestrey
Yarpole
Eye
BERRINGTON HALL
A456
Kinsham
Mortimer's Cross
Lucton
Luston
The Hundred
Leysters Pole
JUDGES LODGING
Byton
Combe Moor
WATER-MILL AND BATTLE CENTRE
Lugg Green
Kimbolton
Combe
Ledicot
Kingsland
Eyton
The Broad
Stockton
Whyle
Grafton
Rodd
Shobdon
Cobnash
Cholstrey
LEOMINSTER
Leominster
Pudleston
Nash
Staunton on Arrow
Shirl Heath
Lawton
Barons Cross
Steen's Bridge
Knill
Titley
Eardisland
Monkland
Ivington
A44
Docklow
Grendon Green
77
Flintsham
Pembridge
BURTON COURT
Ivington Green
Stoke Prior
Humber
OFFA'S DYKE PATH
KINGTON
Marston
DUNKERTONS CIDER
Brierley
Risbury
Marston Stannett
Headbrook
Bearwood
Luntley
Sollers Dilwyn
Aulden
Marlbrook
Newton
Hegdon Hill
Lyonshall
Holme Marsh
Haven
Dilwyn
Upper Hill
Hope under Dinmore
Bowley
Pencombe
Hopley's Green
Broxwood
Knapton Green
Birley
HAMPTON COURT
Wootton
Woonton
Weobley Marsh
Bush Bank
Bodenham
WORKING DAIRY FARM
Almeley
Sarnesford
Weobley
King's Pyon
Westhope
QUEENSWOOD
Bodenham Moor
Ullingswick
Eardisley
Kinnersley
Ledgemoor
Canon Pyon
Urdimarsh
Maund Bryan
Felten
Calver Hill
Wormsley
Wellington
Walker's Green
Willersley
Ailey
Norton Canon
Moorhampton
Yarsop
Tillington Common
A49
Marden
Preston Wynne
Ocle Pychard
Letton
Yazor
Mansel Lacy
Tillington
Moreton on Lugg Pipe and Lyde
Sutton St Nicholas
A438
Staunton on Wye
Mansell Gamage
Brinsop
Burghill
Westhide
Withington
Bredwardine
GARDENS & GALLERY
Monnington on Wye
Bishopstone
Credenhill
Kenchester
Stretton Sugwas
Shelwick
A4103
Shucknall
Brobury
ARTHUR'S STONE
MOCCAS PARK
Byford
Holmer
A4103
Moccas
Preston on Wye
Bridge Sollers
Canon Bridge
King's Acre
HEREFORD
Lugwardine
Hagley
Bartestree
Dorstone
Ploughfield
THE FLITS
Lulham
THE WEIR
Swainshill
Breinton Common
Upper Breinton
CIDER MUSEUM
Hereford
Blakemere
Madley
Eaton Bishop
Breinton
Ruckhall Common
Lower Bullingham
ROTHERWAS
Hampton Bishop
Snodhill
Tyberton
Cublington
Clehonger
Grafton
Dinedor
Mordiford
77
Peterchurch
Shenmore
Kingstone
Portway
Allensmore
Twyford Common
Holme Lacy
Hinton
Vowchurch
Brampton
Callow
A49
Fownhope
Urishay Common
Turnastone
Thruxton
Winnal
Dewshall Court
Aconbury
Bolstone
Upper Maes-coed
St Margaret's
Cockyard
A465
Kivernoll
King's Thorn
Little Dewchurch
Escley
Middle Maes-coed
Newton
Bacton
Kerry's Gate
Didley
St Devereux
Little Birch
Much Birch
Carey
Lower Maes-coed
Wormbridge
ABBEY DORE COURT
Kilpeck
Much Dewchurch
Wormelow Tump
Fawley Chapel
61
Abbey Dore
Howton
KILPECK CHURCH
Ewyas
Orcop Hill
Hoarwithy
Llandinabo
62
King's Caple

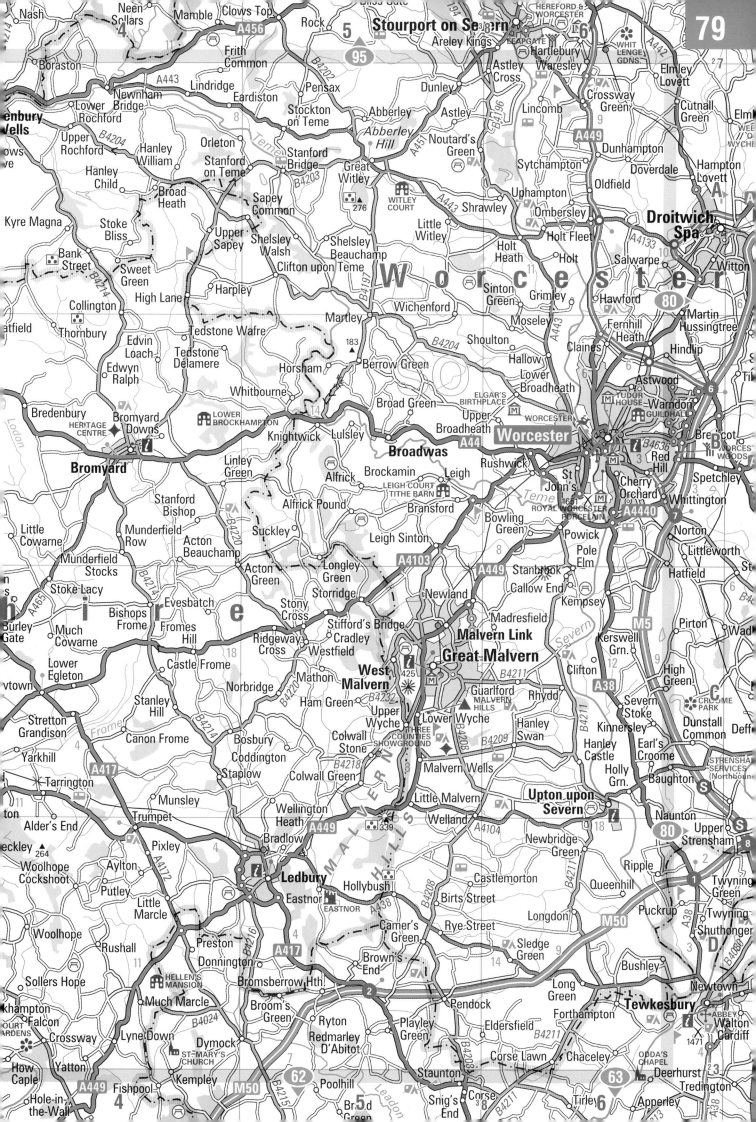

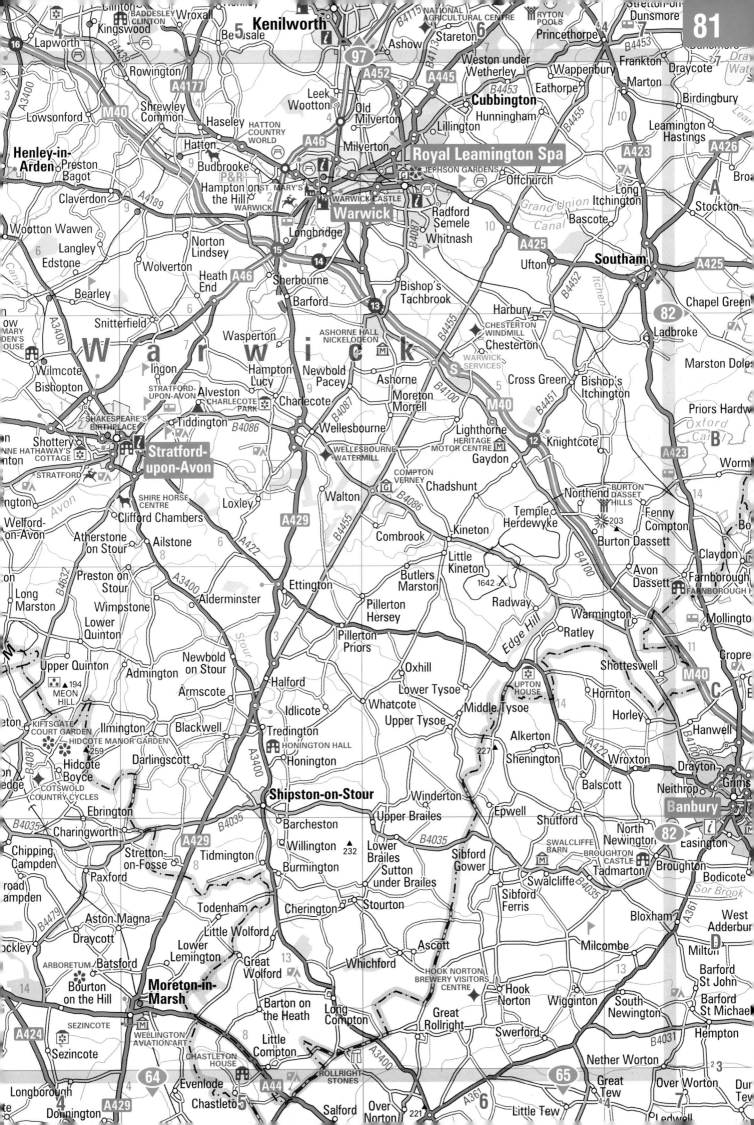

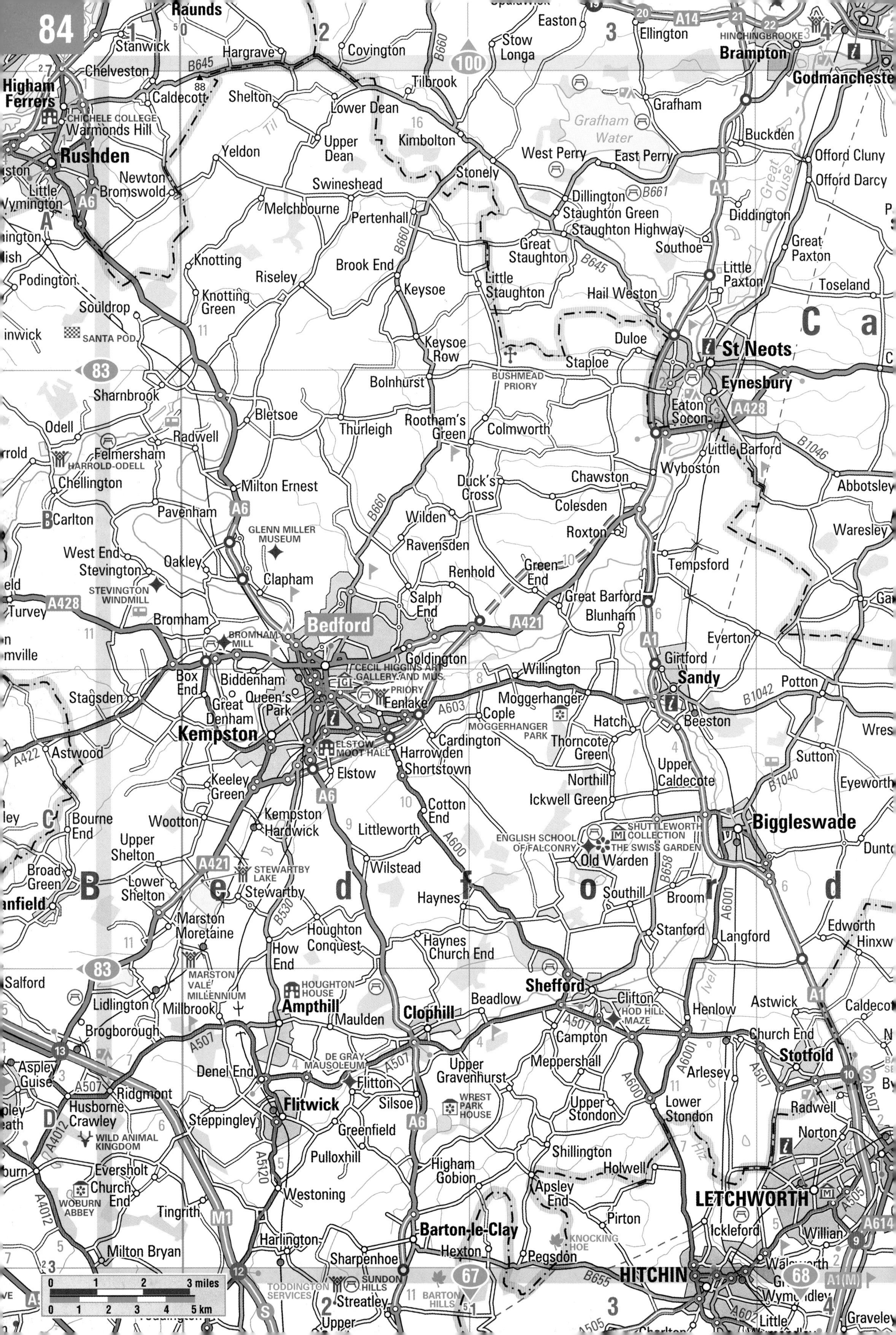

Raunds
Stanwick
Hargrave
Covington
Easton
Stow Longa
Ellington
A14
HINCHINGBROOKE
Brampton
Godmanchester
100
Chelveston
Higham Ferrers
Caldecott
Shelton
Tilbrook
Lower Dean
Grafham
CHICHELE COLLEGE
Warmonds Hill
Upper Dean
Kimbolton
Grafham Water
Buckden
Rushden
Yeldon
West Perry
East Perry
Offord Cluny
Offord Darcy
Newton Bromswold
Swineshead
Stonely
Little Irthlingborough
A6
Melchbourne
Pertenhall
Dillington
B661
Staughton Green
Staughton Highway
Diddington
Southoe
Great Paxton
Great Ouse
Great Staughton
Knotting
Brook End
Podington
Riseley
Keysoe
Little Staughton
B645
Little Paxton
Hail Weston
Toseland
Souldrop
Knotting Green
SANTA POD
Keysoe Row
Duloe
St Neots
Staploe
BUSHMEAD PRIORY
Eynesbury
83
Sharnbrook
Bolnhurst
Eaton Socon
A428
Odell
Bletsoe
Thurleigh
Rootham's Green
Colmworth
Little Barford
Radwell
B1046
Felmersham
HARROLD-ODELL
Chellington
Milton Ernest
Duck's Cross
Chawston
Wyboston
Abbotsley
Pavenham
Colesden
Carlton
B660
Wilden
GLENN MILLER MUSEUM
Roxton
Waresley
West End
Ravensden
Tempsford
Stevington
Oakley
Renhold
Green End
Clapham
STEVINGTON WINDMILL
Turvey
Salph End
Great Barford
Blunham
Bromham
Bedford
A421
BROMHAM MILL
Everton
Goldington
CECIL HIGGINS ART GALLERY AND MUS.
Willington
Gamlingay
Biddenham
Box End
PRIORY
Girtford
Sandy
Potton
B1042
Stagsden
Great Denham
Queen's Park
Fenlake
Moggerhanger
A603
Cople
MOGGERHANGER PARK
Beeston
Hatch
Kempston
Cardington
Thorncote Green
A422
Astwood
ELSTOW MOOT HALL
Harrowden
Shortstown
Sutton
Elstow
Upper Caldecote
Northill
B1040
Eyeworth
Keeley Green
Ickwell Green
Kempston Hardwick
Cotton End
Bourne End
Wootton
SHUTTLEWORTH COLLECTION
Biggleswade
Littleworth
Upper Shelton
ENGLISH SCHOOL OF FALCONRY
THE SWISS GARDEN
Old Warden
Broad Green
STEWARTBY LAKE
A600
Wilstead
B658
Lower Shelton
Stewartby
Haynes
Southill
Broom
Cranfield
A6001
Marston Moretaine
Houghton Conquest
Stanford
Edworth
Hinxworth
Haynes Church End
Langford
How End
Salford
MARSTON VALE MILLENNIUM
HOUGHTON HOUSE
Shefford
Clifton
HOD HILL MAZE
Astwick
Caldecote
Lidlington
Millbrook
Ampthill
Maulden
Clophill
Beadlow
Henlow
Ivel
Brogborough
A507
Campton
Church End
Stotfold
DE GRAY MAUSOLEUM
Meppershall
Upper Gravenhurst
Arlesey
Aspley Guise
Denel End
Flitton
Ridgmont
Husborne Crawley
Flitwick
Silsoe
WREST PARK HOUSE
Upper Stondon
Lower Stondon
Radwell
Steppingley
A4012
WILD ANIMAL KINGDOM
Greenfield
Norton
Shillington
Pulloxhill
A5120
Eversholt
Higham Gobion
Holwell
Hiz
Woburn
Church End
WOBURN ABBEY
Westoning
Apsley End
LETCHWORTH
Tingrith
M1
Pirton
Ickleford
William
A614
Harlington
Barton-le-Clay
KNOCKING HOE
Milton Bryan
Sharpenhoe
Hexton
Pegsdon
Walsworth
Great Wymondley
TODDINGTON SERVICES
SUNDON HILLS
BARTON HILLS
67
B655
HITCHIN
68
A1(M)
Streatley
Upper
A602
Little
Graveley
A505
0 1 2 3 miles
0 1 2 3 4 5 km
B e d f o r d
C a

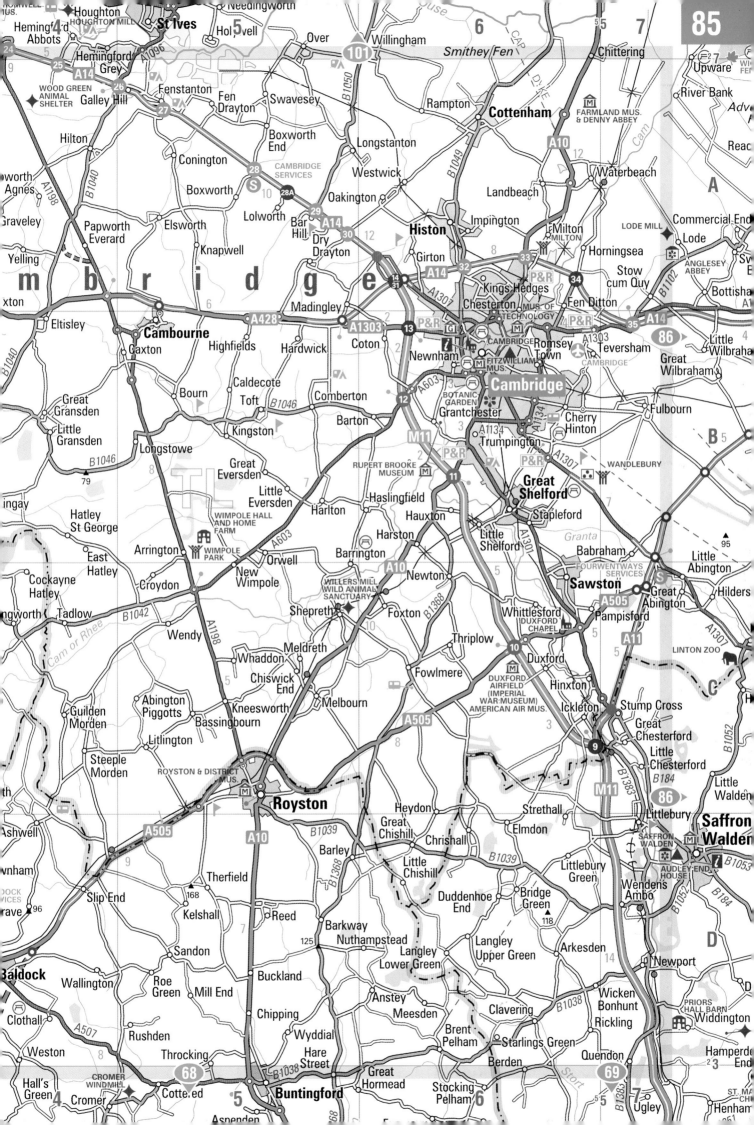

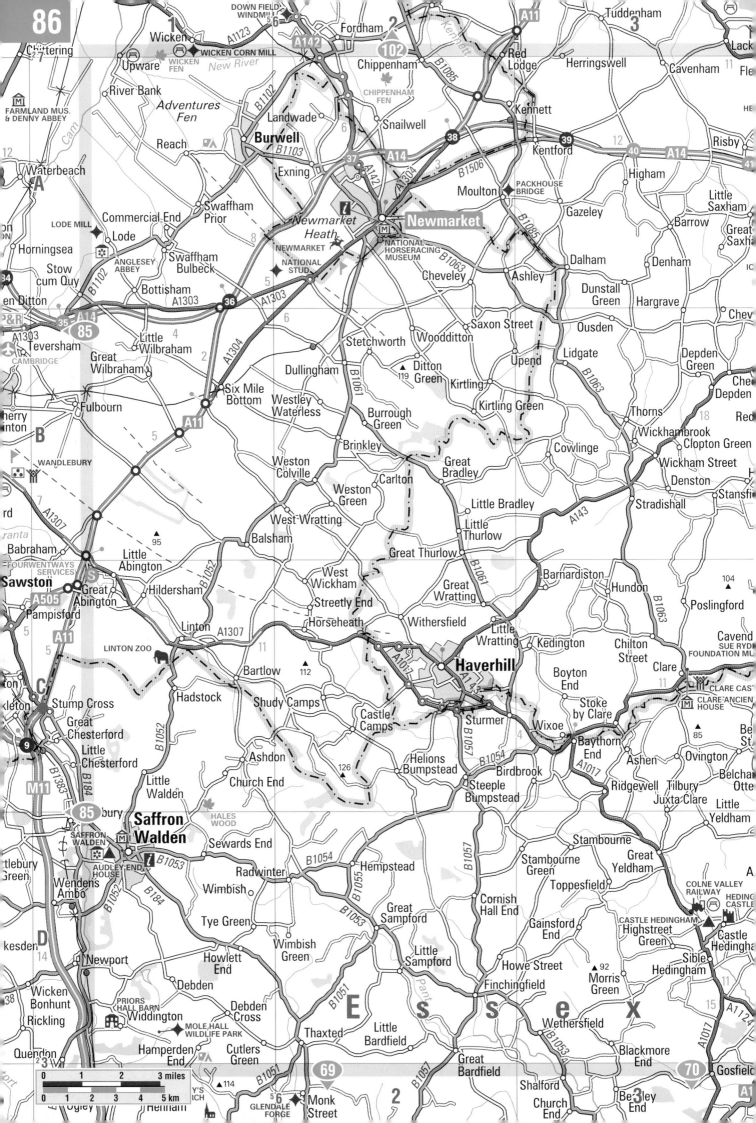

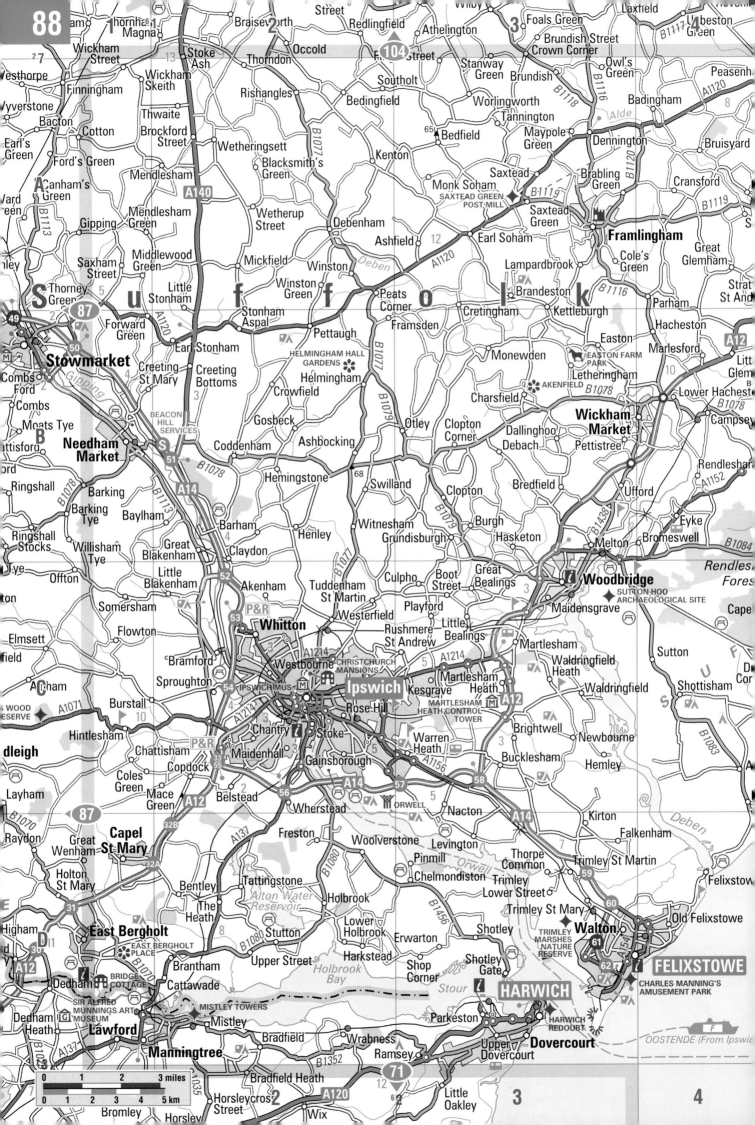

Green
4 High Street
Hemp
Green
Sibton
Yoxford
Rotten End
**A12**
Curlew
Green Kelsale
endham
B1121
Carlton
effling
**Saxmundham**
Benhall
Street
Benhall Green
Sternfield
ord
ew
Friston
Farnham
Gromford
Ash
Tunstall
Blaxhall
B1069
Iken
Tunstall
Forest
Sudbourne
Chillesford
Butley
am
Butley High
Corner
St Andrew
Boyton
Stores
Corner
ck
er
Hollesley
Shingle Street
erton
awdsey
e Ferry

Darsham
2
B1122
Middleton
Moor
North Green
Theberton
B1122
LEISTON
ABBEY
B1121
B1119
Knodishall
Coldfair
Green
B1121
B1069
Snape
SNAPE MALTINGS
RIVERSIDE CENTRE
B1078
B1084
ORFORD
CASTLE
Orford
Westleton
WESTLETON
HEATH
Westleton
Middleton
Eastbridge
**Leiston**
Sizewell
Aldringham
Thorpeness
NORTH WARREN RSPB
NATURE RESERVE
**Aldeburgh**
High
Street
*Aldeburgh Bay*
Alde
Orford Ness
ORFORDNESS-
HAVERGATE
*Hollesley
Bay*

Dunwich
*Forest*
DUNWICH UNDERWATER
EXPLORATION EXHIBITION
Dunwich **105**

A1094
6
B1353
B1122

HEATHS

A L D E

S T

C

6

TM

5 6 6 7 **89**
7
A

B

C

D

CUXHAVEN 16:45
ESBJERG 20:00
HOEK VAN HOLLAND 6:00

HOEK VAN HOLLAND 3:40

GOTHENBURG 38:30
ROTTERDAM 8:00

) 9:00

4 5 6 6 7

SH

A

**Barmouth**
**(Abermaw)**
RNLI LIFEBOAT MUSEUM
BARMOUTH BAY
BAE BERMO
FAIRBOURNE & BARMOUTH
STEAM RAILWAY
Tal-y-bont
Plas-canol
Llanaber
Caerdeon
Cutiau
The Bar
Arthog
Ynysgyf
Fairbourne
Friog
20

SNOWDO
NATION
PARK

B

Llangelynin
Rhoslefain
Llanfendigaid
Tonfanau
**Tywyn**
Llwyngwril
Llanegryn
Peniarth
309
Bryncrug
Pandy
Rhyd-yr-onen
TALYLLYN RAILWAY

C A R D I G A N

Caethle

279

C

B A Y

Aberdovey

Aberdovey Bar
Bae Aberdyfi
DYFI

Ynyslas
Llancynfelyn
BORTH

B A E

Borth
Upper Borth
Tal-y-bo
Dôl-y-Bont

C E R E D I G I O N

Llandre
Pen-y-garn

D

SN

Bow
Street
ARTS CENTRE
NATIONAL
LIBRARY
CLIFF RAILWAY
Clarach
Plas Goge
148
**Aberystwyth**
Comins
Coch
Capel D
P&R
Trefechan
CASTLE
Llanbadarn Fawr
Penparcau
Southgate
Glanrafon
Rhydyfelin
Moriah
Capel
Seion
Llanfarian

0 1 2 3 miles
0 1 2 3 4 5 km

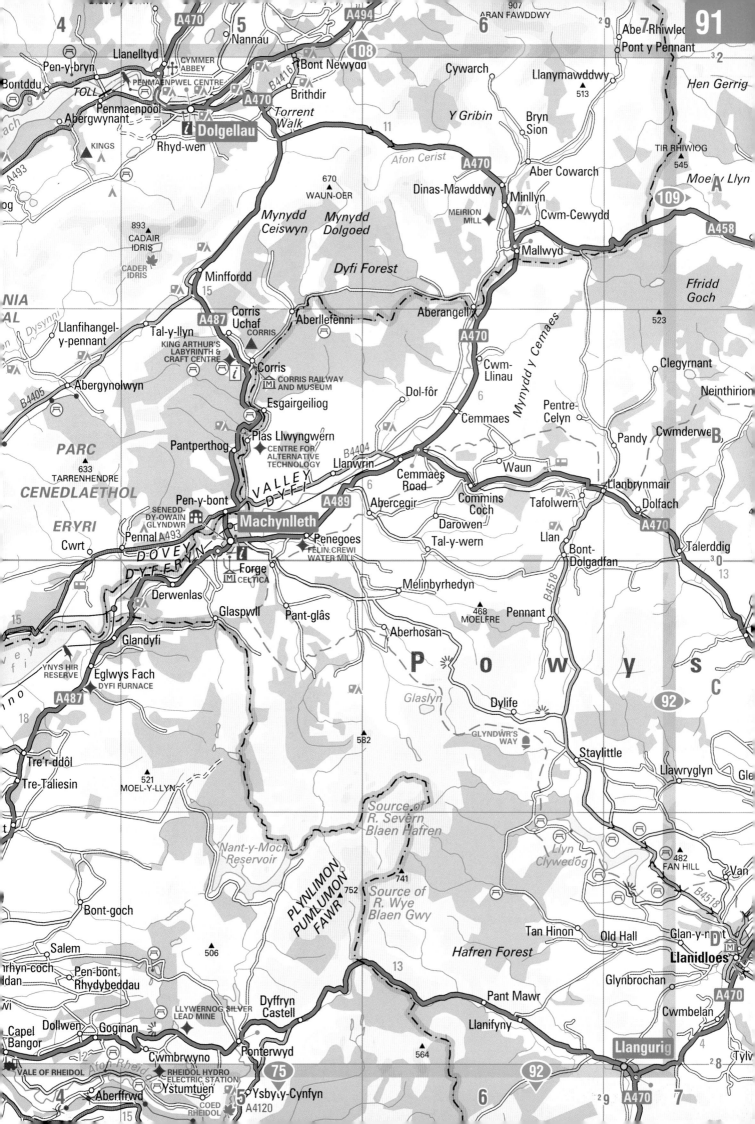

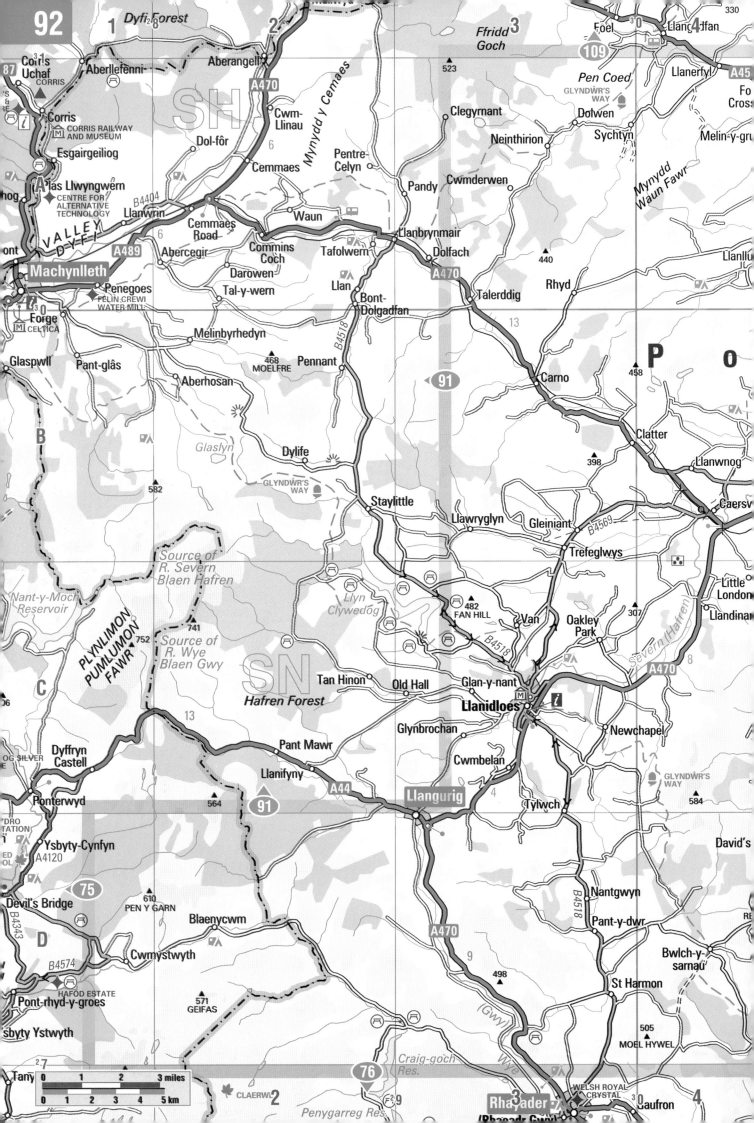

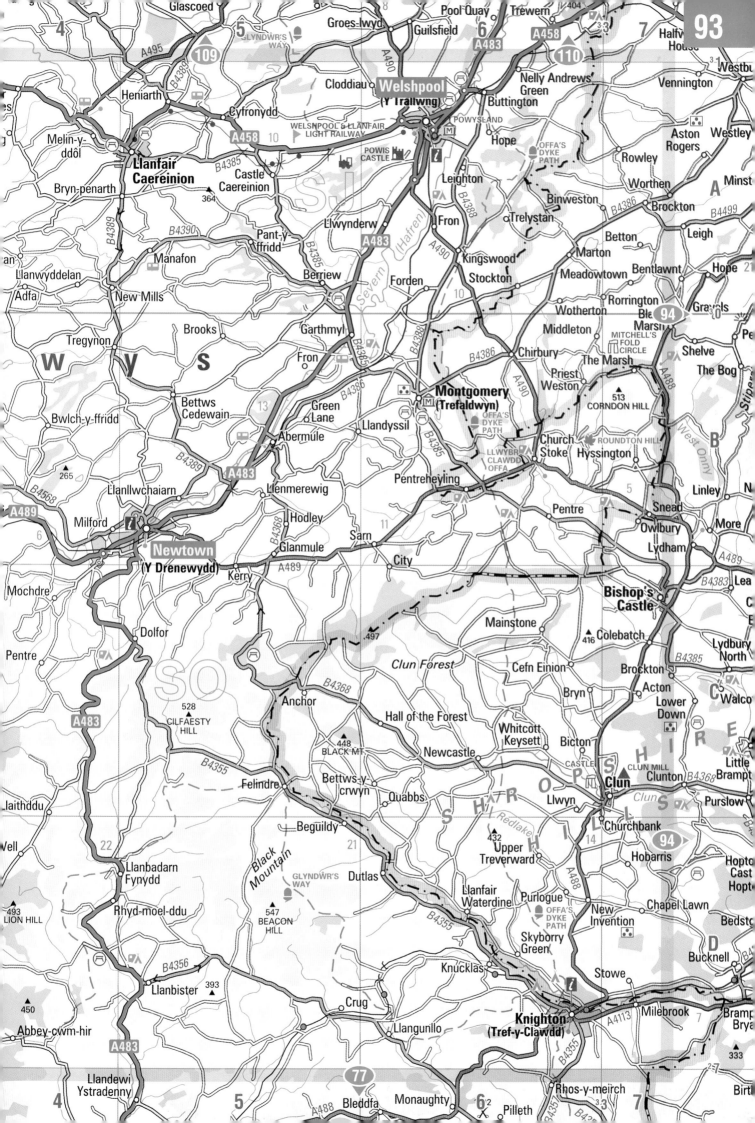

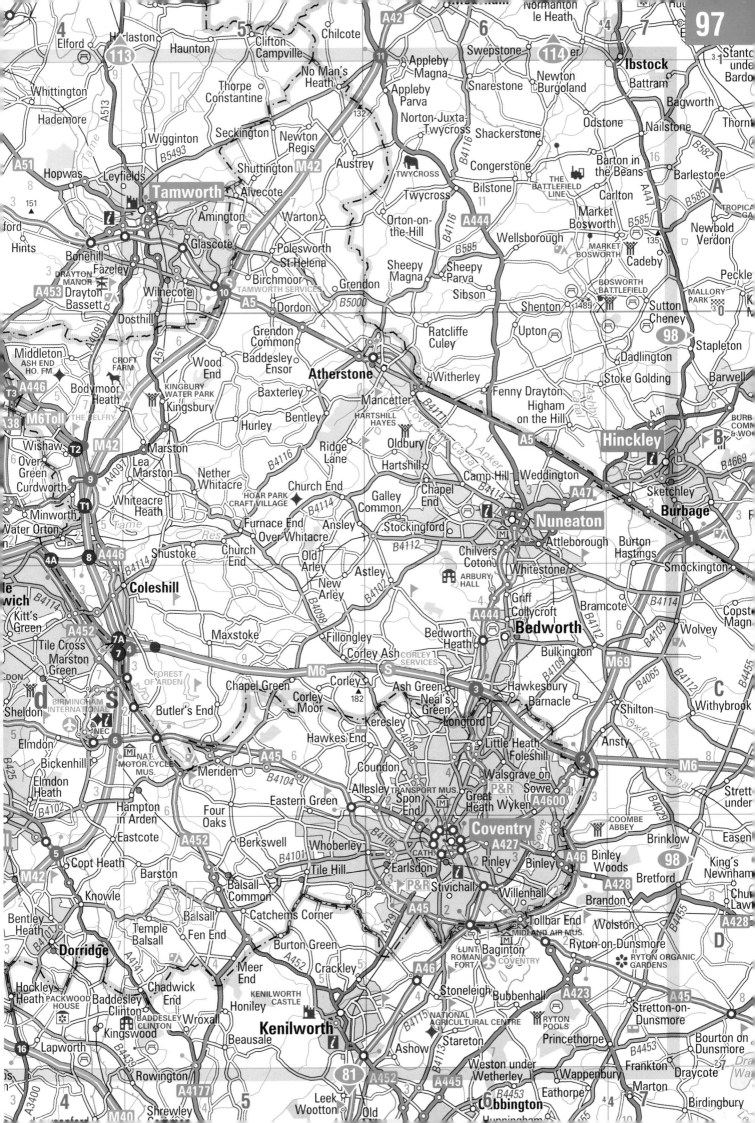

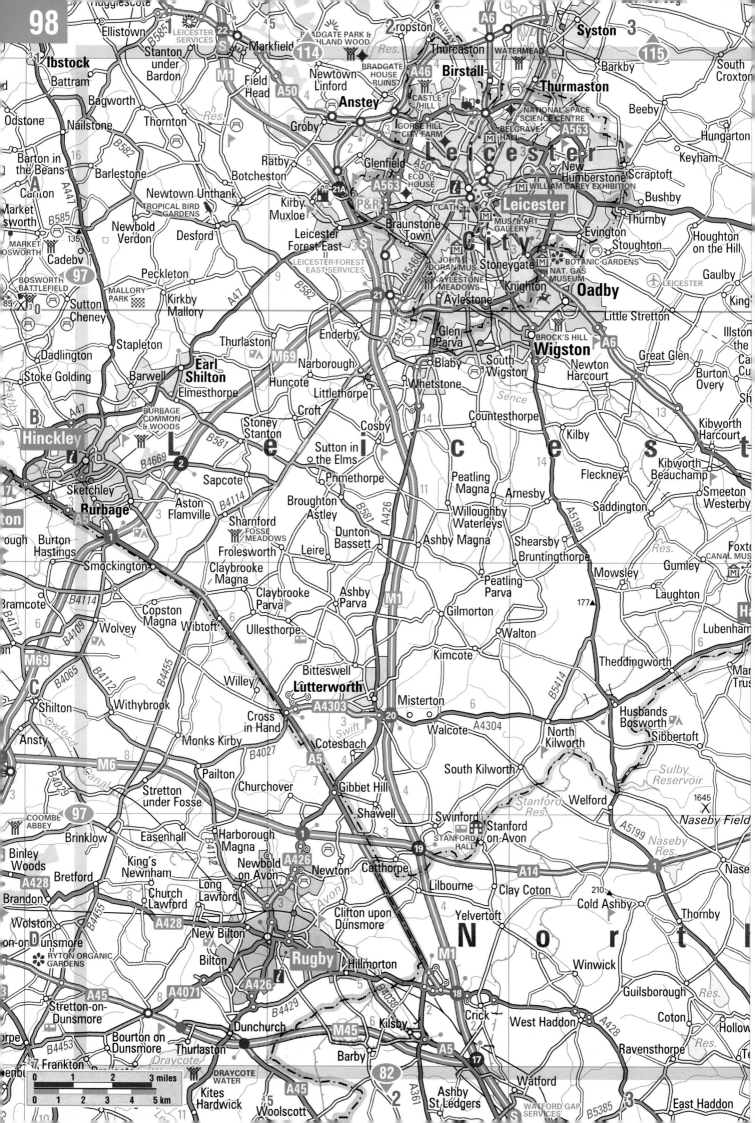

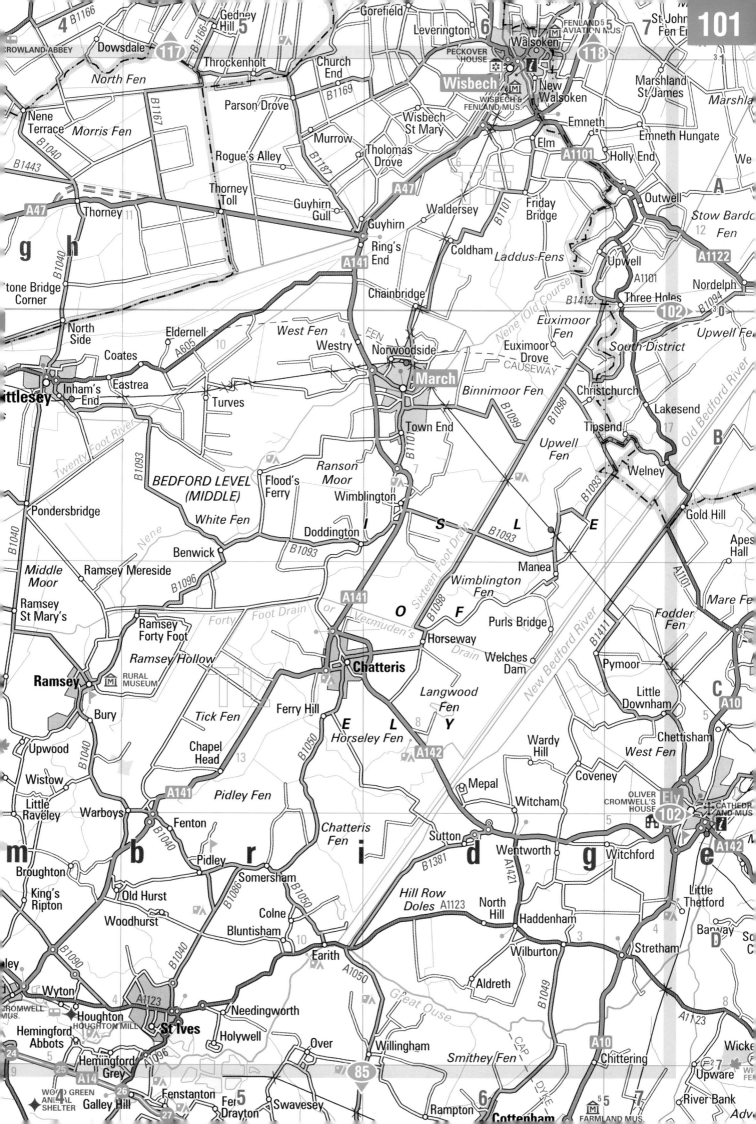

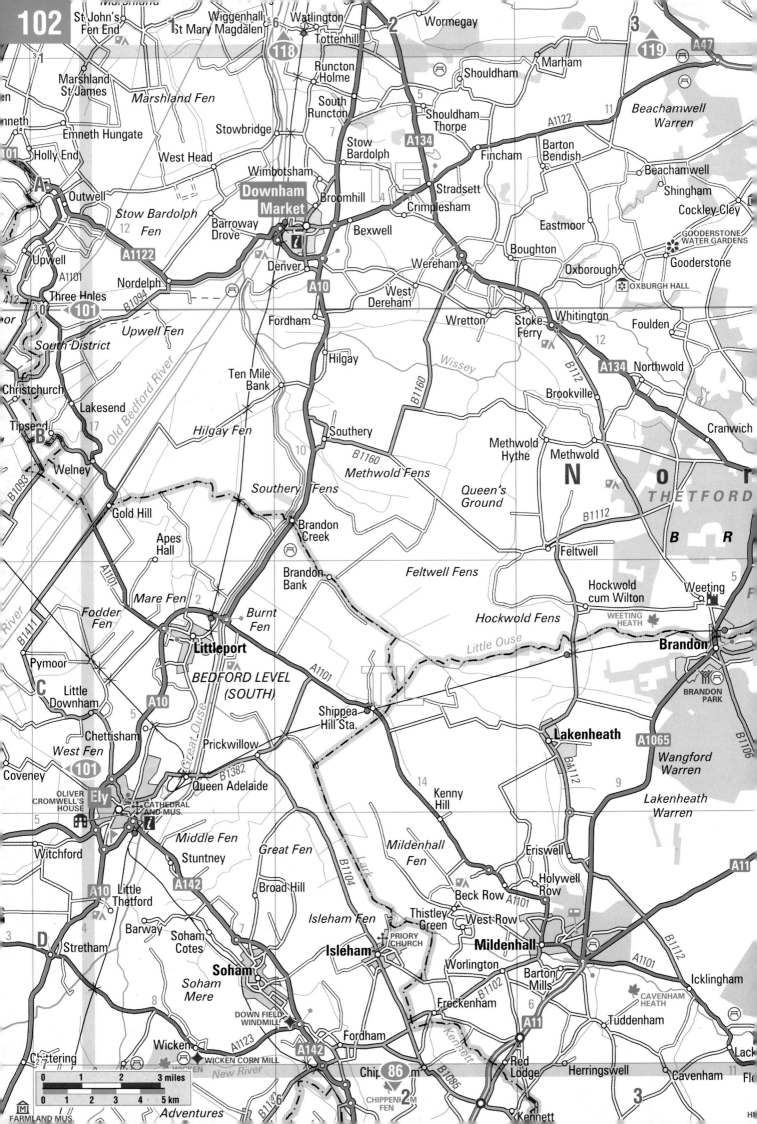

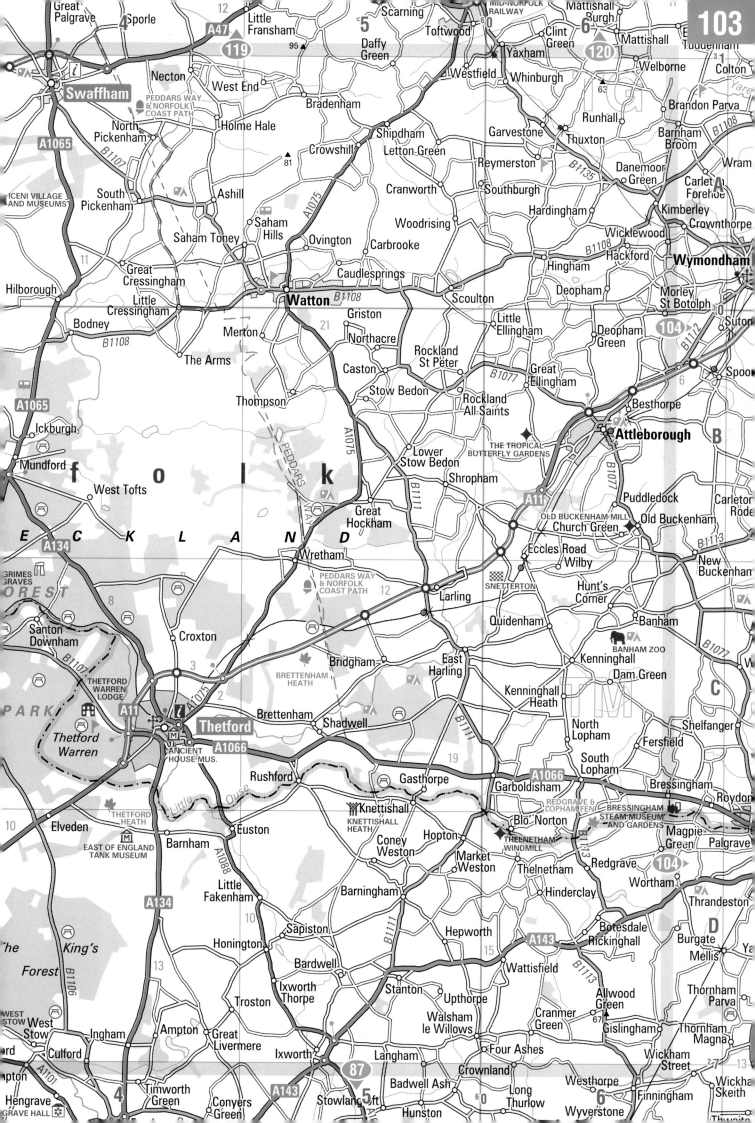

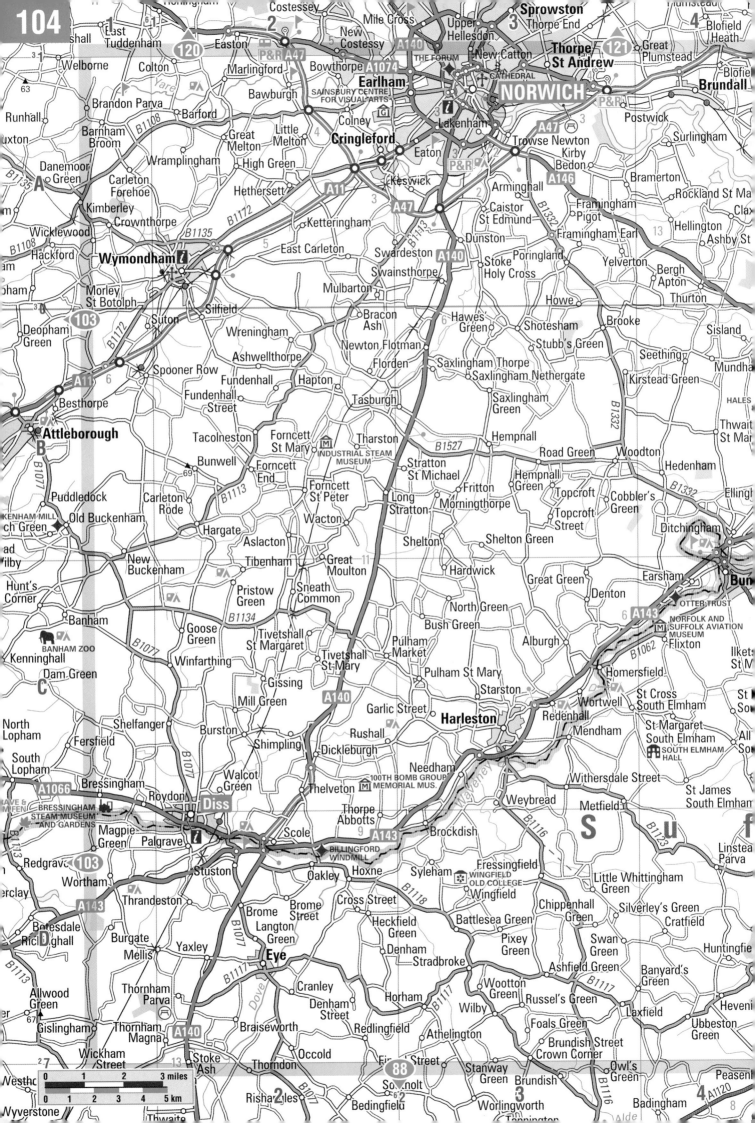

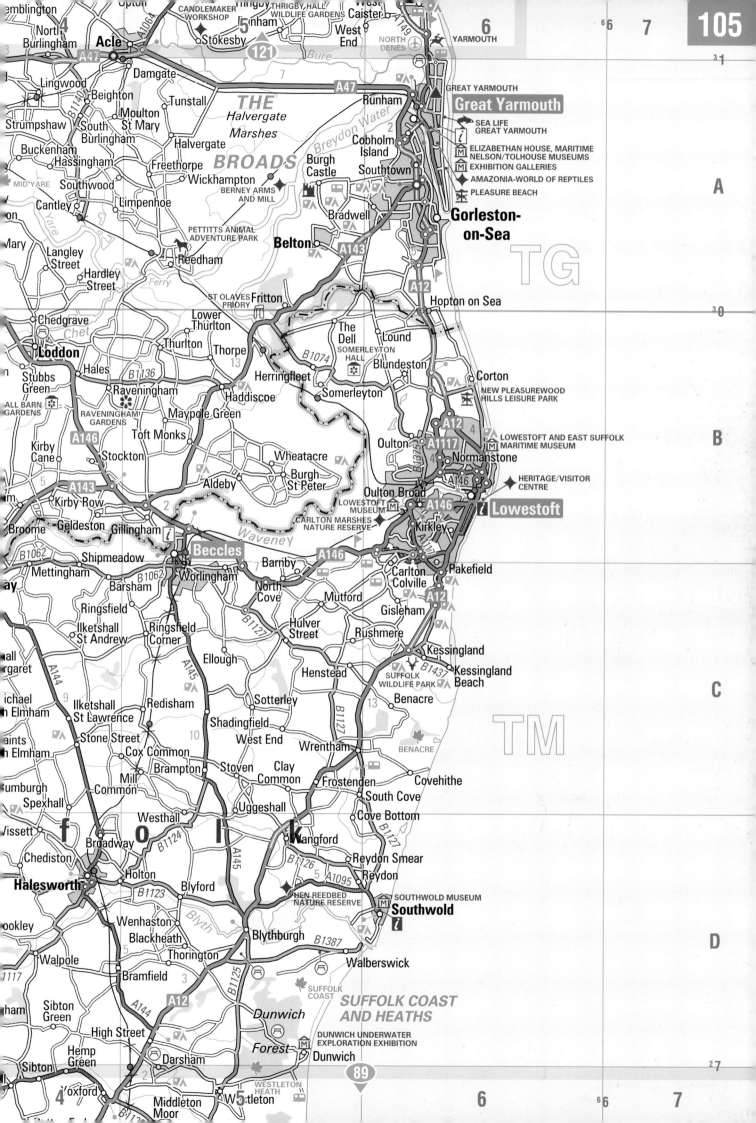

1     2     2     3

122

3 6

*C A E R N A R F O N*

*B A Y*

*B A E*

*C A E R N A R F O N*

Clynn

Gyrn-goc

Bryn-yr-eryr

SH

Trefor

L
L
E
Y
N
Ŷ
N
N

Llana

564 ▲
YR EIFL

GYR

A

Carreg Ddu    Porth
Dinllaen

B4417

6

Llithfaen

B

Pistyll

Llwyndyrys

**Morfa Nefyn**

**Nefyn**

Fron

B4354

Edern

LLEYN HISTORIAL
MARITIME MUSEUM

Rhos-fawr

*Porth Ysgadan*

B4417

Glanrhyd

Tan-y-
graig

A
4
9
7

A

L
L
Y
N

Rhos-y-llan

CORS
GEIRCH

Boduan

Llannor

B4354

Efailnewydd

*Porth Golmon*

14

Tudweiliog

BODVEL HALL
ADVENTURE PARK

Denio

**Pwllheli**

C

Dinas

Rhyd-y-
clafdy

7

Carr

Garnfadryn

South Beach

Bryn-mawr

Llaniestyn

B4415

Penrhos

*Penrhyn Mawr*

Pen-y-graig

P
E
N
R
H
Y
N
  
L
L
Y
N

Rhedyn

Llangwnnadl

Sarn
Meyllteyrn

B4413

Llanbedrog

Ty-hen

Pen-y-
groeslon

Botwnnog

Nanhoron

*Trwyn Llanbedrog*

Methlem

Bryncroes

Mynytho

Rhydlios

Llandegwining

St Tudwal's
Road

Rhoshirwaun

304 ▲
MYNYDD
RHIW

PLAS-YN-
RHIW

Llawr
Dref

*Angorfa St Tudwal*

Capel Carmel

Llangian

**Abersoch**

191 ▲

Rhiw

*Porth Neigwl or
Hell's Mouth*

Llanengan

B4413

St Tudwal's Island East
Ynys St Tudwal Dwyrain

Uwchmynydd

Aberdaron

*Llanfaelrhys*

Sarn Bach

Bwlchtocyn

Marchroes

St Tudwal's Island West
Ynys St Tudwal Gorllewin

D

Bodermid

*Pen-y-cil*

Cilan Uchaf

*Bardsey Sound
Swnt Enlli*

L
L
Y
N
Ŷ
N
N

*Trwyn Cilan*

167 ▲

YNYS ENLLI

**Bardsey
Island
Ynys Enlli**

3 2

L    L    E    L    Ŷ    N

| 0 | 1 | 2 | 3 miles |
| 0 | 1 | 2 | 3 | 4 | 5 km |

2 2

2

3

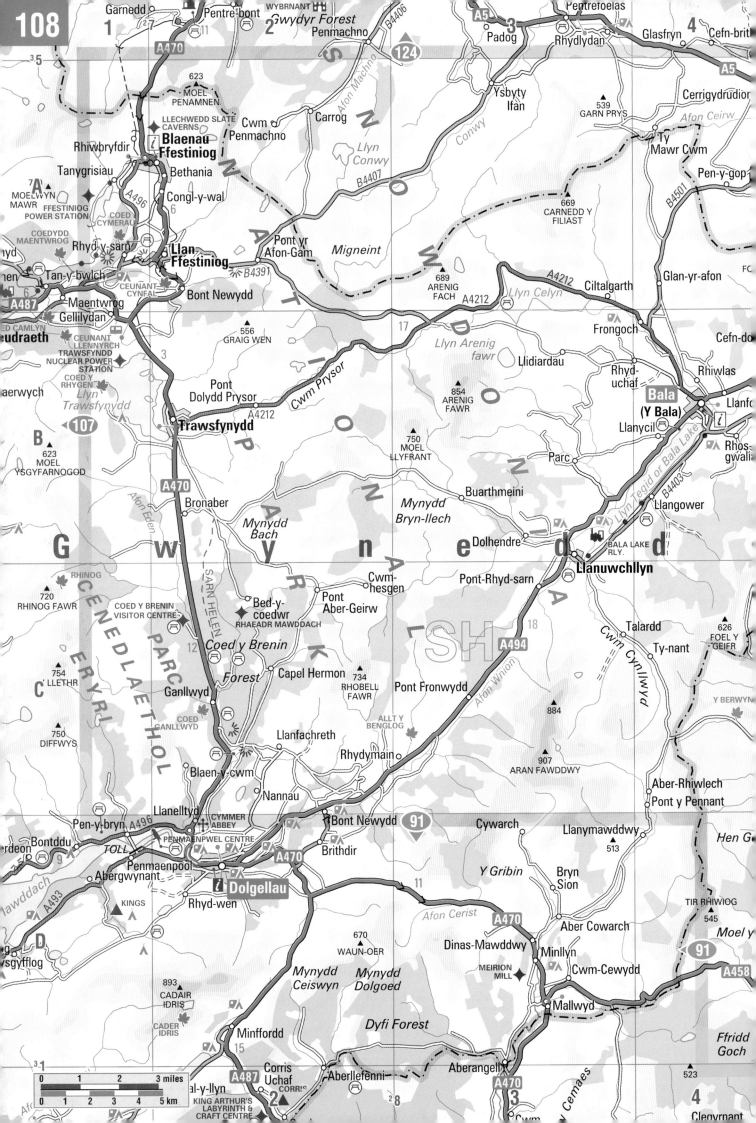

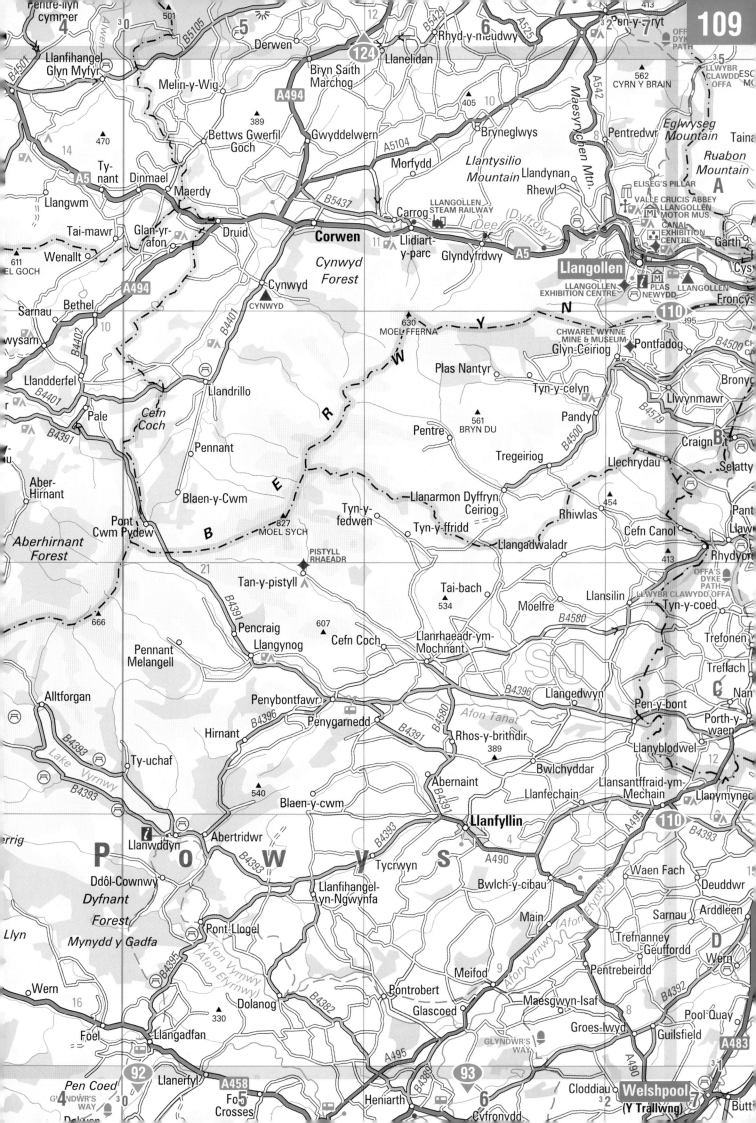

CHOLMONDELEY CASTLE GDNS

Chorley · Larden Green · Nantwich · Shavington · Barthomley · Englesea-brook

127 · Ravensmoor · Butt Green · 128 · Gorsteyhill · Balterley

Hampton Heath · STAPELEY WATER GARDENS · Stapeley · WYBUN MOSS · Hough

Bickley Moss · Sound · Broomhall · Walgherton · Wybunbury · Betley · Wrinehill · Madeley Heath

Man's Heath · Wrenbury · Sound Heath · Hatherton · Hunsterson · Blakenhall · M6 · Silv

Norbury · Aston · Newhall · Hankelow · Checkley · Madeley · Keele

Marbury · Marley Green · Onneley · Madeley Park · Whitmore · 112

Wirswall · 156 · Audlem · Buerton · Woore · Pipe Gate · Aston

Brooklands · Whitchurch · Burleydam · Lightwood Green · Coxbank · Ireland's Cross · Knighton · Willoughbridge · THE DOROTHY CLIVE GARDEN · Baldwi

Redbrook · Waymills · Broughall · Wilkesley · Adderley · Bearstone · Blackbrook · A51

Alkington · Ash Magna · Norton in Hales · Mucklestone · Maer · Chorlton

Tilstock · Ightfield · New Street Lane · Betton · Ashley Heath · Ashley · Podmore · B

Prees Heath · Calverhall · Loggerheads · Hookgate · Chatcull · Stan

Hollinwood · Prees Higher Heath · 1459 · Almington · Wetwood · Croxtonbank

Welsh End · Moreton Say · Longford · Market Drayton · Hales · Fairoak · Croxton · Sugn

Waterloo · Prees · Sandford · Bletchley · Ternhill · The Four Alls · Woodseaves · Cheswardine · Bishop's Offley · Persh

Quina Brook · Prees Lower Heath · Darliston · Fauls · Lostford · Sutton · Rosehill · Chipnall

Edstaston · Prees Green · Wollerton · Stoke Heath · Woodseaves · Soudley · Adbaston

Nem · Weston · Marchamley · Hodnet · HODNET HALL · Wistanswick · GOLDSTONE HALL · Lockleywood · Knighton · High Offley

Aston · Wixhill · HAWKSTONE PARK · 180 · Stoke on Tern · Millgreen · Hinstock · Shebdon · Woodseaves

Lee Brockhurst · Moston · Hopton · High Hatton · Ollerton · Child's Ercall · Ellerton · Weston Jones · Norbury

Preston Brockhurst · Stanton upon Hine Heath · Radmoor · Howle · Sambrook · Pickstock · Sutton · Puleston

Clive · Moreton Corbet · Ellerdine Heath · Eaton on Tern · Forton · 112 · Aqualate Mere

Grinshill · MORETON CORBETT · Great Bolas · Tibberton · Edgmond Marsh

Shawbury · Edgebolton · Cold Hatton · Cherrington · Edgmond · Newport · Outwoods

Hadnall · Muckleton · Great Wytheford · Rowton · Waters Upton · Adeney · Longford · Church Aston · Coto

Astley · Walton · Crudgington · Kynnersley · Brockton · Chetwynd Aston · Moret

Bings Heath · High Ercall · High Ercall · Eyton upon the Weald Moors · Preston upon the Weald Moors · Lilleshall · Orslow

Poynton Green · Roden · B5062 · Telford and Wrekin · A518 · Great

Haughton · Longdon on Tern · Sleapford · HOO FARM ANIMAL KINGDOM · LILLESHALL ABBEY · Heath Hill · reat

Shrewsbury · HAUGHMOND ABBEY · Rodington · Bratton · Muxton · Weston Heath

Upton Magna · Withington · Admaston · Wrockwardine · Donnington · Lilyhurst · Sheriffhales

Preston · Walcot · Hadley · Trench · Donnington Wood · GRANVILLE

Emstrey · ATTINGHAM PARK · Norton · Wellington · Charlton · Ketley · Oakengates · Crackleybank · TELFORD SERVICES

94 · Aston · 95 · Ketley Bank · Priorslee · West

Atcham · Uppington · Rushton · Lawley · Telford · Haughton · Shifnal · M54 · Tong

Wroxeter · WROXETER ROMAN CITY

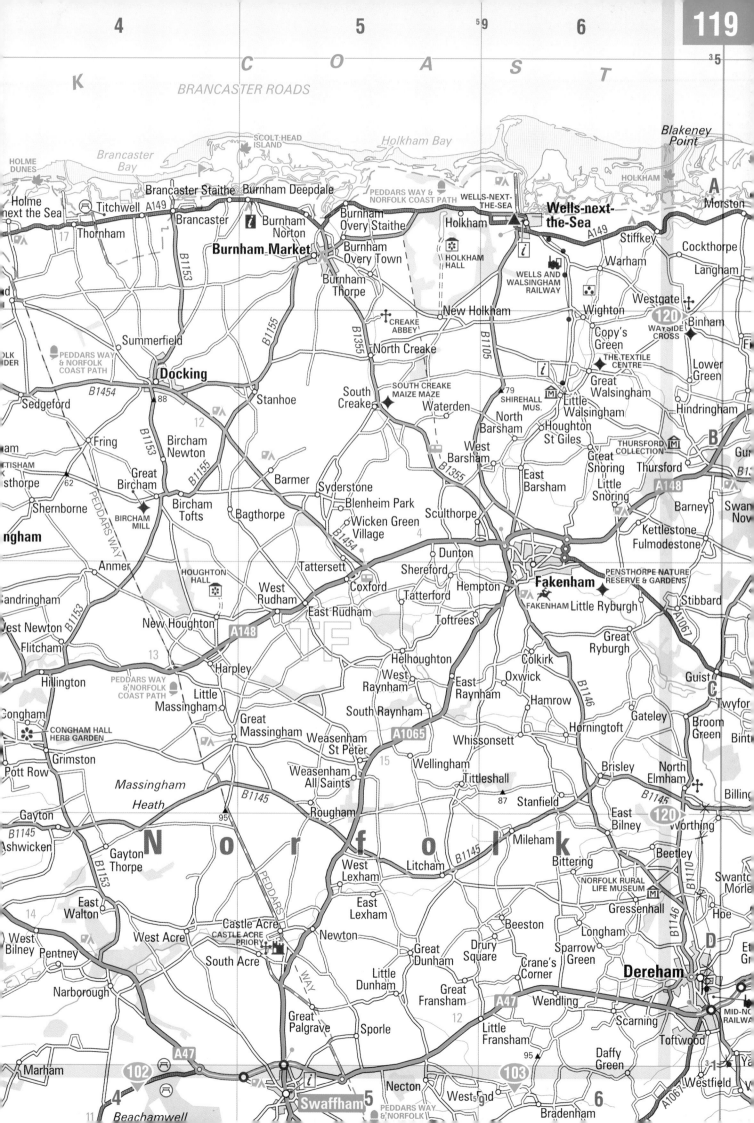

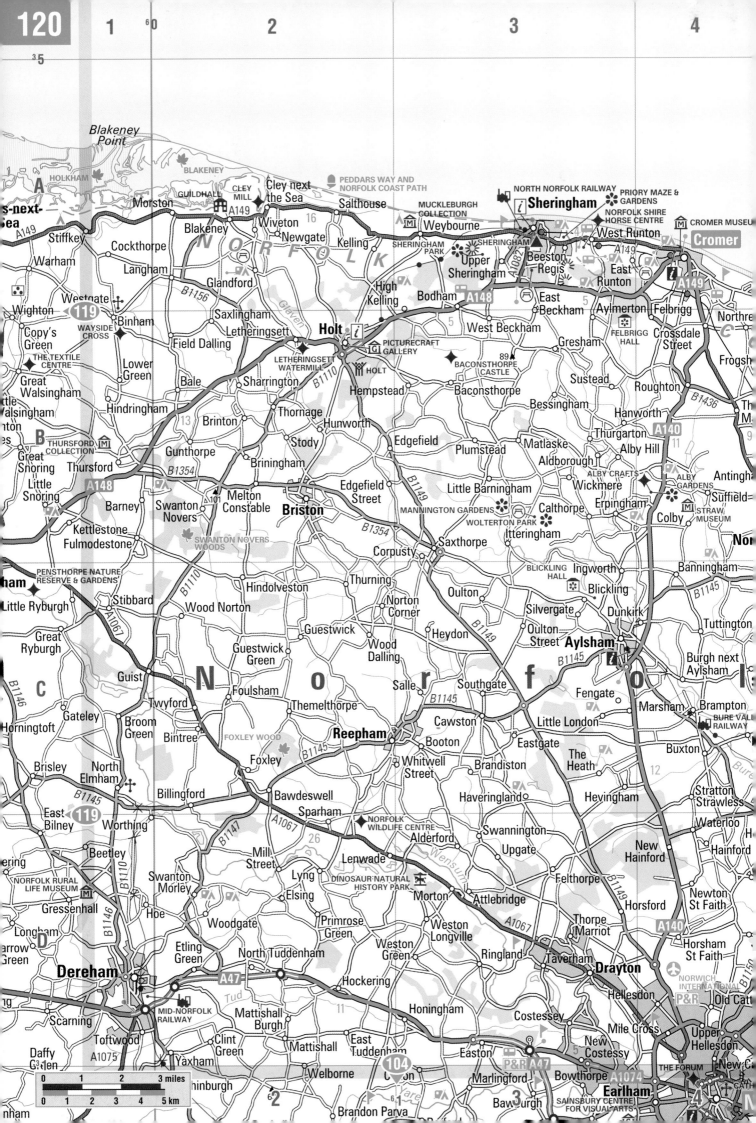

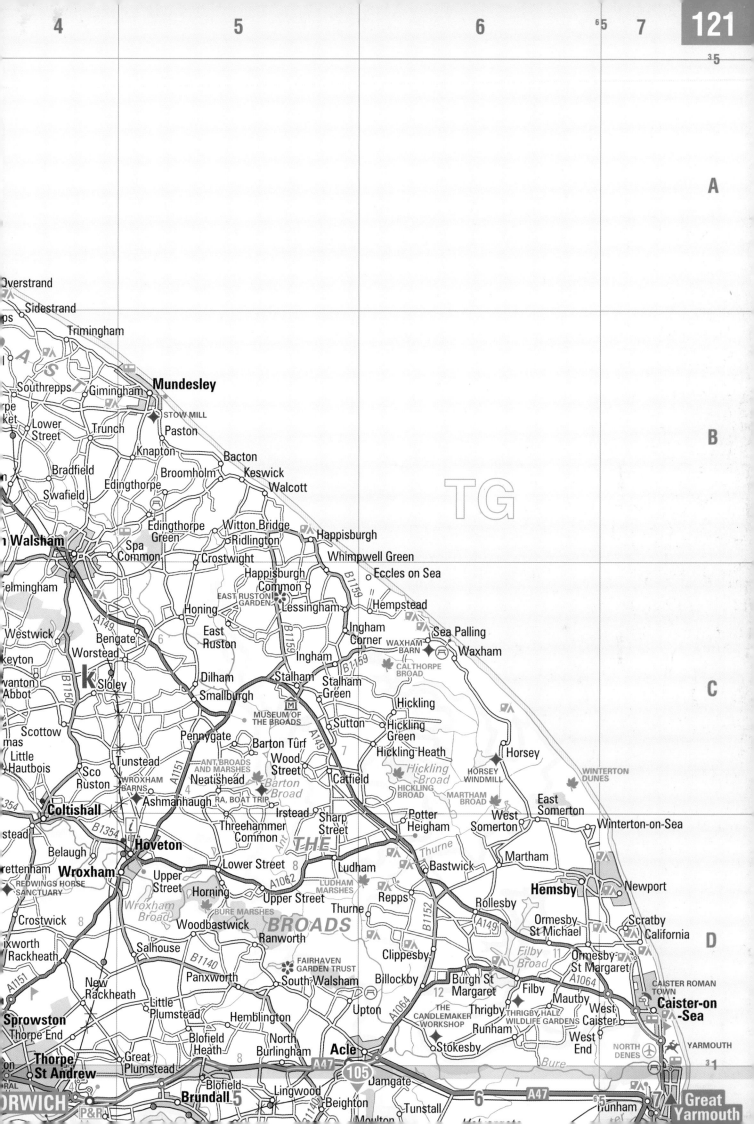

**4** **5** **6** <sup>6</sup>5 **7**

³5

A

B

TG

C

D

Overstrand
Sidestrand
Trimingham
ps
ket
Southrepps
Gimingham
**Mundesley**
STOW MILL
Lower
Street
Trunch
Paston
Bradfield
Knapton
Bacton
Edingthorpe
Broomholm
Keswick
Swafield
Walcott
**Walsham**
Edingthorpe
Green
Witton Bridge
Happisburgh
elmingham
Spa
Common
Ridlington
Crostwight
Whimpwell Green
Happisburgh
Common
Eccles on Sea
B1159
EAST RUSTON
GARDEN
Honing
Lessingham
Hempstead
Westwick
Bengate
East
Ruston
Ingham
Corner
Sea Palling
keyton
Worstead
Ingham
WAXHAM
BARN
Waxham
vanton
Abbot
K
Sloley
Dilham
B1159
CALTHORPE
BROAD
Scottow
mas
Little
Hautbois
Smallburgh
Stalham
Stalham
Green
Hickling
Sco
Ruston
Tunstead
MUSEUM OF
THE BROADS
Sutton
Hickling
Green
Horsey
354
WROXHAM
BARNS
Pennygate
ANT, BROADS
AND MARSHES
Barton Turf
Wood
Street
Catfield
Hickling Heath
Hickling
Broad
HICKLING
BROAD
HORSEY
WINDMILL
WINTERTON
DUNES
Coltishall
Ashmanhaugh
Neatishead
RA, BOAT TRIP
Barton
Broad
Irstead
Sharp
Street
MARTHAM
BROAD
East
Somerton
stead
B1354
Threehammer
Common
Potter
Heigham
West
Somerton
Winterton-on-Sea
Belaugh
i
**Hoveton**
THE
Thurne
Martham
rettenham
**Wroxham**
Upper
Street
Lower Street
Ludham
Bastwick
REDWINGS HORSE
SANCTUARY
Horning
Upper Street
LUDHAM
MARSHES
Repps
**Hemsby**
Newport
Crostwick
Wroxham
Broad
Thurne
B1152
Rollesby
Scratby
California
ixworth
Rackheath
Woodbastwick
BURE MARSHES
**BROADS**
Ranworth
Clippesby
Ormesby
St Michael
Filby
Broad
Ormesby
St Margaret
New
Rackheath
Salhouse
B1140
FAIRHAVEN
GARDEN TRUST
South Walsham
Billockby
Burgh St
Margaret
11
A1064
CAISTER ROMAN
TOWN
**Sprowston**
Little
Plumstead
Panxworth
Upton
A1064
12
THE
CANDLEMAKER
WORKSHOP
Thrigby
THRIGBY HALL
WILDLIFE GARDENS
Filby
Mautby
West
Caister
**Caister-on
-Sea**
Thorpe End
Hemblington
Runham
West
End
**Thorpe
St Andrew**
Great
Plumstead
Blofield
Heath
North
Burlingham
**Acle**
Stokesby
NORTH
DENES
YARMOUTH
RAL
ORWICH
P&R
**Brundall**
Blofield
Lingwood
Damgate
A47
105
Beighton
Moulton
Tunstall
A47
unham
6
5
**Great
Yarmouth**

A149
A1151
B1150
A1151
A1062
A149
A149
B1152
A47

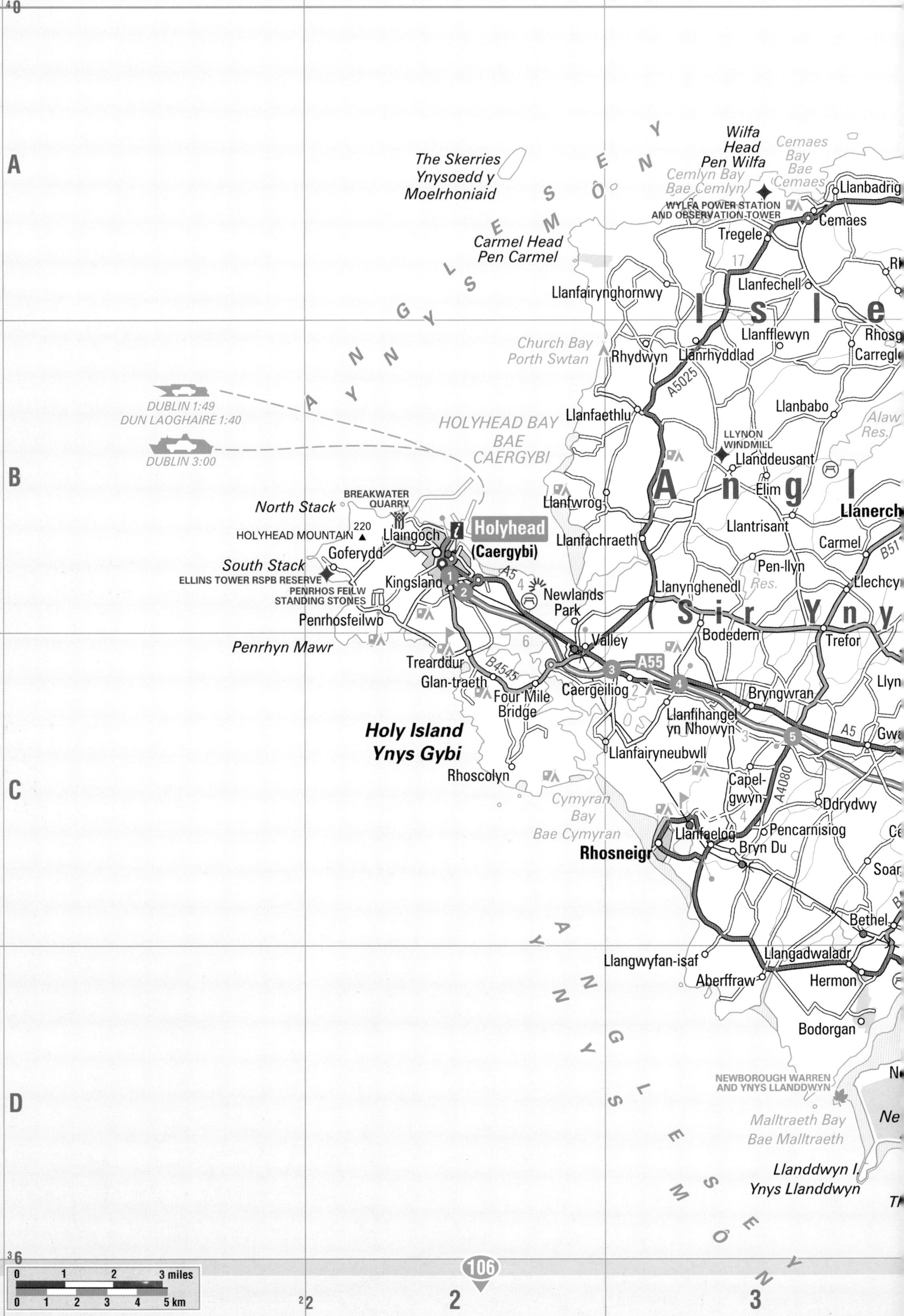

1  2  3

A

The Skerries
Ynysoedd y
Moelrhoniaid

Carmel Head
Pen Carmel

Wilfa
Head
Pen Wilfa

Cemaes
Bay
Bae
Cemaes

Cemlyn Bay
Bae Cemlyn

WYLFA POWER STATION
AND OBSERVATION-TOWER

Llanbadrig

Cemaes

Tregele

Isle

Llanfairynghornwy

Llanff
lewyn

Llanfechell

Rhosg

Carregl

Church Bay
Porth Swtan

Rhydwyn

Llanrhyddlad

17

A5025

Llanbabo

Alaw
Res.

HOLYHEAD BAY
BAE
CAERGYBI

Llanfaethlu

LLYNON
WINDMILL

Llanddeusant

DUBLIN 1:49
DUN LAOGHAIRE 1:40

DUBLIN 3:00

B

North Stack

BREAKWATER
QUARRY

Llanfwrog

Angl

Elim

Llanerch

220

HOLYHEAD MOUNTAIN

Llaingoch

Holyhead
(Caergybi)

Llanfachraeth

Llantrisant

Carmel

B51

South Stack

Goferydd

ELLINS TOWER RSPB RESERVE

Kingsland

PENRHOS FEILW
STANDING STONES

A5

Newlands
Park

Pen-llyn
Res.

Llechcy

Penrhosfeilwo

Llanynghenedl

Sir Y Ny

Penrhyn Mawr

Valley

Bodedern

Trefor

Trearddur

B4545

A55

Glan-traeth

Caergeiliog

3

A55

4

Bryngwran

Llyn

Four Mile
Bridge

Llanfihangel
yn Nhowyn

A5

Gw

5

Holy Island
Ynys Gybi

Rhoscolyn

Llanfairyneubwll

Capel-
gwyn

Ddrydwy

C

Cymyran
Bay
Bae Cymyran

Llanfaelog

4

Pencarnisiog

Ce

Soar

Rhosneigr

Bryn Du

Bethel

Llangwyfan-isaf

Llangadwaladr

Aberffraw

Hermon

F

Bodorgan

NEWBOROUGH WARREN
AND YNYS LLANDDWYN

N

D

Malltraeth Bay
Bae Malltraeth

Ne

Llanddwyn I.
Ynys Llanddwyn

Th

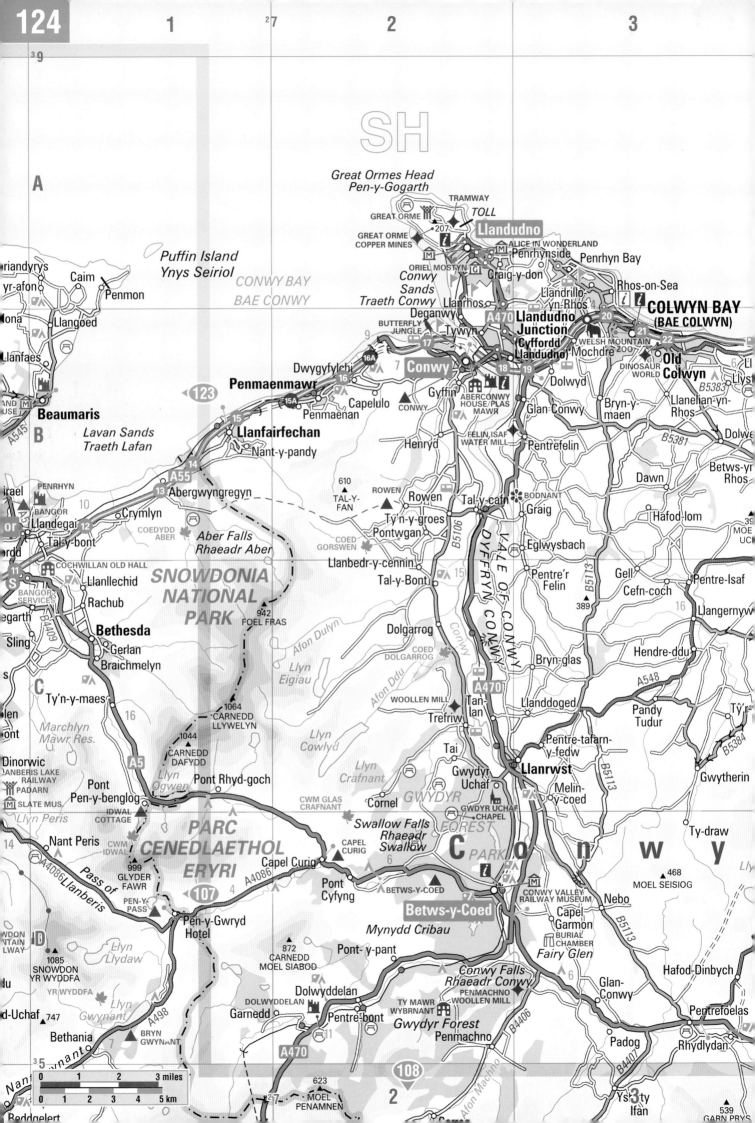

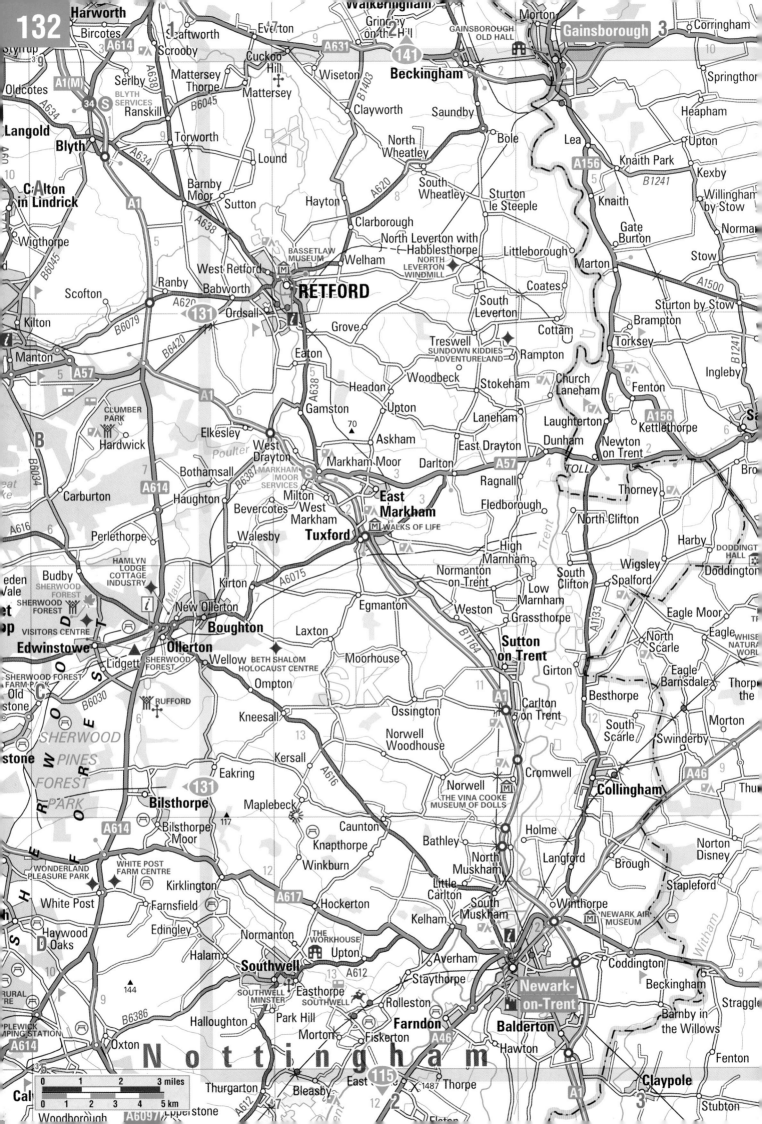

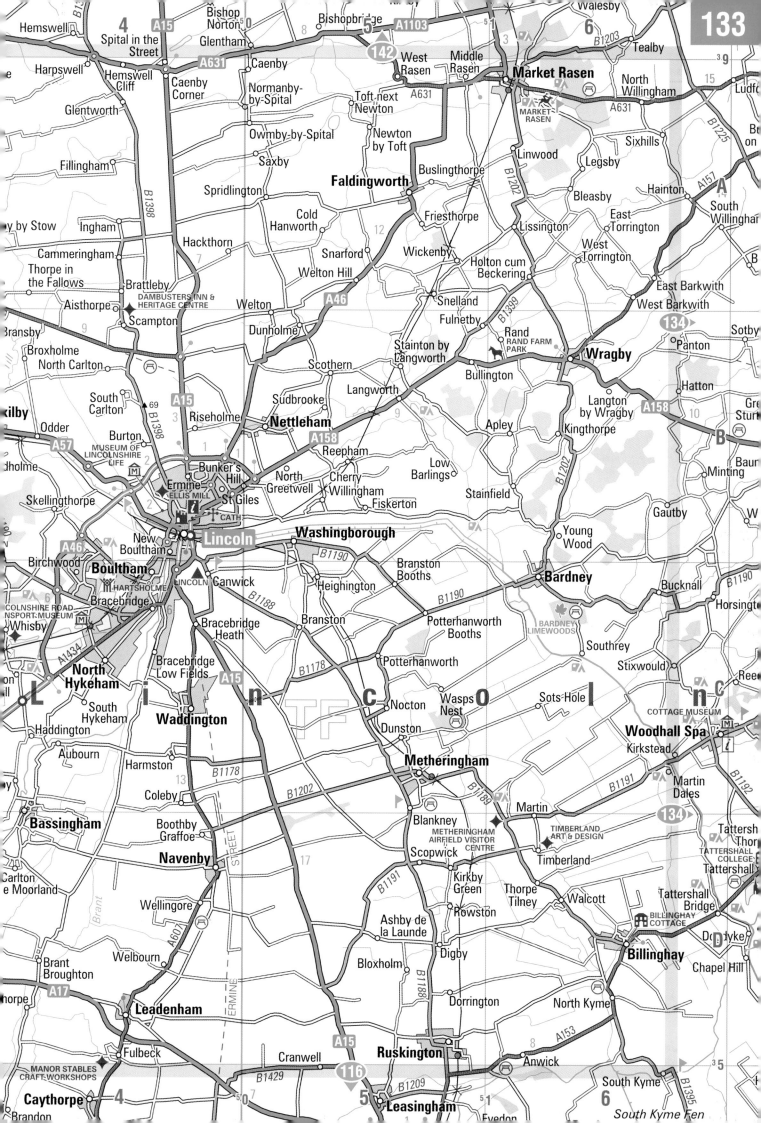

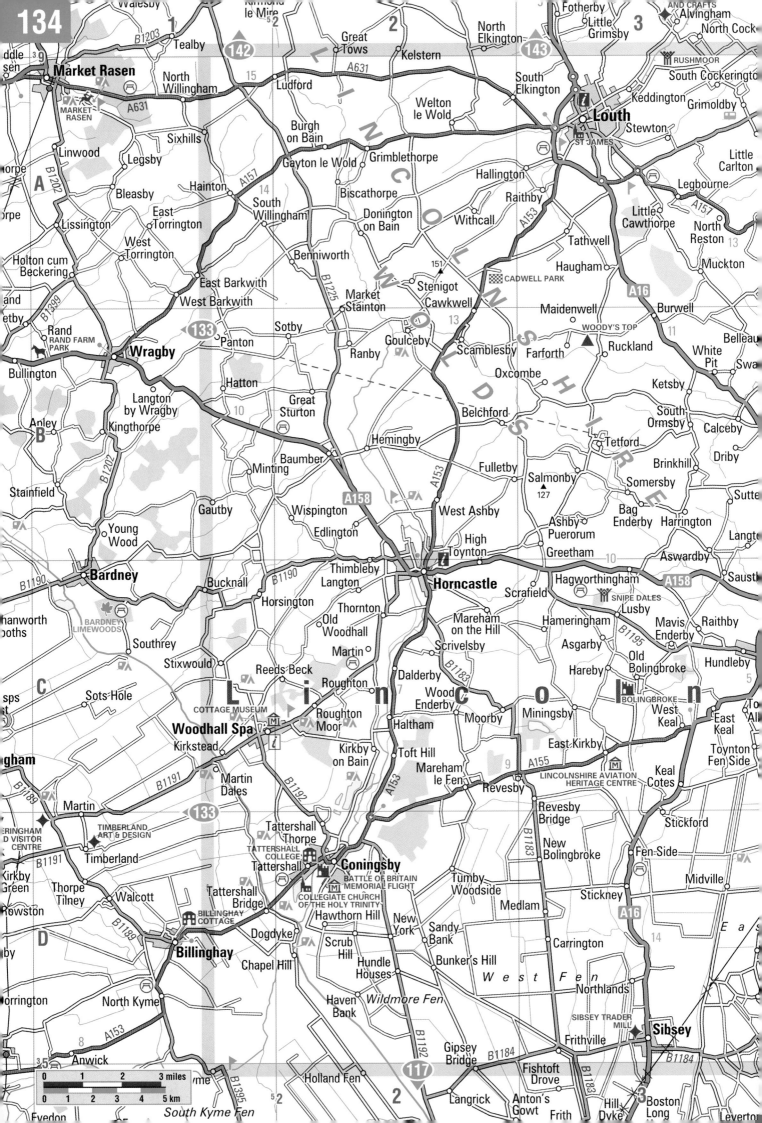

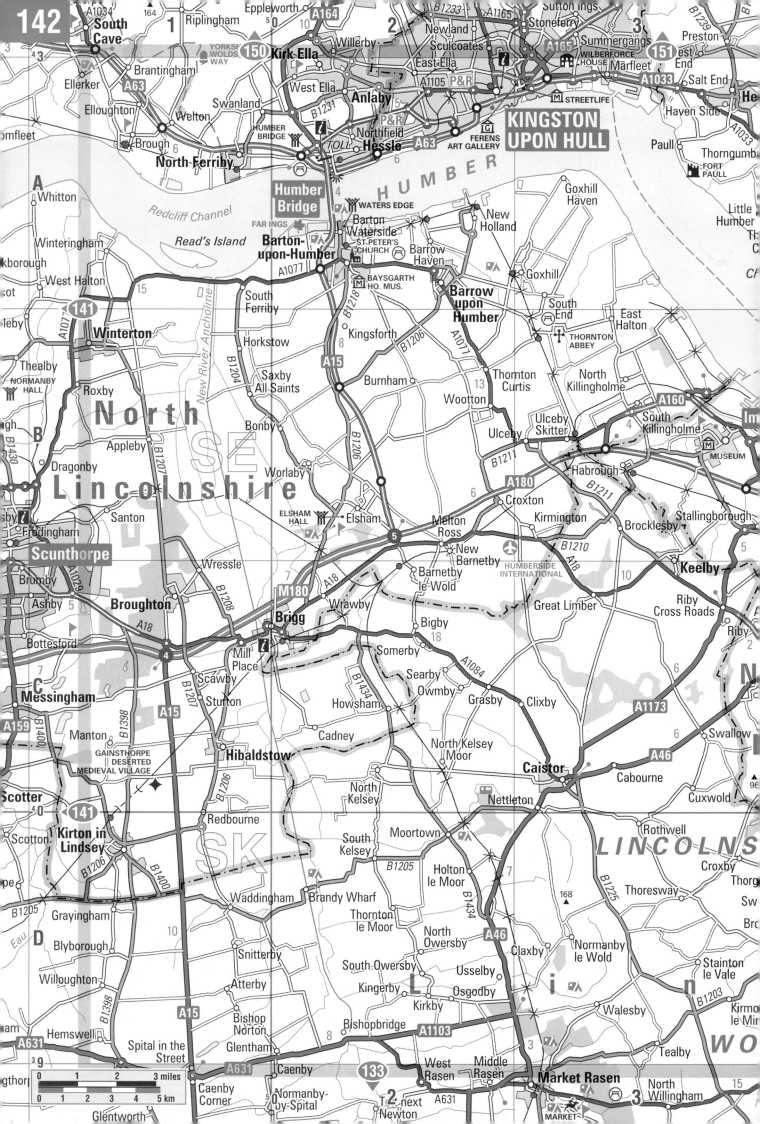

Elstronwick
Tunstall
North End
Roos
151
B1242
Burton Pidsea
4
Waxholme
Owthorne
Withernsea
Rimswell
i
Burstwick
B1362
Halsham
East End
Hollym
Camerton
Keyingham
Ottringham
Holmpton
Ryehill
18
Winestead
A1033
5
A
don
Patrington
Out Newton
Welwick
6
Weeton
B1445
Sunk Island
Skeffling
Easington
orney rofts
erry Cob Sands

ROTTERDAM 12:30
ZEEBRUGGE 12:45
Kilnsea
TA
B

ROTTERDAM
ZEEBRUGGE
SPURN

mingham
HOEK VAN HOLLAND 13:00
OOSTENDE 15:00
SPURN HEAD

A180
Pyewipe
Grimsby
Healing
West Marsh
A180
CLEETHORPES
MOUTH OF THE HUMBER
Great Coates
NATIONAL FISHING HERITAGE CENTRE
Old Clee
i
BREVIK 33:00
CUXHAVEN 22:00
Laceby
Freshney
5
Nunsthorpe
A46
CLEETHORPES COAST LIGHT RAILWAY
ESBJERG 22:00
GOTHENBURG 26:00
KRISTIANSAND 30:00
ROTTERDAM 11:45
ZEEBRUGGE 14:00
C
Scartho
A1098
PLEASURE ISLAND THEME PARK
CLEETHORPES
orth East
A16
Bradley
Humberston
Irby upon Humber
A18
Waltham
B1219
Barnoldby le Beck
9
New Waltham
incolnshire
WALTHAM WINDMILL
Holton le Clay
Tetney Lock
Beelsby
B1208
Brigsley
A1031
North Cotes
Hatcliffe
Ashby cum Fenby
East Ravendale
Waithe
Tetney
10
Grainsby
Marshchapel
40
Donna Nook
TF
B1201
Eskham
North Thoresby
Wragholme
Grainthorpe
25
North Somercotes
Wold Newton
Fulstow
DONNA NOOK
nhope
Ludborough
Covenham St Bartholomew
Conisholme
Skidbrooke North End
D
South Somercotes
Saltfleet
nby
LINCOLNSHIRE WOLDS RLY.
Covenham St Mary
A1031
Binbrook
North Ormsby
Utterby
Yarburgh
Skidbrooke
SALTFLEETB THEDDLETH
C
I
n
Fotherby
ALVINGHAM POTTERY AND CRAFTS
Saltfleetby St Clements
Great Tows
LDS
North Elkington
Little Grimsby
Alvingham
North Cockerington
Saltfleetby All Saints
Kelstern
A631
134
A16
RUSHMOOR
135
Saltfleetby St Peter
Theddlethorpe St Helen
Ludford
South Elkington
i
Keddington
South Cockerington
B1200
Grimoldby
Welton
Theddlethorpe

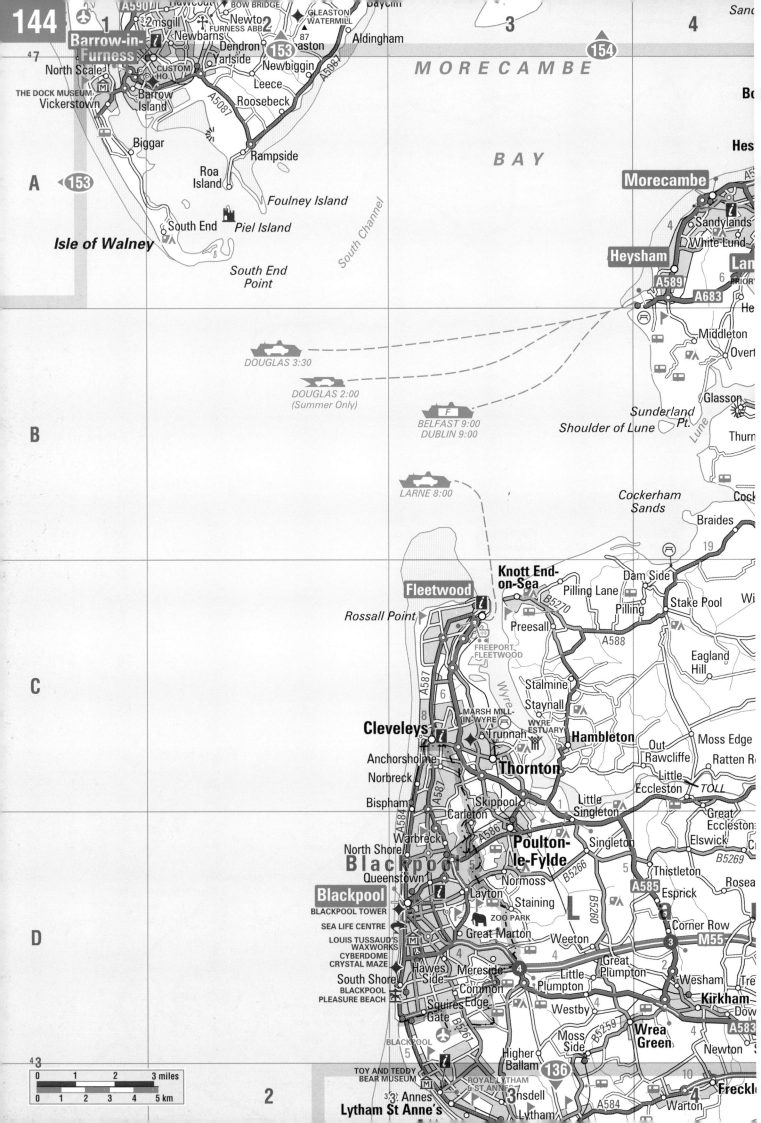

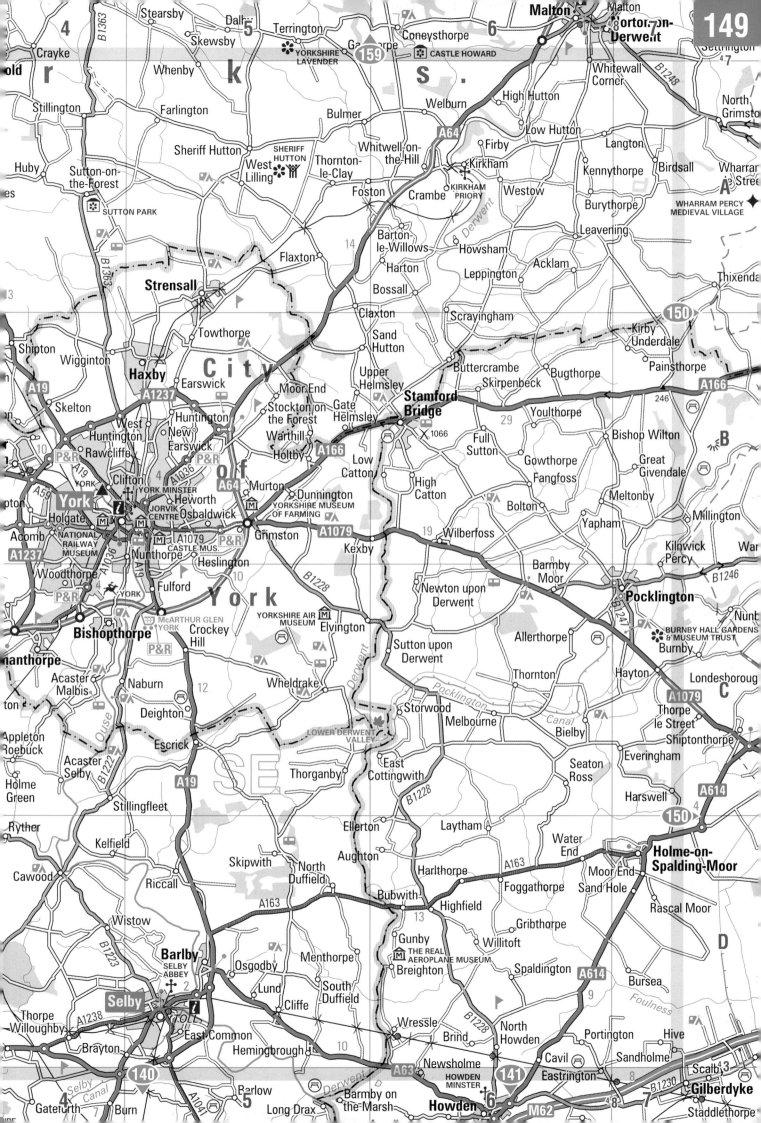

Grindale
A165
4
Flamborough
5
B1255
B1259
FLAMBOROUGH
HEAD
6
161
4 7

Boynton
B1253
SEWERBY HALL AND GARDENS
Sewerby
BONDVILLE MODEL VILLAGE
BAYLE MUSEUM
PRIORY
Bridlington
Bessingby
West Hill
OLD PENNY
MEMORIES
Carnaby
Hilderthorpe
A
Haisthorpe
A614
holme
BRIDLINGTON BAY
PARK ROSE POTTERY
AND LEISURE PARK
Burton Agnes
am

Fraisthorpe

Gransmoor
Barmston

Great Kelk
Lissett
14
Gembling
Ulrome
A165

16
B
CKLEY
AL FARM
SKIPSEA
CASTLE
Skipsea
B1249
Beeford
Skipsea
Brough
North
Frodingham
B1242
Dunnington

Bewholme
Atwick

North Cliff
C
Brandesburton
Hornsea
HORNSEA MUSEUM
Seaton
FREEPORT
HORNSEA
B1244
Hornsea Bridge
Sigglesthorne
Hornsea
Mere
Rolston
e
Catwick
Goxhill
Mappleton
Little
Hatfield
B1243
Rise
Great Hatfield
Great Cowden
ng Riston
A165
Arnold
Withernwick
New
Ellerby
B1242
Meaux
Skirlaugh
Marton
West
Newton
Aldbrough
East Newton
17
Old
Ellerby
BURTON CONSTABLE
HALL
Flinton
13
Coniston
Garton
Swine
Grimston
D
Bransholme
Thirtleby
Sproatley
Humbleton
Fitling
Hilston
Sutton
on Hull
Ganstead
B1238
B1240
Lelley
Owstwick
Tunstall
Bilton
B1237
Sutton Ings
Elstronwick
Stoneferry
B1239
Burton
Pidsea
North End
B1242
Summergangs
Preston
Roos
A165
WILBERFORCE
HOUSE
West
End
142
143
Waxholme
Marfleet
Salt End
STREETLIFE
A1033
4
Hedon
5
B1362
Rimswell
Owt orne
6
Withernsea
4 3

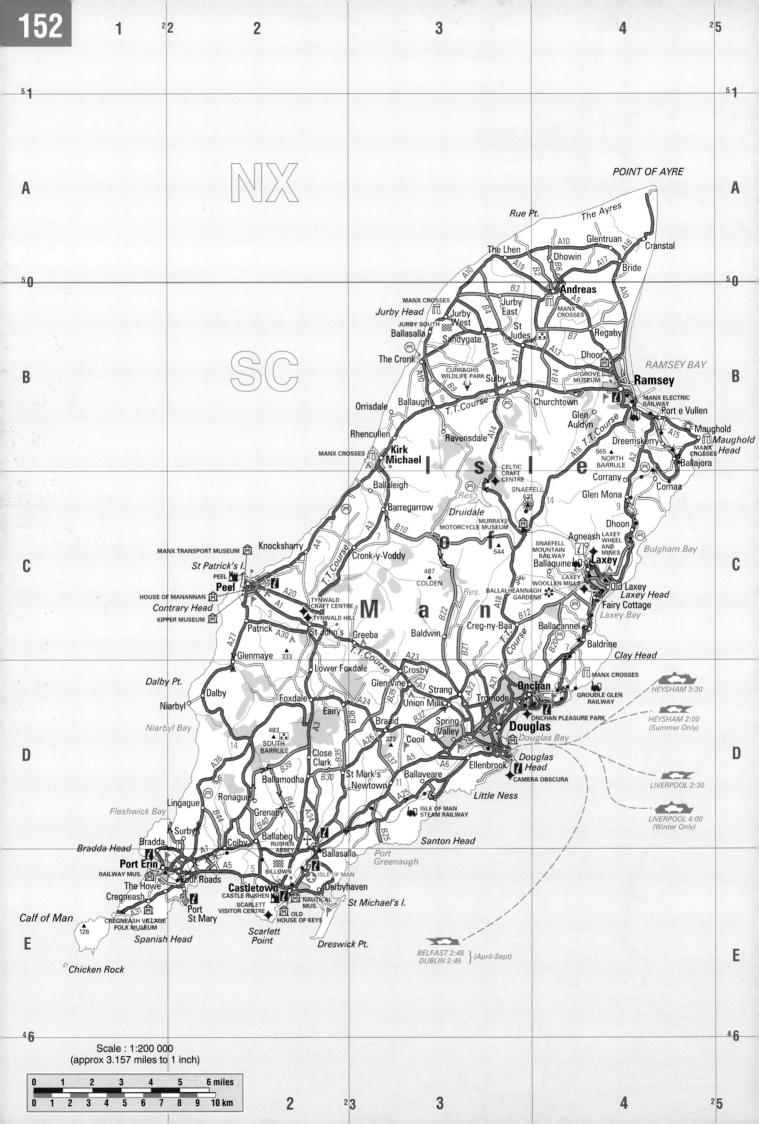

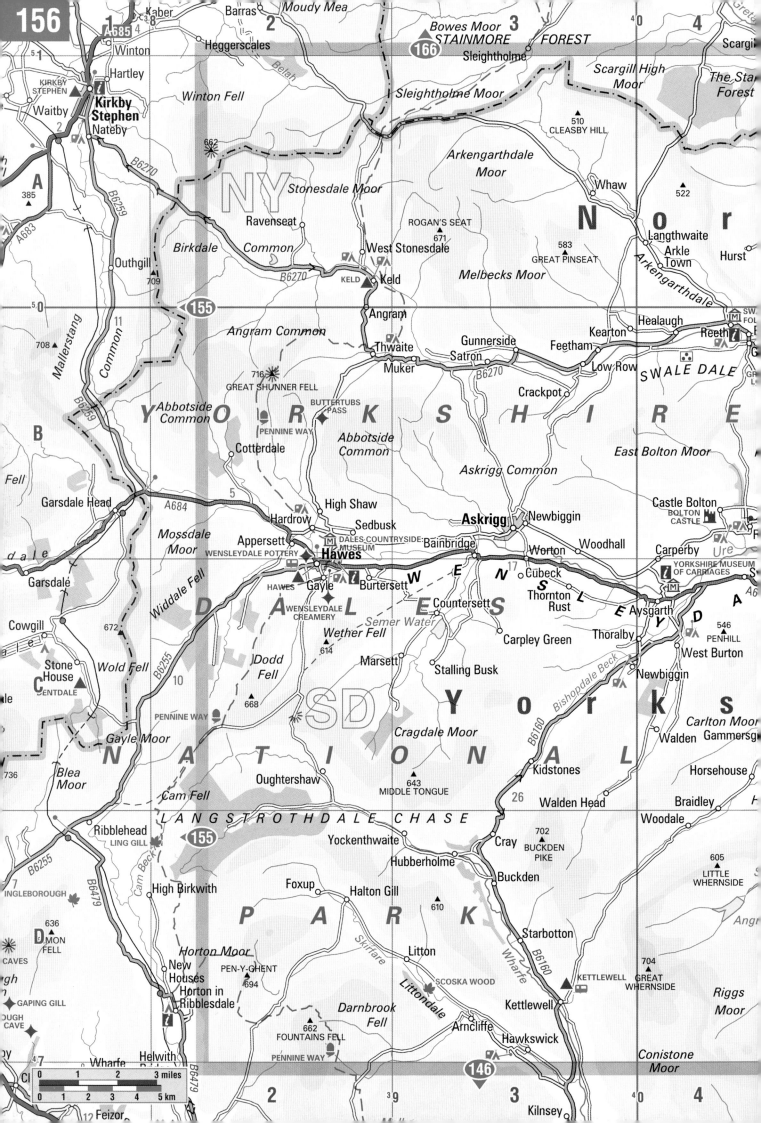

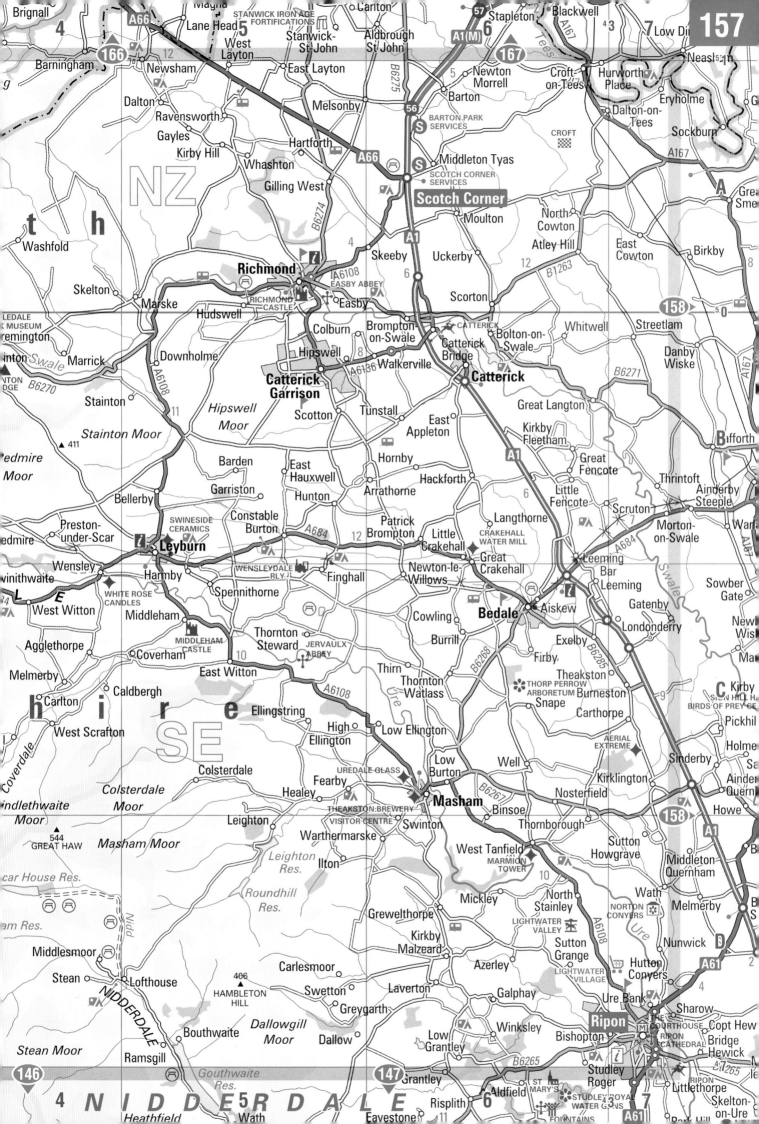

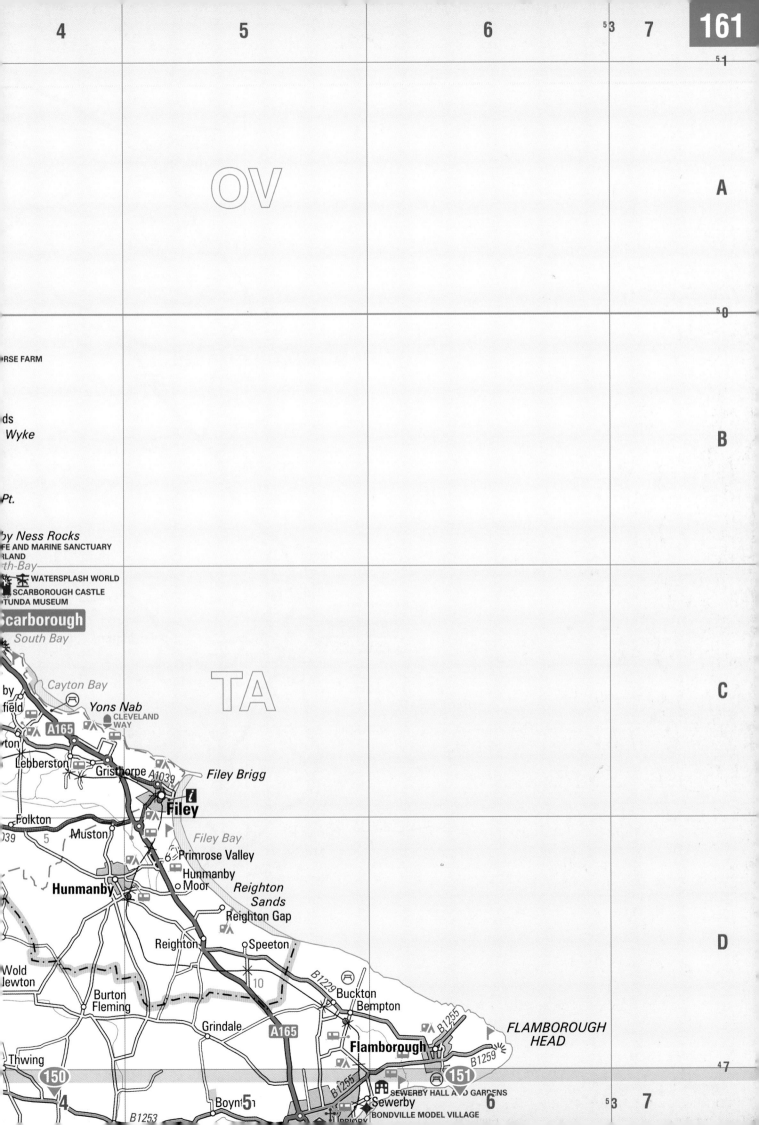

4  5  6  ⁵3  7

OV

A

5 1

5 0

B

RSE FARM

ds

*Wyke*

*Pt.*

*by Ness Rocks*
FE AND MARINE SANCTUARY
RLAND
*th-Bay*

WATERSPLASH WORLD
SCARBOROUGH CASTLE
TUNDA MUSEUM

Scarborough
*South Bay*

TA

C

*Cayton Bay*

**Yons Nab**
CLEVELAND
WAY

by
field

A165

ton

Lebberston

Gristhorpe  A1039

*Filey Brigg*

Folkton

**Filey**

039  5

Muston

*Filey Bay*

Primrose Valley

Hunmanby
Moor

*Reighton
Sands*

**Hunmanby**

Reighton Gap

Reighton

Speeton

Wold
Newton

D

B1229

Burton
Fleming

Buckton
Bempton

10

Grindale

A165

B1255

**FLAMBOROUGH
HEAD**

Thwing

B1259

150

151

4  5  6  ⁵3  7

**Flamborough**

SEWERBY HALL AND GARDENS

B1255

Boyn 5 1

Sewerby
BONDVILLE MODEL VILLAGE

B1253

4 7

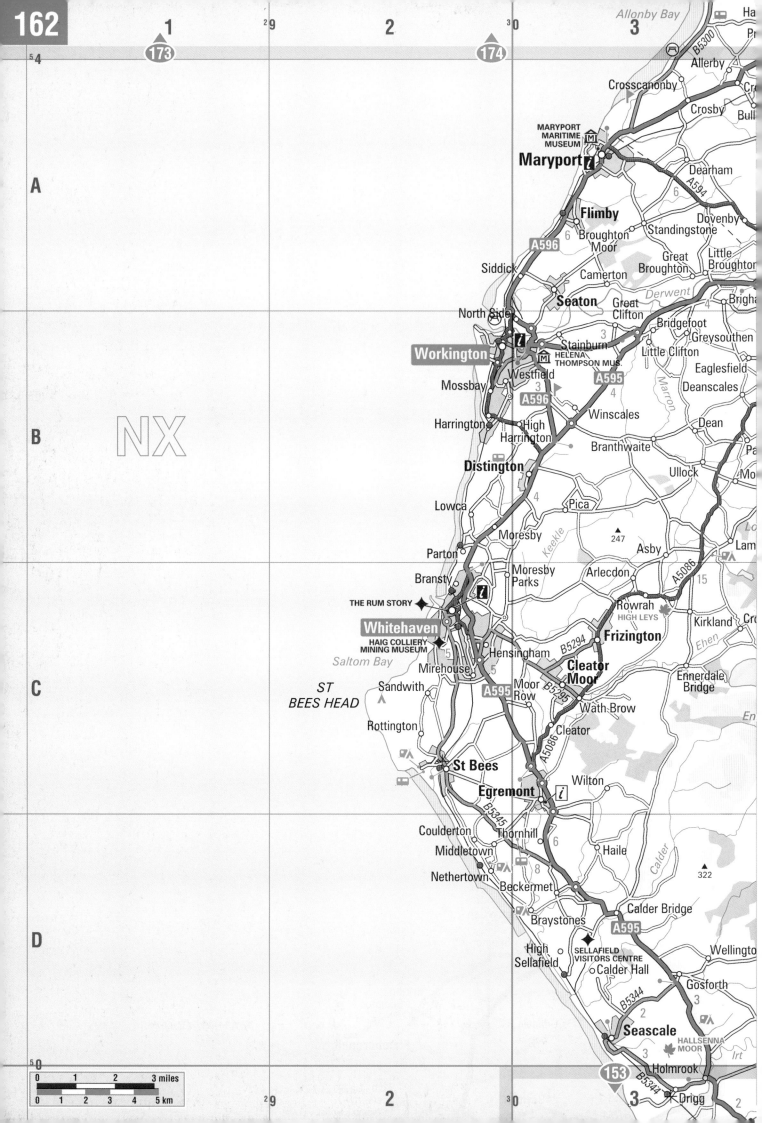

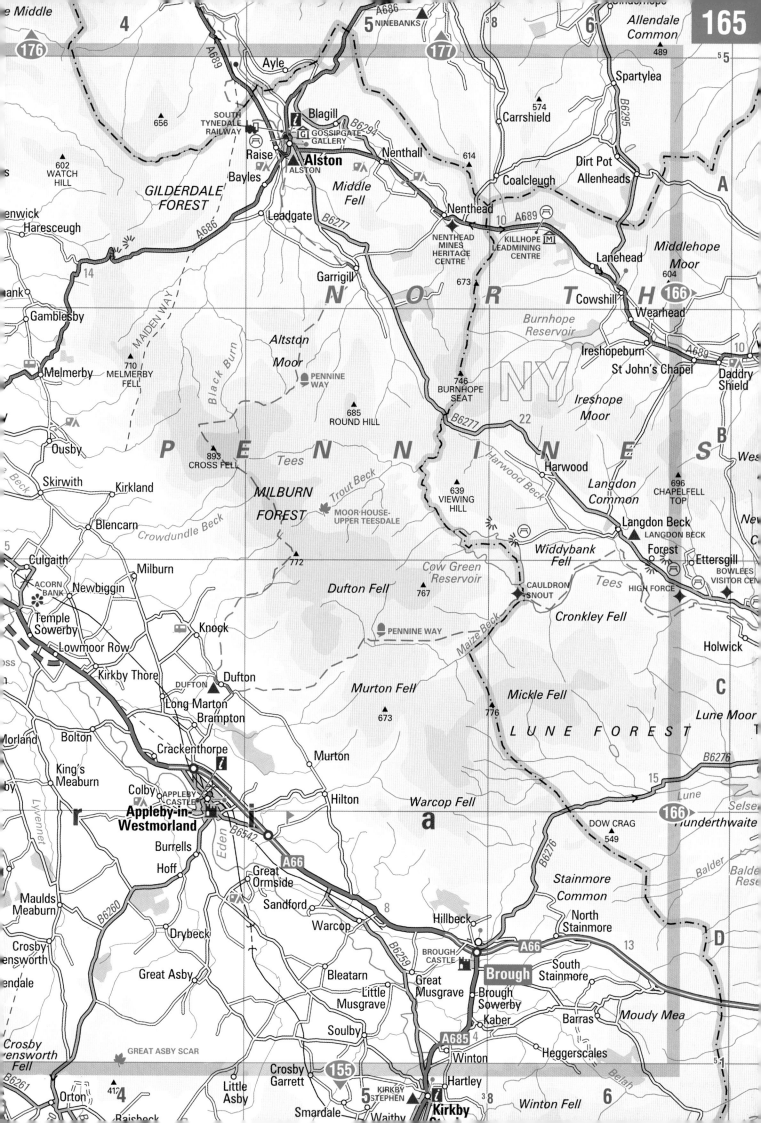

<sup>5</sup>5

**A**

**B**

NZ

**C**

MINIATURE
RAILWAY
TBURN
GLERS
RITAGE
ENTRE
**Saltburn-
by-the-Sea**

CHRIS BIRBECK
INTERNATIONAL RALLY
SCHOOL
166
**Brotton**
Skinningrove

Carlin
How
Boulby
beck
5
**Loftus**    A174    **Staithes**
North
Skelton
Easington
Port Mulgrave
Kilton
Thorpe
Hinderwell                    *Runswick Bay*
Lingdale
Liverton    Roxby
Margrove    Stanghow
Newton    Runswick
Park
Mulgrave    Bay
Ellerby    Kettleness
**D**
n d
Moorsholm
B1366    Goldsborough
9
14
Res.
Scaling
A174    Lythe
n d    A171
Scaling Dam    B1266
Sandsend    THE DRACULA
EXPERIENCE
East    *Sandsend Wyke*    SUTCLIFFE GALLERY
ndale    Scaling    Mickleby    Barnby
Res.
West    East Row    **Whitby**    *Saltwick*
or    Barnby    Dunsley    *Bay*
Commondale    *Danby Low Moor*    Ugthorpe    Newholm    WHITBY ABBEY
*Lealholm*    WHITBY
*Moor*    CAPTAIN COOK
159    E MOORS    299    Ruswarp    MEMORIAL MUSEUM
Danby    CENTRE    Stonegate    160    B1410    Sta    acre
13    Aislaby
High Hawsker

<sup>5</sup>1

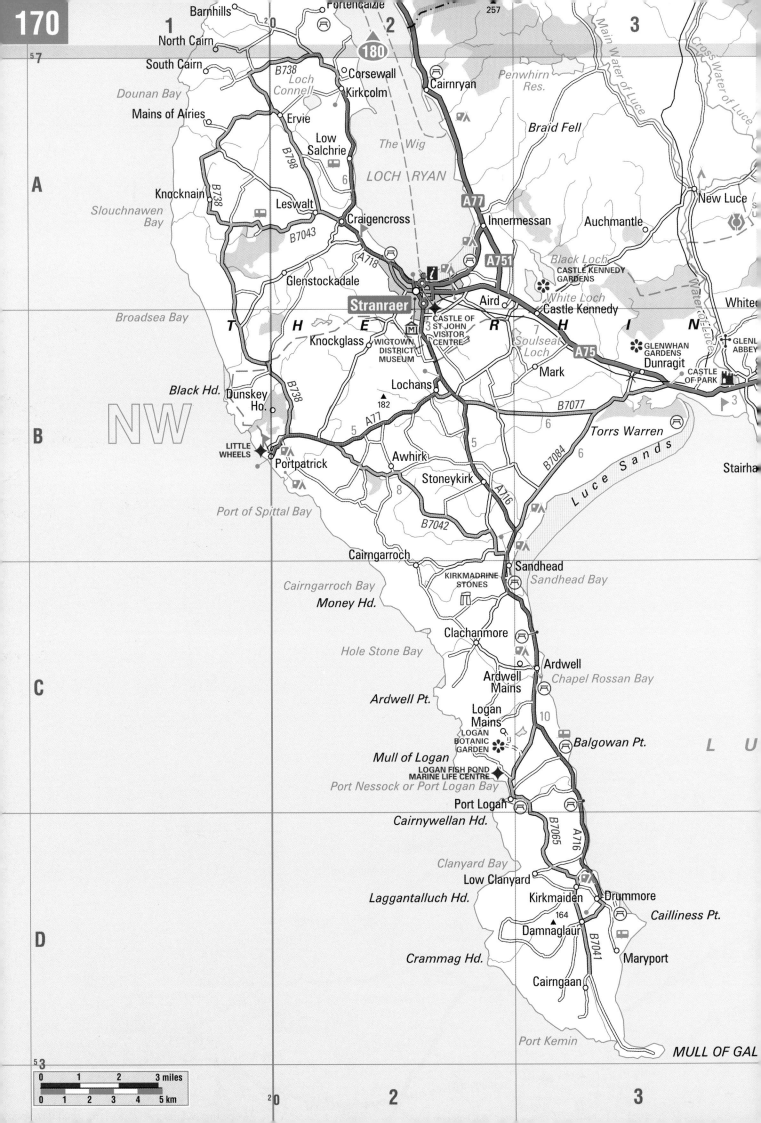

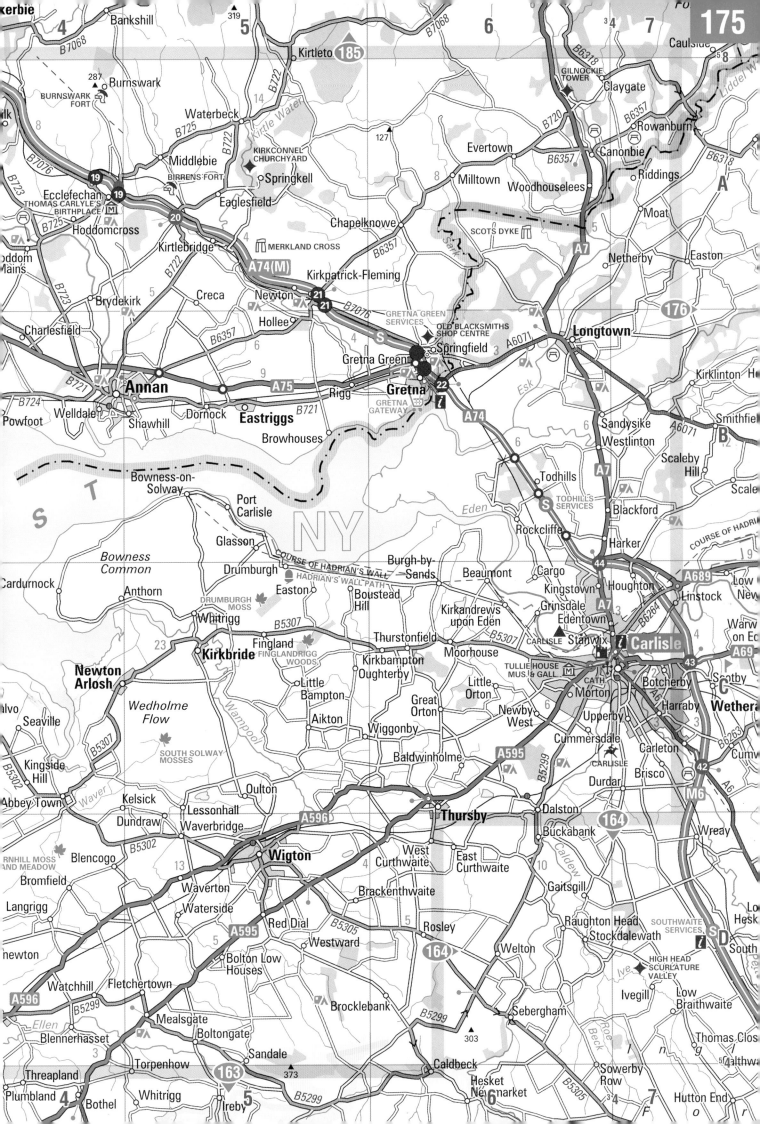

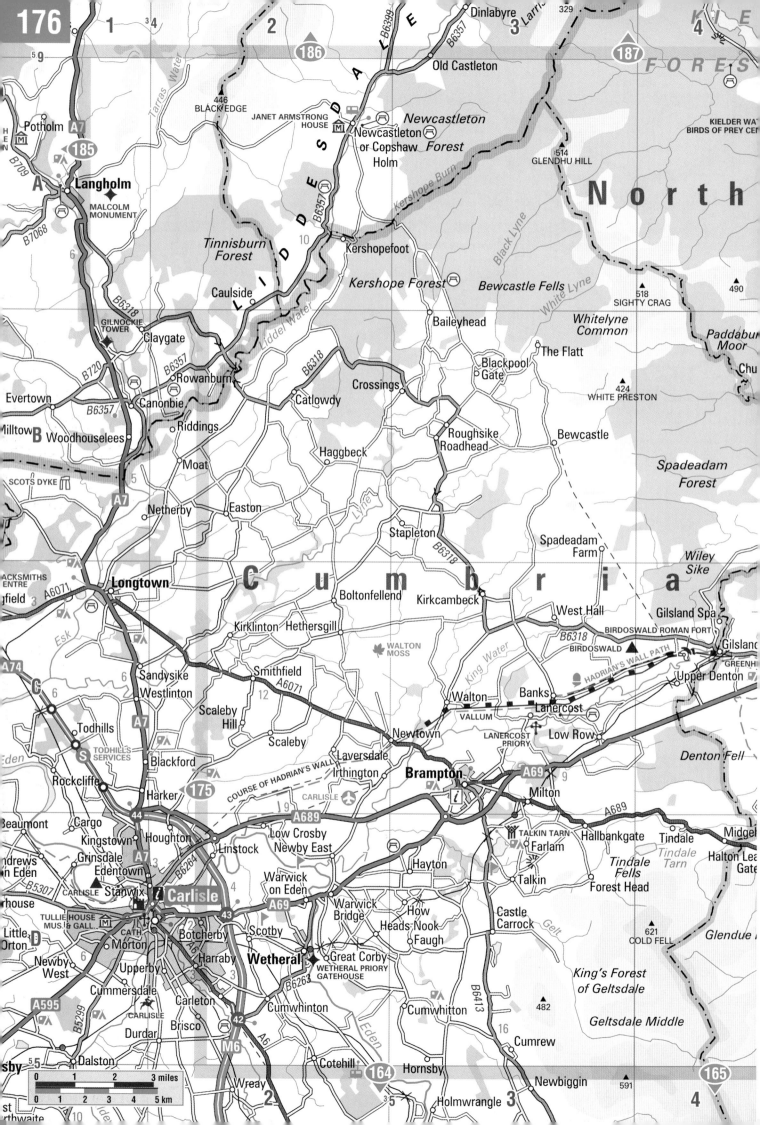

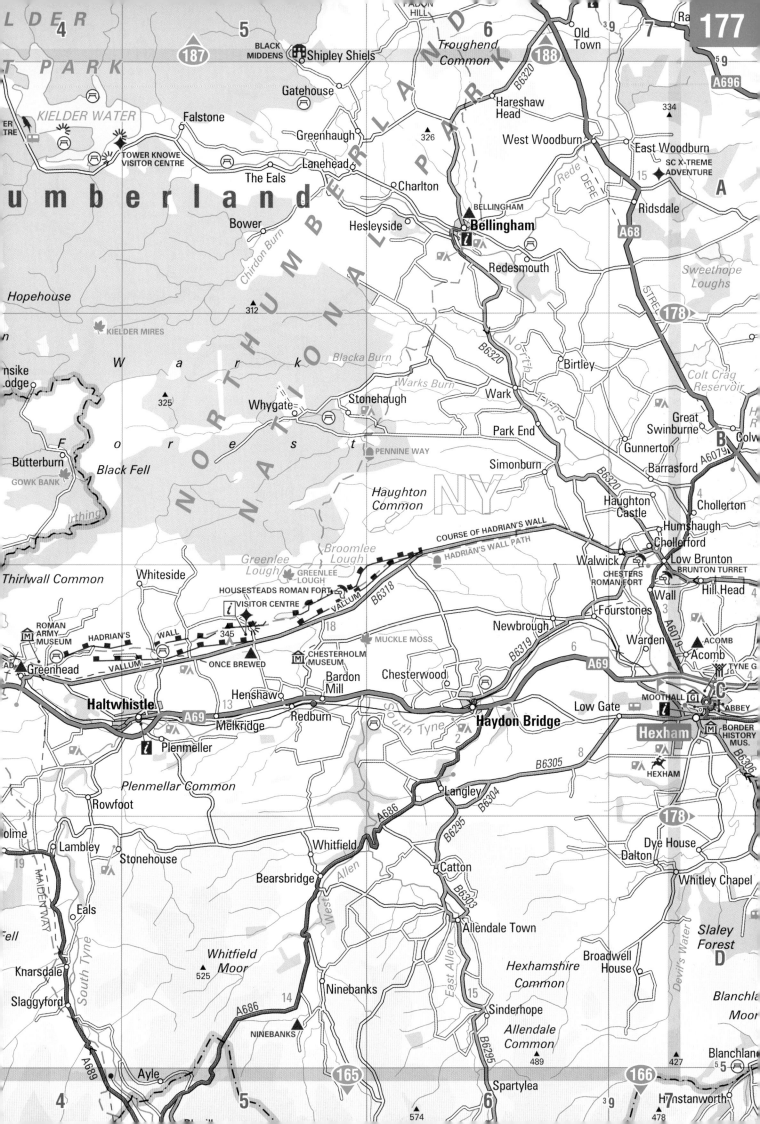

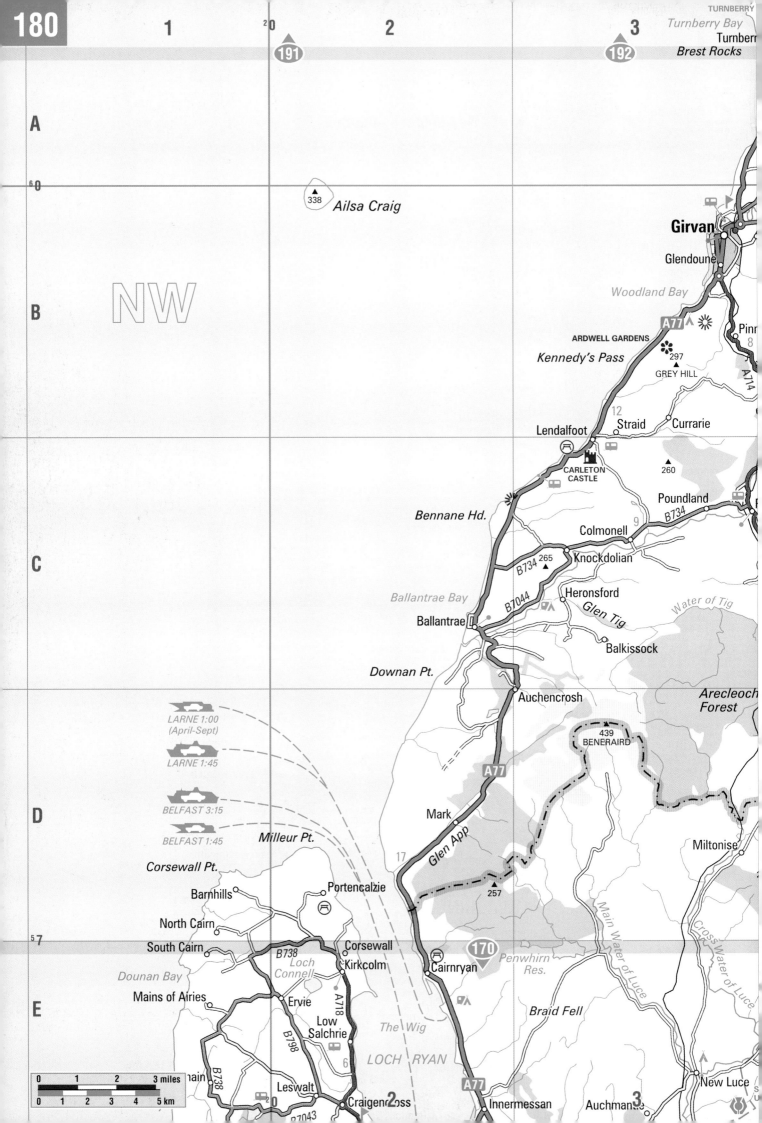

TURNBERRY
*Turnberry Bay*
Turnberr
*Brest Rocks*

191

192

**1**   20   **2**   **3**

A

6 0

▲ 338  *Ailsa Craig*

**NW**

**Girvan**

Glendoune

*Woodland Bay*

B

A77

Pinn
8

**ARDWELL GARDENS**

A714

*Kennedy's Pass*          ✳
297
▲
GREY HILL

12          Straid     Currarie

Lendalfoot

CARLETON
CASTLE          260
▲

Poundland

*Bennane Hd.*          Colmonell          B734

9

C

B734  265
▲
Knockdolian

*Ballantrae Bay*          B7044          Heronsford
Glen Tig          *Water of Tig*

Ballantrae          Balkissock

*Downan Pt.*

Auchencrosh          *Arecleoch
Forest*

439
▲
BENERAIRD

LARNE 1:00
(April-Sept)

LARNE 1:45          A77          Mark          *Miltonise*

BELFAST 3:15

D

BELFAST 1:45          *Milleur Pt.*          *Glen App*

*Corsewall Pt.*          17          257
▲

Barnhills          *Portencalzie*

North Cairn

5 7          South Cairn          Corsewall          170

B738          *Kirkcolm*          Cairnryan          *Penwhirn
Res.*

*Dounan Bay*          *Loch
Connell*

Mains of Airies          A718          *The Wig*          *Braid Fell*

E          Ervie

Low
Salchrie          *LOCH RYAN*

6

| 0 | 1 | 2 | 3 miles |
| 0 | 1 | 2 | 3 | 4 | 5 km |

B738          Leswalt          Craigencross

B738          Innermessan          Auchmant          New Luce

A77          **2**          **3**

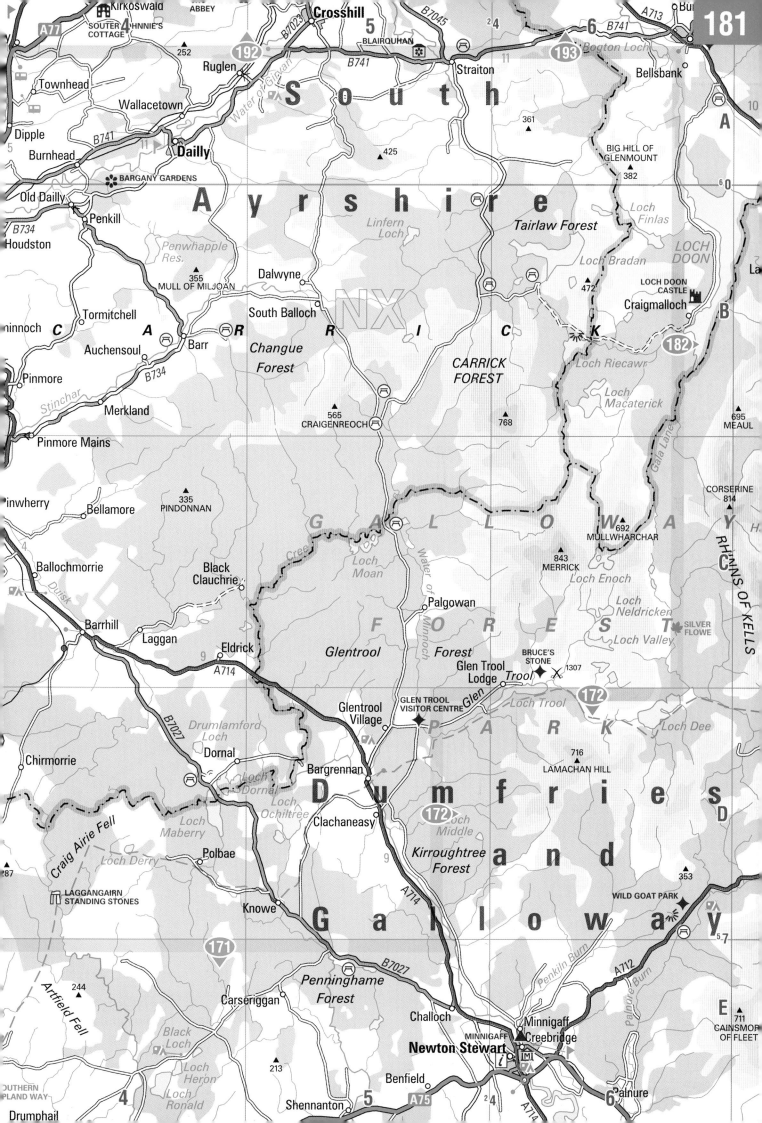

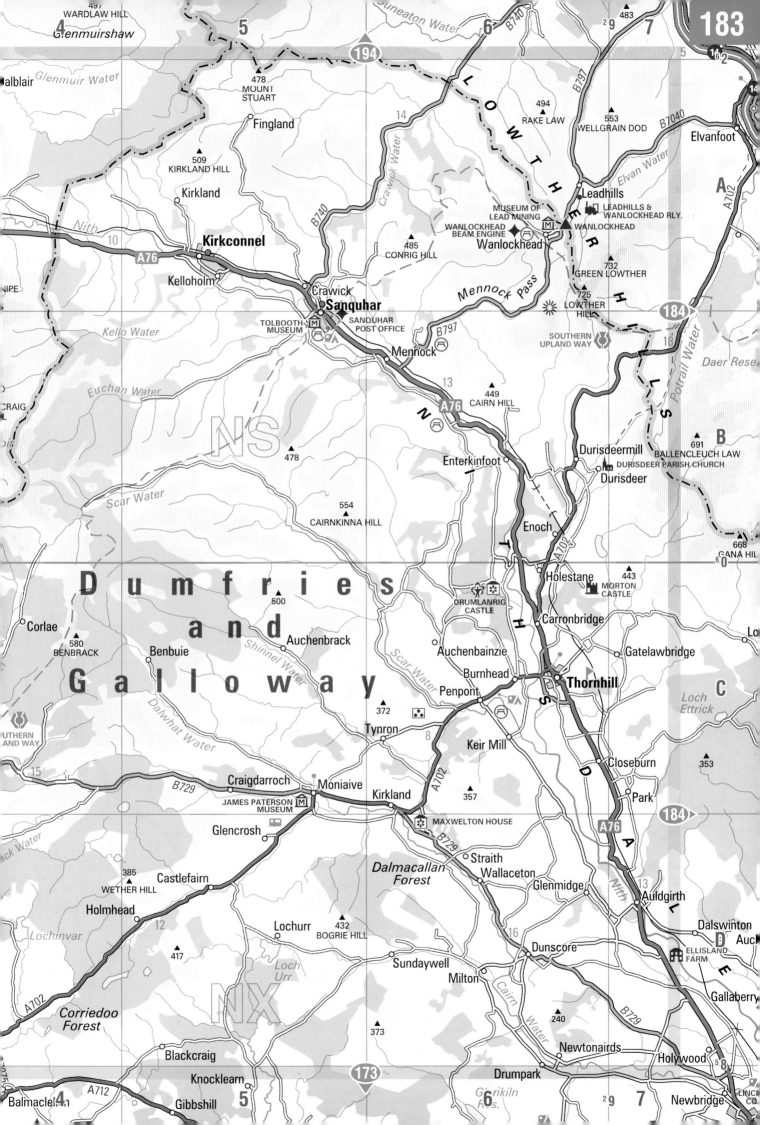

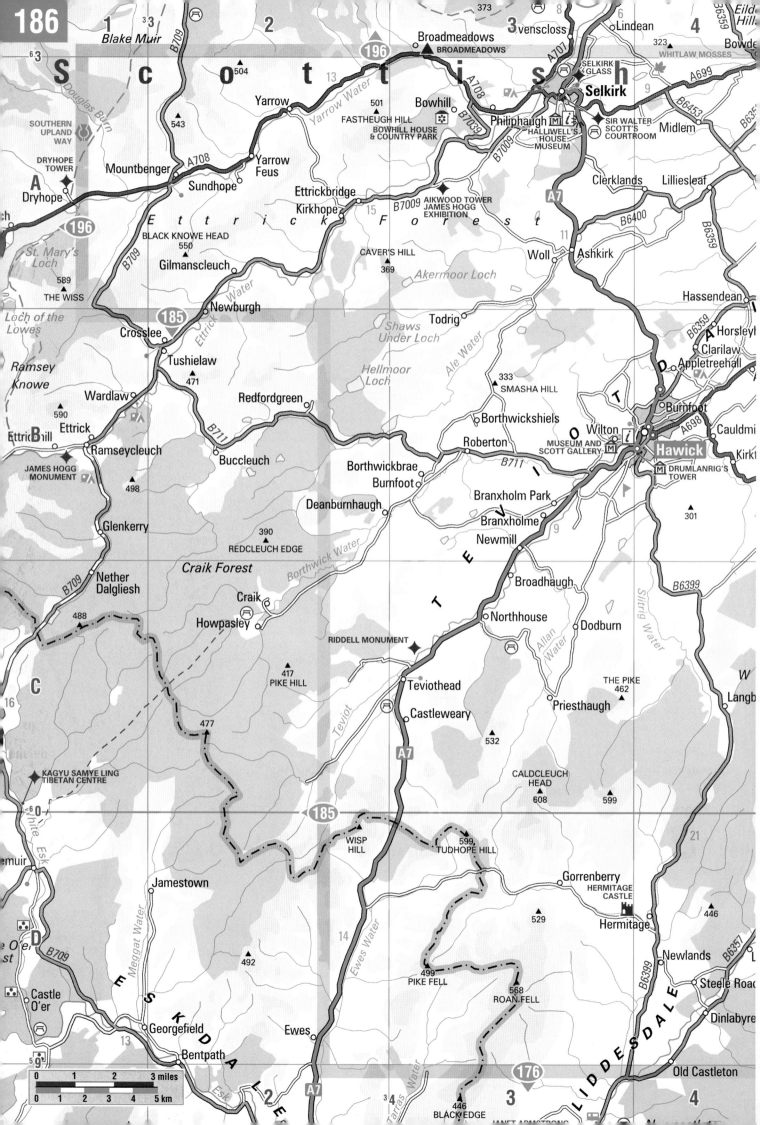

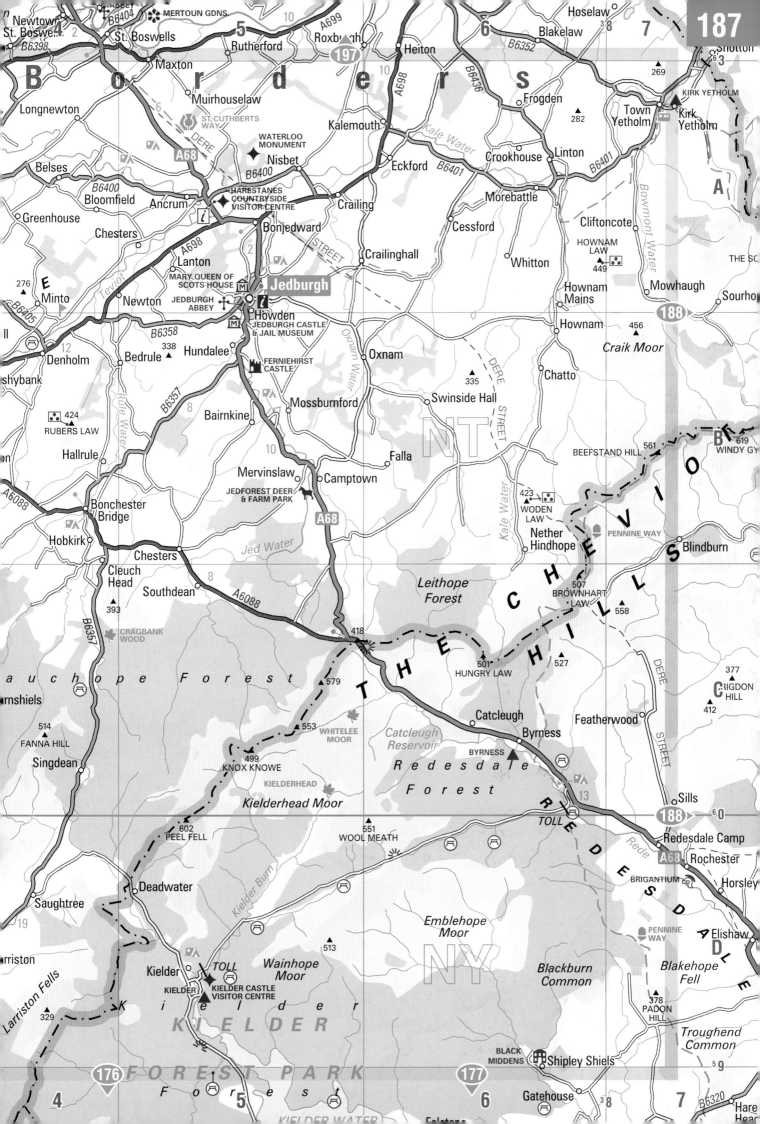

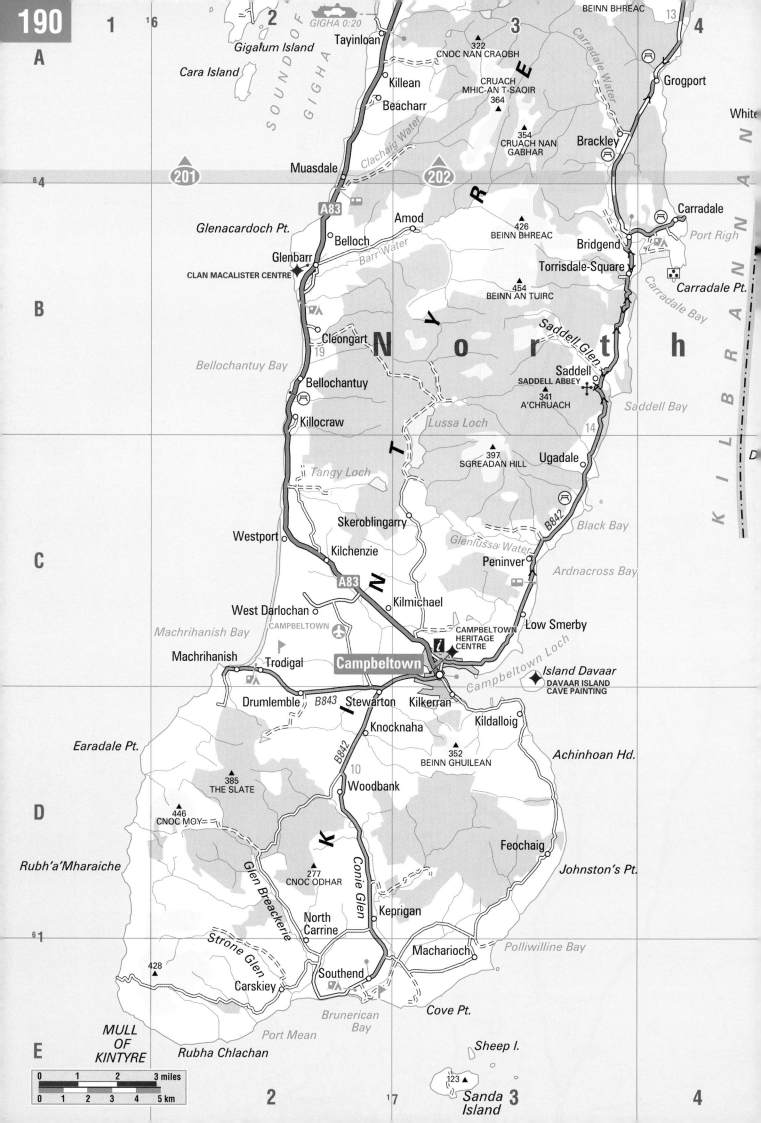

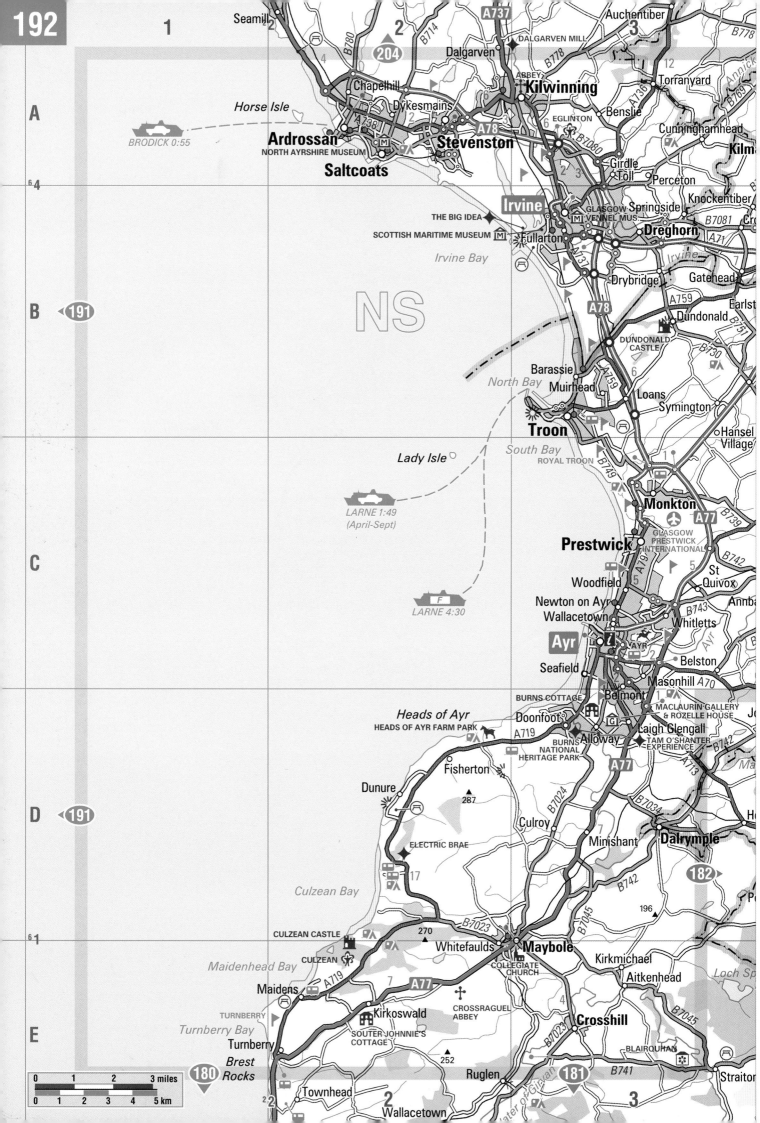

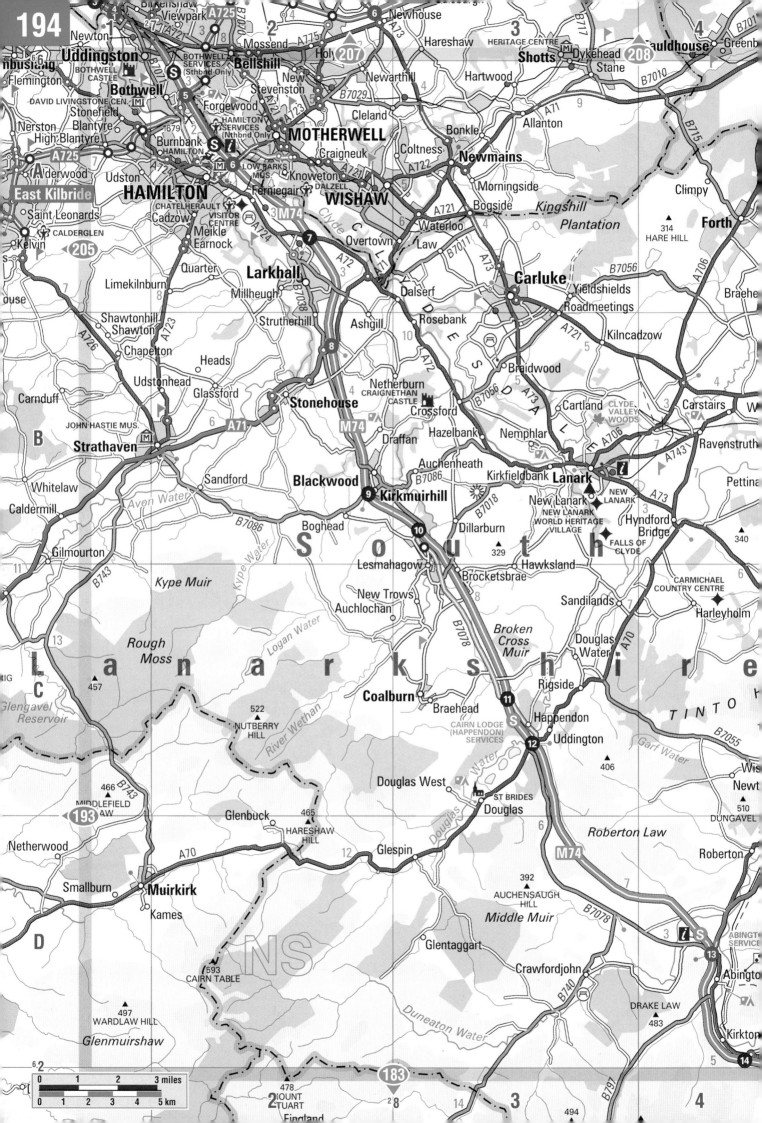

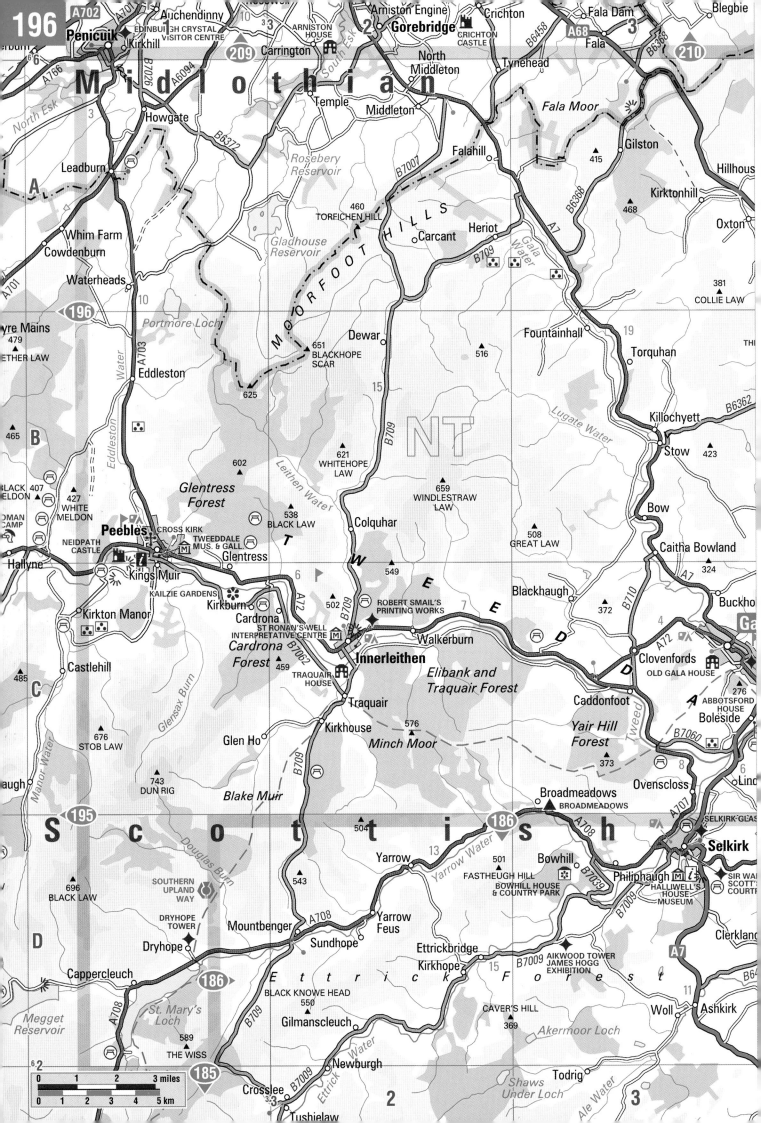

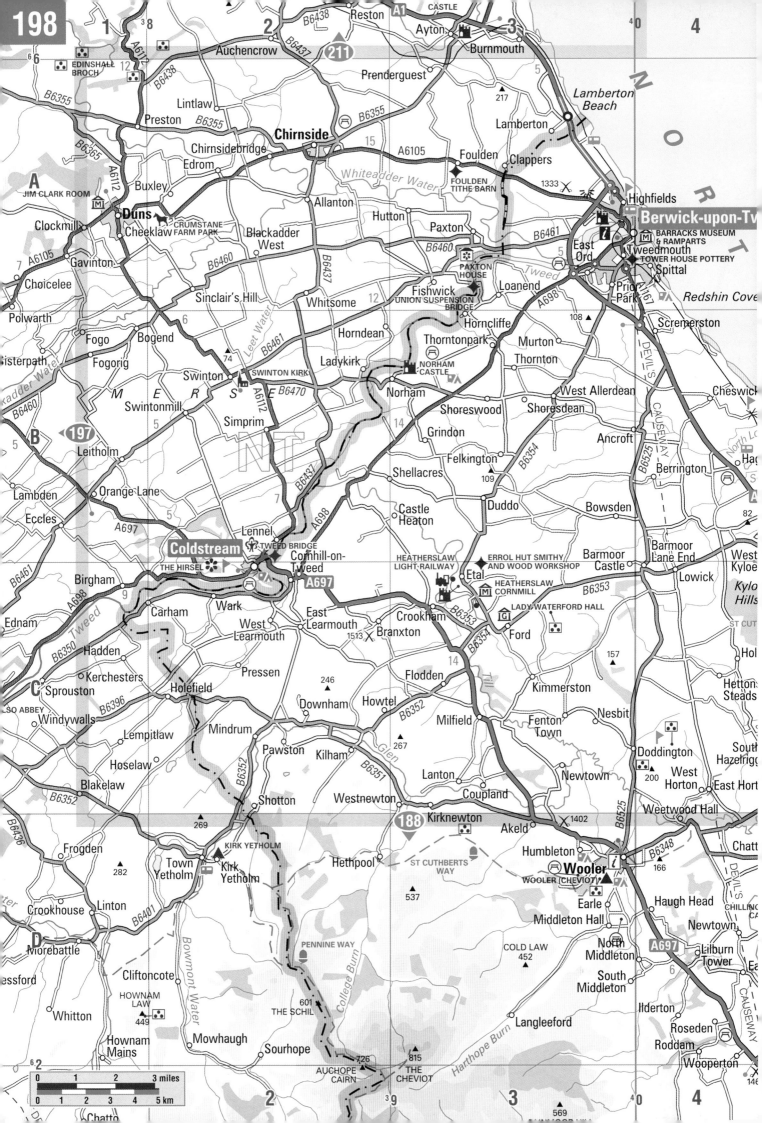

eed

A

B

**NU**

Goswick

gerston

uth Low

Beal

LINDISFARNE

*Emmanuel Hd.*

**Holy Island
(Lindisfarne)**

12

Causeway
Holy
Island
Sands

Holy
Island

LINDISFARNE CASTLE
*Castle Pt.*

HERITAGE
CENTRE

LINDISFARNE
PRIORY

Fenham

*Guile
Pt.*

353

Fenwick

East
Kyloe

Buckton

ERTS
WAY

Elwick

Ross

*Budle
Bay*

*Farne
Islands*

*Staple Sound*

NU

FARNE ISLANDS

*Inner Sound*

C

urn

Detchant

Middleton

Budle

BAMBURGH
CASTLE

211

North Hazelrigg

**Belford**

Easington

B1342

Waren Mill

**Bamburgh**

B1340

Burton

Glororum

B6349

Spindlestone

Mousen

Bradford

B1341

Elford

North
Sunderland

**Seahouses**

10

Bellshill

Warenton

Adderstone

Lucker

NEWHAM
BOG

Newham
Hall

189

**Beadnell**

B6348

Warenford

Swinhoe

Benthall

Greendikes

Newham

Newstead

Fleetham

*Beadnell
Bay*

A1

AM
TLE

Chillingham

CHILLINGHAM
WILD CATTLE

Rosebrough

Ellingham

Preston

Brunton

**High Newton-
by-the-Sea**

315

Hepburn

15

Brockdam

PRESTON TOWER

Low Newton-
by-the-Sea

D

Lilburn

Brownyside

North Charlton

Doxford

Chiston
Bank

*Embleton Bay*

Embleton

Dunstan Steads

*Castle Point*

Old Bewick

West
Ditchburn

South
Charlton

B6347

Rock

DUNSTANBURGH
CASTLE

reamish

B6346

Harehope

B6341

Dunstan

Craster

62

New
Bewick

Eglingham

169

101

Rennington

43

4　　　　　5　　　　　6　　43　7

Beanley

Littlemill

Howick

COAST

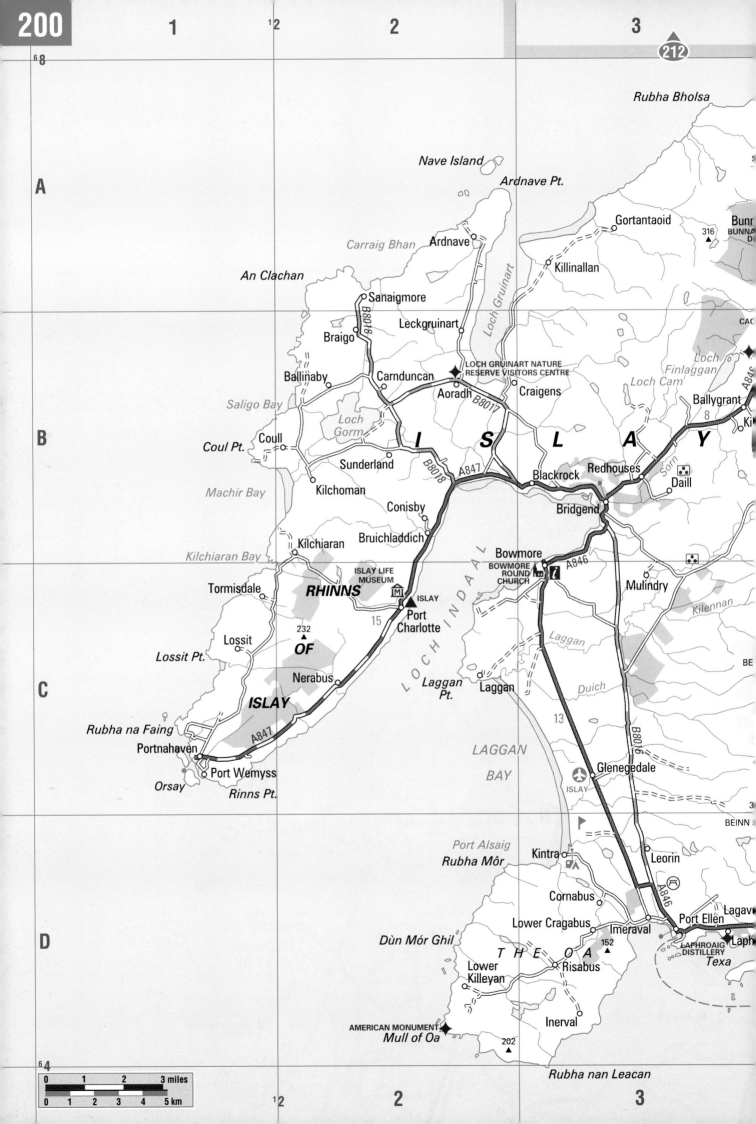

1  2  2  3

A

6 8

B

C

D

6 4

Rubha Bholsa

Nave Island
Ardnave Pt.

Carraig Bhan  Ardnave

Gortantaoid

316
BUNN
BUNNA
D

An Clachan

Killinallan

Loch Gruinart

Sanaigmore

Leckgruinart

Braigo

LOCH GRUINART NATURE
RESERVE VISITORS CENTRE

Loch
Finlaggan

CAC

Ballinaby  Carnduncan

Aoradh  B8017  Craigens

Loch Cam

Saligo Bay

Ballygrant

Loch
Gorm

I  S  L  A  Y

8  Ki

Coul Pt.  Coull

Sunderland

B8018  A847

Blackrock  Redhouses

Sorn

Machir Bay

Kilchoman

Conisby

Bridgend

Daill

Bruichladdich

Kilchiaran

ISLAY LIFE
MUSEUM

Bowmore

Kilchiaran Bay

Tormisdale  RHINNS
M
ISLAY

BOWMORE
ROUND
CHURCH  A846

Mulindry

Kilennan

Port
Charlotte

15

Lossit  232
OF

Loch Indaal

Laggan

Lossit Pt.

Nerabus

Laggan
Pt.  Laggan

Duich

BE

Rubha na Faing  ISLAY

13

Portnahaven  A847

Port Wemyss

LAGGAN  Glenegedale
ISLAY

Orsay  Rinns Pt.

BAY

BEINN

Port Alsaig
Rubha Mòr  Kintra  Leorin

Dùn Mór Ghil

Cornabus

A846

Port Ellen  Lagav

Lower Cragabus  Imeraval  Laph

T H E  O A

152

LAPHROAIG
DISTILLERY  Texa

Lower
Killeyan  Risabus

AMERICAN MONUMENT
Mull of Oa

Inerval

202

Rubha nan Leacan

0  1  2  3 miles
0  1  2  3  4  5 km

2  2  3

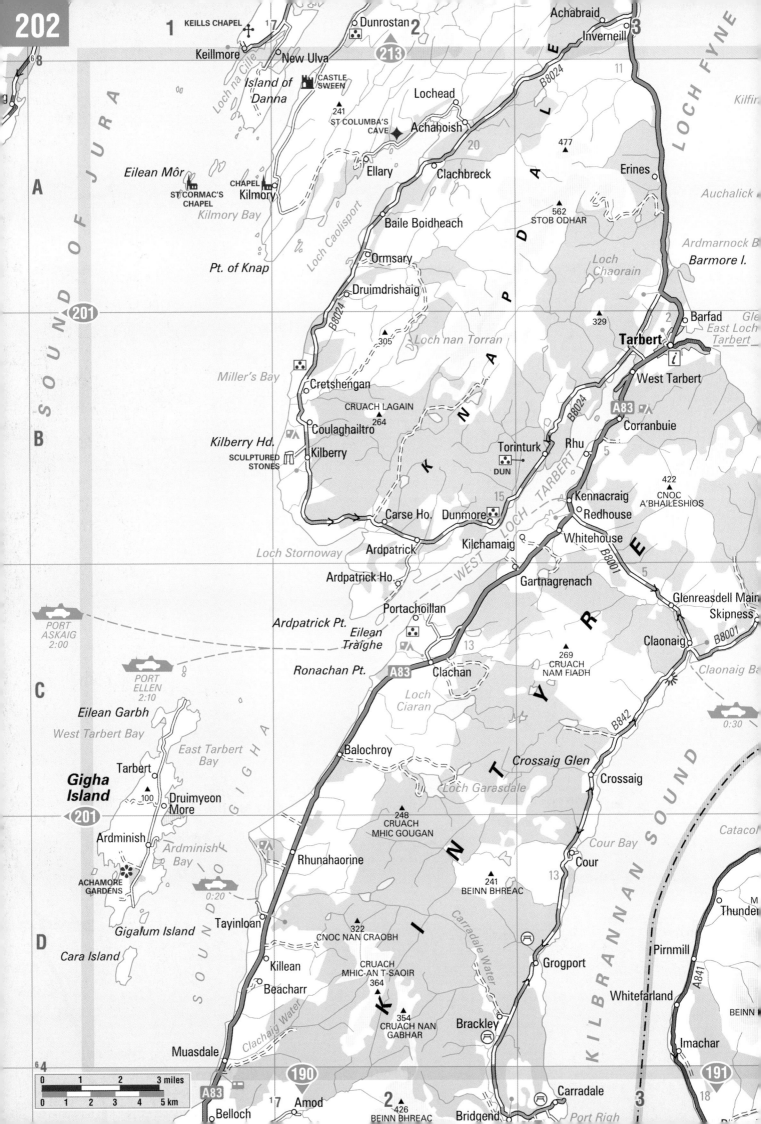

Auchnaha
Auchenbreck
Dalinlongart
Clachaig
Sandbank
Ardnadam
Hunter's Qu
Kirn
Dunoon
Cloch Pt.
A

Kilfinan
CRUACH NAN CAORACH
458
405
214
578
CRUACH NAN CAPULL
Glen Kin
COWAL BIRD GARDEN
ST JOHN'S CHURCH
HIGHLAND MARY'S STATUE

Drum
12
454
BEINN BHREAC
A886
Loch Riddon
Glenstriven
506
BEINN BHREAC
KYLES OF BUTE
Inverchaolain
522
BLACK CRAIG
Bullwood

Melldalloch
B8000
266
Port Driseach
Tighnabruaich
Auchenlochan
Kames
Ardentraive
Colintraive
Algaltraig
Ferry
418
CORLARACH HILL
Corlarach Forest
WAVE WHISPER GALLERY

Asgog Loch
Portavadie
Millhouse
Blair's Ferry
0:25
Glen More
227
WINDY HILL
278
ISLAND
Port Lamont
Newton Park
Innellan
Wemyss Bay
Skelmorlie
Up
Ske
204

Kilbride Bay
Ardlamont Ho.
St Colmac
Ettrick Bay
A844
B875
Port Bannatyne
3
Rothesay Bay
Kames B.
Ardyne Pt.
Toward
Toward Pt.
0:35
Meigle
B

Ardlamont Pt.
OF
ROTHESAY CASTLE
Rothesay
Craigmore
ARDENCRAIG GARDENS
Montford
A78
Route

NR
NS
Rubha Leathan
254
Straad
B878
BUTE
VICTORIAN FERNERY
Ascog
Kerrycroy
Largs Bay
Largs

Inchmarnock
60
Scalpsie
A844
Loch Fad
Loch Quien
7
Scoulag
B881
MOUNT STUART HOUSE AND GARDEN
Tomont End
CHRISTIAN HERITAGE MUSEUM
B896
Downcraig Ferry

SKIPNESS CASTLE
Skipness Pt.
Skipness Bay
Ardscalpsie Pt.
12
Scalpsie Bay
Stravanan Bay
Kingarth
B881
Kilchattan Bay
157
Kilchattan Bay
Great Cumbrae Island
MUSEUM OF THE CUMBRAES
Millport
B889
C

SOUND OF BUTE
Garroch Hd.
ST BLANE'S CHAPEL
The Tan
Fairlie Roads
HUNTERSTON POWER STATION VISITOR CENTRE
Little Cumbrae Island
Farland Hd.
Thirdpart
Portencross
West Kilbride
204
A78

Cock of Arran
LOCHRANZA CASTLE
Lochranza
Catacol
ISLE OF ARRAN DISTILLERY
LOCHRANZA
Millstone Pt.
444
North
FIRTH
Seamill
Horse Isle
D

ISLE
ALL NAN DAMH
570
A841
NORTH SANNOX FARM PARK
Sannox
14
Sannox Bay
Ayrshire

NORTH
OF
573
Loch Tanna
859
Glen Sannox
Corrie
OF
CLYDE

HARRAIN
21
798
CIR MHÒR
BEINN TARSUINN
825
874
GOAT FELL
ARRAN

ARRAN
191
Glen Iorsa
BRODICK
BRODICK
192
4
5
6

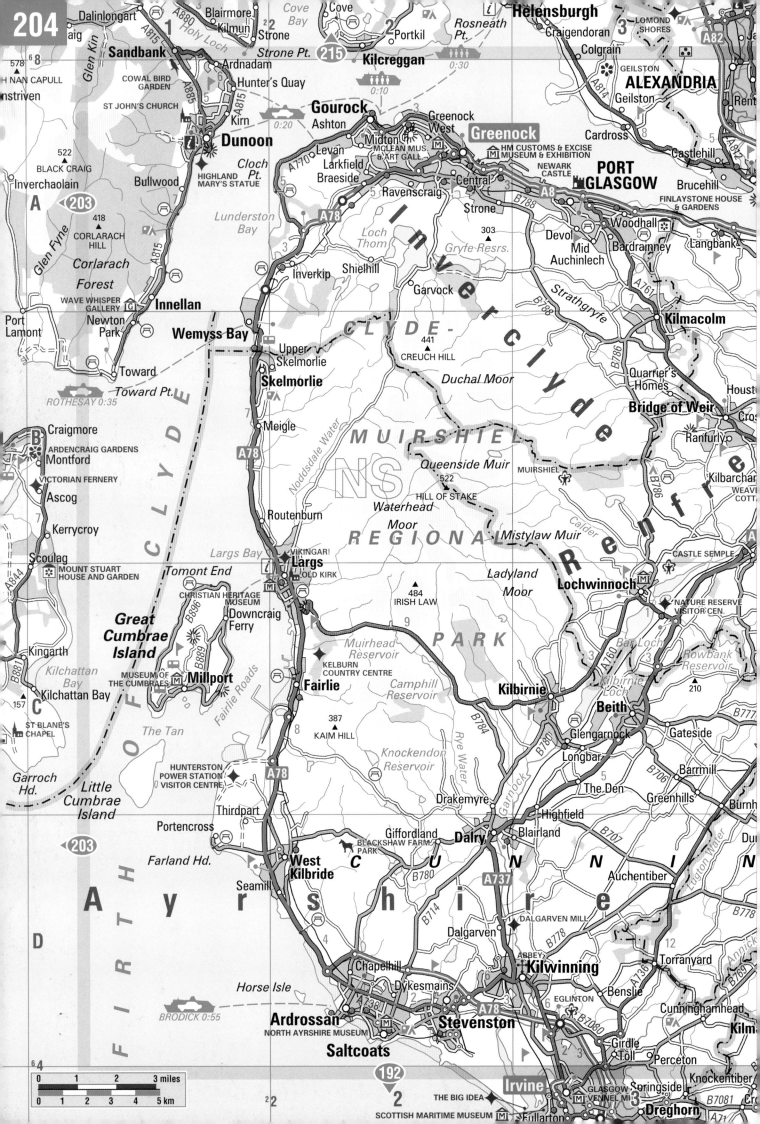

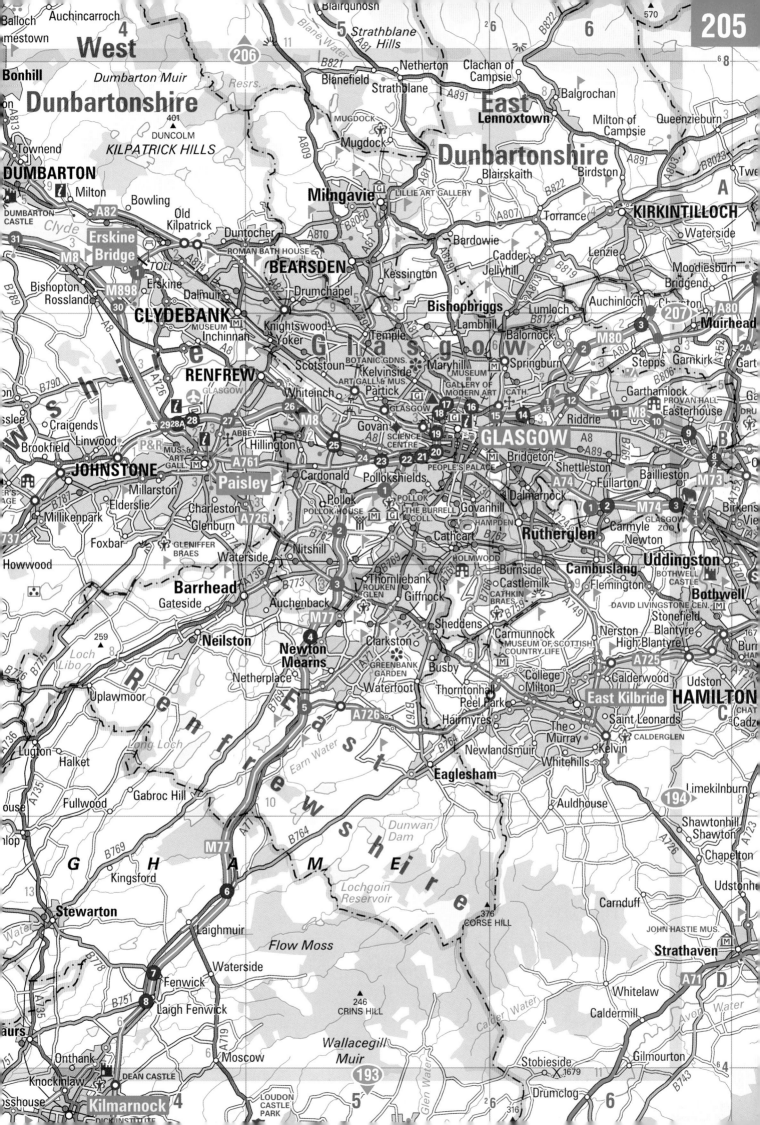

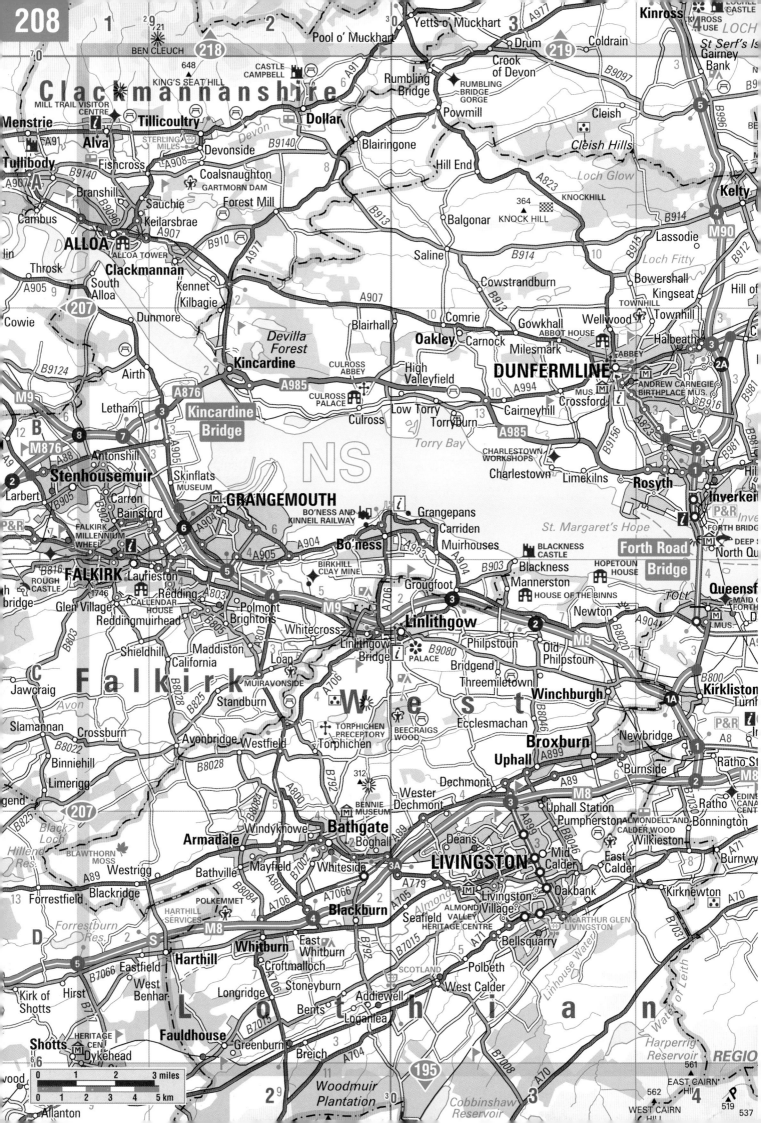

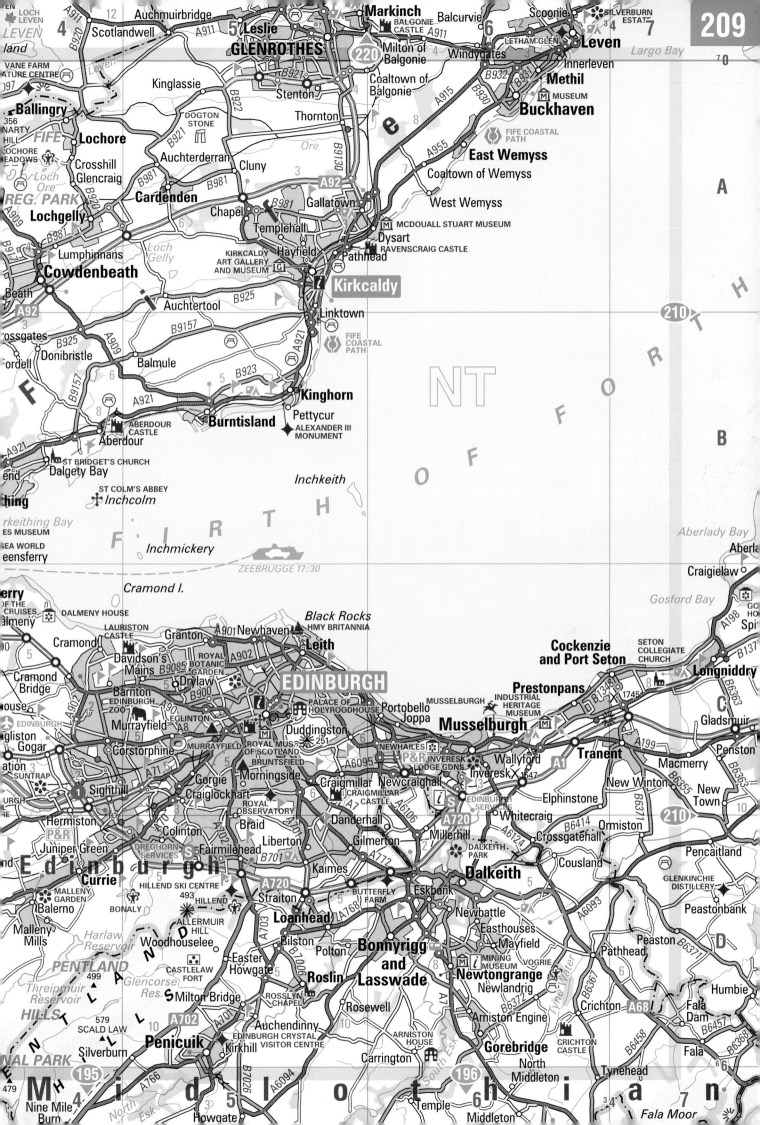

A

NT

B

HOUSE

xburn  *Barns Ness*

East Barns

Skateraw

**A1** 13

TORNESS NUCLEAR POWER
STATION VISTOR CENTRE

C

urn

Innerwick

Thorntonloch

COCKLAW
HILL
319

DUNGLASS
COLLEGIATE
CHURCH

Cove

*Reed Pt.*

Oldhamstocks

Cockburnspath

*Siccar Pt.*

*Wheat Stack*

FAST CASTLE

ST ABB'S HEAD

*St. Abb's Head*

KITTIWAKE GALLERY

Ecclaw

A1107

245

Lumsdaine

Northfield

St. Abb's

*Coldingham Bay*

391
HEART LAW

SOUTHERN
UPLAND WAY

*Coldingham
Moor*

12

B6438

Grantshouse

Huxton

Coldingham

St. Abb's Haven

COLDINGHAM SANDS
COLDINGHAM PRIORY

ynut Water

Nether
Monynut

Houndwood

*Ale Water*

D

*Eye Water*

12

Cairncross

EYEMOUTH MUSEUM

**Eyemouth**

shaws

Abbey
St. Bathans

262

Reston

**A1**

AYTON
CASTLE

B6355

A1107

Ellemford

197

EDINSHALL
BROCH

12

B6438

Auchencrow

B6438

198

Ayton

Burnmouth

66

4 B6355

Lintlaw

5

39

Prenderguest

B6355

6
217

*Lamberton
Beach*

Tiraghoil

Bunessa

Lee

Carsaig

CRUACHAN MIN
376

376

Carsaig
Bay

Rubha
Dubh

A849
224

Loch
Assapol

225

**R O S S   O F   M U L L**

Ardalanish

Uisken

Ardchiavaig

Scoor

CARSAIG ARCHES

Malcolm's Pt.

125

Rubha nam
Braithrean

Eilean
a'Chalmain

Rubh Ardalanish

**A**

OBAN 2:20

**NM**

**B**

Rubh'a'Geadha

Balnahard

Kiloran Bay

KILORAN GARDENS

B8086

Kiloran

Kilchattan

B8087

**COLONSAY**

136

Scalasaig

**NR**

Glendeb

**C**

Loch Staosnaig

Corpach Bay

Garvard

B8085

Rubha Dubh

467
BEINN BH

PRIORY

453

Dubh Eilean

**Oronsay**

RAINBERG
MOR

Shian Bay

Shian

318

Eilean nan Ron

Loch Righ
Mòr

**D**

Rubh'an t-Sàilein

PORT ASKAIG 1:10

Loch Tarbert

Rubha Lang-aoinidh

0    1    2    3 miles

200

201

3

0  1  2  3  4  5 km

Rubha
Bholsa

Rubha a'Mhail

439

Lagg

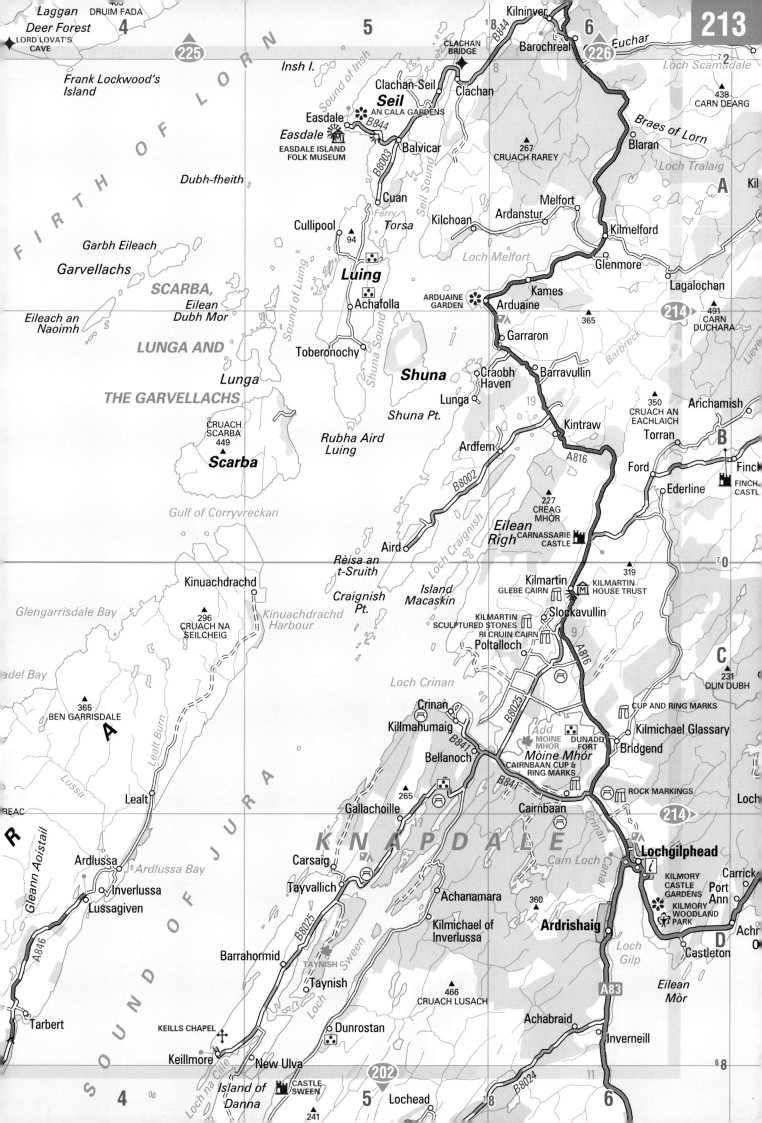

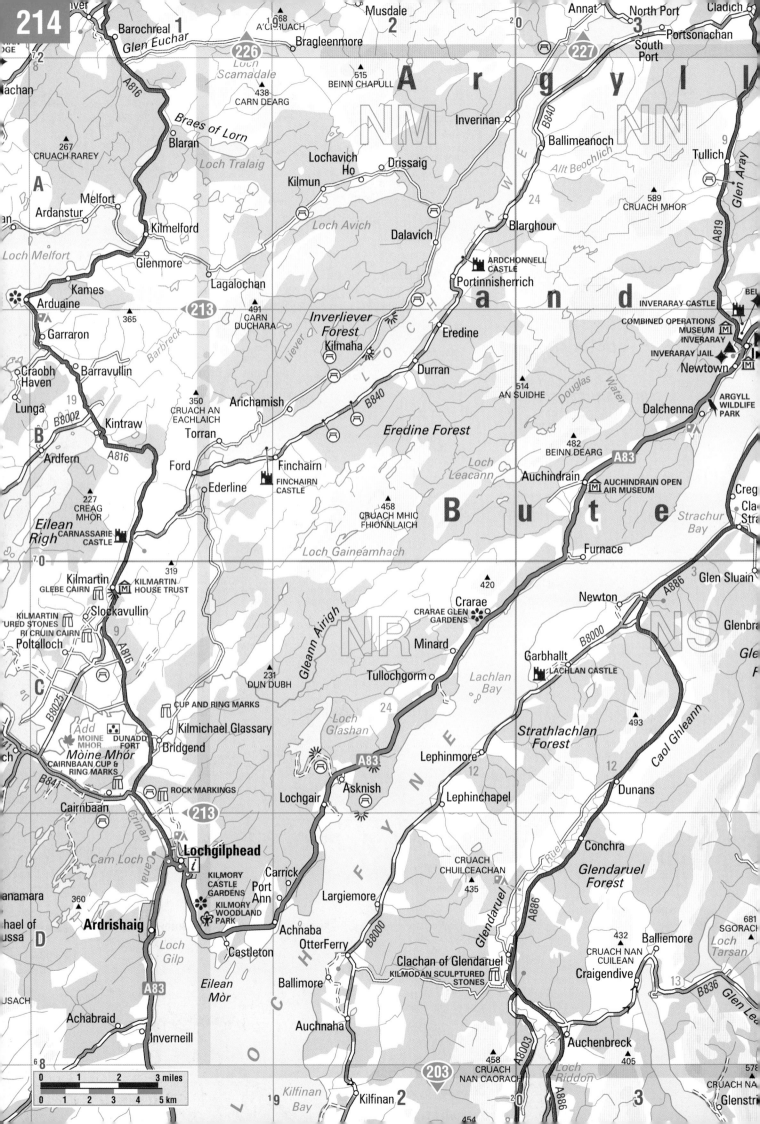

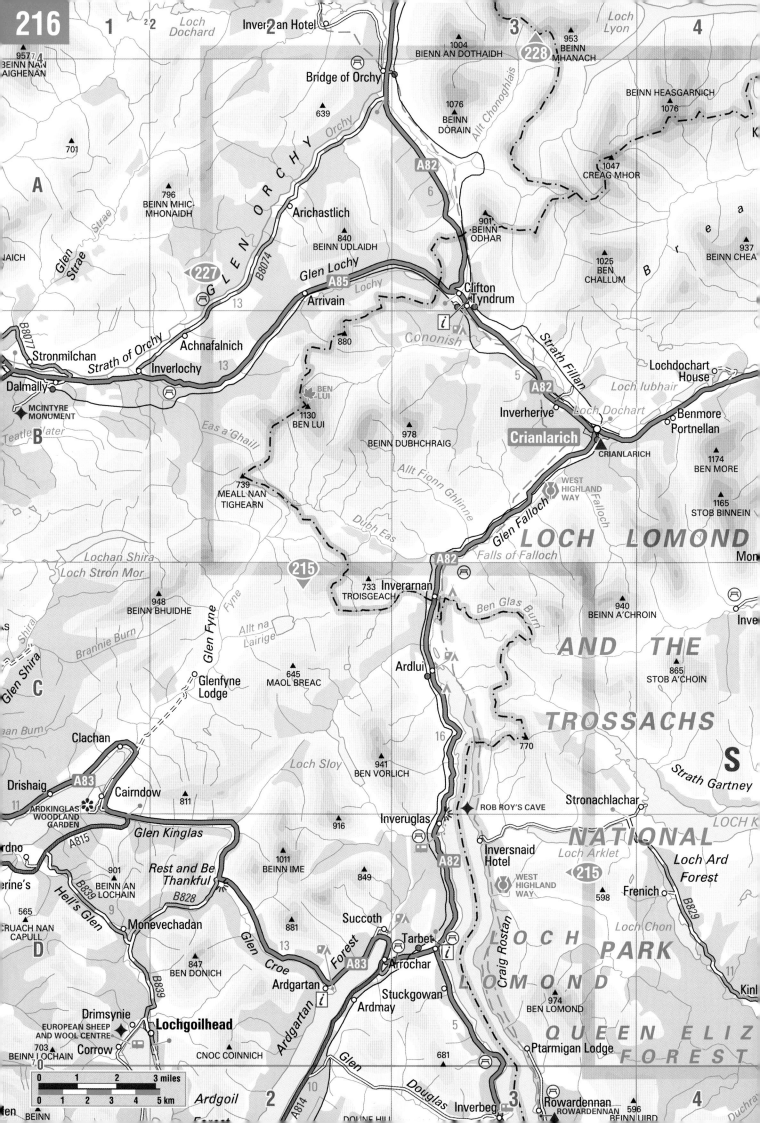

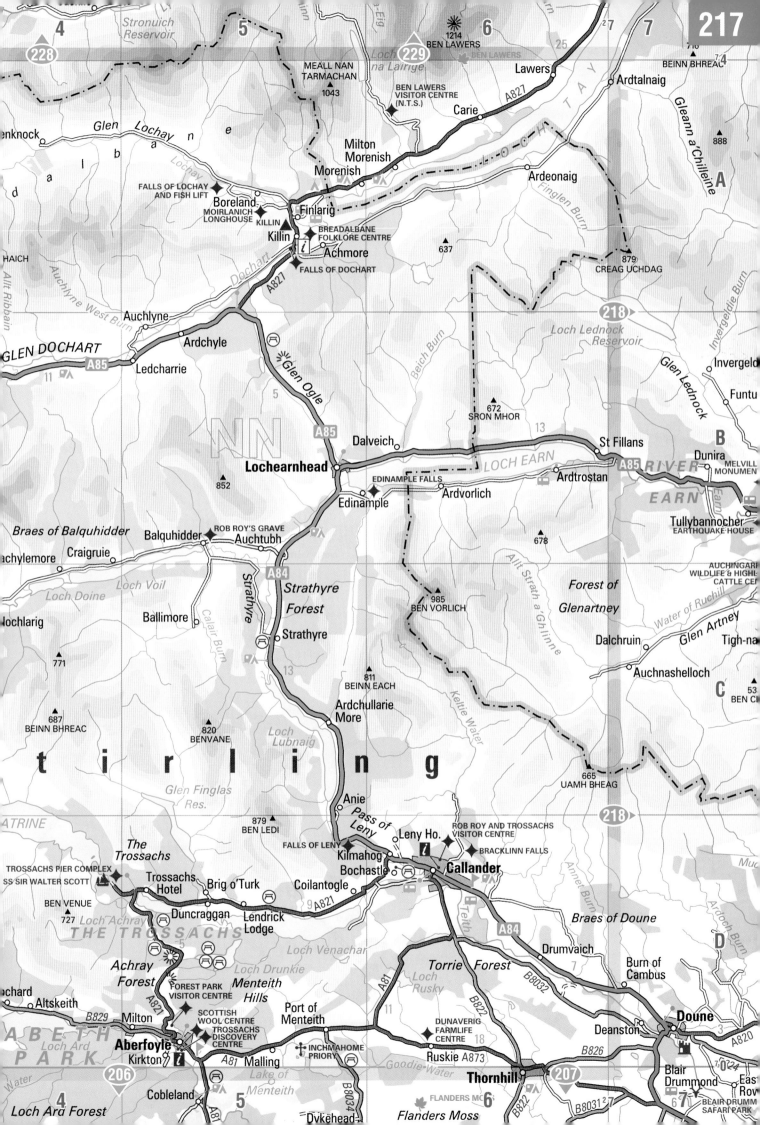

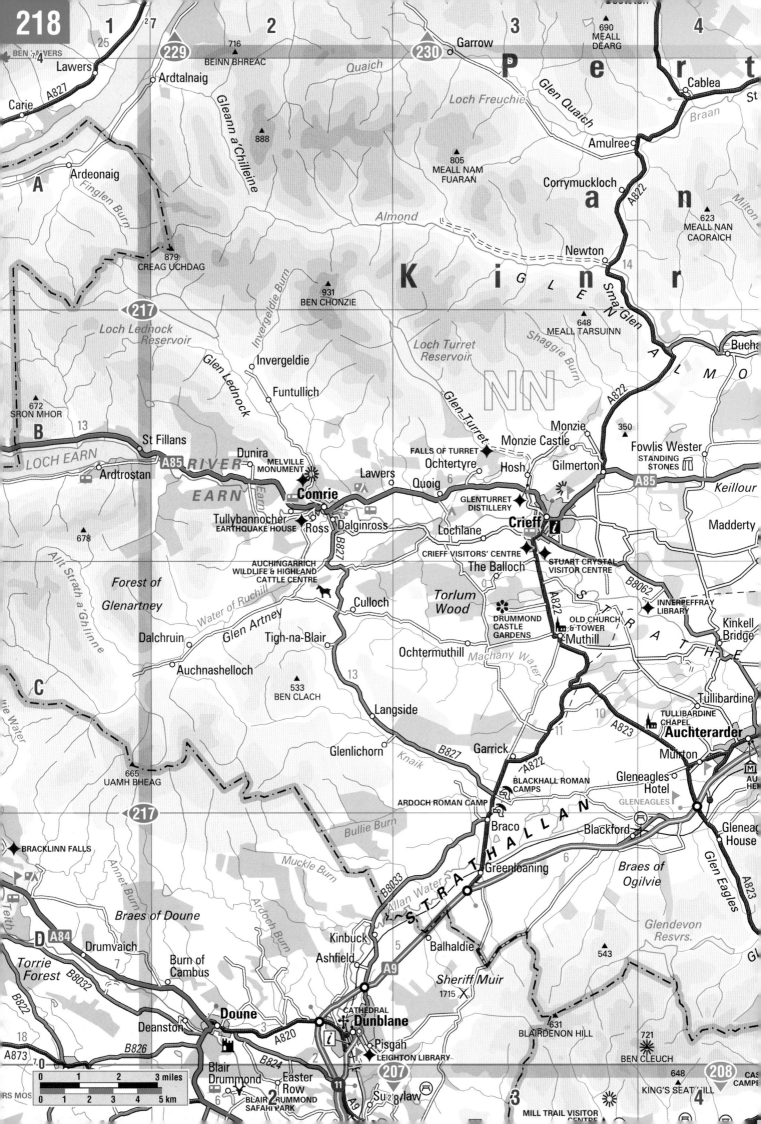

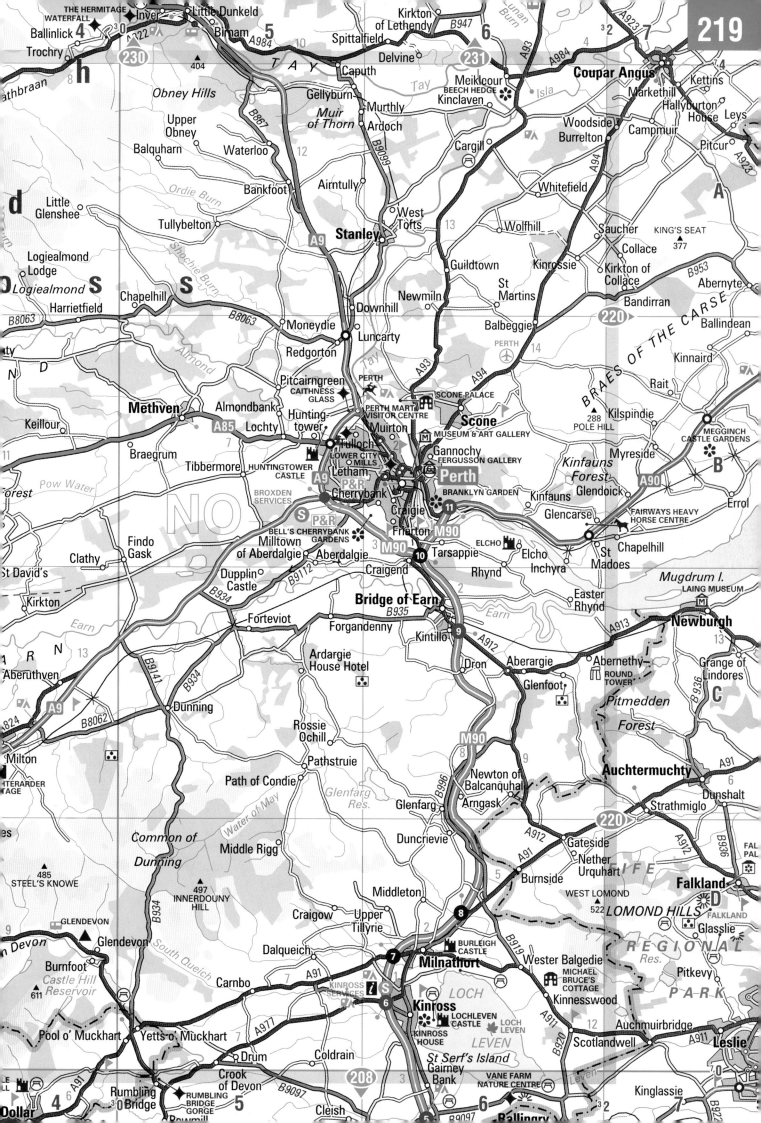

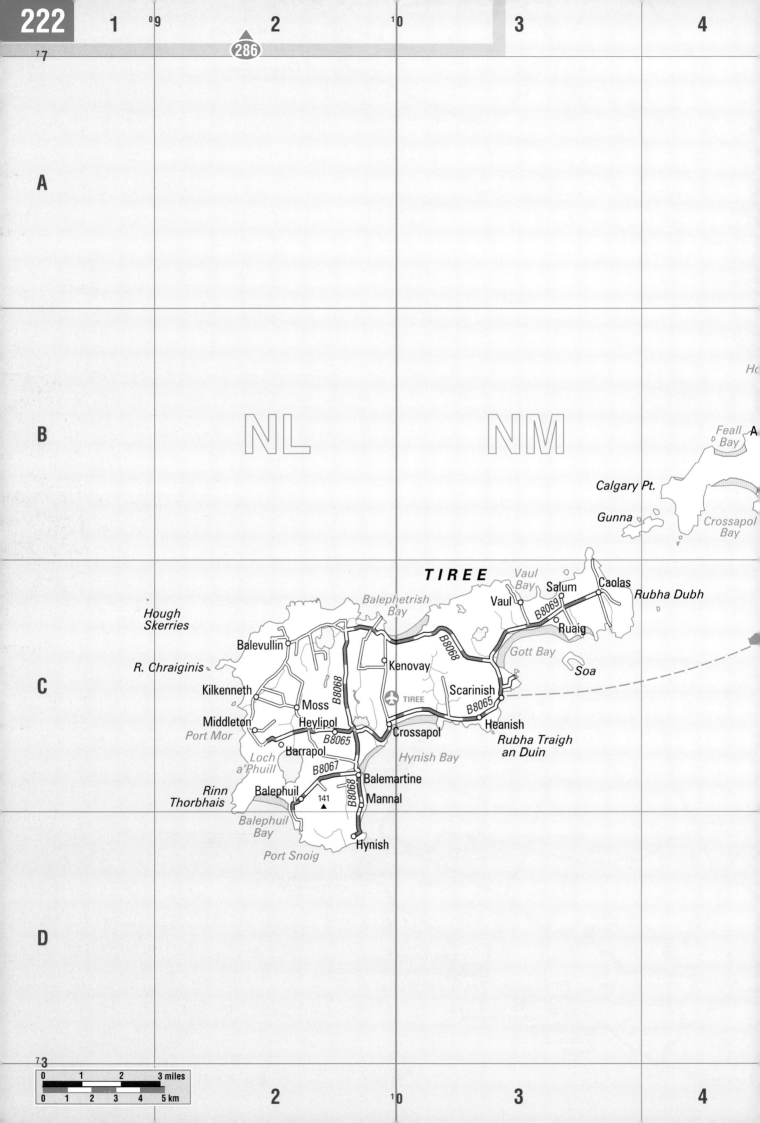

286

7 7

A

B

NL    NM

Feall A
Bay

Calgary Pt.

Gunna    Crossapol
Bay

**TIREE**    Vaul
Bay    Caolas
Salum    Rubha Dubh
Hough    Vaul
Skerries    Balephetrish    B8069
Bay    Ruaig
Balevullin    B8068
Gott Bay
R. Chraiginis    Kenovay    Soa
C    Scarinish
Kilkenneth    B8068
Moss    TIREE    Heanish
Middleton    Heylipol    B8065
Port Mor    Crossapol    Rubha Traigh
an Duin
Loch    B8065    Hynish Bay
a'Phuill    Barrapol
B8067
Rinn    141    Balemartine
Thorbhais    Balephuil    B8068    Mannal
Balephuil
Bay
Port Snoig    Hynish

D

7 3

Sanna Point

Sanna Bay

Sanna

Portuairk

Point of
Ardnamurchan
**ARDNAMURCHAN LIGHTHOUSE**

Achosnic

B8007

**A**

Ormsai

Ormsaigb

An Acairseid

Cairns of Coll

234

Eilean Mor

Rubha Mor

Bousd

Sorisdale

Ardmore
Bay

Cliad Bay

Quinish Pt.

Glengorm
Castle

Arnabost

Gallanach

B8072

Mishnish

Grishipoll

B8071

Rubha
an Aird

Quinish

Ballyhaugh

B8071

Loch
Cliad

▲
73

**COLL**

Caliach Pt.

Sunipol

Mornish

**MULL LITTLE
THEATRE**

**B**

h Bay

▲
104

OBAN 2:40

Penmore
Mill

Dervaig

Achn

Totronald

B8070

Acha

Arinagour

Eilean
Ornsay

Loch Eatharna

Calgary

**THE OLD BYRE
HERITAGE CENTR**

eod

Breachacha
Castle

Friesland

Calgary Bay

Loch Breachacha

Soa

0:55

Ensay

▲ 342
CARN MOR

Achnacr

Treshnish Pt.

Haunn

B8073

**C**

▲ 390

Rubh a'Chaoil

224

Burg

Kilninian

Achleck

23

Fanmore

Ballygown

Treshnish Isles

Fladda

Eilean Dioghlum

**EAS FORS
WATERFALL**

La

Lunga

Gometra

LOCH TUATH

Laggan
Bay

Os

Bearnus ▲ 313

**Ulva**

Bac Mor

Ulva House

Little
Colonsay

INCH KENNETH
CHAPEL

Inch
Kenneth

**D**

Bal

Staffa

**STAFFA**

**FINGAL'S CAVE**

**MACKINNON'S CAVE**

IONA 0:45
(April-Oct)

Erisgeir

▲ 519
BEI**3**N NA SREI

1

2

3

**COLL**

Arnab

Gallanach

B8072

B8071

B8071

73

Loch
Cliad

B8070

Arinagour

Loch Eatharna

OBAN 2:40

**A**

Friesland

Eilean
Ornsay

TIREE 0:55

Quinish Pt.

Ardmore Bay

Ardmore Pt.

Bloody B

Glengorm
Castle

**MULL AND IONA
FOLKLORE MUSEUM** [M]

Rubha
an Aird

Quinish

**Tobermory**

Caliach Pt.

Sunipol

Mornish

Penmore
Mill

Mishnish

'S AIRDE-BEINN

292

MULL LITTLE
THEATRE

B8073

7

Calgary

Dervaig

Achnadrish

Calgary Bay

THE OLD BYRE
HERITAGE CENTRE

SPEINN

4

**B**

Treshnish Pt.

Ensay

342
CARN MOR

Loch Frisa

Let

Haunn

B8073

Burg

Kilninian

Achnacraig

Rubh a'Chaoil

Achleck

Bellart

223

Fanmore

390

Treshnish Isles

Fladda

Ballygown

LOCH TUATH

EAS FORS
WATERFALL

424
BEINN NA DRISE

Eilean Dioghlum

Lunga

Gometra

Bearnus

313

Lagganulva

Laggan
Bay

Oskamull

Killien

U l v a

Ulva House

Sound of Ulva

Bac Mor

LOCH NA KEAL,

Little
Colonsay

Eorsa

ISLE OF

LOCH

17

Derr

INCH KENNETH
CHAPEL

Staffa

STAFFA

Inch
Kenneth

Balnahard

**C**

FINGAL'S CAVE

Erisgeir

MACKINNON'S CAVE

561

519
BEINN NA SREINE

Glen Seilisdeir

(April-Oct)
0:45

**ARDMEANACH**

Ki
H

Kilfinich
Bay

Eilean
Annraidh

MACLEAN'S CROSS

THE BURG

LOCH SCRIDAIN

Rubha nan Cearc

100

IONA ABBEY AND
CATHEDRAL

Kintra

ST COLUMBA EXHIBITION
& WELCOME CENTRE

Loch na
Lathaich

**D**

IONA HERITAGE CENTRE [M]

**Iona**

Baile Mor

Aridhglas

Eorabus

18

Torrans

Stac an
Aoineidh

Sound of Iona

Fionnphort

A849

Lee

BRO

Fidden

Tiraghoil

Bunessan

376
CRUACHAN MIN

0      1      2      3 miles

0   1   2   3   4   5 km

Erraid

212

**R O S S   O F   M U L L**

Ardalanish

Uisken

Scoor

Ardchiavaig

Malcolm's Pt.

2

3

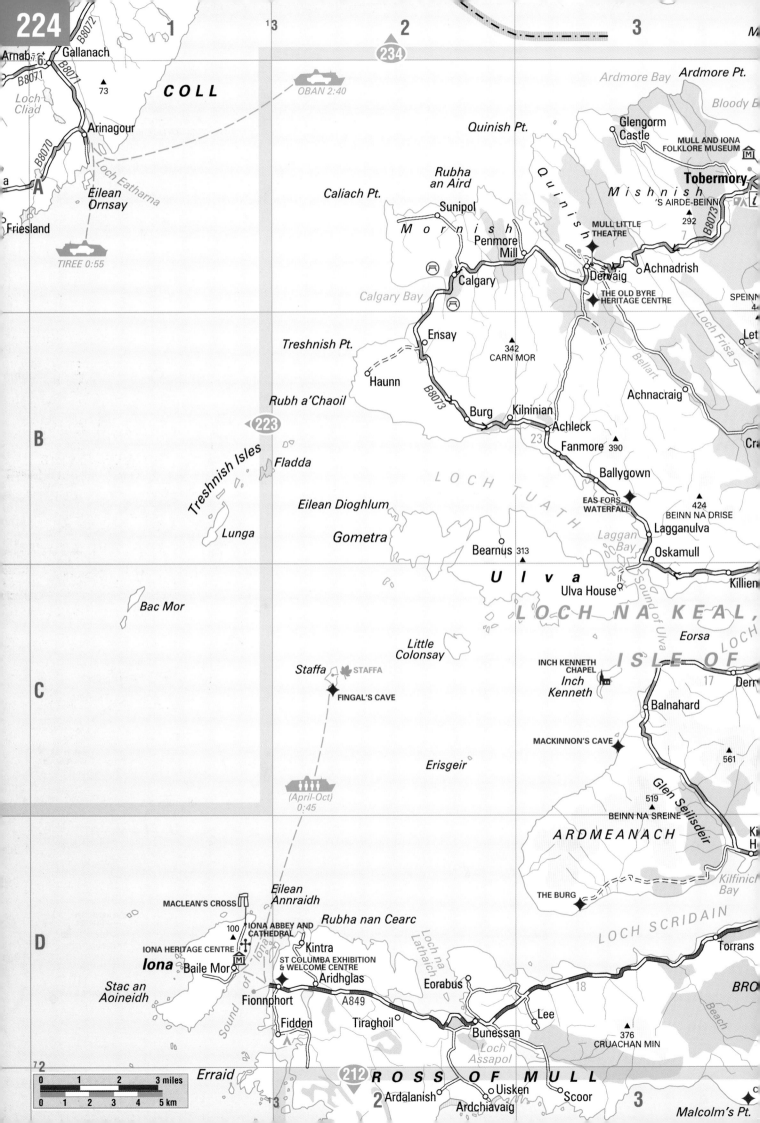

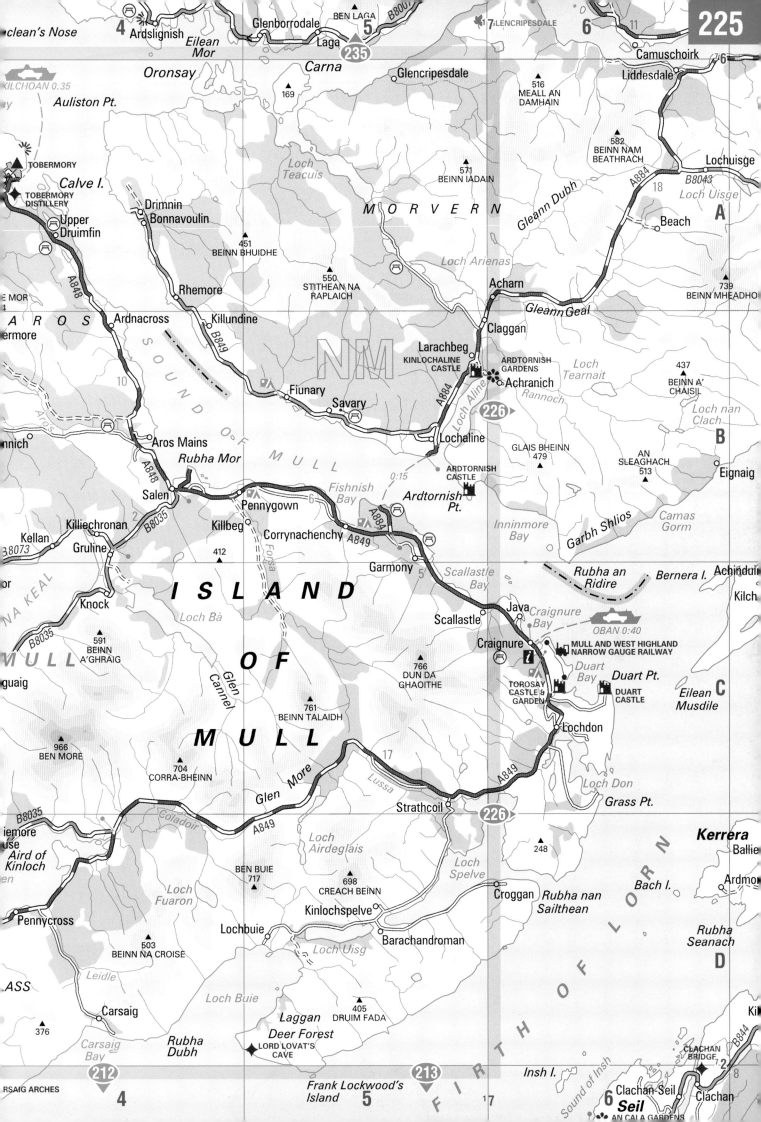

Maclean's Nose
4
Ardslignish
Eilean Mor
Oronsay
Auliston Pt.
KILCHOAN 0:35

BEN LAGA
Glenborrodale
5
Laga
B8007
235
Carna
Glencripesdale
7
Glencripesdale
6
11
Camuschoirk
6
Liddesdale
169
MEALL AN DAMHAIN
516
BEINN NAM BEATHRACH
582
Lochuisge
A884
B8043
18
Loch Uisge
Beach
A

TOBERMORY
Calve I.
TOBERMORY DISTILLERY
Upper Druimfin
Drimnin
Bonnavoulin
MORVERN
Loch Teacuis
BEINN IADAIN
571
BEINN NAM BEATHRACH
Loch Arienas
BEINN A' CHAISIL
437
BEINN MHEADHO
739

BEINN BHUIDHE
451
STITHEAN NA RAPLAICH
550
Acharn
Gleann Geal
AROS
Ardnacross
Rhemore
Killundine
B849
NM
A884
Claggan
Larachbeg
KINLOCHALINE CASTLE
ARDTORNISH GARDENS
Achranich
Loch Tearnait
Rannoch

10
SOUND
Fiunary
Savary
226
GLAIS BHEINN
479
AN SLEAGHACH
513
Eignaig
B

Aros Mains
Rubha Mor
OF
Lochaline
ARDTORNISH CASTLE
Ardtornish Pt.
Inninmore Bay
Garbh Shlios
Camas Gorm

nnich
Salen
A848
MULL
Fishnish Bay
0:15

Kellan
Killiechronan
Gruline
B8073
B8035
2
Pennygown
Killbeg
412
Corrynachenchy
A849
Garmony
5
A884
Scallastle Bay
Rubha an Ridire
Bernera I.
Achindui
Kilch

MULL
Knock
B8035
Loch Bà
ISLAND
Forsa
Scallastle
Java
Craignure Bay
OBAN 0:40
C

BEINN A'GHRAIG
591
OF
Glen Cannel
DUN DA GHAOITHE
766
Craignure
MULL AND WEST HIGHLAND NARROW GAUGE RAILWAY
Duart Bay
Duart Pt.
Eilean Musdile

guaig
BEINN TALAIDH
761
MULL
TOROSAY CASTLE & GARDEN
DUART CASTLE

BEN MORE
966
CORRA-BHEINN
704
Glen More
Lussa
17
A849
Lochdon
Loch Don
Grass Pt.
Kerrera
Ballie

iemore
use
Aird of Kinloch
B8035
Coladoir
A849
Loch Airdeglais
Strathcoil
226
248
Bach I.
Ardmo

Pennycross
BEINN NA CROISE
503
BEN BUIE
717
CREACH BEINN
698
Loch Spelve
Croggan
Rubha nan Sailthean
Rubha Seanach
D

376
Leidle
Loch Buie
Carsaig
Laggan
DRUIM FADA
405
Kinlochspelve
Lochbuie
Barachandroman
Loch Uisg
Insh I.
CLACHAN BRIDGE
B844

ASS
Carsaig Bay
Rubha Dubh
Deer Forest
LORD LOVAT'S CAVE
Frank Lockwood's Island
FIRTH OF LORN
Sound of Insh
Seil
AN CALA GARDENS
Clachan-Seil
Clachan

212
4
213
5
17
6

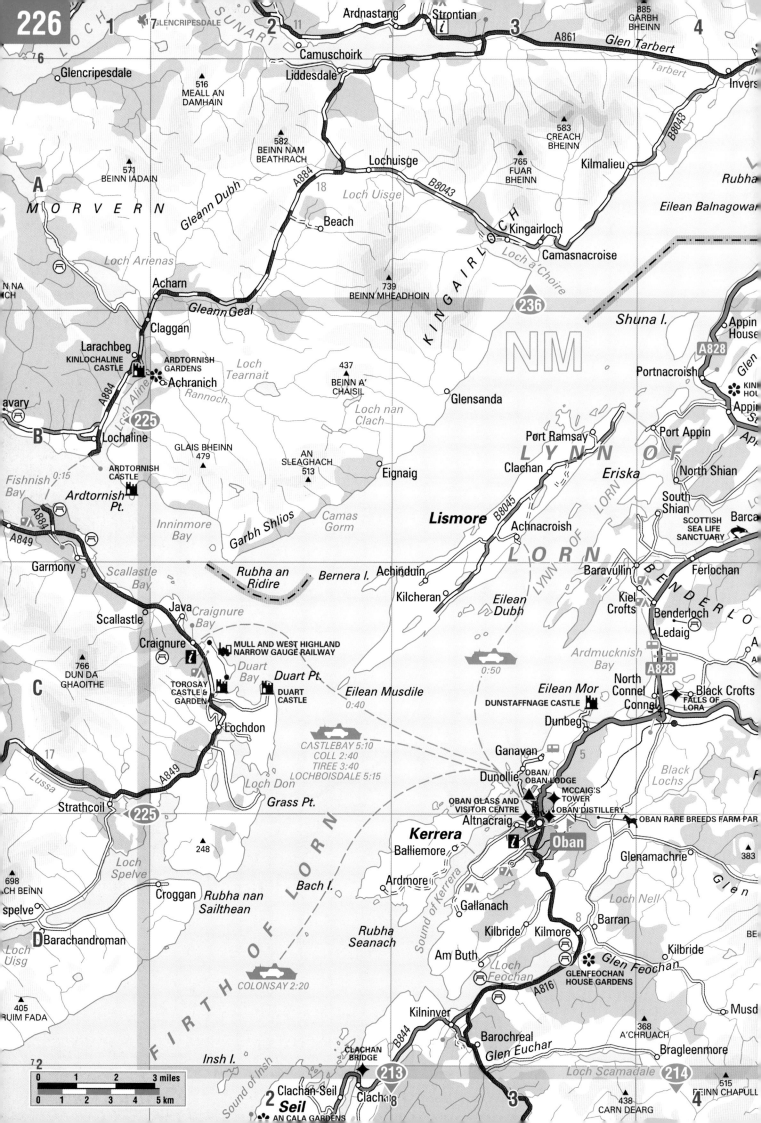

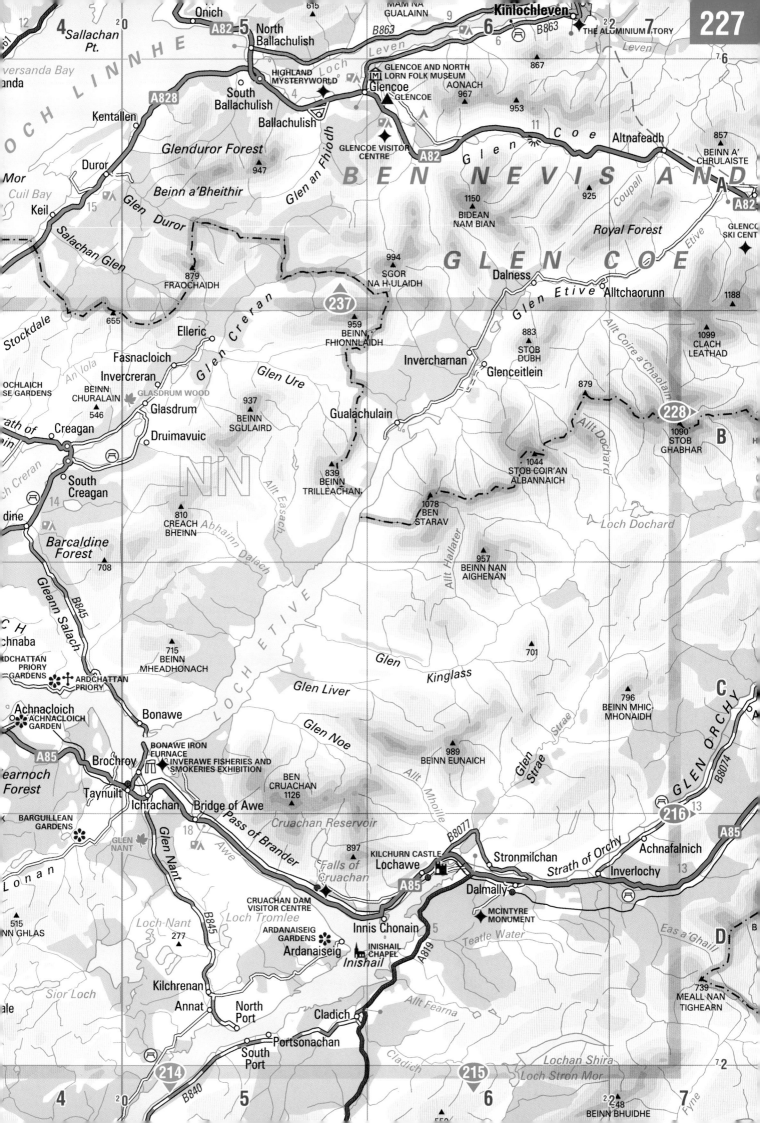

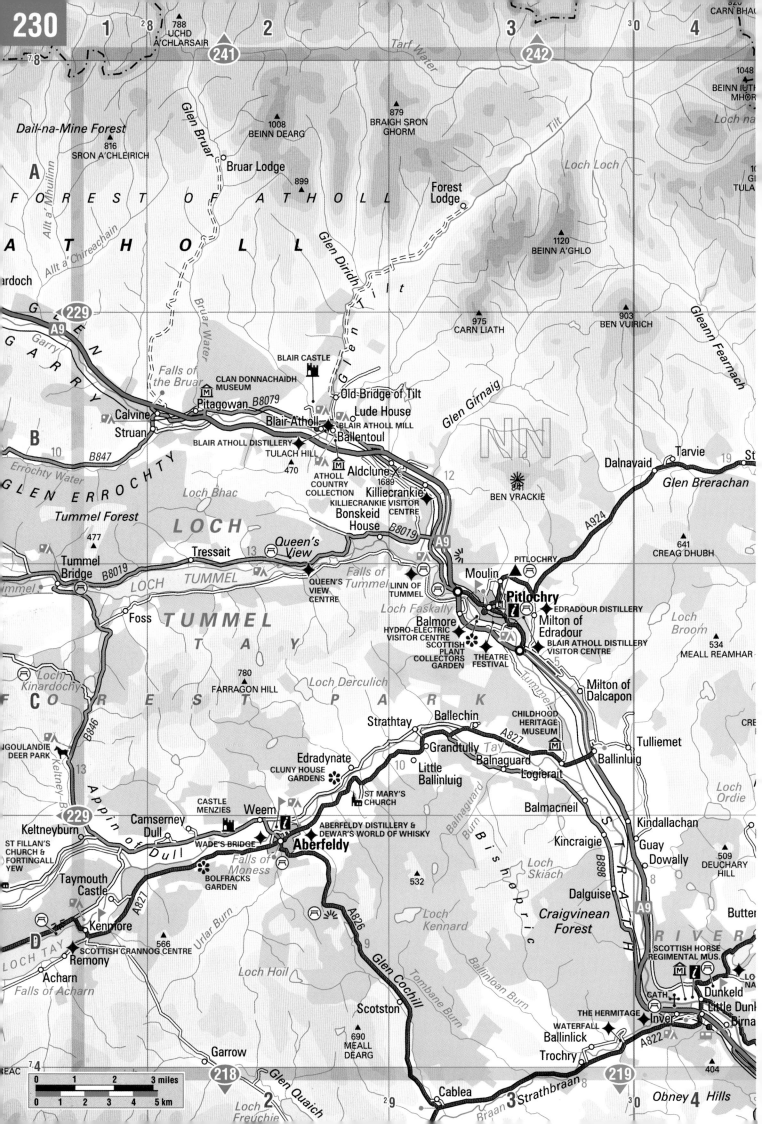

**1**    2⁸ 8 I   788    **2**    **3**    3⁰    **4**

UCHD
A'CHLARSAIR

⁷ 8

CARN BHAC

241    242

1048
BEINN IUTH
MHOR

Tarf Water

Loch na

Dail-na-Mine Forest

816
SRON A'CHLEIRICH

Glen Bruar

1008
BEINN DEARG

879
BRAIGH SRON
GHORM

Loch Loch

Loch
TULA

**A**

FOREST OF ATHOLL

Bruar Lodge

899

Forest
Lodge

975
CARN LIATH

903
BEN VUIRICH

Gleann Fearnach

FOREST

Allt a' Mhuilinn

Allt a' Chireachain

Glen Diridh

Tilt

1120
BEINN A'GHLO

229   A9

GLEN GARRY

Garry

Falls of
the Bruar

BLAIR CASTLE

CLAN DONNACHAIDH
MUSEUM

Old-Bridge of Tilt

Glen

Glen Girnaig

**NN**

B847

Pitagowan   B8079

Lude House

ardoch

Calvine

Struan

Blair-Atholl

BLAIR ATHOLL MILL
Ballentoul

BLAIR ATHOLL DISTILLERY

TULACH HILL

470

ATHOLL
COUNTRY
COLLECTION

Aldclune

1689

Killiecrankie

KILLIECRANKIE VISITOR
CENTRE

12

BEN VRACKIE
841

Dalnavaid

Tarvie

19   St

Glen Brerachan

**B**

10

GLEN ERROCHTY

Errochty Water

Tummel Forest

477

Loch Bhac

LOCH

Tressait

Bonskeid
House

B8019

A9

PITLOCHRY

Moulin

Pitlochry

641
CREAG DHUBH

A924

Tummel
Bridge

B8019

Queen's
View

13

QUEEN'S
VIEW
CENTRE

Falls of
Tummel

Linn of
Tummel

Loch Faskally

Edradour Distillery

Loch
Broom

LOCH TUMMEL

Foss

TUMMEL

TAY

Balmore

HYDRO-ELECTRIC
VISITOR CENTRE

SCOTTISH
PLANT
COLLECTORS
GARDEN

THEATRE
FESTIVAL

Milton of
Edradour

BLAIR ATHOLL DISTILLERY
VISITOR CENTRE

5

534
MEALL REAMHAR

Milton of
Dalcapon

**C**

Loch
Kinardochy

780
FARRAGON HILL

Loch Derculich

FOREST    PARK

Ballechin

Strathtay

CHILDHOOD
HERITAGE
MUSEUM

Tulliemet

CR

B846

ngoulandie
DEER PARK

Keltney B

13

Grandtully

A827

Tay

Balnaguard

Ballinluig

Loch
Ordie

APPIN OF DULL

Edradynate

CLUNY HOUSE
GARDENS

10

Little
Ballinluig

Logierait

Balmacneil

Kindallachan

229

Keltneyburn

ST FILLAN'S
CHURCH &
FORTINGALL
YEW

Camserney
Dull

CASTLE
MENZIES

Weem

St MARY'S
CHURCH

ABERFELDY DISTILLERY &
DEWAR'S WORLD OF WHISKY

Bainaguard
Burn

Kincraigie

Guay

Dowally

509
DEUCHARY
HILL

WADE'S BRIDGE

Aberfeldy

Kincraigie

B898

8

STRATH

A9

**D**

Taymouth
Castle

A827

Kenmore

566

SCOTTISH CRANNOG CENTRE

Remony

Acharn

Falls of Acharn

LOCH TAY

BOLFRACKS
GARDEN

Falls of
Moness

Urlar Burn

532

A826

Loch
Kennard

Loch
Skiach

Dalguise

Craigvinean
Forest

RIVER

SCOTTISH HORSE
REGIMENTAL MUS.

CATH

Dunkeld

Little Dun

Birna

Butter

LO
NA

⁷ 4

EAC

0   1   2   3 miles
0   1   2   3   4   5 km

218

Garrow

Glen Quaich

Loch
Freuchie

2⁹

690
MEALL
DEARG

Scotston

Glen Cochill

Tombane Burn

Ballinloan Burn

Bishopric

THE HERMITAGE

WATERFALL

Ballinlick

Trochry

A822

Inver

219

Cablea

Strathbraan 8

Braan 3

Obney 4 Hills

404

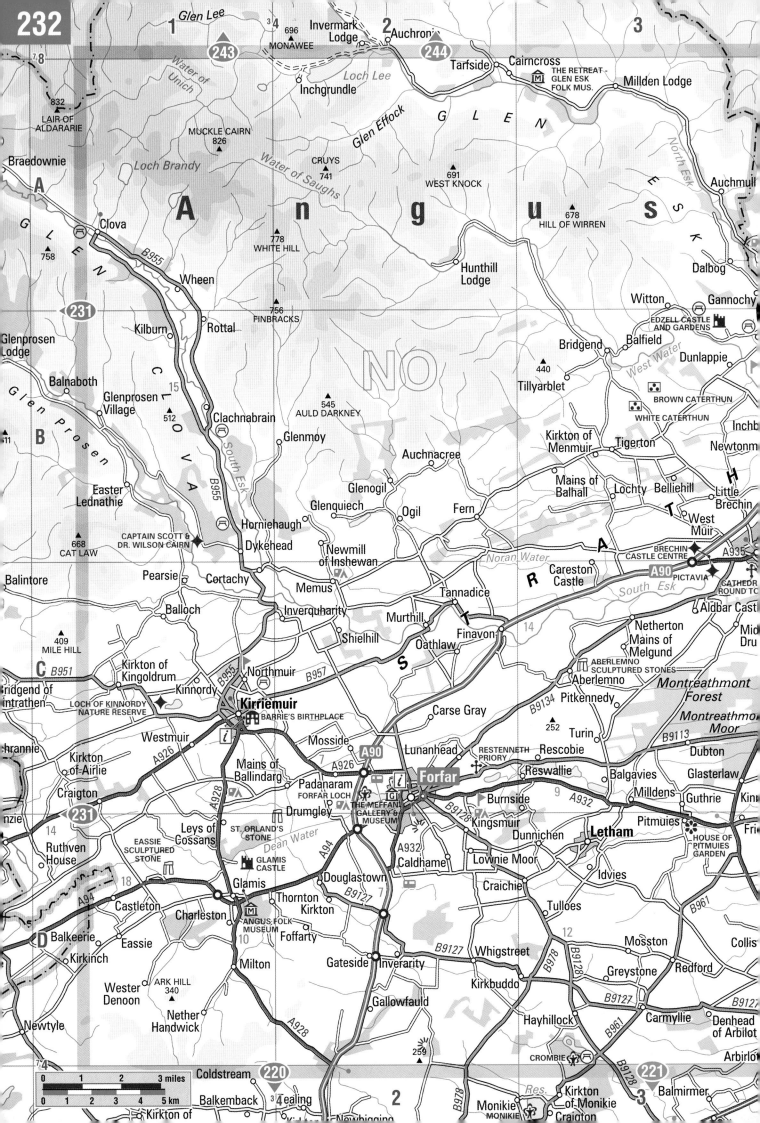

THE SMALL ISLES

1    2    3

A

B

C

D

*Guirdil Bay*

388

246    *Kimory Glen*    *Kinloch Glen*

CANNA 1:15    *Rubha na Roinne*

A'Bhrideanach

Kinloch    *Loch Scresort*

R    Ù    M

571
ORVAL    *RÙM*    KINLOCH
CASTLE    *Rubha Port
na Caranean*

Schooner Pt.

Harris    *Glen Harris*

812
ASKIVAL

1:30

Rubha Sgorr
an t-Snidhe    781
AINSHVAL

1:15

Rubha nam
Meirleach

*SOUND OF RÙM*

*Bay of Laig*    Cleadale

*Rubha an
Fhasaidh*    **Eigg**    Kildo

393
AN SGURR    Galmisc

*Eile*

*SOUND OF EIGG*

*Eilean nan Each*

0:40

137    Port Mor

**Muck**

*Sanna Point*

Sanna

*Sanna Bay*    Portuairk    Achnaha

Point of
Ardnamurchan    Achosnich
ARDNAMURCHAN LIGHTHOUSE

223    Cairns of Coll

223    Ormsaigmore    Kilcho

Rubha Mor    Eilean Mor    B8007    Ormsaigbeg

Sorisdale    *Kilchoan
Bay*

Bousd    *An Acairseid*

B8072

**COLL**

Arnab    Gallanach

B8071

0    1    2    3 miles
0    1    2    3    4    5 km

224    *Ardmore Bay*    *Ardmore Pt.*

*Bloody*

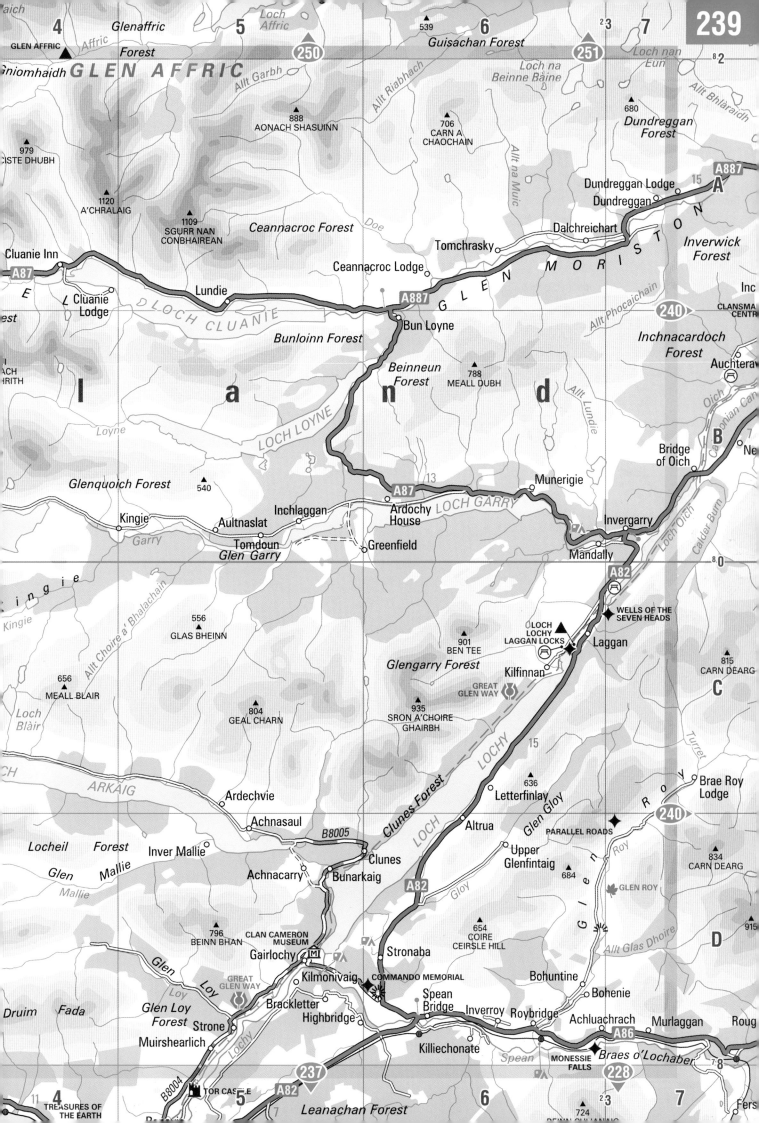

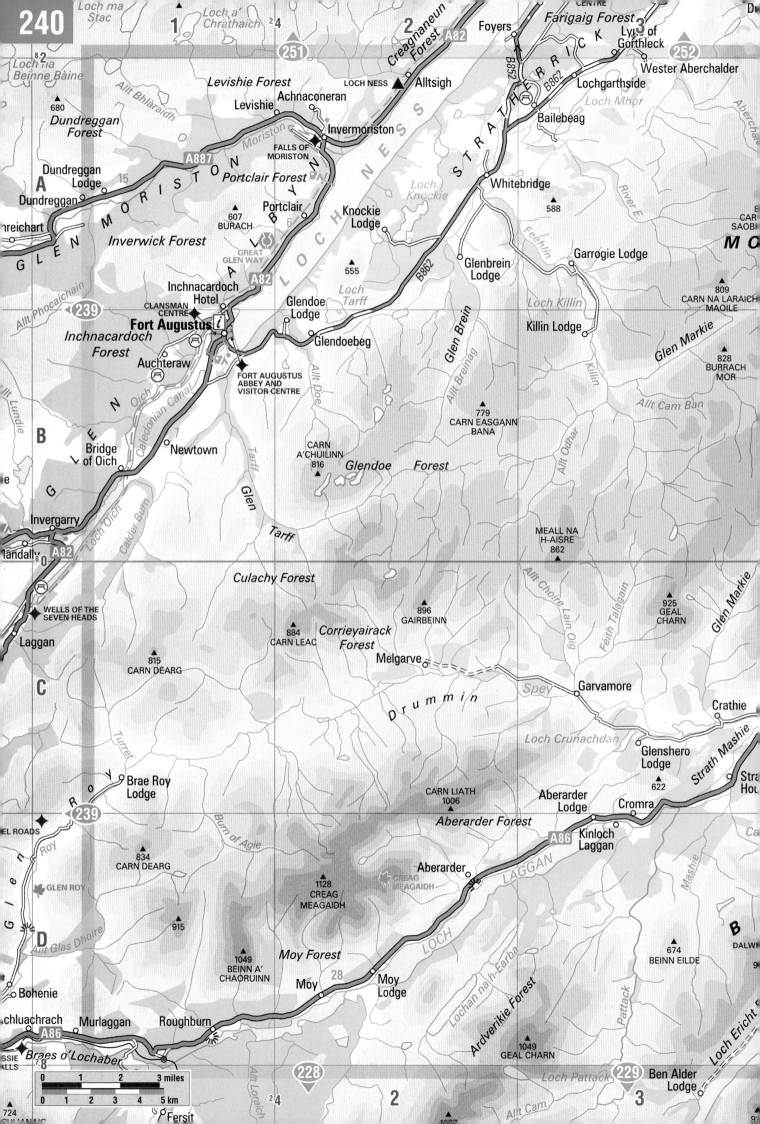

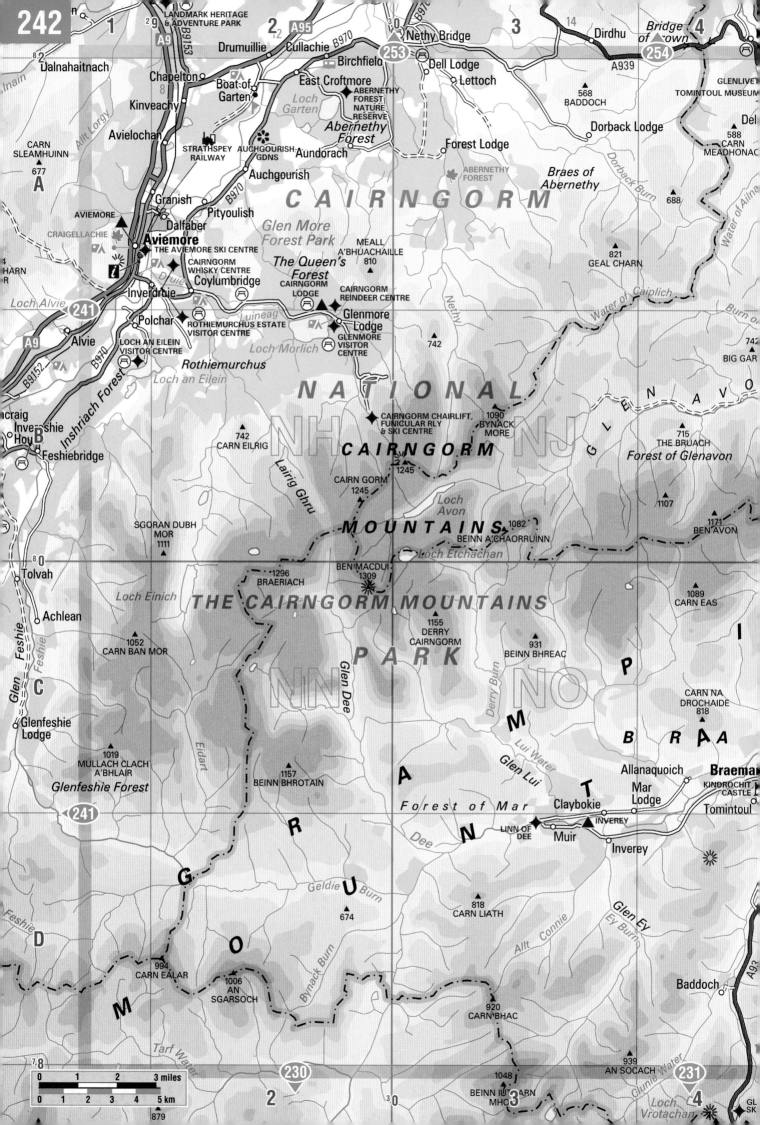

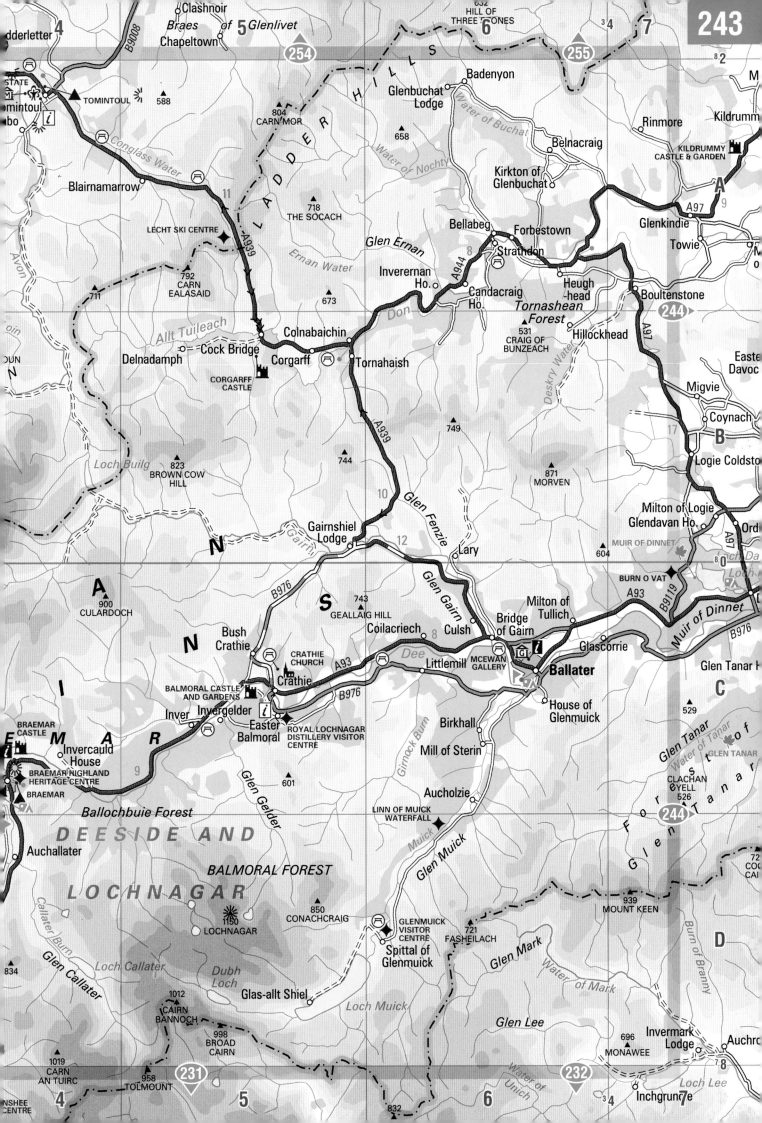

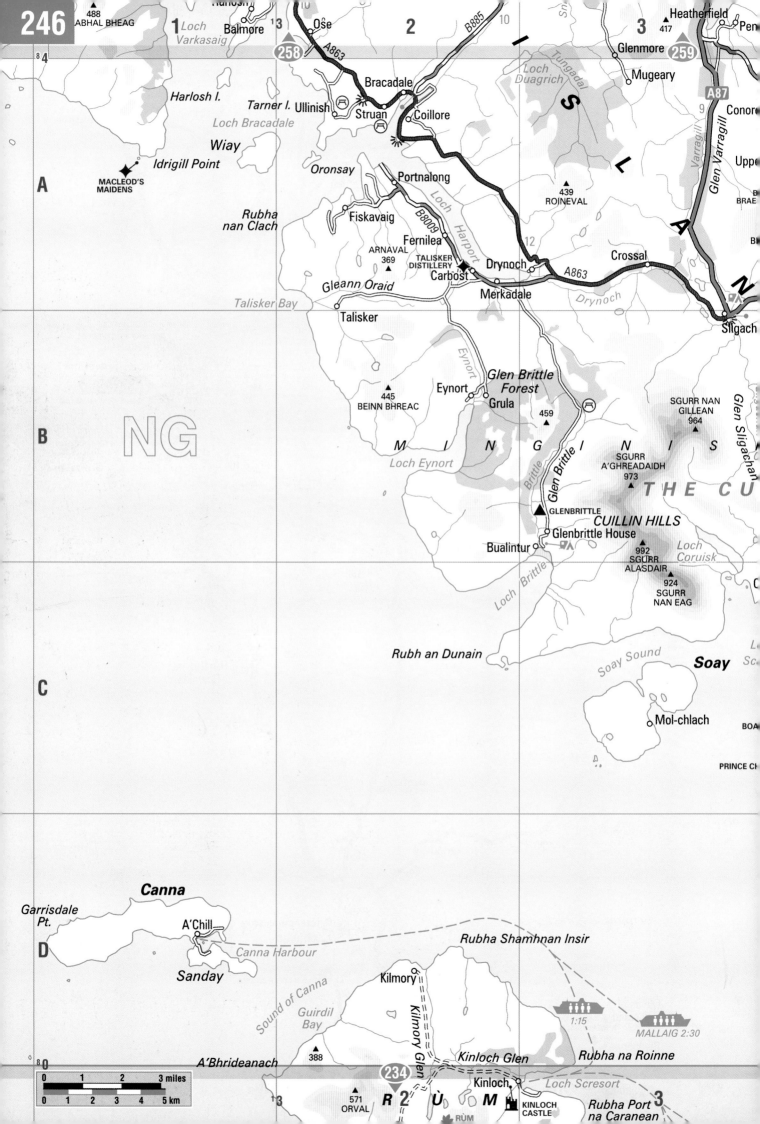

488
ABHAL BHEAG

Loch
Varkasaig
Balmore
13
Ose
**1**
**2**
B885
10
Heatherfield
Pen
417
**3**
259

ISLA

258
A863

B885
10

Loch
Duagrich
Glenmore
Mugeary
A87

Bracadale

Harlosh I.

Tarner I. Ullinish
Struan
Coillore
Glen Varragill
Conor

Upp
BRAE
B

Wiay

*Idrigill Point*

Oronsay

Portnalong

Loch Harport

439
ROINEVAL

Varragill

MACLEOD'S
MAIDENS

**A**

Rubha
nan Clach

Fiskavaig

B8009

Crossal

Talisker
Bay
Fernilea
ARNAVAL
369
TALISKER
DISTILLERY
Carbost
Drynoch
12
A863
Drynoch
Sligach

N

Gleann Oraid
Merkadale

Talisker

Eynort

Eynort

Grula
445
BEINN BHREAC

Glen Brittle
Forest

459

SGURR NAN
GILLEAN
964

Glen Sligachan

NG

**B**

Loch Eynort

Brittle

Glen Brittle

SGURR
A'GHREADAIDH
973

THE CU

I N I S

GLENBRITTLE

CUILLIN HILLS

Glenbrittle House

Bualintur

Loch Brittle

992
SGURR
ALASDAIR

Loch
Coruisk

924
SGURR
NAN EAG

Rubh an Dunain

Soay Sound

**Soay**

L
Sc

**C**

Mol-chlach

BOA

PRINCE CH

*Canna*

Garrisdale
Pt.
A'Chill

Rubha Shamhnan Insir

**D**

Canna Harbour

*Sanday*

Sound of Canna

Kilmory

Kilmory Glen

Guirdil
Bay

Kilmory Glen

388

Kinloch Glen

1:15

MALLAIG 2:30

Rubha na Roinne

A'Bhrideanach

234

Kinloch
KINLOCH
CASTLE

Loch Scresort

**3**

13
571
ORVAL
R 2 Ù
RÙM
M
*Rubha Port
na Caranean*

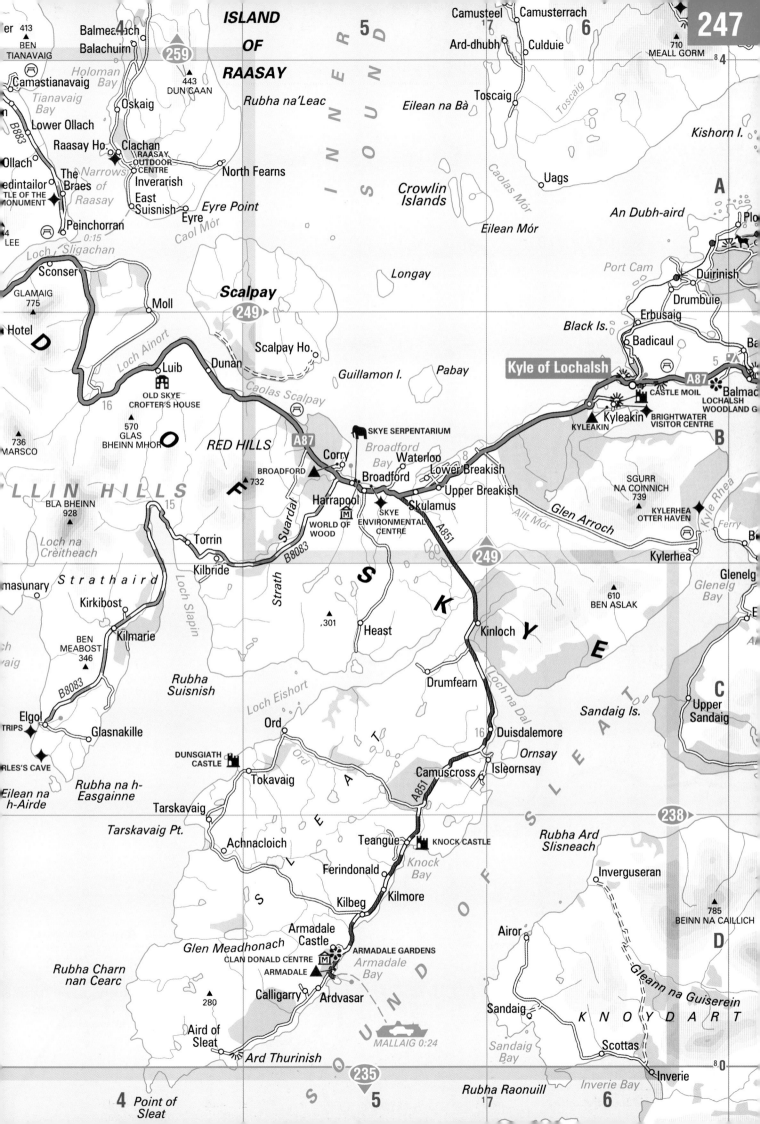

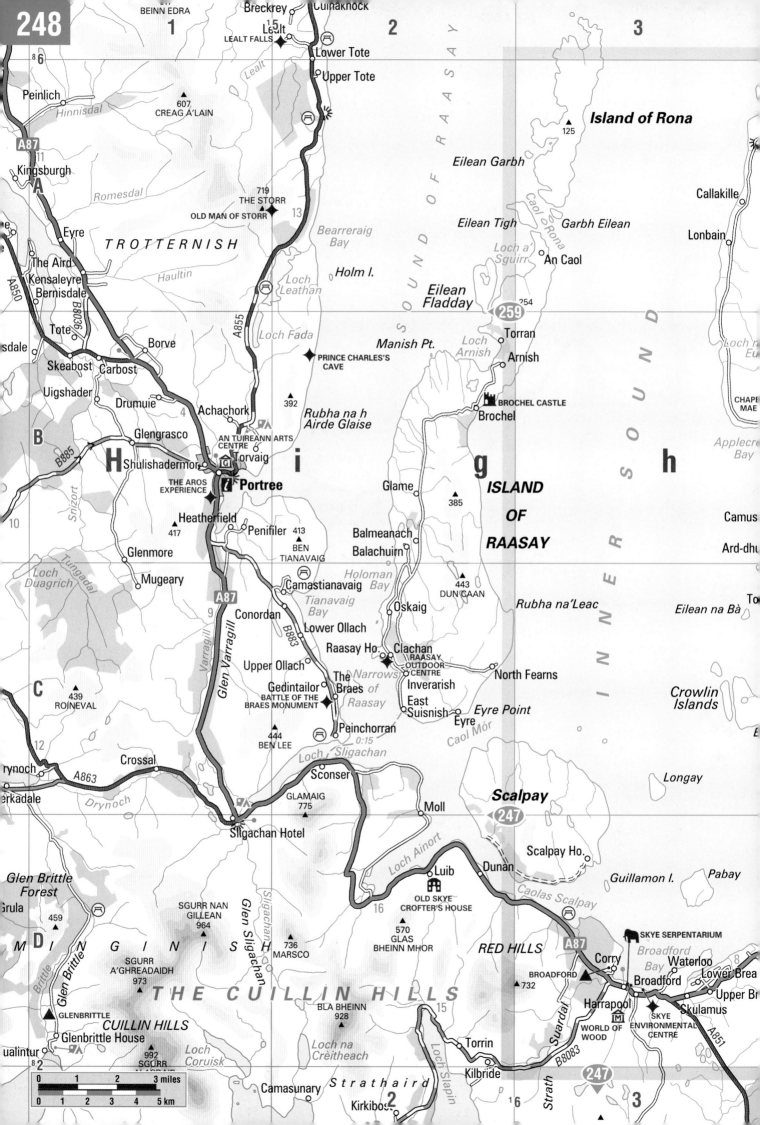

**248**

1    2    3

BEINN EDRA
Breckrey    Cuinaknock

Lealt    Lealt
LEALT FALLS
Lower Tote
Upper Tote

Peinlich
*Hinnisdal*
607
CREAG A'LAIN

**Island of Rona**
125

Eilean Garbh

A87
Kingsburgh

*Romesdal*
THE STORR    719
OLD MAN OF STORR

Eilean Tigh    Garbh Eilean

Callakille
Lonbain

Eyre
The Aird
Kensaleyre
Bernisdale

T R O T T E R N I S H
*Haultin*

*Bearreraig Bay*

Loch Leathan

An Caol

Tote
Borve
Skeabost
Carbost

Loch Fada

*Manish Pt.*
PRINCE CHARLES'S CAVE

Holm I.

Eilean Fladday    259    254

Loch a' Sguirr

Loch Arnish    Torran
Arnish

Uigshader
Drumuie
Achachork    392
*Rubha na h Airde Glaise*

BROCHEL CASTLE
Brochel

CHAPEL MAE

B    B885
Glengrasco
Shulishadermor

AN TUIREANN ARTS CENTRE
Torvaig

i    g    **ISLAND OF RAASAY**    h    *Applecross Bay*

THE AROS EXPERIENCE
**Portree**

Glame    385

Camus
Ard-dhu

Heatherfield    417

Penifiler    413
BEN TIANAVAIG    392

Balmeanach
Balachuirn

Glenmore
Mugeary

*Loch Duagrich*    *Tungadal*

*Holoman Bay*    443    DUN CAAN
*Rubha na'Leac*

*Eilean na Bà*

Camastianavaig
*Tianavaig Bay*

Oskaig

A87    Conordan
Lower Ollach

B883

Raasay Ho.    Clachan
RAASAY OUTDOOR CENTRE

*Crowlin Islands*

C    439
ROINEVAL    Upper Ollach

Gedintailor
BATTLE OF THE BRAES MONUMENT

The Braes    *Narrows of Raasay*

Inverarish
East Suisnish
Eyre    Eyre Point

North Fearns

Crossal
*Drynoch*    A863

444    BEN LEE    Peinchorran    0:15

*Loch Sligachan*

*Caol Mór*

*Longay*

Sconser

GLAMAIG    775    Moll    **Scalpay**    247

*Glen Brittle Forest*    *Sligachan Hotel*

*Loch Ainort*

Scalpay Ho.

Dunan
*Caolas Scalpay*

*Guillamon I.*    *Pabay*

Grula    459

SGURR NAN GILLEAN    964

*Glen Sligachan*

Luib    OLD SKYE CROFTER'S HOUSE

SKYE SERPENTARIUM
*Broadford Bay*
Waterloo
Lower Brea

M    D    I    N    G    I    N    I    S    H    736    MARSCO

570    GLAS BHEINN MHOR

**RED HILLS**    A87    Corry    Broadford

Glenbrittle
CUILLIN HILLS

SGURR A'GHREADAIDH    973

**T H E   C U I L L I N   H I L L S**

BLA BHEINN    928

732    BROADFORD

Harrapool    SKYE ENVIRONMENTAL CENTRE    Skulamus

Glenbrittle House

992    SGURR

*Loch Coruisk*

*Loch na Crèitheach*

Torrin
WORLD OF WOOD    A851

247

0    1    2    3 miles
0    1    2    3    4    5 km

Camasunary    *S t r a t h a i r d*

Kirkibost    Kilbride    *Loch Slapin*    *Strath*    B8083

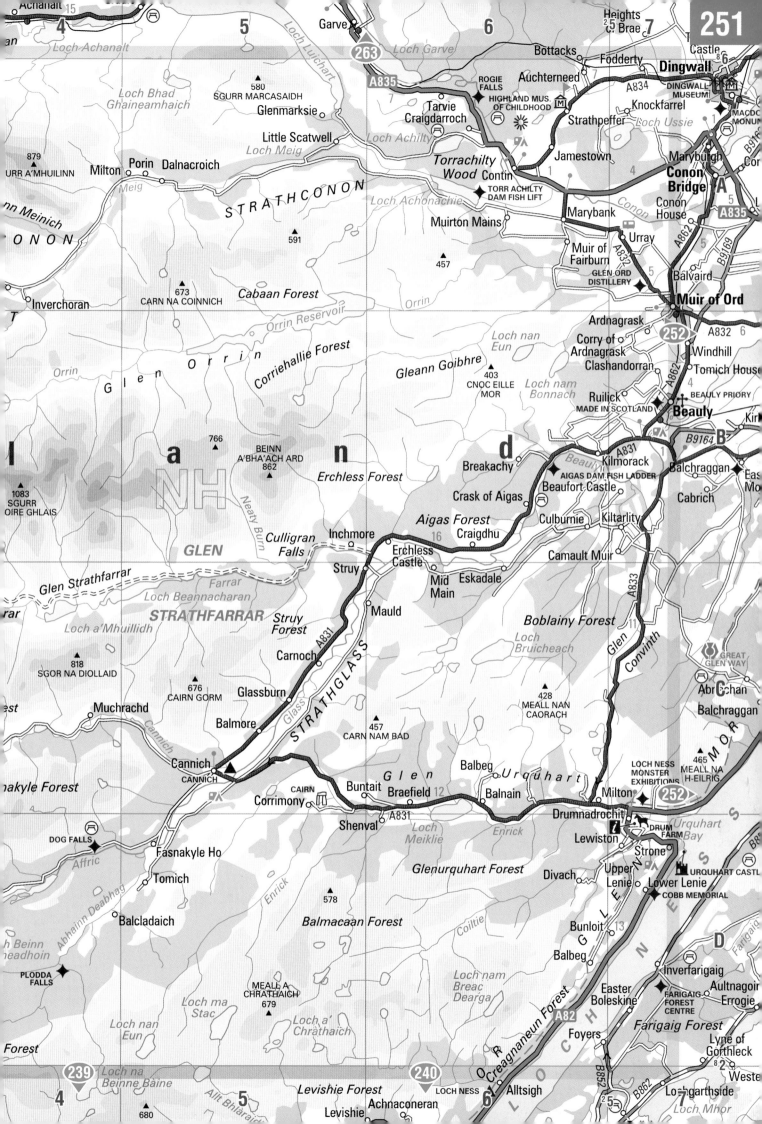

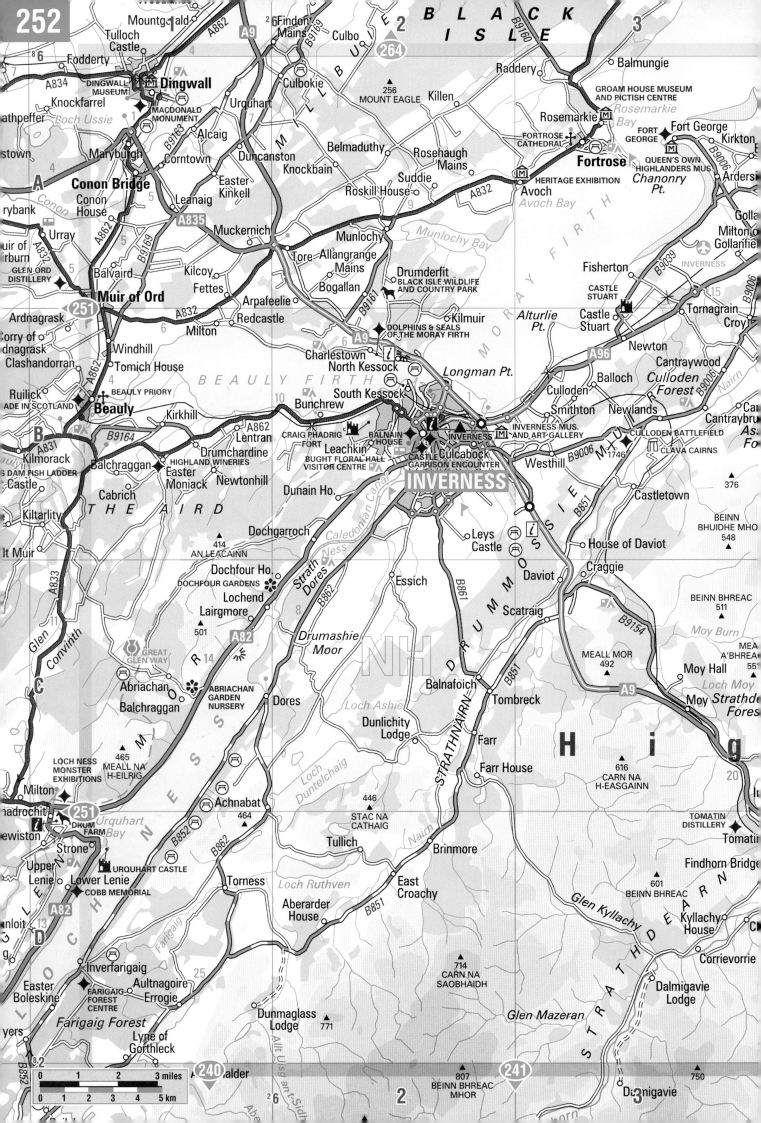

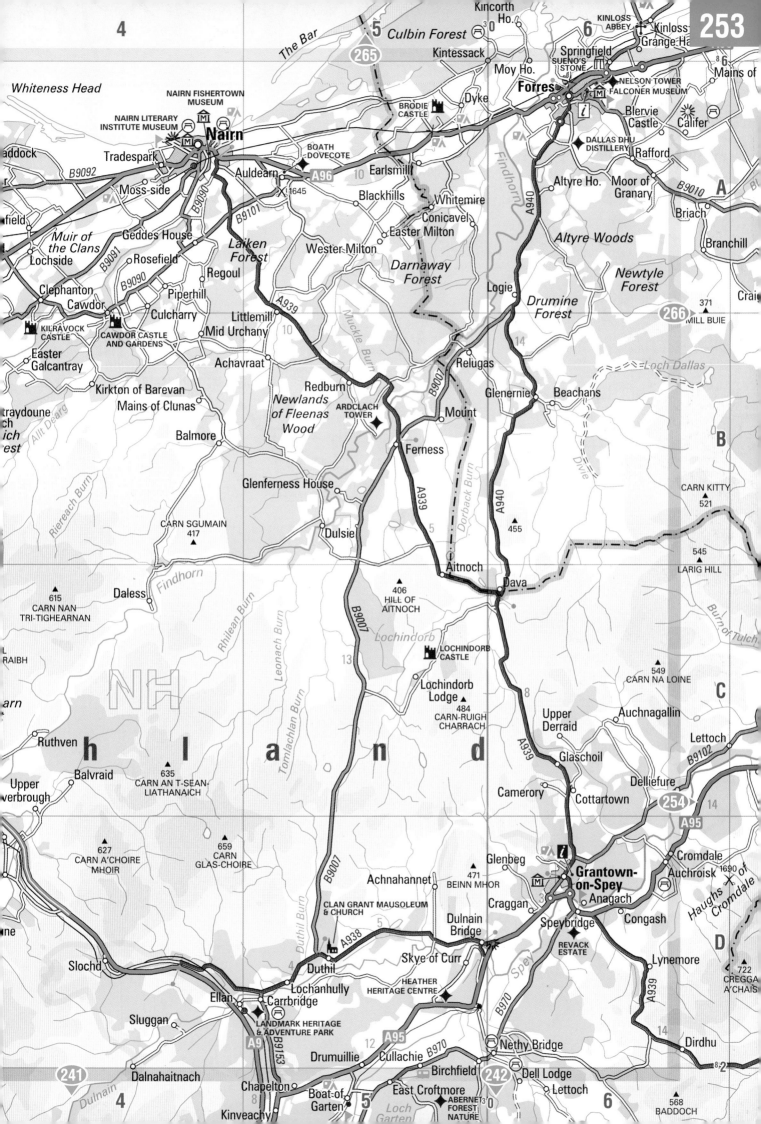

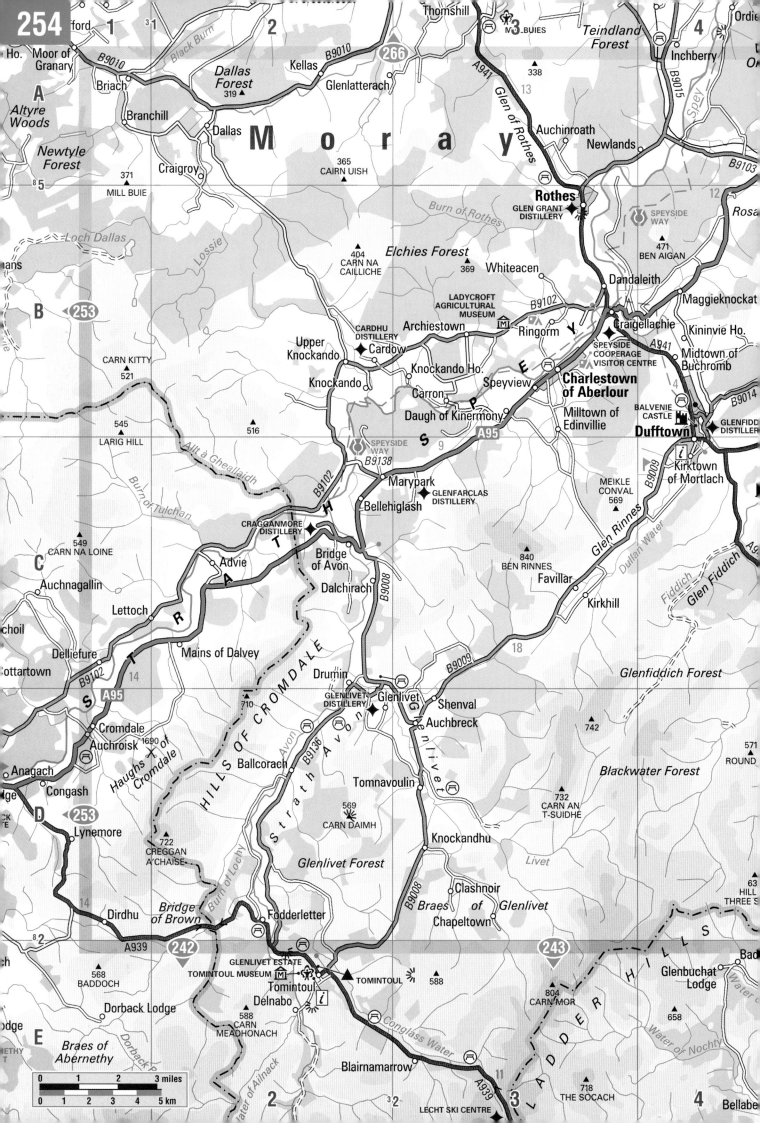

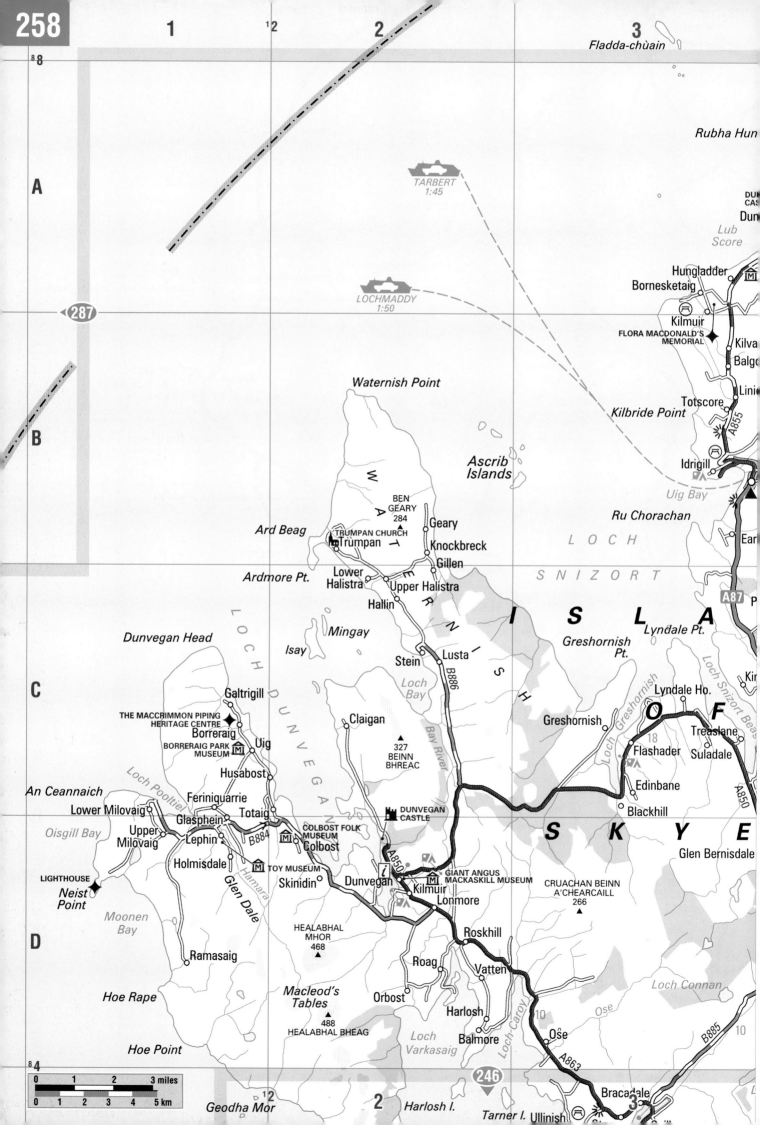

**1** | **2** | **3**

**A**

Fladda-chùain

Rubha Hun

TARBERT
1:45

LOCHMADDY
1:50

**B**

Lub
Score

Hungladder

Bornesketaig

DUN
CAS

Dun

Kilmuir

FLORA MACDONALD'S
MEMORIAL

Kilva

Balgo

Linie

Totscore

Kilbride Point

Idrigill

Uig Bay

Waternish Point

Ascrib
Islands

Ru Chorachan

LOCH

**C**

Ard Beag

BEN
GEARY
284

Geary

TRUMPAN CHURCH

Trumpan

Knockbreck

Gillen

Ardmore Pt.

Lower
Halistra

Upper Halistra

Hallin

SNIZORT

Earl

A87

ISLA

Lyndale Pt.

Dunvegan Head

Isay

Mingay

Loch
Bay

Stein

Lusta

B886

Greshornish
Pt.

O

F

Greshornish

Lyndale Ho.

Loch Snizort Bea

Kir

Galtrigill

THE MACCRIMMON PIPING
HERITAGE CENTRE

Borreraig

BORRERAIG PARK
MUSEUM

Uig

Husabost

Claigan

327
BEINN
BHREAC

Bay River

Loch Greshornish

18

Treaslane

Flashader

Suladale

An Ceannaich

Lower Milovaig

Feriniquarrie

Totaig

Edinbane

Loch Pooltiel

Glasphein

COLBOST FOLK
MUSEUM

Colbost

DUNVEGAN
CASTLE

Blackhill

A850

S K Y E

**D**

Oisgill Bay

Upper
Milovaig

Lephin

B884

TOY MUSEUM

Glen Bernisdale

Holmisdale

Skinidin

Dunvegan

Kilmuir

GIANT ANGUS
MACKASKILL MUSEUM

CRUACHAN BEINN
A'CHEARCAILL
266

LIGHTHOUSE

Neist
Point

Glen Dale

Hamara

A850

Lonmore

Moonen
Bay

Ramasaig

HEALABHAL
MHOR
468

Roskhill

Roag

Vatten

Loch Connan

Hoe Rape

Macleod's
Tables

Orbost

Harlosh

Loch-Caroy

10

Loch Connan

Ose

B885

10

Hoe Point

HEALABHAL BHEAG
488

Loch
Varkasaig

Balmore

Ose

A863

84

0   1   2   3 miles
0 1 2 3 4 5 km

Geodha Mor

2

Harlosh I.

246

Tarner I. Ullinish

Bracadale

3

4 · 5 · 6

8

A

260

261

Eilean Trodday

Rubha na h-Aiseig

TULM
CASTLE
ulm

Balmacqueen

Kilmaluag

20

MUSEUM OF
ISLAND LIFE

Flodigarry

Eilean
Flodigarry

MEALL NA
SUIRAMACH
543

Digg

Staffin I.

Glashvin

Staffin
Bay

THE QUIRAING

Brogaig

ter

Staffin

wn

Stenscholl

TROTTERNISH

Kilt Rock

466
BIOD BUIDHE

Elishader

KILT ROCK & MEALT FALLS

Maligar

Loch Mealt

Valtos

NG

Rha

Marishader

Garros

Rubha nam
Brathairean

Uig

B

JIG

Balnaknock

Conon

611
BEINN EDRA

Breckrey

Culnaknock

sh

Lealt

Lower Tote

LEALT FALLS

Upper Tote

inlich

Hinnisdal

N        D

607
CREAG A'LAIN

11

gsburgh

Romesdal

719
THE STORR

Island of Rona

125

Eilean Garbh

Caol Rona

Callakille

C

Eyre

OLD MAN OF STORR

13

Bearreraig
Bay

Eilean Tigh

Garbh Eilean

Lonbain

The Aird

Haultin

TROTTERNISH

Holm I.

Loch a'
Sguirr

An Caol

Cua

Allt na h-

ensaleyre

Bernisdale

Loch
Leathan

Eilean
Fladday

249

Tote

A855

Loch Fada

Manish Pt.

Loch
Arnish

Torran

Loch nan
Eun

Skeabost

B8036

Borve

PRINCE CHARLES'S
CAVE

Arnish

Carbost

Uigshader

Drumuie

Achachork

392

Rubha na h
Airde Glaise

BROCHEL CASTLE

Brochel

CHAPEL OF ST
MAELRUBHA

D

4

Glengrasco

AN TUIREANN ARTS
CENTRE

Shulishadermor

Torvaig

THE AROS
EXPERIENCE

Portree

ISLAND

Applecross
Bay

Heatherfield

Penifiler

413

Glame

385

OF

RAASAY

Camusteel

417

BEN
TIANAVAIG

Balmeanach

Ard-dhubh

Glenmore

Balachuirn

4

Mugeary

Loch
uagrich

A87

Tungadal

9

Conordan

Camastianavaig

B883

Tianavaig
Bay

Holoman Bay

248

Uskaig

5

DUN CAAN
443

6

Rubha na' Leac

Eilean na Bà

Toscaig

Snizort

1    ¹5    2    3

*Garbh Eilean*

*Eilean Mhuire*

*Eilean an Tighe*

*Na h-Eileanan Mòra (Shiant Islands)*

A

288

288

NG

B

259

*Eilean Trodday*

*Rubha Hunish*

*Rubha na h-Aiseig*

259

**DUN** C **LM CASTLE**

20

Balmacqueen

Duntulm

Kilmaluag

MUSEUM OF ISLAND LIFE

*Eilean Flodigarry*

Flodigarry

MEALL NA SUIRAMACH

543

Diggl

*Staffin I.*

Kilvaxter

Glashvin

*Staffin Bay*

Balgown

THE QUIRAING

Brogaig

Linicro

Stenscholl

Staffin

*TROTTERNISH*

Kilt Rock

KILT ROCK & MEALT FALLS

466

BIOD BUIDHE

D

Elishader

Uig

Maligar

*Loch Mealt*

Marishader

Valtos

UIG

*Rubha nam Brathairean*

Balnaknock

Garros

611

BEINN EDRA

Breckrey

Culnaknock

**Island of Rona**

Earlish

Lealt

LEALT FALLS

⁸6

Lower Tote

0    1    2    3 miles

0  1  2  3  4  5 km

Upper Tote

¹5

2    3

*Uinnisdal*    607
CREAG A'LAIN

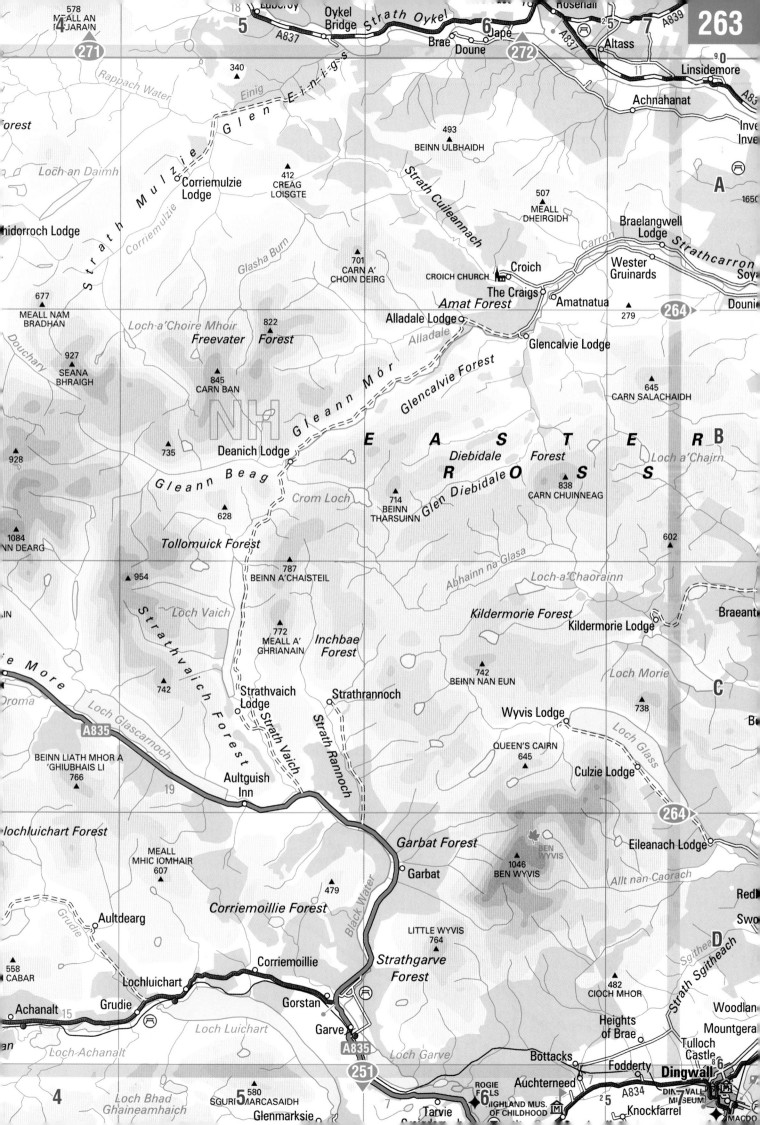

578
M'ALL AN
4 T'JARAIN
271

18
Euberoy
Oykel
Bridge
Strath Oykel
5
A837
6
Jape
Brae
Doune
272
A837
7
A839
25
Rosenall
Altass
11
9 0
Linsidemore
A83
Achnahanat

Inve
Inve

340

Rappach Water

Glen E-in-i-g-s
Einig

493
BEINN ULBHAIDH

507
MEALL
DHEIRGIDH

Carron

A

1650

Strath Mulzie

Corriemulzie
Lodge

412
CREAG
LOISGTE

Strath Cuileannach

Braelangwell
Lodge
Strathcarron

hidorroch Lodge

Corriemulzie

Glasha Burn

701
CARN A'
CHOIN DEIRG

Croich
CROICH CHURCH

The Craigs

Wester
Gruinards

Soy

677
MEALL NAM
BRADHAN

Loch-a'Choire Mhoir
Freevater
822
Forest

Alladale Lodge

Amat Forest

Amatnatua
279

264

Douni

Douchary

927
SEANA
BHRAIGH

845
CARN BAN

NH

Gleann Mór

Alladale

Glencalvie Lodge

Glencalvie Forest

EASTER

645
CARN SALACHAIDH

B
Loch a'Chairn

928

735

Deanich Lodge

R O S S

Diebidale Forest

838
CARN CHUINNEAG

1084
NN DEARG

Gleann Beag

Crom Loch

714
BEINN
THARSUINN

Glen Diebidale

602

954

628

Tollomuick Forest

787
BEINN A'CHAISTEIL

Abhainn na Glasa

Loch-a'Chaorainn

Braeant

Loch Vaich

772
MEALL A'
GHRIANAIN

Inchbae
Forest

Kildermorie Forest

Kildermorie Lodge

Strathvaich Forest

IN

e More
Oroma

Loch Glascarnoch
A835
19

742

Strathvaich
Lodge

Strath Vaich

Strathrannoch

Strath Rannoch

742
BEINN NAN EUN

Wyvis Lodge

Loch Morie

738

C

Be

BEINN LIATH MHOR A
'GHIUBHAIS LI
766

Aultguish
Inn

QUEEN'S CAIRN
645

Loch Glass

Culzie Lodge

264

ochluichart Forest

MEALL
MHIC IOMHAIR
607

479

Garbat Forest

Garbat

BEN
WYVIS

1046
BEN WYVIS

Eileanach Lodge

Allt nan-Caorach

D

Corriemoillie Forest

Black Water

LITTLE WYVIS
764

Strathgarve
Forest

Red
Swo

Grudie

Aultdearg

558
CABAR

Lochluichart

Grudie

Corriemoillie

Gorstan

CIOCH MHOR
482

Strath Sgitheach

Woodlan
Mountgera

Achanalt
15

Loch Luichart

Garve
A835

Loch Garve

Bottacks

Heights
of Brae

Fodderty

Tulloch
Castle
6

DINGWALL

Loch Achanalt

251

Auchterneed

A834

DIN
VALL
MUSEUM
7

Loch Bhad
Ghaineamhaich

4

580
SGURII
MARCASAIDH
5

Glenmarksie

ROGIE
F6LS
HIGHLAND MUS.
OF CHILDHOOD

Tarvie

25

Knockfarrel

MACDO

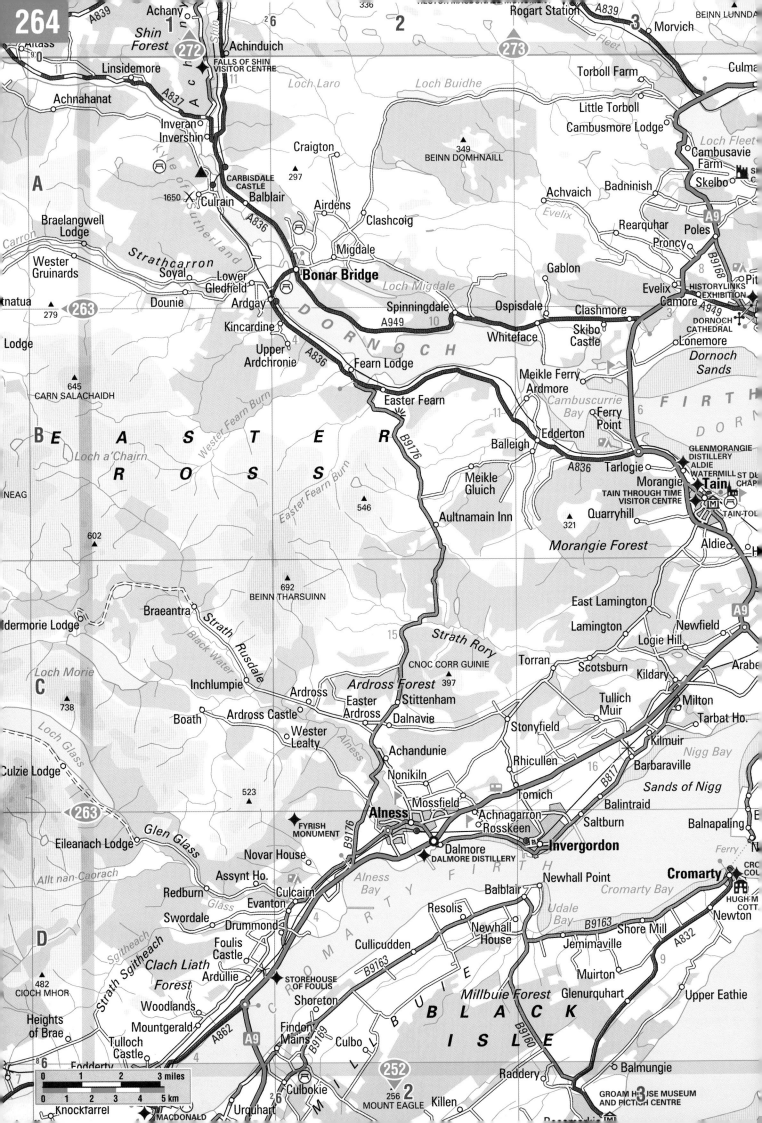

4  A9
**DUNROBIN CASTLE**
**MUSEUM & GARDENS**
**Golspie**

Kirkton

5  274
30  6

NH  NJ  A

LOCH
FLEET
Littleferry

KELBO
ASTLE

Fourpenny

Embo

Embo Street
grudy

WITCHES STONE
OLD POST OFFICE
VISITOR CENTRE
**Dornoch**

LOCH FIRTH

*Whiteness
Sands*

*Tarbat Ness*
**TARBAT NESS LIGHTHOUSE**
Wilkhaven

THUS'S

TARBAT DISCOVERY
CENTRE

Bindal

Portmahomack

Rockfield

Inver

Balnagall
OOTH
Arboll

Lochslin

Tarrel

*Loch
Eye*
Iton

B9165

Rhynie
Geanies House

Fearn Station

B9165

Fearn

Hill of Fearn
B9166

FEARN ABBEY

Hilton of Cadboll

Loans of Tullich

**Balintore**
SHANDWICK STONE
Shandwick

B9175
Ankerville

Chapelhill

*Port an Righ*

Pitcalnie

Nigg

203

*King's Cave*
ount Canisp

Inabruaich

Castlecraig
g Ferry

ARTY
T HOUSE

LER'S
GE
Sutors of Cromarty

266

**Burghead**

*BURGHEAD BAY*

M O R A Y   F I R T H

Findhorn
Lower
Hempriggs

D

*Findhorn
Bay*
B9011

Miltonhill

Kincorth
Ho.
KINLOSS
ABBEY
Kinloss

Grange Hall
A96

The Bar

*Culbin Forest*
Kintessack

Springfield

SUENO'S
STONE

NELSON TOWER
ALCONER MUSEUM

Mains of

253

Moy Ho.
Dyke

**Forres**

*Whiteness Head*  4

5

BRODIE
CASTLE

Blervie

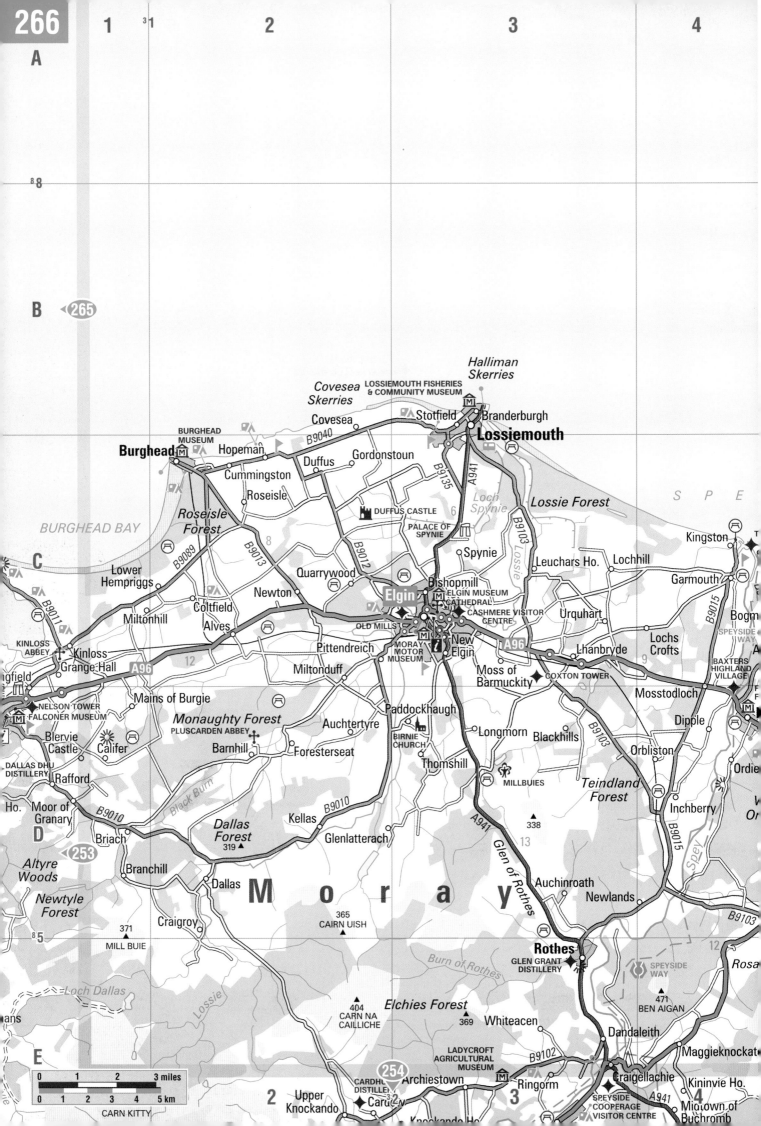

A

B

◁ 265

Halliman
Skerries

Covesea
Skerries

LOSSIEMOUTH FISHERIES
& COMMUNITY MUSEUM

Covesea          Stotfield      Branderburgh

B9040                                 **Lossiemouth**

BURGHEAD
MUSEUM
**Burghead**    Hopeman    Duffus    Gordonstoun

Cummingston                                            Lossie Forest    S P E

Roseisle                                         Loch
Spynie

*Roseisle*                          DUFFUS CASTLE
*Forest*

BURGHEAD BAY                              PALACE OF
SPYNIE                      Kingston

C    Lower                         Spynie       Leuchars Ho.    Lochhill
Hempriggs     Quarrywood                                                  Garmouth
B9089                       Bishopmill
Newton                              ELGIN MUSEUM
Miltonhill    Coltfield                      Elgin  CATHEDRAL    Urquhart       Lochs
B9011              Alves                         CASHMERE VISITOR           Crofts
CENTRE
KINLOSS                      OLD MILLS    New           A96    Lhanbryde
ABBEY         Pittendreich            MORAY    Elgin                                 Mosstodloch
Kinloss                    MOTOR                    Moss of
Grange Hall  A96   Miltonduff   MUSEUM         Barmuckity  COXTON TOWER
field                                                                   Dipple
NELSON TOWER  Mains of Burgie                         Longmorn                Orbliston
FALCONER MUSEUM                      Paddockhaugh                  Blackhills
Blervie     Califer    *Monaughty Forest*   Auchtertyre  BIRNIE                              *Teindland*
Castle            PLUSCARDEN ABBEY          CHURCH                            Inchberry
DALLAS DHU                   Barnhill    Foresterseat        Thomshill      338   *Forest*
DISTILLERY  Rafford                                                MILLBUIES
Ho.  Moor of              B9010   Kellas  B9010           Glen                          Ordie
Granary  Briach           *Dallas Forest*  Glenlatterach  of
D     Branchill    Dallas   319                          Rothes  Auchinroath
*Altyre*  ◁ 253                                                    Newlands
*Woods*                                                A941
*Newtyle*     Craigroy         365
*Forest*                    CAIRN UISH                      13
371
MILL BUIE                                              Rothes
Loch Dallas      Lossie               *Elchies Forest*    GLEN GRANT    SPEYSIDE
404                      DISTILLERY     WAY
E                            CARN NA                    471
CAILLICHE   369  Whiteacen   BEN AIGAN  Dandaleith
LADYCROFT                                       Craigellachie
AGRICULTURAL                                     SPEYSIDE
MUSEUM                                          COOPERAGE

1        2        3        4

0    1    2    3 miles
0  1  2  3  4  5 km
CARN KITTY

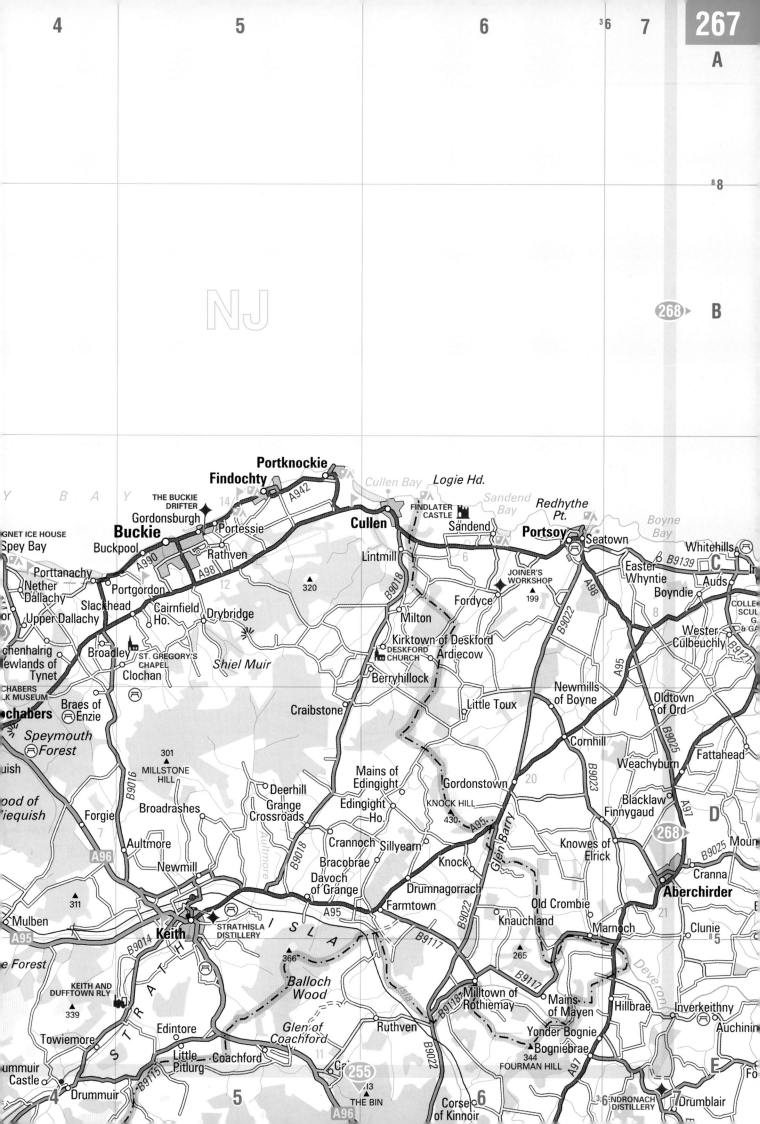

A

4 5 6 ³6 7

NJ

B
268

B

Y   B A Y

**Portknockie**
**Findochty**
THE BUCKIE
DRIFTER
Gordonsburgh
Spey Bay
GNET ICE HOUSE
**Buckie**
Buckpool
Portessie
A942
Cullen Bay
Logie Hd.
FINDLATER
CASTLE
Sandend
Bay
Redhythe
Pt.
Boyne
Bay
Sandend
**Portsoy**
Seatown
Whitehills
C
Porttanachy
Nether
Dallachy
Rathven
A98
**Cullen**
Lintmill
JOINER'S
WORKSHOP
199
B9139
Easter
Whyntie
Auds
Boyndie
Portgordon
A990
12
320
B9018
Milton
Fordyce
B9022
A98
8
A95
COLLE
SCUL
G
G&G
Slackhead
Cairnfield
Ho.
Drybridge
Kirktown of Deskford
DESKFORD
CHURCH
Ardiecow
Wester
Culbeuchly
Upper Dallachy
chenhalrig
ewlands of
Tynet
Broadley
ST. GREGORY'S
CHAPEL
Shiel Muir
Berryhillock
Little Toux
Newmills
of Boyne
Oldtown
of Ord
B9025
Clochan
CHABERS
LK MUSEUM
chabers
Braes of
Enzie
Craibstone
Cornhill
B9023
Weachyburn
Fattahead
Speymouth
Forest
301
MILLSTONE
HILL
Mains of
Edingight
Gordonstown
20
Blacklaw
Finnygaud
D
uish
ood of
iequish
B9016
Deerhill
Grange
Crossroads
Edingight
Ho.
KNOCK HILL
430.
A95
B9022
Knowes of
Elrick
268
B9025
Moun
Forgie
7
Broadrashes
Crannoch
Sillyearn
Knock
Glen Barry
Cranna
Aultmore
Newmill
Bracobrae
Davoch
of Grange
Drumnagorrach
Old Crombie
Aberchirder
A96
311
A95
Farmtown
Knauchland
Marnoch
Clunie
5
Mulben
**Keith**
STRATHISLA
DISTILLERY
ISLA
B9117
265
Hillbrae
Inverkeithny
e Forest
KEITH AND
DUFFTOWN RLY
366
Balloch
Wood
B9118
Milltown of
Rothiemay
Mains
of Mayen
Auchinin
339
Edintore
Glen of
Coachford
Ruthven
B9022
Yonder Bognie
Bogniebrae
344
A97
Drumblair
Towiemore
Little
Pitlurg
Coachford
11
255
FOURMAN HILL
E
ummuir
Castle
Drummuir
4
A96
5
13
THE BIN
Corse
of Kinnoir
6
³6
ENDRONACH
DISTILLERY
Deveron

A

8

NJ

NK

B

C

SANDHAVEN
MEAL MILL

FRASERBURGH
HERITAGE
MUSEUM

Rosehearty          B9031      Pittulie      Fraserburgh

PITSLIGO CASTLE          Sandhaven      Broadsea      Kinnaird Head

Peathill      KINNAIRD CASTLE LIGHTHOUSE &
SCOTLAND'S LIGHTHOUSE MUSEUM

Percyhorner      Pitblae      Fraserburgh
Bay

Coburty      B9032      A90      B9033      B9107      Cairnbulg Pt.

Inverallochy

MAGGIE'S HOOSIE

Upper
Boyndlie      Mid
Ardlaw      Memsie      A981      5      Cairnbulg Castle      St Combs

Tyrie      Gowanhill      Inzie Head

A98      Whitewell      MEMSIE
BURIAL CAIRN      Rathen      Strathellie

10      Cairness      B9033

Loch of
Strathbeg

Hillhead of
Auchentumb      Newburgh      Crimonmogate

16      Lonmay      LOCH OF STRATHBEG
NATURE RESERVE
VISITOR CENTRE      Rattray Head

230
MORMOND
HILL      Crimond

Knowhead      Nether
Park      Old
Rattray

B9093      Strichen      A952      Blackhill

New Leeds      Longhill      A90      D

7      Balearn

Adziel      B9093      Leys      St Fergus
Moss      12      St
Fergus

Little
Skillymarno      Denhead      Backfolds      Kirktown      Scotstown Hd.

North Ugie Water      Fetterangus      Hythie      Rora Moss      North Kirkton

11      Forest
of Deer      Toux      Rora      Lunderton      Kirkton Hd.      8  5

DEER
ABBEY      Dunshillock      Woodside      Ugie

B      U      C      H      A      N      Newseat      Inverugie

Maud      A950      A      Water      INVERUGIE CASTLE

B9029      Old Deer      Mintlaw      Longside      Torterston      UGIE SALMON FISH HOUSE

MAUD
RAILWAY
MUSEUM      B9106      Flushing      A982      Buchanhaven

Backhill of
Clackriach      ABERDEENSHIRE
FARMING
MUSEUM      South Ugie      Peterhead

Stuartfield      ARBUTHNOT MUSEUM & ART GALLERY

Drymuir      Inverquhomery      8      Keith Inch

Bulwark      Crichie      Millbreck      257      Hillhead of
Cocklaw      PETERHEAD MARITIME

Nethermuir      Mains of
Crichie      B9030      Neth      Invernettie

4      Kinnadie      Clola      5      Little Dens      1      Sandford      6
Skelmuir      Kinmundy      Bay      Peterhead Bay

E

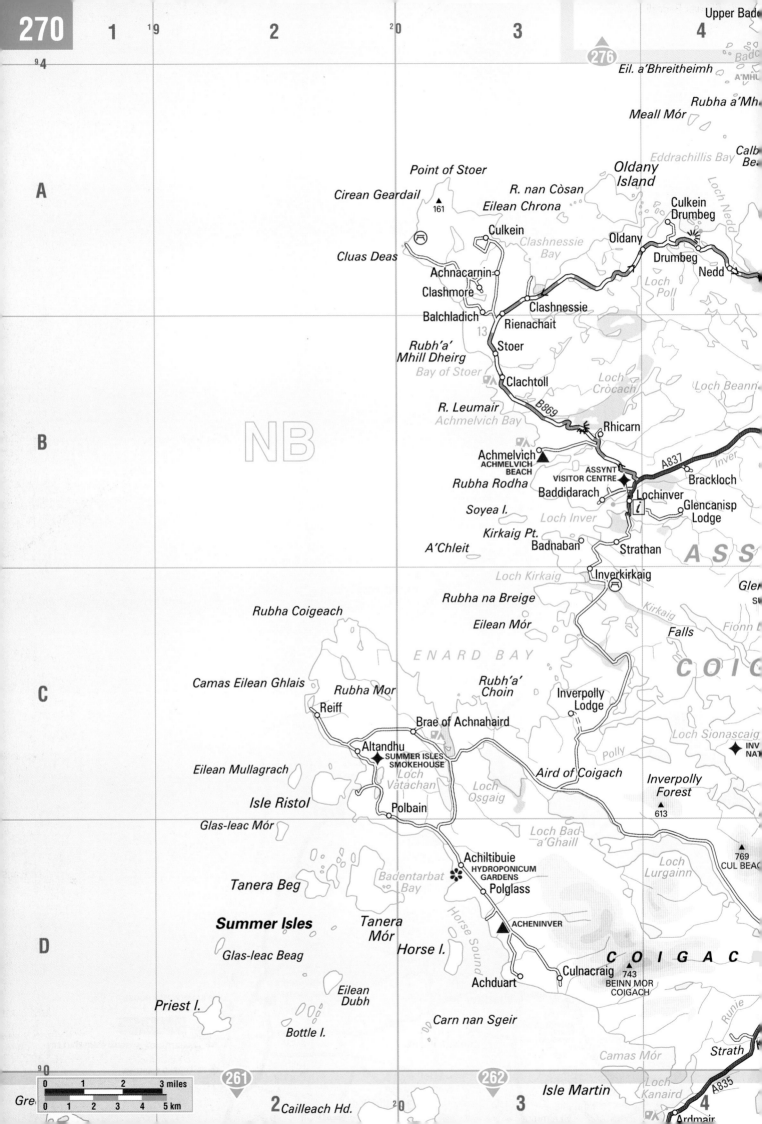

Upper Bad
276
Eil. a'Bhreitheimh
A'MHL
Rubha a'Mh
Meall Mór
Eddrachillis Bay
Calb
Be

**A**

Point of Stoer
Cirean Geardail
R. nan Còsan
Oldany
Island
Eilean Chrona
Culkein
Drumbeg
Culkein
161
Oldany
Clashnessie
Bay
Drumbeg
Loch Nedd
Nedd
Cluas Deas
Loch
Poll
Achnacarnin
Clashmore
Clashnessie
Balchladich
Rienachait
13
Stoer
Rubh 'a'
Mhill Dheirg
Loch
Cròcach
Loch Beann
Bay of Stoer
Clachtoll
B869

**B**

R. Leumair
Achmelvich Bay
Rhicarn
NB
Inver
A837
Achmelvich
ACHMELVICH
BEACH
Brackloch
Rubha Rodha
ASSYNT
VISITOR CENTRE
Baddidarach
Lochinver
Soyea I.
Glencanisp
Lodge
Loch Inver
Kirkaig Pt.
A'Chleit
Badnaban
Strathan
A S S
Loch Kirkaig
Inverkirkaig
Glen
S
Rubha na Breige
Kirkaig
Rubha Coigeach
Eilean Mór
Falls
Fionn
 E N A R D   B A Y
C O I G

**C**

Camas Eilean Ghlais
Rubha Mor
Rubh 'a'
Choin
Inverpolly
Lodge
Loch Sionascaig
Reiff
Brae of Achnahaird
INV
NAT
Altandhu
SUMMER ISLES
SMOKEHOUSE
Aird of Coigach
Inverpolly
Forest
Eilean Mullagrach
Loch
Vatachan
Loch
Osgaig
Polly
Isle Ristol
Polbain
613
Glas-leac Mór
Loch Bad
a'Ghaill
Loch
Lurgainn
769
CUL BEAC
Achiltibuie
HYDROPONICUM
GARDENS
Badentarbat
Bay
Polglass
Tanera Beg
Horse Sound
**Summer Isles**
Tanera
Mór
Acheninver

**D**

Glas-leac Beag
Horse I.
C O I G A C
Culnacraig
Priest I.
Eilean
Dubh
Achduart
743
BEINN MOR
COIGACH
Bottle I.
Carn nan Sgeir
Runie
Camas Mór
Strath
Gre
261
262
Isle Martin
A835
0      1      2      3 miles
0  1  2  3  4  5 km
Cailleach Hd.
2      0
3
Loch
Kanaird
4
Ardmair

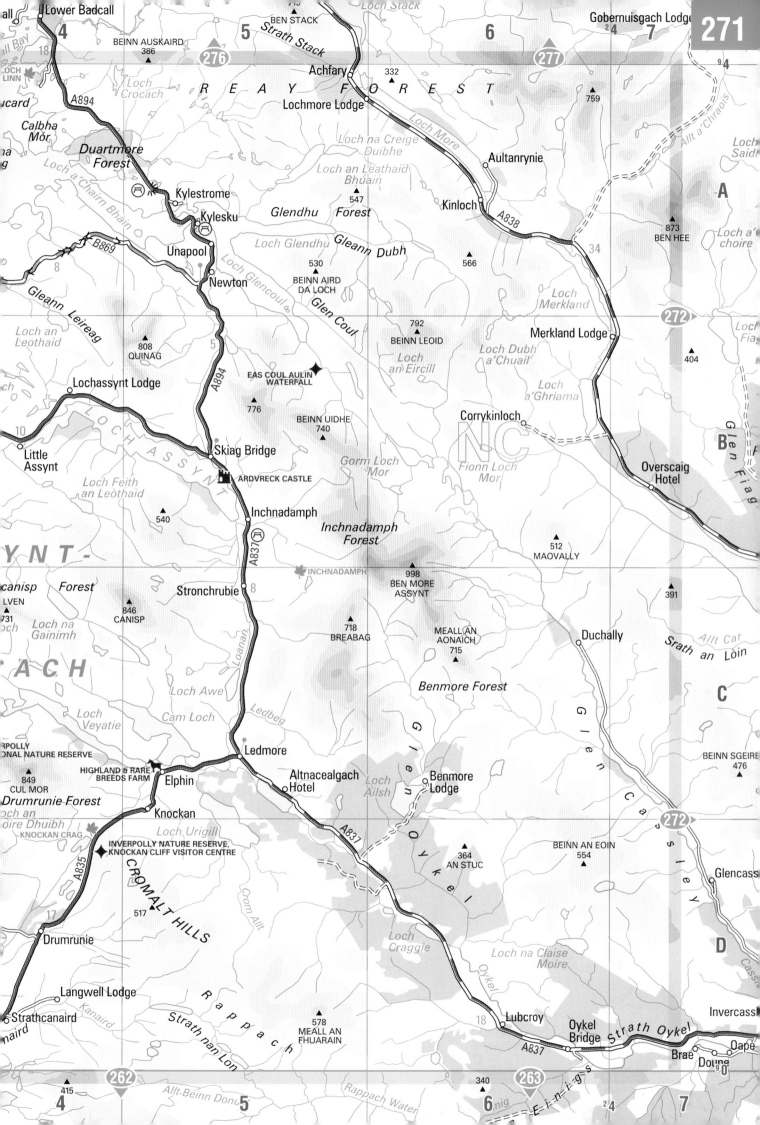

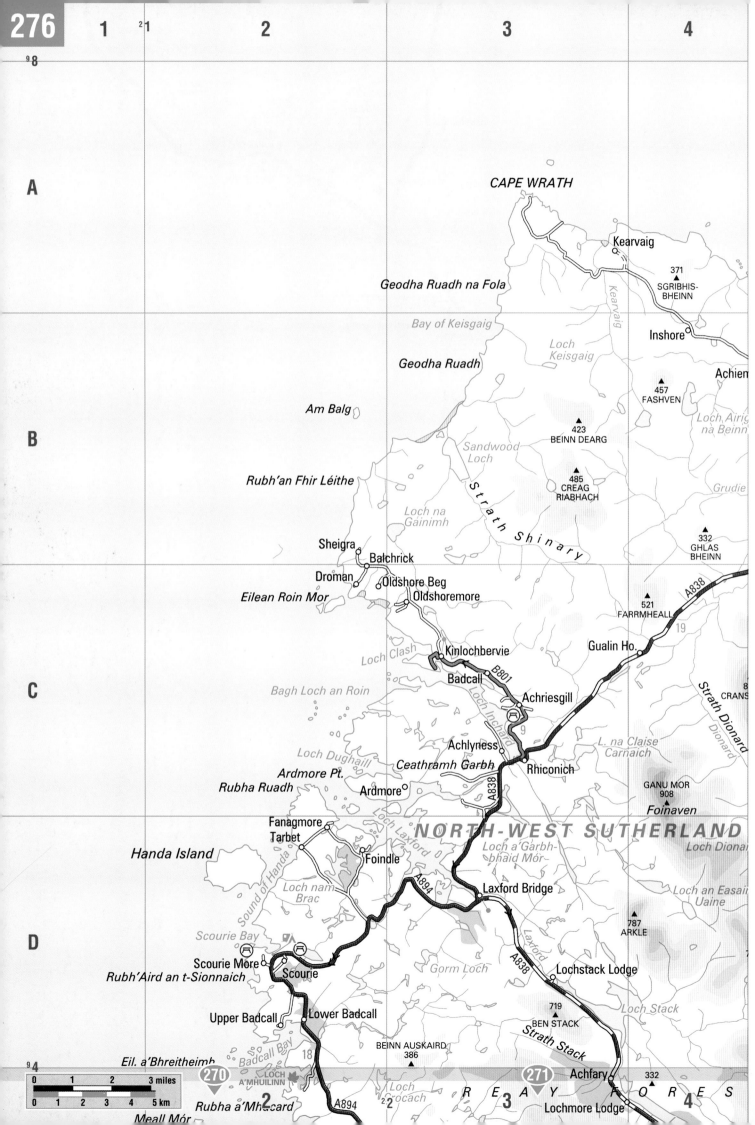

CAPE WRATH

Kearvaig

Geodha Ruadh na Fola

371 ▲ SGRIBHIS-BHEINN

Bay of Keisgaig

Loch Keisgaig

Inshore

Geodha Ruadh

Achiem

457 ▲ FASHVEN

Loch Airig na Beinn

Am Balg

Sandwood Loch

423 ▲ BEINN DEARG

Rubh'an Fhir Léithe

485 ▲ CREAG RIABHACH

Grudie

Loch na Gáinimh

Strath Shinary

332 ▲ GHLAS BHEINN

Sheigra

Balchrick

Droman

Oldshore Beg

Oldshoremore

521 ▲ FARRMHEALL

A838

19

Eilean Roin Mor

Loch Clash

Kinlochbervie

Gualin Ho.

Loch Inchard

Badcall

B801

Strath Dionard

Bagh Loch an Roin

Achriesgill

9

L. na Claise Carnaich

CRANS

Strath Dionard

Loch Dughaill

Achlyness

Ceathramh Garbh

Rhiconich

Ardmore Pt.

Rubha Ruadh

Ardmore

A838

GANU MOR 908

Foinaven

Fanagmore

Tarbet

**NORTH-WEST SUTHERLAND**

Loch Dionar

Handa Island

Loch Laxford

Loch a'Garbh-bhaid Mór

Foindle

Loch an Easair Uaine

Sound of Handa

Loch nam Brac

A894

Laxford Bridge

Scourie Bay

A838

787 ▲ ARKLE

Scourie More

Rubh'Aird an t-Sionnaich

Scourie

Gorm Loch

Lochstack Lodge

Laxford

Upper Badcall

Lower Badcall

719 ▲ BEN STACK

Loch Stack

Eil. a'Bhreitheimh

BEINN AUSKAIRD 386

Strath Stack

Badcall Bay

18

270

271

Achfary

332 ▲

Rubha a'Mhecard

A894

Loch Crocach

REAY FORES

Lochmore Lodge

Meall Mór

0  1  2  3 miles
0  1  2  3  4  5 km

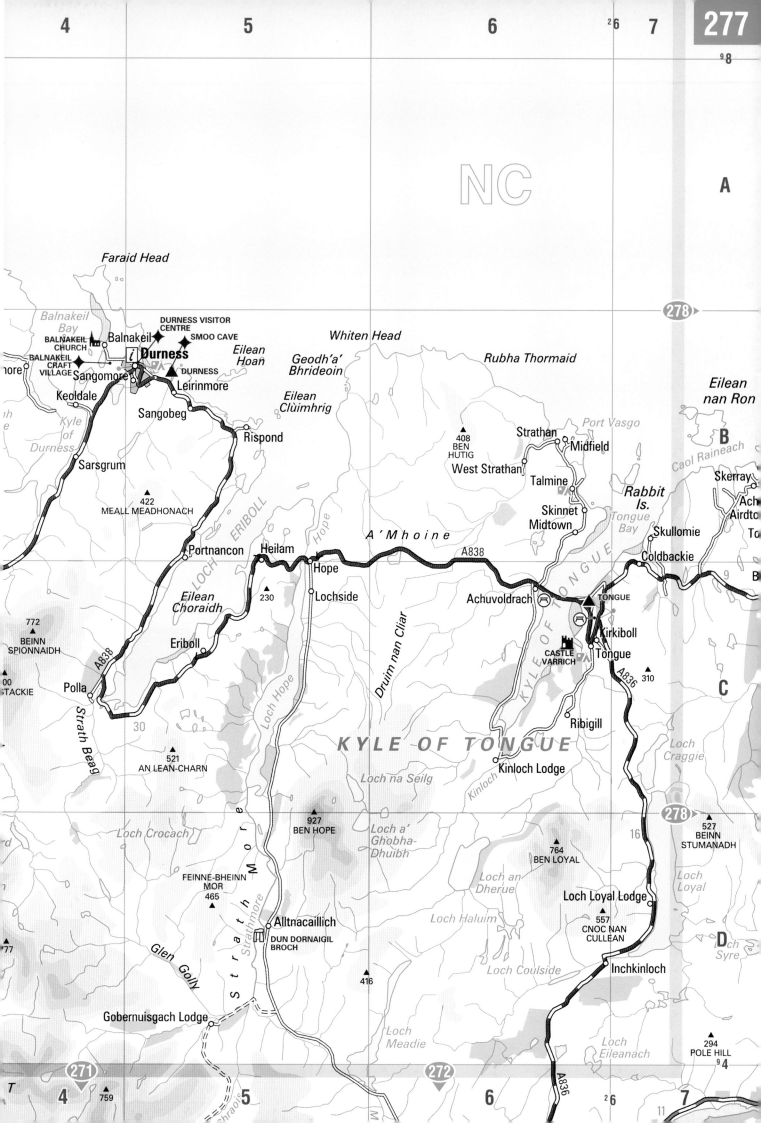

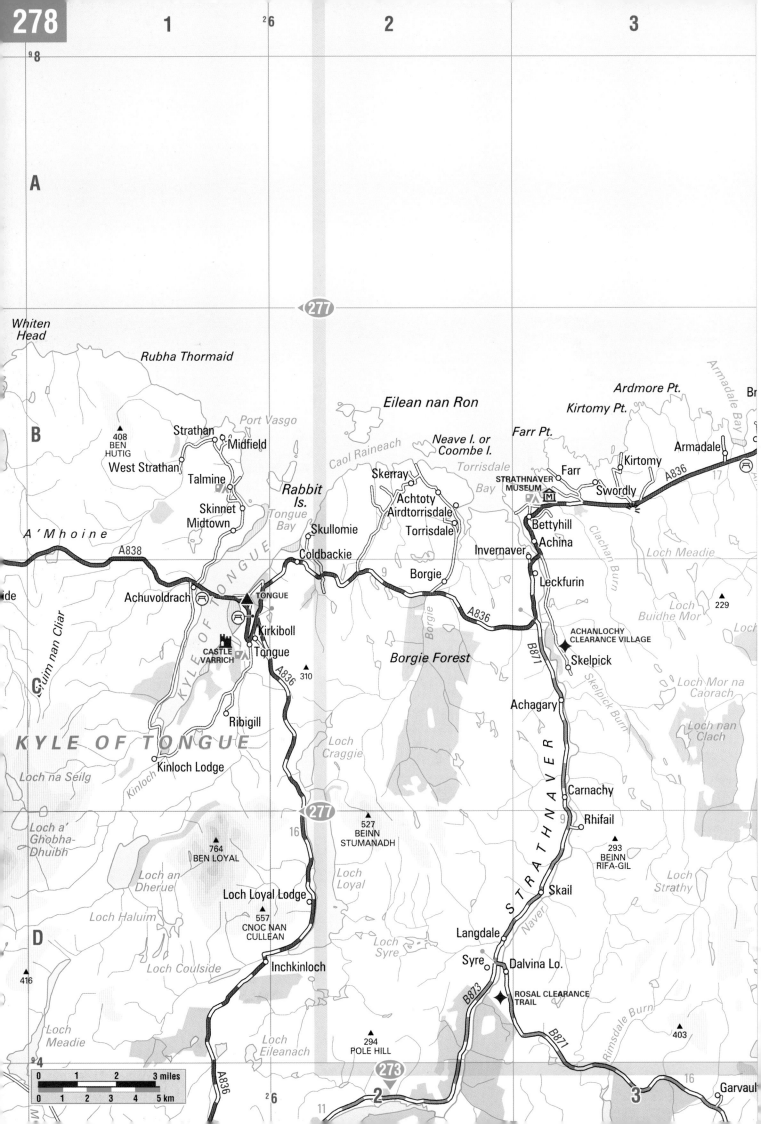

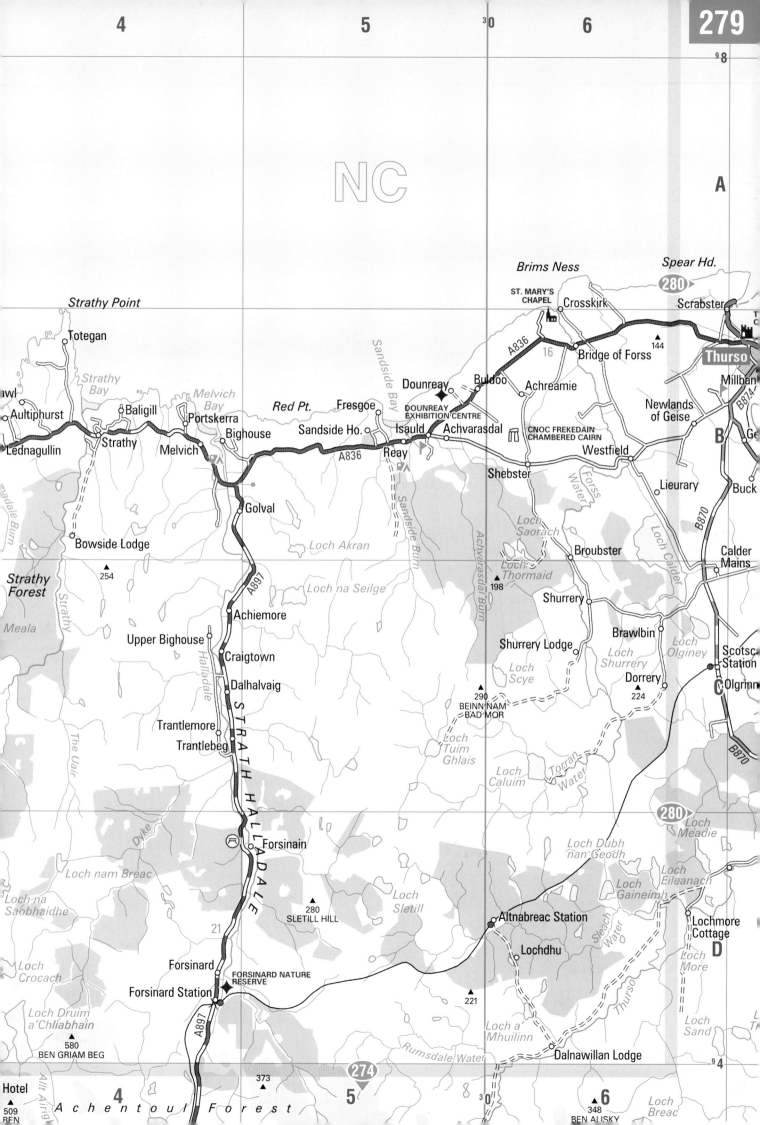

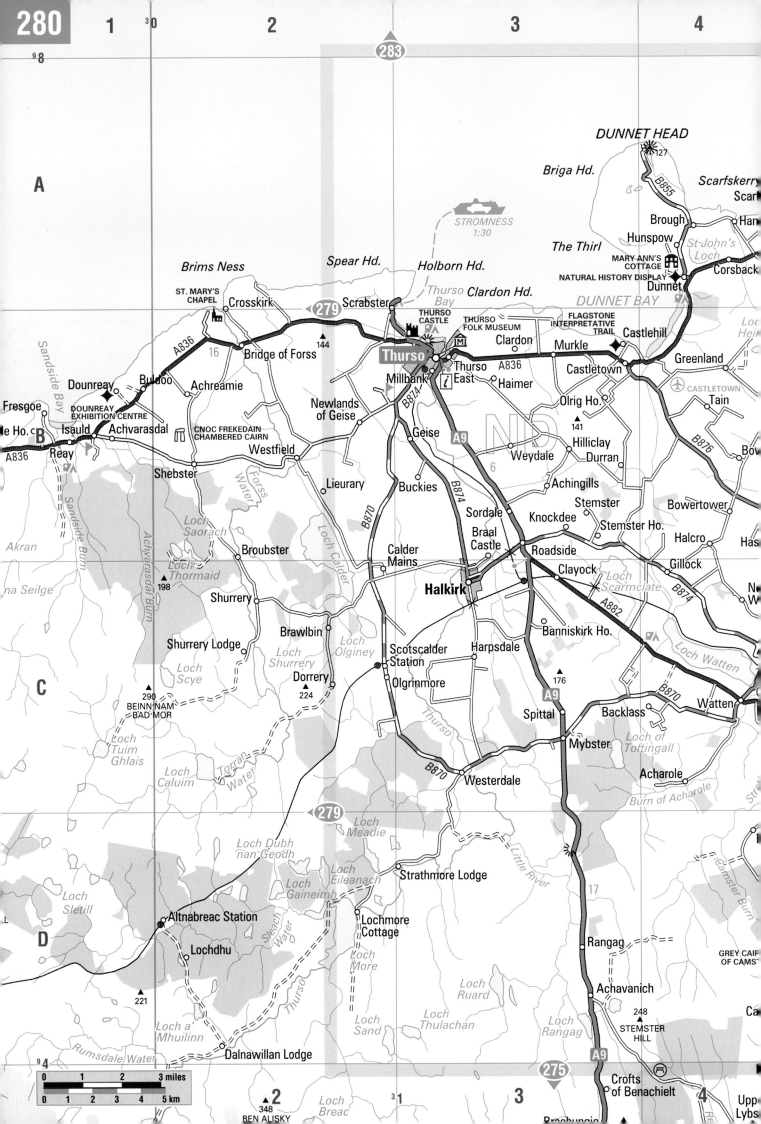

1  ³0  2  3  4

⁹8

A

**DUNNET HEAD**
127
*Briga Hd.*
Scarfskerry
Scar

STROMNESS
1:30
Brough
Han
Hunspow
St John's
MARY ANN'S
COTTAGE
Loch
*The Thirl*
NATURAL HISTORY DISPLAY
Corsback
*Spear Hd.*  *Holborn Hd.*
Dunnet
*Clardon Hd.*
DUNNET BAY
*Brims Ness*
FLAGSTONE
INTERPRETATIVE
ST. MARY'S
CHAPEL  Crosskirk
Scrabster  *Thurso*  TRAIL
279  *Bay*  Castlehill
THURSO CASTLE  THURSO  Clardon  Murkle
FOLK MUSEUM  Loch Hei
A836  Greenland
16  Bridge of Forss  144  Thurso  Castletown  CASTLETOWN
Buldoo  **Thurso**  East  A836  Tain
Dounreay  Achreamie  Millbank  Haimer  Castletown  Bo
Fresgoe  Newlands  Geise  Olrig Ho.  Hilliclay  B876
B  of Geise  141  Durran
Isauld  Achvarasdal  CNOC FREKEDAIN  A9  Weydale
A836  CHAMBERED CAIRN  Westfield  Buckies  Achingills
Reay  Shebster  Lieurary  B870  Sordale  Knockdee  Stemster
Akran  Forss  Calder  Braal  Stemster Ho.
na Seilge  Loch  Water  Mains  Castle  Roadside  Halcro
Saorach  Broubster  Clayock  Has
Loch  **Halkirk**  Gillock
Thormaid  A882  Loch
198  Shurrery  Scarmclate  B874
290  Loch  Banniskirk Ho.  NW
C  Scye  Brawlbin  176
BEINN NAM  Shurrery Lodge  Loch  Scotscalder  Harpsdale  A9  Loch Watten
BAD MOR  Shurrery  Station  Spittal  Backlass  Watten
Loch  Dorrery  Olginmore  Mybster  Loch of
Tuim  224  Loch  Toftingall
Ghlais  Olginey  Acharole
Loch  Thurso  Westerdale  Burn of Acharole
Caluim  Torran  B870
Loch  Water
279

Loch
Meadie
Loch Dubh
nan Geodh
Loch  Little River  17
Loch  Eileanach  Strathmore Lodge
Loch  Gaineimh
Sletill  Lochmore
Cottage
Loch
More  Rangag  GREY CAIR
D  Altnabreac Station  OF CAMS
Lochdhu  Loch
Ruard  Loch  Achavanich
221  Sleach  Thulachan  Ca
Water  248
Loch a'  Loch  STEMSTER
Mhuilinn  Sand  Loch  HILL
⁹4  Rangag
Rumsdale Water  Dalnawillan Lodge  A9
Loch  275
Breac  Crofts  Upp
2  ³1  3  of Benachielt  Lybs
BEN ALISKY  4

0   1   2   3 miles
0  1  2  3  4  5 km

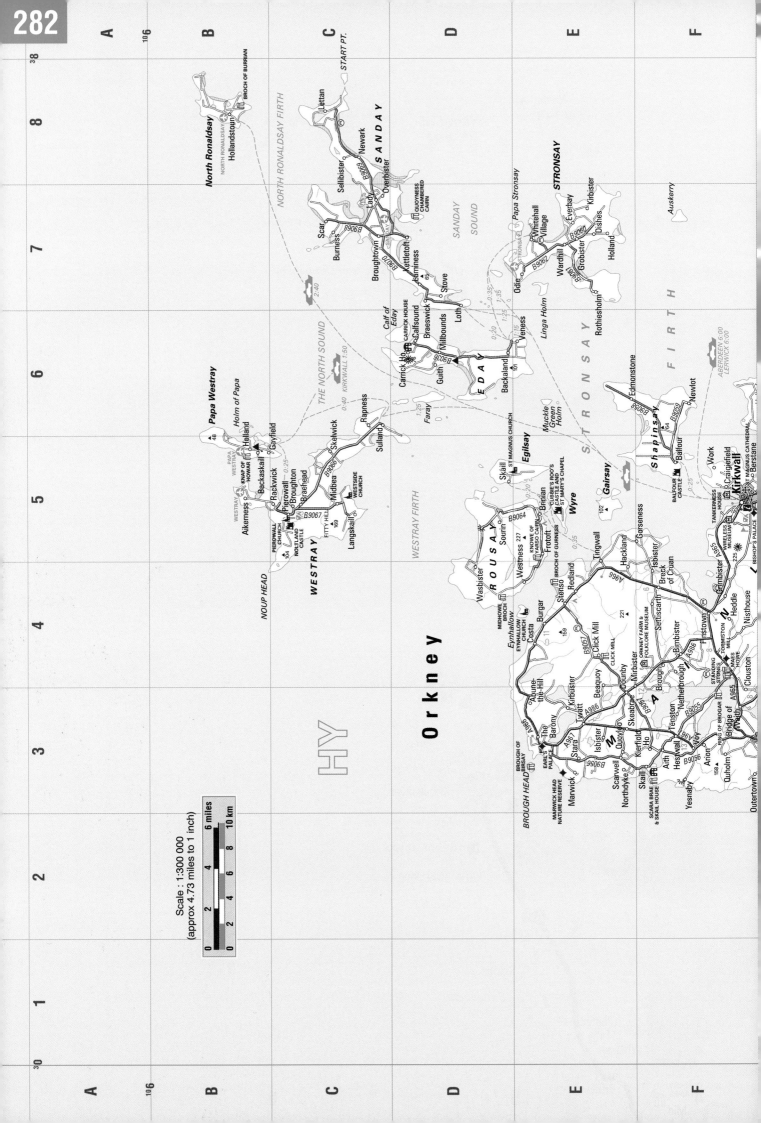

Scale : 1:300 000
(approx 4.73 miles to 1 inch)

6 miles
10 km

HY

Orkney

*North Ronaldsay*

NORTH RONALDSAY

Hollandstoun

BROCH OF BURRIAN

NORTH RONALDSAY FIRTH

START PT.

Lettan

Newark

Sellibister

S A N D A Y

Lady

B9069

Overbister

QUOYNESS
CHAMBERED
CAIRN

Scar

B9068

Burness

SANDAY
SOUND

STRONSAY

Quoyness

Whitehall
Village

Kirbister

Everbay

Papa Stronsay

Odie

B9062

Wardhill

B9060

Grobister

Dishes

Holland

Rothiesholm

STRONSAY
FIRTH

Auskerry

Broughton

B9070

Kettletoft

Lami11ess

Stove

Braeswick

Braemound

Loth

Veness

Calf of
Eday

Carrick Ho.

Carrick House

B9033

Guith

Millbounds

E D A Y

Backaland

Faray

Muckle
Green
Holm

Linga Holm

THE NORTH SOUND

KIRKWALL 1:50

KIRKWALL 1:50

Papa Westray

Holm of Papa

Holland

Gayfield

PAPA
WESTRAY

KNAP OF
HOWAR

Backaskaill

Rapness

Rackwick

Pierowall

Braehead

B9067

Midbea

WESTSIDE
CHURCH

Skelwick

Sulland

Langskaill

WESTRAY FIRTH

ST MAGNUS CHURCH

*Egilsay*

Skaill

Brinian

Sourin

CUBBIE ROO'S
CASTLE AND
ST MARY'S CHAPEL

*Wyre*

*Gairsay*

R O U S A Y

B9064

Westness

KNOWE OF
YARSO CAIRN

Frotoft

BROCH OF GURNESS

Tingwall

SHAPINSAY

Edmonstone

B9058

B9059

Newlot

Work

Balfour

BALFOUR
CASTLE

Craigiefield

ST MAGNUS CATHEDRAL

KIRKWALL

Berstane

BISHOP'S PALACE

EARL'S PALACE

TANKERNESS
HOUSE

WIRELESS
MUSEUM

WESTRAY

Aikerness

NOLTLAND
CASTLE

PIEROWALL
CHURCH

FITTY HILL

NOUP HEAD

Wasbister

MIDHOWE
BROCH

EYNHALLOW
CHURCH

Costa

Burgar

Eynhallow

Hackland

Gorseness

Isbister

Breck
of Cruan

Finstown

Tormiston

Heddle

Nisthouse

BROUGH
OF BIRSAY

BROUGH HEAD

The
Barony

Twatt

Kirbister

Beaquoy

Dounby

CLICK MILL

Click Mill

Mirbister

Settiscarth

ORKNEY FARM &
FOLKLORE MUSEUM

Brough

Netherbrough

STANDING
STONES

MAES
HOWE

RING OF BROGAR

Bridge of
Waith

Clouston

A965

Grimbister

MARWICK HEAD
NATURE RESERVE

Marwick

Scarwell

Northdyke

SCARA BRAE
& SKAIL HOUSE

Skaill

Yesnaby

Stara

Isbister

Quoyloo

B9056

Skeabrae

Kierfiold
Ho.

Aith

Hestwall

Sandwick

A986

Trenston

Quholm

Outertown

A967

Aune-
the-Hill

ABERDEEN 6:00
LERWICK 6:00

F I R T H

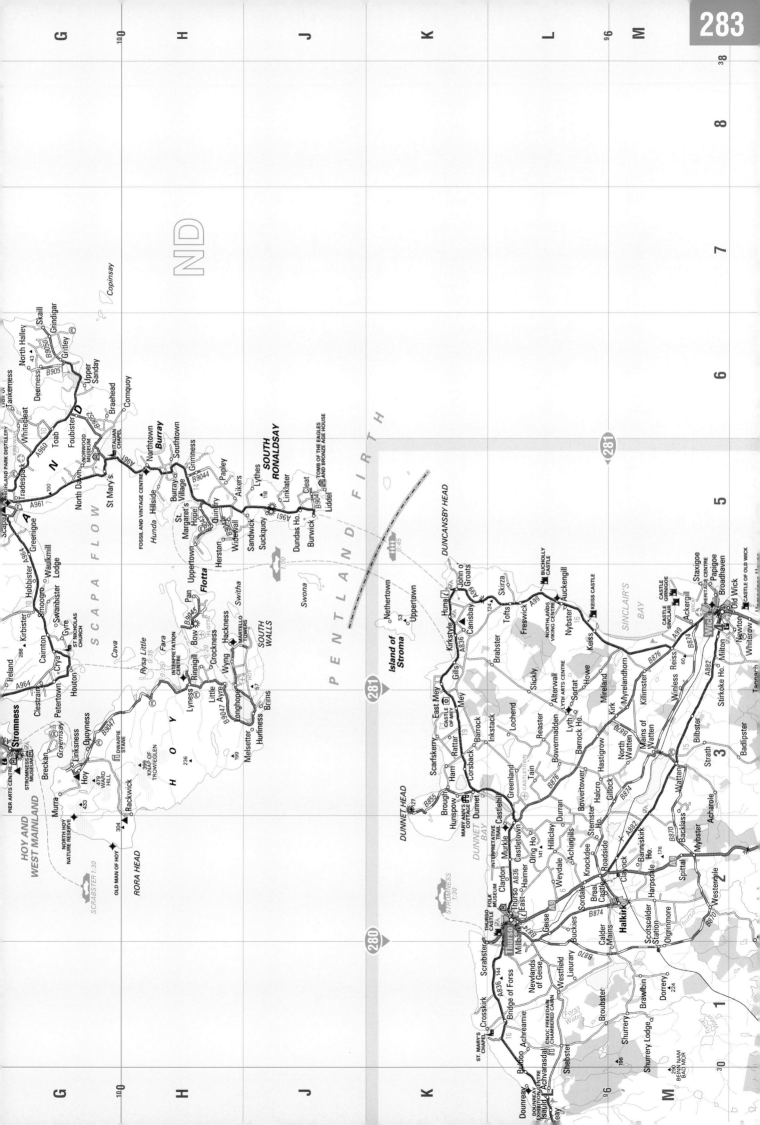

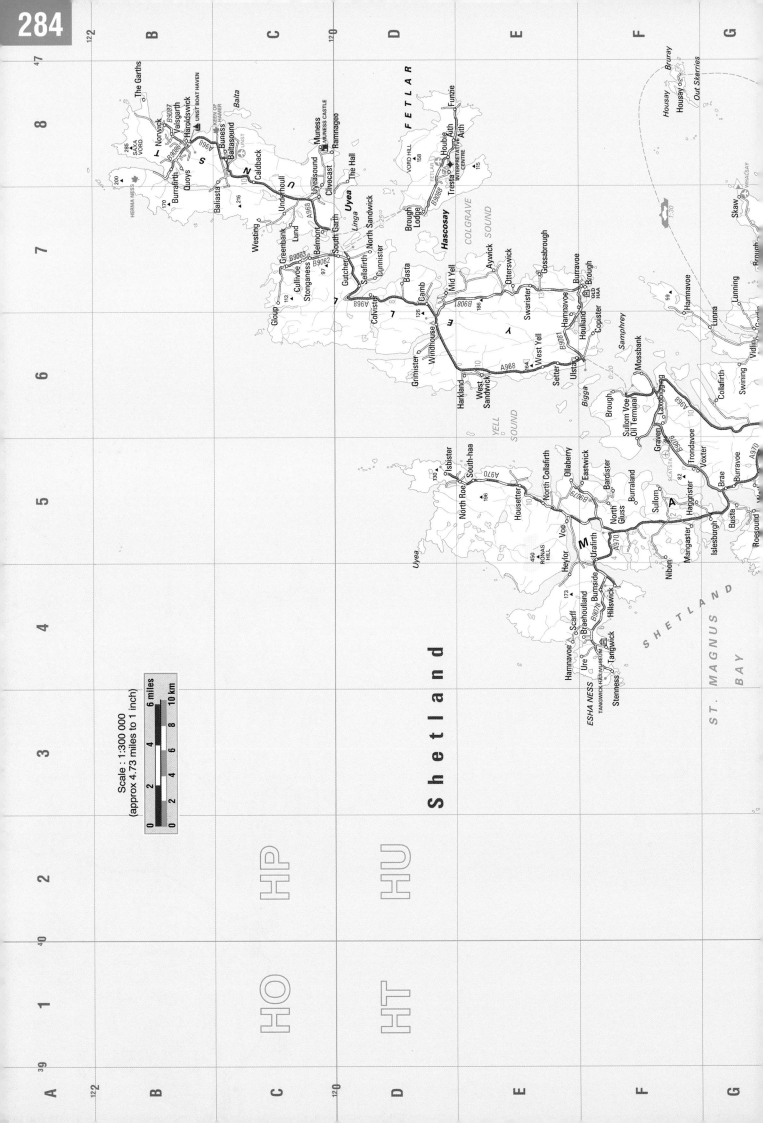

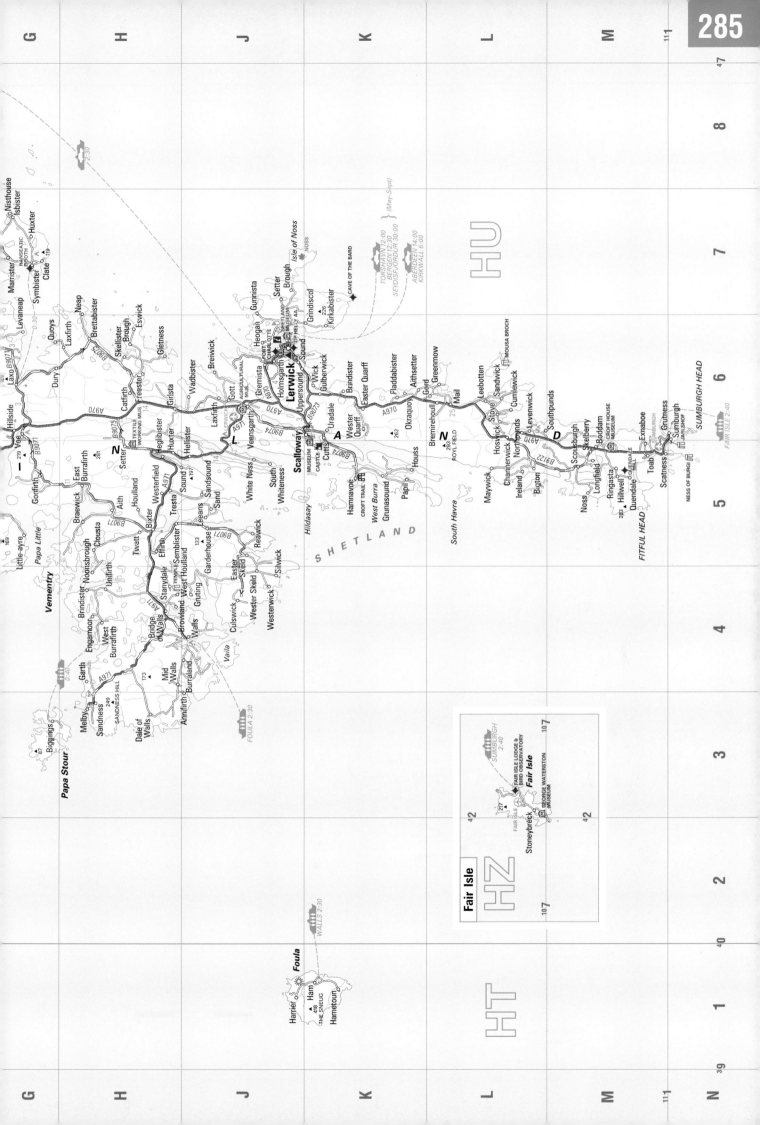

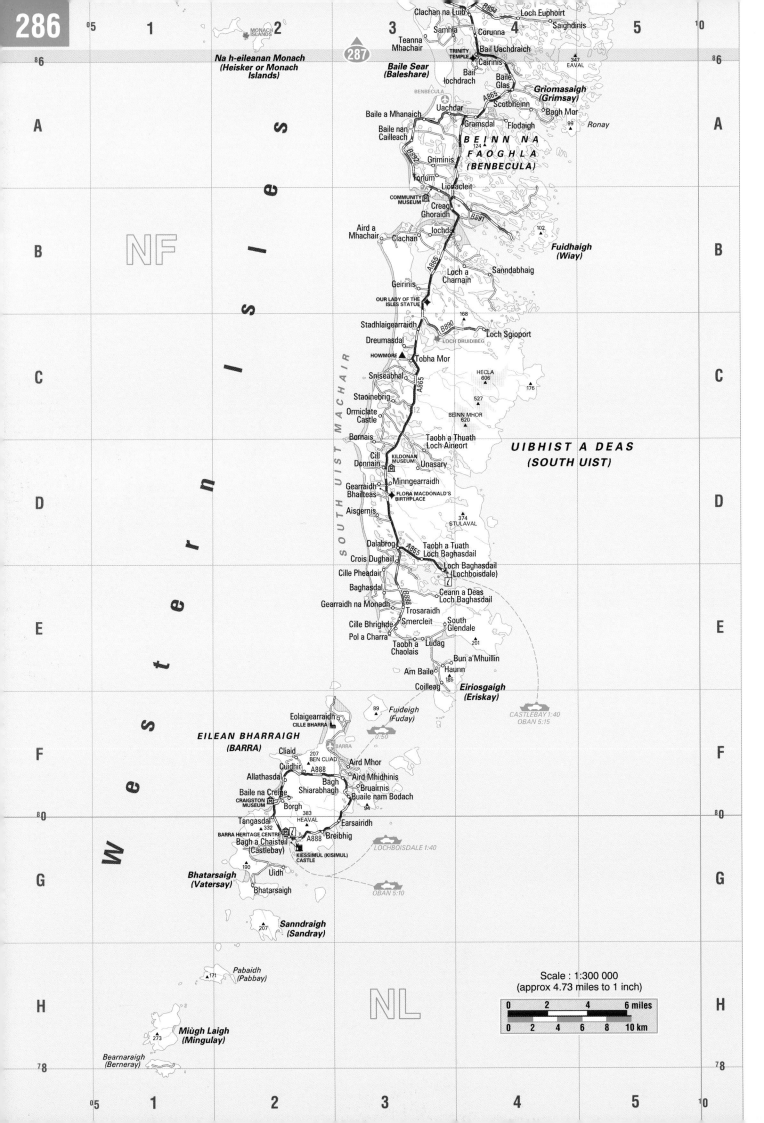

Na h-eileanan Monach
(Heisker or Monach
Islands)

MONACH
ISLANDS

**Western Isles**

NF

NL

Clachan na Luib
Loch Euphoirt
Saighdinis
Samhla
Teanna
Mhachair
Corunna
Bail Uachdraich
TRINITY
TEMPLE
Cairinis
EAVAL
Baile Sear
(Baleshare)
Bail
Iochdrach
Baile
Glas
**Griomasaigh
(Grimsay)**
BENBECULA
Uachdar
Scotbheinn
Bagh Mor
Baile a Mhanaich
Gramsdal
Flodaigh
Baile nan
Cailleach
Ronay
**BEINN NA
FAOGHLA
(BENBECULA)**
Griminis
Torlum
Liniclett
COMMUNITY
MUSEUM
Creag
Ghoraidh
Aird a
Mhachair
Iochdar
Clachan
**Fuidhaigh
(Wiay)**
Geirinis
Loch a
Charnain
Sanndabhaig
OUR LADY OF THE
ISLES STATUE
Stadhlaigearraidh
Loch Sgioport
Dreumasdal
LOCH DRUIDIBEG
HOWMORE
Tobha Mor
HECLA
606
Sniseabhal
Staoinebrig
BEINN MHOR
620
Ormiclate
Castle
Bornais
Taobh a Thuath
Loch Aineort
Cill
Donnain
KILDONAN
MUSEUM
Unasary
**UIBHIST A DEAS
(SOUTH UIST)**
Gearraidh
Bhailteas
Minngearraidh
FLORA MACDONALD'S
BIRTHPLACE
Aisgernis
STULAVAL
Dalabrog
Taobh a Tuath
Loch Baghasdail
Crois Dughaill
Loch Baghasdail
(Lochboisdale)
Cille Pheadair
Ceann a Deas
Loch Baghasdail
Baghasdal
Gearraidh na Monadh
Trosaraidh
Cille Bhrighde
Smercleit
South
Glendale
Pol a Charra
Taobh a
Chaolais
Ludag
Bun a'Mhuillin
Am Baile
Haunn
Coilleag
**Eiriosgaigh
(Eriskay)**
CASTLEBAY 1:40
OBAN 5:15
Fuideigh
(Fuday)
Eolaigearraidh
CILLE BHARRA
Barra
**EILEAN BHARRAIGH
(BARRA)**
Cliaid
BEN CLIAD
Aird Mhor
Cuidhir
Aird Mhidhinis
Allathasdal
Bagh
Shiarabhagh
Bruairnis
Baile na Creige
Buaile nam Bodach
CRAIGSTON
MUSEUM
Borgh
Tangasdal
HEAVAL
Earsairidh
BARRA HERITAGE CENTRE
Breibhig
Bagh a Chaisteil
(Castlebay)
KIESSIMUL (KISIMUL)
CASTLE
LOCHBOISDALE 1:40
**Bhatarsaigh
(Vatersay)**
Uidh
Bhatarsaigh
OBAN 5:10
**Sanndraigh
(Sandray)**
Pabaidh
(Pabbay)
**Miùgh Laigh
(Mingulay)**
Bearnaraigh
(Berneray)

SOUTH UIST MACHAIR

Scale : 1:300 000
(approx 4.73 miles to 1 inch)

0       2       4      6 miles
0    2   4   6   8    10 km

## St. Kilda

Scale : 1:300 000
(approx 4.73 miles to 1 inch)

0   2   4   6 miles
0   2   4   6   8   10 km

NA

NF

CNOC GLAS 376  Soay
CONACHAIR 376
ST KILDA
MULLACH BI 358
St Kilda or Hirta (Hiort)

Boreray 384

ST KILDA

---

AN CAOLAS
IRON AGE HOUSE  Crotha
Tobson
Aird Uig
Bhaltos
205 Cliobh  Breacleit
Timsgearraidh  Miabhig
Cradhlastadh  Riof  Taclet  Barragl
Uigen
Cairisiadar  Crulabha
Mangurstadh  Eadar Dha Fhadhail
429 SUAINAVAL  Geisiadar  256
288
Islibhig  Einacleite
Breanais  574 MEALISVAL  Giosla
397 BEINN MHEADHONACH

Mealasta Island

308  Aird a' Mhul
Scarp  NB
SOUTH LEWIS,  STULAVAL
Huisinis  489  679 TIRGA MOR  UISGNAVAL MORE 729
 ULLAVAL  CLISHAM 799
Gobhaig  HARRIS AND
Abhainn Suidhe  CEANN A TUATH NA HEARADH
Cliasmol  13  Bun Abhainn  A859
Miabhag  Eadarra  559
OLD WHALING STATION  Aird Asaig  3
NORTH UIST
Tarasaigh (Taransay)  436 BEN LUSKENTYRE
Paible  99  Losgaintir  Tairbeart (Tarbert)  467
LUSKENTYRE BEACH  288
Seilebost  A859  Miabh
Borve Lodge  23  NA HEARADH  Aird  Kennacley
Buirgh  (HARRIS)  Mhighe  Greosabhagh
CHAIPAVAL 365  Sgarasta Mhor  386  Liceasto  Leac a Li
398 BLEAVAL  Geocrab  Cliuthar
Beacrabhaic  Caolas
Taobh Tuath  Fleoideabhagh  Stocinis
196  SEALLAM  Manais
Pabaidh (Pabbay)  Aird Mhighe  Cuidhtinis
Fionnsbhagh  Boirseam
Ensay  An t-Ob  459 ROINEABHAL  Lingreabhagh
Eilean  Killegray  (Leverburgh)
Bhearnaraigh  Cairminis  Srahnda
(Berneray)  Ruisigearraidh  ST CLEMENT'S CHURCH  Roghadal
BERNERAY
Boreray  Borgh  Baile
CAOLAS NA HEARADH
1:10

Port nan Long
Vallay  Oronsay  Baile Mhic Phail
B893  190
Scolpaig  Solas  Greinetobht  3
SCOLPAIG TOWER  20 A865  Trumaisgearraidh  Hermetray
Baile Mhartainn  Malacleit  A865
Taigh a Ghearraidh  Hosta  180  154
133  Lochportain
Hogha  Baile  UIBHIST A TUATH  5
Gearraidh  Raghaill  230
BALRANALD NATURE RESERVE  MARRIVAL  Loch nam Madadh (Lochmaddy)
UIST ANIMAL  Claddach-knockline  CHEARSABHAGH  UIG 1:50
Ceann a Bhaigh  VISITOR CENTRE  TAIGH
Paibeil  Baile Mor  (NORTH UIST)  A867  NG
Cladach  BARPA LANGASS CAIRN
Na h-eileanan Monach  Chireboist  250
(Heisker or Monach  Kirkibost Island  Clachan na Luib  281 SOUTH LEE
Islands)  A865  Loch
MONACH  Samhla  B894  Euphoirt  Saighdinis
ISLANDS  Teanna Mhachair  Corunna
Baile Sear  Cairnis  347 EAVAL
(Baleshare)  TRINITY  Bail Uachdraich
TEMPLE  286
Bail  Griomasaigh
Iochdrach  Baile  (Grimsay)
Glas  Scotbheinn
BENBECULA  A865
Uachdar  Bach Mor

AN CAOLAS MHONACH

# Aberdeen

# Bath

## Aberdeen

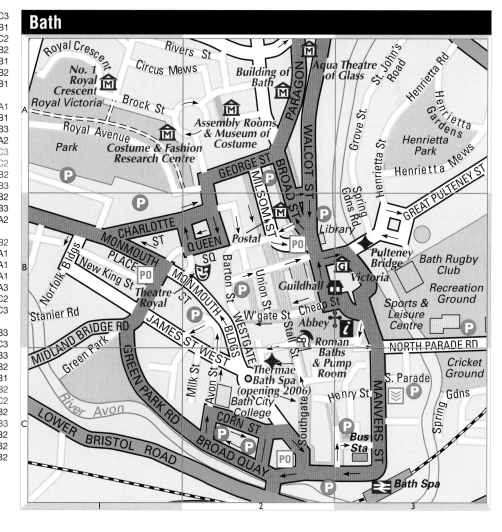

## Bath

# Birmingham

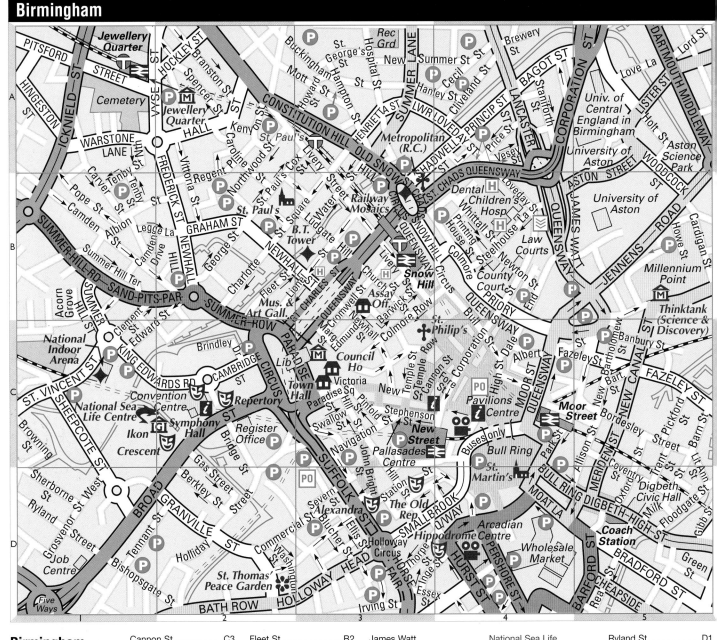

## Birmingham

## Blackpool

## Brighton

## Birmingham continued

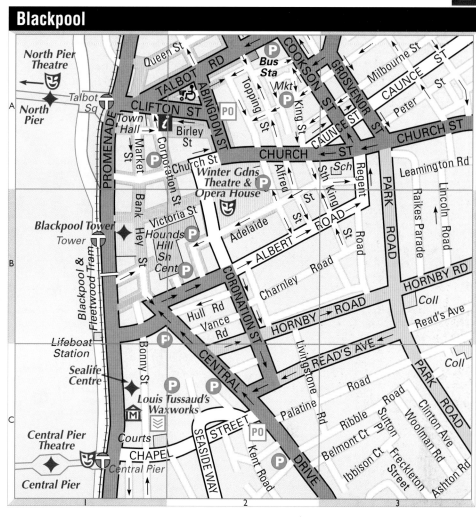

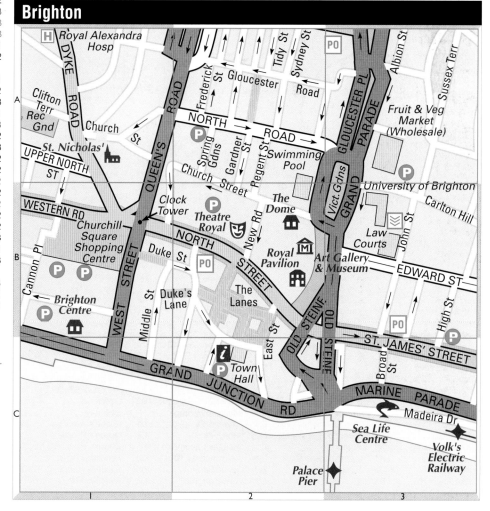

# Bristol

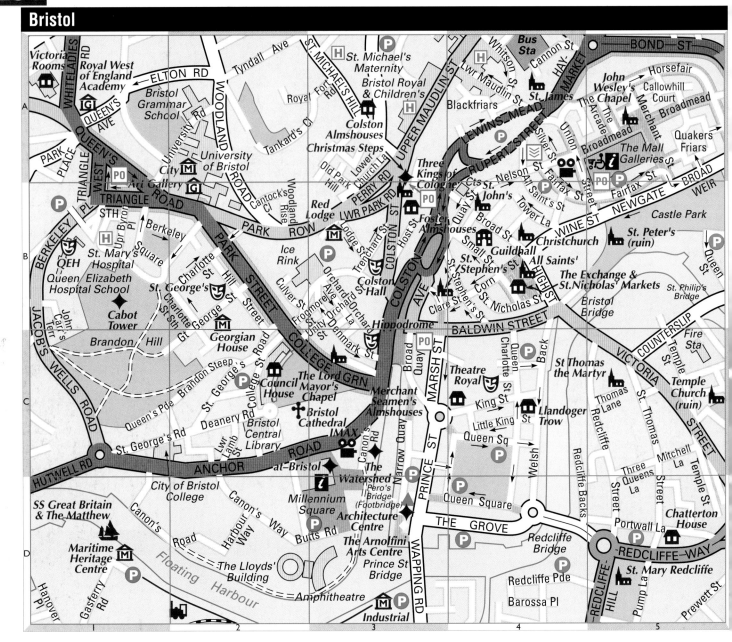

## Bristol

## Cambridge

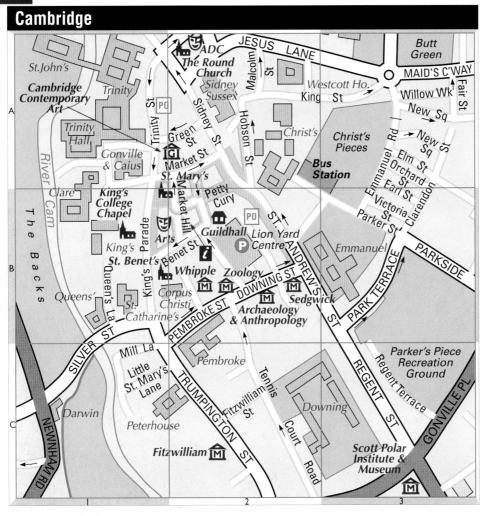

## Canterbury

# Cardiff / Caerdydd

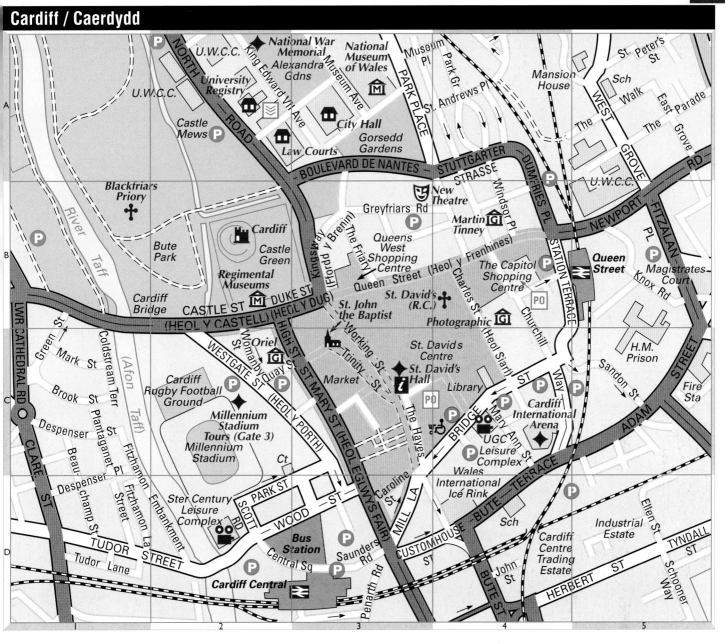

## Cardiff/Caerdydd

# Carlisle

# Chester

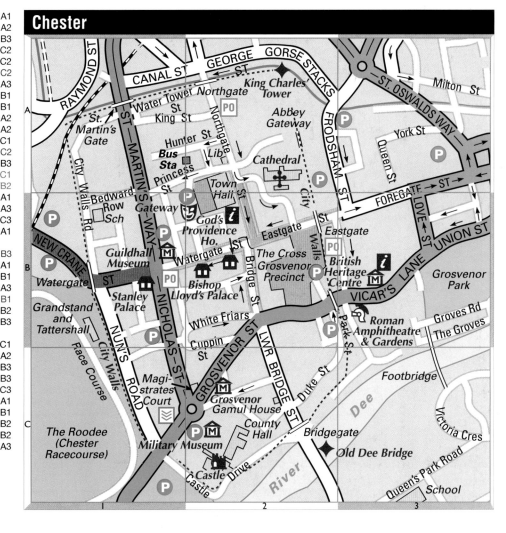

## Coventry

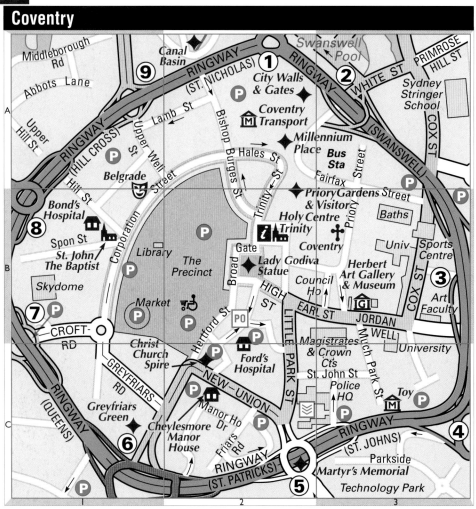

## Derby

# Durham

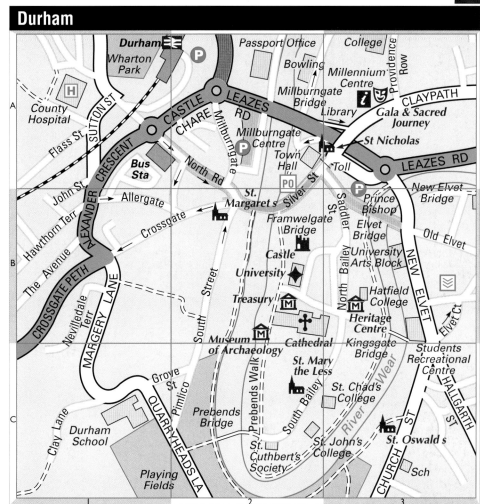

# Exeter

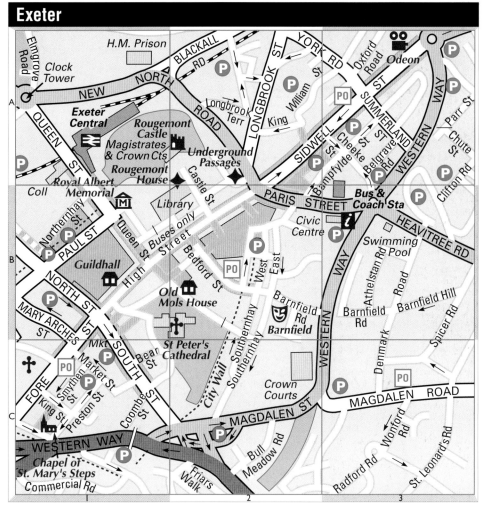

# Edinburgh

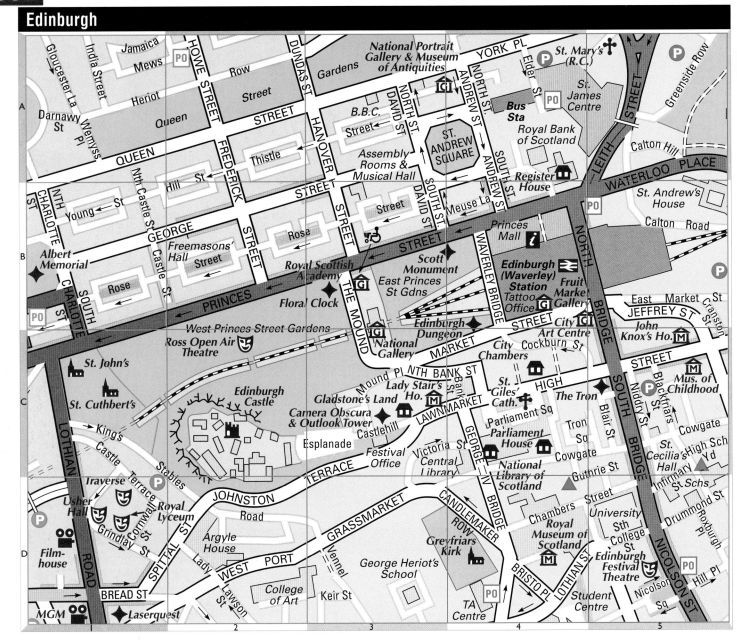

## Edinburgh

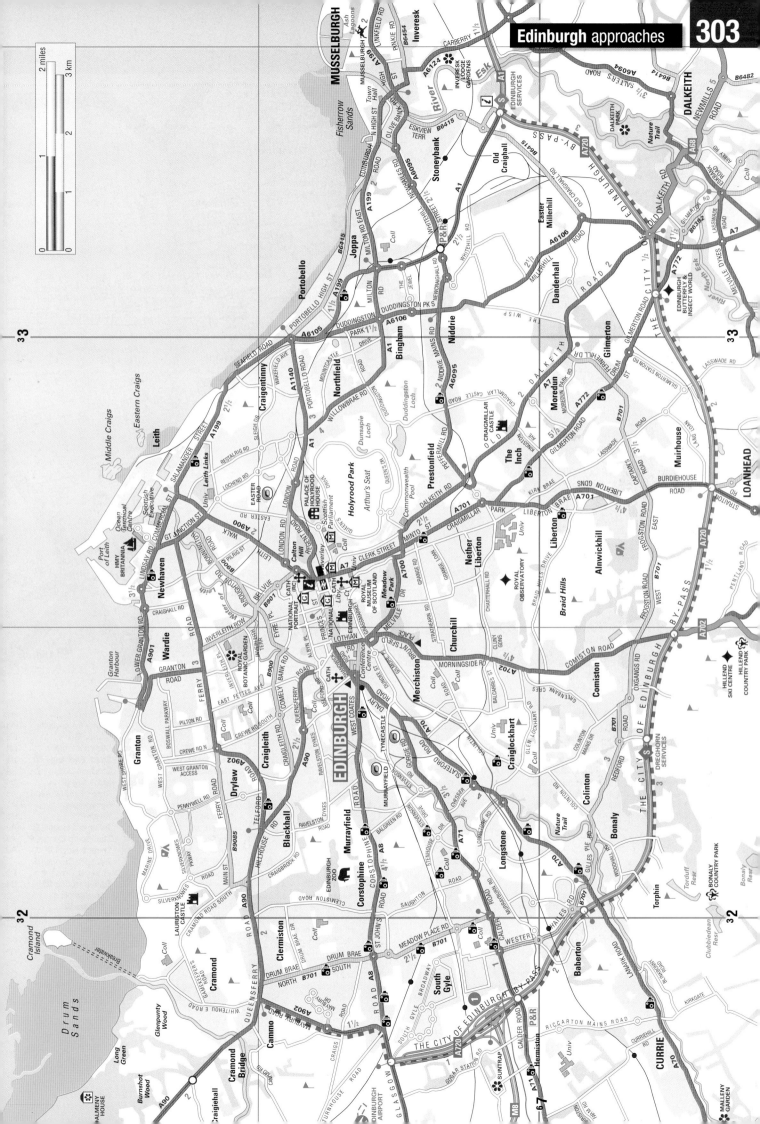

# Glasgow

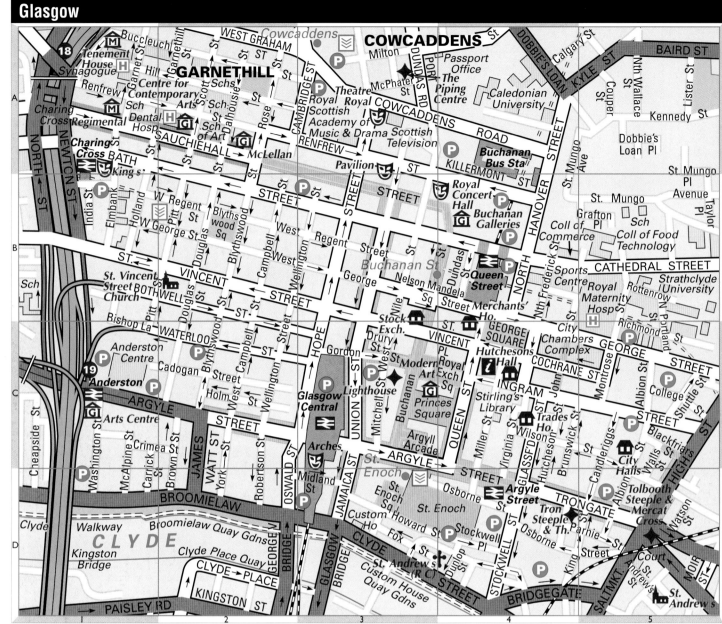

## Glasgow

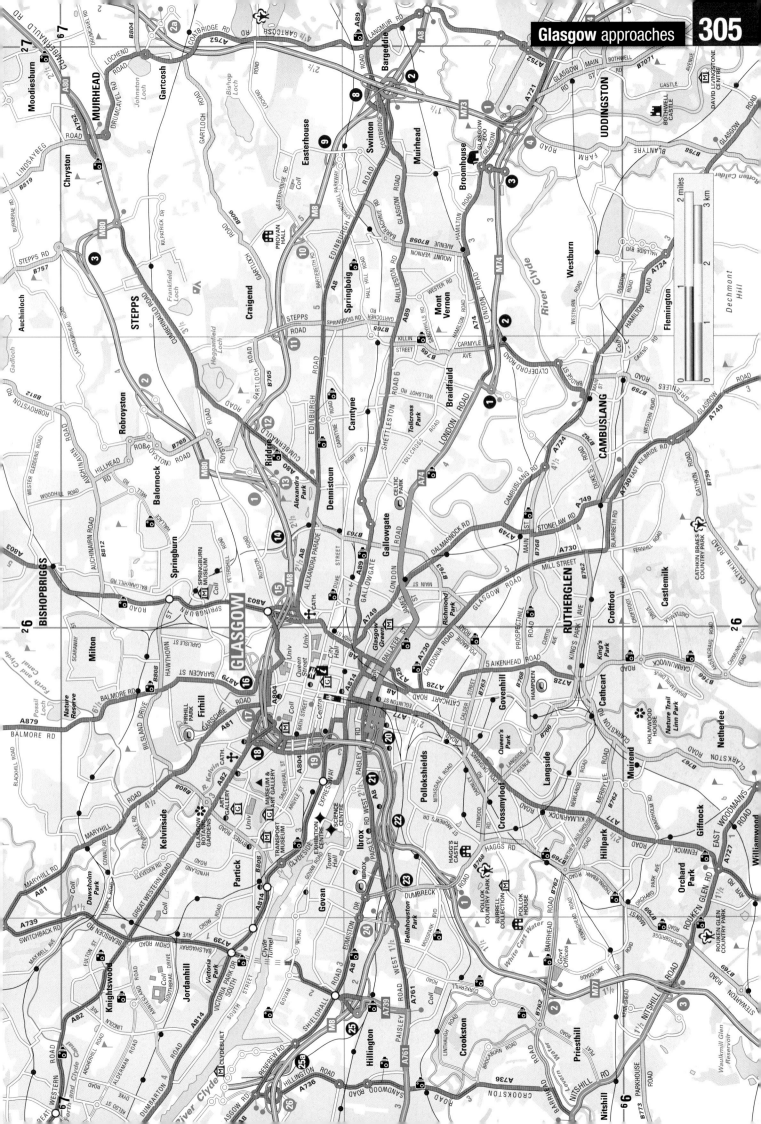

# Gloucester

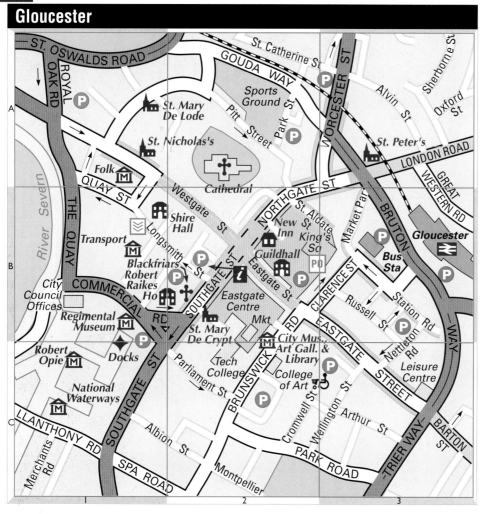

# Leicester

# Leeds

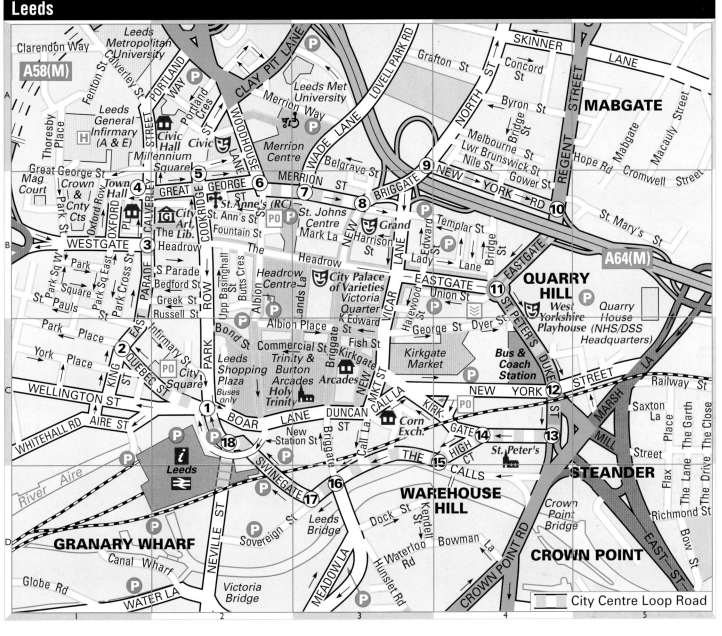

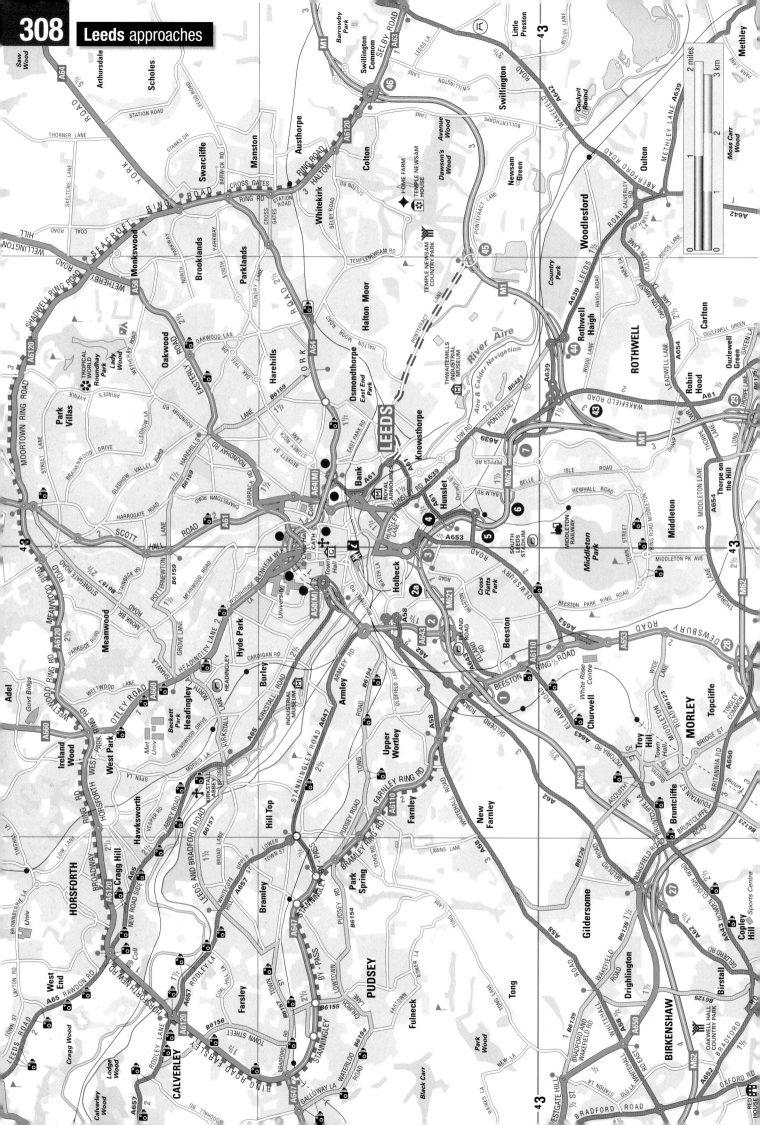

# Liverpool

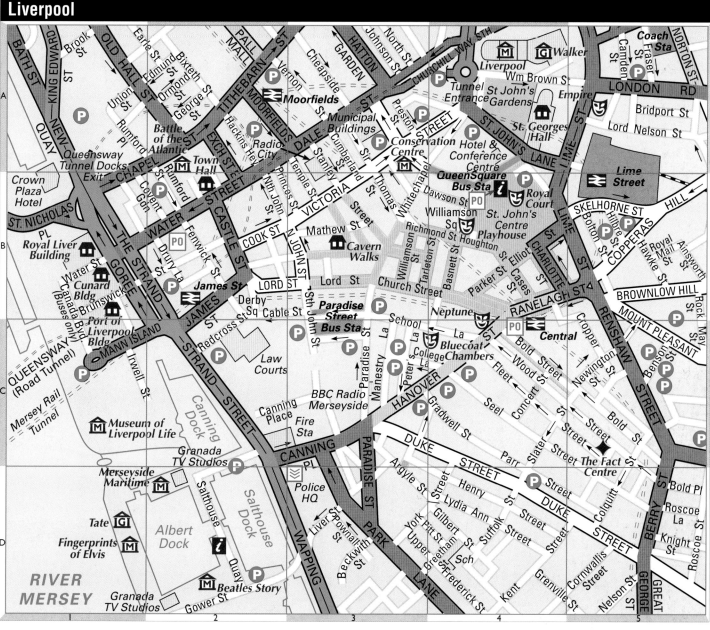

# Liverpool

# London

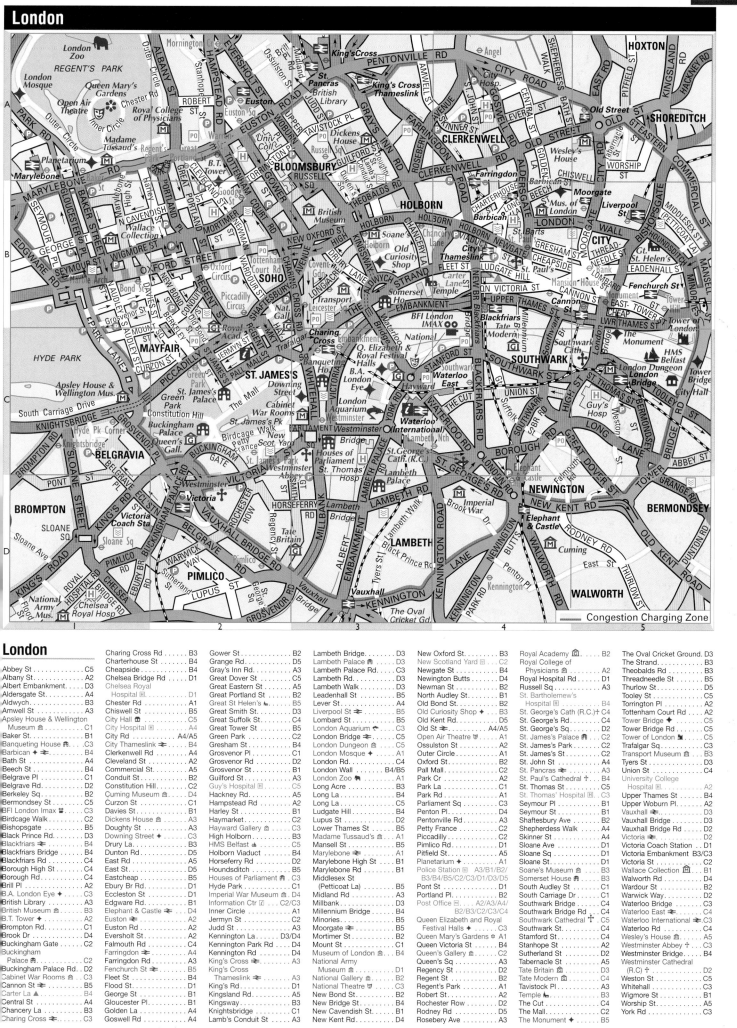

# London

## Manchester

# Newcastle

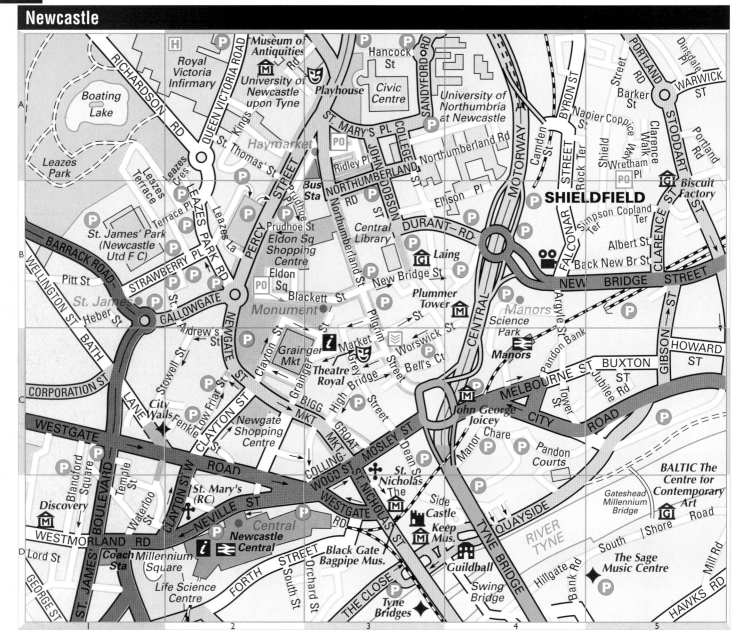

# Newcastle
# upon Tyne

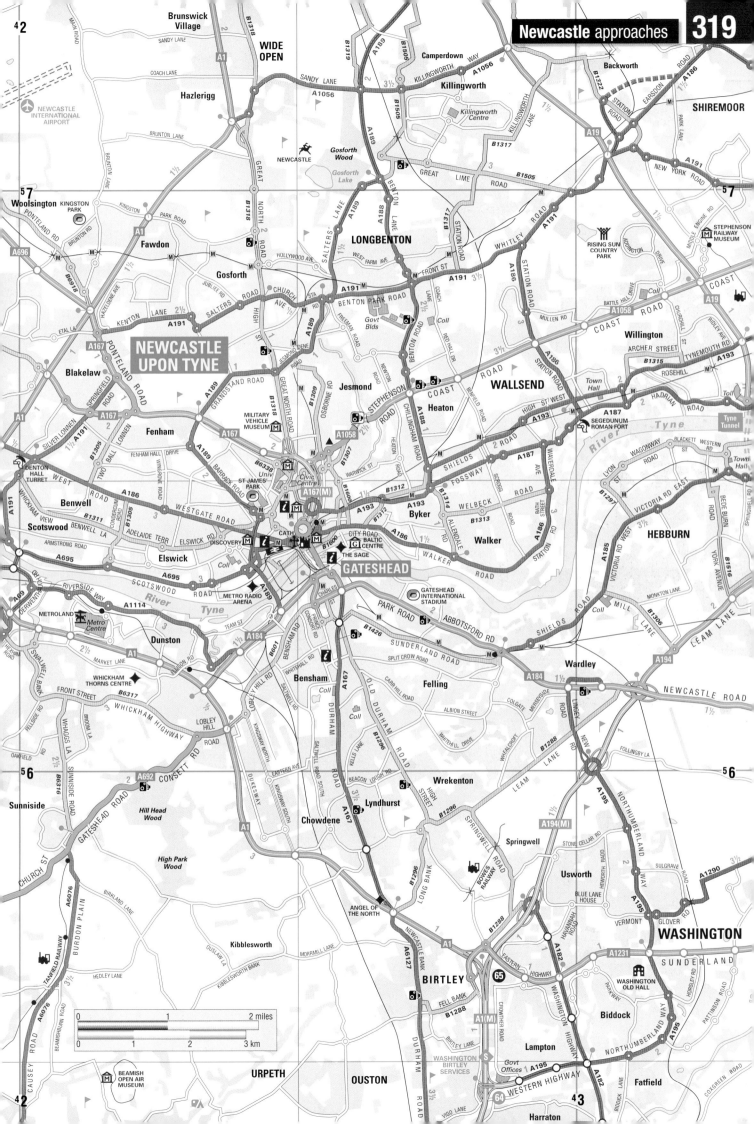

## Norwich

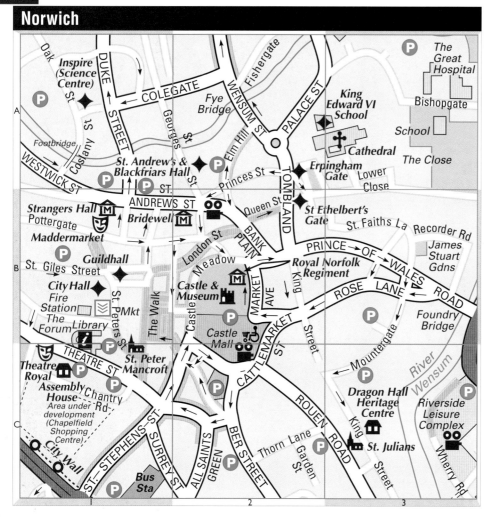

## Nottingham

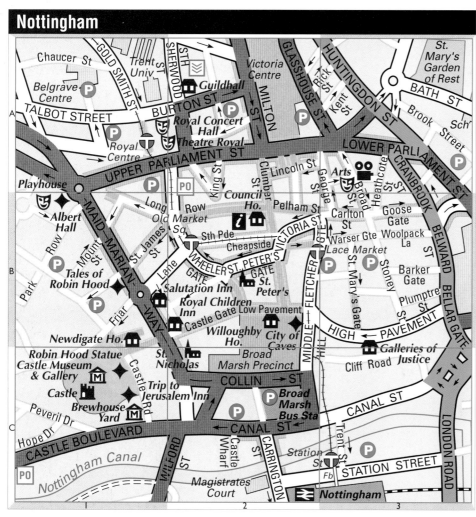

## Oxford

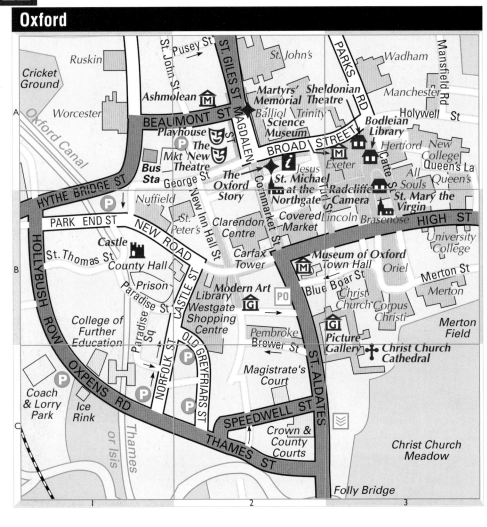

## Plymouth

# Salisbury

# Stratford-upon-Avon

## Salisbury

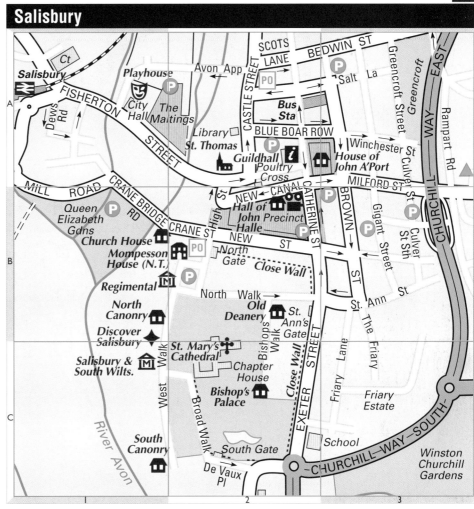

## Stratford-upon-Avon

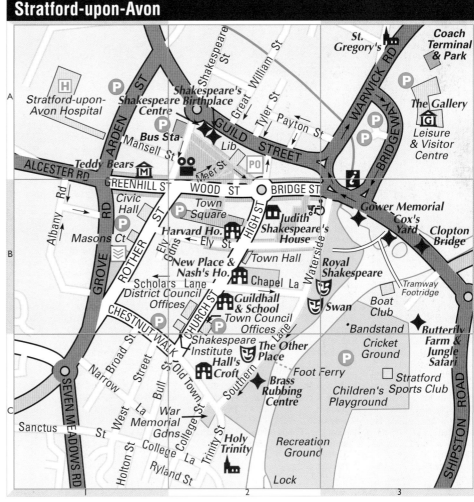

# Sheffield

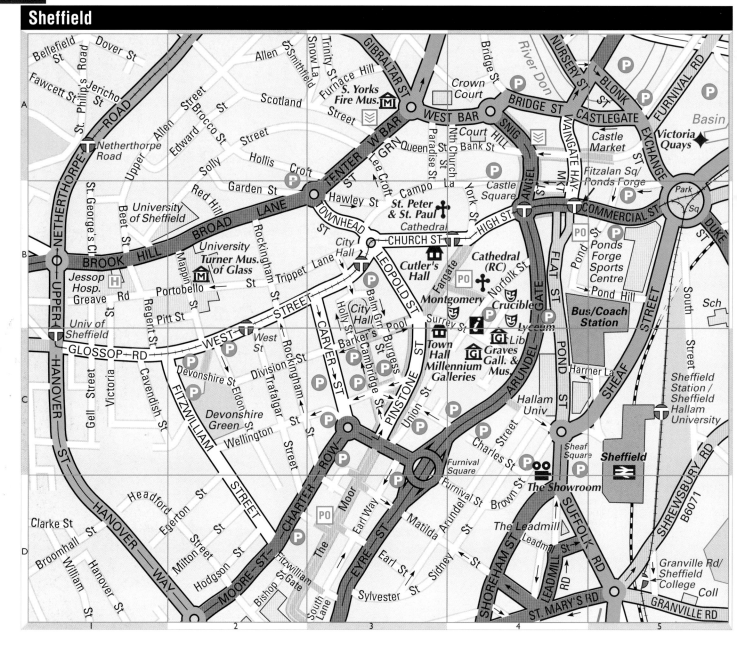

# Swansea / Abertawe

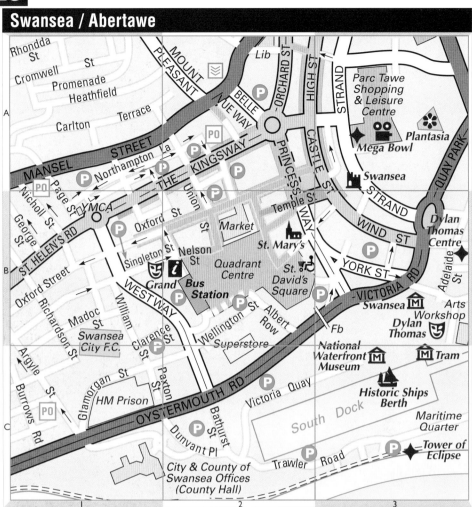

## Swansea/Abertawe

# Winchester

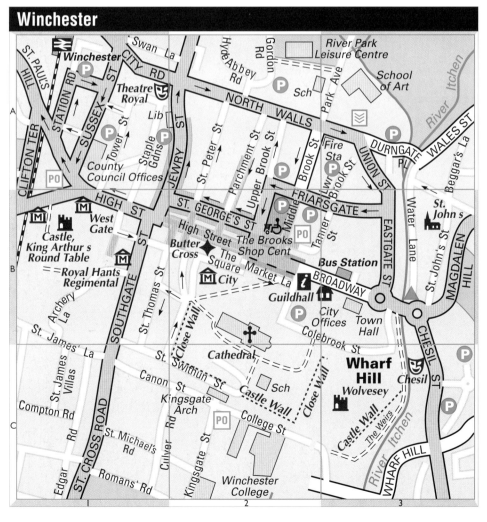

## Winchester

# Worcester

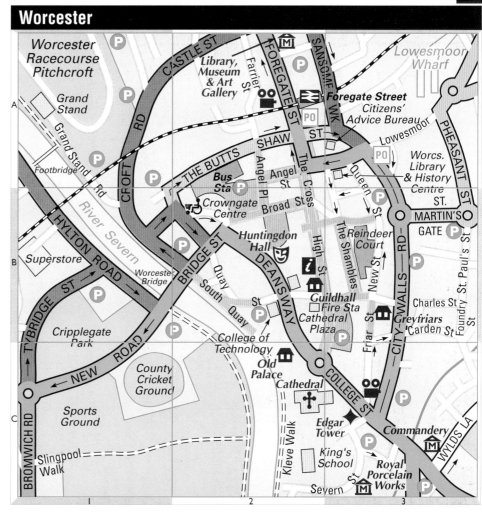

# York

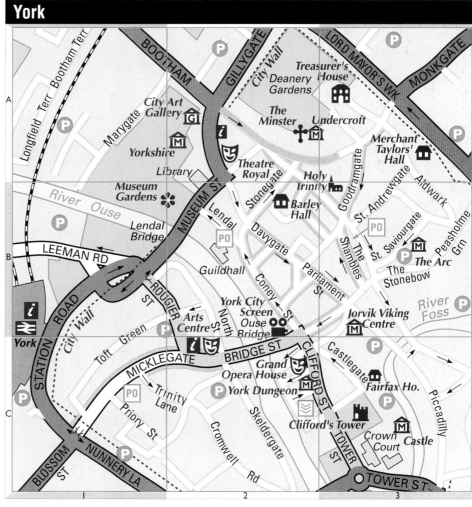

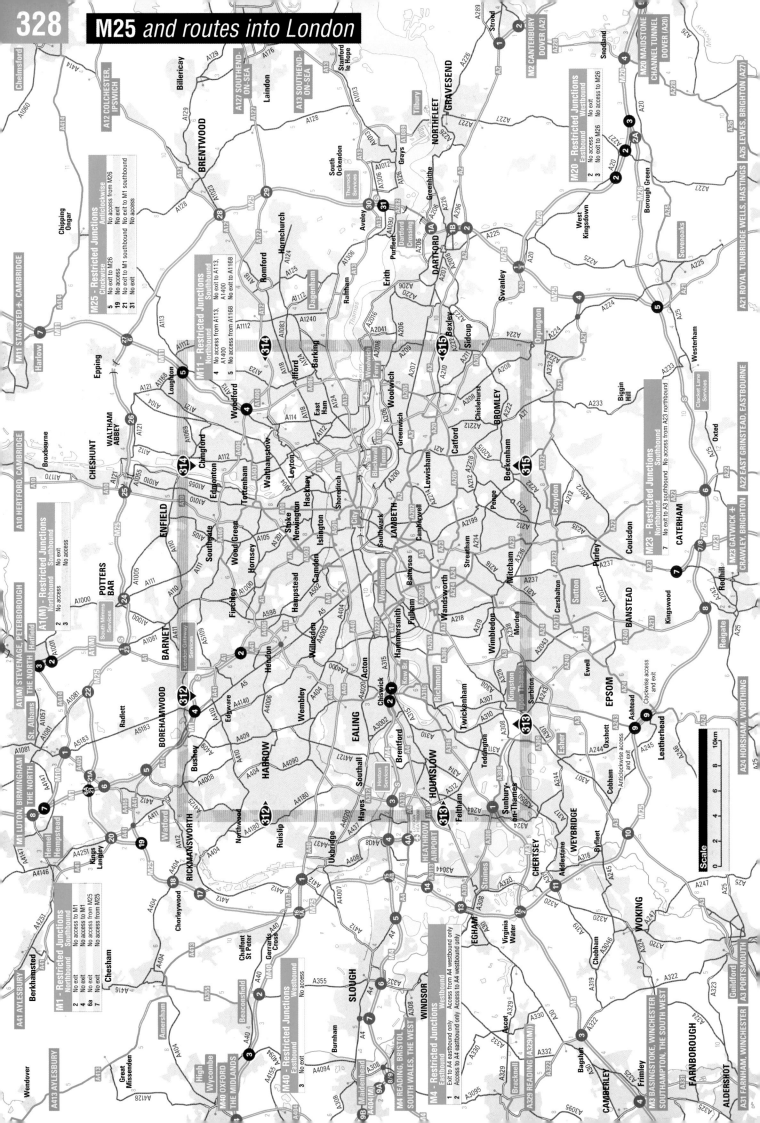

## How to use the index

Example

Adlestrop Glos 64 A3

- grid square
- page number
- county or unitary authority

Places of special interest are highlighted in magenta

## Abbreviations used in the index

| | | | |
|---|---|---|---|
| Aberdeen | Aberdeen City | Bristol | City and County of Bristol |
| Aberds | Aberdeenshire | | |
| Ald | Alderney | Bucks | Buckinghamshire |
| Anglesey | Isle of Anglesey | Caerph | Caerphilly |
| Angus | Angus | Cambs | Cambridgeshire |
| Argyll | Argyll and Bute | Cardiff | Cardiff |
| Bath | Bath and North East Somerset | Carms | Carmarthenshire |
| | | Ceredig | Ceredigion |
| Beds | Bedfordshire | Ches | Cheshire |
| Bl Gwent | Blaenau Gwent | Clack | Clackmannanshire |
| Blkburn | Blackburn with Darwen | Conwy | Conwy |
| | | Corn | Cornwall |
| Blkpool | Blackpool | Cumb | Cumbria |
| Bmouth | Bournemouth | Darl | Darlington |
| Borders | Scottish Borders | Denb | Denbighshire |
| Brack | Bracknell | Derby | City of Derby |
| Bridgend | Bridgend | Derbys | Derbyshire |
| Brighton | City of Brighton and Hove | Devon | Devon |
| | | Dorset | Dorset |

| | | | |
|---|---|---|---|
| Dumfries | Dumfries and Galloway | I o W | Isle of Wight |
| Dundee | Dundee City | Invclyd | Inverclyde |
| Durham | Durham | Jersey | Jersey |
| E Ayrs | East Ayrshire | Kent | Kent |
| E Dunb | East Dunbartonshire | Lancs | Lancashire |
| | | Leicester | City of Leicester |
| E Loth | East Lothian | Leics | Leicestershire |
| E Renf | East Renfrewshire | Lincs | Lincolnshire |
| E Sus | East Sussex | London | Greater London |
| E Yorks | East Riding of Yorkshire | Luton | Luton |
| | | M Keynes | Milton Keynes |
| Edin | City of Edinburgh | M Tydf | Merthyr Tydfil |
| Essex | Essex | M'bro | Middlesbrough |
| Falk | Falkirk | Medway | Medway |
| Fife | Fife | Mers | Merseyside |
| Flint | Flintshire | Midloth | Midlothian |
| Glasgow | City of Glasgow | Mon | Monmouthshire |
| Glos | Gloucesterhire | Moray | Moray |
| Gtr Man | Greater Manchester | N Ayrs | North Ayrshire |
| | | N Lincs | North Lincolnshire |
| Guern | Guernsey | N Lnrk | North Lanarkshire |
| Gwyn | Gwynedd | N Som | North Somerset |
| Halton | Halton | N Yorks | North Yorkshire |
| Hants | Hampshire | NE Lincs | North East Lincolnshire |
| Hereford | Herefordshire | | |
| Herts | Hertfordshire | Neath | Neath Port Talbot |
| Highld | Highland | Newport | City and County of Newport |
| Hrtlpl | Hartlepool | | |
| Hull | Hull | Norf | Norfolk |
| I o M | Isle of Man | Northants | Northamptonshire |
| | | Northumb | Northumberland |

| | | | |
|---|---|---|---|
| Nottingham | City of Nottingham | Stirl | Stirling |
| Notts | Nottinghamshire | Stockton | Stockton-on-Tees |
| Orkney | Orkney | Stoke | Stoke-on-Trent |
| Oxon | Oxfordshire | Suff | Suffolk |
| P'boro | Peterborough | Sur | Surrey |
| Pembs | Pembrokeshire | Swansea | Swansea |
| Perth | Perth and Kinross | T & W | Tyne and Wear |
| Plym | Plymouth | Telford | Telford and Wrekin |
| Poole | Poole | Thamesdown | Thamesdown |
| Powys | Powys | Thurrock | Thurrock |
| Ptsmth | Portsmouth | Torbay | Torbay |
| Reading | Reading | Torf | Torfaen |
| Redcar | Redcar and Cleveland | V Glam | The Vale of Glamorgan |
| Renfs | Renfrewshire | W Berks | West Berkshire |
| Rhondda | Rhondda Cynon Taff | W Dunb | West Dunbartonshire |
| Rutland | Rutland | W Isles | Western Isles |
| S Ayrs | South Ayrshire | W Loth | West Lothian |
| S Glos | South Gloucestershire | W Mid | West Midlands |
| | | W Sus | West Sussex |
| S Lnrk | South Lanarkshire | W Yorks | West Yorkshire |
| S Yorks | South Yorkshire | Warks | Warwickshire |
| Scilly | Scilly | Warr | Warrington |
| Shetland | Shetland | Wilts | Wiltshire |
| Shrops | Shropshire | Windsor | Windsor and Maidenhead |
| Slough | Slough | | |
| Som | Somerset | Wokingham | Wokingham |
| Soton | Southampton | Worcs | Worcestershire |
| Staffs | Staffordshire | Wrex | Wrexham |
| Sthend | Southend-on-Sea | York | City of York |

## A

Alciston E Sus 22 B3
Alcombe Som 27 A4
Alcombe Wilts 44 C2
Alconbury Cambs 100 D3
Alconbury Weston Cambs 100 D3
Aldbar Castle Angus 232 C3
Aldborough Norf 120 B3
Aldborough N Yorks 148 A3
Aldbourne Wilts 45 B6
Aldbrough E Yorks 151 D5
Aldbrough St John N Yorks 167 D5
Aldbury Herts 67 B4
Aldcliffe Lancs 145 A4
Aldclune Perth 230 B3
Aldeburgh Suff 89 B5
Aldeby Norf 105 B5
Aldenham Herts 67 D6
Alderbury Wilts 31 C5
Aldercar Derbys 114 A2
Alderford Norf 120 D3
Alderholt Dorset 31 D5
Alderley Glos 62 D3
Alderley Edge Ches 128 B3
Aldermaston W Berks 46 C3
Aldermaston Wharf W Berks 47 C4
Alderminster Warks 81 C5
Alderney Airport Ald 7
Alder's End Hereford 79 C4
Aldersey Green Ches 127 D4
Aldershot Hants 34 A1
Alderton Glos 80 D3
Alderton Northants 83 C4
Alderton Shrops 110 C3
Alderton Suff 88 C4
Alderton Wilts 44 A2
Alderwasley Derbys 130 D3
Aldfield N Yorks 147 A6
Aldford Ches 127 D4
Aldham Essex 70 A3
Aldham Suff 87 C6
Aldie Highld 264 B3
Aldingbourne W Sus 20 B2
Aldingham Cumb 154 D1
Aldington Kent 38 B2
Aldington Worcs 80 C3
Aldington Frith Kent 38 B2
Aldochlay Argyll 206 A3
Aldreth Cambs 101 D6
Aldridge W Mid 96 A3
Aldringham Suff 89 A5
Aldsworth Glos 64 B2
Aldunie Moray 255 D4
Aldwark Derbys 130 D2
Aldwark N Yorks 148 A3
Aldwick W Sus 20 C2
Aldwincle Northants 100 C2
Aldworth W Berks 46 B3
Alexandria W Dunb 206 C1
Alfardisworthy Devon 24 D3
Alfington Devon 13 B6
Alfold Sur 34 C3
Alfold Bars W Sus 34 C3
Alfold Crossways Sur 34 C3
Alford Aberds 244 A2
Alford Lincs 135 B4
Alford Som 29 B6
Alfreton Derbys 131 D4
Alfrick Worcs 79 B5
Alfrick Pound Worcs 79 B5
Alfriston E Sus 22 B3
Algaltraig Argyll 203 A5
Algarkirk Lincs 117 B5
Alhampton Som 29 B6
Aline Lodge W Isles 288 F2
Alisary Highld 235 C6
Alkborough N Lincs 141 A6
Alkerton Oxon 81 C6
Alkham Kent 39 A4
Alkington Shrops 111 B4
Alkmonton Derbys 113 B5
All Cannings Wilts 45 C4
All Saints Church, Godshill I o W 18 C4
All Saints South Elmham Suff 104 C4
All Stretton Shrops 94 B2
Alladale Lodge Highld 263 B6
Allaleigh Devon 8 B2
Allanaquoich Aberds 242 C4
Allangrange Mains Highld 252 A2
Allanton Borders 198 A2
Allanton N Lnrk 194 A3
Allathasdal W Isles 286 F2
Allendale Town Northumb 177 D6
Allenheads Northumb 165 A6
Allens Green Herts 69 B4
Allensford Durham 178 D2
Allensmore Hereford 78 D2
Allenton Derby 114 B1
Aller Som 28 C4
Allerby Cumb 162 A3
Allerford Som 27 A4
Allerston N Yorks 160 C2
Allerthorpe E Yorks 149 C6
Allerton Mers 127 A4
Allerton W Yorks 147 D5
Allerton Bywater W Yorks 140 A2
Allerton Mauleverer N Yorks 148 B3
Allesley W Mid 97 C6
Allestree Derby 114 B1
Allet Corn 4 C2
Allexton Leics 99 A5
Allgreave Ches 129 C4
Allhallows Medway 51 B5
Allhallows-on-Sea Medway 51 B5
Alligin Shuas Highld 249 A5
Allimore Green Staffs 112 D2
Allington Lincs 115 A6
Allington Wilts 31 B6
Allington Wilts 45 C4
Allithwaite Cumb 154 D2
Alloa Clack 208 A1
Allonby Cumb 174 D3
Alloway S Ayrs 192 D3
Allt Carms 57 B5
Allt na h-Airbhe Highld 262 A3
Allt-nan-sùgh Highld 249 D6
Alltchaorunn Highld 237 D5
Alltforgan Powys 109 C4
Alltmawr Powys 77 C4
Alltnacaillich Highld 277 D5
Alltsigh Highld 240 A2
Alltwalis Carms 58 B1
Alltwen Neath 40 A2
Alltyblaca Ceredig 75 D4
Allwood Green Suff 103 D6
Almeley Hereford 78 B1
Almer Dorset 16 B3
Almholme S Yorks 140 C3
Almington Staffs 111 B6
Alminstone Cross Devon 24 C4
Almondbank Perth 219 B5
Almondbury W Yorks 139 B4
Almondsbury S Glos 43 A5
Alne N Yorks 148 A3
Alness Highld 264 D2
Alnham Northumb 188 B2
Alnmouth Northumb 189 B5
Alnwick Northumb 189 B4
Alperton London 49 A4
Alphamstone Essex 87 D4
Alpheton Suff 87 B4
Alphington Devon 13 B4
Alport Derbys 130 C2
Alpraham Ches 127 D5
Alresford Essex 71 A4
Alrewas Staffs 113 D5
Alsager Ches 128 D2
Alsagers Bank Staffs 112 A2
Alsop en le Dale Derbys 129 D6
Alston Cumb 165 A5
Alston Devon 14 A3
Alstone Glos 80 D2
Alstonefield Staffs 129 D6
Alswear Devon 26 C2
Altandhu Highld 270 C2
Altanduin Highld 274 B2
Altarnun Corn 10 C3
Altass Highld 272 D2
Alterwall Highld 281 B4
Altham Lancs 146 D1
Althorne Essex 70 D3
Althorp House, Great Brington Northants 82 A3
Althorpe N Lincs 141 C6
Alticry Dumfries 171 B4
Altnabreac Station Highld 279 D6
Altnacealgach Hotel Highld 271 C5
Altnacraig Argyll 226 D3
Altnafeadh Highld 237 D6
Altnaharra Highld 272 A3
Altofts W Yorks 139 A6
Alton Derbys 130 C3
Alton Hants 33 B6
Alton Staffs 113 A4
Alton Pancras Dorset 15 A7
Alton Priors Wilts 45 C5
Alton Towers Staffs 113 A4
Altrincham Gtr Man 128 A2
Altrua Highld 239 D6
Altskeith Stirl 217 D4
Altyre Ho. Moray 253 A6
Alva Clack 208 A1
Alvanley Ches 127 B4
Alvaston Derby 114 B1
Alvechurch Worcs 96 D3
Alvecote Warks 97 A5
Alvediston Wilts 30 C3
Alveley Shrops 95 C5
Alverdiscott Devon 25 C6
Alverstoke Hants 19 B5
Alverstone I o W 19 C4
Alverton Notts 115 A5
Alves Moray 266 C2
Alvescot Oxon 64 C3
Alveston S Glos 43 A5
Alveston Warks 81 B5
Alvie Highld 241 B6
Alvingham Lincs 143 D5
Alvington Glos 62 C2
Alwalton Cambs 100 B3
Alweston Dorset 29 D6
Alwinton Northumb 188 C2
Alwoodley W Yorks 148 C1
Alyth Perth 231 D6
Am Baile W Isles 286 E3
Am Buth Argyll 226 D3
Amatnatua Highld 263 A6
Amber Hill Lincs 117 A5
Ambergate Derbys 130 D3
Amberley Glos 63 C4
Amberley W Sus 20 A3
Amble Northumb 189 C5
Amblecote W Mid 96 C1
Ambler Thorn W Yorks 138 A3
Ambleside Cumb 154 A2
Ambleston Pembs 55 B6
Ambrosden Oxon 65 B7
Amcotts N Lincs 141 B6
American Adventure, Ilkeston Derbys 114 A2
American Air Museum, Duxford Cambs 85 C6
Amersham Bucks 67 D4
Amerton Working Farm, Stowe-by-Chartley Staffs 112 C3
Amesbury Wilts 31 A5
Amington Staffs 97 A5
Amisfield Dumfries 184 D2
Amlwch Anglesey 123 A4
Amlwch Port Anglesey 123 A4
Ammanford = Rhydaman Carms 57 A6
Amod Argyll 190 B3
Amotherby N Yorks 159 D6
Ampfield Hants 32 C3
Ampleforth N Yorks 159 D4
Ampney Crucis Glos 63 C6
Ampney St Mary Glos 64 C1
Ampney St Peter Glos 64 C1
Amport Hants 32 A1
Ampthill Beds 84 D2
Ampton Suff 103 D4
Amroth Pembs 56 B1
Amulree Perth 218 A3
An Caol Highld 248 A3
An Cnoc W Isles 288 D5
An Gleann Ur W Isles 288 D5
An t-Ob = Leverburgh W Isles 287 F5
Anagach Highld 253 D6
Anaheilt Highld 236 C2
Anancaun Highld 262 D2
Ancaster Lincs 116 A2
Anchor Shrops 93 C5
Anchorsholme Blkpool 144 C3
Ancroft Northumb 198 B3
Ancrum Borders 187 A5
Anderby Lincs 135 B5
Anderson Dorset 16 B2
Anderton Ches 127 B6
Andover Hants 32 A2
Andover Down Hants 32 A2
Andoversford Glos 63 B6
Andreas I o M 152 B4
Anfield Mers 136 D2
Angersleigh Som 28 D1
Angle Pembs 55 D4
Angmering W Sus 20 B3
Angram N Yorks 148 C4
Angram N Yorks 156 B2
Anie Stirl 217 C5
Ankerville Highld 265 C4
Anlaby E Yorks 142 A2
Anmer Norf 119 C4
Anna Valley Hants 32 A2
Annan Dumfries 175 B4
Annat Argyll 227 D5
Annat Highld 249 A5
Annbank S Ayrs 193 C4
Anne Hathaway's Cottage, Stratford-upon-Avon Warks 81 B4
Annesley Notts 131 D5
Annesley Woodhouse Notts 131 D4
Annfield Plain Durham 178 D3
Annifirth Shetland 285 J3
Annitsford T & W 179 B4
Annscroft Shrops 94 A2
Ansdell Lancs 136 A2
Ansford Som 29 B6
Ansley Warks 97 B5
Anslow Staffs 113 C6
Anslow Gate Staffs 113 C5
Anstey Herts 85 D6
Anstey Leics 98 A2
Anstruther Easter Fife 221 D5
Anstruther Wester Fife 221 D5
Ansty Hants 33 A6
Ansty Warks 97 C6
Ansty Wilts 30 C3
Ansty W Sus 35 D5
Anthill Common Hants 33 D5
Anthorn Cumb 175 C4
Antingham Norf 121 B4
Anton's Gowt Lincs 117 A5
Antonshill Falk 208 B1
Antony Corn 6 B3
Anwick Lincs 133 D6
Anwoth Dumfries 172 C3
Aoradh Argyll 200 B2
Apes Hall Cambs 102 B1
Apethorpe Northants 100 B2
Apeton Staffs 112 D2
Apley Lincs 133 B6
Apperknowle Derbys 130 B3
Apperley Glos 63 A4
Apperley Bridge W Yorks 147 D5
Appersett N Yorks 156 B2
Appin Argyll 226 B4
Appin House Argyll 226 B4
Appleby N Lincs 142 B1
Appleby-in-Westmorland Cumb 165 C4
Appleby Magna Leics 97 A6
Appleby Parva Leics 97 A6
Applecross Highld 249 B4
Applecross Ho. Highld 249 B4
Appledore Devon 25 B5
Appledore Devon 27 D5
Appledore Kent 38 C1
Appledore Heath Kent 38 B1
Appleford Oxon 65 D6
Applegarthtown Dumfries 185 D4
Appleshaw Hants 32 A2
Applethwaite Cumb 163 B5
Appleton Halton 127 A5
Appleton Oxon 65 C5
Appleton-le-Moors N Yorks 159 C6
Appleton-le-Street N Yorks 159 D6
Appleton Roebuck N Yorks 149 C4
Appleton Thorn Warr 127 A6
Appleton Wiske N Yorks 158 A2
Appletreehall Borders 186 B4
Appletreewick N Yorks 147 A4
Appley Som 27 C5
Appley Bridge Lancs 136 C4
Apse Heath I o W 19 C4
Apsley End Beds 84 D3
Apuldram W Sus 20 B1
Aquhythie Aberds 245 A4
Arabella Highld 265 C4
Arbeadie Aberds 244 C3
Arbeia Roman Fort and Museum T & W 179 C5
Arberth = Narberth Pembs 55 C7
Arbirlot Angus 233 D4
Arboll Highld 265 B4
Arborfield Wokingham 47 C5
Arborfield Cross Wokingham 47 C5
Arborfield Garrison Wokingham 47 C5
Arbour-thorne S Yorks 130 A3
Arbroath Angus 233 D4
Arbuthnott Aberds 233 A5
Archiestown Moray 254 B3
Arclid Ches 128 C2
Ard-dhubh Highld 249 B4
Ardachu Highld 273 D4
Ardalanish Argyll 224 E2
Ardanaiseig Argyll 227 D5
Ardaneaskan Highld 249 C5
Ardanstur Argyll 213 A6
Ardargie House Hotel Perth 219 C5
Ardarroch Highld 249 C5
Ardbeg Argyll 201 D4
Ardbeg Argyll 215 D4
Ardbeg Distillery, Port Ellen Argyll 201 D4
Ardcharnich Highld 262 B3
Ardchiavaig Argyll 224 E2
Ardchullarie More Stirl 217 C5
Ardchyle Stirl 217 B5
Arddleen Powys 110 D1
Ardechvie Highld 239 C5
Ardeley Herts 68 A3
Ardelve Highld 249 D5
Arden Argyll 206 B1
Ardens Grafton Warks 80 B4
Ardentinny Argyll 215 D4
Ardentraive Argyll 203 A5
Ardeonaig Stirl 217 A6
Ardersier Highld 252 A3
Ardessie Highld 262 B2
Ardfern Argyll 213 B6
Ardgartan Argyll 215 B5
Ardgay Highld 264 A1
Ardgour Highld 237 C4
Ardheslaig Highld 249 A4
Ardiecow Moray 267 C6
Ardindrean Highld 262 B3
Ardingly W Sus 35 D6
Ardington Oxon 46 A2
Ardlair Aberds 255 D6
Ardlamont Ho. Argyll 203 B4
Ardleigh Essex 71 A4
Ardler Perth 231 D6
Ardley Oxon 65 A6
Ardlui Argyll 215 A6
Ardlussa Argyll 213 D4
Ardmair Highld 262 A3
Ardmay Argyll 215 B5
Ardminish Argyll 202 D1
Ardmolich Highld 235 C6
Ardmore Argyll 226 D2
Ardmore Highld 276 C3
Ardmore Highld 264 B3
Ardnacross Argyll 225 B4
Ardnadam Argyll 203 A6
Ardnagrask Highld 251 B7
Ardnarff Highld 249 C5
Ardnastang Highld 236 C2
Ardnave Argyll 200 A2
Ardno Argyll 215 B4
Ardo Aberds 256 C3
Ardo Ho. Aberds 257 D4
Ardoch Perth 219 A5
Ardochy House Highld 239 B6
Ardoyne Aberds 256 D1
Ardpatrick Argyll 202 B2
Ardpatrick Ho. Argyll 202 C2
Ardpeaton Argyll 215 D5
Ardrishaig Argyll 213 D6
Ardross Fife 221 D5
Ardross Highld 264 C2
Ardross Castle Highld 264 C2
Ardrossan N Ayrs 204 D2
Ardshealach Highld 235 D5
Ardsley S Yorks 140 C1
Ardslignish Highld 235 D4
Ardtalla Argyll 201 C4
Ardtalnaig Perth 218 A2
Ardtoe Highld 235 C5
Ardtrostan Perth 217 B6
Arduaine Argyll 213 A5
Ardullie Highld 264 D1
Ardvasar Highld 247 D5
Ardvorlich Perth 217 B6
Ardwell Dumfries 170 C3
Ardwell Mains Dumfries 170 C3
Ardwick Gtr Man 138 D1
Areley Kings Worcs 95 D6
Arford Hants 34 C1
Argoed Caerph 41 B6
Argoed Mill Powys 76 A3
Argyll & Sutherland Highlanders Museum (See Stirling Castle) Stirl 207 A5
Arichamish Argyll 214 B2
Arichastlich Argyll 216 A2
Aridhglas Argyll 224 D2
Arileod Argyll 223 B4
Arinacrinachd Highld 249 A4
Arinagour Argyll 223 B5
Arion Orkney 282 F3
Arisaig Highld 235 B5
Ariundle Highld 236 C2
Arkendale N Yorks 148 A2
Arkesden Essex 85 D6
Arkholme Lancs 155 D4
Arkle Town N Yorks 156 A4
Arkley London 68 D2
Arksey S Yorks 140 C3
Arkwright Town Derbys 131 B4
Arle Glos 63 A5
Arlecdon Cumb 162 C3
Arlesey Beds 84 D3
Arleston Telford 111 D5
Arley Ches 128 A1
Arlingham Glos 62 B3
Arlington Devon 25 A7
Arlington E Sus 22 B3
Arlington Glos 64 C2
Arlington Court Devon 25 A7
Armadale Highld 278 B3
Armadale W Loth 208 D2
Armadale Castle Highld 247 D5
Armathwaite Cumb 164 A3
Arminghall Norf 104 A3
Armitage Staffs 113 D4
Armley W Yorks 148 D1
Armscote Warks 81 C5
Armthorpe S Yorks 140 C4
Arnabost Argyll 223 B5
Arncliffe N Yorks 156 D3
Arncroach Fife 221 D5
Arne Dorset 16 C3
Arnesby Leics 98 B3
Arngask Perth 219 C6
Arnisdale Highld 238 A2
Arnish Highld 248 B2
Arniston Engine Midloth 209 D6
Arnol W Isles 288 C4
Arnold E Yorks 151 C4
Arnold Notts 114 A3
Arnolfini Gallery Bristol 43 B4
Arnprior Stirl 207 A4
Arnside Cumb 154 D3
Aros Mains Argyll 225 B4
Arowry Wrex 110 B3
Arpafeelie Highld 252 A2
Arrad Foot Cumb 154 C2
Arram E Yorks 150 C3
Arrathorne N Yorks 157 B6
Arreton I o W 18 C4
Arrington Cambs 85 B5
Arrivain Argyll 216 A2
Arrochar Argyll 215 B5
Arrow Warks 80 B3
Arthington W Yorks 147 C6
Arthingworth Northants 99 C4
Arthog Gwyn 90 A4
Arthrath Aberds 257 C4
Arthurstone Perth 231 D6
Artrochie Aberds 257 C5
Arundel W Sus 20 B3
Arundel Castle W Sus 20 B3
Aryhoulan Highld 237 C4
Asby Cumb 162 B3
Ascog Argyll 203 B6
Ascot Windsor 48 C2
Ascot Racecourse Windsor 48 C2
Ascott Warks 81 D6
Ascott-under-Wychwood Oxon 64 B4
Asenby N Yorks 158 D2
Asfordby Leics 115 D5
Asfordby Hill Leics 115 D5
Asgarby Lincs 116 A4
Asgarby Lincs 134 C3
Ash Kent 50 C2
Ash Kent 53 D4
Ash Som 29 C4
Ash Sur 34 A1
Ash Bullayne Devon 12 A2
Ash Green Warks 97 C6
Ash Magna Shrops 111 B4
Ash Mill Devon 26 C2
Ash Priors Som 27 C6
Ash Street Suff 87 C6
Ash Thomas Devon 27 D5
Ash Vale Sur 34 A1
Ashampstead W Berks 46 B3
Ashbocking Suff 88 B2
Ashbourne Derbys 113 A5
Ashbrittle Som 27 C5
Ashburton Devon 7 A6
Ashbury Devon 11 B6
Ashbury Oxon 45 A6
Ashby N Lincs 141 C7
Ashby by Partney Lincs 135 C4
Ashby cum Fenby NE Lincs 143 C4
Ashby de la Launde Lincs 133 D5
Ashby-de-la-Zouch Leics 114 D1
Ashby Folville Leics 115 D5
Ashby Magna Leics 98 B2
Ashby Parva Leics 98 C2
Ashby Puerorum Lincs 134 B3
Ashby St Ledgers Northants 82 A2
Ashby St Mary Norf 104 A4
Ashchurch Glos 80 D2
Ashcombe Devon 13 D4
Ashcott Som 28 B4
Ashdon Essex 86 C1
Ashe Hants 32 A4
Asheldham Essex 70 C3
Ashen Essex 86 C3
Ashendon Bucks 66 B2
Ashfield Carms 58 C3
Ashfield Stirl 218 D2
Ashfield Suff 88 A3
Ashfield Green Suff 104 D3
Ashfold Crossways W Sus 35 D5
Ashford Devon 25 B6
Ashford Hants 31 D5
Ashford Kent 38 A2
Ashford Sur 48 B3
Ashford Bowdler Shrops 94 D3
Ashford Carbonell Shrops 94 D3
Ashford Hill Hants 46 C3
Ashford in the Water Derbys 130 C1
Ashgill S Lnrk 194 B2
Ashill Devon 27 D5
Ashill Norf 103 A4
Ashill Som 28 D3
Ashingdon Essex 70 D2
Ashington Northumb 179 A4
Ashington Som 29 C5
Ashington W Sus 21 A4
Ashintully Castle Perth 231 B5
Ashkirk Borders 186 A3
Ashlett Hants 18 A3

Cors-y-Gedol Gwyn 107 D5
Corsback Highld 280 A4
Corscombe Dorset 15 A5
Corse Aberds 255 B7
Corse Glos 62 A3
Corse Lawn Worcs 79 D6
Corse of Kinnoir Aberds 255 B6
Corsewall Dumfries 170 A2
Corsham Wilts 44 B2
Corsindae Aberds 244 B3
Corsley Wilts 30 A2
Corsley Heath Wilts 30 A2
Corsock Dumfries 173 A5
Corston Bath 43 C5
Corston Wilts 44 A3
Corstorphine Edin 209 C4
Cortachy Angus 232 C1
Corton Suff 105 B6
Corton Wilts 30 A3
Corton Denham Som 29 C6
Coruanan Lodge Highld 237 C4
Corunna W Isles 287 H3
Corwen Denb 109 A5
Coryton Devon 11 C5
Coryton Thurrock 51 A4
Cosby Leics 98 B2
Coseley W Mid 96 B2
Cosgrove Northants 83 C4
Cosham Ptsmth 19 A5
Cosheston Pembs 55 D6
Cossall Notts 114 A2
Cossington Leics 115 D4
Cossington Som 28 A3
Costa Orkney 282 E4
Costessey Norf 120 D3
Costock Notts 114 C3
Coston Leics 115 C6
Cote Oxon 64 C4
Cotebrook Ches 127 C5
Cotehele House Corn 6 A3
Cotehill Cumb 176 D2
Cotes Cumb 154 C3
Cotes Leics 114 C3
Cotes Staffs 112 B2
Cotesbach Leics 98 C2
Cotgrave Notts 115 B4
Cothall Aberds 245 A5
Cotham Notts 115 A5
Cothelstone Som 28 B1
Cotherstone Durham 166 D3
Cothill Oxon 65 D5
Cotleigh Devon 14 A2
Cotmanhay Derbys 114 A2
Cotmaton Devon 13 C6
Coton Cambs 85 B6
Coton Northants 98 D3
Coton Staffs 112 C2
Coton Staffs 112 B3
Coton Clanford Staffs 112 C2
Coton Hill Shrops 110 D3
Coton Hill Staffs 112 B3
Coton in the Elms Derbys 113 D6
Cotswold Wild Life Park, Burford Oxon 64 C3
Cott Devon 8 A1
Cottam E Yorks 150 A2
Cottam Lancs 145 D5
Cottam Notts 132 B3
Cottartown Highld 253 C6
Cottenham Cambs 85 A6
Cotterdale N Yorks 156 B2
Cottered Herts 68 A3
Cotteridge W Mid 96 D3
Cotterstock Northants 100 B2
Cottesbrooke Northants 99 D4
Cottesmore Rutland 116 D2
Cotteylands Devon 27 D4
Cottingham E Yorks 150 D3
Cottingham Northants 99 B5
Cottingley W Yorks 147 D5
Cottisford Oxon 82 D2
Cotton Staffs 113 A4
Cotton Suff 87 A6
Cotton End Beds 84 C2
Cottown Aberds 255 D6
Cottown Aberds 245 A4
Cottown Aberds 256 B3
Cotwalton Staffs 112 B3
Couch's Mill Corn 5 B6
Coughton Hereford 62 A1
Coughton Warks 80 A3
Coulaghailtro Argyll 202 B2
Coulags Highld 249 B6
Coulby Newham M'bro 168 D3
Coulderton Cumb 162 D2
Coulin Highld 250 A2
Coull Aberds 244 B2
Coull Argyll 200 B2
Coulport Argyll 215 D5
Coulsdon London 35 A5
Coulston Wilts 44 D3
Coulter S Lnrk 195 C5
Coulton N Yorks 159 D5
Cound Shrops 94 A3
Coundon Durham 167 C5
Coundon W Mid 97 C6
Coundon Grange Durham 167 C5
Countersett N Yorks 156 C3
Countess Wilts 31 A5
Countess Wear Devon 13 C4
Countesthorpe Leics 98 B2
Countisbury Devon 26 A2
County Oak W Sus 35 C5
Coup Green Lancs 137 A4
Coupar Angus Perth 231 D6
Coupland Northumb 198 C3
Cour Argyll 202 D3
Courance Dumfries 184 C3
Court-at-Street Kent 38 B2
Court Henry Carms 58 C2
Courteenhall Northants 83 B4
Courtsend Essex 71 D4
Courtway Som 28 B2
Cousland Midloth 209 D6
Cousley Wood E Sus 37 C4
Cove Argyll 215 D5
Cove Borders 211 C4
Cove Devon 27 D4
Cove Hants 34 A1
Cove Highld 261 A5
Cove Bay Aberdeen 245 B6
Cove Bottom Suff 105 D5
Covehithe Suff 105 C6
Coven Staffs 96 A2
Coveney Cambs 101 C6
Covenham St Bartholomew Lincs 143 D5
Covenham St Mary Lincs 143 D5
Coventry W Mid 97 D6
Coventry Airport Warks 97 D6
Coventry Cathedral W Mid 97 D6
Coverack Corn 3 D5
Coverham N Yorks 157 C5
Covesea Moray 266 B2
Covington Cambs 100 D2
Covington S Lnrk 195 C4
Cow Ark Lancs 145 C6
Cowan Bridge Lancs 155 D5
Cowbeech E Sus 22 A4
Cowbit Lincs 117 D5
Cowbridge Lincs 117 A6
Cowbridge Som 27 A4
Cowbridge = Y Bont-Faen V Glam 41 D4
Cowdale Derbys 129 B5
Cowden Kent 36 B2
Cowdenbeath Fife 209 A4
Cowdenburn Borders 195 A7
Cowers Lane Derbys 113 A7
Cowes I o W 18 B3
Cowesby N Yorks 158 C3
Cowfold W Sus 35 D5
Cowgill Cumb 155 C6
Cowie Aberds 245 D5
Cowie Stirl 207 B6
Cowley Devon 13 B4
Cowley Glos 63 B5
Cowley London 48 A3
Cowley Oxon 65 C6
Cowleymoor Devon 27 D4
Cowling Lancs 137 B4
Cowling N Yorks 146 C3
Cowling N Yorks 157 C6
Cowlinge Suff 86 B3
Cowpe Lancs 138 A1
Cowpen Northumb 179 A4
Cowpen Bewley Stockton 168 C2
Cowplain Hants 33 D5
Cowshill Durham 165 A6
Cowstrandburn Fife 208 A3
Cowthorpe N Yorks 148 B3
Cox Common Suff 105 C4
Cox Grn. Windsor 48 B1
Cox Moor Notts 131 D5
Coxbank Ches 111 A5
Coxbench Derbys 114 A1
Coxford Norf 119 C5
Coxford Soton 32 D2
Coxheath Kent 37 A5
Coxhill Kent 39 A4
Coxhoe Durham 167 B6
Coxley Som 29 A5
Coxwold N Yorks 158 D4
Coychurch Bridgend 40 D4
Coylton S Ayrs 193 C4
Coylumbridge Highld 242 A2
Coynach Aberds 244 B1
Coynachie Aberds 255 C5
Coytrahen Bridgend 40 C3
Crabadon Devon 7 B6
Crabbs Cross Worcs 80 A3
Crabtree W Sus 35 D5
Crackenthorpe Cumb 165 C4
Crackington Haven Corn 10 B2
Crackley Warks 97 D5
Crackleybank Shrops 111 D6
Crackpot N Yorks 156 B3
Cracoe N Yorks 146 A3
Craddock Devon 27 D5
Cradhlastadh W Isles 287 A5
Cradley Hereford 79 C5
Cradley Heath W Mid 96 C2
Crafthole Corn 6 B2
Cragg Vale W Yorks 138 A3
Craggan Highld 253 D6
Craggie Highld 274 C2
Craggie Highld 252 C3
Craghead Durham 179 D4
Crai Powys 59 C5
Craibstone Moray 267 D5
Craichie Angus 232 D3
Craig Dumfries 173 A4
Craig Dumfries 173 B4
Craig Highld 250 B2
Craig Castle Aberds 255 D5
Craig-cefn-parc Swansea 40 A1
Craig Penllyn V Glam 41 D4
Craig-y-don Conwy 124 A2
Craig-y-nos Powys 59 D5
Craiganor Lodge Perth 229 C5
Craigdam Aberds 256 C3
Craigdarroch Dumfries 183 C5
Craigdarroch Highld 251 A6
Craigdhu Highld 251 B6
Craigearn Aberds 245 A4
Craigellachie Moray 254 B3
Craigencross Dumfries 170 A2
Craigend Perth 219 B6
Craigend Stirl 207 B5
Craigendive Argyll 214 D3
Craigendoran Argyll 215 D6
Craigends Renfs 205 B4
Craigens Argyll 200 B2
Craigens E Ayrs 182 A3
Craighat Stirl 206 B2
Craighead Fife 221 D6
Craighlaw Mains Dumfries 171 A5
Craighouse Argyll 201 B5
Craigie Aberds 245 A6
Craigie Dundee 220 A4
Craigie Perth 219 B6
Craigie Perth 231 D5
Craigie S Ayrs 193 B4
Craigiefield Orkney 282 F5
Craigielaw E Loth 210 C1
Craiglockhart Edin 209 C5
Craigmalloch E Ayrs 182 C2
Craigmaud Aberds 268 D3
Craigmillar Edin 209 C5
Craigmore Argyll 203 B6
Craignant Shrops 110 B1
Craigneuk N Lnrk 194 A2
Craigneuk N Lnrk 207 D5
Craignure Argyll 225 C6
Craigo Angus 233 B4
Craigow Perth 219 D5
Craigrothie Fife 220 C3
Craigroy Moray 266 D2
Craigruie Stirl 217 B4
Craigston Castle Aberds 268 D2
Craigton Aberdeen 245 B5
Craigton Angus 232 C1
Craigton Angus 221 A5
Craigton Highld 264 A2
Craigtown Highld 279 C4
Craik Borders 185 B6
Crail Fife 221 D6
Crailing Borders 187 A5
Crailinghall Borders 187 A5
Craiselound N Lincs 141 D5
Crakehill N Yorks 158 D3
Crakemarsh Staffs 113 B4
Crambe N Yorks 149 A6
Cramlington Northumb 179 B4
Cramond Edin 209 C4
Cramond Bridge Edin 209 C4
Cranage Ches 128 C2
Cranberry Staffs 112 B2
Cranborne Dorset 31 D4
Cranbourne Brack 48 B2
Cranbrook Kent 37 C5
Cranbrook Common Kent 37 C5
Crane Moor S Yorks 139 C6
Crane's Corner Norf 119 D6
Cranfield Beds 83 C6
Cranford London 48 B4
Cranford St Andrew Northants 99 D6
Cranford St John Northants 99 D6
Cranham Glos 63 B4
Cranham London 50 A2
Crank Mers 136 D4
Crank Wood Gtr Man 137 C5
Cranleigh Sur 34 C3
Cranley Suff 104 D2
Cranmer Green Suff 103 D6
Cranmore I o W 18 C2
Cranna Aberds 268 D1
Crannich Argyll 225 B4
Crannoch Moray 267 D5
Cranoe Leics 99 B4
Cransford Suff 88 A4
Cranshaws Borders 210 D3
Cranstal I o M 152 A4
Crantock Corn 4 A2
Cranwell Lincs 116 A3
Cranwich Norf 102 B3
Cranworth Norf 103 A5
Craobh Haven Argyll 213 B5
Crapstone Devon 7 A4
Crarae Argyll 214 C2
Crask Inn Highld 272 B3
Crask of Aigas Highld 251 B6
Craskins Aberds 244 B2
Craster Northumb 189 B5
Craswall Hereford 77 D6
Cratfield Suff 104 D4
Crathes Aberds 245 C4
Crathes Castle and Gardens Aberds 245 C4
Crathie Aberds 243 C5
Crathie Highld 240 C3
Crathorne N Yorks 158 A3
Craven Arms Shrops 94 C2
Crawcrook T & W 178 C3
Crawford Lancs 136 C3
Crawford S Lnrk 195 D4
Crawfordjohn S Lnrk 194 D3
Crawick Dumfries 183 A5
Crawley Hants 32 B3
Crawley Oxon 64 B4
Crawley W Sus 35 C5
Crawley Down W Sus 35 C6
Crawleyside Durham 166 A2
Crawshawbooth Lancs 137 A7
Crawton Aberds 233 A6
Cray N Yorks 156 D3
Cray Perth 231 B5
Crayford London 50 B2
Crayke N Yorks 159 D4
Crays Hill Essex 69 D7
Cray's Pond Oxon 47 A4
Creacombe Devon 26 D3
Creag Ghoraidh W Isles 286 B3
Creagan Argyll 227 B4
Creaguaineach Lodge Highld 228 B2
Creaksea Essex 70 D3
Creaton Northants 99 D4
Creca Dumfries 175 A5
Credenhill Hereford 78 C2
Crediton Devon 12 A3
Creebridge Dumfries 171 A6
Creech Heathfield Som 28 C2
Creech St Michael Som 28 C2
Creed Corn 4 C4
Creekmouth London 50 A1
Creeting Bottoms Suff 88 B2
Creeting St Mary Suff 88 B1
Creeton Lincs 116 C3
Creetown Dumfries 171 B6
Creg-ny-Baa I o M 152 C3
Creggans Argyll 214 B3
Cregneash I o M 152 E1
Cregrina Powys 77 B5
Creich Fife 220 B3
Creigiau Cardiff 41 C5
Cremyll Corn 6 B3
Creslow Bucks 66 A3
Cressage Shrops 94 A3
Cressbrook Derbys 129 B6
Cresselly Pembs 55 D6
Cressing Essex 70 A1
Cresswell Northumb 189 D5
Cresswell Staffs 112 B3
Cresswell Quay Pembs 55 D6
Creswell Derbys 131 B5
Cretingham Suff 88 A3
Cretshengan Argyll 202 B2
Crewe Ches 127 D4
Crewe Ches 128 D2
Crewgreen Powys 110 D2
Crewkerne Som 14 A4
Crianlarich Stirl 216 B3
Cribyn Ceredig 75 C4
Criccieth Gwyn 107 C4
Crich Derbys 130 D3
Crichie Aberds 257 B4
Crichton Midloth 209 D6
Crick Mon 61 D6
Crick Northants 98 D2
Crickadarn Powys 77 C4
Cricket Malherbie Som 28 D3
Cricket St Thomas Som 14 A3
Crickheath Shrops 110 C1
Crickhowell Powys 60 B4
Cricklade Wilts 64 D2
Cricklewood London 49 A5
Cridling Stubbs N Yorks 140 A3
Crieff Perth 218 B3
Crieff Visitors' Centre Perth 218 B3
Criggion Powys 110 D1
Crigglestone W Yorks 139 B6
Crimond Aberds 269 D5
Crimonmogate Aberds 269 D5
Crimplesham Norf 102 A2
Crinan Argyll 213 C5
Cringleford Norf 104 A2
Cringles W Yorks 147 C4
Crinow Pembs 56 A1
Cripplesease Corn 2 B3
Cripplestyle Dorset 31 D4
Cripp's Corner E Sus 37 D5
Croasdale Cumb 162 C3
Crock Street Som 28 D3
Crockenhill Kent 50 C2
Crockernwell Devon 12 B2
Crockerton Wilts 30 A2
Crocketford or Ninemile Bar Dumfries 173 A6
Crockey Hill York 149 C5
Crockham Hill Kent 36 A2
Crockleford Heath Essex 71 A4
Crockness Orkney 283 H4
Croes-goch Pembs 54 A4
Croes-lan Ceredig 73 B6
Croes-y-mwyalch Torf 61 D5
Croeserw Neath 40 B3
Croesor Gwyn 107 B6
Croesyceiliog Carms 57 A4
Croesyceiliog Torf 61 D5
Croesywaun Gwyn 107 A5
Croft Leics 98 B2
Croft Lincs 135 C5
Croft Pembs 73 B4
Croft Warr 137 D5
Croft Motor Racing Circuit N Yorks 157 A6
Croft-on-Tees N Yorks 157 A6
Croftamie Stirl 206 B2
Croftmalloch W Loth 208 D2
Crofton Wilts 45 C6
Crofton W Yorks 140 B1
Crofts of Benachielt Highld 275 A5
Crofts of Haddo Aberds 256 C3
Crofts of Inverthernie Aberds 256 B2
Crofts of Meikle Ardo Aberds 256 B3
Crofty Swansea 57 C5
Croggan Argyll 225 D6
Croglin Cumb 164 A3
Croich Highld 263 A6
Crois Dughaill W Isles 286 D3
Cromarty Highld 264 D3
Cromblet Aberds 256 C2
Cromdale Highld 253 D6
Cromer Herts 68 A2
Cromer Norf 120 A4
Cromford Derbys 130 D2
Cromhall S Glos 62 D2
Cromhall Common S Glos 43 A5
Cromor W Isles 288 E5
Cromra Highld 240 C3
Cromwell Notts 132 C2
Cronberry E Ayrs 193 C6
Crondall Hants 33 A6
Cronk-y-Voddy I o M 152 C3
Cronton Mers 127 A4
Crook Cumb 154 B3
Crook Durham 167 B4
Crook of Devon Perth 219 D5
Crookedholm E Ayrs 193 B4
Crookes S Yorks 130 A3
Crookham Northumb 198 C3
Crookham W Berks 46 C3
Crookham Village Hants 47 D5
Crookhaugh Borders 195 D6
Crookhouse Borders 187 A6
Crooklands Cumb 154 C4
Croome Park, Pershore Worcs 80 C1
Cropredy Oxon 82 C1
Cropston Leics 114 D3
Cropthorne Worcs 80 C2
Cropton N Yorks 159 C6
Cropwell Bishop Notts 115 B4
Cropwell Butler Notts 115 B4
Cros W Isles 288 A6
Crosbost W Isles 288 E4
Crosby Cumb 162 A3
Crosby I o M 152 D3
Crosby N Lincs 141 B6
Crosby Garrett Cumb 155 A6
Crosby Ravensworth Cumb 165 D4
Crosby Villa Cumb 162 A3
Croscombe Som 29 A5
Cross Som 42 D3
Cross Ash Mon 61 B6
Cross-at-Hand Kent 37 B5
Cross Green Devon 11 C4
Cross Green Suff 87 B5
Cross Green Suff 87 B4
Cross Green Warks 81 B6
Cross Hands Carms 57 A5
Cross-hands Carms 73 D4
Cross Hands Pembs 55 C6
Cross Hill Derbys 114 A2
Cross Houses Shrops 94 A3
Cross in Hand E Sus 36 D3
Cross in Hand Leics 98 C2
Cross Inn Ceredig 73 A6
Cross Inn Ceredig 75 B4
Cross Inn Rhondda 41 C5
Cross Keys Kent 36 A3
Cross Lane Head Shrops 95 B5
Cross Lanes Corn 3 C4
Cross Lanes N Yorks 148 A4
Cross Lanes Wrex 110 A2
Cross Oak Powys 60 A3
Cross of Jackston Aberds 256 C2
Cross o'th'hands Derbys 113 A6
Cross Street Suff 104 D2
Crossaig Argyll 202 C3
Crossal Highld 246 A3
Crossapol Argyll 222 C2
Crossburn Falk 207 C6
Crossbush W Sus 20 B3
Crosscanonby Cumb 162 A3
Crossdale Street Norf 120 B4
Crossens Mers 136 B2
Crossflatts W Yorks 147 C5
Crossford Fife 208 B3
Crossford S Lnrk 194 B3
Crossgate Lincs 117 C5
Crossgatehall E Loth 209 D6
Crossgates Fife 208 B4
Crossgates Powys 77 A4
Crossgill Lancs 145 A5
Crosshill E Ayrs 193 C4
Crosshill Fife 209 A4
Crosshill S Ayrs 192 E3
Crosshouse E Ayrs 192 B3
Crossings Cumb 176 B3
Crosskeys Caerph 41 B7
Crosskirk Highld 279 A6
Crosslanes Shrops 110 D2
Crosslee Borders 185 A6
Crosslee Renfs 205 B4
Crossmichael Dumfries 173 B5
Crossmoor Lancs 144 D4
Crossroads Aberds 245 C4
Crossroads E Ayrs 193 B4
Crossway Hereford 79 D4
Crossway Mon 61 B6
Crossway Powys 77 B4
Crossway Green Worcs 79 A6
Crossways Dorset 16 C1
Crosswell Pembs 72 C4
Crosswood Ceredig 75 A5
Crosthwaite Cumb 154 B3
Croston Lancs 136 B3
Crostwick Norf 121 D4
Crostwight Norf 121 C5
Crothair W Isles 288 D2
Crouch Kent 36 A4
Crouch Hill Dorset 29 D7
Crouch House Green Kent 36 B2
Croucheston Wilts 31 C4
Croughton Northants 82 D2
Crovie Aberds 268 C3
Crow Edge S Yorks 139 C4
Crow Hill Hereford 62 A2
Crowan Corn 3 B4
Crowborough E Sus 36 C3
Crowcombe Som 27 B6
Crowdecote Derbys 129 C6
Crowden Derbys 138 D3
Crowell Oxon 66 D2
Crowfield Northants 82 C3
Crowfield Suff 88 B2
Crowhurst E Sus 23 A5
Crowhurst Sur 36 B1
Crowhurst Lane End Sur 36 B1
Crowland Lincs 117 D5
Crowlas Corn 2 B3
Crowle N Lincs 141 B5
Crowle Worcs 80 B2
Crowmarsh Gifford Oxon 47 A4
Crown Corner Suff 104 D3
Crownhill Plym 6 B3
Crownland Suff 103 E6
Crownthorpe Norf 104 A1
Crowntown Corn 3 B4
Crows-an-wra Corn 2 C1
Crowshill Norf 103 A5
Crowsnest Shrops 94 A1
Crowthorne Brack 47 C6
Crowton Ches 127 B5
Croxall Staffs 113 D5
Croxby Lincs 142 D3
Croxdale Durham 167 B5
Croxden Staffs 113 B4
Croxley Green Herts 67 D5
Croxton Cambs 84 A4
Croxton N Lincs 142 B2
Croxton Norf 103 C4
Croxton Staffs 112 B1
Croxton Kerrial Leics 115 C6
Croxtonbank Staffs 112 B1
Croy Highld 252 B3
Croy N Lnrk 207 C5
Croyde Devon 25 B5
Croydon Cambs 85 C5
Croydon London 49 C6
Crubenmore Lodge Highld 241 C4
Cruckmeole Shrops 94 A2
Cruckton Shrops 110 D3

Dingley Northants 99 C4
Dingwall Highld 252 A1
Dinlabyre Borders 186 D4
Dinmael Conwy 109 A5
Dinnet Aberds 244 C1
Dinnington Som 28 D4
Dinnington S Yorks 131 A5
Dinnington T & W 179 B4
Dinorwic Gwyn 123 D5
Dinton Bucks 66 B2
Dinton Wilts 31 B4
Dinwoodie Mains Dumfries 185 C4
Dinworthy Devon 24 D4
Dippen N Ayrs 191 C6
Dippenhall Sur 33 A7
Dipple Moray 266 D4
Dipple S Ayrs 181 A4
Diptford Devon 7 B6
Dipton Durham 178 D3
Dirdhu Highld 254 D1
Dirleton E Loth 210 B2
Dirt Pot Northumb 165 A6
Discoed Powys 77 A6
Discovery Point Dundee 220 B4
Diseworth Leics 114 C2
Dishes Orkney 282 E7
Dishforth N Yorks 158 D2
Disley Ches 129 A4
Diss Norf 104 D2
Disserth Powys 76 B4
Distington Cumb 162 B3
Ditchampton Wilts 31 B4
Ditcheat Som 29 B6
Ditchingham Norf 104 B4
Ditchling E Sus 21 A6
Ditherington Shrops 111 D4
Dittisham Devon 8 B2
Ditton Halton 127 A4
Ditton Kent 37 A5
Ditton Green Cambs 86 B2
Ditton Priors Shrops 95 C4
Divach Highld 251 D6
Divlyn Carms 59 B4
Dixton Glos 80 D2
Dixton Mon 61 B7
Dobcross Gtr Man 138 C2
Dobwalls Corn 5 A7
Doc Penfro = Pembroke Dock Pembs 55 D5
Doccombe Devon 12 C2
Dochfour Ho. Highld 252 C2
Dochgarroch Highld 252 B2
Docking Norf 119 B4
Docklow Hereford 78 B3
Dockray Cumb 164 C1
Dockroyd W Yorks 147 D4
Dodburn Borders 186 C3
Doddinghurst Essex 69 D5
Doddington Cambs 101 B5
Doddington Kent 51 D6
Doddington Lincs 133 B4
Doddington Northumb 198 C3
Doddington Shrops 95 D4
Doddiscombsleigh Devon 12 C3
Dodford Northants 82 A3
Dodford Worcs 96 D2
Dodington S Glos 43 A6
Dodleston Ches 126 C3
Dods Leigh Staffs 112 B4
Dodworth S Yorks 139 C6
Doe Green Warr 127 A5
Doe Lea Derbys 131 C4
Dog Village Devon 13 B4
Dogdyke Lincs 134 D2
Dogmersfield Hants 47 D5
Dogridge Wilts 45 A4
Dogsthorpe P'boro 100 A3
Dol-fôr Powys 91 B6
Dôl-y-Bont Ceredig 90 D4
Dol-y-cannau Powys 77 C6
Dolanog Powys 109 D5
Dolau Powys 77 A5
Dolau Rhondda 41 C4
Dolbenmaen Gwyn 107 B5
Dolfach Powys 91 B7
Dolfor Powys 93 C5
Dolgarrog Conwy 124 C2
Dolgellau Gwyn 91 A5
Dolgran Carms 58 B1
Dolhendre Gwyn 108 B3
Doll Highld 274 D2
Dollar Clack 208 A2
Dolley Green Powys 77 A6
Dollwen Ceredig 91 D4
Dolphin Flint 126 B1
Dolphinholme Lancs 145 B5
Dolphinton S Lnrk 195 B6
Dolton Devon 25 D6
Dolwen Conwy 124 B3
Dolwen Powys 92 A3
Dolwyd Conwy 124 B3
Dolwyddelan Conwy 124 D2
Dolyhir Powys 77 B6
Doncaster S Yorks 140 C3
Doncaster Racecourse S Yorks 140 C4
Dones Green Ches 127 B6
Donhead St Andrew Wilts 30 C3
Donhead St Mary Wilts 30 C3
Donibristle Fife 209 B4
Donington Lincs 117 B5
Donington on Bain Lincs 134 A2
Donington Park Motor Racing Circuit Leics 114 C2
Donington South Ing Lincs 117 B5
Donisthorpe Leics 113 D7
Donkey Town Sur 48 C2
Donnington Glos 64 A2
Donnington Hereford 79 D5
Donnington Shrops 94 A3
Donnington Telford 111 D6
Donnington W Berks 46 C2
Donnington W Sus 20 B1
Donnington Wood Telford 111 D6
Donyatt Som 28 D3
Doonfoot S Ayrs 192 D3
Dorback Lodge Highld 242 A3
Dorchester Dorset 15 B6
Dorchester Oxon 65 D6
Dorchester Abbey, Wallingford Oxon 65 D6
Dordon Warks 97 A5
Dore S Yorks 130 A3
Dores Highld 252 C1
Dorking Sur 35 B4
Dormansland Sur 36 B2
Dormanstown Redcar 168 C3
Dormington Hereford 78 C3
Dormston Worcs 80 B2
Dornal S Ayrs 181 D4
Dorney Bucks 48 B2
Dornie Highld 249 D5
Dornoch Highld 264 B3
Dornock Dumfries 175 B5
Dorrery Highld 279 C6
Dorridge W Mid 97 D4
Dorrington Lincs 133 D5
Dorrington Shrops 94 A2
Dorsington Warks 80 C4
Dorstone Hereford 77 C7
Dorton Bucks 66 B1
Dorusduain Highld 250 D1
Dosthill Staffs 97 B5
Dottery Dorset 15 B4
Doublebois Corn 5 A6
Dougarie N Ayrs 191 B4
Doughton Glos 63 D4
Douglas I o M 152 D3
Douglas S Lnrk 194 C3
Douglas & Angus Dundee 220 A4
Douglas Water S Lnrk 194 C3
Douglas West S Lnrk 194 C3
Douglastown Angus 232 D2
Doulting Som 29 A6
Dounby Orkney 282 E3
Doune Highld 272 D2
Doune Stirl 218 D2
Doune Park Aberds 268 C2
Douneside Aberds 244 B1
Dounie Highld 264 A1
Dounreay Highld 279 B5
Dousland Devon 7 A4
Dovaston Shrops 110 C2
Dove Cottage and Wordsworth Museum Cumb 154 A2
Dove Holes Derbys 129 B5
Dovenby Cumb 162 A3
Dover Kent 39 A5
Dover Castle Kent 39 A5
Dovercourt Essex 88 D3
Doverdale Worcs 79 A6
Doveridge Derbys 113 B5
Doversgreen Sur 35 B5
Dowally Perth 230 D4
Dowbridge Lancs 144 D4
Dowdeswell Glos 63 B5
Dowlais M Tydf 60 C2
Dowland Devon 25 D6
Dowlish Wake Som 28 D3
Down Ampney Glos 64 D2
Down Hatherley Glos 63 A4
Down St Mary Devon 12 A2
Down Thomas Devon 7 B4
Downcraig Ferry N Ayrs 204 C1
Downderry Corn 6 B2
Downe London 50 C1
Downend I o W 18 C4
Downend S Glos 43 B5
Downend W Berks 46 B2
Downfield Dundee 220 A3
Downgate Corn 11 D4
Downham Essex 70 D1
Downham Lancs 146 C1
Downham Northumb 198 C2
Downham Market Norf 102 A2
Downhead Som 29 A6
Downhill Perth 219 A5
Downhill T & W 179 D5
Downholland Cross Lancs 136 C2
Downholme N Yorks 157 B5
Downies Aberds 245 C6
Downley Bucks 66 D3
Downside Som 29 A6
Downside Sur 35 A4
Downton Hants 17 B6
Downton Wilts 31 C5
Downton on the Rock Hereford 94 D2
Dowsby Lincs 116 C4
Dowsdale Lincs 117 D5
Dowthwaitehead Cumb 163 B6
Doxey Staffs 112 C3
Doxford Northumb 189 A4
Doxford Park T & W 179 D5
Doynton S Glos 43 B6
Draffan S Lnrk 194 B2
Dragonby N Lincs 141 B7
Drakeland Corner Devon 7 B4
Drakemyre N Ayrs 204 C2
Drake's Broughton Worcs 80 C2
Drakes Cross Worcs 96 D3
Drakewalls Corn 11 D5
Draughton Northants 99 D4
Draughton N Yorks 147 B4
Drax N Yorks 141 A4
Draycote Warks 98 D1
Draycott Derbys 114 B2
Draycott Glos 81 D4
Draycott Som 42 D3
Draycott in the Clay Staffs 113 C5
Draycott in the Moors Staffs 112 A3
Drayford Devon 26 D2
Drayton Leics 99 B5
Drayton Lincs 117 B5
Drayton Norf 120 D3
Drayton Oxon 82 C1
Drayton Oxon 65 D5
Drayton Ptsmth 19 A5
Drayton Som 28 C4
Drayton Worcs 96 D2
Drayton Bassett Staffs 97 A4
Drayton Beauchamp Bucks 67 B4
Drayton Manor Park, Tamworth Staffs 97 A4
Drayton Parslow Bucks 66 A3
Drayton St Leonard Oxon 65 D6
Dre-fach Ceredig 75 D4
Dre-fach Carms 57 A6
Dreamland Theme Park, Margate Kent 53 B5
Drebley N Yorks 147 B4
Dreemskerry I o M 152 B4
Dreenhill Pembs 55 C5
Drefach Carms 73 C6
Drefach Carms 57 A5
Drefelin Carms 73 C6
Dreghorn N Ayrs 192 B3
Drellingore Kent 39 A4
Drem E Loth 210 C2
Dresden Stoke 112 A3
Dreumasdal W Isles 286 C3
Drewsteignton Devon 12 B2
Driby Lincs 134 B3
Driffield E Yorks 150 B3
Driffield Glos 63 D6
Drigg Cumb 153 A1
Drighlington W Yorks 139 A5
Drimnin Highld 225 A4
Drimpton Dorset 14 A4
Drimsynie Argyll 215 B4
Drinisiadar W Isles 288 H2
Drinkstone Suff 87 A5
Drinkstone Green Suff 87 A5
Drishaig Argyll 215 A4
Drissaig Argyll 214 A2
Drochil Borders 195 B6
Drointon Staffs 112 C4
Droitwich Spa Worcs 80 A1
Droman Highld 276 C2
Dron Perth 219 C6
Dronfield Derbys 130 B3
Dronfield Woodhouse Derbys 130 B3
Drongan E Ayrs 182 A2
Dronley Angus 220 A3
Droxford Hants 33 D5
Droylsden Gtr Man 138 D2
Druid Denb 109 A5
Druidston Pembs 55 C4
Druimarbin Highld 237 B4
Druimavuic Argyll 227 B5
Druimdrishaig Argyll 202 A2
Druimindarroch Highld 235 B5
Druimyeon More Argyll 202 C1
Drum Argyll 203 A4
Drum Perth 219 D5
Drumbeg Highld 270 A4
Drumblade Aberds 255 B6
Drumblair Aberds 256 B1
Drumbuie Dumfries 182 D3
Drumbuie Highld 249 C4
Drumburgh Cumb 175 C5
Drumburn Dumfries 174 B2
Drumchapel Glasgow 205 A5
Drumchardine Highld 252 B1
Drumchork Highld 261 B5
Drumclog S Lnrk 193 B6
Drumderfit Highld 252 A2
Drumeldrie Fife 220 D4
Drumelzier Borders 195 C6
Drumfearn Highld 247 C5
Drumgask Highld 241 C4
Drumgley Angus 232 C2
Drumguish Highld 241 C5
Drumin Moray 254 C2
Drumlasie Aberds 244 B3
Drumlemble Argyll 190 D2
Drumligair Aberds 245 A6
Drumlithie Aberds 245 D4
Drummoddie Dumfries 171 C5
Drummond Highld 264 D2
Drummore Dumfries 170 D3
Drummuir Moray 255 B4
Drummuir Castle Moray 255 B4
Drumnadrochit Highld 251 D7
Drumnagorrach Moray 267 D6
Drumoak Aberds 245 C4
Drumpark Dumfries 183 D6
Drumphail Dumfries 171 A4
Drumrash Dumfries 173 A4
Drumrunie Highld 271 D4
Drums Aberds 257 D4
Drumsallie Highld 236 B3
Drumstinchall Dumfries 173 C6
Drumsturdy Angus 221 A4
Drumtochty Castle Aberds 244 E3
Drumtroddan Dumfries 171 C5
Drumuie Highld 259 D4
Drumuillie Highld 253 D5
Drumvaich Stirl 217 D6
Drumwhindle Aberds 257 C4
Drunkendub Angus 233 D4
Drury Flint 126 C2
Drury Square Norf 119 D6
Drusillas Park, Polegate E Sus 22 B3
Dry Doddington Lincs 115 A6
Dry Drayton Cambs 85 A5
Drybeck Cumb 165 D4
Drybridge Moray 267 C5
Drybridge N Ayrs 192 B3
Drybrook Glos 62 B2
Dryburgh Borders 197 C4
Dryhope Borders 196 D1
Drylaw Edin 209 C5
Drym Corn 3 B4
Drymen Stirl 206 B2
Drymuir Aberds 257 B4
Drynoch Highld 246 A3
Dryslwyn Carms 58 C2
Dryton Shrops 94 A3
Dubford Aberds 268 C3
Dubton Angus 232 C3
Duchally Highld 271 C6
Duchlage Argyll 206 B1
Duck Corner Suff 89 C4
Duckington Ches 127 D4
Ducklington Oxon 65 C4
Duckmanton Derbys 131 B4
Duck's Cross Beds 84 B3
Duddenhoe End Essex 85 D6
Duddingston Edin 209 C5
Duddington Northants 100 A1
Duddleswell E Sus 36 D2
Duddo Northumb 198 B3
Duddon Ches 127 C5
Duddon Bridge Cumb 153 B3
Dudleston Shrops 110 B2
Dudleston Heath Shrops 110 B2
Dudley T & W 179 B4
Dudley W Mid 96 B2
Dudley Port W Mid 96 B2
Dudley Zoological Gardens W Mid 96 B2
Duffield Derbys 114 A1
Duffryn Newport 42 A1
Duffryn Neath 40 B3
Dufftown Moray 254 C4
Duffus Moray 266 C2
Dufton Cumb 165 C4
Duggleby N Yorks 150 A1
Duirinish Highld 249 C4
Duisdalemore Highld 247 C6
Duisky Highld 237 B4
Dukestown Bl Gwent 60 B3
Dukinfield Gtr Man 138 D2
Dulas Anglesey 123 B4
Dulcote Som 29 A5
Dulford Devon 13 A5
Dull Perth 230 D2
Dullatur N Lnrk 207 C5
Dullingham Cambs 86 B2
Dulnain Bridge Highld 253 D5
Duloe Beds 84 A3
Duloe Corn 6 B1
Dulsie Highld 253 B5
Dulverton Som 27 C4
Dulwich London 49 B6
Dumbarton W Dunb 205 A4
Dumbleton Glos 80 D3
Dumcrieff Dumfries 185 B4
Dumfries Dumfries 174 A2
Dumgoyne Stirl 206 B3
Dummer Hants 33 A4
Dumpford W Sus 34 D1
Dumpton Kent 53 C5
Dun Angus 233 C4
Dun Charlabhaigh W Isles 288 C2
Dunain Ho. Highld 252 B2
Dunalastair Perth 229 C6
Dunan Highld 247 B4
Dunans Argyll 214 C3
Dunball Som 28 A3
Dunbar E Loth 210 C3
Dunbeath Highld 275 B5
Dunbeg Argyll 226 C3
Dunblane Stirl 218 D2
Dunbog Fife 220 C2
Duncanston Aberds 255 D6
Duncanston Highld 252 A1
Dunchurch Warks 98 D1
Duncote Northants 82 B3
Duncow Dumfries 184 D2
Duncraggan Stirl 217 D5
Duncrievie Perth 219 D6
Duncton W Sus 20 A2
Dundas Ho. Orkney 283 K5
Dundee Dundee 220 A4
Dundee Airport Dundee 220 B3
Dundeugh Dumfries 182 D3
Dundon Som 29 B4
Dundonald S Ayrs 192 B3
Dundonnell Highld 262 B2
Dundonnell Hotel Highld 262 B2
Dundonnell House Highld 262 B3
Dundraw Cumb 175 D5
Dundreggan Highld 239 A7
Dundreggan Lodge Highld 240 A1
Dundrennan Dumfries 173 D5
Dundry N Som 43 C4
Dunecht Aberds 245 B4
Dunfermline Fife 208 B3
Dunfield Glos 64 D2
Dunford Bridge S Yorks 139 C4
Dungworth S Yorks 130 A2
Dunham Notts 132 B3
Dunham Massey Gtr Man 128 A2
Dunham-on-the-Hill Ches 127 B4
Dunham Town Gtr Man 128 A2
Dunhampton Worcs 79 A6
Dunholme Lincs 133 B5
Dunino Fife 221 C5
Dunipace Falk 207 B6
Dunira Perth 218 B2
Dunkeld Perth 230 D4
Dunkerton Bath 43 D6
Dunkeswell Devon 13 A6
Dunkeswick N Yorks 148 C2
Dunkirk Kent 52 D2
Dunkirk Norf 120 C4
Dunk's Green Kent 36 A4
Dunlappie Angus 232 B3
Dunley Hants 46 D2
Dunley Worcs 79 A5
Dunlichity Lodge Highld 252 C2
Dunlop E Ayrs 205 D4
Dunmaglass Lodge Highld 252 D1
Dunmore Argyll 202 B2
Dunmore Falk 208 B1
Dunnet Highld 280 A4
Dunnichen Angus 232 D3
Dunninald Angus 233 C5
Dunning Perth 219 C5
Dunnington E Yorks 151 B4
Dunnington Warks 80 B3
Dunnington York 149 B5
Dunnockshaw Lancs 137 A7
Dunollie Argyll 226 C3
Dunoon Argyll 203 A6
Dunragit Dumfries 170 B3
Dunrobin Castle Museum & Gardens Highld 274 D2
Dunrostan Argyll 213 D5
Duns Borders 198 A1
Duns Tew Oxon 65 A5
Dunsby Lincs 116 C4
Dunscore Dumfries 183 D6
Dunscroft S Yorks 141 C4
Dunsdale Redcar 168 D4
Dunsden Green Oxon 47 B5
Dunsfold Sur 34 C3
Dunsford Devon 12 C3
Dunshalt Fife 220 C2
Dunshillock Aberds 257 B4
Dunskey Ho. Dumfries 170 B2
Dunsley N Yorks 169 D6
Dunsmore Bucks 66 C3
Dunsop Bridge Lancs 145 B6
Dunstable Beds 67 A5
Dunstall Staffs 113 C5
Dunstall Common Worcs 80 C1
Dunstall Green Suff 86 A3
Dunstan Northumb 189 B5
Dunstan Steads Northumb 189 A5
Dunster Som 27 A4
Dunster Castle, Minehead Som 27 A4
Dunston Lincs 133 C5
Dunston Norf 104 A3
Dunston Staffs 112 D3
Dunston T & W 179 C4
Dunsville S Yorks 140 C4
Dunswell E Yorks 150 D3
Dunsyre S Lnrk 195 B5
Dunterton Devon 11 D4
Duntisbourne Abbots Glos 63 C5
Duntisbourne Leer Glos 63 C5
Duntisbourne Rouse Glos 63 C5
Duntish Dorset 15 A6
Duntocher W Dunb 205 A4
Dunton Beds 84 C4
Dunton Bucks 66 A3
Dunton Norf 119 B5
Dunton Bassett Leics 98 B2
Dunton Green Kent 36 A3
Dunton Wayletts Essex 69 D6
Duntulm Highld 259 A4
Dunure S Ayrs 192 D2
Dunvant Swansea 57 C5
Dunvegan Highld 258 D2
Dunvegan Castle Highld 258 C2
Dunwich Suff 105 D5
Dunwood Staffs 129 D4
Dupplin Castle Perth 219 C5
Durdar Cumb 175 C7
Durgates E Sus 36 C4
Durham Durham 167 A5
Durham Cathedral Durham 167 A5
Durham Tees Valley Airport Stockton 167 D6
Durisdeer Dumfries 183 B6
Durisdeermill Dumfries 183 B6
Durkar W Yorks 139 B6
Durleigh Som 28 B2
Durley Hants 32 D4
Durley Wilts 45 C6
Durnamuck Highld 262 A2
Durness Highld 277 B5
Durno Aberds 256 D2
Duror Highld 236 D3
Durran Argyll 214 B2
Durran Highld 280 B3
Durrington Wilts 31 A5
Durrington W Sus 21 B4
Dursley Glos 62 D3
Durston Som 28 C2
Durweston Dorset 16 A2
Dury Shetland 285 G6
Duston Northants 83 A4
Duthil Highld 253 D5
Dutlas Powys 93 D6
Duton Hill Essex 69 A6
Dutson Corn 10 C4
Dutton Ches 127 B5
Duxford Cambs 85 C6
Duxford Oxon 65 D4
Duxford Airfield (Imperial War Museum), Sawston Cambs 85 C6
Dwygyfylchi Conwy 124 B2
Dwyran Anglesey 123 D4
Dyce Aberdeen 245 A5
Dye House Northumb 178 D1
Dyffryn Bridgend 40 B3
Dyffryn Carms 73 D6
Dyffryn Pembs 72 C2
Dyffryn Ardudwy Gwyn 107 D5
Dyffryn Castell Ceredig 91 D5
Dyffryn Ceidrych Carms 59 C4
Dyffryn Cellwen Neath 59 E5
Dyke Lincs 116 C4
Dyke Moray 253 A5
Dykehead Angus 232 B1
Dykehead N Lnrk 207 E6
Dykehead Stirl 206 A3
Dykelands Aberds 233 B5
Dykends Angus 231 C6
Dykeside Aberds 256 B2
Dykesmains N Ayrs 204 D2
Dylife Powys 91 C6
Dymchurch Kent 38 C2
Dymock Glos 79 D5
Dyrham S Glos 43 B6
Dyrham Park S Glos 43 B6
Dysart Fife 209 A6
Dyserth Denb 125 B5


## E


Eachwick Northumb 178 B3
Eadar Dha Fhadhail W Isles 287 A5
Eagland Hill Lancs 144 C4
Eagle Lincs 132 C3
Eagle Barnsdale Lincs 132 C3

Eagle Moor Lincs 132 C3
Eaglescliffe Stockton 168 D2
Eaglesfield Cumb 162 B3
Eaglesfield Dumfries 175 A5
Eaglesham E Renf 205 C5
Eaglethorpe Northants 100 B2
Eairy I o M 152 D2
Eakley Lanes M Keynes 83 B5
Eakring Notts 132 C1
Ealand N Lincs 141 B5
Ealing London 49 A4
Eals Northumb 177 D4
Eamont Bridge Cumb 164 C3
Earby Lancs 146 C3
Earcroft Blkburn 137 A5
Eardington Shrops 95 B5
Eardisland Hereford 78 B2
Eardisley Hereford 77 C7
Eardiston Shrops 110 C2
Eardiston Worcs 79 A4
Earith Cambs 101 D5
Earl Shilton Leics 98 B1
Earl Soham Suff 88 A3
Earl Sterndale Derbys 129 C5
Earl Stonham Suff 88 B2
Earle Northumb 188 A2
Earley Wokingham 47 B5
Earlham Norf 104 A3
Earlish Highld 258 B3
Earls Barton Northants 83 A5
Earls Colne Essex 70 A2
Earl's Croome Worcs 79 C6
Earl's Green Suff 87 A6
Earlsdon W Mid 97 D6
Earlsferry Fife 221 E4
Earlsfield Lincs 116 B2
Earlsford Aberds 256 C3
Earlsheaton W Yorks 139 A5
Earlsmill Moray 253 A5
Earlston Borders 197 C4
Earlston E Ayrs 193 B4
Earlswood Mon 61 D6
Earlswood Sur 35 B5
Earlswood Warks 96 D4
Earnley W Sus 19 B7
Earsairidh W Isles 286 G3
Earsdon T & W 179 B5
Earsham Norf 104 C4
Earswick York 149 B5
Eartham W Sus 20 B2
Easby N Yorks 159 A4
Easby N Yorks 157 A5
Easdale Argyll 213 A5
Easebourne W Sus 34 D1
Easenhall Warks 98 D1
Eashing Sur 34 B2
Easington Bucks 66 B1
Easington Durham 168 A2
Easington E Yorks 143 B5
Easington Northumb 199 C5
Easington Oxon 82 D1
Easington Oxon 66 D1
Easington Redcar 169 D5
Easington Colliery Durham 168 A2
Easington Lane T & W 167 A6
Easingwold N Yorks 148 A4
Easole Street Kent 53 D4
Eassie Angus 232 D1
East Aberthaw V Glam 41 E5
East Adderbury Oxon 82 D1
East Allington Devon 7 C6
East Anstey Devon 26 C3
East Appleton N Yorks 157 B6
East Ardsley W Yorks 139 A6
East Ashling W Sus 19 A7
East Auchronie Aberds 245 B5
East Ayton N Yorks 160 C3
East Bank Bl Gwent 60 C4
East Barkwith Lincs 133 A6
East Barming Kent 37 A5
East Barnby N Yorks 169 D6
East Barnet London 68 D2
East Barns E Loth 211 C4
East Barsham Norf 119 B6
East Beckham Norf 120 B3
East Bedfont London 48 B3
East Bergholt Suff 87 D6
East Bilney Norf 119 D6
East Blatchington E Sus 22 B2
East Boldre Hants 18 A2
East Brent Som 42 D2
East Bridgford Notts 115 A4
East Buckland Devon 26 B1
East Budleigh Devon 13 C5
East Burrafirth Shetland 285 H5
East Burton Dorset 16 C2
East Butsfield Durham 166 A4
East Butterwick N Lincs 141 C6
East Cairnbeg Aberds 233 A5
East Calder W Loth 208 D3
East Carleton Norf 104 A2
East Carlton Northants 99 C5
East Carlton W Yorks 147 C6
East Chaldon Dorset 16 C1
East Challow Oxon 46 A1
East Chiltington E Sus 21 A6
East Chinnock Som 29 D4
East Chisenbury Wilts 45 D5
East Clandon Sur 34 A3
East Claydon Bucks 66 A2
East Clyne Highld 274 D2
East Coker Som 29 D5
East Combe Som 27 B6
East Common N Yorks 149 D5
East Compton Som 29 A6
East Cottingwith E Yorks 149 C6
East Cowes I o W 18 B4
East Cowick E Yorks 141 A4
East Cowton N Yorks 157 A7
East Cramlington Northumb 179 B4
East Cranmore Som 29 A6
East Creech Dorset 16 C3
East Croachy Highld 252 D2
East Croftmore Highld 242 A2
East Curthwaite Cumb 164 A1
East Dean E Sus 22 C3
East Dean Hants 31 C6
East Dean W Sus 20 A2
East Down Devon 25 A7
East Drayton Notts 132 B2
East Ella Hull 142 A2
East End Dorset 16 B3
East End E Yorks 143 A4
East End Hants 18 B2
East End Hants 33 C5
East End Hants 46 C2
East End Herts 69 A4
East End Kent 37 C6
East End N Som 42 B3
East End Oxon 65 B4
East Farleigh Kent 37 A5
East Farndon Northants 99 C4
East Ferry Lincs 141 D6
East Fortune E Loth 210 C2
East Garston W Berks 46 B1
East Ginge Oxon 46 A2
East Goscote Leics 115 D4
East Grafton Wilts 45 C6
East Grimstead Wilts 31 C6
East Grinstead W Sus 36 C1
East Guldeford E Sus 38 C1
East Haddon Northants 82 A3
East Hagbourne Oxon 46 A3
East Halton N Lincs 142 B3
East Ham London 50 A1
East Hanney Oxon 65 D5
East Hanningfield Essex 70 C1
East Hardwick W Yorks 140 B2
East Harling Norf 103 C5
East Harlsey N Yorks 158 B3
East Harnham Wilts 31 C5
East Harptree Bath 43 D4
East Hartford Northumb 179 B4
East Harting W Sus 33 D6
East Hatley Cambs 85 B4
East Hauxwell N Yorks 157 B5
East Haven Angus 221 A5
East Heckington Lincs 117 A4
East Hedleyhope Durham 167 A4
East Hendred Oxon 46 A2
East Herrington T & W 179 D5
East Heslerton N Yorks 160 D3
East Hoathly E Sus 22 A3
East Horrington Som 29 A5
East Horsley Sur 34 A3
East Horton Northumb 198 C4
East Huntspill Som 28 A3
East Hyde Beds 67 B6
East Ilkerton Devon 26 A2
East Ilsley W Berks 46 A2
East Keal Lincs 134 C3
East Kennett Wilts 45 C5
East Keswick W Yorks 148 C2
East Kilbride S Lnrk 205 C6
East Kirkby Lincs 134 C3
East Knapton N Yorks 160 D2
East Knighton Dorset 16 C2
East Knoyle Wilts 30 B2
East Kyloe Northumb 199 C4
East Lambrook Som 28 D4
East Lamington Highld 264 C3
East Langdon Kent 39 A5
East Langton Leics 99 B4
East Langwell Highld 273 D5
East Lavant W Sus 20 B1
East Lavington W Sus 20 A2
East Layton N Yorks 157 A5
East Leake Notts 114 C3
East Learmouth Northumb 198 C2
East Leigh Devon 12 A1
East Lexham Norf 119 D5
East Lilburn Northumb 188 A3
East Linton E Loth 210 C2
East Liss Hants 33 C6
East Looe Corn 6 B1
East Lound N Lincs 141 D5
East Lulworth Dorset 16 C2
East Lutton N Yorks 150 A2
East Lydford Som 29 B5
East Mains Aberds 244 C3
East Malling Kent 37 A5
East March Angus 220 A4
East Marden W Sus 33 D7
East Markham Notts 132 B2
East Marton N Yorks 146 B3
East Meon Hants 33 C5
East Mere Devon 27 D4
East Mersea Essex 71 B4
East Mey Highld 281 A5
East Molesey Sur 49 C4
East Morden Dorset 16 B3
East Morton W Yorks 147 C4
East Ness N Yorks 159 D5
East Newton E Yorks 151 D5
East Norton Leics 99 A4
East Nynehead Som 27 C6
East Oakley Hants 46 D3
East Ogwell Devon 12 D3
East Orchard Dorset 30 D2
East Ord Northumb 198 A3
East Panson Devon 11 B4
East Peckham Kent 37 B4
East Pennard Som 29 B5
East Perry Cambs 84 A3
East Portlemouth Devon 7 D6
East Prawle Devon 8 D1
East Preston W Sus 20 B3
East Putford Devon 25 D4
East Quantoxhead Som 27 A6
East Rainton T & W 167 A6
East Ravendale NE Lincs 143 D4
East Raynham Norf 119 C5
East Rhidorroch Lodge Highld 262 A4
East Rigton W Yorks 148 C2
East Rounton N Yorks 158 A3
East Row N Yorks 169 D6
East Rudham Norf 119 C5
East Runton Norf 120 A3
East Ruston Norf 121 C5
East Saltoun E Loth 210 D1
East Sleekburn Northumb 179 A4
East Somerton Norf 121 D6
East Stockwith Lincs 141 D5
East Stoke Dorset 16 C2
East Stoke Notts 115 A5
East Stour Dorset 30 C2
East Stourmouth Kent 53 C4
East Stowford Devon 26 C1
East Stratton Hants 32 B4
East Studdal Kent 39 A5
East Suisnish Highld 248 C2
East Taphouse Corn 5 A6
East-the-Water Devon 25 C5
East Thirston Northumb 189 D4
East Tilbury Thurrock 50 B3
East Tisted Hants 33 B6
East Torrington Lincs 133 A6
East Tuddenham Norf 120 D2
East Tytherley Hants 32 C1
East Tytherton Wilts 44 B3
East Village Devon 12 A3
East Wall Shrops 94 B3
East Walton Norf 119 D4
East Wellow Hants 32 C2
East Wemyss Fife 209 A6
East Whitburn W Loth 208 D2
East Williamston Pembs 55 D6
East Winch Norf 118 D3
East Winterslow Wilts 31 B6
East Wittering W Sus 19 B6
East Witton N Yorks 157 C5
East Woodburn Northumb 177 A7
East Woodhay Hants 46 C2
East Worldham Hants 33 B6
East Worlington Devon 26 D2
East Worthing W Sus 21 B4
Eastbourne E Sus 22 C4
Eastbridge Suff 89 A5
Eastburn W Yorks 147 C4
Eastbury Herts 67 D5
Eastbury W Berks 46 B1
Eastby N Yorks 147 B4
Eastchurch Kent 52 B1
Eastcombe Glos 63 C4
Eastcote London 48 A4
Eastcote Northants 82 B3
Eastcote W Mid 97 D4
Eastcott Corn 24 D3
Eastcott Wilts 44 D4
Eastcourt Wilts 63 D5
Eastcourt Wilts 45 C6
Easter Ardross Highld 264 C2
Easter Balmoral Aberds 243 C5
Easter Boleskine Highld 251 D7
Easter Compton S Glos 43 A4
Easter Cringate Stirl 207 B5
Easter Davoch Aberds 244 B1
Easter Earshaig Dumfries 184 B3
Easter Fearn Highld 264 B2
Easter Galcantray Highld 253 B4
Easter Howgate Midloth 209 D5
Easter Howlaws Borders 197 B6
Easter Kinkell Highld 252 A1
Easter Lednathie Angus 232 B1
Easter Milton Highld 253 A5
Easter Moniack Highld 252 B1
Easter Ord Aberds 245 B5
Easter Quarff Shetland 285 K6
Easter Rhynd Perth 219 C6
Easter Row Stirl 207 A5
Easter Silverford Aberds 268 C2
Easter Skeld Shetland 285 J5
Easter Whyntie Aberds 267 C7
Eastergate W Sus 20 B2
Eastern Green W Mid 97 C5
Easterton Wilts 44 D4
Eastertown Som 42 D2
Eastertown of Auchleuchries Aberds 257 C5
Eastfield N Lnrk 208 D1
Eastfield N Yorks 160 C4
Eastfield Hall Northumb 189 C5
Eastgate Durham 166 B2
Eastgate Norf 120 C3
Eastham Mers 126 A3
Eastham Ferry Mers 126 A3
Easthampstead Brack 47 C6
Eastheath Wokingham 47 C6
Easthope Shrops 94 B3
Easthorpe Essex 70 A3
Easthorpe Leics 115 B6
Easthorpe Notts 132 D2
Easthouses Midloth 209 D6
Eastington Devon 12 A2
Eastington Glos 62 C3
Eastington Glos 64 B2
Eastleach Martin Glos 64 C3
Eastleach Turville Glos 64 C2
Eastleigh Devon 25 C5
Eastleigh Hants 32 D3
Eastling Kent 51 D6
Eastmoor Derbys 130 B3
Eastmoor Norf 102 A3
Eastney Ptsmth 19 B5
Eastnor Hereford 79 D5
Eastoft N Lincs 141 B6
Eastoke Hants 19 B6
Easton Cambs 100 D3
Easton Cumb 175 C5
Easton Cumb 176 B2
Easton Devon 12 C2
Easton Dorset 15 D6
Easton Hants 32 B4
Easton Lincs 116 C2
Easton Norf 120 D3
Easton Som 29 A5
Easton Suff 88 B3
Easton Wilts 44 B2
Easton Grey Wilts 44 A2
Easton-in-Gordano N Som 43 B4
Easton Maudit Northants 83 B5
Easton on the Hill Northants 100 A2
Easton Royal Wilts 45 C6
Eastpark Dumfries 174 B3
Eastrea Cambs 101 B4
Eastriggs Dumfries 175 B5
Eastrington E Yorks 141 A5
Eastry Kent 53 D5
Eastville Bristol 43 B5
Eastville Lincs 135 D4
Eastwell Leics 115 C5
Eastwick Herts 68 D4
Eastwick Shetland 284 F5
Eastwood Notts 114 A2
Eastwood Sthend 51 A5
Eastwood W Yorks 138 A2
Eathorpe Warks 81 A6
Eaton Ches 127 C5
Eaton Ches 128 C3
Eaton Leics 115 C5
Eaton Norf 104 A3
Eaton Notts 132 B2
Eaton Oxon 65 C5
Eaton Shrops 94 C1
Eaton Shrops 94 C3
Eaton Bishop Hereford 78 D2
Eaton Bray Beds 67 A4
Eaton Constantine Shrops 94 A3
Eaton Green Beds 67 A4
Eaton Hastings Oxon 64 D3
Eaton on Tern Shrops 111 C5
Eaton Socon Cambs 84 B3
Eavestone N Yorks 147 A6
Ebberston N Yorks 160 C2
Ebbesbourne Wake Wilts 30 C3
Ebbw Vale = Glyn Ebwy Bl Gwent 60 C3
Ebchester Durham 178 D3
Ebford Devon 13 C4
Ebley Glos 63 C4
Ebnal Ches 110 A3
Ebrington Glos 81 C4
Ecchinswell Hants 46 D2
Ecclaw Borders 211 D4
Ecclefechan Dumfries 175 A4
Eccles Borders 197 B6
Eccles Gtr Man 137 D6
Eccles Kent 51 C4
Eccles on Sea Norf 121 C6
Eccles Road Norf 103 B6
Ecclesall S Yorks 130 A3
Ecclesfield S Yorks 139 D6
Ecclesgreig Aberds 233 B5
Eccleshall Staffs 112 C2
Eccleshill W Yorks 147 D5
Ecclesmachan W Loth 208 C3
Eccleston Ches 127 C4
Eccleston Lancs 136 B4
Eccleston Mers 136 D3
Eccleston Park Mers 136 D3
Eccup W Yorks 148 C1
Echt Aberds 245 B4
Eckford Borders 187 A6
Eckington Derbys 131 B4
Eckington Worcs 80 C2
Ecton Northants 83 A5
Edale Derbys 129 A6
Edburton W Sus 21 A5
Edderside Cumb 174 D3
Edderton Highld 264 B3
Eddistone Devon 24 C3
Eddleston Borders 196 B1
Eden Camp Museum, Malton N Yorks 159 D6
Eden Park London 49 C6
Edenbridge Kent 36 B2
Edenfield Lancs 137 B6
Edenhall Cumb 164 B3
Edenham Lincs 116 C3
Edensor Derbys 130 C2
Edentaggart Argyll 215 C6
Edenthorpe S Yorks 140 C4
Edentown Cumb 175 C6
Ederline Argyll 214 B1
Edern Gwyn 106 C2
Edgarley Som 29 B5
Edgbaston W Mid 96 C3
Edgcott Bucks 66 A1
Edgcott Som 26 B3
Edge Shrops 94 A1
Edge End Glos 62 B1
Edge Green Ches 127 D4
Edge Hill Mers 136 E2
Edgebolton Shrops 111 C4
Edgefield Norf 120 B2
Edgefield Street Norf 120 B2
Edgeside Lancs 138 A1
Edgeworth Glos 63 C5
Edgmond Telford 111 D6
Edgmond Marsh Telford 111 C6
Edgton Shrops 94 C1
Edgware London 68 D1
Edgworth Blkburn 137 B6
Edinample Stirl 217 B5
Edinbane Highld 258 C3
Edinburgh Edin 209 C5
Edinburgh Airport Edin 209 C4
Edinburgh Castle Edin 209 C5
Edinburgh Crystal Visitor Centre, Penicuik Midloth 209 D5
Edinburgh Zoo Edin 209 C5
Edingale Staffs 113 D6
Edingight Ho. Moray 267 D6
Edingley Notts 131 D6
Edingthorpe Norf 121 B5
Edingthorpe Green Norf 121 B5
Edington Som 28 B3
Edington Wilts 44 D3
Edintore Moray 255 B5
Edith Weston Rutland 99 A6
Edithmead Som 28 A3
Edlesborough Bucks 67 B4
Edlingham Northumb 189 C4
Edlington Lincs 134 B2
Edmondsham Dorset 31 D4
Edmondsley Durham 167 A5
Edmondthorpe Leics 115 D6
Edmonstone Orkney 282 E6
Edmonton London 68 D3
Edmundbyers Durham 178 D2
Ednam Borders 197 C6
Ednaston Derbys 113 A6
Edradynate Perth 230 C2
Edrom Borders 198 A2
Edstaston Shrops 111 B4
Edstone Warks 81 A4
Edvin Loach Hereford 79 B4
Edwalton Notts 114 B3
Edwardstone Suff 87 C5
Edwinsford Carms 58 B3
Edwinstowe Notts 131 C6
Edworth Beds 84 C4
Edwyn Ralph Hereford 79 B4
Edzell Angus 232 B3
Efail Isaf Rhondda 41 C5
Efailnewydd Gwyn 106 C3
Efailwen Carms 72 D4
Efenechtyd Denb 125 D6
Effingham Sur 35 A4
Effirth Shetland 285 H5
Efford Devon 12 A3
Egdon Worcs 80 B2
Egerton Gtr Man 137 B6
Egerton Kent 37 B7
Egerton Forstal Kent 37 B6
Eggborough N Yorks 140 A3
Eggbuckland Plym 7 B4
Eggington Beds 67 A4
Egginton Derbys 113 C6
Egglescliffe Stockton 168 D2
Eggleston Durham 166 C2
Egham Sur 48 B3
Egleton Rutland 99 A5
Eglingham Northumb 189 B4
Egloshayle Corn 9 D6
Egloskerry Corn 10 C3
Eglwys-Brewis V Glam 41 E5
Eglwys Cross Wrex 110 A3
Eglwys Fach Ceredig 91 C4
Eglwysbach Conwy 124 B3
Eglwyswen Pembs 73 C4
Eglwyswrw Pembs 72 C4
Egmanton Notts 132 C2
Egremont Cumb 162 C3
Egremont Mers 136 D2
Egton N Yorks 159 A7
Egton Bridge N Yorks 159 A7
Eight Ash Green Essex 70 A3
Eignaig Highld 226 B2
Eil Highld 241 A6
Eilanreach Highld 238 A2
Eilean Darach Highld 262 B3
Eileanach Lodge Highld 264 D1
Einacleite W Isles 288 E2
Eisgean W Isles 288 F4
Eisingrug Gwyn 107 C6
Elan Village Powys 76 A3
Elberton S Glos 43 A5
Elburton Plym 7 B4
Elcho Perth 219 B6
Elcombe Thamesdown 45 A5
Eldernell Cambs 101 B5
Eldersfield Worcs 79 D6
Elderslie Renfs 205 B4
Eldon Durham 167 C5
Eldrick S Ayrs 181 C4
Eldroth N Yorks 146 A1
Eldwick W Yorks 147 C5
Elfhowe Cumb 154 B3
Elford Northumb 199 C5
Elford Staffs 113 D5
Elgin Moray 266 C3
Elgol Highld 247 C4
Elham Kent 38 A3
Elie Fife 221 D4
Elim Anglesey 122 B3
Eling Hants 32 D2
Elishader Highld 259 B5
Elishaw Northumb 188 D1
Elkesley Notts 132 B1
Elkstone Glos 63 B5
Ellan Highld 253 D4
Elland W Yorks 139 A4
Ellary Argyll 202 A2
Ellastone Staffs 113 A5
Ellemford Borders 211 D4
Ellenbrook I o M 152 D3
Ellenhall Staffs 112 C2
Ellen's Green Sur 34 C3
Ellerbeck N Yorks 158 B3
Ellerburn N Yorks 160 C2
Ellerby N Yorks 169 D5
Ellerdine Heath Telford 111 C5
Ellerhayes Devon 13 A4
Elleric Argyll 227 B5
Ellerker E Yorks 141 A7
Ellerton E Yorks 149 D6
Ellerton Shrops 111 C6
Ellesborough Bucks 66 C3
Ellesmere Shrops 110 B3
Ellesmere Port Ches 127 B4
Ellingham Norf 105 B4
Ellingham Northumb 189 A4
Ellingstring N Yorks 157 C5
Ellington Cambs 100 D3
Ellington Northumb 189 D5
Elliot Angus 221 A6
Ellisfield Hants 33 A5
Ellistown Leics 114 D2
Ellon Aberds 257 C4
Ellonby Cumb 164 B2
Ellough Suff 105 C5
Elloughton E Yorks 142 A1
Ellwood Glos 62 C1
Elm Cambs 101 A6
Elm Hill Dorset 30 C2
Elm Park London 50 A2
Elmbridge Worcs 80 A2
Elmdon Essex 85 D6
Elmdon W Mid 97 C4
Elmdon Heath W Mid 97 C4
Elmers End London 49 C6
Elmesthorpe Leics 98 B1
Elmfield I o W 19 B5
Elmhurst Staffs 113 D5
Elmley Castle Worcs 80 C2
Elmley Lovett Worcs 79 A6
Elmore Glos 62 B3

Fin – Gar 345


Finchdean Hants 33 D6
Finchingfield Essex 86 D2
Finchley London 68 D2
Findern Derbys 113 B7
Findhorn Moray 265 D6
Findhorn Bridge Highld 253 D4
Findo Gask Perth 219 B5
Findochty Moray 267 C5
Findon Aberds 245 C6
Findon W Sus 21 B4
Findon Mains Highld 264 D2
Findrack Ho. Aberds 244 B3
Finedon Northants 99 D6
Fingal Street Suff 88 A3
Fingask Aberds 256 D2
Fingerpost Worcs 95 D5
Fingest Bucks 66 D2
Finghall N Yorks 157 C5
Fingland Cumb 175 C5
Fingland Dumfries 183 A5
Finglesham Kent 53 D5
Fingringhoe Essex 71 A4
Finlarig Stirl 217 A5
Finmere Oxon 82 D3
Finnart Perth 229 C4
Finningham Suff 87 A6
Finningley S Yorks 141 D4
Finnygaud Aberds 267 D6
Finsbury London 49 A6
Finstall Worcs 80 A2
Finsthwaite Cumb 154 C2
Finstock Oxon 65 B4
Finstown Orkney 282 F4
Fintry Aberds 268 D2
Fintry Dundee 220 A4
Fintry Stirl 207 B4
Finzean Aberds 244 C3
Fionnphort Argyll 224 D2
Fionnsbhagh W Isles 287 F5
Fir Tree Durham 166 B4
Firbeck S Yorks 131 A5
Firby N Yorks 157 C6
Firby N Yorks 149 A6
Firgrove Gtr Man 138 B2
Firsby Lincs 135 C4
Firsdown Wilts 31 B6
First Coast Highld 261 A6
Fishbourne I o W 19 B4
Fishbourne W Sus 20 B1
Fishbourne Palace W Sus 20 B1
Fishburn Durham 167 B6
Fishcross Clack 208 A1
Fisher Place Cumb 163 C6
Fisherford Aberds 256 C1
Fisher's Pond Hants 32 C3
Fisherstreet W Sus 34 C2
Fisherton Highld 252 A3
Fisherton S Ayrs 192 D2
Fishguard = Abergwaun Pembs 72 C2
Fishlake S Yorks 141 B4
Fishleigh Barton Devon 25 C6
Fishponds Bristol 43 B5
Fishpool Glos 62 A2
Fishtoft Lincs 117 A6
Fishtoft Drove Lincs 117 A6
Fishtown of Usan Angus 233 C5
Fishwick Borders 198 A3
Fiskavaig Highld 246 A2
Fiskerton Lincs 133 B5
Fiskerton Notts 132 D2
Fitling E Yorks 151 D5
Fittleton Wilts 31 A5
Fittleworth W Sus 20 A3
Fitton End Cambs 118 D1
Fitz Shrops 110 D3
Fitzhead Som 27 C6
Fitzwilliam W Yorks 140 B2
Fitzwilliam Museum, Cambridge Cambs 85 B6
Fiunary Highld 225 B5
Five Acres Glos 62 B1
Five Ashes E Sus 36 D3
Five Oak Green Kent 36 B4
Five Oaks Jersey 6
Five Oaks W Sus 34 D3
Five Roads Carms 57 B4
Fivecrosses Ches 127 B5
Fivehead Som 28 C3
Flack's Green Essex 70 B1
Flackwell Heath Bucks 48 A1
Fladbury Worcs 80 C2
Fladdabister Shetland 285 K6
Flagg Derbys 129 C6
Flambards Experience, Helston Corn 3 C4
Flamborough E Yorks 161 D6
Flamingo Land, Pickering N Yorks 159 D6
Flamstead Herts 67 B5
Flamstead End Herts 68 C3
Flansham W Sus 20 B2
Flanshaw W Yorks 139 A6
Flasby N Yorks 146 B3
Flash Staffs 129 C5
Flashader Highld 258 C3
Flask Inn N Yorks 160 A3
Flaunden Herts 67 C5
Flawborough Notts 115 A5
Flawith N Yorks 148 A3
Flax Bourton N Som 43 C4
Flaxby N Yorks 148 B2
Flaxholme Derbys 114 A1
Flaxley Glos 62 B2
Flaxpool Som 27 B6
Flaxton N Yorks 149 A5
Fleckney Leics 98 B3
Flecknoe Warks 82 A2
Fledborough Notts 132 B3
Fleet Hants 47 D6
Fleet Hants 19 A6
Fleet Lincs 117 C6
Fleet Air Arm Museum, Yeovil Som 29 C5
Fleet Hargate Lincs 117 C6
Fleetham Northumb 189 A4
Fleetlands Hants 19 A4
Fleetville Herts 67 C6
Fleetwood Lancs 144 C3
Flemingston V Glam 41 D5
Flemington S Lnrk 205 C6
Flempton Suff 87 A4
Fleoideabhagh W Isles 287 F5
Fletchertown Cumb 175 D5
Fletching E Sus 36 D2
Flexbury Corn 10 A3
Flexford Sur 34 B2
Flimby Cumb 162 A3
Flimwell E Sus 37 C5
Flint = Y Fflint Flint 126 B2
Flint Mountain Flint 126 B2
Flintham Notts 115 A5
Flinton E Yorks 151 D5
Flintsham Hereford 77 B7
Flitcham Norf 119 C4
Flitton Beds 84 D2
Flitwick Beds 84 D2
Flixborough N Lincs 141 B6
Flixborough Stather N Lincs 141 B6
Flixton Gtr Man 137 D6
Flixton N Yorks 160 D4
Flixton Suff 104 C4
Flockton W Yorks 139 B5
Flodaigh W Isles 286 A4
Flodden Northumb 198 C3
Flodigarry Highld 259 A4
Flood's Ferry Cambs 101 B5
Flookburgh Cumb 154 D2
Florden Norf 104 B2
Flore Northants 82 A3
Flotterton Northumb 188 C2
Flowton Suff 88 C1
Flush House W Yorks 139 C4
Flushing Aberds 257 B5
Flushing Corn 4 D3
Flyford Flavell Worcs 80 B2
Foals Green Suff 104 D3
Fobbing Thurrock 51 A4
Fochabers Moray 266 D4
Fochriw Caerph 60 C3
Fockerby N Lincs 141 B6
Fodderletter Moray 254 D2
Fodderty Highld 251 A7
Foel Powys 109 D4
Foel-gastell Carms 57 A5
Foffarty Angus 232 D2
Foggathorpe E Yorks 149 D6
Fogo Borders 197 B6
Fogorig Borders 198 B1
Foindle Highld 276 D2
Folda Angus 231 B5
Fole Staffs 112 B4
Foleshill W Mid 97 C6
Folke Dorset 29 D6
Folkestone Kent 39 B4
Folkestone Racecourse Kent 38 B3
Folkingham Lincs 116 B3
Folkington E Sus 22 B3
Folksworth Cambs 100 C3
Folkton N Yorks 161 D4
Folla Rule Aberds 256 C2
Follifoot N Yorks 148 B2
Folly Gate Devon 11 B6
Fonthill Bishop Wilts 30 B3
Fonthill Gifford Wilts 30 B3
Fontmell Magna Dorset 30 D2
Fontwell W Sus 20 B2
Fontwell Park Racecourse W Sus 20 B2
Foolow Derbys 130 B1
Foots Cray London 50 B1
Forbestown Aberds 243 A6
Force Mills Cumb 154 B2
Forcett N Yorks 167 D4
Ford Argyll 214 B1
Ford Bucks 66 C2
Ford Devon 25 C5
Ford Glos 64 A1
Ford Northumb 198 C3
Ford Shrops 110 D3
Ford Staffs 129 D5
Ford Wilts 44 B2
Ford W Sus 20 B2
Ford End Essex 69 B6
Ford Street Som 27 D6
Fordcombe Kent 36 B3
Fordell Fife 209 B4
Forden Powys 93 A6
Forder Grn. Devon 8 A1
Fordham Cambs 102 D2
Fordham Essex 70 A3
Fordham Norf 102 B2
Fordhouses W Mid 96 A2
Fordingbridge Hants 31 D5
Fordon E Yorks 160 D4
Fordoun Aberds 233 A5
Ford's Green Suff 87 A6
Fordstreet Essex 70 A3
Fordwells Oxon 64 B4
Fordwich Kent 52 D3
Fordyce Aberds 267 C6
Forebridge Staffs 112 C3
Forest Durham 165 B6
Forest Becks Lancs 146 B1
Forest Gate London 49 A7
Forest Green Sur 35 B4
Forest Hall Cumb 154 A4
Forest Head Cumb 176 D3
Forest Hill Oxon 65 C6
Forest Lane Head N Yorks 148 B2
Forest Lodge Argyll 228 D1
Forest Lodge Highld 242 A3
Forest Lodge Perth 230 A3
Forest Mill Clack 208 A2
Forest Row E Sus 36 C2
Forest Town Notts 131 C5
Forestburn Gate Northumb 188 D3
Foresterseat Moray 266 D2
Forestside W Sus 33 D6
Forfar Angus 232 C2
Forgandenny Perth 219 C5
Forge Powys 91 C5
Forge Side Torf 60 C4
Forgewood N Lnrk 194 A2
Forgie Moray 267 D4
Forglen Ho. Aberds 268 D1
Formby Mers 136 C2
Forncett End Norf 104 B2
Forncett St Mary Norf 104 B2
Forncett St Peter Norf 104 B2
Forneth Perth 231 D4
Fornham All Saints Suff 87 A4
Fornham St Martin Suff 87 A4
Forres Moray 253 A6
Forrest Lodge Dumfries 182 D3
Forrestfield N Lnrk 207 D6
Forsbrook Staffs 112 A3
Forse Highld 275 A6
Forse Ho. Highld 275 A6
Forsinain Highld 279 D5
Forsinard Highld 279 D4
Forsinard Station Highld 279 D4
Forston Dorset 15 B6
Fort Augustus Highld 240 B1
Fort George Guern 6
Fort George Highld 252 A3
Fort Victoria Country Park & Marine Aquarium I o W 18 C2
Fort William Highld 237 B5
Forteviot Perth 219 C5
Forth S Lnrk 194 A4
Forth Road Bridge Edin 208 C4
Forthampton Glos 79 D6
Fortingall Perth 229 D6
Forton Hants 32 A3
Forton Lancs 145 B4
Forton Shrops 110 D3
Forton Som 14 A3
Forton Staffs 111 C6
Forton Heath Shrops 110 D3
Fortrie Aberds 256 B1
Fortrose Highld 252 A3
Fortuneswell Dorset 15 D6
Forty Green Bucks 67 D4
Forty Hill London 68 D3
Forward Green Suff 88 B1
Fosbury Wilts 45 D7
Fosdyke Lincs 117 B6
Foss Perth 230 C1
Foss Cross Glos 63 C6
Fossebridge Glos 64 B1
Foster Street Essex 69 C4
Fosterhouses S Yorks 141 B4
Foston Derbys 113 B5
Foston Lincs 115 A6
Foston N Yorks 149 A5
Foston on the Wolds E Yorks 151 B4
Fotherby Lincs 143 D5
Fotheringhay Northants 100 B2
Foubister Orkney 283 G6
Foul Mile E Sus 22 A4
Foulby W Yorks 140 B1
Foulden Borders 198 A3
Foulden Norf 102 B3
Foulis Castle Highld 264 D1
Foulridge Lancs 146 C2
Foulsham Norf 120 C2
Fountainhall Borders 196 B3
Fountains Abbey, Ripon N Yorks 147 A6
Four Ashes Staffs 95 C6
Four Ashes Suff 103 D6
Four Crosses Powys 93 A4
Four Crosses Powys 110 D1
Four Crosses Wrex 126 D2
Four Elms Kent 36 B2
Four Forks Som 28 B2
Four Gotes Cambs 118 D1
Four Lane Ends Ches 127 C5
Four Lanes Corn 3 B4
Four Marks Hants 33 B5
Four Mile Bridge Anglesey 122 C2
Four Oaks E Sus 37 D6
Four Oaks W Mid 97 C5
Four Oaks W Mid 96 B4
Four Roads Carms 57 B4
Four Roads I o M 152 E2
Four Throws Kent 37 D5
Fourlane Ends Derbys 130 D3
Fourlanes End Ches 128 D3
Fourpenny Highld 265 A4
Fourstones Northumb 177 C6
Fovant Wilts 31 C4
Foveran Aberds 257 D4
Fowey Corn 5 B6
Fowley Common Warr 137 D5
Fowlis Angus 220 A3
Fowlis Wester Perth 218 B4
Fowlmere Cambs 85 C6
Fownhope Hereford 78 D3
Fox Corner Sur 34 A2
Fox Lane Hants 34 A1
Fox Street Essex 71 A4
Foxbar Renfs 205 B4
Foxcombe Hill Oxon 65 C5
Foxdale I o M 152 D2
Foxearth Essex 87 C4
Foxfield Cumb 153 B3
Foxham Wilts 44 B3
Foxhole Corn 5 B4
Foxhole Swansea 57 C6
Foxholes N Yorks 160 D4
Foxhunt Green E Sus 22 A3
Foxley Norf 120 C2
Foxley Wilts 44 A2
Foxt Staffs 112 A4
Foxton Cambs 85 C6
Foxton Durham 167 C6
Foxton Leics 99 B4
Foxton Canal Locks Leics 98 C3
Foxup N Yorks 156 D2
Foxwist Green Ches 127 C6
Foxwood Shrops 95 D4
Foy Hereford 62 A1
Foyers Highld 251 D6
Fraddam Corn 2 B3
Fraddon Corn 4 B4
Fradley Staffs 113 D5
Fradswell Staffs 112 B3
Fraisthorpe E Yorks 151 A4
Framfield E Sus 36 D2
Framingham Earl Norf 104 A3
Framingham Pigot Norf 104 A3
Framlingham Suff 88 A3
Framlingham Castle Suff 88 A3
Frampton Dorset 15 B6
Frampton Lincs 117 B6
Frampton Cotterell S Glos 43 A5
Frampton Mansell Glos 63 C5
Frampton on Severn Glos 62 C3
Frampton West End Lincs 117 A5
Framsden Suff 88 B2
Framwellgate Moor Durham 167 A5
Franche Worcs 95 D6
Frankby Mers 126 A2
Frankley Worcs 96 C2
Frank's Bridge Powys 77 B5
Frankton Warks 98 D1
Frant E Sus 36 C3
Fraserburgh Aberds 269 C4
Frating Green Essex 71 A4
Fratton Ptsmth 19 B5
Freathy Corn 6 B3
Freckenham Suff 102 D2
Freckleton Lancs 136 A3
Freeby Leics 115 C6
Freehay Staffs 112 A4
Freeland Oxon 65 B5
Freeport Hornsea Outlet Village E Yorks 151 C5
Freester Shetland 285 H6
Freethorpe Norf 105 A5
Freiston Lincs 117 A6
Fremington Devon 25 B6
Fremington N Yorks 156 B4
Frenchay S Glos 43 B5
Frenchbeer Devon 12 C1
Frenich Stirl 216 D4
Frensham Sur 34 B1
Fresgoe Highld 279 B5
Freshfield Mers 136 C1
Freshford Bath 44 C1
Freshwater I o W 18 C2
Freshwater Bay I o W 18 C2
Freshwater East Pembs 55 E6
Fressingfield Suff 104 D3
Freston Suff 88 D2
Freswick Highld 281 B5
Fretherne Glos 62 C3
Frettenham Norf 120 D4
Freuchie Fife 220 D2
Freuchies Angus 231 B6
Freystrop Pembs 55 C5
Friar's Gate E Sus 36 C2
Friarton Perth 219 B6
Friday Bridge Cambs 101 A6
Friday Street E Sus 22 B4
Fridaythorpe E Yorks 150 B1
Friern Barnet London 68 D2
Friesland Argyll 223 B4
Friesthorpe Lincs 133 A5
Frieston Lincs 116 A2
Frieth Bucks 66 D2
Frilford Oxon 65 D5
Frilsham W Berks 46 B3
Frimley Sur 34 A1
Frimley Green Sur 34 A1
Frindsbury Medway 51 B4
Fring Norf 119 B4
Fringford Oxon 65 A7
Frinsted Kent 37 A6
Frinton-on-Sea Essex 71 A6
Friockheim Angus 232 D3
Friog Gwyn 90 A4
Frisby on the Wreake Leics 115 D4
Friskney Lincs 135 D4
Friskney Eaudike Lincs 135 D4
Friskney Tofts Lincs 135 D4
Friston E Sus 22 C3
Friston Suff 89 A5
Fritchley Derbys 130 D3
Frith Bank Lincs 117 A6
Frith Common Worcs 79 A4
Fritham Hants 31 D6
Frithelstock Devon 25 D5
Frithelstock Stone Devon 25 D5
Frithville Lincs 134 D3
Frittenden Kent 37 B6
Frittiscombe Devon 8 C2
Fritton Norf 104 B3
Fritton Norf 105 A5
Fritwell Oxon 65 A6
Frizinghall W Yorks 147 D5
Frizington Cumb 162 C3
Frocester Glos 62 C3
Frodesley Shrops 94 A3
Frodingham N Lincs 141 B6
Frodsham Ches 127 B5
Frogden Borders 187 A6
Froggatt Derbys 130 B2
Froghall Staffs 112 A4
Frogmore Devon 7 C6
Frogmore Hants 34 A1
Frognall Lincs 117 D4
Frogshail Norf 121 B4
Frolesworth Leics 98 B2
Frome Som 30 A1
Frome St Quintin Dorset 15 A5
Fromes Hill Hereford 79 C4
Fron Denb 125 C5
Fron Gwyn 107 A5
Fron Gwyn 106 C3
Fron Powys 77 A4
Fron Powys 93 A6
Fron Powys 93 B5
Froncysyllte Wrex 110 A1
Frongoch Gwyn 108 B4
Frostenden Suff 105 C5
Frosterley Durham 166 B3
Frotoft Orkney 282 E5
Froxfield Wilts 45 C6
Froxfield Green Hants 33 C6
Froyle Hants 33 A6
Fryerning Essex 69 C6
Fryton N Yorks 159 D5
Fulbeck Lincs 133 D4
Fulbourn Cambs 85 B7
Fulbrook Oxon 64 B3
Fulford Som 28 C2
Fulford Staffs 112 B3
Fulford York 149 C5
Fulham London 49 B5
Fulking W Sus 21 A5
Full Sutton E Yorks 149 B6
Fullarton Glasgow 205 B6
Fullarton N Ayrs 192 B3
Fuller Street Essex 70 B1
Fuller's Moor Ches 127 D4
Fullerton Hants 32 B2
Fulletby Lincs 134 B2
Fullwood E Ayrs 205 C4
Fulmer Bucks 48 A2
Fulmodestone Norf 120 B1
Fulnetby Lincs 133 B5
Fulstow Lincs 143 D5
Fulwell T & W 179 D5
Fulwood Lancs 145 D5
Fulwood S Yorks 130 A3
Fundenhall Norf 104 B2
Fundenhall Street Norf 104 B2
Funtington W Sus 19 A6
Funtley Hants 19 A4
Funtullich Perth 218 B2
Funzie Shetland 284 D8
Furley Devon 14 A2
Furnace Argyll 214 B3
Furnace Carms 57 B5
Furnace End Warks 97 B5
Furneaux Pelham Herts 68 A4
Furness Vale Derbys 129 A5
Furze Platt Windsor 48 A1
Furzehill Devon 26 A2
Fyfett Som 28 D2
Fyfield Essex 69 C5
Fyfield Glos 64 C3
Fyfield Hants 32 A1
Fyfield Oxon 65 D5
Fyfield Wilts 45 C5
Fylingthorpe N Yorks 160 A3
Fyvie Aberds 256 C2


## G


Gabhsann bho Dheas W Isles 288 B5
Gabhsann bho Thuath W Isles 288 B5
Gablon Highld 264 A3
Gabroc Hill E Ayrs 205 C4
Gaddesby Leics 115 D4
Gadebridge Herts 67 C5
Gaer Powys 60 A3
Gaerllwyd Mon 61 D6
Gaerwen Anglesey 123 C4
Gagingwell Oxon 65 A5
Gaick Lodge Highld 241 D5
Gailey Staffs 112 D3
Gainford Durham 167 D4
Gainsborough Lincs 141 D6
Gainsborough Suff 88 C2
Gainsford End Essex 86 D3
Gairloch Highld 261 C5
Gairlochy Highld 239 D5
Gairney Bank Perth 208 A4
Gairnshiel Lodge Aberds 243 B5
Gaisgill Cumb 155 A5
Gaitsgill Cumb 164 A1
Galashiels Borders 196 C3
Galgate Lancs 145 B4
Galhampton Som 29 C6
Gallaberry Dumfries 184 D2
Gallachoille Argyll 213 D5
Gallanach Argyll 226 D3
Gallanach Argyll 223 A5
Gallantry Bank Ches 127 D5
Gallatown Fife 209 A5
Galley Common Warks 97 B6
Galley Hill Cambs 85 A5
Galleyend Essex 69 C7
Galleywood Essex 69 C7
Gallin Perth 229 D4
Gallowfauld Angus 232 D2
Gallows Green Staffs 113 A4
Galltair Highld 249 D5
Galmisdale Highld 234 B3
Galmpton Devon 7 C5
Galmpton Torbay 8 B2
Galphay N Yorks 157 D6
Galston E Ayrs 193 B5
Galtrigill Highld 258 C1
Gamblesby Cumb 165 B4
Gamesley Derbys 138 D3
Gamlingay Cambs 84 B4
Gammersgill N Yorks 157 C4
Gamston Notts 132 B2
Ganarew Hereford 62 B1
Ganavan Argyll 226 C3
Gang Corn 6 A2
Ganllwyd Gwyn 108 C2
Gannochy Angus 232 A3
Gannochy Perth 219 B6
Gansclet Highld 281 D5
Ganstead E Yorks 151 D4
Ganthorpe N Yorks 159 D5
Ganton N Yorks 160 D3
Garbat Highld 263 D6
Garbhallt Argyll 214 C3
Garboldisham Norf 103 C6
Garden City Flint 126 C3
Garden Village Wrex 126 D3
Garden Village W Yorks 148 D3
Gardenstown Aberds 268 C2
Garderhouse Shetland 285 J5
Gardham E Yorks 150 C2
Gardin Shetland 284 G6
Gare Hill Som 30 A1
Garelochhead Argyll 215 C5
Garford Oxon 65 D5
Garforth W Yorks 148 D3

Hacton London 50 A2
Hadden Borders 198 C1
Haddenham Bucks 66 C2
Haddenham Cambs 101 D6
Haddington E Loth 210 C2
Haddington Lincs 133 C4
Haddiscoe Norf 105 B5
Haddon Cambs 100 B3
Haddon Ches 129 C4
Haddon Hall Derbys 130 C2
Hade Edge W Yorks 139 C4
Hademore Staffs 97 A4
Hadfield Derbys 138 D3
Hadham Cross Herts 68 B4
Hadham Ford Herts 68 A4
Hadleigh Essex 51 A5
Hadleigh Suff 87 C6
Hadley Telford 111 D5
Hadley End Staffs 113 C5
Hadlow Kent 36 B4
Hadlow Down E Sus 36 D3
Hadnall Shrops 111 D4
Hadstock Essex 86 C1
Hady Derbys 130 B3
Hadzor Worcs 80 A2
Haffenden Quarter Kent 37 B6
Hafod-Dinbych Conwy 124 D3
Hafod-lom Conwy 124 B3
Haggate Lancs 146 D2
Haggbeck Cumb 176 B2
Haggerston Northumb 198 B4
Haggrister Shetland 284 F5
Hagley Hereford 78 C3
Hagley Worcs 96 C2
Hagworthingham Lincs 134 C3
Haigh Gtr Man 137 C5
Haigh S Yorks 139 B5
Haigh Moor W Yorks 139 A5
Haighton Green Lancs 145 D5
Hail Weston Cambs 84 A3
Haile Cumb 162 D3
Hailes Glos 80 D3
Hailey Herts 68 B3
Hailey Oxon 65 B4
Hailsham E Sus 22 B3
Haimer Highld 280 B3
Hainault London 69 D4
Hainford Norf 120 D4
Hainton Lincs 134 A1
Hairmyres S Lnrk 205 C6
Haisthorpe E Yorks 151 A4
Hakin Pembs 55 D4
Halam Notts 132 D1
Halbeath Fife 208 B4
Halberton Devon 27 D5
Halcro Highld 280 B4
Hale Gtr Man 128 A2
Hale Halton 127 A4
Hale Hants 31 D5
Hale Bank Halton 127 A4
Hale Street Kent 37 B4
Halebarns Gtr Man 128 A2
Hales Norf 105 B4
Hales Staffs 111 B6
Hales Place Kent 52 D3
Halesfield Telford 95 A5
Halesgate Lincs 117 C6
Halesowen W Mid 96 C2
Halesworth Suff 105 D4
Halewood Mers 127 A4
Halford Shrops 94 C2
Halford Warks 81 C5
Halfpenny Furze Carms 56 A2
Halfpenny Green Staffs 95 B6
Halfway Carms 58 B3
Halfway Carms 59 B5
Halfway W Berks 46 C2
Halfway Bridge W Sus 34 D2
Halfway House Shrops 110 D2
Halfway Houses Kent 51 B6
Halifax W Yorks 138 A3
Halket E Ayrs 205 C4
Halkirk Highld 280 C3
Halkyn Flint 126 B2
Hall Dunnerdale Cumb 153 A3
Hall Green W Mid 96 C4
Hall Green W Yorks 139 B6
Hall Grove Herts 68 B2
Hall of Tankerness Orkney 283 G6
Hall of the Forest Shrops 93 C6
Halland E Sus 22 A2
Hallaton Leics 99 B4
Hallatrow Bath 43 D5
Hallbankgate Cumb 176 D3
Hallen S Glos 43 A4
Halliburton Borders 197 B5
Hallin Highld 258 C2
Halling Medway 51 C4
Hallington Lincs 134 A3
Hallington Northumb 178 B1
Halliwell Gtr Man 137 B6
Halloughton Notts 132 D1
Hallow Worcs 79 B6
Hallrule Borders 187 B4
Halls E Loth 210 C3
Hall's Green Herts 68 A2
Hallsands Devon 8 D2
Hallthwaites Cumb 153 B2
Hallworthy Corn 10 C2
Hallyburton House Perth 220 A2
Hallyne Borders 195 B6
Halmer End Staffs 112 A1
Halmore Glos 62 C2
Halmyre Mains Borders 195 B6
Halnaker W Sus 20 B2
Halsall Lancs 136 B2
Halse Northants 82 C2
Halse Som 27 C6
Halsetown Corn 2 B3
Halsham E Yorks 143 A4
Halsinger Devon 25 B6
Halstead Essex 87 D4
Halstead Kent 50 C1
Halstead Leics 99 A4
Halstock Dorset 15 A5
Haltham Lincs 134 C2
Haltoft End Lincs 117 A6
Halton Bucks 66 B3
Halton Halton 127 A5
Halton Lancs 145 A5
Halton Northumb 178 C1
Halton Wrex 110 B2
Halton W Yorks 148 D2
Halton East N Yorks 147 B4
Halton Gill N Yorks 156 D2
Halton Holegate Lincs 135 C4
Halton Lea Gate Northumb 176 D4
Halton West N Yorks 146 B2
Haltwhistle Northumb 177 C5
Halvergate Norf 105 A5
Halwell Devon 8 B1
Halwill Devon 11 B5
Halwill Junction Devon 11 A5
Ham Devon 14 A2
Ham Glos 62 D2
Ham London 49 B4
Ham Highld 280 A4
Ham Kent 53 D5
Ham Shetland 285 K1
Ham Wilts 46 C1
Ham Common Dorset 30 C2
Ham Green Hereford 79 C5
Ham Green Kent 37 D6
Ham Green Kent 51 C5
Ham Green N Som 43 B4
Ham Green Worcs 80 A3
Ham Street Som 29 B5
Hamble-le-Rice Hants 18 A3
Hambleden Bucks 47 A5
Hambledon Hants 33 D5
Hambledon Sur 34 C2
Hambleton Lancs 144 C3
Hambleton N Yorks 149 D4
Hambridge Som 28 C3
Hambrook S Glos 43 B5
Hambrook W Sus 19 A6
Hameringham Lincs 134 C3
Hamerton Cambs 100 D3
Hametoun Shetland 285 K1
Hamilton S Lnrk 194 A2
Hamilton Park Racecourse S Lnrk 194 A2
Hammer W Sus 34 C1
Hammerpot W Sus 20 B3
Hammersmith London 49 B5
Hammerwich Staffs 96 A3
Hammerwood E Sus 36 C2
Hammond Street Herts 68 C3
Hammoon Dorset 30 D2
Hamnavoe Shetland 284 E4
Hamnavoe Shetland 285 K5
Hamnavoe Shetland 284 E6
Hamnavoe Shetland 284 F6
Hampden National Stadium Glasgow 205 B5
Hampden Park E Sus 22 B4
Hamperden End Essex 86 D1
Hampnett Glos 64 B1
Hampole S Yorks 140 B3
Hampreston Dorset 17 B4
Hampstead London 49 A5
Hampstead Norreys W Berks 46 B3
Hampsthwaite N Yorks 147 B6
Hampton London 48 C4
Hampton Shrops 95 C5
Hampton Worcs 80 C3
Hampton Bishop Hereford 78 D3
Hampton Court Palace, Teddington London 52 C3
Hampton Heath Ches 110 A3
Hampton in Arden W Mid 97 C5
Hampton Loade Shrops 95 C5
Hampton Lovett Worcs 80 A1
Hampton Lucy Warks 81 B5
Hampton on the Hill Warks 81 A5
Hampton Poyle Oxon 65 B6
Hamrow Norf 119 C6
Hamsey E Sus 22 A2
Hamsey Green Sur 35 A6
Hamstall Ridware Staffs 113 D5
Hamstead I o W 18 B3
Hamstead W Mid 96 B3
Hamstead Marshall W Berks 46 C2
Hamsterley Durham 166 B4
Hamsterley Durham 178 D3
Hamstreet Kent 38 B2
Hamworthy Poole 16 B3
Hanbury Staffs 113 C5
Hanbury Worcs 80 A2
Hanbury Woodend Staffs 113 C5
Hanby Lincs 116 B3
Hanchurch Staffs 112 A2
Handbridge Ches 127 C4
Handcross W Sus 35 D5
Handforth Ches 128 A3
Handley Ches 127 D4
Handsacre Staffs 113 D4
Handsworth S Yorks 131 A4
Handsworth W Mid 96 B3
Handy Cross Devon 25 C5
Hanford Stoke 112 A2
Hanging Langford Wilts 31 B4
Hangleton W Sus 20 B3
Hanham S Glos 43 B5
Hankelow Ches 111 A5
Hankerton Wilts 63 D5
Hankham E Sus 22 B4
Hanley Stoke 112 A2
Hanley Castle Worcs 79 C6
Hanley Child Worcs 79 A4
Hanley Swan Worcs 79 C6
Hanley William Worcs 79 A4
Hanlith N Yorks 146 A3
Hanmer Wrex 110 B3
Hannah Lincs 135 B5
Hannington Hants 46 D3
Hannington Northants 99 D5
Hannington Thamesdown 64 D2
Hannington Wick Thamesdown 64 D2
Hansel Village S Ayrs 192 B3
Hanslope M Keynes 83 C5
Hanthorpe Lincs 116 C3
Hanwell London 49 A4
Hanwell Oxon 82 C1
Hanwood Shrops 94 A2
Hanworth London 48 B4
Hanworth Norf 120 B3
Happendon S Lnrk 194 C3
Happisburgh Norf 121 B5
Happisburgh Common Norf 121 C5
Hapsford Ches 127 B4
Hapton Lancs 146 D1
Hapton Norf 104 B2
Harberton Devon 8 B1
Harbertonford Devon 8 B1
Harbledown Kent 52 D3
Harborne W Mid 96 C3
Harborough Magna Warks 98 D1
Harbottle Northumb 188 C2
Harbour Park, Littlehampton W Sus 20 C3
Harbury Warks 81 B6
Harby Leics 115 B5
Harby Notts 132 B3
Harcombe Devon 13 B6
Harden W Mid 96 A3
Harden W Yorks 147 D4
Hardenhuish Wilts 44 B3
Hardgate Aberds 245 B4
Hardham W Sus 20 A3
Hardingham Norf 103 A6
Hardingstone Northants 83 B4
Hardington Som 43 D6
Hardington Mandeville Som 29 D5
Hardington Marsh Som 15 A5
Hardley Hants 18 A3
Hardley Street Norf 105 A4
Hardmead M Keynes 83 C6
Hardrow N Yorks 156 B2
Hardstoft Derbys 131 C4
Hardway Hants 19 A5
Hardway Som 29 B7
Hardwick Bucks 66 B3
Hardwick Cambs 85 B5
Hardwick Norf 118 D3
Hardwick Norf 104 C3
Hardwick Notts 131 B6
Hardwick Northants 83 A5
Hardwick Oxon 65 C4
Hardwick Oxon 65 A6
Hardwick W Mid 96 B3
Hardwick Hall Derbys 131 C4
Hardwicke Glos 62 B3
Hardwicke Glos 63 A5
Hardwicke Hereford 77 C6
Hardy's Green Essex 70 A3
Hare Green Essex 71 A4
Hare Hatch Wokingham 47 B6
Hare Street Herts 68 A3
Hareby Lincs 134 C3
Hareden Lancs 145 B6
Harefield London 67 D5
Harehills W Yorks 148 D2
Harehope Northumb 188 A3
Haresceugh Cumb 165 A4
Harescombe Glos 63 B4
Haresfield Glos 63 B4
Hareshaw N Lnrk 207 D6
Hareshaw Head Northumb 177 A6
Harewood W Yorks 148 C2
Harewood End Hereford 62 A1
Harewood House, Wetherby W Yorks 148 C2
Harford Carms 58 A3
Harford Devon 7 B5
Hargate Norf 104 B2
Hargatewall Derbys 129 B6
Hargrave Ches 127 C4
Hargrave Northants 100 D2
Hargrave Suff 86 B3
Harker Cumb 175 B6
Harkland Shetland 284 E6
Harkstead Suff 88 D2
Harlaston Staffs 113 D6
Harlaw Ho. Aberds 256 D2
Harlaxton Lincs 116 B1
Harle Syke Lancs 146 D2
Harlech Gwyn 107 C5
Harlech Castle Gwyn 107 C5
Harlequin Notts 115 B4
Harlescott Shrops 111 D4
Harlesden London 49 A5
Harleston Devon 8 C1
Harleston Norf 104 C3
Harleston Suff 87 B6
Harlestone Northants 83 A4
Harley Shrops 94 A3
Harley S Yorks 139 D6
Harleyholm S Lnrk 194 C4
Harlington Beds 84 D2
Harlington London 48 B3
Harlington S Yorks 140 C2
Harlosh Highld 258 D2
Harlow Essex 69 B4
Harlow Carr RHS Garden, Harrogate N Yorks 148 B1
Harlow Hill Northumb 178 C2
Harlow Hill N Yorks 148 B1
Harlthorpe E Yorks 149 D6
Harlton Cambs 85 B5
Harman's Cross Dorset 16 C3
Harmby N Yorks 157 C5
Harmer Green Herts 68 B2
Harmer Hill Shrops 110 C3
Harmondsworth London 48 B3
Harmston Lincs 133 C4
Harnham Northumb 178 B2
Harnhill Glos 63 C6
Harold Hill London 69 D5
Harold Wood London 69 D5
Haroldston West Pembs 55 C4
Haroldswick Shetland 284 B8
Harome N Yorks 159 C5
Harpenden Herts 67 B6
Harpford Devon 13 B5
Harpham E Yorks 150 A3
Harpley Norf 119 C4
Harpley Worcs 79 A4
Harpole Northants 82 A3
Harpsdale Highld 280 C3
Harpsden Oxon 47 A5
Harpswell Lincs 133 A4
Harpur Hill Derbys 129 B5
Harpurhey Gtr Man 138 C1
Harraby Cumb 175 C7
Harrapool Highld 247 B5
Harrier Shetland 285 J1
Harrietfield Perth 219 B4
Harrietsham Kent 37 A6
Harrington Cumb 162 B2
Harrington Lincs 134 B3
Harrington Northants 99 C4
Harringworth Northants 99 B6
Harris Highld 234 A2
Harris Museum, Preston Lancs 136 A4
Harrogate N Yorks 148 B2
Harrold Beds 83 B6
Harrow London 49 A4
Harrow on the Hill London 49 A4
Harrow Street Suff 87 D5
Harrow Weald London 67 D6
Harrowbarrow Corn 6 A2
Harrowden Beds 84 C2
Harrowgate Hill Darl 167 D5
Harston Cambs 85 B6
Harston Leics 115 B6
Harswell E Yorks 150 C1
Hart Hrtlpl 168 B2
Hart Common Gtr Man 137 C5
Hart Hill Luton 67 A6
Hart Station Hrtlpl 168 B2
Hartburn Northumb 178 A2
Hartburn Stockton 168 D2
Hartest Suff 87 B4
Hartfield E Sus 36 C2
Hartford Cambs 101 D4
Hartford Ches 127 B6
Hartford End Essex 69 B6
Hartfordbridge Hants 47 D5
Hartforth N Yorks 157 A5
Harthill Ches 127 D5
Harthill N Lnrk 208 D2
Harthill S Yorks 131 A4
Hartington Derbys 129 C6
Hartland Devon 24 C3
Hartlebury Worcs 95 D6
Hartlepool Hrtlpl 168 B3
Hartley Cumb 155 A6
Hartley Kent 50 C3
Hartley Kent 37 C5
Hartley Northumb 179 B5
Hartley Westpall Hants 47 D4
Hartley Wintney Hants 47 D5
Hartlip Kent 51 C5
Hartoft End N Yorks 159 B6
Harton N Yorks 149 A6
Harton Shrops 94 C2
Harton T & W 179 C5
Hartpury Glos 62 A3
Hartshead W Yorks 139 A4
Hartshill Warks 97 B6
Hartshorne Derbys 113 C7
Hartsop Cumb 164 D2
Hartwell Northants 83 B4
Hartwood N Lnrk 194 A3
Harvieston Stirl 206 B3
Harvington Worcs 80 C3
Harvington Cross Worcs 80 C3
Harwell Oxon 46 A2
Harwich Essex 88 D3
Harwood Durham 165 B6
Harwood Gtr Man 137 B6
Harwood Dale N Yorks 160 B3
Harworth Notts 140 D4
Hasbury W Mid 96 C2
Hascombe Sur 34 B2
Haselbech Northants 99 D4
Haselbury Plucknett Som 29 D4
Haseley Warks 81 A5
Haselor Warks 80 B4
Hasfield Glos 63 A4
Hasguard Pembs 55 D4
Haskayne Lancs 136 C2
Hasketon Suff 88 B3
Hasland Derbys 130 C3
Haslemere Sur 34 C2
Haslingden Lancs 137 A6
Haslingfield Cambs 85 B6
Haslington Ches 128 D2
Hassall Ches 128 D2
Hassall Green Ches 128 D2
Hassell Street Kent 38 A2
Hassendean Borders 186 A4
Hassingham Norf 105 A4
Hassocks W Sus 21 A5
Hassop Derbys 130 B2
Hastigrow Highld 281 B4
Hastingleigh Kent 38 A2
Hastings E Sus 23 B6
Hastings Castle E Sus 23 A6
Hastings Sea Life Centre E Sus 23 B6
Hastingwood Essex 69 C4
Hastoe Herts 67 C4
Haswell Durham 167 A6
Haswell Plough Durham 167 A6
Hatch Beds 84 C3
Hatch Hants 47 D4
Hatch Wilts 30 C3
Hatch Beauchamp Som 28 C3
Hatch End London 67 D6
Hatch Green Som 28 D3
Hatchet Gate Hants 18 A2
Hatching Green Herts 67 B6
Hatchmere Ches 127 B5
Hatcliffe NE Lincs 143 C4
Hatfield Hereford 78 B3
Hatfield Herts 68 C2
Hatfield S Yorks 141 C4
Hatfield Worcs 80 B1
Hatfield Broad Oak Essex 69 B5
Hatfield Garden Village Herts 68 C2
Hatfield Heath Essex 69 B5
Hatfield House Herts 68 C2
Hatfield Hyde Herts 68 B2
Hatfield Peverel Essex 70 B1
Hatfield Woodhouse S Yorks 141 C4
Hatford Oxon 64 D4
Hatherden Hants 46 D1
Hatherleigh Devon 11 A6
Hathern Leics 114 C2
Hatherop Glos 64 C2
Hathersage Derbys 130 A2
Hathershaw Gtr Man 138 C2
Hatherton Ches 111 A5
Hatherton Staffs 112 D3
Hatley St George Cambs 85 B4
Hatt Corn 6 A2
Hattingley Hants 33 B5
Hatton Aberds 257 C5
Hatton Derbys 113 C6
Hatton Lincs 134 B1
Hatton Shrops 94 B2
Hatton Warks 81 A5
Hatton Warr 127 A5
Hatton Castle Aberds 256 B2
Hatton Country World Warks 81 A5
Hatton Heath Ches 127 C4
Hatton of Fintray Aberds 245 A5
Hattoncrook Aberds 256 D3
Haugh E Ayrs 193 C4
Haugh Gtr Man 138 B2
Haugh Lincs 135 B4
Haugh Head Northumb 188 A3
Haugh of Glass Moray 255 C5
Haugh of Urr Dumfries 173 B6
Haugham Lincs 134 A3
Haughley Suff 87 A6
Haughley Green Suff 87 A6
Haughs of Clinterty Aberdeen 245 A5
Haughton Notts 132 B1
Haughton Shrops 95 B4
Haughton Shrops 110 C2
Haughton Shrops 111 D4
Haughton Shrops 95 A5
Haughton Staffs 112 C2
Haughton Castle Northumb 177 B7
Haughton Grn. Gtr Man 138 D2
Haughton Le Skerne Darl 167 D6
Haughton Moss Ches 127 D5
Haultwick Herts 68 A3
Haunn Argyll 224 B2
Haunn W Isles 286 E3
Haunton Staffs 113 D6
Hauxley Northumb 189 C5
Hauxton Cambs 85 B6
Havant Hants 19 A6
Haven Hereford 78 B2
Haven Bank Lincs 134 D2
Haven Side E Yorks 142 A3
Havenstreet I o W 19 B4
Havercroft W Yorks 140 B1
Haverfordwest = Hwlfordd Pembs 55 C5
Haverhill Suff 86 C2
Haverigg Cumb 153 C2
Havering-atte-Bower London 69 D5
Haveringland Norf 120 C3
Haversham M Keynes 83 C5
Haverthwaite Cumb 154 C2
Haverton Hill Stockton 168 C2
Hawarden = Penarlâg Flint 126 C3
Hawcoat Cumb 153 C3
Hawen Ceredig 73 B6
Hawes N Yorks 156 C2
Hawes Side Blkpool 144 D3
Hawes'Green Norf 104 B3
Hawford Worcs 79 A6
Hawick Borders 186 B4
Hawk Green Gtr Man 129 A4
Hawkchurch Devon 14 A3
Hawkedon Suff 86 B3
Hawkenbury Kent 37 B6
Hawkenbury Kent 36 C3
Hawkeridge Wilts 44 D2
Hawkerland Devon 13 C5
Hawkes End W Mid 97 C6
Hawkesbury S Glos 43 A6
Hawkesbury Warks 97 C6
Hawkesbury Upton S Glos 44 A1
Hawkhill Northumb 189 B5
Hawkhurst Kent 37 C5
Hawkinge Kent 39 B4
Hawkley Hants 33 C6
Hawkridge Som 26 B3
Hawkshead Cumb 154 B2
Hawkshead Hill Cumb 154 B2
Hawksland S Lnrk 194 C3
Hawkswick N Yorks 156 D3
Hawksworth Notts 115 A5
Hawksworth W Yorks 147 C5
Hawksworth W Yorks 147 D6
Hawkwell Essex 70 D2
Hawley Hants 34 A1
Hawley Kent 50 B2
Hawling Glos 63 A6
Hawnby N Yorks 158 C4
Haworth W Yorks 147 D4
Hawstead Suff 87 B4
Hawthorn Durham 168 A2
Hawthorn Rhondda 41 C6
Hawthorn Wilts 44 C2
Hawthorn Hill Brack 48 B1
Hawthorn Hill Lincs 134 D2
Hawthorpe Lincs 116 C3
Hawton Notts 132 D2

Haxby York 149 B5
Haxey N Lincs 141 C5
Hay Green Norf 118 D2
Hay-on-Wye = Y Gelli Gandryll Powys 77 C6
Hay Street Herts 68 A3
Haydock Mers 137 D4
Haydock Park Racecourse Mers 137 D4
Haydon Dorset 29 D6
Haydon Bridge Northumb 177 C6
Haydon Wick Thamesdown 45 A5
Haye Corn 6 A2
Hayes London 49 C7
Hayes London 48 A4
Hayfield Derbys 129 A5
Hayfield Fife 209 A5
Hayhill E Ayrs 182 A2
Hayhillock Angus 232 D3
Hayle Corn 2 B3
Haynes Beds 84 C2
Haynes Church End Beds 84 C2
Hayscastle Pembs 55 B4
Hayscastle Cross Pembs 55 B5
Hayshead Angus 233 D4
Hayton Aberdeen 245 B6
Hayton Cumb 174 D4
Hayton Cumb 176 D3
Hayton E Yorks 149 C7
Hayton Notts 132 A2
Hayton's Bent Shrops 94 C3
Haytor Vale Devon 12 D2
Haywards Heath W Sus 35 D6
Haywood S Yorks 140 B3
Haywood Oaks Notts 131 D6
Hazel Grove Gtr Man 129 A4
Hazel Street Kent 37 C4
Hazelbank S Lnrk 194 B3
Hazelbury Bryan Dorset 16 A1
Hazeley Hants 47 D5
Hazelhurst Gtr Man 138 C2
Hazelslade Staffs 112 D4
Hazelton Glos 64 B1
Hazelton Walls Fife 220 B3
Hazelwood Derbys 114 A1
Hazlemere Bucks 66 D3
Hazlerigg T & W 179 B4
Hazlewood N Yorks 147 B4
Hazon Northumb 189 C4
Heacham Norf 118 B3
Head of Muir Falk 207 B6
Headbourne Worthy Hants 32 B3
Headbrook Hereford 77 B7
Headcorn Kent 37 B6
Headingley W Yorks 148 D1
Headington Oxon 65 C6
Headlam Durham 167 D4
Headless Cross Worcs 80 A3
Headley Hants 46 C3
Headley Hants 33 B7
Headley Sur 35 A5
Headon Notts 132 B2
Heads S Lnrk 194 B2
Heads Nook Cumb 176 D2
Heage Derbys 130 D3
Healaugh N Yorks 148 C3
Healaugh N Yorks 156 B4
Heald Green Gtr Man 128 A3
Heale Devon 26 A1
Heale Som 29 A6
Healey Gtr Man 138 B1
Healey Northumb 178 D2
Healey N Yorks 157 C5
Healing NE Lincs 143 B4
Heamoor Corn 2 B2
Heanish Argyll 222 C3
Heanor Derbys 114 A2
Heanton Punchardon Devon 25 B6
Heapham Lincs 132 A3
Heart of the National Forest Leics 113 D7
Hearthstane Borders 195 D6
Heasley Mill Devon 26 B2
Heast Highld 247 C5
Heath Cardiff 41 D6
Heath Derbys 131 C4
Heath and Reach Beds 67 A4
Heath End Hants 46 C3
Heath End Sur 34 B1
Heath End Warks 81 A5
Heath Hayes Staffs 112 D4
Heath Hill Shrops 111 D6
Heath House Som 28 A4
Heath Town W Mid 96 B2
Heathcote Derbys 129 C6
Heather Leics 114 D1
Heatherfield Highld 259 D4
Heathfield Devon 12 D3
Heathfield E Sus 36 D3
Heathfield Som 27 C6
Heathhall Dumfries 174 A2
Heathrow Airport London 48 B3
Heathstock Devon 14 A2
Heathton Shrops 95 B6
Heatley Warr 128 A2
Heaton Lancs 144 A4
Heaton Staffs 129 C4
Heaton T & W 179 C4
Heaton W Yorks 147 D5
Heaton Moor Gtr Man 138 D1
Heaverham Kent 36 A3
Heaviley Gtr Man 129 A4
Heavitree Devon 13 B4
Hebburn T & W 179 C5
Hebden N Yorks 147 A4
Hebden Bridge W Yorks 138 A2
Hebron Anglesey 123 B4
Hebron Carms 73 D4
Hebron Northumb 178 A3
Heck Dumfries 184 D3
Heckfield Hants 47 C5
Heckfield Green Suff 104 D2
Heckfordbridge Essex 70 A3
Heckington Lincs 116 A4
Heckmondwike W Yorks 139 A5
Heddington Wilts 44 C3
Heddle Orkney 282 F4
Heddon-on-the-Wall Northumb 178 C3
Hedenham Norf 104 B4
Hedge End Hants 32 D3
Hedgerley Bucks 48 A2
Hedging Som 28 C3
Hedley on the Hill Northumb 178 D2
Hednesford Staffs 112 D3
Hedon E Yorks 142 A3
Hedsor Bucks 48 A2
Hedworth T & W 179 C5
Heeley City Farm, Sheffield S Yorks 130 A3
Hegdon Hill Hereford 78 B3
Heggerscales Cumb 165 D6
Heglibister Shetland 285 H5
Heighington Darl 167 C5
Heighington Lincs 133 C5
Heights of Brae Highld 263 D7
Heights of Kinlochewe Highld 262 D2
Heilam Highld 277 B5
Heiton Borders 197 C6
Hele Devon 25 A6
Hele Devon 13 A4
Helensburgh Argyll 215 D5
Helford Corn 3 C5
Helford Passage Corn 3 C5
Helhoughton Norf 119 C5
Helions Bumpstead Essex 86 C2
Hellaby S Yorks 140 D3
Helland Corn 10 D1
Hellesdon Norf 120 D4
Hellidon Northants 82 B2
Hellifield N Yorks 146 B2
Hellingly E Sus 22 A3
Hellington Norf 104 A4
Hellister Shetland 285 J5
Helm Northumb 189 D4
Helmdon Northants 82 C2
Helmingham Suff 88 B2
Helmington Row Durham 167 B4
Helmsdale Highld 274 C4
Helmshore Lancs 137 A6
Helmsley N Yorks 159 C5
Helperby N Yorks 148 A3
Helperthorpe N Yorks 160 D3
Helpringham Lincs 116 A4
Helpston P'boro 100 A3
Helsby Ches 127 B4
Helsey Lincs 135 B5
Helston Corn 3 C4
Helstone Corn 10 C1
Helton Cumb 164 C3
Helwith Bridge N Yorks 146 A2
Hemblington Norf 121 D5
Hemel Hempstead Herts 67 C5
Hemingbrough N Yorks 149 D5
Hemingby Lincs 134 B2
Hemingford Abbots Cambs 101 D4
Hemingford Grey Cambs 101 D4
Hemingstone Suff 88 B2
Hemington Leics 114 C2
Hemington Northants 100 C2
Hemington Som 43 D6
Hemley Suff 88 C3
Hemlington M'bro 168 D3
Hemp Green Suff 89 A4
Hempholme E Yorks 150 B3
Hempnall Norf 104 B3
Hempnall Green Norf 104 B3
Hempriggs House Highld 281 D5
Hempstead Essex 86 D2
Hempstead Medway 51 C4
Hempstead Norf 120 B3
Hempstead Norf 121 C6
Hempsted Glos 63 B4
Hempton Norf 119 C6
Hempton Oxon 82 D1
Hemsby Norf 121 D6
Hemswell Lincs 142 D1
Hemswell Cliff Lincs 133 A4
Hemsworth W Yorks 140 B2
Hemyock Devon 27 D6
Hen-feddau fawr Pembs 73 C5
Henbury Bristol 43 B4
Henbury Ches 128 B3
Hendon London 49 A5
Hendon T & W 179 D6
Hendre Flint 126 C1
Hendre-ddu Conwy 124 C3
Hendreforgan Rhondda 41 C4
Hendy Carms 57 B5
Heneglwys Anglesey 123 C4
Henfield W Sus 21 A5
Henford Devon 11 B4
Henghurst Kent 38 B1
Hengoed Caerph 41 B6
Hengoed Powys 77 B6
Hengoed Shrops 110 B1
Hengrave Suff 87 A4
Henham Essex 69 A5
Heniarth Powys 93 A5
Henlade Som 28 C2
Henley Shrops 94 D3
Henley Som 28 B4
Henley Suff 88 B2
Henley W Sus 34 D1
Henley-in-Arden Warks 81 A4
Henley-on-Thames Oxon 47 A5
Henley's Down E Sus 23 A5
Henllan Ceredig 73 B6
Henllan Denb 125 C5
Henllan Amgoed Carms 73 D4
Henllys Torf 61 D4
Henlow Beds 84 D3
Hennock Devon 12 C3
Henny Street Essex 87 D4
Henryd Conwy 124 B2
Henry's Moat Pembs 55 B6
Hensall N Yorks 140 A3
Henshaw Northumb 177 C5
Hensingham Cumb 162 C2
Henstead Suff 105 C5
Henstridge Som 30 D1
Henstridge Ash Som 29 C7
Henstridge Marsh Som 30 C1
Henton Oxon 66 C2
Henton Som 29 A4
Henwood Corn 10 D3
Heogan Shetland 285 J6
Heol-las Swansea 40 B1
Heol Senni Powys 59 C6
Heol-y-Cyw Bridgend 40 C4
Hepburn Northumb 188 A3
Hepple Northumb 188 C2
Hepscott Northumb 179 A4
Heptonstall W Yorks 138 A2
Hepworth Suff 103 D5
Hepworth W Yorks 139 C4
Herbrandston Pembs 55 D4
Hereford Hereford 78 C3
Hereford Cathedral Hereford 78 D3
Hereford Racecourse Hereford 78 C3
Heriot Borders 196 A2
Heritage Motor Centre, Gaydon Warks 81 B6
Hermiston Edin 209 C4
Hermitage Borders 186 D4
Hermitage Dorset 15 A6
Hermitage W Berks 46 B3
Hermitage W Sus 19 A6
Hermon Anglesey 122 D3
Hermon Carms 73 C6
Hermon Carms 58 C3
Hermon Pembs 73 C5
Herne Kent 52 C3
Herne Bay Kent 52 C3
Herner Devon 25 C6
Hernhill Kent 52 C2
Herodsfoot Corn 5 A7
Herongate Essex 69 D6
Heronsford S Ayrs 180 C3
Herriard Hants 33 A5
Herringfleet Suff 105 B5
Herringswell Suff 102 D3
Hersden Kent 53 C4
Hersham Corn 10 A3
Hersham Sur 48 C4
Herstmonceux E Sus 22 A4
Herston Orkney 283 H5
Hertford Herts 68 B3
Hertford Heath Herts 68 B3
Hertingfordbury Herts 68 B3
Hesket Newmarket Cumb 163 A6
Hesketh Bank Lancs 136 A3
Hesketh Lane Lancs 145 C6
Heskin Green Lancs 136 B4
Hesleden Durham 168 B2
Hesleyside Northumb 177 A6
Heslington York 149 B5
Hessay York 148 B4
Hessenford Corn 6 B2
Hessett Suff 87 A5
Hessle E Yorks 142 A2
Hest Bank Lancs 145 A4
Heston London 48 B4
Hestwall Orkney 282 F3
Heswall Mers 126 A2
Hethe Oxon 65 A6
Hethersett Norf 104 A2
Hethersgill Cumb 176 C2
Hethpool Northumb 188 A1
Hett Durham 167 B5
Hetton N Yorks 146 B3
Hetton-le-Hole T & W 167 A6
Hetton Steads Northumb 198 C4
Heugh Northumb 178 B2
Heugh-head Aberds 243 A6
Heveningham Suff 104 D4
Hever Kent 36 B2
Hever Castle and Gardens Kent 36 B2
Heversham Cumb 154 C3
Hevingham Norf 120 C3
Hewas Water Corn 5 C4
Hewelsfield Glos 62 C1
Hewish N Som 42 C3
Hewish Som 14 A4
Heworth York 149 B5
Hexham Northumb 178 C1
Hexham Abbey Northumb 178 C1
Hexham Racecourse Northumb 177 C7
Hextable Kent 50 B2
Hexton Herts 84 D3
Hexworthy Devon 12 D1
Hey Lancs 146 C2
Heybridge Essex 69 D6
Heybridge Essex 70 C2
Heybridge Basin Essex 70 C2
Heybrook Bay Devon 7 C4
Heydon Cambs 85 C6
Heydon Norf 120 C3
Heydour Lincs 116 B3
Heylipol Argyll 222 C2
Heylor Shetland 284 E4
Heysham Lancs 144 A4
Heyshott W Sus 20 A1
Heyside Gtr Man 138 C2
Heytesbury Wilts 30 A3
Heythrop Oxon 64 A4
Heywood Gtr Man 138 B1
Heywood Wilts 44 D2
Hibaldstow N Lincs 142 C1
Hickleton S Yorks 140 C2
Hickling Norf 121 C6
Hickling Notts 115 C4
Hickling Green Norf 121 C6
Hickling Heath Norf 121 C6
Hickstead W Sus 35 D5
Hidcote Boyce Glos 81 C4
Hidcote Manor Garden, Moreton-in-Marsh Glos 81 C4
High Ackworth W Yorks 140 B2
High Angerton Northumb 178 A2
High Bankhill Cumb 164 A3
High Barnes T & W 179 D5
High Beach Essex 68 D4
High Bentham N Yorks 145 A6
High Bickington Devon 25 C7
High Birkwith N Yorks 155 D6
High Blantyre S Lnrk 194 A1
High Bonnybridge Falk 207 C6
High Bradfield S Yorks 139 D5
High Bray Devon 26 B1
High Brooms Kent 36 B3
High Bullen Devon 25 C6
High Buston Northumb 189 C5
High Callerton Northumb 178 B3
High Catton E Yorks 149 B6
High Cogges Oxon 65 C4
High Coniscliffe Darl 167 D5
High Cross Hants 33 C6
High Cross Herts 68 B3
High Easter Essex 69 B6
High Eggborough N Yorks 140 A3
High Ellington N Yorks 157 C5
High Ercall Telford 111 D4
High Etherley Durham 167 C4
High Garrett Essex 70 A1
High Grange Durham 167 B4
High Green Norf 104 A2
High Green S Yorks 139 D6
High Green Worcs 80 C1
High Halden Kent 37 C6
High Halstow Medway 51 B4
High Ham Som 28 B4
High Harrington Cumb 162 B3
High Hatton Shrops 111 C5
High Hawsker N Yorks 160 A3
High Hesket Cumb 164 A2
High Hesleden Durham 168 B2
High Hoyland S Yorks 139 B5
High Hunsley E Yorks 150 D2
High Hurstwood E Sus 36 D2
High Hutton N Yorks 149 A6
High Ireby Cumb 163 A5
High Kelling Norf 120 A3
High Kilburn N Yorks 158 D4
High Lands Durham 166 C4
High Lane Gtr Man 129 A4
High Lane Hereford 79 A4
High Laver Essex 69 C5
High Legh Ches 128 A2
High Leven Stockton 168 D2
High Littleton Bath 43 D5
High Lorton Cumb 163 B4
High Marishes N Yorks 159 D7
High Marnham Notts 132 B3
High Melton S Yorks 140 C3
High Mickley Northumb 178 C2
High Mindork Dumfries 171 B5
High Moorland Visitor Centre, Princetown Devon 11 D6
High Newton Cumb 154 C3
High Newton-by-the-Sea Northumb 189 A5
High Nibthwaite Cumb 154 C1
High Offley Staffs 112 C1
High Ongar Essex 69 C5
High Onn Staffs 112 D2
High Roding Essex 69 B6
High Row Cumb 163 A6
High Salvington W Sus 21 B4
High Sellafield Cumb 162 D3
High Shaw N Yorks 156 B2
High Spen T & W 178 D3
High Stoop Durham 166 A4
High Street Corn 5 B4
High Street Kent 37 C5
High Street Suff 89 B5
High Street Suff 105 D5
High Street Suff 87 C4
High Street Green Suff 87 B6
High Throston Hrtlpl 168 B2
High Toynton Lincs 134 C2
High Trewhitt Northumb 188 C3
High Valleyfield Fife 208 B3
High Westwood Durham 178 D3
High Wray Cumb 154 B2
High Wych Herts 69 B4
High Wycombe Bucks 66 D3
Higham Derbys 130 D3
Higham Kent 51 B4
Higham Lancs 146 D2
Higham Suff 87 D6
Higham Suff 86 A3
Higham Dykes Northumb 178 B3
Higham Ferrers Northants 83 A6
Higham Gobion Beds 84 D3
Higham on the Hill Leics 97 B6
Higham Wood Kent 36 B3
Highampton Devon 11 A5
Highbridge Highld 239 D5
Highbridge Som 28 A3
Highbrook W Sus 35 C6
Highburton W Yorks 139 B4
Highbury Som 29 A6
Highclere Hants 46 C2
Highcliffe Dorset 17 B6
Higher Ansty Dorset 16 A1
Higher Ashton Devon 12 C3
Higher Ballam Lancs 144 D3
Higher Bartle Lancs 145 D5
Higher Boscaswell Corn 2 B1
Higher Burwardsley Ches 127 D5
Higher Clovelly Devon 24 C4
Higher End Gtr Man 136 C4
Higher Kinnerton Flint 126 C3
Higher Penwortham Lancs 136 A4
Higher Town Scilly 2 E4
Higher Walreddon Devon 11 D5
Higher Walton Lancs 137 A4
Higher Walton Warr 127 A5
Higher Wheelton Lancs 137 A5
Higher Whitley Ches 127 A6
Higher Wincham Ches 128 B1
Higher Wych Ches 110 A3
Highfield E Yorks 149 D6
Highfield Gtr Man 137 C6
Highfield N Ayrs 204 C3
Highfield Oxon 65 A6
Highfield S Yorks 130 A3
Highfield T & W 178 D3
Highfields Cambs 85 B5
Highfields Northumb 198 A3
Highgate London 49 A5
Highland Folk Museum, Aultlairie Highld 241 C5
Highland Folk Museum, Kingussie Highld 241 B5
Highlane Ches 128 C3
Highlane Derbys 131 A4
Highlaws Cumb 174 D4
Highleadon Glos 62 A3
Highleigh W Sus 20 C1
Highley Shrops 95 C5
Highmoor Cross Oxon 47 A5
Highmoor Hill Mon 42 A3
Highnam Glos 62 B3
Highnam Green Glos 62 A3
Highsted Kent 51 C6
Highstreet Green Essex 86 D3
Hightae Dumfries 174 A3
Hightown Ches 128 C3
Hightown Mers 136 C2
Hightown Green Suff 87 B5
Highway Wilts 44 B4
Highweek Devon 12 D3
Highworth Thamesdown 64 D3
Hilborough Norf 103 A4
Hilcote Derbys 131 D4
Hilcott Wilts 45 D5
Hilden Park Kent 36 B3
Hildenborough Kent 36 B3
Hildersham Cambs 86 C1
Hilderstone Staffs 112 B3
Hilderthorpe E Yorks 151 A4
Hilfield Dorset 15 A6
Hilgay Norf 102 B2
Hill Pembs 55 D7
Hill S Glos 62 D2
Hill W Mid 96 B4
Hill Brow W Sus 33 C6
Hill Dale Lancs 136 B3
Hill Dyke Lincs 117 A6
Hill End Durham 166 B3
Hill End Fife 208 A3
Hill End N Yorks 147 B4
Hill Head Hants 18 A4
Hill Head Northumb 178 C1
Hill Mountain Pembs 55 D5
Hill of Beath Fife 209 A4
Hill of Fearn Highld 265 C4
Hill of Mountblairy Aberds 268 D1
Hill Ridware Staffs 113 D4
Hill Top Durham 166 C2
Hill Top Hants 18 A3
Hill Top W Mid 96 B2
Hill Top W Yorks 139 B6
Hill Top, Sawrey Cumb 154 B2
Hill View Dorset 16 B3
Hillam N Yorks 140 A3
Hillbeck Cumb 165 D5
Hillborough Kent 53 C4
Hillbrae Aberds 256 D2
Hillbrae Aberds 255 B7
Hillbutts Dorset 16 A3
Hillclifflane Derbys 113 A6
Hillcommon Som 27 C6
Hillend Fife 208 B4
Hillerton Devon 12 B2
Hillesden Bucks 66 A1
Hillesley Glos 43 A6
Hillfarance Som 27 C6
Hillhead Aberds 255 C6
Hillhead Devon 8 B3
Hillhead S Ayrs 182 A2
Hillhead of Auchentumb Aberds 269 D4
Hillhead of Cocklaw Aberds 257 B5
Hillhouse Borders 197 A4
Hilliclay Highld 280 B3
Hillier Gardens and Arboretum Hants 32 C2
Hillingdon London 48 A3
Hillington Glasgow 205 B5
Hillington Norf 119 C4
Hillmorton Warks 98 D2
Hillockhead Aberds 244 A1
Hillockhead Aberds 243 B6
Hillside Aberds 245 C6
Hillside Angus 233 B5
Hillside Mers 136 B2
Hillside Orkney 283 H5
Hillside Shetland 285 G6
Hillswick Shetland 284 F4
Hillway I o W 19 C5
Hillwell Shetland 285 M5
Hilmarton Wilts 44 B4
Hilperton Wilts 44 D2
Hilsea Ptsmth 19 A5
Hilston E Yorks 151 D5
Hilton Aberds 257 C4
Hilton Cambs 85 A4
Hilton Cumb 165 C5
Hilton Derbys 113 B6
Hilton Dorset 16 A1
Hilton Durham 167 C4
Hilton Highld 264 B3
Hilton Shrops 95 B5
Hilton Stockton 168 D2
Hilton of Cadboll Highld 265 C4
Himbleton Worcs 80 B2
Himley Staffs 96 B1
Hincaster Cumb 154 C4
Hinckley Leics 98 B1
Hinderclay Suff 103 D6
Hinderton Ches 126 B3
Hinderwell N Yorks 169 D5
Hindford Shrops 110 B2
Hindhead Sur 34 C1
Hindley Gtr Man 137 C5
Hindley Green Gtr Man 137 C5

Hurst Som 29 D4
Hurst Wokingham 47 B5
Hurst Green E Sus 37 D5
Hurst Green Lancs 145 D6
Hurst Wickham W Sus 21 A5
Hurstbourne Priors Hants 32 A3
Hurstbourne Tarrant Hants 46 D1
Hurstpierpoint W Sus 21 A5
Hurstway Common Hereford 77 C6
Hurstwood Lancs 146 D2
Hurtmore Sur 34 B2
Hurworth Place Darl 157 A6
Hury Durham 166 D2
Husabost Highld 258 C2
Husbands Bosworth Leics 98 C3
Husborne Crawley Beds 83 D6
Husthwaite N Yorks 158 D4
Hutchwns Bridgend 40 D3
Huthwaite Notts 131 D4
Huttoft Lincs 135 B5
Hutton Borders 198 A3
Hutton Cumb 164 C2
Hutton E Yorks 150 B3
Hutton Essex 69 D6
Hutton Lancs 136 A3
Hutton N Som 42 D2
Hutton Buscel N Yorks 160 C3
Hutton Conyers N Yorks 158 D2
Hutton Cranswick E Yorks 150 B3
Hutton End Cumb 164 B2
Hutton Gate Redcar 168 D3
Hutton Henry Durham 168 B2
Hutton-le-Hole N Yorks 159 B6
Hutton Magna Durham 166 D4
Hutton Roof Cumb 163 A6
Hutton Roof Cumb 155 D4
Hutton Rudby N Yorks 158 A3
Hutton Sessay N Yorks 158 D3
Hutton Village Redcar 168 D3
Hutton Wandesley N Yorks 148 B4
Huxley Ches 127 C5
Huxter Shetland 285 H5
Huxter Shetland 285 G7
Huxton Borders 211 D5
Huyton Mers 136 D3
Hwlfforrdd = Haverfordwest Pembs 55 C5
Hycemoor Cumb 153 B1
Hyde Glos 63 C4
Hyde Gtr Man 138 D2
Hyde Hants 31 D5
Hyde Heath Bucks 67 C4
Hyde Park S Yorks 140 C3
Hydestile Sur 34 B2
Hylton Castle T & W 179 D5
Hyndford Bridge S Lnrk 194 B4
Hynish Argyll 222 D2
Hyssington Powys 93 B7
Hythe Hants 18 A3
Hythe Kent 38 B3
Hythe End Windsor 48 B3
Hythie Aberds 269 D5

## I

Ibberton Dorset 16 A1
Ible Derbys 130 D2
Ibsley Hants 17 A5
Ibstock Leics 114 D2
Ibstone Bucks 66 D2
Ibthorpe Hants 46 D1
Ibworth Hants 46 D3
Ichrachan Argyll 227 C5
Ickburgh Norf 103 B4
Ickenham London 48 A3
Ickford Bucks 66 C1
Ickham Kent 53 D4
Ickleford Herts 84 D3
Icklesham E Sus 23 A6
Ickleton Cambs 85 C6
Icklingham Suff 102 D3
Ickwell Green Beds 84 C3
Ickworth House Suff 87 A4
Icomb Glos 64 A3
Idbury Oxon 64 B3
Iddesleigh Devon 11 A6
Ide Devon 12 B3
Ide Hill Kent 36 A2
Ideford Devon 12 D3
Iden E Sus 37 D7
Iden Green Kent 37 C6
Iden Green Kent 37 C5
Idle W Yorks 147 D5
Idlicote Warks 81 C5
Idmiston Wilts 31 B5
Idole Carms 57 A4
Idridgehay Derbys 113 A6
Idrigill Highld 258 B3
Idstone Oxon 45 A6
Idvies Angus 232 D3
Iffley Oxon 65 C6
Ifield W Sus 35 C5
Ifold W Sus 34 C3
Iford E Sus 22 B2
Ifton Heath Shrops 110 B2
Ightfield Shrops 111 B4
Ightham Kent 36 A3
Ightham Mote, Sevenoaks Kent 49 B6
Iken Suff 89 B5
Ilam Staffs 129 D6
Ilchester Som 29 C5
Ilderton Northumb 188 A3
Ilford London 50 A1
Ilfracombe Devon 25 A6
Ilkeston Derbys 114 A2
Ilketshall St Andrew Suff 105 C4
Ilketshall St Lawrence Suff 105 C4
Ilketshall St Margaret Suff 104 C4
Ilkley W Yorks 147 C5
Illey W Mid 96 C2
Illingworth W Yorks 138 A3
Illogan Corn 3 A4
Illston on the Hill Leics 99 B4
Ilmer Bucks 66 C2
Ilmington Warks 81 C5
Ilminster Som 28 D3
Ilsington Devon 12 D2
Ilston Swansea 57 C5
Ilton N Yorks 157 D5
Ilton Som 28 D3
Imachar N Ayrs 202 D3
Imeraval Argyll 200 D3
Immingham NE Lincs 142 B3
Imperial War Museum London 36 A3
Imperial War Museum North Gtr Man 137 D7
Impington Cambs 85 A6
Ince Ches 127 B4
Ince Blundell Mers 136 C2
Ince in Makerfield Gtr Man 137 C4
Inch of Arnhall Aberds 233 A4
Inchbare Angus 233 B4
Inchberry Moray 266 D4
Inchbraoch Angus 233 C5
Incheril Highld 262 D2
Inchgrundle Angus 232 A2
Inchina Highld 261 A6
Inchinnan Renfs 205 B4
Inchkinloch Highld 277 D6
Inchlaggan Highld 239 B5
Inchlumpie Highld 264 C1
Inchmore Highld 251 B5
Inchnacardoch Hotel Highld 240 A1
Inchnadamph Highld 271 B5
Inchree Highld 237 C4
Inchture Perth 220 B2
Inchyra Perth 219 B6
Indian Queens Corn 4 B4
Inerval Argyll 200 D3
Ingatestone Essex 69 D6
Ingbirchworth S Yorks 139 C5
Ingestre Staffs 112 C3
Ingham Lincs 133 A4
Ingham Norf 121 C5
Ingham Suff 103 D4
Ingham Corner Norf 121 C5
Ingleborough Norf 118 D1
Ingleby Derbys 114 C1
Ingleby Lincs 132 B3
Ingleby Arncliffe N Yorks 158 A3
Ingleby Barwick Stockton 168 D2
Ingleby Greenhow N Yorks 159 A4
Inglemire Hull 150 D3
Inglesbatch Bath 43 C6
Inglesham Thamesdown 64 D3
Ingleton Durham 167 C4
Ingleton N Yorks 155 D5
Inglewhite Lancs 145 C5
Ingliston Edin 208 C4
Ingoe Northumb 178 B2
Ingol Lancs 145 D5
Ingoldisthorpe Norf 118 B3
Ingoldmells Lincs 135 C5
Ingoldsby Lincs 116 B3
Ingon Warks 81 B5
Ingram Northumb 188 B3
Ingrave Essex 69 D6
Ingrow W Yorks 147 D4
Ings Cumb 154 B3
Ingst S Glos 43 A4
Ingworth Norf 120 C3
Inham's End Cambs 101 B4
Inkberrow Worcs 80 B3
Inkpen W Berks 46 C1
Inkstack Highld 281 A4
Inn Cumb 154 A3
Innellan Argyll 203 A6
Innerleithen Borders 196 C2
Innerleven Fife 220 D3
Innermessan Dumfries 170 A2
Innerwick E Loth 211 C4
Innerwick Perth 229 D4
Innis Chonain Argyll 227 D6
Insch Aberds 256 D1
Insh Highld 241 B6
Inshore Highld 276 B1
Inskip Lancs 145 D4
Instoneville S Yorks 140 B3
Instow Devon 25 B5
Intake S Yorks 140 C3
Inver Aberds 243 C5
Inver Highld 265 B4
Inver Perth 230 D4
Inver Mallie Highld 239 D5
Inverailort Highld 235 B6
Inveraldie Angus 220 A4
Inveralligin Highld 249 A5
Inverallochy Aberds 269 C5
Inveran Highld 264 A1
Inveraray Argyll 214 B3
Inveraray Jail Argyll 214 B3
Inverarish Highld 248 C2
Inverarity Angus 232 D2
Inverarnan Stirl 215 A6
Inverasdale Highld 261 B5
Inverbeg Argyll 206 A1
Inverbervie Aberds 233 A6
Inverboyndie Aberds 268 C1
Inverbroom Highld 262 B3
Invercassley Highld 272 D2
Invercauld House Aberds 243 C4
Inverchaolain Argyll 203 A5
Invercharnan Highld 227 B6
Inverchoran Highld 251 A4
Invercreran Argyll 227 B5
Inverdruie Highld 242 A2
Inverebrie Aberds 257 C4
Invereck Argyll 215 D4
Inverernan Ho. Aberds 243 A6
Invereshie House Highld 241 B6
Inveresk E Loth 209 C6
Inverewe Gardens, Gairloch Highld 261 B5
Inverey Aberds 242 D3
Inverfarigaig Highld 251 D7
Invergarry Highld 239 B7
Invergelder Aberds 243 C5
Invergeldie Perth 218 B2
Invergordon Highld 264 D3
Invergowrie Perth 220 A3
Inverguseran Highld 247 D6
Inverhadden Perth 229 C5
Inverharroch Moray 255 C4
Inverherive Stirl 216 B3
Inverie Highld 247 E6
Inverinan Argyll 214 A2
Inverinate Highld 249 D6
Inverkeilor Angus 233 D4
Inverkeithing Fife 208 B4
Inverkeithny Aberds 256 B1
Inverkip Invclyd 204 A2
Inverkirkaig Highld 270 C3
Inverlael Highld 262 B3
Inverlochlarig Stirl 216 C4
Inverlochy Argyll 227 D6
Inverlochy Highld 237 B5
Inverlussa Argyll 213 D4
Invermark Lodge Angus 244 D1
Invermoidart Highld 235 C5
Invermoriston Highld 240 A2
Invernaver Highld 278 B3
Inverneill Argyll 213 D6
Inverness Highld 252 B2
Inverness Airport Highld 252 A3
Invernettie Aberds 257 B6
Invernoaden Argyll 215 C4
Inveroran Hotel Argyll 228 D1
Inverpolly Lodge Highld 270 C3
Inverquharity Angus 232 C2
Inverquhomery Aberds 257 B5
Inverroy Highld 239 D6
Inversanda Highld 236 D3
Invershiel Highld 238 A3
Invershin Highld 264 A1
Inversnaid Hotel Stirl 215 B6
Inverugie Aberds 257 B6
Inveruglas Argyll 215 B6
Inveruglass Highld 241 B6
Inverurie Aberds 256 D2
Invervar Perth 229 D5
Inverythan Aberds 256 B2
Inwardleigh Devon 11 B6
Inworth Essex 70 B2
Iochdar W Isles 286 B3
Iona Abbey and Cathedral Argyll 224 D1
Iping W Sus 34 D1
Ipplepen Devon 8 A2
Ipsden Oxon 47 A4
Ipsley Worcs 80 A3
Ipstones Staffs 129 D5
Ipswich Suff 88 C2
Irby Mers 126 A2
Irby in the Marsh Lincs 135 C4
Irby upon Humber NE Lincs 142 C3
Irchester Northants 83 A6
Ireby Cumb 163 A5
Ireby Lancs 155 D5
Ireland Orkney 283 G4
Ireland Shetland 285 L5
Ireland's Cross Shrops 111 A6
Ireleth Cumb 153 C3
Ireshopeburn Durham 165 B6
Irlam Gtr Man 137 D6
Irnham Lincs 116 C3
Iron Acton S Glos 43 A5
Iron Cross Warks 80 B3
Ironbridge Telford 95 A4
Ironbridge Gorge Museum, Telford Shrops 95 A4
Ironmacannie Dumfries 173 A4
Ironside Aberds 268 D3
Ironville Derbys 131 D4
Irstead Norf 121 C5
Irthington Cumb 176 C2
Irthlingborough Northants 99 D6
Irton N Yorks 160 C4
Irvine N Ayrs 192 B3
Isauld Highld 279 B5
Isbister Orkney 282 E3
Isbister Orkney 282 F4
Isbister Shetland 284 D5
Isbister Shetland 285 G7
Isfield E Sus 22 A2
Isham Northants 99 D5
Islay Airport Argyll 200 C3
Isle Abbotts Som 28 C3
Isle Brewers Som 28 C3
Isle of Man Airport I o M 152 E2
Isle of Man Steam Railway I o M 152 E1
Isle of Whithorn Dumfries 171 D6
Isleham Cambs 102 D2
Isleornsay Highld 247 C6
Islesburgh Shetland 284 G5
Islesteps Dumfries 174 A2
Isleworth London 49 B4
Isley Walton Leics 114 C2
Islibhig W Isles 287 B4
Islington London 49 A6
Islip Northants 100 D1
Islip Oxon 65 B6
Istead Rise Kent 50 C3
Isycoed Wrex 127 D4
Itchen Soton 32 D3
Itchen Abbas Hants 32 B4
Itchen Stoke Hants 33 B4
Itchingfield W Sus 35 D4
Itchington S Glos 43 A5
Itteringham Norf 120 B3
Itton Devon 12 B1
Itton Common Mon 61 D6
Ivegill Cumb 164 A2
Iver Bucks 48 A3
Iver Heath Bucks 48 A3
Iveston Durham 178 D3
Ivinghoe Bucks 67 B4
Ivinghoe Aston Bucks 67 B4
Ivington Hereford 78 B2
Ivington Green Hereford 78 B2
Ivy Chimneys Essex 68 C4
Ivy Cross Dorset 30 C2
Ivy Hatch Kent 36 A3
Ivybridge Devon 7 B5
Ivychurch Kent 38 C2
Iwade Kent 51 C6
Iwerne Courtney or Shroton Dorset 30 D2
Iwerne Minster Dorset 30 D2
Ixworth Suff 103 D5
Ixworth Thorpe Suff 103 D5

## J

Jack Hill N Yorks 147 B6
Jack in the Green Devon 13 B5
Jacksdale Notts 131 D4
Jackstown Aberds 256 C2
Jacobstow Corn 10 B2
Jacobstowe Devon 11 A6
Jameston Pembs 55 E6
Jamestown Dumfries 185 C6
Jamestown Highld 251 A6
Jamestown W Dunb 206 B1
Jarlshof Prehistoric Site Shetland 285 N5
Jarrow T & W 179 C5
Jarvis Brook E Sus 36 D3
Jasper's Green Essex 69 A7
Java Argyll 225 C6
Jawcraig Falk 207 C6
Jaywick Essex 71 B5
Jealott's Hill Brack 47 B6
Jedburgh Borders 187 A5
Jeffreyston Pembs 55 D6
Jellyhill E Dunb 205 A6
Jemimaville Highld 264 D3
Jersey Airport Jersey 6
Jersey Farm Herts 67 C6
Jersey Zoo & Wildlife Park Jersey 6
Jesmond T & W 179 C4
Jevington E Sus 22 B3
Jockey End Herts 67 B5
Jodrell Bank Visitor Centre, Holmes Chapel Ches 128 B2
John o'Groats Highld 281 A5
Johnby Cumb 164 B2
John's Cross E Sus 37 D5
Johnshaven Aberds 233 B5
Johnston Pembs 55 C5
Johnstone Renfs 205 B4
Johnstonebridge Dumfries 184 C3
Johnstown Carms 57 A4
Johnstown Wrex 110 A2
Joppa Edin 209 C6
Joppa S Ayrs 182 A2
Jordans Bucks 67 D4
Jordanthorpe S Yorks 130 A3
Jorvik Centre York 149 B5
Judges Lodging, Presteigne Powys 77 A7
Jump S Yorks 140 C1
Jumpers Green Dorset 17 B5
Juniper Green Edin 209 D4
Jurby East I o M 152 B3
Jurby South Motor Racing Circuit I o M 152 B3
Jurby West I o M 152 B3

## K

Kaber Cumb 165 D5
Kaimend S Lnrk 195 B4
Kaimes Edin 209 D5
Kalemouth Borders 187 A6
Kames Argyll 203 A4
Kames Argyll 213 A6
Kames E Ayrs 194 D1
Kea Corn 4 C3
Keadby N Lincs 141 B6
Keal Cotes Lincs 134 C3
Kearsley Gtr Man 137 C6
Kearstwick Cumb 155 C5
Kearton N Yorks 156 B3
Kearvaig Highld 276 A3
Keasden N Yorks 145 A7
Keckwick Halton 127 A5
Keddington Lincs 134 A3
Kedington Suff 86 C3
Kedleston Derbys 113 A7
Kedleston Hall Derbys 113 A7
Keelby Lincs 142 B3
Keele Staffs 112 A2
Keeley Green Beds 84 C2
Keeston Pembs 55 C5
Keevil Wilts 44 D3
Kegworth Leics 114 C2
Kehelland Corn 3 A4
Keig Aberds 244 A3
Keighley W Yorks 147 C4
Keighley and Worth Valley Railway W Yorks 147 D4
Keil Highld 236 D3
Keilarsbrae Clack 208 A1
Keilhill Aberds 268 D2
Keillmore Argyll 213 D4
Keillor Perth 231 D6
Keillour Perth 219 B4
Keills Argyll 201 B4
Keils Argyll 201 B5
Keinton Mandeville Som 29 B5
Keir Mill Dumfries 183 C6
Keisby Lincs 116 C3
Keiss Highld 281 B5
Keith Moray 267 D5
Keith Inch Aberds 257 B6
Keithock Angus 233 B4
Kelbrook Lancs 146 C3
Kelby Lincs 116 A3
Keld Cumb 164 D3
Keld N Yorks 156 A2
Keldholme N Yorks 159 C6
Kelfield N Lincs 141 C6
Kelfield N Yorks 149 D4
Kelham Notts 132 D2
Kellan Argyll 225 B4
Kellas Angus 221 A4
Kellas Moray 266 D2
Kellaton Devon 8 D2
Kelleth Cumb 155 A5
Kelleythorpe E Yorks 150 B2
Kelling Norf 120 A2
Kellingley N Yorks 140 A3
Kellington N Yorks 140 A3
Kelloe Durham 167 B6
Kelloholm Dumfries 183 A5
Kelly Devon 11 C4
Kelly Bray Corn 11 D4
Kelmarsh Northants 99 D4
Kelmscot Oxon 64 D3
Kelsale Suff 89 A4
Kelsall Ches 127 C5
Kelsall Hill Ches 127 C5
Kelshall Herts 85 D5
Kelsick Cumb 175 C4
Kelso Borders 197 C6
Kelso Racecourse Borders 197 C6
Kelstedge Derbys 130 C3
Kelstern Lincs 143 D4
Kelston Bath 43 C6
Keltneyburn Perth 229 D6
Kelton Dumfries 174 A2
Kelty Fife 208 A4
Kelvedon Essex 70 B2
Kelvedon Hatch Essex 69 D5
Kelvin S Lnrk 205 C6
Kelvinside Glasgow 205 B5
Kelynack Corn 2 B1
Kemback Fife 220 C4
Kemberton Shrops 95 A5
Kemble Glos 63 D5
Kemerton Worcs 80 D2
Kemeys Commander Mon 61 C5
Kemnay Aberds 245 A4
Kemp Town Brighton 21 B6
Kempley Glos 62 A2
Kemps Green Warks 96 D4
Kempsey Worcs 79 C6
Kempsford Glos 64 D2
Kempshott Hants 47 D4
Kempston Beds 84 C2
Kempston Hardwick Beds 84 C2
Kempton Shrops 94 C1
Kempton Park Racecourse Sur 48 B4
Kemsing Kent 36 A3
Kemsley Kent 51 C6
Kenardington Kent 38 B1
Kenchester Hereford 78 C2
Kencot Oxon 64 C3
Kendal Cumb 154 B4
Kendoon Dumfries 182 D4
Kendray S Yorks 139 C6
Kenfig Bridgend 40 C3
Kenfig Hill Bridgend 40 C3
Kenilworth Warks 97 D5
Kenilworth Castle Warks 97 D5
Kenknock Stirl 217 A4
Kenley London 35 A6
Kenley Shrops 94 A3
Kenmore Highld 249 A4
Kenmore Perth 230 D1
Kenn Devon 13 C4
Kenn N Som 42 C3
Kennacley W Isles 288 H2
Kennacraig Argyll 202 B3
Kennerleigh Devon 12 A3
Kennet Clack 208 A2
Kennethmont Aberds 255 D6
Kennett Cambs 86 A2
Kennford Devon 13 C4
Kenninghall Norf 103 C6
Kenninghall Heath Norf 103 C6
Kennington Kent 38 A2
Kennington Oxon 65 C6
Kennoway Fife 220 D3
Kenny Hill Suff 102 D2
Kennythorpe N Yorks 149 A6
Kenovay Argyll 222 C2
Kensaleyre Highld 259 C4
Kensington London 49 B5
Kensworth Beds 67 B5
Kensworth Common Beds 67 B5
Kent International Airport Kent 53 C5
Kent Street E Sus 23 A5
Kent Street Kent 37 A4
Kent Street W Sus 35 D5
Kentallen Highld 237 D4
Kentchurch Hereford 61 A6
Kentford Suff 86 A3
Kentisbeare Devon 13 A5
Kentisbury Devon 25 A7
Kentisbury Ford Devon 25 A7
Kentmere Cumb 154 A3
Kenton Devon 13 C4
Kenton Suff 88 A2
Kenton T & W 179 C4
Kenton Bankfoot T & W 179 C4
Kentra Highld 235 D5
Kents Bank Cumb 154 D2
Kent's Green Glos 62 A3
Kent's Oak Hants 32 C2
Kenwick Shrops 110 B3
Kenwyn Corn 4 C3
Keoldale Highld 277 B4
Keppanach Highld 237 C4
Keppoch Highld 249 D6
Keprigan Argyll 190 D2
Kepwick N Yorks 158 B3
Kerchesters Borders 197 C6
Keresley W Mid 97 C6
Kernborough Devon 8 C1
Kerne Bridge Hereford 62 B1
Kerris Corn 2 C2
Kerry Powys 93 C5
Kerrycroy Argyll 203 B6

Kerry's Gate Hereford 78 D1
Kerrysdale Highld 261 C5
Kersall Notts 132 C2
Kersey Suff 87 C6
Kershopefoot Cumb 176 A2
Kersoe Worcs 80 D2
Kerswell Devon 13 A5
Kerswell Grn. Worcs 79 C6
Kesgrave Suff 88 C3
Kessingland Suff 105 C6
Kessingland Beach Suff 105 C6
Kessington E Dunb 205 A5
Kestle Corn 5 C4
Kestle Mill Corn 4 B3
Keston London 49 C7
Keswick Cumb 163 B5
Keswick Norf 104 A3
Keswick Norf 121 B5
Ketley Telford 111 D5
Ketley Bank Telford 111 D5
Ketsby Lincs 134 B3
Kettering Northants 99 D5
Ketteringham Norf 104 A2
Kettins Perth 220 A2
Kettlebaston Suff 87 B5
Kettlebridge Fife 220 D3
Kettleburgh Suff 88 A3
Kettlehill Fife 220 D3
Kettleholm Dumfries 174 A4
Kettleness N Yorks 169 D6
Kettleshume Ches 129 B4
Kettlesing Bottom N Yorks 147 B6
Kettlesing Head N Yorks 147 B6
Kettlestone Norf 119 B6
Kettlethorpe Lincs 132 B3
Kettletoft Orkney 282 D7
Kettlewell N Yorks 156 D3
Ketton Rutland 100 A1
Kew London 49 B4
Kew Br. London 49 B4
Kew Gardens London 48 B4
Kewstoke N Som 42 C2
Kexbrough S Yorks 139 C6
Kexby Lincs 132 A3
Kexby York 149 B6
Key Green Ches 128 C3
Keyham Leics 98 A3
Keyhaven Hants 18 B2
Keyingham E Yorks 143 A4
Keymer W Sus 21 A6
Keynsham Bath 43 C5
Keysoe Beds 84 A2
Keysoe Row Beds 84 A2
Keyston Cambs 100 D2
Keyworth Notts 115 B4
Kibblesworth T & W 179 D4
Kibworth Beauchamp Leics 98 B3
Kibworth Harcourt Leics 98 B3
Kidbrooke London 49 B7
Kiddemore Green Staffs 95 A6
Kidderminster Worcs 95 D6
Kiddington Oxon 65 A5
Kidlington Oxon 65 B5
Kidmore End Oxon 47 B4
Kidsgrove Staffs 128 D3
Kidstones N Yorks 156 C3
Kidwelly = Cydweli Carms 57 B4
Kiel Crofts Argyll 226 C4
Kielder Northumb 187 D5
Kielder Castle Visitor Centre Northumb 187 D5
Kierfiold Ho Orkney 282 F3
Kilbagie Clack 208 B2
Kilbarchan Renfs 205 B4
Kilbeg Highld 247 D5
Kilberry Argyll 202 B2
Kilbirnie N Ayrs 204 C3
Kilbride Argyll 226 D3
Kilbride Argyll 226 D4
Kilbride Highld 247 B4
Kilburn Angus 232 B1
Kilburn Derbys 114 A1
Kilburn London 49 A5
Kilburn N Yorks 158 D4
Kilby Leics 98 B3
Kilchamaig Argyll 202 B3
Kilchattan Argyll 212 C1
Kilchattan Bay Argyll 203 C6
Kilchenzie Argyll 190 C2
Kilcheran Argyll 226 C3
Kilchiaran Argyll 200 B2
Kilchoan Argyll 213 A5
Kilchoan Highld 234 D3
Kilchoman Argyll 200 B2
Kilchrenan Argyll 227 D5
Kilconquhar Fife 221 D4
Kilcot Glos 62 A2
Kilcoy Highld 252 A1
Kilcreggan Argyll 215 D5
Kildale N Yorks 159 A5
Kildalloig Argyll 190 D3
Kildary Highld 264 C3
Kildermorie Lodge Highld 263 C7
Kildonan N Ayrs 191 C6
Kildonan Lodge Highld 274 B3
Kildonnan Highld 234 B3
Kildrummy Aberds 244 A1
Kildwick N Yorks 147 C4
Kilfinan Argyll 203 A4
Kilfinnan Highld 239 C6
Kilgetty Pembs 56 B1
Kilgwrrwg Common Mon 61 D6
Kilham E Yorks 150 A3
Kilham Northumb 198 C2
Kilkenneth Argyll 222 C2
Kilkerran Argyll 190 D3
Kilkhampton Corn 24 D3
Killamarsh Derbys 131 A4
Killay Swansea 57 C6
Killbeg Argyll 225 B5
Killean Argyll 202 D1
Killearn Stirl 206 B3
Killen Highld 252 A2
Killerby Darl 167 D4
Killerton House, Exeter Devon 13 A4
Killichonan Perth 229 C4
Killiechonate Highld 239 D6
Killiechronan Argyll 225 B4
Killiecrankie Perth 230 B3
Killiemor Argyll 224 C3
Killiemore House Argyll 224 D3
Killilan Highld 249 C6
Killimster Highld 281 C5
Killin Stirl 217 A5
Killin Lodge Highld 240 B3
Killinallan Argyll 200 A3
Killinghall N Yorks 148 B1
Killington Cumb 155 C5
Killingworth T & W 179 B4
Killmahumaig Argyll 213 C5
Killochyett Borders 196 B3
Killocraw Argyll 190 B2
Killundine Highld 225 B4
Kilmacolm Invclyd 204 B3
Kilmaha Argyll 214 B2
Kilmahog Stirl 217 D6
Kilmalieu Highld 236 D2
Kilmaluag Highld 259 A4
Kilmany Fife 220 B3
Kilmarie Highld 247 C4
Kilmarnock E Ayrs 193 B4
Kilmaron Castle Fife 220 C3
Kilmartin Argyll 213 C6
Kilmaurs E Ayrs 205 D4
Kilmelford Argyll 213 A6
Kilmeny Argyll 200 B3
Kilmersdon Som 43 D5
Kilmeston Hants 33 C4
Kilmichael Argyll 190 C2
Kilmichael Glassary Argyll 214 C1
Kilmichael of Inverlussa Argyll 213 D5
Kilmington Devon 14 B2
Kilmington Wilts 30 B1
Kilmonivaig Highld 239 D5
Kilmorack Highld 251 B6
Kilmore Argyll 226 D3
Kilmore Highld 247 D5
Kilmory Argyll 202 A2
Kilmory Highld 235 C4
Kilmory Highld 246 D2
Kilmory N Ayrs 191 C5
Kilmuir Highld 258 D2
Kilmuir Highld 252 B2
Kilmuir Highld 264 C3
Kilmuir Highld 258 A3
Kilmun Argyll 215 D4
Kilmun Argyll 214 A2
Kiln Pit Hill Northumb 178 D2
Kilncadzow S Lnrk 194 B3
Kilndown Kent 37 C5
Kilnhurst S Yorks 140 D2
Kilninian Argyll 224 B2
Kilninver Argyll 226 D3
Kilnsea E Yorks 143 B6
Kilnsey N Yorks 146 A3
Kilnwick E Yorks 150 C2
Kilnwick Percy E Yorks 149 B1
Kiloran Argyll 212 C1
Kilpatrick N Ayrs 191 C5
Kilpeck Hereford 78 D2
Kilphedir Highld 274 C3
Kilpin E Yorks 141 A5
Kilpin Pike E Yorks 141 A5
Kilrenny Fife 221 D5
Kilsby Northants 98 D2
Kilspindie Perth 220 B2
Kilsyth N Lnrk 207 C5
Kiltarlity Highld 251 B7
Kilton Notts 131 B5
Kilton Som 27 A6
Kilton Thorpe Redcar 169 D4
Kilvaxter Highld 258 B3
Kilve Som 27 A6
Kilvington Notts 115 A5
Kilwinning N Ayrs 204 D3
Kimber worth S Yorks 140 D2
Kimberley Norf 103 A6
Kimberley Notts 114 A3
Kimble Wick Bucks 66 C3
Kimblesworth Durham 167 A5
Kimbolton Cambs 84 A2
Kimbolton Hereford 78 A3
Kimcote Leics 98 C2
Kimmeridge Dorset 16 D3
Kimmerston Northumb 198 C3
Kimpton Hants 32 A1
Kimpton Herts 68 B1
Kinbrace Highld 274 A2
Kinbuck Stirl 218 D2
Kincaple Fife 221 C4
Kincardine Fife 208 B2
Kincardine Highld 264 B2
Kincardine Bridge Falk 208 B2
Kincardine O'Neil Aberds 244 C2
Kinclaven Perth 219 A6
Kincorth Aberdeen 245 B6
Kincorth Ho. Moray 265 D6
Kincraig Highld 241 B6
Kincraigie Perth 230 D3
Kindallachan Perth 230 D3
Kinderland, Scarborough N Yorks 160 B4
Kineton Glos 64 A1
Kineton Warks 81 B6
Kinfauns Perth 219 B6
King Edward Aberds 268 D2
King Sterndale Derbys 129 B5
Kingairloch Highld 236 D2
Kingarth Argyll 203 C5
Kingcoed Mon 61 C6
Kingerby Lincs 142 D2
Kingham Oxon 64 A3
Kingholm Quay Dumfries 174 A2
Kinghorn Fife 209 B5
Kingie Highld 239 B5
Kinglassie Fife 209 A5
Kingoodie Perth 220 B3
King's Acre Hereford 78 C2
King's Bromley Staffs 113 D5
King's Caple Hereford 62 A1
King's Cliffe Northants 100 B2
Kings College Chapel, Cambridge Cambs 85 B6
King's Coughton Warks 80 B3
King's Heath W Mid 96 C3
Kings Hedges Cambs 85 A6
Kings Langley Herts 67 C5
King's Lynn Norf 118 C3
King's Meaburn Cumb 165 C4
King's Mills Wrex 110 A2
Kings Muir Borders 196 C1
King's Newnham Warks 98 D1
King's Newton Derbys 114 C1
King's Norton Leics 98 A3
King's Norton W Mid 96 D3
King's Nympton Devon 26 D1
King's Pyon Hereford 78 B2
King's Ripton Cambs 101 D4
King's Somborne Hants 32 B2
King's Stag Dorset 30 D1
King's Stanley Glos 63 C4
King's Sutton Northants 82 D1
King's Thorn Hereford 78 D3
King's Walden Herts 67 A6
Kings Worthy Hants 32 B3
Kingsand Corn 6 B3
Kingsbarns Fife 221 C5
Kingsbridge Devon 7 C6
Kingsbridge Som 27 B4
Kingsburgh Highld 258 C3
Kingsbury London 49 A5
Kingsbury Warks 97 B5
Kingsbury Episcopi Som 28 C4
Kingsclere Hants 46 D3
Kingscote Glos 63 D4
Kingscott Devon 25 D6
Kingscross N Ayrs 191 C6
Kingsdon Som 29 C5
Kingsdown Kent 39 A5
Kingseat Fife 208 A4
Kingsey Bucks 66 C2
Kingsfold W Sus 35 C4
Kingsford E Ayrs 205 D4
Kingsford Worcs 95 C6
Kingsforth N Lincs 142 B2
Kingsgate Kent 53 B5
Kingsheanton Devon 25 B6
Kingshouse Hotel Highld 237 D6
Kingside Hill Cumb 175 C4
Kingskerswell Devon 8 A2
Kingskettle Fife 220 D3
Kingsland Anglesey 122 B2
Kingsland Hereford 78 A2
Kingsley Ches 127 B5
Kingsley Hants 33 B6
Kingsley Staffs 112 A4
Kingsley Green W Sus 34 C1
Kingsley Holt Staffs 112 A4
Kingsley Park Northants 83 A4
Kingsmuir Angus 232 D2
Kingsmuir Fife 221 D5
Kingsnorth Kent 38 B2
Kingstanding W Mid 96 B3
Kingsteignton Devon 12 D3
Kingsthorpe Northants 83 A4
Kingston Cambs 85 B5
Kingston Devon 7 C5
Kingston Dorset 16 A1
Kingston Dorset 16 D3
Kingston E Loth 210 B2
Kingston Hants 17 A5
Kingston I o W 18 C3
Kingston Kent 52 D3
Kingston Moray 266 C4
Kingston Bagpuize Oxon 65 D5
Kingston Blount Oxon 66 D2
Kingston by Sea W Sus 21 B5
Kingston Deverill Wilts 30 B2
Kingston Gorse W Sus 20 B3
Kingston Lacy, Wimborne Minster Dorset 16 A3
Kingston Lisle Oxon 45 A7
Kingston Maurward Dorset 15 B7
Kingston near Lewes E Sus 22 B1
Kingston on Soar Notts 114 C3
Kingston Russell Dorset 15 B5
Kingston St Mary Som 28 C2
Kingston Seymour N Som 42 C3
Kingston Upon Hull Hull 142 A2
Kingston upon Thames London 49 C4
Kingston Vale London 49 B5
Kingstone Hereford 78 D2
Kingstone Som 28 D3
Kingstone Staffs 113 C4
Kingstown Cumb 175 C6
Kingswear Devon 8 B2
Kingswells Aberdeen 245 B5
Kingswinford W Mid 96 C1
Kingswood Bucks 66 B1
Kingswood Glos 62 D3
Kingswood Hereford 77 B6
Kingswood Kent 37 A6
Kingswood Powys 93 A6
Kingswood S Glos 43 B5
Kingswood Sur 35 A5
Kingswood Warks 97 D4
Kingthorpe Lincs 133 B6
Kington Hereford 77 B6
Kington Worcs 80 B2
Kington Langley Wilts 44 B3
Kington Magna Dorset 30 C1
Kington St Michael Wilts 44 B3
Kingussie Highld 241 B5
Kingweston Som 29 B5
Kininvie Ho. Moray 254 B4
Kinkell Bridge Perth 218 C4
Kinknockie Aberds 257 B5
Kinlet Shrops 95 C5
Kinloch Fife 220 C2
Kinloch Highld 234 A2
Kinloch Highld 271 A6
Kinloch Highld 247 C5
Kinloch Perth 231 D5
Kinloch Perth 231 D6
Kinloch Hourn Highld 238 B3
Kinloch Laggan Highld 240 D3
Kinloch Lodge Highld 277 C6
Kinloch Rannoch Perth 229 C5
Kinlochan Highld 236 C2
Kinlochard Stirl 217 D4
Kinlochbeoraid Highld 238 D2
Kinlochbervie Highld 276 C3
Kinlocheil Highld 236 B3
Kinlochewe Highld 262 D2
Kinlochleven Highld 237 C5
Kinlochmoidart Highld 235 C6
Kinlochmorar Highld 238 C2
Kinlochmore Highld 237 C5
Kinlochspelve Argyll 225 D5
Kinloid Highld 235 B5
Kinloss Moray 265 D6
Kinmel Bay Conwy 125 A4
Kinmuck Aberds 256 E3
Kinmundy Aberds 245 A5
Kinnadie Aberds 257 B4
Kinnaird Perth 220 B2
Kinnaird Castle Angus 233 C4
Kinneff Aberds 233 A6
Kinnelhead Dumfries 184 B3
Kinnell Angus 233 C4
Kinnerley Shrops 110 C2
Kinnersley Hereford 78 C1
Kinnersley Worcs 79 C6
Kinnerton Powys 77 A6
Kinnesswood Perth 219 D6
Kinninvie Durham 166 C3
Kinnordy Angus 232 C1
Kinoulton Notts 115 B4
Kinross Perth 219 D6
Kinrossie Perth 219 A6
Kinsbourne Green Herts 67 B6
Kinsey Heath Ches 111 A5
Kinsham Hereford 78 A1
Kinsham Worcs 80 D2
Kinsley W Yorks 140 B2
Kinson Bmouth 17 B4
Kintbury W Berks 46 C1
Kintessack Moray 265 D5
Kintillo Perth 219 C6
Kintocher Aberds 244 B2
Kinton Hereford 94 D2
Kinton Shrops 110 D2
Kintore Aberds 245 A4
Kintour Argyll 201 C4
Kintra Argyll 224 D2
Kintra Argyll 200 D3
Kintraw Argyll 213 B6
Kinuachdrachd Argyll 213 C5
Kinveachy Highld 242 A2
Kinver Staffs 95 C6
Kippax W Yorks 148 D3
Kippen Stirl 207 A4
Kippford or Scaur Dumfries 173 C6
Kirbister Orkney 283 G4
Kirbister Orkney 282 E7
Kirbuster Orkney 282 E3
Kirby Bedon Norf 104 A3
Kirby Bellars Leics 115 D5
Kirby Cane Norf 105 B4
Kirby Cross Essex 71 A6
Kirby Grindalythe N Yorks 150 A2
Kirby Hill N Yorks 148 A2
Kirby Hill N Yorks 157 A5
Kirby Knowle N Yorks 158 C3
Kirby-le-Soken Essex 71 A6
Kirby Misperton N Yorks 159 D6
Kirby Muxloe Leics 98 A2
Kirby Overblow N Yorks 148 C2
Kirby Row Norf 105 B4
Kirby Sigston N Yorks 158 B3
Kirby Underdale E Yorks 149 B7
Kirby Wiske N Yorks 158 C2
Kirdford W Sus 34 D3
Kirk Highld 281 C4
Kirk Bramwith S Yorks 140 B4
Kirk Deighton N Yorks 148 B2
Kirk Ella E Yorks 142 A2
Kirk Hallam Derbys 114 A2
Kirk Hammerton N Yorks 148 B3
Kirk Ireton Derbys 130 D2
Kirk Langley Derbys 113 B6
Kirk Merrington Durham 167 B5
Kirk Michael I o M 152 B3
Kirk of Shotts N Lnrk 207 D6
Kirk Sandall S Yorks 140 C4
Kirk Smeaton N Yorks 140 B3
Kirk Yetholm Borders 188 A1
Kirkabister Shetland 285 K6
Kirkandrews Dumfries 172 D4
Kirkandrews upon Eden Cumb 175 C6
Kirkbampton Cumb 175 C6
Kirkbean Dumfries 174 C2
Kirkbride Cumb 175 C5
Kirkbuddo Angus 232 D3
Kirkburn Borders 196 C1
Kirkburn E Yorks 150 B2
Kirkburton W Yorks 139 B4
Kirkby Lincs 142 D2
Kirkby Mers 136 D3
Kirkby N Yorks 158 A4
Kirkby Fleetham N Yorks 157 B6
Kirkby Green Lincs 133 D5
Kirkby In Ashfield Notts 131 D5
Kirkby-in-Furness Cumb 153 B3
Kirkby la Thorpe Lincs 116 A4
Kirkby Lonsdale Cumb 155 D5
Kirkby Malham N Yorks 146 A2
Kirkby Mallory Leics 98 A1
Kirkby Malzeard N Yorks 157 D6
Kirkby Mills N Yorks 159 C6
Kirkby on Bain Lincs 134 C2
Kirkby Stephen Cumb 155 A6
Kirkby Thore Cumb 165 C4
Kirkby Underwood Lincs 116 C3
Kirkby Wharfe N Yorks 148 C4
Kirkbymoorside N Yorks 159 C5
Kirkcaldy Fife 209 A5
Kirkcambeck Cumb 176 C3
Kirkcarswell Dumfries 173 D5
Kirkcolm Dumfries 170 A2
Kirkconnel Dumfries 183 A5
Kirkconnell Dumfries 174 B2
Kirkcowan Dumfries 171 A5
Kirkcudbright Dumfries 173 C4
Kirkdale Mers 136 D2
Kirkfieldbank S Lnrk 194 B3
Kirkgunzeon Dumfries 173 B6
Kirkham Lancs 144 D4
Kirkham N Yorks 149 A6
Kirkhamgate W Yorks 139 A5
Kirkharle Northumb 178 A2
Kirkheaton Northumb 178 B2
Kirkheaton W Yorks 139 B4
Kirkhill Angus 233 B4
Kirkhill Highld 252 B1
Kirkhill Midloth 209 D5
Kirkhill Moray 254 C3
Kirkhope Borders 186 A2
Kirkhouse Borders 196 C2
Kirkiboll Highld 277 C6
Kirkibost Highld 247 C4
Kirkinch Angus 231 D7
Kirkinner Dumfries 171 B6
Kirkintilloch E Dunb 205 A6
Kirkland Cumb 162 C3
Kirkland Cumb 165 B4
Kirkland Dumfries 183 C6
Kirkland Dumfries 183 A5
Kirkleatham Redcar 168 C3
Kirklevington Stockton 158 A3
Kirkley Suff 105 B6
Kirklington Notts 132 D1
Kirklington N Yorks 157 C7
Kirklinton Cumb 176 C2
Kirkliston Edin 208 C4
Kirkmaiden Dumfries 170 D3
Kirkmichael Perth 231 C4
Kirkmichael S Ayrs 192 E3
Kirkmuirhill S Lnrk 194 B2
Kirknewton Northumb 198 C3
Kirknewton W Loth 208 D4
Kirkney Aberds 255 C6
Kirkoswald Cumb 164 A3
Kirkoswald S Ayrs 192 E2
Kirkpatrick Durham Dumfries 173 A5
Kirkpatrick-Fleming Dumfries 175 A5
Kirksanton Cumb 153 B2
Kirkstall W Yorks 147 D6
Kirkstead Lincs 134 C1
Kirkstile Aberds 255 C6
Kirkstyle Highld 281 A5
Kirkton Aberds 256 D1
Kirkton Aberds 268 E1
Kirkton Angus 232 D2
Kirkton Angus 220 A4
Kirkton Borders 186 B4
Kirkton Dumfries 184 D2
Kirkton Fife 220 B3
Kirkton Highld 249 D5
Kirkton Highld 249 B6
Kirkton Highld 265 A4
Kirkton Highld 252 A3
Kirkton Perth 219 C4
Kirkton S Lnrk 194 D4
Kirkton Stirl 217 D5
Kirkton Manor Borders 195 C7
Kirkton of Airlie Angus 231 C7
Kirkton of Auchterhouse Angus 220 A3
Kirkton of Auchterless Aberds 256 B2
Kirkton of Barevan Highld 253 B4
Kirkton of Bourtie Aberds 256 D3
Kirkton of Collace Perth 219 A6
Kirkton of Craig Angus 233 C5
Kirkton of Culsalmond Aberds 256 C1
Kirkton of Durris Aberds 245 C4
Kirkton of Glenbuchat Aberds 243 A6
Kirkton of Glenisla Angus 231 B6
Kirkton of Kingoldrum Angus 232 C1
Kirkton of Largo Fife 220 D4
Kirkton of Lethendy Perth 231 D5
Kirkton of Logie Buchan Aberds 257 D4
Kirkton of Maryculter Aberds 245 C5
Kirkton of Menmuir Angus 232 B3
Kirkton of Monikie Angus 221 A5
Kirkton of Oyne Aberds 256 D1
Kirkton of Rayne Aberds 256 D1
Kirkton of Skene Aberds 245 B5
Kirkton of Tough Aberds 244 A3
Kirktonhill Borders 196 A3
Kirktown Aberds 269 D5
Kirktown of Alvah Aberds 268 C1
Kirktown of Deskford Moray 267 C6
Kirktown of Fetteresso Aberds 245 D5
Kirktown of Mortlach Moray 254 C4
Kirktown of Slains Aberds 257 D5
Kirkurd Borders 195 B6
Kirkwall Orkney 282 F5
Kirkwall Airport Orkney 283 G5
Kirkwhelpington Northumb 178 A1
Kirmington N Lincs 142 B3
Kirmond le Mire Lincs 142 D3
Kirn Argyll 203 A6
Kirriemuir Angus 232 C1

Lelley E Yorks 151 D5
Lem Hill Worcs 95 D5
Lemmington Hall Northumb 189 B4
Lempitlaw Borders 198 C1
Lenchwick Worcs 80 C3
Lendalfoot S Ayrs 180 C3
Lendrick Lodge Stirl 217 D5
Lenham Kent 37 A6
Lenham Heath Kent 37 B7
Lennel Borders 198 B2
Lennoxtown E Dunb 205 A6
Lenton Lincs 116 B3
Lenton Nottingham 114 B3
Lentran Highld 252 B1
Lenwade Norf 120 D2
Leny Ho. Stirl 217 D6
Lenzie E Dunb 205 A6
Leoch Angus 220 A3
Leochel-Cushnie Aberds 244 A2
Leominster Hereford 78 B2
Leonard Stanley Glos 63 C4
Leonardslee Gardens W Sus 35 D5
Leorin Argyll 200 D3
Lepe Hants 18 B3
Lephin Highld 258 D1
Lephinchapel Argyll 214 C2
Lephinmore Argyll 214 C2
Leppington N Yorks 149 A6
Lepton W Yorks 139 B5
Lerryn Corn 5 B6
Lerwick Shetland 285 J6
Lerwick (Tingwall) Airport Shetland 285 J6
Lesbury Northumb 189 B5
Leslie Aberds 255 D6
Leslie Fife 220 D2
Lesmahagow S Lnrk 194 C3
Lesnewth Corn 10 B2
Lessendrum Aberds 255 B6
Lessingham Norf 121 C5
Lessonhall Cumb 175 C5
Leswalt Dumfries 170 A2
Letchmore Heath Herts 67 D6
Letchworth Herts 84 D4
Letcombe Bassett Oxon 46 A1
Letcombe Regis Oxon 46 A1
Letham Angus 232 D3
Letham Falk 208 B1
Letham Fife 220 C3
Letham Perth 219 B5
Letham Grange Angus 233 D4
Lethenty Aberds 256 B3
Letheringham Suff 88 B3
Letheringsett Norf 120 B2
Lettaford Devon 12 C2
Lettan Orkney 282 C8
Letterewe Highld 261 C6
Letterfearn Highld 249 D5
Letterfinlay Highld 239 C6
Lettermorar Highld 235 B6
Lettermore Argyll 224 B3
Letters Highld 262 B3
Letterston Pembs 55 B5
Lettoch Highld 242 A3
Lettoch Highld 254 C1
Letton Hereford 78 C1
Letton Hereford 94 D1
Letton Green Norf 103 A5
Letty Green Herts 68 B2
Letwell S Yorks 131 A5
Leuchars Fife 221 B4
Leuchars Ho. Moray 266 C3
Leumrabhagh W Isles 288 F4
Levan Invclyd 204 A2
Levaneap Shetland 285 G6
Levedale Staffs 112 D2
Leven E Yorks 151 C4
Leven Fife 220 D3
Levencorroch N Ayrs 191 C6
Levens Cumb 154 C3
Levens Green Herts 68 A3
Levenshulme Gtr Man 138 D1
Levenwick Shetland 285 L6
Leverburgh = An t-Ob W Isles 287 F5
Leverington Cambs 118 D1
Leverton Lincs 117 A7
Leverton Highgate Lincs 117 A7
Leverton Lucasgate Lincs 117 A7
Leverton Outgate Lincs 117 A7
Levington Suff 88 D3
Levisham N Yorks 160 B2
Levishie Highld 240 A2
Lew Oxon 64 C4
Lewannick Corn 10 C3
Lewdown Devon 11 C5
Lewes E Sus 22 A2
Leweston Pembs 55 B5
Lewisham London 49 B6
Lewiston Highld 251 D7
Lewistown Bridgend 40 C4
Lewknor Oxon 66 D2
Leworthy Devon 10 A4
Leworthy Devon 26 B1
Lewtrenchard Devon 11 C5
Lexden Essex 70 A3
Ley Aberds 244 A2
Ley Corn 5 A6
Leybourne Kent 37 A4
Leyburn N Yorks 157 B5
Leyfields Staffs 97 A5
Leyhill Bucks 67 C4
Leyland Lancs 136 A4
Leylodge Aberds 245 A4
Leymoor W Yorks 139 B4
Leys Aberds 269 D5
Leys Perth 220 A2
Leys Castle Highld 252 B2
Leys of Cossans Angus 232 D1
Leysdown-on-Sea Kent 52 B2
Leysmill Angus 233 D4
Leysters Pole Hereford 78 A3
Leyton London 49 A6
Leytonstone London 49 A6
Lezant Corn 10 D4
Leziate Norf 118 D3
Lhanbryde Moray 266 C3
Liatrie Highld 250 C4
Libanus Powys 60 A1
Libberton S Lnrk 195 B4
Liberton Edin 209 D5
Liceasto W Isles 288 H2
Lichfield Staffs 96 A4
Lichfield Cathedral Staffs 113 D5
Lickey Worcs 96 D2
Lickey End Worcs 96 D2
Lickfold W Sus 34 D2
Liddel Orkney 283 K5
Liddesdale Highld 236 D1
Liddington Thamesdown 45 A6
Lidgate Suff 86 B3
Lidget S Yorks 141 C4
Lidget Green W Yorks 147 D5
Lidgett Notts 131 C6
Lidlington Beds 84 D1
Lidstone Oxon 65 A4
Lieurary Highld 279 B6
Liff Angus 220 A3
Lifton Devon 11 C4
Liftondown Devon 11 C4
Lighthorne Warks 81 B6
Lightwater Sur 48 C2
Lightwater Valley N Yorks 157 D6
Lightwood Stoke 112 A3
Lightwood Green Ches 111 A5
Lightwood Green Wrex 110 A2
Lilbourne Northants 98 D2
Lilburn Tower Northumb 188 A3
Lilleshall Telford 111 D6
Lilley Herts 67 A6
Lilley W Berks 46 B2
Lilliesleaf Borders 186 A4
Lillingstone Dayrell Bucks 83 D4
Lillingstone Lovell Bucks 83 C4
Lillington Dorset 29 D6
Lillington Warks 81 A6
Lilliput Poole 17 B4
Lilstock Som 27 A6
Lilyhurst Shrops 111 D6
Limbury Luton 67 A5
Limebrook Hereford 78 A1
Limefield Gtr Man 137 B7
Limekilnburn S Lnrk 194 A2
Limekilns Fife 208 B3
Limerigg Falk 207 C6
Limerstone I o W 18 C3
Limington Som 29 C5
Limpenhoe Norf 105 A4
Limpley Stoke Wilts 44 C1
Limpsfield Sur 36 A2
Limpsfield Chart Sur 36 A2
Linby Notts 131 D5
Linchmere W Sus 34 C1
Lincluden Dumfries 174 A2
Lincoln Lincs 133 B4
Lincoln Castle Lincs 133 B4
Lincoln Cathedral Lincs 133 B4
Lincomb Worcs 79 A6
Lincombe Devon 7 B6
Lindal in Furness Cumb 153 C3
Lindale Cumb 154 C3
Lindean Borders 196 C3
Lindfield W Sus 35 D6
Lindford Hants 33 B7
Lindifferon Fife 220 C3
Lindisfarne Priory, Holy Island Northumb 199 B5
Lindley W Yorks 139 B4
Lindley Green N Yorks 147 C6
Lindores Fife 220 C2
Lindridge Worcs 79 A4
Lindsell Essex 69 A6
Lindsey Suff 87 C5
Linford Hants 17 A5
Linford Thurrock 50 B3
Lingague I o M 152 D2
Lingards Wood W Yorks 138 B3
Lingbob W Yorks 147 D4
Lingdale Redcar 169 D4
Lingen Hereford 78 A1
Lingfield Sur 36 B1
Lingfield Park Racecourse Sur 36 B1
Lingreabhagh W Isles 287 F5
Lingwood Norf 105 A4
Linicro Highld 258 B3
Linkenholt Hants 46 D1
Linkhill Kent 37 D6
Linkinhorne Corn 10 D4
Linklater Orkney 283 K5
Linksness Orkney 283 G3
Linktown Fife 209 A5
Linley Shrops 94 B1
Linley Green Hereford 79 B4
Linlithgow W Loth 208 C3
Linlithgow Bridge W Loth 208 C2
Linshiels Northumb 188 C1
Linsiadar W Isles 288 D3
Linsidemore Highld 264 A1
Linslade Beds 67 A4
Linstead Parva Suff 104 D4
Linstock Cumb 176 D2
Linthwaite W Yorks 139 B4
Lintlaw Borders 198 A2
Lintmill Moray 267 C6
Linton Borders 187 A6
Linton Cambs 86 C1
Linton Derbys 113 D6
Linton Hereford 62 A2
Linton Kent 37 B5
Linton Northumb 189 D5
Linton N Yorks 146 A3
Linton W Yorks 148 C2
Linton-on-Ouse N Yorks 148 A3
Linwood Hants 17 A5
Linwood Lincs 133 A6
Linwood Renfs 205 B4
Lionacleit W Isles 286 B3
Lional W Isles 288 A6
Liphook Hants 34 C1
Liscard Mers 136 D2
Liscombe Som 26 B3
Liskeard Corn 6 A1
L'Islet Guern 6
Liss Hants 33 C6
Liss Forest Hants 33 C6
Lissett E Yorks 151 B4
Lissington Lincs 133 A6
Lisvane Cardiff 41 C6
Liswerry Newport 42 A2
Litcham Norf 119 D5
Litchborough Northants 82 B3
Litchfield Hants 46 D2
Litherland Mers 136 D2
Litlington Cambs 85 C5
Litlington E Sus 22 B3
Little Abington Cambs 86 C1
Little Addington Northants 99 D6
Little Alne Warks 80 A4
Little Altcar Mers 136 C2
Little Asby Cumb 155 A5
Little Assynt Highld 271 B4
Little Aston Staffs 96 A3
Little Atherfield I o W 18 C3
Little Ayre Orkney 283 H4
Little-ayre Shetland 285 G5
Little Ayton N Yorks 168 D3
Little Baddow Essex 70 C1
Little Badminton S Glos 44 A2
Little Ballinluig Perth 230 C3
Little Bampton Cumb 175 C5
Little Bardfield Essex 86 D2
Little Barford Beds 84 B3
Little Barningham Norf 120 B3
Little Barrington Glos 64 B3
Little Barrow Ches 127 B4
Little Barugh N Yorks 159 D6
Little Bavington Northumb 178 B1
Little Bealings Suff 88 C3
Little Bedwyn Wilts 45 C6
Little Bentley Essex 71 A5
Little Berkhamsted Herts 68 C2
Little Billing Northants 83 A5
Little Birch Hereford 78 D3
Little Blakenham Suff 88 C2
Little Blencow Cumb 164 B2
Little Bollington Ches 128 A2
Little Bookham Sur 35 A4
Little Bowden Leics 99 C4
Little Bradley Suff 86 B2
Little Brampton Shrops 94 C1
Little Brechin Angus 232 B3
Little Brickhill M Keynes 83 D6
Little Brington Northants 82 A3
Little Bromley Essex 71 A4
Little Broughton Cumb 162 A3
Little Budworth Ches 127 C5
Little Burstead Essex 69 D6
Little Bytham Lincs 116 D3
Little Carlton Lincs 134 A3
Little Carlton Notts 132 D2
Little Casterton Rutland 100 A2
Little Cawthorpe Lincs 134 A3
Little Chalfont Bucks 67 D4
Little Chart Kent 38 A1
Little Chesterford Essex 85 C7
Little Cheverell Wilts 44 D3
Little Chishill Cambs 85 D6
Little Clacton Essex 71 B5
Little Clifton Cumb 162 B3
Little Colp Aberds 256 B2
Little Comberton Worcs 80 C2
Little Common E Sus 23 B5
Little Compton Warks 81 D5
Little Cornard Suff 87 D4
Little Cowarne Hereford 79 B4
Little Coxwell Oxon 64 D3
Little Crakehall N Yorks 157 B6
Little Cressingham Norf 103 A4
Little Crosby Mers 136 C2
Little Dalby Leics 115 D5
Little Dawley Telford 95 A4
Little Dens Aberds 257 B5
Little Dewchurch Hereford 78 D3
Little Downham Cambs 101 C7
Little Driffield E Yorks 150 B3
Little Dunham Norf 119 D5
Little Dunkeld Perth 230 D4
Little Dunmow Essex 69 A6
Little Easton Essex 69 A6
Little Eaton Derbys 114 A1
Little Eccleston Lancs 144 C4
Little Ellingham Norf 103 B6
Little End Essex 69 C5
Little Eversden Cambs 85 B5
Little Fakenham Suff 103 D5
Little Faringdon Oxon 64 C3
Little Fencote N Yorks 157 B6
Little Fenton N Yorks 148 D4
Little Finborough Suff 87 B6
Little Fransham Norf 119 D6
Little Gaddesden Herts 67 B4
Little Gidding Cambs 100 C3
Little Glemham Suff 88 B4
Little Glenshee Perth 219 A4
Little Gransden Cambs 85 B4
Little Green Som 29 A7
Little Grimsby Lincs 143 D5
Little Gruinard Highld 261 B6
Little Habton N Yorks 159 D6
Little Hadham Herts 68 A4
Little Hale Lincs 116 A4
Lit. Hallingbury Essex 69 B4
Little Hampden Bucks 66 C3
Little Harrowden Northants 99 D5
Little Haseley Oxon 66 C1
Little Hatfield E Yorks 151 C4
Little Hautbois Norf 121 C4
Little Haven Pembs 55 C4
Little Hay Staffs 96 A4
Little Hayfield Derbys 129 A5
Little Haywood Staffs 112 C4
Little Heath W Mid 97 C6
Little Hereford Hereford 78 A3
Little Horkesley Essex 87 D5
Little Horsted E Sus 22 A2
Little Horton W Yorks 147 D5
Little Horwood Bucks 83 D4
Little Houghton Northants 83 B5
Little Houghton S Yorks 140 C2
Little Hucklow Derbys 129 B6
Little Hulton Gtr Man 137 C6
Little Humber E Yorks 142 A3
Little Hungerford W Berks 46 B3
Little Irchester Northants 83 A6
Little Kimble Bucks 66 C3
Little Kineton Warks 81 B6
Little Kingshill Bucks 66 D3
Little Langdale Cumb 154 A2
Little Langford Wilts 31 B4
Little Laver Essex 69 C5
Little Leigh Ches 127 B6
Little Leighs Essex 69 B7
Little Lever Gtr Man 137 C6
Little London Bucks 66 B1
Little London E Sus 22 A3
Little London Hants 32 A2
Little London Hants 47 D4
Little London Lincs 117 C5
Little London Lincs 118 C1
Little London Norf 120 C3
Little London Powys 92 C4
Little Longstone Derbys 130 B1
Little Lynturk Aberds 244 A2
Little Malvern Worcs 79 C5
Little Maplestead Essex 87 D4
Little Marcle Hereford 79 D4
Little Marlow Bucks 47 A6
Little Marsden Lancs 146 D2
Little Massingham Norf 119 C4
Little Melton Norf 104 A2
Little Mill Mon 61 C5
Little Milton Oxon 65 C7
Little Missenden Bucks 67 D4
Little Musgrave Cumb 165 D5
Little Ness Shrops 110 D3
Little Neston Ches 126 B2
Little Newcastle Pembs 55 B5
Little Newsham Durham 166 D4
Little Oakley Essex 71 A6
Little Oakley Northants 99 C5
Little Orton Cumb 175 C6
Little Ouseburn N Yorks 148 A3
Little Paxton Cambs 84 A3
Little Petherick Corn 9 D5
Little Pitlurg Moray 255 B5
Little Plumpton Lancs 144 D3
Little Plumstead Norf 121 D5
Little Ponton Lincs 116 B2
Little Raveley Cambs 101 D4
Little Reedness E Yorks 141 A6
Little Ribston N Yorks 148 B2
Little Rissington Glos 64 B2
Little Ryburgh Norf 119 C6
Little Ryle Northumb 188 B3
Little Salkeld Cumb 164 B3
Little Sampford Essex 86 D2
Little Sandhurst Brack 47 C6
Little Saxham Suff 86 A3
Little Scatwell Highld 251 A5
Little Sessay N Yorks 158 D3
Little Shelford Cambs 85 B6
Little Singleton Lancs 144 D3
Little Skillymarno Aberds 269 D4
Little Smeaton N Yorks 140 B3
Little Snoring Norf 119 B6
Little Sodbury S Glos 43 A6
Little Somborne Hants 32 B2
Little Somerford Wilts 44 A3
Little Stainforth N Yorks 146 A2
Little Stainton Darl 167 C6
Little Stanney Ches 127 B4
Little Staughton Beds 84 A3
Little Steeping Lincs 135 C4
Little Stoke Staffs 112 B3
Little Stonham Suff 88 A2
Little Stretton Leics 98 A3
Little Stretton Shrops 94 B2
Little Strickland Cumb 164 D3
Little Stukeley Cambs 100 D4
Little Sutton Ches 126 B3
Little Tew Oxon 65 A4
Little Thetford Cambs 102 D1
Little Thirkleby N Yorks 158 D3
Little Thurlow Suff 86 B2
Little Thurrock Thurrock 50 B3
Little Torboll Highld 264 A3
Little Torrington Devon 25 D5
Little Totham Essex 70 B2
Little Toux Aberds 267 D6
Little Town Cumb 163 C5
Little Town Lancs 145 D6
Little Urswick Cumb 153 C3
Little Wakering Essex 51 A6
Little Walden Essex 86 C1
Little Waldingfield Suff 87 C5
Little Walsingham Norf 119 B6
Little Waltham Essex 69 B7
Little Warley Essex 69 D6
Little Weighton E Yorks 150 D2
Little Weldon Northants 99 C6
Little Welnetham Suff 87 A4
Little Wenlock Telford 95 A4
Little Whittingham Green Suff 104 D3
Little Wilbraham Cambs 86 B1
Little Wishford Wilts 31 B4
Little Witley Worcs 79 A5
Little Wittenham Oxon 65 D6
Little Wolford Warks 81 D5
Little Wratting Suff 86 C2
Little Wymington Beds 83 A6
Little Wymondley Herts 68 A2
Little Wyrley Staffs 96 A3
Little Yeldham Essex 86 D3
Littlebeck N Yorks 160 A2
Littleborough Gtr Man 138 B2
Littleborough Notts 132 A3
Littlebourne Kent 53 D4
Littlebredy Dorset 15 C5
Littlebury Essex 85 D7
Littlebury Green Essex 85 D6
Littledean Glos 62 B2
Littleferry Highld 265 A4
Littleham Devon 13 C5
Littleham Devon 25 C5
Littlehampton W Sus 20 B3
Littlehempston Devon 8 A2
Littlehoughton Northumb 189 B5
Littlemill Aberds 243 C6
Littlemill E Ayrs 182 A2
Littlemill Highld 253 A5
Littlemill Northumb 189 B5
Littlemoor Dorset 15 C6
Littlemore Oxon 65 C6
Littleover Derby 114 B1
Littleport Cambs 102 C1
Littlestone on Sea Kent 38 C2
Littlethorpe Leics 98 B2
Littlethorpe N Yorks 148 A2
Littleton Ches 127 C4
Littleton Hants 32 B3
Littleton Perth 220 A2
Littleton Som 29 B4
Littleton Sur 48 C3
Littleton Sur 34 B2
Littleton Drew Wilts 44 A2
Littleton-on-Severn S Glos 43 A4
Littleton Pannell Wilts 44 D4
Littletown Durham 167 A6
Littlewick Green Windsor 47 B6
Littleworth Beds 84 C2
Littleworth Glos 63 C4
Littleworth Oxon 64 D4
Littleworth Staffs 112 D4
Littleworth Worcs 80 B1
Litton Derbys 129 B6
Litton N Yorks 156 D3
Litton Som 43 D4
Litton Cheney Dorset 15 B5
Liurbost W Isles 288 E4
Liverpool Mers 136 D2
Liverpool Airport Mers 127 A4
Liverpool Cathedral (C of E) Mers 126 A3
Liverpool Cathedral (RC) Mers 136 D2
Liverpool John Lennon Airport Mers 127 A4
Liversedge W Yorks 139 A5
Liverton Devon 12 D3
Liverton Redcar 169 D5
Livingston W Loth 208 D3
Livingston Village W Loth 208 D3
Lixwm Flint 125 B6
Lizard Corn 3 D5
Llaingoch Anglesey 122 B2
Llaithddu Powys 93 C4
Llan Powys 91 B6
Llan Ffestiniog Gwyn 108 A2
Llan-y-pwll Wrex 126 D3
Llanaber Gwyn 90 A4
Llanaelhaearn Gwyn 106 B3
Llanafan Ceredig 75 A5
Llanafan-fawr Powys 76 B3
Llanallgo Anglesey 123 B4
Llanandras = Presteigne Powys 77 A7
Llanarmon Gwyn 107 C4
Llanarmon Dyffryn Ceiriog Wrex 109 B6
Llanarmon-yn-Ial Denb 126 D1
Llanarth Ceredig 73 A7
Llanarth Mon 61 B5
Llanarthne Carms 58 C2
Llanasa Flint 125 A6
Llanbabo Anglesey 122 B3
Llanbadarn Fawr Ceredig 90 D4
Llanbadarn Fynydd Powys 93 D5
Llanbadarn-y-Garreg Powys 77 C5
Llanbadoc Mon 61 C5
Llanbadrig Anglesey 122 A3
Llanbeder Newport 61 D5
Llanbedr Gwyn 107 D5
Llanbedr Powys 77 C5
Llanbedr Powys 60 A4
Llanbedr-Dyffryn-Clwyd Denb 125 D6
Llanbedr Pont Steffan = Lampeter Ceredig 75 D4
Llanbedr-y-cennin Conwy 124 C2
Llanbedrgoch Anglesey 123 B5
Llanbedrog Gwyn 106 C3
Llanberis Gwyn 123 D5
Llanbethêry V Glam 41 E5
Llanbister Powys 93 D5
Llanblethian V Glam 41 D4
Llanboidy Carms 73 D5
Llanbradach Caerph 41 B6
Llanbrynmair Powys 91 B6
Llancarfan V Glam 41 D5
Llancayo Mon 61 C5
Llancloudy Hereford 61 A6
Llancynfelyn Ceredig 90 C4
Llandaff Cardiff 41 D6
Llandanwg Gwyn 107 D5
Llandarcy Neath 40 B2
Llandawke Carms 56 A2
Llanddaniel Fab Anglesey 123 C4
Llanddarog Carms 57 A5
Llanddeiniol Ceredig 75 A4
Llanddeiniolen Gwyn 123 D5
Llandderfel Gwyn 109 B4
Llanddeusant Anglesey 122 B3
Llanddeusant Carms 59 C4
Llanddew Powys 77 D4
Llanddewi Swansea 57 D4
Llanddewi-Brefi Ceredig 75 C5
Llanddewi Rhydderch Mon 61 B5
Llanddewi Velfrey Pembs 56 A1

356 Lon – Man


Longridge Staffs 112 D3
Longridge W Loth 208 D2
Longriggend N Lnrk 207 C6
Longsdon Staffs 129 D4
Longshaw Gtr Man 136 C4
Longside Aberds 257 B5
Longstanton Cambs 85 A5
Longstock Hants 32 B2
Longstone Pembs 56 B1
Longstowe Cambs 85 B5
Longthorpe P'boro 100 B3
Longthwaite Cumb 164 C2
Longton Lancs 136 A3
Longton Stoke 112 A3
Longtown Cumb 175 B6
Longtown Hereford 61 A5
Longview Mers 136 D3
Longville in the Dale Shrops 94 B3
Longwick Bucks 66 C2
Longwitton Northumb 178 A2
Longwood Shrops 95 A4
Longworth Oxon 65 D4
Longyester E Loth 210 D2
Lonmay Aberds 269 D5
Lonmore Highld 258 D2
Looe Corn 6 B1
Loose Kent 37 A5
Loosley Row Bucks 66 C3
Lopcombe Corner Wilts 31 B6
Lopen Som 28 D4
Loppington Shrops 110 C3
Lopwell Devon 6 A3
Lorbottle Northumb 188 C3
Lorbottle Hall Northumb 188 C3
Lord's Cricket Ground London 49 A5
Lornty Perth 231 D5
Loscoe Derbys 114 A2
Losgaintir W Isles 287 E5
Lossiemouth Moray 266 B3
Lossit Argyll 200 C1
Lostford Shrops 111 B5
Lostock Gralam Ches 128 B1
Lostock Green Ches 128 B1
Lostock Hall Lancs 136 A4
Lostock Junction Gtr Man 137 C5
Lostwithiel Corn 5 B6
Loth Orkney 282 D7
Lothbeg Highld 274 C3
Lothersdale N Yorks 146 C3
Lothmore Highld 274 C3
Loudwater Bucks 67 D4
Loughborough Leics 114 D3
Loughor Swansea 57 C5
Loughton Essex 68 D4
Loughton M Keynes 83 D5
Loughton Shrops 95 C4
Louis Tussaud's Waxworks Blkpool 144 D3
Lound Lincs 116 D3
Lound Notts 132 A1
Lound Suff 105 B6
Lount Leics 114 D1
Louth Lincs 134 A3
Love Clough Lancs 137 A7
Lovedean Hants 33 D5
Lover Wilts 31 C6
Loversall S Yorks 140 D3
Loves Green Essex 69 C6
Lovesome Hill N Yorks 158 B2
Loveston Pembs 55 D6
Lovington Som 29 B5
Low Ackworth W Yorks 140 B2
Low Barlings Lincs 133 B5
Low Bentham N Yorks 145 A6
Low Bradfield S Yorks 139 D5
Low Bradley N Yorks 147 C4
Low Braithwaite Cumb 164 A2
Low Brunton Northumb 177 B7
Low Burnham N Lincs 141 C5
Low Burton N Yorks 157 C6
Low Buston Northumb 189 C5
Low Catton E Yorks 149 B6
Low Clanyard Dumfries 170 D3
Low Coniscliffe Darl 167 D5
Low Crosby Cumb 176 D2
Low Dalby N Yorks 160 C2
Low Dinsdale Darl 167 D6
Low Ellington N Yorks 157 C6
Low Etherley Durham 167 C4
Low Fell T & W 179 D4
Low Fulney Lincs 117 C5
Low Garth N Yorks 159 A6
Low Gate Northumb 177 C7
Low Grantley N Yorks 157 D6
Low Habberley Worcs 95 D6
Low Ham Som 28 C4
Low Hesket Cumb 164 A2
Low Hesleyhurst Northumb 188 D3
Low Hutton N Yorks 149 A6
Low Laithe N Yorks 147 A5
Low Leighton Derbys 129 A5
Low Lorton Cumb 163 B4
Low Marishes N Yorks 159 D7
Low Marnham Notts 132 C3
Low Mill N Yorks 159 B5
Low Moor Lancs 146 C1
Low Moor W Yorks 139 A4
Low Moorsley T & W 167 A6
Low Newton Cumb 154 C3
Low Newton-by-the-Sea Northumb 189 A5
Low Row Cumb 163 A6
Low Row Cumb 176 C3
Low Row N Yorks 156 B3
Low Salchrie Dumfries 170 A2
Low Smerby Argyll 190 C3
Low Torry Fife 208 B3
Low Worsall N Yorks 158 A2
Low Wray Cumb 154 A2
Lowbridge House Cumb 154 A4
Lowca Cumb 162 B2
Lowdham Notts 115 A4
Lowe Shrops 111 B4
Lowe Hill Staffs 129 D4
Lower Aisholt Som 28 B2
Lower Arncott Oxon 65 B7
Lower Ashton Devon 12 C3
Lower Assendon Oxon 47 A5
Lower Badcall Highld 276 D2
Lower Bartle Lancs 145 D4
Lower Basildon W Berks 47 B4
Lower Beeding W Sus 35 D5
Lower Benefield Northants 100 C1
Lower Boddington Northants 82 B1
Lower Brailes Warks 81 D6
Lower Breakish Highld 247 B5
Lower Broadheath Worcs 79 B6
Lower Bullingham Hereford 78 D3
Lower Cam Glos 62 C3
Lower Chapel Powys 76 D4
Lower Chute Wilts 45 D7
Lower Cragabus Argyll 200 D3
Lower Crossings Derbys 129 A5
Lower Cumberworth W Yorks 139 C5
Lower Cwm-twrch Powys 59 D4
Lower Darwen Blkburn 137 A5
Lower Dean Beds 84 A2
Lower Diabaig Highld 261 D4
Lower Dicker E Sus 22 A3
Lower Dinchope Shrops 94 C2
Lower Down Shrops 94 C1
Lower Drift Corn 2 C2
Lower Dunsforth N Yorks 148 A3
Lower Egleton Hereford 79 C4
Lower Elkstone Staffs 129 D5
Lower End Beds 67 A4
Lower Everleigh Wilts 45 D5
Lower Farringdon Hants 33 B6
Lower Foxdale I o M 152 D2
Lower Frankton Shrops 110 B2
Lower Froyle Hants 33 A6
Lower Gledfield Highld 264 A1
Lower Green Norf 120 B1
Lower Hacheston Suff 88 B4
Lower Halistra Highld 258 C2
Lower Halstow Kent 51 C5
Lower Hardres Kent 52 D3
Lower Hawthwaite Cumb 153 B3
Lower Heath Ches 128 C3
Lower Hempriggs Moray 266 C2
Lower Hergest Hereford 77 B6
Lower Heyford Oxon 65 A5
Lower Higham Kent 51 B4
Lower Holbrook Suff 88 D2
Lower Hordley Shrops 110 C2
Lower Horsebridge E Sus 22 A3
Lower Killeyan Argyll 200 D2
Lower Kingswood Sur 35 A5
Lower Kinnerton Ches 126 C3
Lower Langford N Som 42 C3
Lower Largo Fife 220 D4
Lower Leigh Staffs 112 B4
Lower Lemington Glos 81 D5
Lower Lenie Highld 251 D7
Lower Lydbrook Glos 62 B1
Lower Lye Hereford 78 A2
Lower Machen Newport 42 A1
Lower Maes-coed Hereford 78 D1
Lower Mayland Essex 70 C3
Lower Midway Derbys 113 C7
Lower Milovaig Highld 258 C1
Lower Moor Worcs 80 C2
Lower Nazeing Essex 68 C3
Lower Netchwood Shrops 95 B4
Lower Ollach Highld 247 A4
Lower Penarth V Glam 41 D6
Lower Penn Staffs 95 B6
Lower Pennington Hants 18 B2
Lower Peover Ches 128 B2
Lower Pexhill Ches 128 B3
Lower Place Gtr Man 138 B2
Lower Quinton Warks 81 C4
Lower Rochford Worcs 79 A4
Lower Seagry Wilts 44 A3
Lower Shelton Beds 84 C1
Lower Shiplake Oxon 47 B5
Lower Shuckburgh Warks 82 A1
Lower Slaughter Glos 64 A2
Lower Stanton St Quintin Wilts 44 A3
Lower Stoke Medway 51 B5
Lower Stondon Beds 84 D3
Lower Stow Bedon Norf 103 B5
Lower Street Norf 121 B4
Lower Street Norf 121 D5
Lower Strensham Worcs 80 C2
Lower Stretton Warr 127 A6
Lower Sundon Beds 67 A5
Lower Swanwick Hants 18 A3
Lower Swell Glos 64 A2
Lower Tean Staffs 112 B4
Lower Thurlton Norf 105 B5
Lower Tote Highld 259 B5
Lower Town Pembs 72 C2
Lower Tysoe Warks 81 C6
Lower Upham Hants 32 D4
Lower Vexford Som 27 B6
Lower Weare Som 42 D3
Lower Welson Hereford 77 B6
Lower Whitley Ches 127 B6
Lower Wield Hants 33 A5
Lower Winchendon Bucks 66 B2
Lower Withington Ches 128 C3
Lower Woodend Bucks 47 A6
Lower Woodford Wilts 31 B5
Lower Wyche Worcs 79 C5
Lowesby Leics 99 A4
Lowestoft Suff 105 B6
Loweswater Cumb 163 B4
Lowford Hants 32 D3
Lowgill Cumb 155 B5
Lowgill Lancs 145 A6
Lowick Northants 100 C1
Lowick Northumb 198 C4
Lowick Bridge Cumb 154 C1
Lowick Green Cumb 154 C1
Lowlands Torf 61 D4
Lowmoor Row Cumb 165 C4
Lownie Moor Angus 232 D2
Lowsonford Warks 81 A4
Lowther Cumb 164 C3
Lowthorpe E Yorks 150 A3
Lowton Gtr Man 137 D5
Lowton Common Gtr Man 137 D5
Loxbeare Devon 27 D4
Loxhill Sur 34 C3
Loxhore Devon 25 B7
Loxley Warks 81 B5
Loxton N Som 42 D2
Loxwood W Sus 34 C3
Lubcroy Highld 271 D6
Lubenham Leics 99 C4
Luccombe Som 27 A4
Luccombe Village I o W 19 D4
Lucker Northumb 199 C5
Luckett Corn 11 D4
Luckington Wilts 44 A2
Lucklawhill Fife 220 B4
Luckwell Bridge Som 27 B4
Lucton Hereford 78 A2
Ludag W Isles 286 E3
Ludborough Lincs 143 D4
Ludchurch Pembs 56 A1
Luddenden W Yorks 138 A3
Luddenden Foot W Yorks 138 A3
Luddesdown Kent 50 C3
Luddington N Lincs 141 B6
Luddington Warks 81 B4
Luddington in the Brook Northants 100 C3
Lude House Perth 230 B2
Ludford Lincs 134 A2
Ludford Shrops 94 D3
Ludgershall Bucks 66 B1
Ludgershall Wilts 45 D6
Ludgvan Corn 2 B3
Ludham Norf 121 D5
Ludlow Shrops 94 D3
Ludlow Racecourse Shrops 94 D2
Ludwell Wilts 30 C3
Ludworth Durham 167 A6
Luffincott Devon 10 B4
Lugar E Ayrs 193 C5
Lugg Green Hereford 78 A2
Luggate Burn E Loth 210 C3
Luggiebank N Lnrk 207 C5
Lugton E Ayrs 205 C4
Lugwardine Hereford 78 C3
Luib Highld 247 B4
Lulham Hereford 78 C2
Lullenden Sur 36 B2
Lullington Derbys 113 D6
Lullington Som 44 D1
Lulsgate Bottom N Som 43 C4
Lulsley Worcs 79 B5
Lulworth Castle Dorset 16 C2
Lumb W Yorks 138 A3
Lumby N Yorks 148 D3
Lumloch E Dunb 205 B6
Lumphanan Aberds 244 B2
Lumphinnans Fife 209 A4
Lumsdaine Borders 211 D5
Lumsden Aberds 255 D5
Lunan Angus 233 C4
Lunanhead Angus 232 C2
Luncarty Perth 219 B5
Lund E Yorks 150 C2
Lund N Yorks 149 D5
Lund Shetland 284 C7
Lunderton Aberds 269 E6
Lundie Angus 220 A2
Lundie Highld 239 A5
Lundin Links Fife 220 D4
Lunga Argyll 213 B5
Lunna Shetland 284 G6
Lunning Shetland 284 G7
Lunnon Swansea 57 D5
Lunsford's Cross E Sus 23 A5
Lunt Mers 136 C2
Luntley Hereford 78 B1
Luppitt Devon 13 A6
Lupset W Yorks 139 B6
Lupton Cumb 155 C4
Lurgashall W Sus 34 D2
Lusby Lincs 134 C3
Luson Devon 7 C5
Luss Argyll 206 A1
Lussagiven Argyll 213 D4
Lusta Highld 258 C3
Lustleigh Devon 12 C2
Luston Hereford 78 A2
Luthermuir Aberds 233 B4
Luthrie Fife 220 C3
Luton Devon 13 D4
Luton Luton 67 A5
Luton Medway 51 C4
Lutterworth Leics 98 C2
Lutton Devon 7 B4
Lutton Lincs 118 C1
Lutton Northants 100 C3
Lutworthy Devon 26 D2
Luxborough Som 27 B4
Luxulyan Corn 5 B5
Lybster Highld 275 A6
Lydbury North Shrops 94 C1
Lydcott Devon 26 B1
Lydd Kent 38 C2
Lydd on Sea Kent 38 C2
Lydden Kent 39 A4
Lydden Motor Racing Circuit Kent 39 A4
Lyddington Rutland 99 B5
Lyde Green Hants 47 D5
Lydeard St Lawrence Som 27 B6
Lydford Devon 11 C6
Lydford-on-Fosse Som 29 B5
Lydgate W Yorks 138 A2
Lydham Shrops 94 B1
Lydiard Green Wilts 45 A4
Lydiard Millicent Wilts 45 A4
Lydiate Mers 136 C2
Lydlinch Dorset 30 D1
Lydney Glos 62 C2
Lydstep Pembs 55 E6
Lye W Mid 96 C2
Lye Cross N Som 42 C3
Lye Green Bucks 67 C4
Lye Green E Sus 36 C3
Lyford Oxon 65 D4
Lymbridge Green Kent 38 A3
Lyme Park, Disley Ches 129 A4
Lyme Regis Dorset 14 B3
Lyminge Kent 38 A3
Lymington Hants 18 B2
Lyminster W Sus 20 B3
Lymm Warr 128 A1
Lymore Hants 18 B1
Lympne Kent 38 B3
Lympsham Som 42 D2
Lympstone Devon 13 C4
Lynchat Highld 241 B5
Lyndale Ho. Highld 258 C3
Lyndhurst Hants 18 A2
Lyndon Rutland 99 A6
Lyne Sur 48 C3
Lyne Down Hereford 79 D4
Lyne of Gorthleck Highld 252 D1
Lyne of Skene Aberds 245 A4
Lyneal Shrops 110 B3
Lyneham Oxon 64 A3
Lyneham Wilts 44 B4
Lynemore Highld 253 D6
Lynemouth Northumb 189 D5
Lyness Orkney 283 H4
Lyng Norf 120 D2
Lyng Som 28 C3
Lynmouth Devon 26 A2
Lynsted Kent 51 C6
Lynton Devon 26 A2
Lynton & Lynmouth Cliff Railway Devon 26 A2
Lyon's Gate Dorset 15 A6
Lyonshall Hereford 78 B1
Lytchett Matravers Dorset 16 B3
Lytchett Minster Dorset 16 B3
Lyth Highld 281 B4
Lytham Lancs 136 A2
Lytham St Anne's Lancs 136 A2
Lythe N Yorks 169 D6
Lythes Orkney 283 K5

## M

Mabe Burnthouse Corn 4 D2
Mabie Dumfries 174 A2
Mablethorpe Lincs 135 A5
Macclesfield Ches 129 B4
Macclesfield Forest Ches 129 B4
Macduff Aberds 268 C2
Mace Green Suff 88 C2
Macharioch Argyll 190 E3
Machen Caerph 41 C7
Machrihanish Argyll 190 C2
Machynlleth Powys 91 B5
Machynys Carms 57 C5
Mackerel's Common W Sus 34 D3
Mackworth Derbys 113 B7
Macmerry E Loth 210 C1
Madame Tussaud's and Planetarium London 49 B5
Madderty Perth 219 B4
Maddiston Falk 208 C2
Madehurst W Sus 20 A2
Madeley Staffs 111 A6
Madeley Telford 95 A4
Madeley Heath Staffs 112 A1
Madeley Park Staffs 112 A1
Madingley Cambs 85 A5
Madley Hereford 78 D2
Madresfield Worcs 79 C6
Madron Corn 2 B2
Maen-y-groes Ceredig 73 A6
Maenaddwyn Anglesey 123 B4
Maenclochog Pembs 55 B6
Maendy V Glam 41 D5
Maentwrog Gwyn 107 B6
Maer Staffs 112 B1
Maerdy Conwy 109 A5
Maerdy Rhondda 41 B4
Maes-Treylow Powys 77 A6
Maesbrook Shrops 110 C1
Maesbury Shrops 110 C2
Maesbury Marsh Shrops 110 C2
Maesgwyn-Isaf Powys 109 D6
Maesgwynne Carms 73 D5
Maeshafn Denb 126 C2
Maesllyn Ceredig 73 B6
Maesmynis Powys 76 C4
Maesteg Bridgend 40 B3
Maestir Ceredig 75 D4
Maesy cwmmer Caerph 41 B6
Maesybont Carms 57 A5
Maesycrugiau Carms 58 A1
Maesymeillion Ceredig 73 B7
Magdalen Laver Essex 69 C5
Maggieknockater Moray 254 B4
Magham Down E Sus 22 A4
Maghull Mers 136 C2
Magna Science Adventure Centre, Rotherham S Yorks 140 D2
Magor Mon 42 A3
Magpie Green Suff 104 D1
Maiden Bradley Wilts 30 B2
Maiden Law Durham 167 A4
Maiden Newton Dorset 15 B5
Maiden Wells Pembs 55 E5
Maidencombe Torbay 8 A3
Maidenhall Suff 88 C2
Maidenhead Windsor 48 A1
Maidens S Ayrs 192 E2
Maiden's Green Brack 48 B1
Maidensgrave Suff 88 C3
Maidenwell Corn 10 D2
Maidenwell Lincs 134 B3
Maidford Northants 82 B3
Maids Moreton Bucks 83 D4
Maidstone Kent 37 A5
Maidwell Northants 99 D4
Mail Shetland 285 L6
Main Powys 109 D6
Maindee Newport 42 A2
Mains of Airies Dumfries 170 A1
Mains of Allardice Aberds 233 A6
Mains of Annochie Aberds 257 B4
Mains of Ardestie Angus 221 A5
Mains of Balhall Angus 232 B3
Mains of Ballindarg Angus 232 C2
Mains of Balnakettle Aberds 233 A4
Mains of Birness Aberds 257 C4
Mains of Burgie Moray 266 D1
Mains of Clunas Highld 253 B4
Mains of Crichie Aberds 257 B4
Mains of Dalvey Highld 254 C2
Mains of Dellavaird Aberds 245 D4
Mains of Drum Aberds 245 C5
Mains of Edingight Moray 267 D6
Mains of Fedderate Aberds 268 E3
Mains of Inkhorn Aberds 257 C4
Mains of Mayen Moray 255 B6
Mains of Melgund Angus 232 C3
Mains of Thornton Aberds 233 A4
Mains of Watten Highld 281 C4
Mainsforth Durham 167 B6
Mainsriddle Dumfries 174 C2
Mainstone Shrops 93 C6
Maisemore Glos 63 A4
Malacleit W Isles 287 G2
Malborough Devon 7 D6
Malcoff Derbys 129 A5
Maldon Essex 70 C2
Malham N Yorks 146 A3
Maligar Highld 259 B4
Mallaig Highld 235 A5
Malleny Mills Edin 209 D4
Malling Stirl 217 D5
Mallory Park Motor Racing Circuit Leics 98 A1
Malltraeth Anglesey 123 D4
Mallwyd Gwyn 91 A6
Malmesbury Wilts 44 A3
Malmsmead Devon 26 A2
Malpas Ches 110 A3
Malpas Corn 4 C3
Malpas Newport 61 D5
Malswick Glos 62 A3
Maltby Stockton 168 D2
Maltby S Yorks 140 D3
Maltby le Marsh Lincs 135 A4
Malting Green Essex 70 A3
Maltman's Hill Kent 37 B7
Malton N Yorks 159 D6
Malvern Link Worcs 79 C5
Malvern Wells Worcs 79 C5
Mamble Worcs 95 D4
Man-moel Caerph 41 A6
Manaccan Corn 3 C5
Manafon Powys 93 A5
Manar Ho. Aberds 256 D2
Manaton Devon 12 C2
Manby Lincs 134 A3
Mancetter Warks 97 B6
Manchester Gtr Man 138 D1
Manchester Airport Gtr Man 128 A3
Manchester National Velodrome Gtr Man 138 D1
Mancot Flint 126 C3
Mandally Highld 239 B6
Manea Cambs 101 C6
Manfield N Yorks 167 D5
Mangaster Shetland 284 F5
Mangotsfield S Glos 43 B5
Mangurstadh W Isles 287 A5
Mankinholes W Yorks 138 A2
Manley Ches 127 B5
Mannal Argyll 222 C2
Mannerston W Loth 208 C3
Manningford Bohune Wilts 45 D5
Manningford Bruce Wilts 45 D5
Manningham W Yorks 147 D5
Mannings Heath W Sus 35 D5
Mannington Dorset 17 A4
Manningtree Essex 88 D1
Mannofield Aberdeen 245 B6
Manor Estate S Yorks 130 A3
Manor Park London 50 A1
Manorbier Pembs 55 E6
Manordeilo Carms 58 C3
Manorhill Borders 197 C5
Manorowen Pembs 72 C2
Mansel Lacy Hereford 78 C2
Manselfield Swansea 57 D5
Mansell Gamage Hereford 78 C1
Mansergh Cumb 155 C5
Mansfield E Ayrs 182 A4
Mansfield Notts 131 C5
Mansfield Woodhouse Notts 131 C5
Mansriggs Cumb 154 C1
Manston Dorset 30 D2
Manston Kent 53 C5
Manston W Yorks 148 D2
Manswood Dorset 16 A3
Manthorpe Lincs 116 D3
Manthorpe Lincs 116 B2
Manton N Lincs 142 C1
Manton Notts 131 B5
Manton Rutland 99 A5
Manton Wilts 45 C5
Manuden Essex 69 A4

Norwell Woodhouse Notts 132 C2
Norwich Norf 104 A3
Norwich Castle Museum Norf 104 A3
Norwich Cathedral Norf 104 A3
Norwich International Airport Norf 120 D4
Norwick Shetland 284 B8
Norwood Derbys 131 A4
Norwood Hill Sur 35 B5
Norwoodside Cambs 101 B6
Noseley Leics 99 B4
Noss Shetland 285 M5
Noss Mayo Devon 7 C4
Nosterfield N Yorks 157 C6
Nostie Highld 249 D5
Notgrove Glos 64 A2
Nothe Fort, Weymouth Dorset 15 D6
Nottage Bridgend 40 D3
Nottingham Nottingham 114 B3
Nottingham Castle Museum Nottingham 114 B3
Nottingham East Midlands Airport Leics 114 C2
Nottingham Racecourse Nottingham 114 B3
Nottington Dorset 15 C6
Notton Wilts 44 C3
Notton W Yorks 139 B6
Nounsley Essex 70 B1
Noutard's Green Worcs 79 A5
Novar House Highld 264 D2
Nox Shrops 110 D3
Nuffield Oxon 47 A4
Nun Hills Lancs 138 A1
Nun Monkton N Yorks 148 B4
Nunburnholme E Yorks 150 C1
Nuncargate Notts 131 D5
Nuneaton Warks 97 B6
Nuneham Courtenay Oxon 65 D6
Nunney Som 30 A1
Nunnington N Yorks 159 D5
Nunnykirk Northumb 188 D3
Nunsthorpe NE Lincs 143 C4
Nunthorpe M'bro 168 D3
Nunthorpe York 149 B5
Nunton Wilts 31 C5
Nunwick N Yorks 157 D7
Nupend Glos 62 C3
Nursling Hants 32 D2
Nursted Hants 33 C6
Nutbourne W Sus 20 A3
Nutbourne W Sus 19 A6
Nutfield Sur 35 A6
Nuthall Notts 114 A3
Nuthampstead Herts 85 D6
Nuthurst W Sus 35 D4
Nutley E Sus 36 D2
Nutley Hants 33 A5
Nutwell S Yorks 140 C4
Nybster Highld 281 B5
Nyetimber W Sus 20 C1
Nyewood W Sus 33 C7
Nymans Garden, Crawley W Sus 35 D5
Nymet Rowland Devon 12 A2
Nymet Tracey Devon 12 A2
Nympsfield Glos 63 C4
Nynehead Som 27 C6
Nyton W Sus 20 B2

## O

Oad Street Kent 51 C5
Oadby Leics 98 A3
Oak Cross Devon 11 B6
Oakamoor Staffs 113 A4
Oakbank W Loth 208 D3
Oakdale Caerph 41 B6
Oake Som 27 C6
Oaken Staffs 95 A6
Oakenclough Lancs 145 C5
Oakengates Telford 111 D6
Oakenholt Flint 126 B2
Oakenshaw Durham 167 B5
Oakenshaw W Yorks 139 A4
Oakerthorpe Derbys 130 D3
Oakes W Yorks 139 B4
Oakfield Torf 61 D5
Oakford Ceredig 74 C3
Oakford Devon 27 C4
Oakfordbridge Devon 27 C4
Oakgrove Ches 129 C4
Oakham Rutland 99 A5
Oakhanger Hants 33 B6
Oakhill Som 29 A6
Oakhurst Kent 36 A3
Oakington Cambs 85 A6
Oaklands Herts 68 B2
Oaklands Powys 76 B4
Oakle Street Glos 62 B3
Oakley Beds 84 B2
Oakley Bucks 66 B1
Oakley Fife 208 B3
Oakley Hants 46 D3
Oakley Oxon 66 C2
Oakley Poole 17 B4
Oakley Suff 104 D2
Oakley Green Windsor 48 B2
Oakley Park Powys 92 C3
Oakmere Ches 127 C5
Oakridge Glos 63 C5
Oakridge Hants 47 D4
Oaks Shrops 94 A2
Oaks Green Derbys 113 B5
Oaksey Wilts 63 D5
Oakthorpe Leics 113 D7
Oakwood Adventure Park, Narberth Pembs 55 C6
Oakwoodhill Sur 35 C4
Oakworth W Yorks 147 D4
Oape Highld 272 D2
Oare Kent 52 C2
Oare Som 26 A3
Oare W Berks 46 B3
Oare Wilts 45 C5
Oasby Lincs 116 B3
Oathlaw Angus 232 C2
Oatlands N Yorks 148 B2
Oban Argyll 226 D3
Oban Highld 238 D2
Oborne Dorset 29 D6
Obthorpe Lincs 116 D3
Occlestone Green Ches 128 C1
Occold Suff 104 D2
Ocean Beach Amusement Park, Rhyl Denb 125 A4
Ochiltree E Ayrs 193 C5
Ochtermuthill Perth 218 C3
Ochtertyre Perth 218 B3
Ockbrook Derbys 114 B2
Ockham Sur 34 A3
Ockle Highld 235 C4
Ockley Sur 35 C4
Ocle Pychard Hereford 78 C3
Octon E Yorks 150 A3
Octon Cross Roads E Yorks 150 A3
Odcombe Som 29 D5
Odd Down Bath 43 C6
Oddendale Cumb 164 D3
Odder Lincs 133 B4
Oddingley Worcs 80 B2
Oddington Glos 64 A3
Oddington Oxon 65 B6
Odell Beds 83 B6
Odie Orkney 282 E7
Odiham Hants 47 D5
Odstock Wilts 31 C5
Odstone Leics 97 A6
Offchurch Warks 81 A6
Offenham Worcs 80 C3
Offham E Sus 22 A1
Offham Kent 37 A4
Offham W Sus 20 B3
Offord Cluny Cambs 84 A4
Offord Darcy Cambs 84 A4
Offton Suff 87 C6
Offwell Devon 14 B1
Ogbourne Maizey Wilts 45 B5
Ogbourne St Andrew Wilts 45 B5
Ogbourne St George Wilts 45 B6
Ogil Angus 232 B2
Ogle Northumb 178 B3
Ogmore V Glam 40 D3
Ogmore-by-Sea V Glam 40 D3
Ogmore Vale Bridgend 40 B4
Okeford Fitzpaine Dorset 30 D2
Okehampton Devon 11 B6
Okehampton Camp Devon 11 B6
Okraquoy Shetland 285 K6
Old Northants 99 D4
Old Aberdeen Aberdeen 245 B6
Old Alresford Hants 33 B4
Old Arley Warks 97 B5
Old Basford Nottingham 114 A3
Old Basing Hants 47 D4
Old Bewick Northumb 188 A3
Old Blacksmith's Shop Centre, Gretna Green Dumfries 175 B6
Old Bolingbroke Lincs 134 C3
Old Bramhope W Yorks 147 C6
Old Brampton Derbys 130 B3
Old Bridge of Tilt Perth 230 B2
Old Bridge of Urr Dumfries 173 B5
Old Buckenham Norf 103 B6
Old Burghclere Hants 46 D2
Old Byland N Yorks 159 C4
Old Cassop Durham 167 B6
Old Castleton Borders 186 D4
Old Catton Norf 120 D4
Old Clee NE Lincs 143 C4
Old Cleeve Som 27 A5
Old Clipstone Notts 131 C6
Old Colwyn Conwy 124 B3
Old Coulsdon London 35 A6
Old Crombie Aberds 267 D6
Old Dailly S Ayrs 181 B4
Old Dalby Leics 115 C4
Old Deer Aberds 257 B4
Old Denaby S Yorks 140 D2
Old Edlington S Yorks 140 D3
Old Eldon Durham 167 C5
Old Ellerby E Yorks 151 D4
Old Felixstowe Suff 88 D4
Old Fletton P'boro 100 B3
Old Glossop Derbys 138 D3
Old Goole E Yorks 141 A5
Old Hall Powys 91 D7
Old Heath Essex 71 A4
Old Heathfield E Sus 36 D3
Old Hill W Mid 96 C2
Old House, Rochford Essex 70 D2
Old Hunstanton Norf 118 A3
Old Hurst Cambs 101 D4
Old Hutton Cumb 155 C4
Old Kea Corn 4 C3
Old Kilpatrick W Dunb 205 A4
Old Kinnernie Aberds 245 B4
Old Knebworth Herts 68 A2
Old Langho Lancs 145 D7
Old Laxey I o M 152 C4
Old Leake Lincs 135 D4
Old Malton N Yorks 159 D6
Old Micklefield W Yorks 148 D3
Old Milton Hants 17 B6
Old Milverton Warks 81 A5
Old Monkland N Lnrk 207 D5
Old Netley Hants 18 A3
Old Philpstoun W Loth 208 C3
Old Quarrington Durham 167 B6
Old Radnor Powys 77 B6
Old Rattray Aberds 269 D5
Old Rayne Aberds 256 D1
Old Romney Kent 38 C2
Old Sarum, Salisbury Wilts 31 B5
Old Sodbury S Glos 43 A6
Old Somerby Lincs 116 B2
Old Stratford Northants 83 C4
Old Thirsk N Yorks 158 C3
Old Town Cumb 164 A2
Old Town Cumb 155 C4
Old Town Northumb 188 D1
Old Town Scilly 2 E4
Old Trafford Gtr Man 137 D7
Old Tupton Derbys 130 C3
Old Warden Beds 84 C3
Old Weston Cambs 100 D2
Old Whittington Derbys 130 B3
Old Wick Highld 281 C5
Old Windsor Windsor 48 B2
Old Wives Lees Kent 52 D2
Old Woking Sur 34 A3
Old Woodhall Lincs 134 C2
Oldany Highld 270 A4
Oldberrow Warks 80 A4
Oldborough Devon 12 A2
Oldbury Shrops 95 B5
Oldbury Warks 97 B6
Oldbury W Mid 96 C2
Oldbury-on-Severn S Glos 62 D2
Oldbury on the Hill Glos 44 A2
Oldcastle Bridgend 40 D4
Oldcastle Mon 61 A5
Oldcotes Notts 131 A5
Oldfallow Staffs 112 D3
Oldfield Worcs 79 A6
Oldford Som 44 D1
Oldham Gtr Man 138 C2
Oldhamstocks E Loth 211 C4
Oldland S Glos 43 B5
Oldmeldrum Aberds 256 D3
Oldshore Beg Highld 276 C2
Oldshoremore Highld 276 C3
Oldstead N Yorks 158 C4
Oldtown Aberds 255 D6
Oldtown of Ord Aberds 267 D7
Oldway Swansea 57 D5
Oldways End Devon 26 C3
Oldwhat Aberds 268 D3
Olgrinmore Highld 280 C2
Oliver's Battery Hants 32 C3
Ollaberry Shetland 284 E5
Ollerton Ches 128 B2
Ollerton Notts 131 C6
Ollerton Shrops 111 C5
Olmarch Ceredig 75 C5
Olney M Keynes 83 B5
Olrig Ho. Highld 280 B3
Olton W Mid 96 C4
Olveston S Glos 43 A5
Olwen Ceredig 75 D4
Ombersley Worcs 79 A6
Ompton Notts 132 C1
Onchan I o M 152 D3
Onecote Staffs 129 D5
Onen Mon 61 B6
Ongar Hill Norf 118 C2
Ongar Street Hereford 78 A1
Onibury Shrops 94 D2
Onich Highld 237 C4
Onllwyn Neath 59 D5
Onneley Staffs 111 A6
Onslow Village Sur 34 B2
Onthank E Ayrs 205 D4
Openwoodgate Derbys 114 A1
Opinan Highld 261 A5
Opinan Highld 261 C4
Orange Lane Borders 198 B1
Orange Row Norf 118 C2
Orasaigh W Isles 288 F4
Orbliston Moray 266 D4
Orbost Highld 258 D2
Orby Lincs 135 C4
Orchard Hill Devon 25 C5
Orchard Portman Som 28 C2
Orcheston Wilts 31 A4
Orcop Hereford 61 A6
Orcop Hill Hereford 61 A6
Ord Highld 247 C5
Ordhead Aberds 244 A3
Ordie Aberds 244 B1
Ordiequish Moray 266 D4
Ordsall Notts 132 A1
Ore E Sus 23 A6
Oreton Shrops 95 C4
Orford Suff 89 C5
Orford Warr 137 D5
Orgreave Staffs 113 D5
Orlestone Kent 38 B1
Orleton Hereford 78 A2
Orleton Worcs 79 A4
Orlingbury Northants 99 D5
Ormesby Redcar 168 D3
Ormesby St Margaret Norf 121 D6
Ormesby St Michael Norf 121 D6
Ormiclate Castle W Isles 286 C3
Ormiscaig Highld 261 A5
Ormiston E Loth 209 D7
Ormsaigbeg Highld 234 D3
Ormsaigmore Highld 234 D3
Ormsary Argyll 202 A2
Ormsgill Cumb 153 C2
Ormskirk Lancs 136 C3
Orpington London 50 C1
Orrell Gtr Man 136 C4
Orrell Mers 136 D2
Orrisdale I o M 152 B3
Orroland Dumfries 173 D5
Orsett Thurrock 50 A3
Orslow Staffs 112 D2
Orston Notts 115 A5
Orthwaite Cumb 163 A5
Ortner Lancs 145 B5
Orton Cumb 155 A5
Orton Northants 99 D5
Orton Longueville P'boro 100 B3
Orton-on-the-Hill Leics 97 A6
Orton Waterville P'boro 100 B3
Orwell Cambs 85 B5
Osbaldeston Lancs 145 D6
Osbaldwick York 149 B5
Osbaston Shrops 110 C2
Osborne House I o W 18 B4
Osbournby Lincs 116 B3
Oscroft Ches 127 C5
Ose Highld 258 D3
Osgathorpe Leics 114 D2
Osgodby Lincs 142 D2
Osgodby N Yorks 149 D5
Osgodby N Yorks 161 C4
Oskaig Highld 248 C2
Oskamull Argyll 224 B3
Osmaston Derbys 113 A6
Osmaston Derby 114 B1
Osmington Dorset 16 C1
Osmington Mills Dorset 16 C1
Osmotherley N Yorks 158 B3
Ospisdale Highld 264 B3
Ospringe Kent 52 C2
Ossett W Yorks 139 A5
Ossington Notts 132 C2
Ostend Essex 70 D3
Oswaldkirk N Yorks 159 D5
Oswaldtwistle Lancs 137 A6
Oswestry Shrops 110 C1
Otford Kent 36 A3
Otham Kent 37 A5
Othery Som 28 B3
Otley Suff 88 B3
Otley W Yorks 147 C6
Otter Ferry Argyll 214 D2
Otterbourne Hants 32 C3
Otterburn Northumb 188 D1
Otterburn N Yorks 146 B2
Otterburn Camp Northumb 188 D1
Otterham Corn 10 B2
Otterhampton Som 28 A2
Ottershaw Sur 48 C3
Otterswick Shetland 284 E7
Otterton Devon 13 C5
Ottery St Mary Devon 13 B6
Ottinge Kent 38 A3
Ottringham E Yorks 143 A4
Oughterby Cumb 175 C5
Oughtershaw N Yorks 156 C2
Oughterside Cumb 174 D4
Oughtibridge S Yorks 139 D6
Oughtrington Warr 128 A1
Oulston N Yorks 158 D4
Oulton Cumb 175 C5
Oulton Norf 120 C3
Oulton Staffs 112 B3
Oulton Suff 105 B6
Oulton W Yorks 139 A6
Oulton Broad Suff 105 B6
Oulton Park Motor Racing Circuit Ches 127 C5
Oulton Street Norf 120 C3
Oundle Northants 100 C2
Ousby Cumb 165 B4
Ousdale Highld 275 B4
Ousden Suff 86 B3
Ousefleet E Yorks 141 A6
Ouston Durham 179 D4
Ouston Northumb 178 B2
Out Newton E Yorks 143 A5
Out Rawcliffe Lancs 144 C4
Outertown Orkney 282 F3
Outgate Cumb 154 B2
Outhgill Cumb 155 A6
Outlane W Yorks 138 B3
Outwell Norf 101 A7
Outwick Hants 31 D5
Outwood Sur 35 B6
Outwood W Yorks 139 A6
Outwoods Staffs 112 D1
Ovenden W Yorks 138 A3
Ovenscloss Borders 196 C3
Over Cambs 101 D5
Over Ches 127 C6
Over S Glos 43 A4
Over Compton Dorset 29 D5
Over Green W Mid 97 B4
Over Haddon Derbys 130 C2
Over Hulton Gtr Man 137 C5
Over Kellet Lancs 154 D4
Over Kiddington Oxon 65 A5
Over Knutsford Ches 128 B2
Over Monnow Mon 61 B7
Over Norton Oxon 64 A4
Over Peover Ches 128 B2
Over Silton N Yorks 158 B3
Over Stowey Som 28 B1
Over Stratton Som 28 D4
Over Tabley Ches 128 A2
Over Wallop Hants 32 B1
Over Whitacre Warks 97 B5
Over Worton Oxon 65 A5
Overbister Orkney 282 C7
Overbury Worcs 80 D2
Overcombe Dorset 15 C6
Overgreen Derbys 130 B3
Overleigh Som 29 B4
Overley Green Warks 80 B3
Overpool Ches 126 B3
Overscaig Hotel Highld 271 B7
Overseal Derbys 113 D6
Oversland Kent 52 D2
Overstone Northants 83 A5
Overstrand Norf 120 A4
Overthorpe Northants 82 C1
Overton Aberdeen 245 A5
Overton Ches 127 B5
Overton Dumfries 174 B2
Overton Hants 32 A4
Overton Lancs 144 B4
Overton N Yorks 149 B4
Overton Shrops 94 D3
Overton Swansea 57 D4
Overton W Yorks 139 B5
Overton = Owrtyn Wrex 110 A2
Overton Bridge Wrex 110 A2
Overtown N Lnrk 194 A3
Oving Bucks 66 A2
Oving W Sus 20 B2
Ovingdean Brighton 21 B6
Ovingham Northumb 178 C2
Ovington Durham 166 D4
Ovington Essex 86 C3
Ovington Hants 33 B4
Ovington Norf 103 A5
Ovington Northumb 178 C2
Ower Hants 32 D2
Owermoigne Dorset 16 C1
Owlbury Shrops 93 B7
Owler Bar Derbys 130 B2
Owlerton S Yorks 130 A3
Owl's Green Suff 88 A3
Owlswick Bucks 66 C2
Owmby Lincs 142 C2
Owmby-by-Spital Lincs 133 A5
Owrtyn = Overton Wrex 110 A2
Owslebury Hants 32 C4
Owston Leics 99 A4
Owston S Yorks 140 B3
Owston Ferry N Lincs 141 C6
Owstwick E Yorks 151 D5
Owthorne E Yorks 143 A5
Owthorpe Notts 115 B4
Oxborough Norf 102 A3
Oxburgh Hall Norf 102 A3
Oxcombe Lincs 134 B3
Oxen Park Cumb 154 C2
Oxenholme Cumb 154 C4
Oxenhope W Yorks 147 D4
Oxenton Glos 80 D2
Oxenwood Wilts 45 D7
Oxford Oxon 65 C6
Oxford University Botanic Garden Oxon 65 C6
Oxhey Herts 67 D6
Oxhill Warks 81 C6
Oxley W Mid 96 A2
Oxley Green Essex 70 B3
Oxley's Green E Sus 37 D4
Oxnam Borders 187 B6
Oxshott Sur 48 C4
Oxspring S Yorks 139 C5
Oxted Sur 36 A1
Oxton Borders 196 A3
Oxton Notts 131 D6
Oxwich Swansea 57 D4
Oxwick Norf 119 C6
Oykel Bridge Highld 271 D6
Oyne Aberds 256 D1

## P

Pabail Iarach W Isles 288 D6
Pabail Uarach W Isles 288 D6
Pace Gate N Yorks 147 B5
Packington Leics 114 D1
Padanaram Angus 232 C2
Padbury Bucks 83 D4
Paddington London 49 A5
Paddlesworth Kent 38 B3
Paddock Wood Kent 37 B4
Paddockhaugh Moray 266 D3
Paddockhole Dumfries 185 D5
Padfield Derbys 138 D3
Padiham Lancs 146 D1
Padog Conwy 124 D3
Padside N Yorks 147 B5
Padstow Corn 9 D5
Padworth W Berks 47 C4
Page Bank Durham 167 B5
Pagelsham Eastend Essex 70 D3
Pagham W Sus 20 C1
Paglesham Churchend Essex 70 D3
Paibeil W Isles 287 H2
Paible W Isles 287 E5
Paignton Torbay 8 A2
Paignton & Dartmouth Steam Railway Devon 8 A2
Paignton Zoo Devon 8 B2
Pailton Warks 98 C1
Painscastle Powys 77 C5
Painshawfield Northumb 178 C2
Painsthorpe E Yorks 149 B7
Painswick Glos 63 C4
Pairc Shiaboist W Isles 288 C3
Paisley Renfs 205 B4
Pakefield Suff 105 B6
Pakenham Suff 87 A5
Palace House, Beaulieu Hants 18 A2
Palace of Holyroodhouse Edin 209 C5
Pale Gwyn 109 B4
Palestine Hants 31 A6
Paley Street Windsor 47 B6
Palfrey W Mid 96 B3
Palgowan Dumfries 181 C5
Palgrave Suff 104 D2
Pallion T & W 179 D5
Palmarsh Kent 38 B3
Palnackie Dumfries 173 C6
Palnure Dumfries 171 A6
Palterton Derbys 131 C4
Pamber End Hants 47 D4
Pamber Green Hants 47 D4
Pamber Heath Hants 47 C4
Pamphill Dorset 16 A3
Pampisford Cambs 85 C6
Pan Orkney 283 H4
Panbride Angus 221 A5
Pancrasweek Devon 10 A3
Pandy Gwyn 90 B4
Pandy Mon 61 A5
Pandy Powys 91 B7
Pandy Wrex 109 B6
Pandy Tudur Conwy 124 C3
Panfield Essex 70 A1
Pangbourne W Berks 47 B4
Pannal N Yorks 148 B2
Panshanger Herts 68 B2
Pant Shrops 110 C1
Pant-glas Carms 58 C2
Pant-glas Gwyn 107 B4
Pant-glâs Powys 91 C5

Pant-glas Shrops 110 B1
Pant gwyn Carms 58 C2
Pant Mawr Powys 91 D6
Pant-teg Carms 58 C1
Pant-y-Caws Carms 73 D4
Pant-y-dwr Powys 92 D3
Pant-y-ffridd Powys 93 A5
Pant-y-Wacco Flint 125 B6
Pant-yr-awel Bridgend 40 C4
Pantgwyn Ceredig 73 B5
Pantlasau Swansea 57 C6
Panton Lincs 134 B1
Pantperthog Gwyn 91 B5
Pantyffynnon Carms 57 A6
Pantymwyn Flint 126 C1
Panxworth Norf 121 D5
Papa Westray Airport Orkney 282 B5
Papcastle Cumb 163 A4
Papigoe Highld 281 C5
Papil Shetland 285 K5
Papley Orkney 283 H5
Papple E Loth 210 C2
Papplewick Notts 131 D5
Papworth Everard Cambs 85 A4
Papworth St Agnes Cambs 85 A4
Par Corn 5 B5
Paradise Wildlife Park, Broxbourne Herts 68 C3
Parbold Lancs 136 B3
Parbrook Som 29 B5
Parbrook W Sus 34 D3
Parc Gwyn 108 B3
Parc-Seymour Newport 61 D6
Parc-y-rhôs Carms 75 D4
Parcllyn Ceredig 73 A5
Pardshaw Cumb 162 B3
Parham Suff 88 A4
Park Dumfries 183 C7
Park Corner Oxon 47 A4
Park Corner Windsor 47 A6
Park End M'bro 168 D3
Park End Northumb 177 B6
Park Gate Hants 18 A4
Park Hill Notts 132 D1
Park Hill N Yorks 148 A2
Park Rose Pottery and Leisure Park, Bridlington E Yorks 151 A4
Park Street W Sus 35 C4
Parkend Glos 62 C2
Parkeston Essex 88 D3
Parkgate Ches 126 B2
Parkgate Dumfries 184 D3
Parkgate Kent 37 C6
Parkgate Sur 35 B5
Parkham Devon 25 C4
Parkham Ash Devon 25 C4
Parkhill Ho. Aberds 245 A5
Parkhouse Mon 61 C6
Parkhouse Green Derbys 131 C4
Parkhurst I o W 18 B3
Parkmill Swansea 57 D5
Parkneuk Aberds 233 A5
Parkstone Poole 17 B4
Parley Cross Dorset 17 B4
Parracombe Devon 26 A1
Parrog Pembs 72 C3
Parsley Hay Derbys 129 C6
Parson Cross S Yorks 139 D6
Parson Drove Cambs 101 A5
Parsonage Green Essex 69 C7
Parsonby Cumb 163 A4
Parson's Heath Essex 71 A4
Partick Glasgow 205 B5
Partington Gtr Man 137 D6
Partney Lincs 135 C4
Parton Cumb 162 B2
Parton Dumfries 173 A4
Parton Glos 63 A4
Partridge Green W Sus 21 A4
Parwich Derbys 130 D1
Passenham Northants 83 D4
Paston Norf 121 B5
Patchacott Devon 11 B5
Patcham Brighton 21 B6
Patching W Sus 20 B3
Patchole Devon 25 A7
Patchway S Glos 43 A5
Pateley Bridge N Yorks 147 A5
Paternoster Heath Essex 70 B3
Path of Condie Perth 219 C5
Pathe Som 28 B3
Pathhead Aberds 233 B5
Pathhead E Ayrs 182 A4
Pathhead Fife 209 A5
Pathhead Midloth 209 D6
Pathstruie Perth 219 C5
Patmore Heath Herts 68 A4
Patna E Ayrs 182 A2
Patney Wilts 45 D4
Patrick I o M 152 C2
Patrick Brompton N Yorks 157 B6
Patrington E Yorks 143 A5
Patrixbourne Kent 52 D3
Patterdale Cumb 164 D1
Pattingham Staffs 95 B6
Pattishall Northants 82 B3
Pattiswick Green Essex 70 A2
Patton Bridge Cumb 155 B4
Paul Corn 2 C2
Paulerspury Northants 83 C4
Paull E Yorks 142 A3
Paulton Bath 43 D5
Paultons Park, Totton Hants 32 D2
Pavenham Beds 84 B1
Pawlett Som 28 A3
Pawston Northumb 198 C2
Paxford Glos 81 D4
Paxton Borders 198 A3
Payhembury Devon 13 A5
Paythorne Lancs 146 B2
Peacehaven E Sus 22 B2
Peak Dale Derbys 129 B5
Peak Forest Derbys 129 B6
Peakirk P'boro 100 A3
Pearsie Angus 232 C1
Pease Pottage W Sus 35 C5
Peasedown St John Bath 43 D6
Peasemore W Berks 46 B2
Peasenhall Suff 89 A4
Peaslake Sur 34 B3
Peasley Cross Mers 136 D4
Peasmarsh E Sus 37 D6
Peaston E Loth 210 D1
Peastonbank E Loth 210 D1
Peat Inn Fife 221 D4
Peathill Aberds 269 C4
Peatling Magna Leics 98 B2
Peatling Parva Leics 98 C2
Peaton Shrops 94 C3
Peats Corner Suff 88 A2
Pebmarsh Essex 87 D4
Pebworth Worcs 80 C4
Pecket Well W Yorks 138 A2
Peckforton Ches 127 D5
Peckham London 49 B6
Peckleton Leics 98 A1
Pedlinge Kent 38 B3
Pedmore W Mid 96 C2
Pedwell Som 28 B4
Peebles Borders 196 B1
Peel I o M 152 C2
Peel Common Hants 19 A4
Peel Park S Lnrk 205 C6
Peening Quarter Kent 37 D6
Pegsdon Beds 84 D3
Pegswood Northumb 179 A4
Pegwell Kent 53 C5
Peinchorran Highld 247 A4
Peinlich Highld 259 C4
Pelaw T & W 179 C4
Pelcomb Bridge Pembs 55 C5
Pelcomb Cross Pembs 55 C5
Peldon Essex 70 B3
Pellon W Yorks 138 A3
Pelsall W Mid 96 A3
Pelton Durham 179 D4
Pelutho Cumb 174 D4
Pelynt Corn 5 B7
Pemberton Gtr Man 137 C4
Pembrey Carms 57 B4
Pembrey Motor Racing Circuit Carms 57 B4
Pembridge Hereford 78 B1
Pembroke = Penfro Pembs 55 D5
Pembroke Castle Pembs 55 D5
Pembroke Dock = Doc Penfro Pembs 55 D5
Pembury Kent 36 B4
Pen-bont Rhydybeddau Ceredig 91 D4
Pen-clawdd Swansea 57 C5
Pen-ffordd Pembs 55 B6
Pen-groes-oped Mon 61 C5
Pen-llyn Anglesey 122 B3
Pen-lon Anglesey 123 D4
Pen-sarn Gwyn 107 B4
Pen-sarn Gwyn 107 D5
Pen-twyn Mon 61 C7
Pen-y-banc Carms 58 C3
Pen-y-bont Carms 73 D6
Pen-y-bont Gwyn 91 B5
Pen-y-bont Gwyn 107 D6
Pen-y-bont Powys 109 C7
Pen-y-bont ar Ogwr = Bridgend Bridgend 40 D4
Pen-y-bryn Gwyn 91 A4
Pen-y-bryn Pembs 73 B4
Pen-y-cae Powys 59 D5
Pen-y-cae-mawr Mon 61 D6
Pen-y-cefn Flint 125 B6
Pen-y-clawdd Mon 61 C6
Pen-y-coedcae Rhondda 41 C5
Pen-y-fai Bridgend 40 C3
Pen-y-garn Ceredig 90 D4
Pen-y-garn Carms 58 B2
Pen-y-garnedd Anglesey 123 C5
Pen-y-gop Conwy 108 A4
Pen-y-graig Gwyn 106 C1
Pen-y-groes Carms 57 A5
Pen-y-groeslon Gwyn 106 C2
Pen-y-Gwryd Hotel Gwyn 107 A6
Pen-y-stryt Denb 126 D1
Pen-yr-heol Mon 61 B6
Pen-yr-Heolgerrig M Tydf 60 C2
Penallt Mon 61 B7
Penally Pembs 55 E7
Penalt Hereford 62 A1
Penare Corn 5 C4
Penarlâg = Hawarden Flint 126 C3
Penarth V Glam 41 D6
Penbryn Ceredig 73 A5
Pencader Carms 58 B1
Pencaenewydd Gwyn 107 B4
Pencaitland E Loth 210 D1
Pencarnisiog Anglesey 122 C3
Pencarreg Carms 75 D4
Pencelli Powys 60 A2
Pencoed Bridgend 41 C4
Pencombe Hereford 78 B3
Pencoyd Hereford 61 A7
Pencraig Hereford 62 A1
Pencraig Powys 109 C5
Pendeen Corn 2 B1
Pendennis Castle Corn 4 D3
Penderyn Rhondda 59 E6
Pendine Carms 56 B2
Pendlebury Gtr Man 137 C6
Pendleton Lancs 146 D1
Pendock Worcs 79 D5
Pendoggett Corn 9 D6
Pendomer Som 29 D5
Pendoylan V Glam 41 D5
Pendre Bridgend 40 C4
Penegoes Powys 91 B5
Penfro = Pembroke Pembs 55 D5
Pengam Caerph 41 B6
Penge London 49 B6
Pengenffordd Powys 77 D5
Pengorffwysfa Anglesey 123 A4
Pengover Green Corn 6 A1
Penhale Corn 3 D4
Penhale Corn 4 B4
Penhalvaen Corn 4 D2
Penhill Thamesdown 45 A5
Penhow Newport 61 D6
Penhurst E Sus 23 A4
Peniarth Gwyn 90 B4
Penicuik Midloth 209 D5
Peniel Carms 58 C1
Peniel Denb 125 C5
Penifiler Highld 259 D4
Peninver Argyll 190 C3
Penisarwaun Gwyn 123 D5
Penistone S Yorks 139 C5
Penjerrick Corn 4 D2
Penketh Warr 127 A5
Penkill S Ayrs 181 B4
Penkridge Staffs 112 D3
Penley Wrex 110 B3
Penllergaer Swansea 57 C6
Penllyn V Glam 41 D4
Penmachno Conwy 124 D2
Penmaen Swansea 57 D5
Penmaenan Conwy 124 B2
Penmaenmawr Conwy 124 B2
Penmaenpool Gwyn 91 A4
Penmark V Glam 41 E5
Penmarth Corn 4 D2
Penmon Anglesey 123 B6
Penmore Mill Argyll 224 A3
Penmorfa Ceredig 73 A6
Penmorfa Gwyn 107 B5
Penmynydd Anglesey 123 C5
Penn Bucks 67 D4
Penn W Mid 96 B1
Penn Street Bucks 67 D4
Pennal Gwyn 91 B5
Pennan Aberds 268 C3
Pennant Ceredig 75 B4
Pennant Denb 109 B5
Pennant Denb 125 D5
Pennant Powys 91 C6
Pennant Melangell Powys 109 C5
Pennar Pembs 55 D5
Pennard Swansea 57 D5
Pennerley Shrops 94 B1
Pennington Cumb 153 C3
Pennington Gtr Man 137 D5
Pennington Hants 18 B2
Penny Bridge Cumb 154 C2
Pennycross Argyll 225 D4
Pennygate Norf 121 C5
Pennygown Argyll 225 B4
Pennymoor Devon 26 D3
Pennywell T & W 179 D5
Penparc Ceredig 73 B5
Penparc Pembs 55 A4
Penparcau Ceredig 90 D3
Penperlleni Mon 61 C5
Penpillick Corn 5 B5
Penpol Corn 4 D3
Penpoll Corn 5 B6
Penpont Dumfries 183 C6
Penpont Powys 59 C6
Penrherber Carms 73 C5
Penrhiw goch Carms 57 A5
Penrhiw-llan Ceredig 73 B6
Penrhiw-pâl Ceredig 73 B6
Penrhiwceiber Rhondda 41 B5
Penrhos Gwyn 106 C3
Penrhôs Mon 61 B6
Penrhos Powys 59 D4
Penrhosfeilwo Anglesey 122 B2
Penrhyn Bay Conwy 124 A3
Penrhyn Castle Gwyn 123 C6
Penrhyn-coch Ceredig 90 D4
Penrhyndeudraeth Gwyn 107 C6
Penrhynside Conwy 124 A3
Penrice Swansea 57 D4
Penrith Cumb 164 B3
Penrose Corn 9 D4
Penruddock Cumb 164 C2
Penryn Corn 4 D2
Pensarn Carms 57 A4
Pensarn Conwy 125 B4
Pensax Worcs 79 A5
Pensby Mers 126 A2
Penselwood Som 30 B1
Pensford Bath 43 C5
Penshaw T & W 179 D5
Penshurst Kent 36 B3
Pensilva Corn 6 A1
Penston E Loth 210 C1
Pentewan Corn 5 C5
Pentir Gwyn 123 D5
Pentire Corn 4 A2
Pentlow Essex 87 C4
Pentney Norf 119 D4
Penton Mewsey Hants 32 A2
Pentraeth Anglesey 123 C5
Pentre Carms 57 A5
Pentre Powys 93 C4
Pentre Powys 93 B6
Pentre Rhondda 41 B4
Pentre Shrops 110 D2
Pentre Wrex 110 A1
Pentre Wrex 109 B6
Pentre-bâch Ceredig 75 D4
Pentre-bach Powys 59 B6
Pentre Berw Anglesey 123 C4
Pentre-bont Conwy 124 D2
Pentre-celyn Denb 125 D6
Pentre-Celyn Powys 91 B6
Pentre-chwyth Swansea 57 C6
Pentre-cwrt Carms 73 C6
Pentre Dolau-Honddu Powys 76 C3
Pentre-dwr Swansea 40 B1
Pentre-galar Pembs 73 C4
Pentre-Gwenlais Carms 57 A6
Pentre Gwynfryn Gwyn 107 D5
Pentre Halkyn Flint 126 B2
Pentre-Isaf Conwy 124 C3
Pentre Llanrhaeadr Denb 125 C5
Pentre-llwyn-llŵyd Powys 76 B3
Pentre-llyn Ceredig 75 A5
Pentre-llyn cymmer Conwy 125 D4
Pentre Meyrick V Glam 41 D4
Pentre-poeth Newport 42 A1
Pentre-rhew Ceredig 75 C5
Pentre-tafarn-y-fedw Conwy 124 C3
Pentre-ty-gwyn Carms 59 B5
Pentrebach M Tydf 41 A5
Pentrebach Swansea 57 B6
Pentrebeirdd Powys 109 D6
Pentrecagal Carms 73 B6
Pentredwr Denb 109 A6
Pentrefelin Ceredig 75 D5
Pentrefelin Carms 58 C2
Pentrefelin Conwy 124 B3
Pentrefelin Gwyn 107 C5
Pentrefoelas Conwy 124 D3
Pentregat Ceredig 73 A6
Pentreheyling Shrops 93 B6
Pentre'r Felin Conwy 124 C3
Pentre'r-felin Powys 59 B6
Pentrich Derbys 130 D3
Pentridge Dorset 31 D4
Pentyrch Cardiff 41 C6
Penuchadre V Glam 40 D3
Penuwch Ceredig 75 B4
Penwithick Corn 5 B5
Penwyllt Powys 59 D5
Penybanc Carms 57 A6
Penybont Powys 77 A5
Penybontfawr Powys 109 C5
Penycae Wrex 110 A1
Penycwm Pembs 54 B4
Penyffordd Flint 126 C3
Penyffridd Gwyn 107 A5
Penygarnedd Powys 109 C6
Penygraig Rhondda 41 B4
Penygroes Gwyn 107 A4
Penygroes Pembs 73 C4
Penyrheol Caerph 41 C6
Penysarn Anglesey 123 A4
Penywaun Rhondda 41 A4
Penzance Corn 2 B2
Penzance Heliport Corn 2 B2
People's Palace Glasgow 205 B6
Peopleton Worcs 80 B2
Peover Heath Ches 128 B2
Peper Harow Sur 34 B2
Perceton N Ayrs 204 D3
Percie Aberds 244 C2
Percyhorner Aberds 269 C4
Periton Som 27 A4
Perivale London 49 A4
Perkinsville Durham 179 D4
Perlethorpe Notts 131 B6
Perranarworthal Corn 4 D2
Perranporth Corn 4 B2
Perranuthnoe Corn 2 C3
Perranzabuloe Corn 4 B2
Perry Barr W Mid 96 B3
Perry Green Herts 68 B4
Perry Green Wilts 44 A3
Perry Street Kent 50 B3
Perryfoot Derbys 129 A6
Pershall Staffs 112 B2
Pershore Worcs 80 C2
Pert Angus 233 B4
Pertenhall Beds 84 A2
Perth Perth 219 B6
Perth Racecourse Perth 219 B6
Perthy Shrops 110 B2
Perton Staffs 95 B6
Pertwood Wilts 30 B2
Peter Tavy Devon 11 D6
Peterborough P'boro 100 B3
Peterborough Cathedral P'boro 100 B3
Peterburn Highld 261 B4
Peterchurch Hereford 78 D1
Peterculter Aberdeen 245 B5
Peterhead Aberds 257 B6
Peterlee Durham 168 A2
Peter's Green Herts 67 B6
Peters Marland Devon 25 D5
Petersfield Hants 33 C6
Peterston super-Ely V Glam 41 D5
Peterstone Wentlooge Newport 42 A1
Peterstow Hereford 62 A1
Petertown Orkney 283 G4
Petham Kent 52 D3
Petrockstow Devon 11 A6
Pett E Sus 23 A6
Pettaugh Suff 88 B2
Petteridge Kent 37 B4
Pettinain S Lnrk 195 B4
Pettistree Suff 88 B3
Petton Devon 27 C5
Petton Shrops 110 C3
Petts Wood London 50 C1
Petty Aberds 256 C2
Pettycur Fife 209 B5
Pettymuick Aberds 257 D4
Petworth W Sus 34 D2
Petworth House W Sus 34 D2
Pevensey E Sus 22 B4
Pevensey Bay E Sus 23 B4
Pewsey Wilts 45 C5
Philham Devon 24 C3
Philiphaugh Borders 186 A3
Phillack Corn 2 B3
Philleigh Corn 4 D3
Philpstoun W Loth 208 C3
Phocle Green Hereford 62 A2
Phoenix Green Hants 47 D5
Pica Cumb 162 B3
Piccotts End Herts 67 C5
Pickering N Yorks 159 C6
Picket Piece Hants 32 A2
Picket Post Hants 17 A5
Pickhill N Yorks 158 C2
Picklescott Shrops 94 B2
Pickletillem Fife 220 B4
Pickmere Ches 128 B1
Pickney Som 28 C1
Pickstock Telford 111 C6
Pickwell Devon 25 A5
Pickwell Leics 115 D5
Pickworth Lincs 116 B3
Pickworth Rutland 116 D2
Picton Ches 127 B4
Picton Flint 125 A6
Picton N Yorks 158 A3
Piddinghoe E Sus 22 B2
Piddington Northants 83 B5
Piddington Oxon 66 B1
Piddlehinton Dorset 15 B7
Piddletrenthide Dorset 15 B7
Pidley Cambs 101 D5
Piece Hall Art Gallery, Halifax W Yorks 138 A3
Piercebridge Darl 167 D5
Pierowall Orkney 282 C5
Pigdon Northumb 178 A3
Pikehall Derbys 130 D1
Pilgrims Hatch Essex 69 D5
Pilham Lincs 141 D6
Pill N Som 43 B4
Pillaton Corn 6 A2
Pillerton Hersey Warks 81 C6
Pillerton Priors Warks 81 C5
Pilleth Powys 77 A6
Pilley Hants 18 B2
Pilley S Yorks 139 C6
Pilling Lancs 144 C4
Pilling Lane Lancs 144 C3
Pillowell Glos 62 C2
Pillwell Dorset 30 D1
Pilning S Glos 43 A4
Pilsbury Derbys 129 C6
Pilsdon Dorset 14 B4
Pilsgate P'boro 100 A2
Pilsley Derbys 130 B2
Pilsley Derbys 131 C4
Pilton Devon 25 B6
Pilton Northants 100 C2
Pilton Rutland 99 A6
Pilton Som 29 A5
Pilton Green Swansea 57 D4
Pimperne Dorset 16 A3
Pinchbeck Lincs 117 C5
Pinchbeck Bars Lincs 117 C4
Pinchbeck West Lincs 117 C5
Pincheon Green S Yorks 141 B4
Pinehurst Thamesdown 45 A5
Pinfold Lancs 136 B2
Pinged Carms 57 B4
Pinhoe Devon 13 B4
Pinkneys Grn. Windsor 47 A6
Pinley W Mid 97 D6
Pinmill Suff 88 D3
Pinminnoch S Ayrs 180 B3
Pinmore S Ayrs 181 B4
Pinmore Mains S Ayrs 181 B4
Pinner London 48 A4
Pinvin Worcs 80 C2
Pinwherry S Ayrs 180 C3
Pinxton Derbys 131 D4
Pipe and Lyde Hereford 78 C3
Pipe Gate Shrops 111 A6
Piperhill Highld 253 A4
Piper's Pool Corn 10 C3
Pipewell Northants 99 C5
Pippacott Devon 25 B6
Pipton Powys 77 D5
Pirbright Sur 34 A2
Pirnmill N Ayrs 202 D3
Pirton Herts 84 D3
Pirton Worcs 80 C1
Pisgah Ceredig 75 A5
Pisgah Stirl 218 D2
Pishill Oxon 47 A5
Pistyll Gwyn 106 B3
Pitagowan Perth 230 B2
Pitblae Aberds 269 C4
Pitcairngreen Perth 219 B5
Pitcalnie Highld 265 C4
Pitcaple Aberds 256 D2
Pitch Green Bucks 66 C2
Pitch Place Sur 34 A2
Pitchcombe Glos 63 C4
Pitchcott Bucks 66 A2
Pitchford Shrops 94 A3
Pitcombe Som 29 B6
Pitcorthie Fife 221 D5
Pitcox E Loth 210 C3
Pitcur Perth 220 A2
Pitfichie Aberds 244 A3
Pitforthie Aberds 233 A6
Pitgrudy Highld 264 A3
Pitkennedy Angus 232 C3
Pitkevy Fife 220 D2
Pitkierie Fife 221 D5
Pitlessie Fife 220 D3
Pitlochry Perth 230 C3
Pitmachie Aberds 256 D1
Pitmain Highld 241 B5
Pitmedden Aberds 256 D3
Pitminster Som 28 D2
Pitmuies Angus 232 D3
Pitmunie Aberds 244 A3
Pitney Som 29 C4
Pitscottie Fife 220 C4
Pitsea Essex 51 A4
Pitsford Northants 83 A4
Pitsmoor S Yorks 130 A3
Pitstone Bucks 67 B4
Pitstone Green Bucks 67 B4
Pitt Rivers Museum (See University Museum) Oxon 65 C6
Pittendreich Moray 266 C2
Pittentrail Highld 273 D5
Pittenweem Fife 221 D5
Pittington Durham 167 A6
Pittodrie Aberds 256 D1

Queniborough Leics 115 D4
Quenington Glos 64 C2
Quernmore Lancs 145 B5
Quethiock Corn 6 A2
Quholm Orkney 282 F3
Quicks Green W Berks 46 B3
Quidenham Norf 103 C6
Quidhampton Hants 46 D3
Quidhampton Wilts 31 B5
Quilquox Aberds 257 C4
Quina Brook Shrops 111 B4
Quindry Orkney 283 H5
Quinton Northants 83 B4
Quinton W Mid 96 C2
Quintrell Downs Corn 4 A3
Quixhill Staffs 113 A5
Quoditch Devon 11 B5
Quoig Perth 218 B3
Quorndon Leics 114 D3
Quothquan S Lnrk 195 C4
Quoyloo Orkney 282 E3
Quoyness Orkney 283 G3
Quoys Shetland 284 B8
Quoys Shetland 285 G6


## R


Raasay Ho. Highld 248 C2
Rabbit's Cross Kent 37 B5
Raby Mers 126 B3
Rachan Mill Borders 195 C6
Rachub Gwyn 123 D6
Rackenford Devon 26 D3
Rackham W Sus 20 A3
Rackheath Norf 121 D4
Racks Dumfries 174 A3
Rackwick Orkney 283 H3
Rackwick Orkney 282 C5
Radbourne Derbys 113 B6
Radcliffe Gtr Man 137 C6
Radcliffe Northumb 189 C5
Radcliffe on Trent Notts 115 B4
Radclive Bucks 82 D3
Radcot Oxon 64 D3
Raddery Highld 252 A3
Radernie Fife 221 D4
Radford Semele Warks 81 A6
Radipole Dorset 15 C6
Radlett Herts 67 D6
Radley Oxon 65 D6
Radmanthwaite Notts 131 C5
Radmoor Shrops 111 C5
Radmore Green Ches 127 D5
Radnage Bucks 66 D2
Radstock Bath 43 D5
Radstone Northants 82 C2
Radway Warks 81 C6
Radway Green Ches 128 D2
Radwell Beds 84 B2
Radwell Herts 84 D4
Radwinter Essex 86 D2
Radyr Cardiff 41 C6
RAF Museum, Cosford Shrops 95 A5
RAF Museum, Hendon London 49 A5
Rafford Moray 253 A6
Ragdale Leics 115 D4
Raglan Mon 61 C6
Ragley Hall Warks 80 B3
Ragnall Notts 132 B3
Rahane Argyll 215 D5
Rainford Mers 136 C3
Rainford Junction Mers 136 C3
Rainham London 50 A2
Rainham Medway 51 C5
Rainhill Mers 136 D3
Rainhill Stoops Mers 136 D4
Rainow Ches 129 B4
Rainton N Yorks 158 D2
Rainworth Notts 131 D5
Raisbeck Cumb 155 A5
Raise Cumb 165 A5
Rait Perth 220 B2
Raithby Lincs 134 A3
Raithby Lincs 134 C3
Rake W Sus 33 C7
Rakewood Gtr Man 138 B2
Ram Carms 75 D4
Ram Lane Kent 38 A1
Ramasaig Highld 258 D1
Rame Corn 4 D2
Rame Corn 6 C3
Rameldry Mill Bank Fife 220 D3
Ramnageo Shetland 284 C8
Rampisham Dorset 15 A5
Rampside Cumb 153 D3
Rampton Cambs 85 A6
Rampton Notts 132 B2
Ramsbottom Gtr Man 137 B6
Ramsbury Wilts 45 B6
Ramscraigs Highld 275 B5
Ramsdean Hants 33 C6
Ramsdell Hants 46 D3
Ramsden Oxon 65 B4
Ramsden Bellhouse Essex 69 D7
Ramsden Heath Essex 69 D7
Ramsey Cambs 101 C4
Ramsey Essex 88 D3
Ramsey I o M 152 B4
Ramsey Forty Foot Cambs 101 C5
Ramsey Heights Cambs 101 C4
Ramsey Island Essex 70 C3
Ramsey Mereside Cambs 101 C4
Ramsey St Mary's Cambs 101 C4
Ramseycleuch Borders 185 A5
Ramsgate Kent 53 C5
Ramsgill N Yorks 157 D5
Ramshorn Staffs 113 A4
Ramsnest Common Sur 34 C2
Ranais W Isles 288 E5
Ranby Lincs 134 B2
Ranby Notts 131 A6
Rand Lincs 133 B6
Randwick Glos 63 C4
Ranfurly Renfs 204 B3
Rangag Highld 280 D3
Rangemore Staffs 113 C5
Rangeworthy S Glos 43 A5
Rankinston E Ayrs 182 A2
Ranmoor S Yorks 130 A3
Ranmore Common Sur 35 A4
Rannerdale Cumb 163 C4
Rannoch Station Perth 228 C3
Ranochan Highld 238 D2
Ranskill Notts 131 A6
Ranton Staffs 112 C2
Ranworth Norf 121 D5
Raploch Stirl 207 A5
Rapness Orkney 282 C6
Rascal Moor E Yorks 149 D7
Rascarrel Dumfries 173 D5
Rashiereive Aberds 257 D4
Raskelf N Yorks 158 D3
Rassau Bl Gwent 60 B3
Rastrick W Yorks 139 A4
Ratagan Highld 238 A3
Ratby Leics 98 A2
Ratcliffe Culey Leics 97 B6
Ratcliffe on Soar Leics 114 C2
Ratcliffe on the Wreake Leics 115 D4
Rathen Aberds 269 C5
Rathillet Fife 220 B3
Rathmell N Yorks 146 B2
Ratho Edin 208 C4
Ratho Station Edin 208 C4
Rathven Moray 267 C5
Ratley Warks 81 C6
Ratlinghope Shrops 94 B2
Rattar Highld 281 A4
Ratten Row Lancs 144 C4
Rattery Devon 7 A6
Rattlesden Suff 87 B5
Rattray Perth 231 D5
Raughton Head Cumb 164 A1
Raunds Northants 100 D1
Ravenfield S Yorks 140 D2
Ravenglass Cumb 153 A1
Ravenglass and Eskdale Railway & Museum Cumb 153 A1
Raveningham Norf 105 B4
Ravenscar N Yorks 160 A3
Ravenscraig Invclyd 204 A2
Ravensdale I o M 152 B3
Ravensden Beds 84 B2
Ravenseat N Yorks 156 A2
Ravenshead Notts 131 D5
Ravensmoor Ches 127 D6
Ravensthorpe Northants 98 D3
Ravensthorpe W Yorks 139 A5
Ravenstone Leics 114 D2
Ravenstone M Keynes 83 B5
Ravenstonedale Cumb 155 A6
Ravenstown Cumb 154 D2
Ravenstruther S Lnrk 194 B4
Ravensworth N Yorks 157 A5
Raw N Yorks 160 A3
Rawcliffe E Yorks 141 A4
Rawcliffe York 149 B4
Rawcliffe Bridge E Yorks 141 A4
Rawdon W Yorks 147 D6
Rawmarsh S Yorks 140 D2
Rawreth Essex 70 D1
Rawridge Devon 14 A2
Rawtenstall Lancs 137 A7
Raxton Aberds 256 C3
Raydon Suff 87 D6
Raylees Northumb 188 D2
Rayleigh Essex 70 D2
Rayne Essex 70 A1
Rayners Lane London 48 A4
Raynes Park London 49 C5
Reach Cambs 86 A1
Read Lancs 146 D1
Reading Reading 47 B5
Reading Street Kent 37 C7
Reagill Cumb 165 D4
Rearquhar Highld 264 A3
Rearsby Leics 115 D4
Reaster Highld 281 B4
Reawick Shetland 285 J5
Reay Highld 279 B5
Rechullin Highld 249 A5
Reculver Kent 53 C4
Red Dial Cumb 175 D5
Red Hill Worcs 79 B6
Red House Glass Cone, Wordsley W Mid 96 C1
Red Houses Jersey 6
Red Lodge Suff 102 D2
Red Rail Hereford 62 A1
Red Rock Gtr Man 137 C4
Red Roses Carms 56 A2
Red Row Northumb 189 D5
Red Street Staffs 128 D3
Red Wharf Bay Anglesey 123 B5
Redberth Pembs 55 D6
Redbourn Herts 67 B6
Redbourne N Lincs 142 D1
Redbrook Glos 62 B1
Redbrook Wrex 111 A4
Redburn Highld 264 D1
Redburn Highld 253 B5
Redburn Northumb 177 C5
Redcar Redcar 168 C4
Redcar Racecourse Redcar 168 C4
Redcastle Angus 233 C4
Redcastle Highld 252 B1
Redcliff Bay N Som 42 B3
Redding Falk 208 C2
Reddingmuirhead Falk 208 C2
Reddish Gtr Man 138 D1
Redditch Worcs 80 A3
Rede Suff 87 B4
Redenhall Norf 104 C3
Redesdale Camp Northumb 187 D7
Redesmouth Northumb 177 A6
Redford Aberds 233 A5
Redford Angus 232 D3
Redford Durham 166 B3
Redfordgreen Borders 185 A6
Redgorton Perth 219 B5
Redgrave Suff 103 D6
Redhill Aberds 256 C1
Redhill Aberds 245 B4
Redhill N Som 42 C3
Redhill Sur 35 A5
Redhouse Argyll 202 B3
Redhouses Argyll 200 B3
Redisham Suff 105 C5
Redland Bristol 43 B4
Redland Orkney 282 E4
Redlingfield Suff 104 D2
Redlynch Som 29 B7
Redlynch Wilts 31 C6
Redmarley D'Abitot Glos 79 D5
Redmarshall Stockton 167 C6
Redmile Leics 115 B5
Redmire N Yorks 156 B4
Redmoor Corn 5 A5
Rednal Shrops 110 C2
Redpath Borders 197 C4
Redpoint Highld 261 D4
Redruth Corn 3 A4
Redvales Gtr Man 137 C7
Redwick Newport 42 A3
Redwick S Glos 43 A4
Redworth Darl 167 C5
Reed Herts 85 D5
Reedham Norf 105 A5
Reedness E Yorks 141 A5
Reeds Beck Lincs 134 C2
Reepham Lincs 133 B5
Reepham Norf 120 C2
Reeth N Yorks 156 B4
Regaby I o M 152 B4
Regoul Highld 253 A4
Reiff Highld 270 C2
Reigate Sur 35 A5
Reighton N Yorks 161 D5
Reighton Gap N Yorks 161 D5
Reinigeadal W Isles 288 G3
Reiss Highld 281 C5
Rejerrah Corn 4 B2
Releath Corn 3 B4
Relubbus Corn 2 B3
Relugas Moray 253 B5
Remenham Wokingham 47 A5
Remenham Hill Wokingham 47 A5
Remony Perth 229 D6
Rempstone Notts 114 C3
Rendcomb Glos 63 C6
Rendham Suff 88 A4
Rendlesham Suff 88 B4
Renfrew Renfs 205 B5
Renhold Beds 84 B2
Renishaw Derbys 131 B4
Rennington Northumb 189 B5
Renton W Dunb 206 C1
Renwick Cumb 164 A3
Repps Norf 121 D6
Repton Derbys 113 C7
Reraig Highld 249 D5
Rescobie Angus 232 C3
Resipole Highld 235 D6
Resolis Highld 264 D2
Resolven Neath 40 A3
Reston Borders 211 D5
Reswallie Angus 232 C3
Retew Corn 4 B4
Retford Notts 132 A2
Rettendon Essex 70 D1
Rettendon Place Essex 70 D1
Revesby Lincs 134 C2
Revesby Bridge Lincs 134 C3
Rew Street I o W 18 B3
Rewe Devon 13 B4
Reydon Suff 105 D5
Reydon Smear Suff 105 D5
Reymerston Norf 103 A6
Reynalton Pembs 55 D6
Reynoldston Swansea 57 C4
Rezare Corn 11 D4
Rhaeadr Gwy = Rhayader Powys 76 A3
Rhandirmwyn Carms 59 A4
Rhayader = Rhaeadr Gwy Powys 76 A3
Rhedyn Gwyn 106 C2
Rhemore Highld 225 A4
Rhencullen I o M 152 B3
Rhes-y-cae Flint 126 B1
Rhewl Denb 125 C6
Rhewl Denb 109 A6
Rhian Highld 272 C3
Rhicarn Highld 270 B3
Rhiconich Highld 276 C3
Rhicullen Highld 264 C2
Rhidorroch Ho. Highld 262 A3
Rhifail Highld 278 D3
Rhigos Rhondda 59 E6
Rhilochan Highld 273 D5
Rhiroy Highld 262 B3
Rhisga = Risca Caerph 60 D4
Rhiw Gwyn 106 D2
Rhiwabon = Ruabon Wrex 110 A2
Rhiwbina Cardiff 41 C6
Rhiwbryfdir Gwyn 107 B6
Rhiwderin Newport 42 A1
Rhiwlas Gwyn 123 D5
Rhiwlas Gwyn 108 B4
Rhiwlas Powys 109 B6
Rhodes Gtr Man 138 C1
Rhodes Minnis Kent 38 A3
Rhodesia Notts 131 B5
Rhodiad Pembs 54 B3
Rhondda Rhondda 41 B4
Rhonehouse or Kelton Hill Dumfries 173 C5
Rhoose = Y Rhws V Glam 41 E5
Rhôs Carms 73 C6
Rhôs Neath 40 A2
Rhos-fawr Gwyn 106 C3
Rhos-hill Pembs 73 B4
Rhos-on-Sea Conwy 124 A3
Rhos-y-brithdir Powys 109 C6
Rhos-y-garth Ceredig 75 A5
Rhos-y-gwaliau Gwyn 108 B4
Rhos-y-llan Gwyn 106 C2
Rhos-y-Madoc Wrex 110 A2
Rhos-y-meirch Powys 77 A6
Rhosaman Carms 59 D4
Rhosbeirio Anglesey 122 A3
Rhoscefnhir Anglesey 123 C5
Rhoscolyn Anglesey 122 C2
Rhoscrowther Pembs 55 D5
Rhosesmor Flint 126 C2
Rhosgadfan Gwyn 107 A5
Rhosgoch Anglesey 123 B4
Rhosgoch Powys 77 C5
Rhoshirwaun Gwyn 106 D1
Rhoslan Gwyn 107 B4
Rhoslefain Gwyn 90 B3
Rhosllanerchrugog Wrex 110 A1
Rhosmaen Carms 58 C3
Rhosmeirch Anglesey 123 C4
Rhosneigr Anglesey 122 C3
Rhosnesni Wrex 126 D3
Rhosrobin Wrex 126 D3
Rhossili Swansea 57 D4
Rhosson Pembs 54 B3
Rhostryfan Gwyn 107 A4
Rhostyllen Wrex 110 A2
Rhosybol Anglesey 123 B4
RHS Garden, Wisley Sur 34 A3
Rhu Argyll 202 B3
Rhu Argyll 215 D5
Rhuallt Denb 125 B5
Rhuddall Heath Ches 127 C5
Rhuddlan Ceredig 58 A1
Rhuddlan Denb 125 B5
Rhue Highld 262 A2
Rhulen Powys 77 B5
Rhunahaorine Argyll 202 D2
Rhuthun = Ruthin Denb 125 D6
Rhyd Gwyn 107 B6
Rhyd Powys 92 A3
Rhyd-Ddu Gwyn 107 A5
Rhyd-moel-ddu Powys 93 D4
Rhyd-Rosser Ceredig 75 B4
Rhyd-uchaf Gwyn 108 B4
Rhyd-wen Gwyn 91 A5
Rhyd-y-clafdy Gwyn 106 C3
Rhŷd-y-foel Conwy 125 B4
Rhyd-y-fro Neath 59 E4
Rhyd-y-gwin Swansea 57 B6
Rhyd-y-meirch Mon 61 C5
Rhyd-y-meudwy Denb 125 D6
Rhyd-y-pandy Swansea 57 B6
Rhyd-y-sarn Gwyn 107 B6
Rhyd-yr-onen Gwyn 90 B4
Rhydaman = Ammanford Carms 57 A6
Rhydargaeau Carms 58 C1
Rhydcymerau Carms 58 B2
Rhydd Worcs 79 C6
Rhydding Neath 40 B2
Rhydfudr Ceredig 75 B4
Rhydlewis Ceredig 73 B6
Rhydlios Gwyn 106 C1
Rhydlydan Conwy 124 D3
Rhydness Powys 77 C5
Rhydowen Ceredig 74 D3
Rhydspence Hereford 77 C6
Rhydtalog Flint 126 D2
Rhydwyn Anglesey 122 B3
Rhydycroesau Shrops 110 B1
Rhydyfelin Ceredig 75 A4
Rhydyfelin Rhondda 41 C5
Rhydymain Gwyn 108 C3
Rhydymwyn Flint 126 C2
Rhyl = Y Rhyl Denb 125 A5
Rhymney = Rhymni Caerph 60 C3
Rhymni = Rhymney Caerph 60 C3
Rhynd Fife 221 B4
Rhynd Perth 219 B6
Rhynie Aberds 255 D5
Rhynie Highld 265 C4
Ribbesford Worcs 95 D5
Ribblehead N Yorks 155 D6
Ribbleton Lancs 145 D5
Ribchester Lancs 145 D6
Ribigill Highld 277 C6
Riby Lincs 142 C3
Riby Cross Roads Lincs 142 C3
Riccall N Yorks 149 D5
Riccarton E Ayrs 193 B4
Richards Castle Hereford 78 A2
Richings Park Bucks 48 B3
Richmond London 49 B4
Richmond N Yorks 157 A5
Rickarton Aberds 245 D5
Rickinghall Suff 103 D6
Rickleton T & W 179 D4
Rickling Essex 85 D6
Rickmansworth Herts 67 D5
Riddings Cumb 175 A7
Riddings Derbys 131 D4
Riddlecombe Devon 25 D7
Riddlesden W Yorks 147 C4
Riddrie Glasgow 205 B6
Ridge Dorset 16 C3
Ridge Hants 32 D2
Ridge Wilts 30 B3
Ridge Green Sur 35 B6
Ridge Lane Warks 97 B5
Ridgebourne Powys 77 A4
Ridgehill N Som 43 C4
Ridgeway Cross Hereford 79 C5
Ridgewell Essex 86 C3
Ridgewood E Sus 22 A2
Ridgmont Beds 84 D1
Riding Mill Northumb 178 C2
Ridleywood Wrex 127 D4
Ridlington Norf 121 B5
Ridlington Rutland 99 A5
Ridsdale Northumb 177 A7
Riechip Perth 231 D4
Riemore Perth 230 D4
Rienachait Highld 270 A3
Rievaulx N Yorks 159 C4
Rievaulx Abbey N Yorks 159 C4
Rift House Hrtlpl 168 B2
Rigg Dumfries 175 B5
Riggend N Lnrk 207 C5
Rigsby Lincs 135 B4
Rigside S Lnrk 194 C3
Riley Green Lancs 137 A5
Rileyhill Staffs 113 D5
Rilla Mill Corn 10 D3
Rillington N Yorks 160 D2
Rimington Lancs 146 C2
Rimpton Som 29 C6
Rimswell E Yorks 143 A5
Rinaston Pembs 55 B5
Ringasta Shetland 285 M5
Ringford Dumfries 173 C4
Ringinglow S Yorks 130 A2
Ringland Norf 120 D3
Ringles Cross E Sus 36 D2
Ringmer E Sus 22 A2
Ringmore Devon 7 C5
Ringorm Moray 254 B3
Ring's End Cambs 101 A5
Ringsfield Suff 105 C5
Ringsfield Corner Suff 105 C5
Ringshall Herts 67 B4
Ringshall Suff 87 B6
Ringshall Stocks Suff 87 B6
Ringstead Norf 119 A4
Ringstead Northants 100 D1
Ringwood Hants 17 A5
Ringwould Kent 39 A5
Rinmore Aberds 243 A7
Rinnigill Orkney 283 H4
Rinsey Corn 2 C3
Riof W Isles 288 D2
Ripe E Sus 22 A3
Ripley Derbys 130 D3
Ripley Hants 17 B5
Ripley N Yorks 148 A1
Ripley Sur 34 A3
Riplingham E Yorks 150 D2
Ripon N Yorks 157 D7
Ripon Cathedral N Yorks 157 D7
Ripon Racecourse N Yorks 148 A2
Rippingale Lincs 116 C3
Ripple Kent 39 A5
Ripple Worcs 79 D6
Ripponden W Yorks 138 B3
Rireavach Highld 262 A2
Risabus Argyll 200 D3
Risbury Hereford 78 B3
Risby Suff 86 A3
Risca = Rhisga Caerph 60 D4
Rise E Yorks 151 C4
Riseden E Sus 36 C4
Risegate Lincs 117 C5
Riseholme Lincs 133 B4
Riseley Beds 84 A2
Riseley Wokingham 47 C5
Rishangles Suff 88 A2
Rishton Lancs 146 D1
Rishworth W Yorks 138 B3
Rising Bridge Lancs 137 A6
Risley Derbys 114 B2
Risley Warr 137 D5
Risplith N Yorks 147 A6
Rispond Highld 277 B5
Rivar Wilts 45 C7
Rivenhall End Essex 70 B2
River Bank Cambs 86 A1
Riverhead Kent 36 A3
Rivington Lancs 137 B5
Roa Island Cumb 153 D3
Roachill Devon 26 C3
Road Green Norf 104 B3
Roade Northants 83 B4
Roadhead Cumb 176 B3
Roadmeetings S Lnrk 194 B3
Roadside Highld 280 B3
Roadside of Catterline Aberds 233 A6
Roadside of Kinneff Aberds 233 A6
Roadwater Som 27 B5
Roag Highld 258 D2
Roath Cardiff 41 D6
Rob Roy and Trossachs Visitor Centre, Callander Stirl 217 D6
Robert Burns Centre, Dumfries Dumfries 174 A2
Roberton Borders 186 B3
Roberton S Lnrk 194 D4
Robertsbridge E Sus 37 D5
Roberttown W Yorks 139 A4
Robeston Cross Pembs 55 D4
Robeston Wathen Pembs 55 C6
Robin Hood W Yorks 139 A6
Robin Hood Doncaster Sheffield Airport S Yorks 141 D4
Robin Hood's Bay N Yorks 160 A3
Roborough Devon 25 D6
Roborough Devon 7 A4
Roby Mers 136 D3
Roby Mill Lancs 136 C4
Rocester Staffs 113 B5
Roch Pembs 55 B4
Roch Gate Pembs 55 B4
Rochdale Gtr Man 138 B1
Roche Corn 5 A4
Rochester Medway 51 C4
Rochester Northumb 188 D1
Rochester Castle Medway 51 C4
Rochester Cathedral Medway 51 C4
Rochford Essex 70 D2
Rock Corn 9 D5
Rock Northumb 189 A5
Rock Worcs 95 D5
Rock W Sus 21 A4
Rock Ferry Mers 126 A3

Upshire Essex 68 C4
Upstreet Kent 53 C4
Upthorpe Suff 103 D5
Upton Cambs 100 D3
Upton Ches 127 C4
Upton Corn 10 A3
Upton Dorset 16 C1
Upton Dorset 16 B3
Upton Hants 32 D2
Upton Hants 46 D1
Upton Leics 97 B6
Upton Lincs 132 A3
Upton Mers 126 A2
Upton Norf 121 D5
Upton Notts 132 D2
Upton Notts 132 B2
Upton Northants 83 A4
Upton Oxon 46 A3
Upton P'boro 100 A3
Upton Slough 48 B2
Upton Som 27 C4
Upton W Yorks 140 B2
Upton Bishop Hereford 62 A2
Upton Cheyney S Glos 43 C5
Upton Cressett Shrops 95 B4
Upton Cross Corn 10 D3
Upton Grey Hants 33 A5
Upton Hellions Devon 12 A3
Upton House Warks 81 C6
Upton Lovell Wilts 30 A3
Upton Magna Shrops 111 D4
Upton Noble Som 29 B7
Upton Pyne Devon 13 B4
Upton St Leonard's Glos 63 B4
Upton Scudamore Wilts 30 A2
Upton Snodsbury Worcs 80 B2
Upton upon Severn Worcs 79 C6
Upton Warren Worcs 80 A2
Upwaltham W Sus 20 A2
Upware Cambs 102 D1
Upwell Norf 101 A6
Upwey Dorset 15 C6
Upwood Cambs 101 C4
Uradale Shetland 285 K6
Urafirth Shetland 284 F5
Urchfont Wilts 44 D4
Urdimarsh Hereford 78 C3
Ure Shetland 284 F4
Ure Bank N Yorks 157 D7
Urgha W Isles 288 H2
Urishay Common Hereford 77 D7
Urlay Nook Stockton 167 D6
Urmston Gtr Man 137 D6
Urpeth Durham 179 D4
Urquhart Highld 252 A1
Urquhart Moray 266 C3
Urquhart Castle, Drumnadrochit Highld 252 D1
Urra N Yorks 159 A4
Urray Highld 251 A7
Ushaw Moor Durham 167 A5
Usk = Brynbuga Mon 61 C5
Usselby Lincs 142 D2
Usworth T & W 179 D5
Utkinton Ches 127 C5
Utley W Yorks 147 C4
Uton Devon 12 B3
Utterby Lincs 143 D5
Uttoxeter Staffs 113 B4
Uttoxeter Racecourse Staffs 113 B5
Uwchmynydd Gwyn 106 D1
Uxbridge London 48 A3
Uyeasound Shetland 284 C7
Uzmaston Pembs 55 C5

## V

Valley Anglesey 122 C2
Valley Truckle Corn 10 C1
Valleyfield Dumfries 173 C4
Valsgarth Shetland 284 B8
Valtos Highld 259 B5
Van Powys 92 C3
Vange Essex 51 A4
Varteg Torf 61 C4
Vatten Highld 258 D2
Vaul Argyll 222 C3
Vaynor M Tydf 60 B2
Veensgarth Shetland 285 J6
Velindre Powys 77 D5
Vellow Som 27 B5
Veness Orkney 282 E6
Venn Green Devon 25 D4
Venn Ottery Devon 13 B5
Vennington Shrops 94 A1
Venny Tedburn Devon 12 B3
Ventnor I o W 19 D4
Ventnor Botanic Garden I o W 19 D4
Vernham Dean Hants 46 D1
Vernham Street Hants 46 D1
Vernolds Common Shrops 94 C2
Verwood Dorset 17 A4
Veryan Corn 4 D4
Vicarage Devon 14 C2
Vickerstown Cumb 153 D2
Victoria Corn 5 A4
Victoria S Yorks 139 C4
Victoria and Albert Museum London 49 B5
Vidlin Shetland 284 G6
Viewpark N Lnrk 207 D5
Vigo Village Kent 50 C3
Vinehall Street E Sus 37 D5
Vine's Cross E Sus 22 A3
Viney Hill Glos 62 C2
Virginia Water Sur 48 C3
Virginstow Devon 11 B4
Vobster Som 29 A7
Voe Shetland 285 G6
Voe Shetland 284 E5
Vowchurch Hereford 78 D1
Voxter Shetland 284 F5
Voy Orkney 282 F3

## W

Wackerfield Durham 167 C4
Wacton Norf 104 B2
Wadbister Shetland 285 J6
Wadborough Worcs 80 C2
Waddesdon Bucks 66 B2
Waddesdon Manor, Aylesbury Bucks 66 B2
Waddingham Lincs 142 D1
Waddington Lancs 146 C1
Waddington Lincs 133 C4
Wadebridge Corn 9 D5
Wadeford Som 28 D3
Wadenhoe Northants 100 C2
Wadesmill Herts 68 B3
Wadhurst E Sus 36 C4
Wadshelf Derbys 130 B3
Wadsley S Yorks 139 D6
Wadsley Bridge S Yorks 139 D6
Wadworth S Yorks 140 D3
Waen Denb 125 C6
Waen Denb 125 C4
Waen Fach Powys 109 D7
Waen Goleugoed Denb 125 B5
Wag Highld 274 B4
Wainfleet All Saints Lincs 135 D4
Wainfleet Bank Lincs 135 D4
Wainfleet St Mary Lincs 135 D5
Wainfleet Tofts Lincs 135 D4
Wainhouse Corner Corn 10 B2
Wainscott Medway 51 B4
Wainstalls W Yorks 138 A3
Waitby Cumb 155 A6
Waithe Lincs 143 C4
Wake Lady Green N Yorks 159 B5
Wakefield W Yorks 139 A6
Wakehurst Place Garden, Crawley W Sus 35 C6
Wakerley Northants 99 B6
Wakes Colne Essex 70 A2
Walberswick Suff 105 D5
Walberton W Sus 20 B2
Walbottle T & W 178 C3
Walcot Lincs 116 B3
Walcot N Lincs 141 A6
Walcot Shrops 94 C1
Walcot Telford 111 D4
Walcot Thamesdown 45 A5
Walcot Green Norf 104 C2
Walcote Leics 98 C2
Walcote Warks 80 B4
Walcott Lincs 133 D6
Walcott Norf 121 B5
Walden N Yorks 156 C4
Walden Head N Yorks 156 C3
Walden Stubbs N Yorks 140 B3
Waldersey Cambs 101 A6
Walderslade Medway 51 C4
Walderton W Sus 33 D6
Walditch Dorset 15 B4
Waldley Derbys 113 B5
Waldridge Durham 179 D4
Waldringfield Suff 88 C3
Waldringfield Heath Suff 88 C3
Waldron E Sus 22 A3
Wales S Yorks 131 A4
Walesby Lincs 142 D3
Walesby Notts 132 B1
Walford Hereford 94 D1
Walford Hereford 62 A1
Walford Shrops 110 C3
Walford Heath Shrops 110 D3
Walgherton Ches 111 A5
Walgrave Northants 99 D5
Walhampton Hants 18 B2
Walk Mill Lancs 146 D2
Walkden Gtr Man 137 C6
Walker T & W 179 C4
Walker Art Gallery Mers 136 D2
Walker Barn Ches 129 B4
Walker Fold Lancs 145 C6
Walkerburn Borders 196 C2
Walkeringham Notts 141 D5
Walkerith Lincs 141 D5
Walkern Herts 68 A2
Walker's Green Hereford 78 C3
Walkerville N Yorks 157 B6
Walkford Dorset 17 B6
Walkhampton Devon 7 A4
Walkington E Yorks 150 D2
Walkley S Yorks 130 A3
Walkley Clogs, Hebden Bridge W Yorks 138 A3
Wall Northumb 177 C7
Wall Staffs 96 A4
Wall Bank Shrops 94 B3
Wall Heath W Mid 96 C1
Wall under Heywood Shrops 94 B3
Wallaceton Dumfries 183 D6
Wallacetown S Ayrs 181 A4
Wallacetown S Ayrs 192 C3
Wallands Park E Sus 22 A2
Wallasey Mers 136 D2
Wallcrouch E Sus 37 C4
Wallingford Oxon 47 A4
Wallington London 49 C5
Wallington Hants 19 A4
Wallington Herts 85 D4
Wallington House, Ponteland Northumb 178 A2
Wallis Pembs 55 B6
Walliswood Sur 35 C4
Walls Shetland 285 J4
Wallsend T & W 179 C4
Wallston V Glam 41 D6
Wallyford E Loth 209 C6
Walmer Kent 53 D5
Walmer Bridge Lancs 136 A3
Walmersley Gtr Man 137 B7
Walmley W Mid 96 B4
Walney Island Airport Cumb 153 C2
Walpole Suff 105 D4
Walpole Cross Keys Norf 118 D2
Walpole Highway Norf 118 D2
Walpole Marsh Norf 118 D1
Walpole St Andrew Norf 118 D2
Walpole St Peter Norf 118 D2
Walsall W Mid 96 B3
Walsall Arboretum W Mid 96 B3
Walsall Wood W Mid 96 A3
Walsden W Yorks 138 A2
Walsgrave on Sowe W Mid 97 C6
Walsham le Willows Suff 103 D5
Walshaw Gtr Man 137 B6
Walshford N Yorks 148 B3
Walsoken Cambs 118 D1
Walston S Lnrk 195 B5
Walsworth Herts 84 D4
Walters Ash Bucks 66 D3
Walterston V Glam 41 D5
Walterstone Hereford 61 A5
Waltham Kent 38 A3
Waltham NE Lincs 143 C4
Waltham Abbey Essex 68 C3
Waltham Chase Hants 33 D4
Waltham Cross Herts 68 C3
Waltham on the Wolds Leics 115 C6
Waltham St Lawrence Windsor 47 B6
Walthamstow London 49 A6
Walton Cumb 176 C3
Walton Derbys 130 C3
Walton Leics 98 C2
Walton Mers 136 D2
Walton M Keynes 83 D5
Walton P'boro 100 A3
Walton Powys 77 B6
Walton Som 29 B4
Walton Staffs 112 B2
Walton Suff 88 D3
Walton Telford 111 D4
Walton Warks 81 B5
Walton W Yorks 139 B6
Walton W Yorks 148 C3
Walton Cardiff Glos 80 D2
Walton East Pembs 55 B6
Walton Hall Warr 127 A6
Walton-in-Gordano N Som 42 B3
Walton-le-Dale Lancs 137 A4
Walton-on-Thames Sur 48 C4
Walton on the Hill Staffs 112 C3
Walton on the Hill Sur 35 A5
Walton-on-the-Naze Essex 71 A6
Walton on the Wolds Leics 114 D3
Walton-on-Trent Derbys 113 D6
Walton West Pembs 55 C4
Walwen Flint 126 B2
Walwick Northumb 177 B7
Walworth Darl 167 D5
Walworth Gate Darl 167 C5
Walwyn's Castle Pembs 55 C4
Wambrook Som 14 A2
Wanborough Sur 34 B2
Wanborough Thamesdown 45 A6
Wandsworth London 49 B5
Wangford Suff 105 D5
Wanlockhead Dumfries 183 A6
Wansford E Yorks 150 B3
Wansford P'boro 100 B2
Wanstead London 49 A7
Wanstrow Som 29 A7
Wanswell Glos 62 C2
Wantage Oxon 46 A1
Wapley S Glos 43 B6
Wappenbury Warks 81 A6
Wappenham Northants 82 C3
Warbleton E Sus 22 A4
Warblington Hants 19 A6
Warborough Oxon 65 D6
Warboys Cambs 101 C5
Warbreck Blkpool 144 D3
Warbstow Corn 10 B3
Warburton Gtr Man 128 A2
Warcop Cumb 165 D5
Ward End W Mid 96 C4
Ward Green Suff 87 A6
Warden Kent 52 B2
Warden Northumb 177 C7
Wardhill Orkney 282 E7
Wardington Oxon 82 C1
Wardlaw Borders 185 A5
Wardle Ches 127 D6
Wardle Gtr Man 138 B2
Wardley Rutland 99 A5
Wardlow Derbys 130 B1
Wardy Hill Cambs 101 C6
Ware Herts 68 B3
Ware Kent 53 C4
Wareham Dorset 16 C3
Warehorne Kent 38 B1
Waren Mill Northumb 199 C5
Warenford Northumb 189 A4
Warenton Northumb 199 C5
Wareside Herts 68 B3
Waresley Cambs 84 B4
Waresley Worcs 95 D6
Warfield Brack 48 B1
Warfleet Devon 8 B2
Wargrave Wokingham 47 B5
Warham Norf 119 A6
Warhill Gtr Man 138 D2
Wark Northumb 177 B6
Wark Northumb 198 C2
Warkleigh Devon 26 C1
Warkton Northants 99 D5
Warkworth Northants 82 C1
Warkworth Northumb 189 C5
Warlaby N Yorks 158 B2
Warland W Yorks 138 A2
Warleggan Corn 5 A6
Warlingham Sur 35 A6
Warmfield W Yorks 140 A1
Warmingham Ches 128 C2
Warmington Northants 100 B2
Warmington Warks 81 C7
Warminster Wilts 30 A2
Warmlake Kent 37 A6
Warmley S Glos 43 B5
Warmley Tower S Glos 43 B5
Warmonds Hill Northants 83 A6
Warmsworth S Yorks 140 C3
Warmwell Dorset 16 C1
Warndon Worcs 80 B1
Warnford Hants 33 C5
Warnham W Sus 35 C4
Warninglid W Sus 35 D5
Warren Ches 128 B3
Warren Pembs 55 E5
Warren Heath Suff 88 C3
Warren Row Windsor 47 A6
Warren Street Kent 51 D6
Warrington M Keynes 83 B5
Warrington Warr 127 A6
Warsash Hants 18 A3
Warslow Staffs 129 D5
Warter E Yorks 150 B1
Warthermarske N Yorks 157 D6
Warthill N Yorks 149 B5
Wartling E Sus 23 B4
Wartnaby Leics 115 C5
Warton Lancs 136 A3
Warton Lancs 154 D3
Warton Northumb 188 C3
Warton Warks 97 A5
Warwick Warks 81 A5
Warwick Bridge Cumb 176 D2
Warwick Castle Warks 81 A5
Warwick on Eden Cumb 176 D2
Warwick Racecourse Warks 81 A5
Wasbister Orkney 282 D4
Wasdale Head Cumb 163 D4
Wash Common W Berks 46 C2
Washaway Corn 5 A5
Washbourne Devon 8 B1
Washfield Devon 27 D4
Washfold N Yorks 157 A4
Washford Som 27 A5
Washford Pyne Devon 26 D3
Washingborough Lincs 133 B5
Washington T & W 179 D5
Washington W Sus 21 A4
Wasing W Berks 46 C3
Waskerley Durham 166 A3
Wasperton Warks 81 B5
Wasps Nest Lincs 133 C5
Wass N Yorks 159 D4
Watchet Som 27 A5
Watchfield Oxon 64 D3
Watchfield Som 28 A3
Watchgate Cumb 154 B4
Watchhill Cumb 175 D4
Watcombe Torbay 8 A3
Watendlath Cumb 163 C5
Water Devon 12 C2
Water Lancs 138 A1
Water End E Yorks 149 D6
Water End Herts 67 B5
Water End Herts 68 C2
Water Newton Cambs 100 B3
Water Orton Warks 97 B4
Water Stratford Bucks 82 D3
Water Yeat Cumb 154 C1
Waterbeach Cambs 85 A6
Waterbeck Dumfries 175 A5
Watercress Line (Mid Hants Railway), Alton Hants 33 B5
Waterden Norf 119 B5
Waterfall Staffs 129 D5
Waterfoot E Renf 205 C5
Waterfoot Lancs 138 A1
Waterford Hants 18 B2
Waterford Herts 68 B3
Waterhead Cumb 154 A2
Waterhead Dumfries 185 C4
Waterheads Borders 196 A1
Waterhouses Durham 167 A4
Waterhouses Staffs 129 D5
Wateringbury Kent 37 A4
Waterloo Gtr Man 138 C2
Waterloo Highld 247 B5
Waterloo Mers 136 D2
Waterloo N Lnrk 194 A3
Waterloo Norf 120 D4
Waterloo Perth 219 A5
Waterloo Poole 17 B4
Waterloo Shrops 111 B4
Waterloo Port Gwyn 123 D4
Waterlooville Hants 19 A5
Watermeetings S Lnrk 184 A2
Watermillock Cumb 164 C2
Watermouth Castle, Ilfracombe Devon 25 A6
Waterperry Oxon 66 C1
Waterrow Som 27 C5
Water's Nook Gtr Man 137 C5
Waters Upton Telford 111 D5
Watersfield W Sus 20 A3
Watershed Mill Visitor Centre, Settle N Yorks 146 A2
Waterside Aberds 257 D5
Waterside Blkburn 137 A6
Waterside Cumb 175 D5
Waterside E Ayrs 182 B2
Waterside E Ayrs 205 D4
Waterside E Dunb 207 C4
Waterside E Renf 205 C5
Waterstock Oxon 66 C1
Waterston Pembs 55 D5
Watford Herts 67 D6
Watford Northants 82 A3
Watford Gap W Mid 96 A4
Wath N Yorks 147 A5
Wath N Yorks 157 D7
Wath N Yorks 159 D5
Wath Brow Cumb 162 C3
Wath upon Dearne S Yorks 140 C2
Watley's End S Glos 43 A5
Watlington Norf 118 D3
Watlington Oxon 66 D1
Watnall Notts 114 A3
Watten Highld 280 C4
Wattisfield Suff 103 D6
Wattisham Suff 87 B6
Wattlesborough Heath Shrops 110 D2
Watton E Yorks 150 B3
Watton Norf 103 A5
Watton at Stone Herts 68 B3
Wattston N Lnrk 207 C5
Wattstown Rhondda 41 B5
Wauchan Highld 238 D3
Waulkmill Lodge Orkney 283 G4
Waun Powys 91 B6
Waun-y-clyn Carms 57 B4
Waunarlwydd Swansea 57 C6
Waunclunda Carms 58 B3
Waunfawr Gwyn 107 A5
Waungron Swansea 57 B5
Waunlwyd Bl Gwent 60 C3
Wavendon M Keynes 83 D6
Waverbridge Cumb 175 D5
Waverton Ches 127 C4
Waverton Cumb 175 D5
Wavertree Mers 126 A3
Wawne E Yorks 150 D3
Waxham Norf 121 C6
Waxholme E Yorks 143 A5
Way Kent 53 C5
Way Village Devon 26 D3
Wayfield Medway 51 C4
Wayford Som 14 A4
Waymills Shrops 111 A4
Wayne Green Mon 61 B6
Wdig = Goodwick Pembs 72 C2
Weachyburn Aberds 268 D1
Weald Oxon 64 C4
Weald and Downland Open Air Museum, Chichester W Sus 20 A1
Wealdstone London 49 A4
Weardley W Yorks 148 C1
Weare Som 42 D3
Weare Giffard Devon 25 C5
Wearhead Durham 165 B6
Weasdale Cumb 155 A5
Weasenham All Saints Norf 119 C5
Weasenham St Peter Norf 119 C5
Weatherhill Sur 35 B6
Weaverham Ches 127 B6
Weaverthorpe N Yorks 160 D3
Webheath Worcs 80 A3
Wedderlairs Aberds 256 C3
Wedderlie Borders 197 A5
Weddington Warks 97 B6
Wedgwood Visitor Centre, Barlaston Staffs 112 B2
Wedhampton Wilts 45 D4
Wedmore Som 28 A4
Wednesbury W Mid 96 B2
Wednesfield W Mid 96 A2
Weedon Bucks 66 B3
Weedon Bec Northants 82 B3
Weedon Lois Northants 82 C3
Weeford Staffs 96 A4
Week Devon 26 D2
Week St Mary Corn 10 B3
Weeke Hants 32 B3
Weekley Northants 99 C5
Weel E Yorks 150 D3
Weeley Essex 71 A5
Weeley Heath Essex 71 A5
Weem Perth 230 D2
Weeping Cross Staffs 112 C3
Weethley Gate Warks 80 B3
Weeting Norf 102 C3
Weeting Heath NNR Norf 102 C3
Weeton E Yorks 143 A5
Weeton Lancs 144 D3
Weeton N Yorks 148 C1
Weetwood Hall Northumb 188 A3
Weir Lancs 138 A1
Weir Quay Devon 6 A3
Welborne Norf 120 E2
Welbourn Lincs 133 D4
Welburn N Yorks 149 A6
Welburn N Yorks 159 C5
Welbury N Yorks 158 A2
Welby Lincs 116 B2
Welches Dam Cambs 101 C6
Welcombe Devon 24 D3
Weld Bank Lancs 137 B4
Weldon Northumb 189 D4
Welford Northants 98 C3
Welford W Berks 46 B2
Welford-on-Avon Warks 81 B4
Welham Leics 99 B4
Welham Notts 132 A2
Welham Green Herts 68 C2
Well Hants 33 A6
Well Lincs 135 B4
Well N Yorks 157 C6
Well End Bucks 48 A1
Well Heads W Yorks 147 D4
Well Hill Kent 50 C1
Well Town Devon 13 A4
Welland Worcs 79 C5
Wellbank Angus 221 A4
Welldale Dumfries 175 B4
Wellesbourne Warks 81 B5
Welling London 50 B1
Wellingborough Northants 83 A5
Wellingham Norf 119 C5
Wellingore Lincs 133 D4
Wellington Cumb 162 D3
Wellington Hereford 78 C2
Wellington Som 27 C6
Wellington Telford 111 D5
Wellington Heath Hereford 79 C5

Wellington Hill W Yorks 148 D2
Wellow Bath 43 D6
Wellow I o W 18 C2
Wellow Notts 131 C6
Wellpond Green Herts 68 A4
Wells Som 29 A5
Wells Cathedral Som 29 A5
Wells Green Ches 128 D1
Wells-next-the-Sea Norf 119 A6
Wellsborough Leics 97 A6
Wellswood Torbay 8 A3
Wellwood Fife 208 B3
Welney Norf 102 B1
Welsh Bicknor Hereford 62 B1
Welsh End Shrops 111 B4
Welsh Frankton Shrops 110 B2
Welsh Highland Railway, Caernarfon Gwyn 123 D4
Welsh Highland Railway, Porthmadog Gwyn 107 C5
Welsh Hook Pembs 55 B5
Welsh National Velodrome Newport 42 A2
Welsh Newton Hereford 61 B6
Welsh St Donats V Glam 41 D5
Welshampton Shrops 110 B3
Welshpool = Y Trallwng Powys 93 A6
Welton Cumb 164 A1
Welton E Yorks 142 A1
Welton Lincs 133 B5
Welton Northants 82 A2
Welton Hill Lincs 133 A5
Welton le Marsh Lincs 135 C4
Welton le Wold Lincs 134 A2
Welwick E Yorks 143 A5
Welwyn Herts 68 B2
Welwyn Garden City Herts 68 B2
Wem Shrops 111 C4
Wembdon Som 28 B2
Wembley London 49 A4
Wembley Stadium London 49 A4
Wembury Devon 7 C4
Wembworthy Devon 12 A1
Wemyss Bay Invclyd 204 B1
Wenallt Ceredig 75 A5
Wenallt Gwyn 109 A4
Wendens Ambo Essex 85 D7
Wendlebury Oxon 65 B6
Wendling Norf 119 D6
Wendover Bucks 66 C3
Wendron Corn 3 B4
Wendy Cambs 85 C5
Wenfordbridge Corn 10 D1
Wenhaston Suff 105 D5
Wennington Cambs 100 D4
Wennington London 50 A2
Wennington Lancs 155 D5
Wensley Derbys 130 C2
Wensley N Yorks 157 C4
Wentbridge W Yorks 140 B2
Wentnor Shrops 94 B1
Wentworth Cambs 101 D6
Wentworth S Yorks 140 D1
Wenvoe V Glam 41 D6
Weobley Hereford 78 B2
Weobley Marsh Hereford 78 B2
Wereham Norf 102 A2
Wergs W Mid 95 A6
Wern Powys 109 D4
Wern Powys 110 D1
Wernffrwd Swansea 57 C5
Wernyrheolydd Mon 61 B5
Werrington Corn 10 C4
Werrington P'boro 100 A3
Werrington Staffs 112 A3
Wervin Ches 127 B4
Wesham Lancs 144 D4
Wessington Derbys 130 D3
West Acre Norf 119 D4
West Adderbury Oxon 82 D1
West Allerdean Northumb 198 B3
West Alvington Devon 7 C6
West Amesbury Wilts 31 A5
West Anstey Devon 26 C3
West Ashby Lincs 134 B2
West Ashling W Sus 19 A7
West Ashton Wilts 44 D2
West Auckland Durham 167 C4
West Ayton N Yorks 160 C3
West Bagborough Som 27 B6
West Barkwith Lincs 133 A6
West Barnby N Yorks 169 D6
West Barns E Loth 210 C3
West Barsham Norf 119 B6
West Bay Dorset 15 B4
West Beckham Norf 120 B3
West Bedfont Sur 48 B3
West Benhar N Lnrk 208 D1
West Bergholt Essex 70 A3
West Bexington Dorset 15 C5
West Bilney Norf 119 D4
West Blatchington Brighton 21 B5
West Bowling W Yorks 147 D5
West Bradford Lancs 146 C1
West Bradley Som 29 B5
West Bretton W Yorks 139 B5
West Bridgford Notts 114 B3
West Bromwich W Mid 96 B3
West Buckland Devon 26 B1
West Buckland Som 28 C1
West Burrafirth Shetland 285 H4
West Burton N Yorks 156 C4
West Burton W Sus 20 A2
West Butterwick N Lincs 141 C6
West Byfleet Sur 48 C3
West Caister Norf 121 D7
West Calder W Loth 208 D3
West Camel Som 29 C5
West Challow Oxon 46 A1
West Chelborough Dorset 15 A5
West Chevington Northumb 189 D5
West Chiltington W Sus 20 A3
West Chinnock Som 29 D4
West Chisenbury Wilts 45 D5
West Clandon Sur 34 A3
West Cliffe Kent 39 A5
West Clyne Highld 274 D2
West Clyth Highld 275 A6
West Coker Som 29 D5
West Compton Dorset 15 B5
West Compton Som 29 A5
West Cowick E Yorks 140 A4
West Cranmore Som 29 A6
West Cross Swansea 57 D6
West Cullery Aberds 245 B4
West Curry Corn 10 B3
West Curthwaite Cumb 175 D6
West Darlochan Argyll 190 C2
West Dean Wilts 31 C6
West Dean W Sus 20 A1
West Deeping Lincs 100 A3
West Derby Mers 136 D2
West Dereham Norf 102 A2
West Didsbury Gtr Man 138 D1
West Ditchburn Northumb 189 A4
West Down Devon 25 A6
West Drayton London 48 B3
West Drayton Notts 132 B2
West Ella E Yorks 142 A2
West End Beds 84 B1
West End E Yorks 150 D2
West End E Yorks 151 D4
West End Hants 32 D3
West End Lancs 137 A6
West End Norf 103 A5
West End Norf 121 D7
West End N Som 42 C3
West End N Yorks 147 B5
West End Oxon 65 C5
West End S Lnrk 195 B4
West End Suff 105 C5
West End Sur 48 C2
West End S Yorks 141 C4
West End Wilts 30 C3
West End Wilts 44 B3
West End W Sus 21 A5
West End Green Hants 47 C4
West Farleigh Kent 37 A5
West Felton Shrops 110 C2
West Fenton E Loth 210 B1
West Ferry Dundee 221 A4
West Firle E Sus 22 B2
West Ginge Oxon 46 A2
West Grafton Wilts 45 C6
West Green Hants 47 D5
West Greenskares Aberds 268 C2
West Grimstead Wilts 31 C6
West Grinstead W Sus 35 D4
West Haddlesey N Yorks 140 A3
West Haddon Northants 98 D3
West Hagbourne Oxon 46 A3
West Hagley Worcs 96 C2
West Hall Cumb 176 C3
West Hallam Derbys 114 A2
West Halton N Lincs 141 A7
West Ham London 49 A7
West Handley Derbys 130 B3
West Hanney Oxon 65 D5
West Hanningfield Essex 70 D1
West Hardwick W Yorks 140 B2
West Harnham Wilts 31 C5
West Harptree Bath 43 D4
West Hatch Som 28 C2
West Head Norf 102 A1
West Heath Ches 128 C3
West Heath Hants 34 A1
West Heath Hants 46 D3
West Helmsdale Highld 274 C4
West Hendred Oxon 46 A2
West Heslerton N Yorks 160 D3
West Hill Devon 13 B5
West Hill E Yorks 151 A4
West Hill N Som 42 B3
West Hoathly W Sus 35 C6
West Holme Dorset 16 C2
West Horndon Essex 50 A3
West Horrington Som 29 A5
West Horsley Sur 34 A3
West Horton Northumb 198 C4
West Hougham Kent 39 A4
West Houlland Shetland 285 H4
West-houses Derbys 131 D4
West Huntington York 149 B5
West Hythe Kent 38 B3
West Ilsley W Berks 46 A2
West Itchenor W Sus 19 A6
West Keal Lincs 134 C3
West Kennett Wilts 45 C5
West Kilbride N Ayrs 204 D2
West Kingsdown Kent 50 C2
West Kington Wilts 44 B2
West Kinharrachie Aberds 257 C4
West Kirby Mers 126 A2
West Knapton N Yorks 160 D2
West Knighton Dorset 16 C1
West Knoyle Wilts 30 B2
West Kyloe Northumb 199 B4
West Lambrook Som 28 D4
West Langdon Kent 39 A5
West Langwell Highld 273 D4
West Lavington Wilts 44 D4
West Lavington W Sus 34 D1
West Layton N Yorks 157 A5
West Lea Durham 168 A2
West Leake Notts 114 C3
West Learmouth Northumb 198 C2
West Leigh Devon 12 A1
West Lexham Norf 119 D5
West Lilling N Yorks 149 A5
West Linton Borders 195 A6
West Liss Hants 33 C6
West Littleton S Glos 43 B6
West Looe Corn 6 B1
West Luccombe Som 26 A3
West Lulworth Dorset 16 C2
West Lutton N Yorks 150 A2
West Lydford Som 29 B5
West Lyng Som 28 C3
West Lynn Norf 118 C3
West Malling Kent 37 A4
West Malvern Worcs 79 C5
West Marden W Sus 33 D6
West Marina E Sus 23 B5
West Markham Notts 132 B2
West Marsh NE Lincs 143 B4
West Marton N Yorks 146 B2
West Meon Hants 33 C5
West Mersea Essex 71 B4
West Midlands Safari Park, Kidderminster Worcs 95 D6
West Milton Dorset 15 B5
West Minster Kent 51 B6
West Molesey Sur 48 C4
West Monkton Som 28 C2
West Moors Dorset 17 A4
West Morriston Borders 197 B5
West Muir Angus 232 B3
West Ness N Yorks 159 D5
West Newham Northumb 178 B2
West Newton E Yorks 151 D4
West Newton Norf 118 C3
West Norwood London 49 B6
West Ogwell Devon 12 D3
West Orchard Dorset 30 D2
West Overton Wilts 45 C5
West Park Hrtlpl 168 B2
West Parley Dorset 17 B4
West Peckham Kent 36 A4
West Pelton Durham 179 D4
West Pennard Som 29 B5
West Pentire Corn 4 A2
West Perry Cambs 84 A3
West Putford Devon 25 D4
West Quantoxhead Som 27 A6
West Rainton Durham 167 A6
West Rasen Lincs 133 A5
West Raynham Norf 119 C5
West Retford Notts 132 A1
West Rounton N Yorks 158 A3
West Row Suff 102 D2
West Rudham Norf 119 C5
West Runton Norf 120 A3
West Saltoun E Loth 210 D1
West Sandwick Shetland 284 E6
West Scrafton N Yorks 157 C4
West Sleekburn Northumb 179 A4
West Somerset Railway, Minehead Som 27 A4
West Somerton Norf 121 D6
West Stafford Dorset 16 C1
West Stockwith Notts 141 D5
West Stoke W Sus 20 B1
West Stonesdale N Yorks 156 A2
West Stoughton Som 28 A4
West Stour Dorset 30 C1
West Stourmouth Kent 53 C4
West Stow Suff 103 D4
West Stowell Wilts 45 C5
West Strathan Highld 277 B6
West Stratton Hants 32 A4
West Street Kent 37 A7
West Tanfield N Yorks 157 D6
West Taphouse Corn 5 A6
West Tarbert Argyll 202 B3
West Thirston Northumb 189 D4
West Thorney W Sus 19 A6
West Thurrock Thurrock 50 B2
West Tilbury Thurrock 50 B3
West Tisted Hants 33 C5
West Tofts Norf 103 B4
West Tofts Perth 219 A6
West Torrington Lincs 133 A6
West Town Hants 19 B6
West Town N Som 42 C3
West Tytherley Hants 32 C1
West Tytherton Wilts 44 B3
West Walton Norf 118 D1
West Walton Highway Norf 118 D1
West Wellow Hants 32 D1
West Wemyss Fife 209 A6
West Wick N Som 42 C2
West Wickham Cambs 86 C2
West Wickham London 49 C6
West Williamston Pembs 55 D6
West Willoughby Lincs 116 A2
West Winch Norf 118 D3
West Winterslow Wilts 31 B6
West Wittering W Sus 19 B6
West Witton N Yorks 157 C4
West Woodburn Northumb 177 A6
West Woodhay W Berks 46 C1
West Woodlands Som 30 A1
West Worldham Hants 33 B6
West Worlington Devon 26 D2
West Worthing W Sus 21 B4
West Wratting Cambs 86 B2
West Wycombe Bucks 66 D3
West Wylam Northumb 178 C3
West Yell Shetland 284 E6
Westacott Devon 25 B6
Westbere Kent 52 C3
Westborough Lincs 115 A6
Westbourne Bmouth 17 B4
Westbourne Suff 88 C2
Westbourne W Sus 19 A6
Westbrook W Berks 46 B2
Westbury Bucks 82 D3
Westbury Shrops 94 A1
Westbury Wilts 44 D2
Westbury Leigh Wilts 44 D2
Westbury-on-Severn Glos 62 B3
Westbury on Trym Bristol 43 B4
Westbury-sub-Mendip Som 29 A5
Westby Lancs 144 D3
Westcliff-on-Sea Sthend 51 A5
Westcombe Som 29 B6
Westcote Glos 64 A3
Westcott Bucks 66 B2
Westcott Devon 13 A5
Westcott Sur 35 B4
Westcott Barton Oxon 65 A5
Westdean E Sus 22 C3
Westdene Brighton 21 B5
Wester Aberchalder Highld 252 D1
Wester Balgedie Perth 219 D6
Wester Culbeuchly Aberds 268 C1
Wester Dechmont W Loth 208 D3
Wester Denoon Angus 232 D1
Wester Fintray Aberds 245 A5
Wester Gruinards Highld 263 A7
Wester Lealty Highld 264 C2
Wester Milton Highld 253 A5
Wester Newburn Fife 220 D4
Wester Quarff Shetland 285 K6
Wester Skeld Shetland 285 J4
Westerdale Highld 280 C3
Westerdale N Yorks 159 A5
Westerfield Shetland 285 H5
Westerfield Suff 88 C2
Westergate W Sus 20 B2
Westerham Kent 36 A2
Westerhope T & W 178 C3
Westerleigh S Glos 43 B6
Westerton Angus 233 C4
Westerton Durham 167 B5
Westerton W Sus 20 B1
Westerwick Shetland 285 J4
Westfield Cumb 162 B2
Westfield E Sus 23 A6
Westfield Hereford 79 C5
Westfield Highld 279 B6
Westfield N Lnrk 207 C5
Westfield Norf 103 A5
Westfield W Loth 208 C2
Westfields Dorset 15 A7
Westfields of Rattray Perth 231 D5
Westgate Durham 166 B2
Westgate N Lincs 141 C5
Westgate Norf 119 A6
Westgate on Sea Kent 53 B5
Westhall Aberds 256 D1
Westhall Suff 105 C5
Westham Dorset 15 D6
Westham E Sus 22 B4
Westham Som 28 A4
Westhampnett W Sus 20 B1
Westhay Som 28 A4
Westhead Lancs 136 C3
Westhide Hereford 78 C3
Westhill Aberds 245 B5
Westhill Highld 252 B3
Westhope Hereford 78 B2
Westhope Shrops 94 C2
Westhorpe Lincs 117 B5
Westhorpe Suff 87 A6
Westhoughton Gtr Man 137 C5
Westhouse N Yorks 155 D5
Westhumble Sur 35 A4
Westing Shetland 284 C7
Westlake Devon 7 B5
Westleigh Devon 25 C5
Westleigh Devon 27 D5
Westleigh Gtr Man 137 C5
Westleton Suff 89 A5
Westley Shrops 94 A1
Westley Suff 87 A4
Westley Waterless Cambs 86 B2
Westlington Bucks 66 B2
Westlinton Cumb 175 B6
Westmarsh Kent 53 C4
Westmeston E Sus 21 A6
Westmill Herts 68 A3
Westminster London 49 B6
Westminster Cathedral London 49 B5
Westmuir Angus 232 C1
Westness Orkney 282 E4
Westnewton Cumb 174 D4
Westnewton Northumb 198 C3
Westoe T & W 179 C5
Weston Bath 43 C6
Weston Ches 128 D2
Weston Devon 13 C6
Weston Dorset 15 D6
Weston Halton 127 A5
Weston Hants 33 C6
Weston Herts 85 D4
Weston Lincs 117 C5
Weston Notts 132 C2
Weston Northants 82 C2
Weston N Yorks 147 C5
Weston Shrops 94 B3
Weston Shrops 111 C4
Weston Staffs 112 C3
Weston W Berks 46 B1
Weston Beggard Hereford 78 C3
Weston by Welland Northants 99 B4
Weston Colville Cambs 86 B2
Weston Coyney Stoke 112 A3
Weston Favell Northants 83 A4
Weston Green Cambs 86 B2
Weston Green Norf 120 D3
Weston Heath Shrops 112 D1
Weston Hills Lincs 117 C5
Weston-in-Gordano N Som 42 B3
Weston Jones Staffs 111 C6
Weston Longville Norf 120 D3
Weston Lullingfields Shrops 110 C3
Weston-on-the-Green Oxon 65 B6
Weston-on-Trent Derbys 114 C2
Weston Park Staffs 112 D2
Weston Patrick Hants 33 A5
Weston Rhyn Shrops 110 B1
Weston-Sub-Edge Glos 80 C4
Weston-super-Mare N Som 42 C2
Weston Turville Bucks 66 B3
Weston under Lizard Staffs 112 D2
Weston under Penyard Hereford 62 A2
Weston under Wetherley Warks 81 A6
Weston Underwood Derbys 113 A6
Weston Underwood M Keynes 83 B5
Westonbirt Glos 44 A2
Westonbirt Arboretum, Tetbury Glos 44 A2
Westoncommon Shrops 110 C3
Westoning Beds 84 D2
Westonzoyland Som 28 B3
Westow N Yorks 149 A6
Westport Argyll 190 C2
Westport Som 28 D3
Westray Airport Orkney 282 B5
Westrigg W Loth 208 D2
Westruther Borders 197 B5
Westry Cambs 101 B5
Westville Notts 114 A3
Westward Cumb 175 D5
Westward Ho! Devon 25 C5
Westwell Kent 38 A1
Westwell Oxon 64 C3
Westwell Leacon Kent 38 A1
Westwick Cambs 85 A6
Westwick Durham 166 D3
Westwick Norf 121 C4
Westwood Devon 13 B5
Westwood Wilts 44 D2
Westwoodside N Lincs 141 D5
Wetheral Cumb 176 D2
Wetherby W Yorks 148 C3
Wetherby Racecourse W Yorks 148 C3
Wetherden Suff 87 A6
Wetheringsett Suff 88 A2
Wethersfield Essex 86 D3
Wethersta Shetland 284 G5
Wetherup Street Suff 88 A2
Wetley Rocks Staffs 112 A3
Wettenhall Ches 127 C6
Wetton Staffs 129 D6
Wetwang E Yorks 150 B2
Wetwood Staffs 111 B6
Wexcombe Wilts 45 D6
Wexham Street Bucks 48 A2
Weybourne Norf 120 A3
Weybread Suff 104 C3
Weybridge Sur 48 C3
Weycroft Devon 14 B3
Weydale Highld 280 B3
Weyhill Hants 32 A2
Weymouth Dorset 15 D6
Weymouth Sea Life Park Dorset 15 C6
Whaddon Bucks 83 D5
Whaddon Cambs 85 C5
Whaddon Glos 63 B4
Whaddon Wilts 31 C5
Whale Cumb 164 C3
Whaley Derbys 131 B5
Whaley Bridge Derbys 129 A5
Whaley Thorns Derbys 131 B5
Whaligoe Highld 281 D5
Whalley Lancs 146 D1
Whalsay Airport Shetland 284 G7
Whalton Northumb 178 A3
Wham N Yorks 146 A1
Whaplode Lincs 117 C6
Whaplode Drove Lincs 117 D6
Whaplode St Catherine Lincs 117 C6
Wharfe N Yorks 146 A1
Wharles Lancs 144 D4
Wharncliffe Side S Yorks 139 D5
Wharram le Street N Yorks 150 A1
Wharton Ches 127 C6
Wharton Green Ches 127 C6
Whashton N Yorks 157 A5
Whatcombe Dorset 16 A2
Whatcote Warks 81 C6
Whatfield Suff 87 C6
Whatley Som 14 A3
Whatley Som 30 A1
Whatlington E Sus 23 A5
Whatstandwell Derbys 130 D3
Whatton Notts 115 B5
Whauphill Dumfries 171 C6
Whaw N Yorks 156 A3
Wheatacre Norf 105 B5
Wheatcroft Derbys 130 D3
Wheathampstead Herts 68 B1
Wheathill Shrops 95 C4
Wheatley Devon 13 B4
Wheatley Hants 33 A6
Wheatley Oxon 65 C6
Wheatley S Yorks 140 C3
Wheatley W Yorks 138 A3
Wheatley Hill Durham 167 B6
Wheaton Aston Staffs 112 D2
Wheddon Cross Som 27 B4
Wheedlemont Aberds 255 D5
Wheelerstreet Sur 34 B2
Wheelock Ches 128 D2
Wheelock Heath Ches 128 D2
Wheelton Lancs 137 A5
Wheen Angus 232 A1
Wheldrake York 149 C5
Whelford Glos 64 D2
Whelpley Hill Bucks 67 C4
Whempstead Herts 68 A3
Whenby N Yorks 149 A5
Whepstead Suff 87 B4
Wherstead Suff 88 C2
Wherwell Hants 32 A2
Wheston Derbys 129 B6
Whetsted Kent 37 B4

Whetstone Leics 98 B2
Whicham Cumb 153 B2
Whichford Warks 81 D6
Whickham T & W 179 C4
Whiddon Down Devon 12 B1
Whigstreet Angus 232 D2
Whilton Northants 82 A3
Whim Farm Borders 195 A7
Whimble Devon 11 A4
Whimple Devon 13 B5
Whimpwell Green Norf 121 C5
Whinburgh Norf 103 A6
Whinnieliggate Dumfries 173 C5
Whinnyfold Aberds 257 C5
Whippingham I o W 18 B4
Whipsnade Beds 67 B5
Whipsnade Wild Animal Park, Dunstable Beds 67 B5
Whipton Devon 13 B4
Whirlow S Yorks 130 A3
Whisby Lincs 133 C4
Whissendine Rutland 115 D6
Whissonsett Norf 119 C6
Whistlefield Argyll 215 C4
Whistlefield Argyll 215 C5
Whistley Green Wokingham 47 B5
Whiston Mers 136 D3
Whiston Northants 83 A5
Whiston Staffs 112 D2
Whiston Staffs 112 A4
Whiston S Yorks 131 A4
Whitbeck Cumb 153 B2
Whitbourne Hereford 79 B5
Whitbread Hop Farm, Beltring Kent 37 B4
Whitburn T & W 179 C6
Whitburn W Loth 208 D2
Whitburn Colliery T & W 179 C6
Whitby Ches 126 B3
Whitby N Yorks 169 D6
Whitby Abbey N Yorks 169 D7
Whitbyheath Ches 126 B3
Whitchurch Bath 43 C5
Whitchurch Bucks 66 A2
Whitchurch Cardiff 41 C6
Whitchurch Devon 11 D5
Whitchurch Hants 32 A3
Whitchurch Hereford 62 B1
Whitchurch Oxon 47 B4
Whitchurch Pembs 54 B3
Whitchurch Shrops 111 A4
Whitchurch Canonicorum Dorset 14 B3
Whitchurch Hill Oxon 47 B4
Whitcombe Dorset 15 C7
Whitcott Keysett Shrops 93 C6
White Coppice Lancs 137 B5
White Lackington Dorset 15 B7
White Ladies Aston Worcs 80 B2
White Lund Lancs 144 A4
White Mill Carms 58 C1
White Ness Shetland 285 J5
White Notley Essex 70 B1
White Pit Lincs 134 B3
White Post Notts 131 D6
White Post Farm Centre, Farnsfield Notts 131 D6
White Rocks Hereford 61 A6
White Roding Essex 69 B5
White Waltham Windsor 47 B6
Whiteacen Moray 254 B3
Whiteacre Heath Warks 97 B5
Whitebridge Highld 240 A2
Whitebrook Mon 62 C1
Whiteburn Borders 197 B4
Whitecairn Dumfries 171 B4
Whitecairns Aberds 245 A6
Whitecastle S Lnrk 195 B5
Whitechapel Lancs 145 C5
Whitecleat Orkney 283 G6
Whitecraig E Loth 209 C6
Whitecroft Glos 62 C2
Whitecross Corn 9 D5
Whitecross Falk 208 C2
Whitecross Staffs 112 C2
Whiteface Highld 264 B3
Whitefarland N Ayrs 202 D3
Whitefaulds S Ayrs 192 E2
Whitefield Gtr Man 137 C7
Whitefield Perth 219 A6
Whiteford Aberds 256 D2
Whitegate Ches 127 C6
Whitehall Blkburn 137 A5
Whitehall W Sus 35 D4
Whitehall Village Orkney 282 E7
Whitehaven Cumb 162 C2
Whitehill Hants 33 B6
Whitehills Aberds 268 C1
Whitehills S Lnrk 205 C6
Whitehough Derbys 129 A5
Whitehouse Aberds 244 A3
Whitehouse Argyll 202 B3
Whiteinch Glasgow 205 B5
Whitekirk E Loth 210 B2
Whitelaw S Lnrk 205 D6
Whiteleas T & W 179 C5
Whiteley Bank I o W 19 C4
Whiteley Green Ches 129 B4
Whiteley Village Sur 48 C3
Whitemans Green W Sus 35 D6
Whitemire Moray 253 A5
Whitemoor Corn 5 B4
Whitemore Staffs 128 C3
Whitenap Hants 32 C2
Whiteoak Green Oxon 64 B4
Whiteparish Wilts 31 C6
Whiterashes Aberds 256 D3
Whiterow Highld 281 D5
Whiteshill Glos 63 C4
Whiteside Northumb 177 C5
Whiteside W Loth 208 D2
Whitesmith E Sus 22 A3
Whitestaunton Som 28 D2
Whitestone Devon 12 B3
Whitestone Devon 25 A5
Whitestone Warks 97 C6
Whitestones Aberds 268 D3
Whitestreet Green Suff 87 D5
Whitewall Corner N Yorks 159 D6
Whiteway Glos 63 D4
Whiteway Glos 63 B5
Whitewell Aberds 269 C4
Whitewell Lancs 145 C6
Whitewell Bottom Lancs 138 A1
Whiteworks Devon 11 D7
Whitfield Kent 39 A5
Whitfield Northants 82 D3
Whitfield Northumb 177 D5
Whitfield S Glos 62 D2
Whitford Devon 14 B2
Whitford Flint 125 B6
Whitgift E Yorks 141 A6
Whitgreave Staffs 112 C2
Whithorn Dumfries 171 C6
Whiting Bay N Ayrs 191 C6
Whitington Norf 102 B3
Whitkirk W Yorks 148 D2
Whitland Carms 56 A1
Whitletts S Ayrs 192 C3
Whitley N Yorks 140 A3
Whitley Reading 47 B5
Whitley Wilts 44 C2
Whitley Bay T & W 179 B5
Whitley Chapel Northumb 178 D1
Whitley Lower W Yorks 139 B5
Whitley Row Kent 36 A2
Whitlock's End W Mid 96 D4
Whitminster Glos 62 C3
Whitmore Staffs 112 A2
Whitnage Devon 27 D5
Whitnash Warks 81 A6
Whitney Hereford 77 C6
Whitrigg Cumb 163 A5
Whitrigg Cumb 175 C5
Whitsbury Hants 31 D5
Whitsome Borders 198 A2
Whitson Newport 42 A2
Whitstable Kent 52 C3
Whitstone Corn 10 B3
Whittingham Northumb 188 B3
Whittingslow Shrops 94 C2
Whittington Glos 63 A6
Whittington Lancs 155 D5
Whittington Shrops 110 B2
Whittington Staffs 95 C6
Whittington Staffs 97 A4
Whittington Worcs 80 B1
Whittle-le-Woods Lancs 137 A4
Whittlebury Northants 82 C3
Whittlesey Cambs 101 B4
Whittlesford Cambs 85 C6
Whittlestone Head Blkburn 137 B6
Whitton Borders 187 A6
Whitton N Lincs 141 A7
Whitton Northumb 188 C3
Whitton Powys 77 A6
Whitton Shrops 94 D3
Whitton Stockton 167 C6
Whitton Suff 88 C2
Whittonditch Wilts 45 B6
Whittonstall Northumb 178 D2
Whitway Hants 46 D2
Whitwell Derbys 131 B5
Whitwell Herts 68 A1
Whitwell I o W 18 D4
Whitwell N Yorks 157 B6
Whitwell Rutland 99 A6
Whitwell-on-the-Hill N Yorks 149 A6
Whitwell Street Norf 120 C3
Whitwick Leics 114 D2
Whitwood W Yorks 140 A2
Whitworth Lancs 138 B1
Whixall Shrops 111 B4
Whixley N Yorks 148 B3
Whoberley W Mid 97 D6
Whorlton Durham 166 D4
Whorlton N Yorks 158 A3
Whygate Northumb 177 B5
Whyle Hereford 78 A3
Whyteleafe Sur 35 A6
Wibdon Glos 62 D1
Wibsey W Yorks 147 D5
Wibtoft Leics 98 C1
Wichenford Worcs 79 A5
Wichling Kent 37 A7
Wick Bmouth 17 B5
Wick Devon 13 A6
Wick Highld 281 C5
Wick S Glos 43 B6
Wick Shetland 285 K6
Wick V Glam 40 D4
Wick Wilts 31 C5
Wick Worcs 80 C2
Wick W Sus 20 B3
Wick Airport Highld 281 C5
Wick Hill Wokingham 47 C5
Wick St Lawrence N Som 42 C2
Wicken Cambs 102 D1
Wicken Northants 83 D4
Wicken Bonhunt Essex 85 D6
Wicken Green Village Norf 119 B5
Wickenby Lincs 133 A5
Wickersley S Yorks 140 D2
Wickford Essex 70 D1
Wickham Hants 33 D4
Wickham W Berks 46 B1
Wickham Bishops Essex 70 B2
Wickham Market Suff 88 B4
Wickham St Paul Essex 87 D4
Wickham Skeith Suff 88 A1
Wickham Street Suff 86 B3
Wickham Street Suff 88 A1
Wickhambreux Kent 53 D4
Wickhambrook Suff 86 B3
Wickhamford Worcs 80 C3
Wickhampton Norf 105 A5
Wicklewood Norf 104 A1
Wickmere Norf 120 B3
Wicksteed Park, Kettering Northants 99 D5
Wickwar S Glos 43 A6
Widdington Essex 86 D1
Widdrington Northumb 189 D5
Widdrington Station Northumb 189 D5
Wide Open T & W 179 B4
Widecombe in the Moor Devon 12 D2
Widegates Corn 6 B1
Widemouth Bay Corn 10 A3
Widewall Orkney 283 H5
Widford Essex 69 C6
Widford Herts 68 B4
Widham Wilts 45 A4
Widmer End Bucks 66 D3
Widmerpool Notts 115 C4
Widnes Halton 127 A5
Wigan Gtr Man 137 C4
Wigan Pier Gtr Man 137 C4
Wiggaton Devon 13 B6
Wiggenhall St Germans Norf 118 D2
Wiggenhall St Mary Magdalen Norf 118 D2
Wiggenhall St Mary the Virgin Norf 118 D2
Wigginton Herts 67 B4
Wigginton Oxon 81 D6
Wigginton Staffs 97 A5
Wigginton York 149 B4
Wigglesworth N Yorks 146 B2
Wiggonby Cumb 175 C5
Wiggonholt W Sus 20 A3
Wighill N Yorks 148 C3
Wighton Norf 119 B6
Wigley Hants 32 D2
Wigmore Hereford 78 A2
Wigmore Medway 51 C5
Wigsley Notts 132 B3
Wigsthorpe Northants 100 C2
Wigston Leics 98 B3
Wigthorpe Notts 131 A5
Wigtoft Lincs 117 B5
Wigton Cumb 175 D5
Wigtown Dumfries 171 B6
Wigtwizzle S Yorks 139 D5
Wike W Yorks 148 C2
Wike Well End S Yorks 141 B4
Wilbarston Northants 99 C5
Wilberfoss E Yorks 149 B6
Wilberlee W Yorks 138 B3
Wilburton Cambs 101 D6
Wilby Norf 103 C6
Wilby Northants 83 A5
Wilby Suff 104 D3
Wilcot Wilts 45 C5
Wilcott Shrops 110 D2
Wilcrick Newport 42 A3
Wilday Green Derbys 130 B3
Wildboarclough Ches 129 C4
Wilden Beds 84 B2
Wilden Worcs 95 D6
Wildfowl and Wetland Centre, Martin Mere Lancs 136 B3
Wildhern Hants 46 D1
Wildhill Herts 68 C2
Wildlife & Dinosaur Park, Combe Martin Devon 25 A6
Wildmoor Worcs 96 D2
Wildsworth Lincs 141 D6
Wilford Notts 114 B3
Wilkesley Ches 111 A5
Wilkhaven Highld 265 B5
Wilkieston W Loth 208 D4
Willand Devon 27 D5
Willaston Ches 126 B3
Willaston Ches 128 D1
Willen M Keynes 83 C5
Willenhall W Mid 97 D6
Willenhall W Mid 96 B2
Willerby E Yorks 150 D3
Willerby N Yorks 160 D4
Willersey Glos 80 D4
Willersley Hereford 77 C7
Willesborough Kent 38 A2
Willesborough Lees Kent 38 A2
Willesden London 49 A5
Willett Som 27 B6
Willey Shrops 95 B4
Willey Warks 98 C1
Willey Green Sur 34 A2
Williamscott Oxon 82 C1
Willian Herts 84 D4
Willingale Essex 69 C5
Willingdon E Sus 22 B3
Willingham Cambs 101 D6
Willingham by Stow Lincs 132 A3
Willington Beds 84 C3
Willington Derbys 113 C6
Willington Durham 167 B4
Willington T & W 179 C5
Willington Warks 81 D5
Willington Corner Ches 127 C5
Willisham Tye Suff 87 B6
Willitoft E Yorks 149 D6
Williton Som 27 A5
Willoughbridge Staffs 111 A6
Willoughby Lincs 135 B4
Willoughby Warks 82 A2
Willoughby-on-the-Wolds Notts 115 C4
Willoughby Waterleys Leics 98 B2
Willoughton Lincs 142 D1
Willows Grn. Essex 69 B7
Willsbridge S Glos 43 B5
Willsworthy Devon 11 C6
Wilmcote Warks 81 B4
Wilmington Devon 14 B2
Wilmington E Sus 22 B3
Wilmington Kent 50 B2
Wilminstone Devon 11 D5
Wilmslow Ches 128 A3
Wilnecote Staffs 97 A5
Wilpshire Lancs 145 D6
Wilsden W Yorks 147 D4
Wilsford Lincs 116 A3
Wilsford Wilts 45 D5
Wilsford Wilts 31 B5
Wilsill N Yorks 147 A5
Wilsley Pound Kent 37 C5
Wilsom Hants 33 B6
Wilson Leics 114 C2
Wilsontown S Lnrk 195 A4
Wilstead Beds 84 C2
Wilsthorpe Lincs 116 D3
Wilstone Herts 67 B4
Wilton Borders 186 B3
Wilton Cumb 162 C3
Wilton N Yorks 160 C2
Wilton Redcar 168 D3
Wilton Wilts 31 B4
Wilton Wilts 45 C6
Wilton House, Salisbury Wilts 31 B5
Wimbish Essex 86 D1
Wimbish Green Essex 86 D2
Wimblebury Staffs 112 D4
Wimbledon London 49 B5
Wimbledon All England Tennis Club London 49 B5
Wimblington Cambs 101 B6
Wimborne Minster Dorset 17 B4
Wimborne Minster Dorset 17 B4
Wimborne St Giles Dorset 31 D4
Wimbotsham Norf 102 A2
Wimpole Hall and Home Farm, Royston Cambs 85 B5
Wimpson Soton 32 D2
Wimpstone Warks 81 C5
Wincanton Som 29 C7
Wincanton Racecourse Som 29 C7
Wincham Ches 128 B1
Winchburgh W Loth 208 C3
Winchcombe Glos 63 A6
Winchelsea E Sus 23 A7
Winchelsea Beach E Sus 23 A7
Winchester Hants 32 C3
Winchester Cathedral Hants 32 C3
Winchet Hill Kent 37 B5
Winchfield Hants 47 D5
Winchmore Hill Bucks 67 D4
Winchmore Hill London 68 D3
Wincle Ches 129 C4
Wincobank S Yorks 140 D1
Windermere Cumb 154 B3
Winderton Warks 81 C6
Windhill Highld 252 B1
Windhouse Shetland 284 D6
Windlehurst Gtr Man 129 A4
Windlesham Sur 48 C2
Windley Derbys 113 A7
Windmill Hill E Sus 22 A4
Windmill Hill Som 28 D3
Windrush Glos 64 B2
Windsor N Lincs 141 B5
Windsor Windsor 48 B2
Windsor Castle Windsor 48 B2
Windsor Racecourse Windsor 48 B2
Windsoredge Glos 63 C4
Windygates Fife 220 D3
Windyknowe W Loth 208 D2
Windywalls Borders 197 C6
Wineham W Sus 35 D5
Winestead E Yorks 143 A4
Winewall Lancs 146 C3
Winfarthing Norf 104 C2
Winford I o W 19 C4
Winford N Som 43 C4
Winforton Hereford 77 C6
Winfrith Newburgh Dorset 16 C2
Wing Bucks 66 A3
Wing Rutland 99 A5
Wingate Durham 168 B2
Wingates Gtr Man 137 C5
Wingates Northumb 189 D4
Wingerworth Derbys 130 C3
Wingfield Beds 67 A5
Wingfield Suff 104 D3
Wingfield Wilts 44 D2
Wingham Kent 53 D4
Wingmore Kent 38 A3
Wingrave Bucks 66 B3
Winkburn Notts 132 D2
Winkfield Brack 48 B2
Winkfield Row Brack 48 B1
Winkhill Staffs 129 D5
Winklebury Hants 47 D4
Winkleigh Devon 12 A1
Winksley N Yorks 157 D6
Winkton Dorset 17 B5
Winlaton T & W 178 C3
Winless Highld 281 C5
Winmarleigh Lancs 145 C4
Winnal Hereford 78 D2
Winnall Hants 32 C3
Winnersh Wokingham 47 B5
Winscales Cumb 162 B3
Winscombe N Som 42 D3
Winsford Ches 127 C6
Winsford Som 27 B4
Winsham Som 14 A3
Winshill Staffs 113 C6
Winskill Cumb 164 B3
Winslade Hants 33 A5
Winsley Wilts 44 C2
Winslow Bucks 66 A2
Winson Glos 64 C1
Winson Grn. W Mid 96 C3
Winsor Hants 32 D2
Winster Cumb 154 B3
Winster Derbys 130 C2
Winston Durham 166 D4
Winston Suff 88 A2
Winston Green Suff 88 A2
Winstone Glos 63 C5
Winswell Devon 25 D5
Winter Gardens Essex 51 A4
Winterborne Bassett Wilts 45 B5
Winterborne Clenston Dorset 16 A2
Winterborne Herringston Dorset 15 C6
Winterborne Houghton Dorset 16 A2
Winterborne Kingston Dorset 16 B2
Winterborne Monkton Dorset 15 C6
Winterborne Monkton Wilts 45 B5
Winterborne Stickland Dorset 16 A2
Winterborne Whitechurch Dorset 16 A2
Winterborne Zelston Dorset 16 B2
Winterbourne S Glos 43 A5
Winterbourne W Berks 46 B2
Winterbourne Abbas Dorset 15 B6
Winterbourne Dauntsey Wilts 31 B5
Winterbourne Down S Glos 43 B5
Winterbourne Earls Wilts 31 B5
Winterbourne Gunner Wilts 31 B5
Winterbourne Steepleton Dorset 15 C6
Winterbourne Stoke Wilts 31 A4
Winterburn N Yorks 146 B3
Winteringham N Lincs 142 A1
Winterley Ches 128 D2
Wintersett W Yorks 140 B1
Wintershill Hants 32 D4
Winterton N Lincs 142 B1
Winterton-on-Sea Norf 121 D6
Winthorpe Lincs 135 C5
Winthorpe Notts 132 D3
Winton Bmouth 17 B4
Winton Cumb 165 D5
Winton N Yorks 158 B3
Wintringham N Yorks 160 D2
Winwick Cambs 100 C3
Winwick Northants 98 D3
Winwick Warr 137 D5
Wirksworth Derbys 130 D2
Wirksworth Moor Derbys 130 D3
Wirswall Ches 111 A4
Wisbech Cambs 101 A6
Wisbech St Mary Cambs 101 A6
Wisborough Green W Sus 34 D3
Wiseton Notts 132 A2
Wishaw N Lnrk 194 A2
Wishaw Warks 97 B4
Wisley Sur 34 A3
Wispington Lincs 134 B2
Wissenden Kent 37 B7
Wissett Suff 105 D4
Wistanstow Shrops 94 C2
Wistanswick Shrops 111 C5
Wistaston Ches 128 D1
Wistaston Green Ches 128 D1
Wiston Pembs 55 C6
Wiston S Lnrk 195 C4
Wiston W Sus 21 A4
Wistow Cambs 101 C4
Wistow N Yorks 149 D4
Wiswell Lancs 146 D1
Witcham Cambs 101 C6
Witchampton Dorset 16 A3
Witchford Cambs 101 D7
Witham Essex 70 B2
Witham Friary Som 30 A1
Witham on the Hill Lincs 116 D3
Withcall Lincs 134 A2
Withdean Brighton 21 B6
Witherenden Hill E Sus 36 D4
Witheridge Devon 26 D3
Witherley Leics 97 B6
Withern Lincs 135 A4
Withernsea E Yorks 143 A5
Withernwick E Yorks 151 C4
Withersdale Street Suff 104 C3
Withersfield Suff 86 C2
Witherslack Cumb 154 C3
Withiel Corn 5 A4
Withiel Florey Som 27 B4
Withington Glos 63 B6
Withington Gtr Man 138 D1
Withington Hereford 78 C3
Withington Shrops 111 D4
Withington Staffs 112 B4
Withington Green Ches 128 B3
Withleigh Devon 27 D4
Withnell Lancs 137 A5
Withybrook Warks 98 C1
Withycombe Som 27 A5
Withycombe Raleigh Devon 13 C5
Withyham E Sus 36 C2
Withypool Som 26 B3
Witley Sur 34 C2
Witnesham Suff 88 B2
Witney Oxon 65 B4
Wittering P'boro 100 A2
Wittersham Kent 37 D6
Witton Angus 232 A3
Witton Worcs 80 A1
Witton Bridge Norf 121 B5
Witton Gilbert Durham 167 A5
Witton-le-Wear Durham 166 B4
Witton Park Durham 167 B4
Wiveliscombe Som 27 C5

**Y**

**Z**